T0236223

Lecture Notes in Artificial Intelligence　　9743

Subseries of Lecture Notes in Computer Science

More information about this series at http://www.springer.com/series/1244

Dylan D. Schmorrow · Cali M. Fidopiastis (Eds.)

Foundations of Augmented Cognition: Neuroergonomics and Operational Neuroscience

10th International Conference, AC 2016
Held as Part of HCI International 2016
Toronto, ON, Canada, July 17–22, 2016
Proceedings, Part I

 Springer

Editors
Dylan D. Schmorrow
Soar Technology Inc.
Vienna, VA
USA

Cali M. Fidopiastis
Design Interactive, Inc.
Orlando, FL
USA

ISSN 0302-9743   ISSN 1611-3349 (electronic)
Lecture Notes in Artificial Intelligence
ISBN 978-3-319-39954-6   ISBN 978-3-319-39955-3 (eBook)
DOI 10.1007/978-3-319-39955-3

Library of Congress Control Number: 2016940364

LNCS Sublibrary: SL7 – Artificial Intelligence

Printed on acid-free paper

This Springer imprint is published by Springer Nature
The registered company is Springer International Publishing AG Switzerland

Foreword

The 18th International Conference on Human-Computer Interaction, HCI International 2016, was held in Toronto, Canada, during July 17–22, 2016. The event incorporated the 15 conferences/thematic areas listed on the following page.

A total of 4,354 individuals from academia, research institutes, industry, and governmental agencies from 74 countries submitted contributions, and 1,287 papers and 186 posters have been included in the proceedings. These papers address the latest research and development efforts and highlight the human aspects of the design and use of computing systems. The papers thoroughly cover the entire field of human-computer interaction, addressing major advances in knowledge and effective use of computers in a variety of application areas. The volumes constituting the full 27-volume set of the conference proceedings are listed on pages IX and X.

I would like to thank the program board chairs and the members of the program boards of all thematic areas and affiliated conferences for their contribution to the highest scientific quality and the overall success of the HCI International 2016 conference.

This conference would not have been possible without the continuous and unwavering support and advice of the founder, Conference General Chair Emeritus and Conference Scientific Advisor Prof. Gavriel Salvendy. For his outstanding efforts, I would like to express my appreciation to the communications chair and editor of *HCI International News*, Dr. Abbas Moallem.

April 2016   Constantine Stephanidis

HCI International 2016 Thematic Areas
and Affiliated Conferences

Thematic areas:

- Human-Computer Interaction (HCI 2016)
- Human Interface and the Management of Information (HIMI 2016)

Affiliated conferences:

- 13th International Conference on Engineering Psychology and Cognitive Ergonomics (EPCE 2016)
- 10th International Conference on Universal Access in Human-Computer Interaction (UAHCI 2016)
- 8th International Conference on Virtual, Augmented and Mixed Reality (VAMR 2016)
- 8th International Conference on Cross-Cultural Design (CCD 2016)
- 8th International Conference on Social Computing and Social Media (SCSM 2016)
- 10th International Conference on Augmented Cognition (AC 2016)
- 7th International Conference on Digital Human Modeling and Applications in Health, Safety, Ergonomics and Risk Management (DHM 2016)
- 5th International Conference on Design, User Experience and Usability (DUXU 2016)
- 4th International Conference on Distributed, Ambient and Pervasive Interactions (DAPI 2016)
- 4th International Conference on Human Aspects of Information Security, Privacy and Trust (HAS 2016)
- Third International Conference on HCI in Business, Government, and Organizations (HCIBGO 2016)
- Third International Conference on Learning and Collaboration Technologies (LCT 2016)
- Second International Conference on Human Aspects of IT for the Aged Population (ITAP 2016)

Conference Proceedings Volumes Full List

Augmented Cognition

Program Board Chairs: **Dylan D. Schmorrow, USA,**
Cali M. Fidopiastis, USA

- Robert Abbott, USA
- Rosario Bruno Cannavò, Italy
- David Combs, USA
- Andrew J. Cowell, USA
- Martha Crosby, USA
- Priya Ganapathy, USA
- Rodolphe Gentili, USA
- Michael W. Hail, USA
- Monte Hancock, USA
- Ion Juvina, USA
- Philip Mangos, USA
- David Martinez, USA
- Santosh Mathan, USA
- Chang Soo Nam, USA
- Banu Onaral, USA
- Robinson Pino, USA
- Lauren Reinerman-Jones, USA
- Victoria Romero, USA
- Jose Rouillard, USA
- Amela Sadagic, USA
- Patricia Shewokis, USA
- Paula Alexandra Silva, USA
- Anna Skinner, USA
- Robert Sottilare, USA
- Ann Speed, USA
- Roy Stripling, USA
- Eric Vorm, USA
- Peter Walker, USA

The full list with the program board chairs and the members of the program boards of all thematic areas and affiliated conferences is available online at:

http://www.hci.international/2016/

HCI International 2017

The 19th International Conference on Human-Computer Interaction, HCI International 2017, will be held jointly with the affiliated conferences in Vancouver, Canada, at the Vancouver Convention Centre, July 9–14, 2017. It will cover a broad spectrum of themes related to human-computer interaction, including theoretical issues, methods, tools, processes, and case studies in HCI design, as well as novel interaction techniques, interfaces, and applications. The proceedings will be published by Springer. More information will be available on the conference website: http://2017. hci.international/.

General Chair
Prof. Constantine Stephanidis
University of Crete and ICS-FORTH
Heraklion, Crete, Greece
E-mail: general_chair@hcii2017.org

http://2017.hci.international/

Contents – Part I

Electroencephalography and Brain Activity Measurement

Cognitive Modelling and Physiological Measuring

Contents – Part II

Human Cognition and Behavior in Complex Tasks and Environments

Interaction in Augmented Cognition

Social Cognition

Brain-Computer Interfaces

Developing an Optical Brain-Computer Interface for Humanoid Robot Control

Alyssa M. Batula[1]($\boxtimes$), Jesse Mark[2], Youngmoo E. Kim[1],
and Hasan Ayaz[2,3,4]

[1] Department of Electrical and Computer Engineering,
Drexel University, Philadelphia, PA, USA
{batulaa,ykim}@drexel.edu
[2] School of Biomedical Engineering, Science and Health Systems,
Drexel University, Philadelphia, PA, USA
{jesse.alexander.mark,hasan.ayaz}@drexel.edu
[3] Department of Family and Community Health,
University of Pennsylvania, Philadelphia, PA, USA
[4] Division of General Pediatrics, Children's Hospital of Philadelphia,
Philadelphia, PA, USA

Abstract. This work evaluates the feasibility of a motor imagery-based optical brain-computer interface (BCI) for humanoid robot control. The functional near-infrared spectroscopy (fNIRS) based BCI-robot system developed in this study operates through a high-level control mechanism where user specifies a target action through the BCI and the robot performs the set of micro operations necessary to fulfill the identified goal. For the evaluation of the system, four motor imagery tasks (left hand, right hand, left foot, and right foot) were mapped to operational commands (turn left, turn right, walk forward, walk backward) that were sent to the robot in real time to direct the robot navigating a small room. An ecologically valid offline analysis with minimal preprocessing shows that seven subjects could achieve an average accuracy of 32.5 %. This was increased to 43.6 % just by including calibration data from the same day of the robot control using the same cap setup, indicating that day-of calibration following the initial training may be important for BCI control.

Keywords: BCI · fNIRS · Motor imagery · Motor cortex · Humanoid robot control · Teleoperation

1 Introduction

Brain-computer interface (BCI) systems attempt to augment or expand a user's control capabilities whereby the user controls a computer directly with his or her thoughts [1]. Direct use of captured brain signals allows a BCI to bypass the neuromuscular system, providing a promising research avenue for restoring communication or movement in patients suffering from injury or neuromuscular diseases [1]. This could take the form of a robotic wheelchair [2], a remotely-controlled assistive robot that navigates a building [3], or even a prosthetic limb that responds to neural signals like a biological limb [4]. BCIs could also prove useful to fully-abled users for teleoperating a robot in a

© Springer International Publishing Switzerland 2016
D.D. Schmorrow and C.M. Fidopiastis (Eds.): AC 2016, Part I, LNAI 9743, pp. 3–13, 2016.
DOI: 10.1007/978-3-319-39955-3_1

remote location, potentially providing faster and more intuitive control either alone or as an enhancement to traditional interfaces such as joysticks, voice control, or typing commands into a computer terminal.

The ideal, field-deployable BCI system should be safe, intuitive, and practical to use. Functional near-infrared spectroscopy (fNIRS) is an emerging optical neuroimaging technique that can be applied as wearable and battery-operated miniaturized devices [5]. Imagined body movements (motor imagery) are frequently used in BCI and are regarded as an intuitive control method. This work outlines the development of a four-class, motor-imagery-based optical BCI to control a small bipedal humanoid robot, the DARwIn-OP.

Four mental tasks are mapped to navigation commands: turn right, turn left, move forwards, and move backwards. Visual feedback is provided via a first-person view of the room through either a virtual representation or a camera in the robot's head presented on a computer monitor. The fNIRS-BCI-robot system developed here serves as a prototype for a telepresence or assistance robot navigating in remote and/or inaccessible locations. To our knowledge, this is the first report of a four-class motor-imagery-based fNIRS BCI-robot system.

2   Background

2.1   Motor Imagery, Movement, and the Motor Cortex

Motor movement (or motor execution) is the process of physically moving an area of the body, such as finger tapping. Motor imagery is an imagined movement of the body during which the muscles remain inactive. It is a conscious utilization of the unconscious motor preparation performed before a motor movement [6]. Because of this close association between motor imagery and naturally produced movement preparation, motor imagery could provide an intuitive mapping for BCI commands.

The primary motor cortex (M1) of the brain is the main control area where a one-to-one relationship between motor movement and brain activation exists, and is subdivided into sections responsible for control of the different areas of the body (the cortical homunculus) [7]. Some studies have shown motor imagery to have a similar activation pattern to motor execution, although the signals are significantly weaker [8, 9].

The brain's hemodynamic response is the rapid delivery of oxygen-rich blood via the hemoglobin protein in red blood cells in response to the immediate need of the brain tissue and is correlated with functional activity such as cognitive tasks and motor activity [10, 11]. Oxygenated hemoglobin (HbO) and deoxygenated hemoglobin (HbR) levels in cortical tissue can be measured to track the flow of blood throughout the brain. Both motor imagery and motor movements cause a rise in HbO and decrease in HbR, although the motor imagery response is slower in time and smaller in scale [12, 13].

2.2   Functional Near-Infrared Spectroscopy (fNIRS)

Functional near-infrared spectroscopy (fNIRS) is a noninvasive optical brain imaging technique that has shown promise for BCI applications [14–17], including the detection of motor movements [18, 19] and motor imagery [20, 21]. It uses near infrared light to measure changes in HbO and HbR levels due to the hemodynamic response. In the common configuration, light sources and detectors are placed on the scalp and two wavelengths of light are transmitted through the top layer of the cerebral cortex. Light at wavelengths between approximately 700–900 nm can pass through skin, bone, and water, but is absorbed mainly by HbO and HbR and at different rates [22]. The relative change in HbO and HbR, and therefore the oxygenation of the tissue, can be calculated from changes in the reflected light using the modified Beer-Lambert law [23].

Many fNIRS devices are relatively low-cost, portable, and potentially wireless [5]. This allows them to be used in more natural settings, such as sitting at a desk, rather than in restricted and artificial lab environments. Despite the time delay due to the slow hemodynamic response, fNIRS provides a unique trade-off between time and spatial resolution and is free from most artifacts, such as muscle activity and eye blinks. It can also be used with other measurements, such as physiological signals [24] and electroencephalography (EEG) [25–27].

2.3 Motor Imagery and Robot-Control BCIs

Overall, preliminary studies show promise for fNIRS-based BCIs. fNIRS has higher spatial resolution than EEG and higher time resolution than fMRI, which provides a balanced trade-off. Several EEG- or fMRI-based studies have used motor imagery as the sole input method with up to four different tasks [28, 29]. It may also be possible to distinguish between simple and compound motor imagery (e.g. moving right hand vs. right hand and foot together) [30]. Many fNIRS motor imagery experiments focus on detecting imagery from a single hand vs. resting state [20], left hand vs. right hand [21, 31], or three motor imagery tasks and rest [32].

Robot control is a natural application of BCIs, and previous BCIs have controlled flying [33], wheeled [2, 34], and humanoid [3, 35–37] robots. Incorporating robot control into a BCI provides visual feedback and can increase subject motivation during use. Improved motivation and feedback, both visual and auditory, have demonstrated promise for reducing subject training time and improving BCI accuracy [38, 39]. While many studies have focused on EEG or fMRI as a control method, fNIRS has also been used for robot control, although previous studies have focused on motor movement or other mental tasks [40–43].

3 Methods

3.1 Participants

Eleven healthy participants volunteered in the experiment. Subjects were aged 18–35, right-handed, English speaking, and with vision correctable to 20/20. No subjects reported any physical or neurological disorders, or were on medication. The experiment was approved by the Drexel University institutional review board, and subjects were informed of the experimental procedure and provided written consent prior to participating.

3.2   Data Acquisition and Protocol

Motor imagery and motor movement data were recorded in three one-hour-long sessions over the course of three days. The first two sessions are training days, used to collect initial data to train a classifier, and the third day is used to test the BCI by navigating a robot within a room containing a goal location and an obstacle to be avoided. A total of 80 motor imagery and 32 motor movement trials were collected for each subject over the course of the two training days, with an additional 40 motor imagery trials collected during the robot-control day. The four tasks were the (actual or imagined) tapping of the right hand, left hand, right foot, and left foot. Preliminary results for three subjects using the two training days have been reported previously [44].

Twenty-four optodes (physical locations) over the motor cortex were recorded using a Hitachi ETG-4000 optical topography system, as shown in Fig. 1(A). HbO and HbR levels were recorded at each location at a sampling rate of 10 Hz.

The timings for training and robot-control days are shown in Fig. 1(B). Each trial began with 6 s of rest followed by a cue to indicate the upcoming task. For the two training sessions this text indicated a specific task (e.g. left foot), while during the robot-control task it read "free choice", indicating the subject should choose the task corresponding to the desired action of the robot. Subjects then performed the designated task for 30 s. During the robot control session, the task was followed by a pause so that the subject could indicate which task they had performed. All trials ended with a 15-s period indicating the task was over. On the robot control day, the time during the results stage was used by a support vector machine (SVM) which had been trained on data from the two training sessions to predict the task being performed. The corresponding command was sent to the robot, which took the corresponding action.

Each day was split into two runs, as shown in Fig. 2. There was a brief pause between the runs until the participant indicated they were ready to continue. The two training days began with 16 motor movement trials, followed by 40 motor imagery trials. Motor movement was performed before motor imagery in order to improve the subject's ability to imagine performing the task. Each training session run had an equal number of the four tasks (motor execution or motor imagery of the right hand, left hand, right foot, and left foot) in a randomized order.

For the third day (robot control), the two runs were identical, except that in the first run they were controlling a virtual robot and in the second they controlled an actual robot. Subjects selected a motor imagery task corresponding to the desired action of the (virtual or physical) robot. The task-to-command mappings are: left foot/walk forward, left hand/turn left 90°, right hand/turn right 90°, and right foot/walk backward. These four tasks were chosen to emulate a common arrow-pad setup, and so that each action had a corresponding opposite action that could undo a movement.

Robot-Control Task. The robot-control session had two parts, beginning with control of a virtual robot and followed by control of an actual robot. During the first run, a second monitor displayed a first-person view of a virtual maze using the Maze Suite program [45], as shown in Fig. 3(A). During the second run, this monitor displayed a first person view recorded from a camera located in the head of the DARwIn-OP, a small humanoid robot [46], shown in the experiment setup in Fig. 3(B). DARwIn-OP

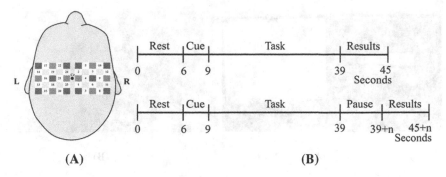

Fig. 1. (A) Sensor layout showing light sources (red squares) and detectors (blue squares). Optodes are numbered 1–24. Adjacent sources and detectors are 3 cm apart. **(B)** Trial timing diagrams for training days 1 & 2 (top) and robot control (bottom). The variable n represents the length of time taken to record participant's intended task. (Color figure online)

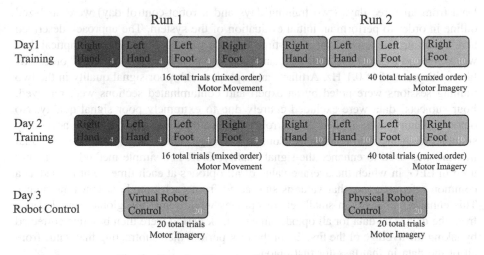

Fig. 2. Experiment protocol and trial organization

is 0.455 m tall, has 20 degrees of freedom, and walks on two legs in a similar manner to humans. The objective in both runs was to use the BCI to navigate through a series of three room designs, in which there was a single goal location (a green cube) and an obstacle (a red cube). The room layouts for the virtual and physical robots were designed to be as similar as possible. This allowed the subjects to acquaint themselves with the new robot-control paradigm before adding the complexities inherent in using a real robot.

A room was successfully completed if the user navigated to the green cube, and it was failed if the user touched the red cube. After completion or failure of a room, the subject would advance to the next room. The run ended if the subject completed (or failed) all three rooms or reached the maximum of 20 trials.

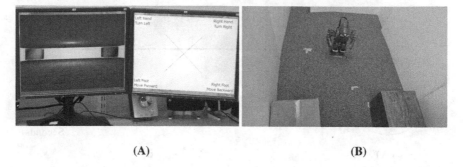

(A)   **(B)**

Fig. 3. View of **(A)** virtual room and task screen and **(B)** the physical robot setup. (Color figure online)

3.3   Data Analysis

Data from all three days (two training days and a robot-control day) were analyzed offline in order to perform an initial evaluation of the system. The approach described here could also be applied for a real-time BCI for robot control. The raw optical data was converted to HbO and HbR data, and then low-pass filtered using a 20th order FIR filter with a cutoff of 0.1 Hz. Artifacts and optodes with poor signal quality in the two training sessions were noted by an expert and contaminated sections were removed. Four subjects' data were excluded entirely due to extremely poor signal quality. No optode cleaning was applied to the robot-control data, in order to more accurately simulate real-time field conditions. Common average referencing (CAR) based spatial filtering was used to enhance the signal quality. CAR is a simple method, commonly used in EEG, in which the average value of all optodes at each time point is used as a common reference (i.e. that value is subtracted from each optode at that time point). This enhances changes in small sets of optodes while removing global spatial trends from the data. The data for all optodes in each task period were then baseline corrected by taking the average of the first 2 s of the task period, then subtracting that value from all of the data in that task for that optode.

Features were calculated on the total hemoglobin (HbT) at each optode, as this outperformed HbO, HbR, and Oxy (the difference between HbO and HbR), on average across subjects in a preliminary analysis on the first two days [44]. The average value for each optode was calculated for each task period from 9–15 s after the start of the task as this period is the expected peak activation.

The features were classified using a linear support vector machine (SVM) using the scikit-learn package [47]. Results are reported as accuracy (average number of correct classifications), precision (positive prediction value), recall (sensitivity or true positive rate), and F-score (the balance between precision and recall). The F-score is calculated as shown in Eq. 1.

$$\text{F-score} = 2 \times \frac{\text{precision} \times \text{recall}}{\text{precision} + \text{recall}} \tag{1}$$

4   Results

Table 1 shows the offline results of the robot-control data (Day 3) using a classifier trained using the training sessions (Day 1 and 2). To reduce the effect of running the experiment across multiple days, half of the robot-control data (randomly selected, evenly distributed across tasks) was added to the training data from the first two days to calibrate the classifier to the new cap position. Figure 4 and Table 2 show the results after 10 repetitions of randomly assigning the robot-control data between training and test sets. The results shown in Tables 1 and 2 were compared to test the significance of adding same-day calibration trials to the training data. Four paired, one-sided t-tests indicated significant improvement as reported in Table 3.

Table 1. Results for robot control using day 1 & day 2 as training data

	S0	S1	S2	S3	S4	S5	S6	Avg.
Accuracy	60.00	27.50	37.50	25.00	25.00	30.00	22.50	32.50
Precision	0.52	0.27	0.30	0.17	0.21	0.23	0.17	0.27
Recall	0.52	0.30	0.33	0.20	0.25	0.23	0.24	0.30
F-Score	0.52	0.29	0.31	0.18	0.23	0.23	0.20	0.28

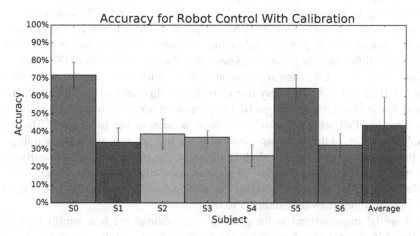

Fig. 4. Accuracy using days 1, 2, and half of the robot control data for training. Error bars show the standard deviation across 10 repetitions, with the error bar for average showing the standard deviation of the accuracy across subjects.

5   Discussion

This is the first study to our knowledge that attempts to create a four-class motor imagery fNIRS BCI for robot control. The preliminary results show that seven subjects achieved an average accuracy of 32.5 % on a four-class fNIRS BCI robot control task with minimal preprocessing to reflect field conditions. Including a portion of the data

Table 2. Results using days 1, 2, and half of the robot control data for training

	S0	S1	S2	S3	S4	S5	S6	Avg.
Accuracy	71.87	33.96	38.75	36.94	26.49	64.51	32.51	43.58
Precision	0.66	0.30	0.36	0.36	0.23	0.19	0.31	0.34
Recall	0.62	0.30	0.35	0.38	0.24	0.21	0.32	0.34
F-Score	0.64	0.30	0.35	0.37	0.23	0.20	0.31	0.34

Table 3. Results (p-values and 95 % confidence intervals) for one-sided paired t-tests comparing accuracy measures with and without same-day calibration data included in the training data

	p-value	Confidence interval
Accuracy	0.02	$(-\infty, -2.80)$
Precision	0.01	$(-\infty, -0.03)$
Recall	0.04	$(-\infty, -0.00)$
F-Score	0.02	$(-\infty, -0.01)$

from day 3 (robot control) into the classifier significantly improved the accuracy for several subjects, increasing the average accuracy to 43.6 %. There was a great deal of variability in performance between subjects, with subject S0 achieving 60 % or higher accuracy using both methods, and subject S5 achieving over 60 % accuracy with the addition of same-day calibration data. Many factors could account for this variability, including differences in participants' ability to perform motor imagery as well as physiological differences (e.g. hair thickness) that can interfere with fNIRS recordings.

Table 3 shows that the improvement on all four metrics was statistically significant (using $\alpha = 0.05$ and false discovery rate correction). This indicates that the inclusion of a calibration session prior to using a BCI improves the accuracy by adding examples to the training set that are more similar to those present in the testing set. These new examples would have the same cap position as the test set data, while the training data from previous days may have a slightly different cap placement. Additionally, brain functionality in individuals varies over time, potentially causing changes in the recorded data across days. Inclusion of calibration tasks immediately before the BCI could provide more relevant examples to the classifier.

A potential improvement to the protocol is to shorten the task length from 30 to 15 s. Preliminary analyses show that using all 30 s of the task did not improve results, and several participants self-reported mental strain caused by sustaining the same imagery for 30 s. The shorter time window would also allow for nearly twice the amount of viable data taken within the same session time period.

Brain-computer interfaces using fNIRS show great promise for both the neuro-muscularly disabled as well as the healthy user. They have far-reaching applications in the fields of computing, telepresence robotics, and prosthetic control, and are becoming increasingly common. Our pilot study demonstrates the feasibility of using a four-class motor imagery-based fNIRS BCI to control a humanoid robot. Additionally, the use of more data and a calibration session immediately prior to the use of the BCI may improve accuracy.

Acknowledgements. This work was supported in part by the National Science Foundation Graduate Research Fellowship under Grant No. DGE-1002809. Work reported here was run on hardware supported by Drexel's University Research Computing Facility.

References

1. Wolpaw, J.R., Birbaumer, N., McFarland, D.J., Pfurtscheller, G., Vaughan, T.M.: Brain–computer interfaces for communication and control. Clin. Neurophysiol. **113**, 767–791 (2002)
2. Leeb, R., Friedman, D., Müller-Putz, G.R., Scherer, R., Slater, M., Pfurtscheller, G.: Self-paced (asynchronous) BCI control of a wheelchair in virtual environments: a case study with a tetraplegic. Comput. Intell. Neurosci. **2007**, 79642 (2007)
3. Chae, Y., Jeong, J., Jo, S.: Toward brain-actuated humanoid robots: asynchronous direct control using an EEG-based BCI. IEEE Trans. Robot. **28**, 1131–1144 (2012)
4. Hochberg, L.R., Bacher, D., Jarosiewicz, B., Masse, N.Y., Simeral, J.D., Vogel, J., Haddadin, S., Liu, J., Cash, S.S., van der Smagt, P., Donoghue, J.P.: Reach and grasp by people with tetraplegia using a neurally controlled robotic arm. Nature **485**, 372–375 (2012)
5. Ayaz, H., Onaral, B., Izzetoglu, K., Shewokis, P.A., McKendrick, R., Parasuraman, R.: Continuous monitoring of brain dynamics with functional near infrared spectroscopy as a tool for neuroergonomic research: empirical examples and a technological development. Front. Hum. Neurosci. **7**, 871 (2013)
6. Jeannerod, M.: Mental imagery in the motor context. Neuropsychologia **33**, 1419–1432 (1995)
7. Naseer, N., Hong, K.-S.: Functional near-infrared spectroscopy based brain activity classification for development of a brain-computer interface. In: International Conference on Robotics and Artificial Intelligence (ICRAI), pp. 174–178 (2012)
8. Lotze, M., Halsband, U.: Motor imagery. J. Physiol. **99**, 386–395 (2006)
9. Miller, K.J., Schalk, G., Fetz, E.E., den Nijs, M., Ojemann, J.G., Rao, R.P.N.: Cortical activity during motor execution, motor imagery, and imagery-based online feedback. Proc. Nat. Acad. Sci. **107**, 4430–4435 (2010)
10. Ayaz, H., Shewokis, P.A., Bunce, S., Izzetoglu, K., Willems, B., Onaral, B.: Optical brain monitoring for operator training and mental workload assessment. Neuroimage **59**, 36–47 (2012)
11. Rodrigo, A.H., Di Domenico, S.I., Ayaz, H., Gulrajani, S., Lam, J., Ruocco, A.C.: Differentiating functions of the lateral and medial prefrontal cortex in motor response inhibition. Neuroimage. **85(Part 1)**, 423–431 (2014)
12. Wriessnegger, S.C., Kurzmann, J., Neuper, C.: Spatio-temporal differences in brain oxygenation between movement execution and imagery: a multichannel near-infrared spectroscopy study. Int. J. Psychophysiol. **67**, 54–63 (2008)
13. Leff, D.R., Orihuela-Espina, F., Elwell, C.E., Athanasiou, T., Delpy, D.T., Darzi, A.W., Yang, G.-Z.: Assessment of the cerebral cortex during motor task behaviours in adults: a systematic review of functional near infrared spectroscopy (fNIRS) studies. Neuroimage **54**, 2922–2936 (2011)
14. Power, S.D., Kushki, A., Chau, T.: Towards a system-paced near-infrared spectroscopy brain–computer interface: differentiating prefrontal activity due to mental arithmetic and mental singing from the no-control state. J. Neural Eng. **8**, 66004 (2011)

15. Ayaz, H., Shewokis, P.A., Bunce, S., Onaral, B.: An optical brain computer interface for environmental control. In: Annual International Conference of the IEEE Engineering in Medicine and Biology Society (EMBC), Boston, MA, pp. 6327–6330 (2011)
16. Ayaz, H., Shewokis, P.A., Bunce, S., Schultheis, M., Onaral, B.: Assessment of cognitive neural correlates for a functional near infrared-based brain computer interface system. In: Schmorrow, D.D., Estabrooke, I.V., Grootjen, M. (eds.) FAC 2009. LNCS, vol. 5638, pp. 699–708. Springer, Heidelberg (2009)
17. Gateau, T., Durantin, G., Lancelot, F., Scannella, S., Dehais, F.: Real-time state estimation in a flight simulator using fNIRS. PLoS ONE 10, e0121279 (2015)
18. Abdelnour, A.F., Huppert, T.: Real-time imaging of human brain function by near-infrared spectroscopy using an adaptive general linear model. Neuroimage 46, 133–143 (2009)
19. Shin, J., Jeong, J.: Multiclass classification of hemodynamic responses for performance improvement of functional near-infrared spectroscopy-based brain–computer interface. J. Biomed. Opt. 19, 67009 (2014)
20. Coyle, S.M., Ward, T.E., Markham, C.M.: Brain-computer interface using a simplified functional near-infrared spectroscopy system. J. Neural Eng. 4, 219 (2007)
21. Naseer, N., Hong, K.-S.: Classification of functional near-infrared spectroscopy signals corresponding to the right- and left-wrist motor imagery for development of a brain–computer interface. Neurosci. Lett. 553, 84–89 (2013)
22. Ayaz, H., Izzetoglu, M., Bunce, S., Heiman-Patterson, T., Onaral, B.: Detecting cognitive activity related hemodynamic signal for brain computer interface using functional near infrared spectroscopy. In: 3rd International IEEE/EMBS Conference on Neural Engineering, Kohala Coast, Hawaii, pp. 342–345 (2007)
23. Villringer, A., Chance, B.: Non-invasive optical spectroscopy and imaging of human brain function. Trends Neurosci. 20, 435–442 (1997)
24. Zimmermann, R., Marchal-Crespo, L., Edelmann, J., Lambercy, O., Fluet, M.-C., Riener, R., Wolf, M., Gassert, R.: Detection of motor execution using a hybrid fNIRS-biosignal BCI: a feasibility study. J. Neuroeng. Rehabil. 10, 4 (2013)
25. Fazli, S., Mehnert, J., Steinbrink, J., Curio, G., Villringer, A., Müller, K.-R., Blankertz, B.: Enhanced performance by a hybrid NIRS-EEG brain computer interface. Neuroimage 59, 519–529 (2012)
26. Liu, Y., Ayaz, H., Curtin, A., Onaral, B., Shewokis, P.A.: Towards a hybrid P300-based BCI using simultaneous fNIR and EEG. In: Schmorrow, D.D., Fidopiastis, C.M. (eds.) AC 2013. LNCS, vol. 8027, pp. 335–344. Springer, Heidelberg (2013)
27. Koo, B., Lee, H.-G., Nam, Y., Kang, H., Koh, C.S., Shin, H.-C., Choi, S.: A hybrid NIRS-EEG system for self-paced brain computer interface with online motor imagery. J. Neurosci. Meth. 244, 26–32 (2015)
28. Doud, A.J., Lucas, J.P., Pisansky, M.T., He, B.: Continuous three-dimensional control of a virtual helicopter using a motor imagery based brain-computer interface. PLoS ONE 6, e26322 (2011)
29. Ge, S., Wang, R., Yu, D.: Classification of four-class motor imagery employing single-channel electroencephalography. PLoS ONE 9, e98019 (2014)
30. Yi, W., Zhang, L., Wang, K., Xiao, X., He, F., Zhao, X., Qi, H., Zhou, P., Wan, B., Ming, D.: Evaluation and comparison of effective connectivity during simple and compound limb motor imagery. In: Annual International Conference of the IEEE Engineering in Medicine and Biology Society (EMBC). IEEE, Chicago (2014)
31. Sitaram, R., Zhang, H., Guan, C., Thulasidas, M., Hoshi, Y., Ishikawa, A., Shimizu, K., Birbaumer, N.: Temporal classification of multichannel near-infrared spectroscopy signals of motor imagery for developing a brain-computer interface. Neuroimage 34, 1416–1427 (2007)

32. Ito, T., Akiyama, H., Hirano, T.: Brain machine interface using portable near-infrared spectroscopy - improvement of classification performance based on ICA analysis and self-proliferating LVQ. In: IEEE/RSJ International Conference on Intelligent Robots and Systems, Tokyo, Japan, pp. 851–858 (2013)

33. LaFleur, K., Cassady, K., Doud, A., Shades, K., Rogin, E., He, B.: Quadcopter control in three-dimensional space using a noninvasive motor imagery-based brain–computer interface. J. Neural Eng. **10**, 46003 (2013)

34. Barbosa, A.O.G., Achanccaray, D.R., Meggiolaro, M.A.: Activation of a mobile robot through a brain computer interface. In: IEEE International Conference on Robotics and Automation (ICRA), Anchorage, Alaska, pp. 4815–4821 (2010)

35. Li, W., Li, M., Zhao, J.: Control of humanoid robot via motion-onset visual evoked potentials. Front. Syst. Neurosci. **8**, 247 (2015)

36. Choi, B., Jo, S.: A low-cost EEG system-based hybrid brain-computer interface for humanoid robot navigation and recognition. PLoS ONE **8**, e74583 (2013)

37. Cohen, O., Druon, S., Lengagne, S., Mendelsohn, A., Malach, R., Kheddar, A., Friedman, D.: fMRI robotic embodiment: a pilot study. In: 4th IEEE RAS/EMBS International Conference on Biomedical Robotics and Biomechatronics (BioRob), pp. 314–319 (2012)

38. Ahn, M., Jun, S.C.: Performance variation in motor imagery brain–computer interface: a brief review. J. Neurosci. Meth. **243**, 103–110 (2015)

39. Tidoni, E., Gergondet, P., Kheddar, A., Aglioti, S.M.: Audio-visual feedback improves the BCI performance in the navigational control of a humanoid robot. Front. Neurorobot. **8**, 20 (2014)

40. Canning, C., Scheutz, M.: Functional near-infrared spectroscopy in human-robot interaction. J. Human-Robot Interact. **2**, 62–84 (2013)

41. Kishi, S., Luo, Z., Nagano, A., Okumura, M., Nagano, Y., Yamanaka, Y.: On NIRS-based BRI for a human-interactive robot RI-MAN. In: Joint 4th International Conference on Soft Computing and Intelligent Systems and 9th International Symposium on Advanced Intelligent Systems (SCIS & ISIS), Nagoya, Japan, pp. 124–129 (2008)

42. Takahashi, K., Maekawa, S., Hashimoto, M.: Remarks on fuzzy reasoning-based brain activity recognition with a compact near infrared spectroscopy device and its application to robot control interface. In: International Conference on Control, Decision and Information Technologies (CoDIT), pp. 615–620. IEEE, Metz (2014)

43. Tumanov, K., Goebel, R., Möckel, R., Sorger, B., Weiss, G.: fNIRS-based BCI for robot control. In: Proceedings of the 2015 International Conference on Autonomous Agents and Multiagent Systems. International Foundation for Autonomous Agents and Multiagent Systems, pp. 1953–1954 (2015)

44. Batula, A.M., Ayaz, H., Kim, Y.E.: Evaluating a four-class motor-imagery-based optical brain-computer interface. In: Proceedings of the Annual International Conference of the IEEE Engineering in Medicine and Biology Society, pp. 2000–2003. IEEE, Chicago (2014)

45. Ayaz, H., Allen, S.L., Platek, S.M., Onaral, B.: Maze Suite 1.0: A complete set of tools to prepare, present, and analyze navigational and spatial cognitive neuroscience experiments. Behav. Res. Meth. **40**, 353–359 (2008)

46. Ha, I., Tamura, Y., Asama, H., Han, J., Hong, D.W.: Development of open humanoid platform DARwIn-OP. In: Proceedings of SICE Annual Conference, Tokyo, Japan, pp. 2178–2181 (2011)

47. Pedregosa, F., Varoquaux, G., Gramfort, A., Michel, V., Thirion, B., Grisel, O., Blondel, M., Prettenhofer, P., Weiss, R., Dubourg, V., Vanderplas, J., Passos, A., Cournapeau, D., Brucher, M., Perrot, M., Duchesnay, E.: Scikit-learn: machine learning in python. J. Mach. Learn. Res. **12**, 2825–2830 (2011)

Using Motor Imagery to Control Brain-Computer Interfaces for Communication

Jonathan S. Brumberg[1,2]([✉]), Jeremy D. Burnison[2], and Kevin M. Pitt[1]

[1] Department of Speech-Language-Hearing: Sciences & Disorders,
University of Kansas, Lawrence, KS, USA
{brumberg,kmp4}@ku.edu
[2] Neuroscience Graduate Program, University of Kansas, Lawrence, KS, USA
jburnison@ku.edu

Abstract. Brain-computer interfaces (BCI) as assistive devices are designed to provide access to communication, navigation, locomotion and environmental interaction to individuals with severe motor impairment. In the present paper, we discuss two approaches to communication using a non-invasive BCI via recording of neurological activity related to motor imagery. The first approach uses modulations of the sensorimotor rhythm related to limb movement imagery to continuously modify the output of an artificial speech synthesizer. The second approach detects event-related changes to neurological activity during single trial motor imagery attempts to control a commercial augmentative and alternative communication device. These two approaches represent two extremes for BCI-based communication ranging from simple, "button-click" operation of a speech generating communication device to continuous modulation of an acoustic output speech synthesizer. The goal of developing along a continuum is to facilitate adoption and use of communication BCIs to a heterogeneous target user population.

Keywords: BCI · Brain-computer interface · Motor imagery · AAC

1 Introduction

Since developing the first computers, technologists have been trying to reduce the separation between users and their devices. Moving from punch cards to keyboards was a dramatic advance, and today we now have reliable voice control, touch screens and adaptive keyboards with language prediction. In addition to improving the manner in which people interact with computers, these new methods are quite useful for providing access to communication systems for individuals with mild to moderate speech and movement disorders. Still, these methods require manual or spoken input, which may not be available to individuals with severe motor impairment and paralysis, specifically, those with locked-in syndrome (LIS) [1] due to stroke and neurodegenerative disorders (e.g., amyotrophic lateral sclerosis, ALS). Locked-in syndrome is characterized by near total paralysis, including the limbs and face, with some remaining eye

© Springer International Publishing Switzerland 2016
D.D. Schmorrow and C.M. Fidopiastis (Eds.): AC 2016, Part I, LNAI 9743, pp. 14–25, 2016.
DOI: 10.1007/978-3-319-39955-3_2

movements and significant amounts of sensation and cognition [2]. Therefore, individuals with LIS require alternative means for accessing language and communication that does not require overt motor control. For those with reliable eye movement control, eye-gaze tracking hardware can be used to control high-tech augmentative and alternative communication devices (AAC), in addition to other user-customized input methods [3,4]. For individuals without reliable oculomotor control, brain-computer interfaces (BCI) may be the only method available to provide access to computers and communication.

The idea behind all BCIs is a straightforward extension of existing assistive technology, albeit to an extreme degree. Consider the case of spelling on a keyboard using an eye-gaze tracker. In this scenario, the user must first determine a desired message, identify all the required elements on the communication display, attend to each element, and make an appropriate oculomotor action to move the eyes and drive the eye-gaze tracking pointer. For an individual with LIS, the final oculomotor stage is impaired to such a degree that eye-gaze tracking is either impossible or unreliable. Individuals who use a button or mouse click to make communication device item selections using linear scanning follow a similar strategy; desired items are identified and attended to, then cortical motor commands are issued to activate limb muscles necessary to activate the selection device. Here too, the final stage of motor command transmission to the periphery is impaired or absent in individuals with LIS. In both examples, the goal of a BCI is to intercept the last reliable neurological control signal available prior to attempted activation of the disordered periphery. For the visual attention example, it is possible to elicit and record the P300 event-related potential (ERP) [5–9], and in the button-click example neurological markers of motor planning and execution for use in communication interfaces [10–14]. A major research area now is focused on translating BCIs from research settings into practical user settings [15,16]. One barrier to this translation process arises since most BCIs use custom communication interface software that may not necessarily be compatible with existing high-tech AAC devices that are already supported by commercial and clinical professionals. In this paper, we describe two motor imagery based BCIs for communication in which one system directly interfaces with existing AAC devices and the other provides direct speech output without the need for a separate communication device.

2   BCI as an AAC Device

One barrier to clinical translation of BCI devices is the reliance on custom communication interfaces that often are not compatible with existing AAC devices. We therefore designed a BCI that does not rely on its own visual interface, rather, it uses existing AAC devices and software to help elicit neurological activity used for BCI control. Electroencephalography (EEG) signals are obtained as participants make covert (or imagined) motor movements of the limbs as they interact with a Tobii C15 communication device (Tobii-DynaVox). The presentation of communication items in a linear scanning protocol is expected to generate neurological signals related to both movement preparation and movement execution.

Specifically, the BCI detects both the contingent negative variation (CNV), a potential related to the preparation of an upcoming, cued movement [17–19], and the event-related (de)synchronization (ERD/S), a change in the sensorimotor rhythm spectral power related to the preparation and execution of overt and covert movement [10–12].

The CNV is an event-related negativity normally elicited in a cue-response paradigm in which a warning stimulus alerts the participant to an upcoming event and a following imperative stimulus instructs the participant to produce a known motor command [17,18]. The linear scanning interface used for this experiment automatically advances sequentially, therefore, all non-target rows and columns can be considered as "warning" stimuli[1] and the target row or column is the "imperative" stimulus. The ERD/S is elicited in response to the preparation and execution of overt and covert motor commands, and are not dependent on a warning stimulus. Typically, an ERD is observed in the μ and β bands (8–14 Hz, 15–25 Hz, respectively) as an attenuation in spectral power around the onset of the intended action. Our BCI uses both movement-related signals to classify neurological activity into intended or unintended actions that are used to send a simulated button-press to the AAC device for item selection, though we only discuss the CNV results below.

2.1   Methods

Six individuals without neurological impairment and one individual with advanced ALS participated in the AAC-based BCI experiment. EEG was recorded continuously from each participant from 62 active electrodes (g.HIAmp, g.tec) at a sampling rate of 512 Hz with notch filters at 58–62 Hz. Participants were seated in a sound-treated booth in front of a simulated AAC device that displayed a preprogrammed communication interface page. The device was configured to automatically highlight each communication item sequentially with a red box (2.5 s interval) and the name of the item was played over the AAC device speakers. Participants were provided with a randomly selected target item and instructed to imagine a movement of their dominant hand every time it was highlighted. EEG signals were bandpass filtered from 0.5–8 Hz to obtain the CNV.

Offline classification of the CNV that preceded overt and covert movement for selecting communication items was accomplished using linear discriminant analysis (LDA) of the average EEG amplitude from -0.23 s to -0.03 s relative to the onset of item highlighting[2]. Bipolar surface electromyography was also collected from the limbs to ensure participants adhered to the motor imagery instructions. Data was collected from 80 item highlighting trials per condition (overt and covert) and performance of the LDA classifier was evaluated using a 2-fold cross validation. In this procedure, the first 40 trials per condition were used to train the classifier and the second 40 trials used for validation, then

---

[1] Though likely strongest for the immediately preceding row or column.

[2] Specifically the auditory signal onset.

the training and validation sets were switched to obtain a full estimate of the performance.

2.2 Results

Analysis of the EEG data indicated that the CNV was present (statistically significantly less than zero, 1-tailed t-test, fdr corrected $p < 0.05$) and spatially located primarily over bilateral parietal electrodes for all participants (see Figs. 1 and 2). In the overt condition, the CNV was characterized by a slow negativity followed by a peak negativity immediately prior to auditory stimulus in the overt condition for participants without neurological impairments. In the covert condition, only the peak negativity prior to auditory stimulus onset was observed for participants without neurological impairments. For the participant with ALS, the overt condition did not elicit demonstrable negativity prior to the auditory stimulus onset, however a slight negativity was observed immediately prior to the auditory stimulus onset in the covert condition.

The cross-validation accuracy of the LDA classifier was 64 % in the overt condition for participants without neurological impairment and 60 % in the covert condition. The cross-validation accuracy of the LDA classifier for the individual with ALS was 63 % in the covert condition, and was not attempted in the overt condition due to the lack of statistically significant CNV response. Table 1 includes a summary of individual and average classification accuracy. For all participants, the classification was based on a 0.2 s window prior to the auditory stimulus onset, however, the number of electrodes differed based on the location of the peak CNV negativity on the scalp. In general, the electrodes were chosen from the CP, P and PO locations, and more electrodes passed our inclusion criteria in the overt condition (average: 3.5, range: 2–7) than the covert condition (average: 1.8, range: 1–3). A similar CNV topography was observed for the individual with ALS, and two electrodes from the CP region were used for decoding.

Table 1. A summary of offline decoding accuracy for all participants, with (P1–6) and without (ALS1) neuromotor impairment in the overt and covert production tasks.

	P1	P2	P3	P4	P5	P6	Average	ALS1
Overt	75.4 %	61.1 %	56.8 %	65.8 %	66.4 %	59.3 %	64.1 %	NA
Covert	60.0 %	55.7 %	58.9 %	60.4 %	63.5 %	61.3 %	60.0 %	62.6 %

2.3 Discussion

The AAC-BCI device described in this experiment is designed to simplify BCI control as much as possible for individuals who already use, or may use BCI in the future. Our approach for achieving this aim is to rely on existing AAC

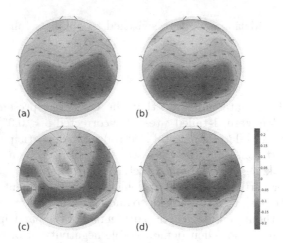

Fig. 1. The topography of average normalized EEG amplitudes in the 200 ms prior to auditory stimulus onset. The average for all participants without impairment in the overt condition is shown in (a) and covert in (b). For both conditions, there is a strong bilateral parietal distribution of negative amplitudes. Similarly, the patterns of negativity for the participant with ALS show bilateral posterior negativity in both the overt (c) and covert (d) conditions, with a slightly right-lateralized response in the covert condition.

technology and techniques that may be most familiar to both users of AAC (who are also potential users of BCI), and AAC professionals. One of the most basic ways for controlling AAC devices is through the use of a physical button and a visual interface with automatically advancing scanning of communication icons. Such a device can be used by individuals with disordered, but present motor control. In this experiment, we extend the existing AAC paradigm to BCI by replacing the AAC item selection mechanism with a "brain switch" controlled using a neurological potential related to motor planning and motor execution in a mental button pressing task.

The contingent negative variation is a very well known neurological potential that precedes movement in a cued paradigm. Classically, this potential is strongest when individuals know they will be required to make a movement in the near future, but both the action and its timing are uncertain [17,18]. In this experiment, however, only a portion of these classical factors used to elicit the CNV are met: (1) movements are made in a cued paradigm and (2) individuals know they will make movements in the near future. The third factor, uncertainty of both action and timing, is not met because the AAC device automatically scans through all available communication items at a predictable rate. Our preliminary results show that the third requirement is not necessary for eliciting the CNV; it is present in our paradigm for both individuals with and without neurological impairments. Further, our offline classification results show it is possible to accurately predict the occurrence of CNVs in a cued motor control paradigm. On average, the LDA classifier performed better in the overt

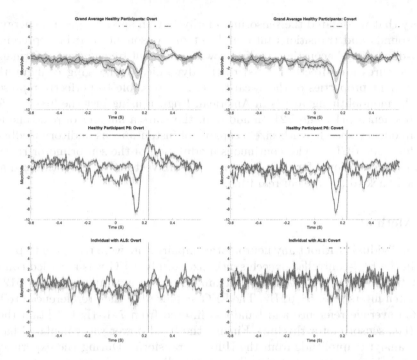

Fig. 2. A graphical summary of average CNV amplitudes for overt (left column) and covert (right column) movements in the AAC selection paradigm. The top row represents average CNVs over all healthy participants (N = 6), the middle row is the average CNV for one healthy participant and the bottom row is the average CNV for one participant with ALS. *: indicates statistically significant differences between target trials (blue) and non-target trials (red), and the shaded ranges indicate the 95 % confidence intervals. (Color figure online)

condition than the covert for individuals without neuromotor impairments. Additionally, the decoder performed marginally better for in the covert condition for the individual with ALS compared to the participants without impairment, though no statistical analysis of these differences was performed. These are promising results that warrant further study of an online decoder for controlling an AAC device in real-time.

3 BCI-Controlled Speech Synthesizer

Our second BCI implementation provides continuous control over a formant frequency based speech synthesizer through detection of modulations to the sensorimotor rhythm [20]. The primary advantage of this system is the distinct lack of a communication interface, rather the user is directly in control of acoustic speech output. This BCI is based on prior work decoding continuous, two-dimensional control signals from the EEG sensorimotor rhythm [14]. In previous studies, participants learned to control a two-dimensional cursor by performing limb motor imagery that modulated the sensorimotor rhythm. In speech, spectral energy of vowel sounds and transitions into, and out of, consonants can be represented by low-dimensional acoustic features known as formant frequencies, or formants. These features are directly related to the dynamically changing configuration and resonant properties of the vocal tract. It is possible to perfectly represent all of the monophthong vowels in American English using just the first two formant frequencies (F1 and F2). In addition, there are a number of real-time formant frequency speech synthesizers capable of instantaneous auditory feedback. Therefore, our BCI decodes continuous modulation of the sensorimotor rhythm into a two-dimensional formant frequency feature vector that is synthesized and provided back to the user in real-time.

3.1   Methods

Three individuals without any neuromotor impairments were recruited to participate in the BCI-controlled speech synthesizer study. EEG was recorded continuously from 62 active electrodes (g.HIAmp, g.tec) at a sampling rate of 512 Hz with notch filters from 58–62 Hz. The EEG signals were then rereferenced to the common average reference and bandpass filtered from 7–15 Hz to obtain the μ band (i.e., sensorimotor rhythm). Finally, the band power was calculated based on the analytic amplitude from the Hilbert transform. During the experiment, vowel sounds were presented visually as a two-dimensional cursor position on a display with the positions of the three test vowels (/a/, /u/ and /i/). Auditory stimuli (and BCI feedback) were synthesized in real-time using the Snack Sound Toolkit (KTH Royal Institute of Technology) and played through pneumatic insert earphones (ER1, Etymotic, Inc.). Participants were instructed to imagine moving their right hand when presented with an /a/ stimulus, their left hand for the /u/ stimulus and their feet for the /i/ stimulus.

During training, participants were asked to imagine the appropriate movement throughout the entire 3 s stimulus period. A total of 135 trials were presented (45 trials per vowel) with vowels in random order. The sensorimotor bandpower and target vowel formant frequency velocities (bark/s) were used to estimate the state and likelihood models of a Kalman filter decoder. Formant velocities are taken as the change in formant frequency over time. Offline training and performance was evaluated using a two-fold cross-validation of the correlation coefficient of each formant velocity trajectory to the target vector, and the combined 2D formant velocity trajectories.

3.2   Results

The procedure for training the Kalman filter decoder revealed asymmetric linear model weights over the left and right sensorimotor areas (C, CP and FC electrodes) contralateral to the intended movement imagery. In contrast, the model weights for relating sensorimotor rhythm modulations to the second formant

Table 2. Pearson's correlation coefficient (r) of the Kalman filter decoder for predicting formant frequency velocities in the synthesizer BCI.

	F1	F2	Combined
Training set	0.50	0.68	0.66
Validation set	0.35	0.62	0.51

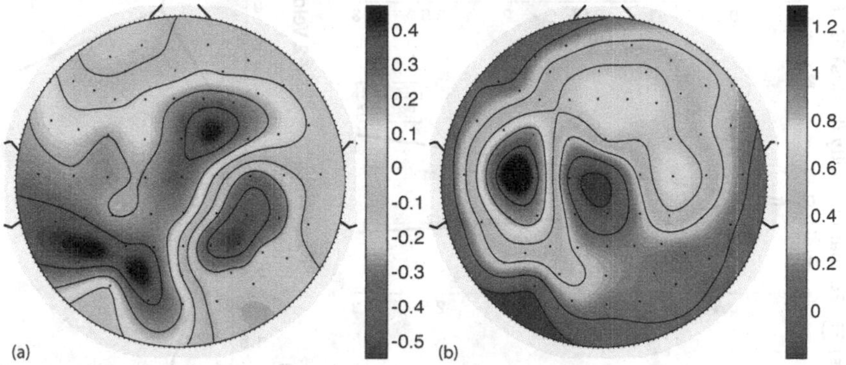

Fig. 3. The Kalman filter decoder linear model weights for each formant velocity dimension reveal contribution of the sensorimotor electrodes to the motor imagery task. (a) The model weights for F1 velocities show asymmetric model weights with sign contralateral to the intended left or right limb movement imagery (/u/ and /a/ vowels). (b) The model weights for F2 velocities show symmetric model weights for the bilateral foot movement imagery task (/i/ sound)

frequency are symmetric and bilateral. The model weights are shown graphically in Fig. 3 and confirm the involvement of sensorimotor areas in the motor imagery task.

A two-fold cross-validation procedure was used to evaluate the offline performance of the trained Kalman filter decoder. The model predicted formant velocities are shown graphically in Fig. 4. In this figure, the average predicted formant frequency velocities are shown on the left for /i/ (top), /a/ (middle) and /u/ (bottom) with 95 % confidence intervals (shaded regions) and velocity targets in black. These trajectories are shown on the 2D formant velocity plane in Fig. 4(d) for the /i/ (blue), /a/ (red) and /u/ (yellow) vowels. From this view, it is possible to observe a more faithful prediction of /i/ vowel velocities compared to the /a/ and /u/ vowels; however, there is greater overall congruence when the velocities are integrated in time to obtain final predicted formant frequencies (Fig. 4(d)). These results, quantitatively summarized in Table 2, indicate a moderate (r = 0.51) correlation between the predicted and target 2D formant velocity trajectories as well as the correlations of the individual formants to their targets (F1: r= 0.35, F2: r = 0.62).

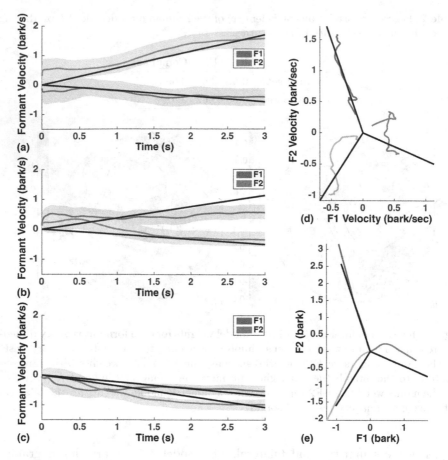

Fig. 4. (Left) A graphical summary of the first and second formant frequency velocities (F1 blue, F2 red) for the /i/, /a/ and /u/ vowels, respectively in subfigures (a), (b) and (c). Shaded regions represent the 95 % confidence interval and the black lines represent target formant velocity trajectories. (right) A graphical summary of the predicted formant frequency velocities (d) and integrated formants (e) on the 2D formant plane. Here, the blue line is the average predicted model response for /i/, the red line for /a/ and the yellow line for /u/. The black lines are the target formant responses. Note, the integrated formants are centered based on the average of the three tested vowels. (Color figure online)

3.3   Discussion

The BCI-controlled speech synthesizer is fundamentally a limb motor imagery based BCI for decoding a continuous 2D output vector (similar to [14]), but in both auditory and visual feedback domains related to speech. Therefore, we can examine the results of our single pilot participant to determine whether our protocol, paradigm and BCI algorithms are functioning appropriately. Specifically, we can examine the Kalman filter linear model weights, which represent the relationship between modulations in the 7–15 Hz sensorimotor rhythm and target formant velocity for each vowel production – motor imagery trial. In this way, the model weights themselves are informative for determining the spatial topography of EEG activity participants use to complete the vowel synthesizer task.

The results of our offline decoding analysis reveal a scalp topography of model weights that reflect differential activation for the control of the first formant frequency, and coordinated activation for controlling the second formant frequency. This asymmetric response is expected because we asked participants to use contralateral limb motor imagery for the vowels /a/ and /u/ which differ almost entirely in the first formant. Similarly, a coordinated, bilateral topography for controlling the second format agrees with the instructed task for associating bilateral foot movement imagery with productions of the vowel /i/, which primarily differs from /a/ and /u/ in the second formant. Finally, the moderate correlation of predicted formant frequency velocities to targets is promising for continued investigation in an online control paradigm. The addition of closed-loop feedback of audio and visual information, should help to generate error control signals used to improve the continuous BCI control for the production of the vowels /a/, /i/ and /u/.

4   Conclusions

In the present paper, we examine two BCIs for communication using two separate control techniques. In the first example, we extend existing AAC input signal designs for accessing communication software programs using a "brain switch." This approach decodes and uses the neurological potentials related to a mental button pressing task to select items on a communication interface. Our preliminary evidence provides some encouraging results for continuing to explore this BCI application in real-time with additional participants with and without neurological impairments. In the second example, we validated our approach for decoding continuously varying two-dimensional formant frequencies from sensorimotor rhythm modulations. Our modeling results are compatible with past studies of SMR-based BCIs for 2D cursor control, and the offline prediction of formant frequencies is reliable enough for additional study of online control of a speech synthesizer via BCI.

Acknowledgments. This work was supported in part by the National Institutes of Health (R03-DC011304), the University of Kansas New Faculty General Research Fund and the American Speech-Language-Hearing Foundation.

24   J.S. Brumberg et al.

References

1. Plum, F., Posner, J.B.: The diagnosis of stupor and coma. Contemp. Neurol. Ser. **10**, 1–286 (1972)
2. Bauer, G., Gerstenbrand, F., Rumpl, E.: Varieties of the locked-in syndrome. J. Neurol. **221**(2), 77–91 (1979)
3. Beukelman, D., Fager, S., Nordness, A.: Communication support for people with ALS. Neurol. Res. Int. **2011**, 714693 (2011)
4. Fager, S., Beukelmanm, D.R., Fried-Oken, M., Jakobs, T., Baker, J.: Access interface strategies. Assistive Technol. Official J. RESNA **24**(1), 25–33 (2012)
5. Donchin, E., Spencer, K.M., Wijesinghe, R.: The mental prosthesis: assessing the speed of a P300-based brain-computer interface. IEEE Trans. Rehabil. Eng. **8**(2), 174–179 (2000)
6. Acqualagna, L., Blankertz, B.: Gaze-independent BCI-spelling using rapid serial visual presentation (RSVP). Clin. Neurophysiol. **124**(5), 901–908 (2013)
7. Krusienski, D.J., Sellers, E.W., McFarland, D.J., Vaughan, T.M., Wolpaw, J.R.: Toward enhanced P300 speller performance. J. Neurosci. Meth. **167**(1), 15–21 (2008)
8. Nijboer, F., Sellers, E.W., Mellinger, J., Jordan, M.A., Matuz, T., Furdea, A., Halder, S., Mochty, U., Krusienski, D.J., Vaughan, T.M., Wolpaw, J.R., Birbaumer, N., Kübler, A.: A P300-based brain-computer interface for people with amyotrophic lateral sclerosis. Clin. Neurophysiol. **119**(8), 1909–1916 (2008)
9. Oken, B.S., Orhan, U., Roark, B., Erdogmus, D., Fowler, A., Mooney, A., Peters, B., Miller, M., Fried-Oken, M.B.: Brain-computer interface with language model-electroencephalography fusion for locked-in syndrome. Neurorehabilitation Neural Repair **28**(4), 387–394 (2014)
10. Pfurtscheller, G., Neuper, C.: Motor imagery and direct brain-computer communication. Proc. IEEE **89**(7), 1123–1134 (2001)
11. Blankertz, B., Dornhege, G., Krauledat, M., Müller, K.R., Kunzmann, V., Losch, F., Curio, G.: The Berlin brain-computer interface: EEG-based communication without subject training. IEEE Trans. Neural Syst. Rehabil. Eng. **14**(2), 147–152 (2006)
12. Neuper, C., Müller-Putz, G.R., Scherer, R., Pfurtscheller, G.: Motor imagery and EEG-based control of spelling devices and neuroprostheses. Prog. Brain Res. **159**, 393–409 (2006)
13. Ramoser, H., Müller-Gerking, J., Pfurtscheller, G.: Optimal spatial filtering of single trial EEG during imagined hand movement. IEEE Trans. Rehabil. Eng. **8**(4), 441–446 (2000)
14. Wolpaw, J.R., McFarland, D.J.: Control of a two-dimensional movement signal by a noninvasive brain-computer interface in humans. Proc. Nat. Acad. Sci. U.S.A **101**(51), 17849 (2004)
15. Kleih, S.C., Kaufmann, T., Zickler, C., Halder, S., Leotta, F., Cincotti, F., Aloise, F., Riccio, A., Herbert, C., Mattia, D., Kübler, A.: Out of the frying pan into the fire-the P300-based BCI faces real-world challenges. In: Schouenborg, J., Garwicz, M., Danielsen, N. (eds.) Progress in Brain Research, vol. 194, 1st edn, pp. 27–46. Elsevier B.V., New York (2011). Chap. 2
16. Vaughan, T.M., McFarland, D.J., Schalk, G., Sarnacki, W.A., Krusienski, D.J., Sellers, E.W., Wolpaw, J.R.: The wadsworth BCI research and development program: at home with BCI. IEEE Trans. Neural Syst. Rehabil. Eng. **14**(2), 229–233 (2006)

17. Walter, W.G., Cooper, R., Aldridge, V.J., McCALLUM, W.C., Winter, A.L.: Contingent negative variation : an electric sign of sensori-motor association and expectancy in the human brain. Nature **203**(4943), 380–384 (1964)
18. Rohrbaugh, J.W., Syndulko, K., Lindsley, D.B.: Brain wave components of the contingent negative variation in humans. Science (New York, N.Y.) **191**(4231), 1055–1057 (1976)
19. Funderud, I., Lindgren, M., Løvstad, M., Endestad, T., Voytek, B., Knight, R.T., Solbakk, A.K.: Differential Go/NoGo activity in both contingent negative variation and spectral power. PLoS ONE **7**(10), e48504 (2012)
20. Guenther, F.H., Brumberg, J.S.: Brain-machine interfaces for real-time speech synthesis. In: Proceedings of the 33rd Annual International Conference of the IEEE Engineering in Medicine and Biology Society (EMBC 2011), Boston, MA (2011)

An Online Gaze-Independent BCI System Used Dummy Face with Eyes Only Region as Stimulus

Long Chen, Brendan Z. Allison, Yu Zhang, Xingyu Wang$^{(\boxtimes)}$, and Jing Jin$^{(\boxtimes)}$

Key Laboratory of Advanced Control and Optimization for Chemical Processes, Ministry of Education, East China University of Science and Technology, Shanghai, China
xywang_ecust@126.com, jinjingat@gmail.com

Abstract. The gaze-independent brain-computer interface (BCI) based on rapid serial visual presentation (RSVP) is an extension of the oddball paradigm, and can facilitate communication for people with severe neuromuscular disorders. Some studies suggested that a face with eyes only (without other facial features) could evoke ERPs as high as a complete face. To evaluate the performance of a BCI system, an online system is needed. In this paper, we compared two types of stimuli: a dummy face with eyes only and a colored circle. Ten healthy subjects (8 male, aged 24–28 years, mean 26 ± 1.5) participated in our experiment. The results showed that the dummy face with eyes only had substantial advantages in online classification accuracy ($t = 2.3$, $p = 0.04$) and information transfer rate ($t = 3.4$, $p = 0.003$). Results from users' feedback also showed that the dummy face with eyes only stimulus was more easily accepted ($t = 4.12$, $p < 0.001$).

Keywords: Event-related potentials · Brain-computer interface (BCI) · Dummy face with eyes only · Gaze-independent

1 Introduction

Brain-computer interfaces (BCI) create a new link between the brain and an external device, which provides an alternative means of device control for people with severe paralysis [1–3]. The P300 is an endogenous component of the event-related potential (ERP) that reflects cognitive process such as attention and working memory [4]. With some paradigms, P300 differences can be elicited without shifting gaze, because attention can be oriented separately from eye movement [5]. This is the reason that the classical speller is considered independent [6]. However, Treder and Blankertz (2010) addressed this question by conducting experiments in both overt and covert attention conditions [7]. Brunner et al. (2010) also indicated that successful operation of the classical P300 speller substantially depends on gaze direction. However, the accuracies of the subjects were also very low [8]. Acqualagna et al. introduced and evaluated a gaze-independent BCI based on RSVP with overt attention and feature attention conditions [9]. The RSVP speller is suitable for patients with deterioration of oculomotor control. Recently, Daly

© Springer International Publishing Switzerland 2016
D.D. Schmorrow and C.M. Fidopiastis (Eds.): AC 2016, Part I, LNAI 9743, pp. 26–34, 2016.
DOI: 10.1007/978-3-319-39955-3_3

et al. reported that the gaze-independent BCIs based on RSVP used dummy face pictures as stimuli obtained high performance [10]. However, in the research of gaze-independent BCIs based on RSVP, the users' fatigue had not been taken seriously. Therefore, an improved paradigm with assessment of subjective user factors was needed, which could improve the performance of BCIs and make users more relaxed. Itier et al. reported that face-specific effects were mediated by the eye region when faces were used as stimuli [11]. That is, compared with mouths and noses, the eyes play more important roles when human faces are as stimuli in BCIs. So in terms of evoking distinct ERPs for BCIs, complete faces have no decisive advantage over faces stimuli with eyes only region [12].

In this paper, to further assess the performance of the online gaze-independent BCI system with the dummy face with eyes only approach, we explored two paradigms. These were called the "colored circle pattern (CCP)" paradigm and "dummy face with eyes only pattern (DFP)" paradigm. We assessed online and offline performance, including subjective measures (via questionnaires) as well as objective results. Two types of stimuli were colored circle and dummy faces with eyes only region, respectively.

2   Materials and Methods

2.1   Subjects

Ten healthy subjects (8 male, aged 24–28 years, mean 26 ± 1.5) participated in this study, and are designated P1 … P10. All subjects signed a written consent form prior to this experiment and were paid for their participation.

2.2   Stimuli and Procedure

Before recording began, subjects were prepared for EEG recording. We recorded from 14 EEG electrode positions based on the extended International 10–20 system [13–15]. These electrodes were Cz, Pz, Oz, Fz, F3, F4, C3, C4, P3, P4, P7, P8, PO7 and PO8. The right mastoid electrode was used as the reference and the front electrode (FPz) was used as the ground. EEG signals were recorded with a g.USBamp and a g.EEGcap (Guger Technologies, Graz, Austria) with a sensitivity of 100 μV, band pass filtered between 0.1 and 30 Hz [16–18].

After electrode preparation, we explained the task to the subjects. Their task was to silently count each time a specific "target" stimulus flashed. We explained that all stimuli would flash sequentially, always in the center of the monitor, and that subjects would sometimes have breaks during which the flashes stopped (see Fig. 2). During these breaks, subjects would be asked to report the number of flashes, and then the procedure would repeat with a new target (Fig. 1).

This study used had two conditions, which differed only in the stimuli used. One condition used the colored circle paradigm (CCP), while the other condition used the dummy face paradigm (DFP). Each condition used six different stimuli (see Fig. 2). The CCP paradigm used colored circles, while the DFP condition used cartoon faces.

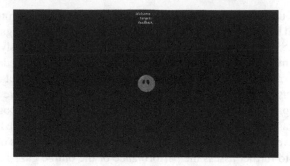

Fig. 1. One example of a flash in the DFP condition. The CCP condition was similar, but used colored circles without the cartoon eyes. (Color figure online)

All twelve of these stimuli were the same size and brightness, and were developed through Photoshop.

Throughout this paper, the term 'flash' refers to each brief stimulus presentation. Stimuli were flashed for 200 ms, with a 100 ms delay between flashes (see Fig. 2). Thus, each trial (meaning a sequence of six flashes) lasted 1.8 s. A trial block refers to a group of trials with the same target. During offline testing, there were 16 trials per trial block and each run consisted of 5 trial blocks, each of which used a different target. During online testing, the number of trials per trial block was adaptive, as described below.

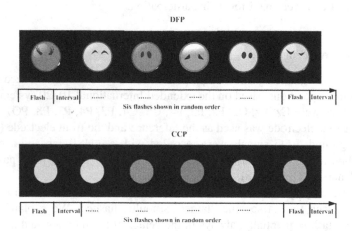

Fig. 2. The timing of each trial. DFP is the dummy face paradigm; CCP is the colored circle paradigm. One trial consists of 6 'image' phases and 6 'interval' phases, and one trial block for choosing one picture consists of several repetitions of the trial. The durations of the 'image' and 'interval' phases are 200 and 100 ms, respectively. The DFP and CCP conditions were identical in terms of timing. (Color figure online)

Prior to each trial block, one of the six stimuli used in that condition was presented in the center of the screen for 3 s, and subjects were told that this stimulus was the new target. Subjects had a 5 min break after each offline run. We first completed two offline runs, and then used the data to train two classifiers (one for each condition). Subjects then had a 3 min break, followed by an online experiment for one condition, then 5 min break, and then an online experiment for another condition. The order of the conditions was determined pseudorandomly. Subjects attempted to identify 24 targets during online testing.

2.3 Data Processing

The first 800 ms of EEG after each flash was used for feature extraction. A pre-stimulus interval of 100 ms was used for baseline correction of single trials. The raw feature matrix is 14×204 for each single flash, since there were 14 channels and 204 samples per trial. Raw features from each channel were down-sampled from 256 Hz to 64 Hz by selecting every fourth sample from the filtered EEG. The size of the resulting feature vector was 14×51 (14 channels by 51 time points). No special signal pre-processing in addition to conventional filtering. We performed a third order Butterworth filter (1–30 Hz). Classification relied on Bayesian linear discriminant analysis (BLDA). BLDA is an extension of Fisher's linear discriminant analysis (FLDA) that avoids over fitting and possibly noisy datasets. The detail of the algorithm can be found in [15]. The online runs used an adaptive strategy with a variable number of trials per average [18].

2.4 Subjective Report

After completing the last online run, each subject was asked two questions (in Chinese) about each of the two conditions. These questions could be answered on a 1–5 scale indicating strong disagreement, moderate disagreement, neutrality, moderate agreement, or strong agreement. The two questions were:

1. Did this paradigm make you tired?
2. Was this paradigm hard?

3 Results

3.1 Objective Results - ERPs

Figure 3 shows the amplitude differences for the target vs. non-target comparison for each of the ten subjects across the three peaks studied in both conditions. These differences are presented at the electrode sites selected for statistical analysis. Electrode site P7 was selected for the N200 analysis. Electrode site Pz was selected for the P300 analysis because it is commonly largest at Pz. Electrode site Cz was selected for the N400 analysis because it typically contains the largest N400. The peak values of the difference ERPs (target minus non-target) with specific time windows were compared

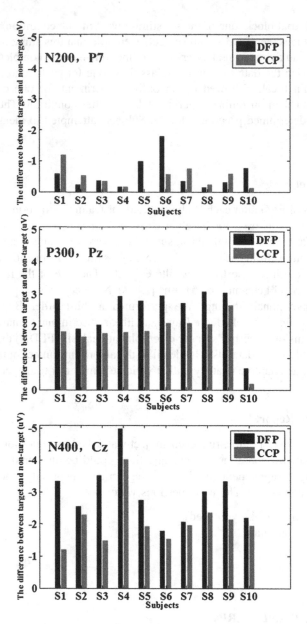

Fig. 3. Upper panel: The amplitude difference of the N200 between target and non-target ERP amplitudes at electrode P7 across 10 subjects (μV); Middle panel: The amplitude difference of the P300 between target and non-target ERP amplitudes at electrode Pz across 10 subjects (μV); Lower panel: The amplitude difference of the N400 between target and non-target ERP amplitudes at electrode Cz across 10 subjects (μV). (Color figure online)

between the two conditions over all subjects by using paired samples t-tests. The time windows were: N200 (150 to 280 ms); P300 (280 to 450 ms), and N400 (450 to 710 ms). At site P7, N200 amplitude (target minus non-target) showed no statistically significant difference between the two conditions (t = 0.62, p = 0.54). At site Pz, P300 amplitude (target minus non-target) was significantly larger (more positive) for DFP compared to CCP (t = 2.27, p = 0.04). At electrode Cz, the N400 amplitude (target minus non-target) was significantly larger (more negative) for DFP compared to CCP (t = 2.29, p = 0.03).

Table 1 shows online classification accuracy, information transfer rate, and number of trials per average for each condition. Paired samples t-tests were used to examine differences between the DFP and CCP. Classification accuracy and information transfer rate were significantly higher for the DFP condition than the CCP condition (t = 2.3, p = 0.03 and t = 3.4, p = 0.003 respectively). The DFP condition required significantly fewer trials per average than the CCP condition (t = 2.4, p = 0.04).

Table 1. Classification accuracy, raw bit rate and number of trials based on averaged data from online experiments. In this table, 'Acc' refers to classification accuracy, 'RBR' refers to raw bit rate, measured in bits/min, and 'NT' refers to number of trials. 'DFP' denotes the dummy face with eyes only region pattern and 'CCP' denotes colored circle pattern.

		S1	S2	S3	S4	S5	S6	S7	S8	S9	S10	Average
Acc (%)	DFP	100	79.1	91.7	95.8	100	95.8	75	95.8	91.7	100	92.5 ± 8.7
	CCP	70.8	33.3	62.5	75	87.5	95.8	83.3	83.3	91.7	20.8	70.4 ± 25.0
RBR	DF-P	40.6	17.9	32.3	31.4	40.5	37.2	15.4	35.1	27.8	41.4	32 ± 9.2
	CCP	13.4	1.7	10.5	16.5	23.7	33.1	21.7	21.4	25.9	0.1	16 ± 10.6
NT	DFP	2.1	2.5	2	2.3	2.1	2.2	2.8	2.1	2.3	2.1	2.3 ± 0.3
	CCP	2.6	2.3	2.4	2.4	2.5	2.3	2.4	2.4	2.5	2.8	2.5 ± 0.2

3.2 Objective Results – BCI Performance

Figure 4 shows the mean classification accuracies based on offline data from each subjects using 15-fold cross-validation. The mean classification accuracy was calculated based on single-trial (not averaged) data. This analysis showed that the DFP is higher than the CCP in classification accuracy (t = 3.86, p < 0.001). The overall mean classification accuracies of all subjects based on single-trial data were 73.5 % ± 10 % (DFP) and 51.6 % ± 12 % (CCP).

3.3 Subjective Results – Questionnaire Replies

Table 2 shows subjects' responses to the two questions. A paired-samples t-test was used to examine mean differences between the DFP and CCP. Subjects reported lower fatigue in the DFP condition than in the CCP condition (t = 4.98, p < 0.001). Subjects also reported that the DFP condition was less difficult than the CCP condition (t = 4.12, p < 0.001).

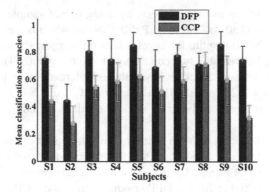

Fig. 4. Mean single-trial classification accuracies across 10 subjects. (Color figure online)

Table 2. Fatigue level and difficulty level of the two conditions, based on subjective report. In this table, 'FL' refers to fatigue level, and 'DL' refers to difficulty level. 'DFP' denotes the dummy face pattern, and 'CCP' denotes the circle pattern.

		S1	S2	S3	S4	S5	S6	S7	S8	S9	S10	Average
DFP	FL	2.5	2	3.5	3	2	2	1.5	2	2	0.5	2.10 ± 0.81
	DL	1	0.5	0.5	2.5	1.5	0.5	1	1	0.5	1.5	1.05 ± 0.64
CCP	FL	4	4.5	4.5	4	2.5	4	3	4	3	4.5	2.85 ± 0.78
	DL	2	3.5	2	2	2	1	3.5	2	3	3	2.40 ± 0.80

4 Discussions

For gaze-independent BCIs based on RSVP, users' subjective report had not been fully considered. Therefore, we assessed users' fatigue and perceived task difficulty, as well as objective performance. Itier et al. had proved that face elicited high event related potential were mediated by the eye region [10]. That is, the eyes may be central to what makes faces so special [10]. We suggested that the dummy face with eyes only was better suited than a completed dummy face for a gaze-independent BCI based on RSVP, since the dummy face with eyes only approach could be simpler and less distracting. However, we had not explored explore this approach online.

The offline results showed that, relative to CCP, DFP elicited a higher P300 (target minus non-target, $p < 0.05$) at Pz and N400 (target minus non-target, $p < 0.05$) at Cz. The DFP had no significant advantage in terms of the N200 (target minus non-target, $p > 0.05$) at P7 compared to the CCP pattern. The DFP had an advantage over CCP in terms of offline classification accuracies ($p < 0.05$). The online results showed that the online classification accuracies ($p < 0.05$) and information transfer rates ($p < 0.05$) of DFP were better than CCP. We also explored the number of trials required per selection in the online condition, and DFP required fewer trials per average ($p < 0.05$).

The main goal of this study was to identify the key characteristics of stimuli that can elicit large ERP differences for a BCI. However, the results are also interesting in their implications for human face processing. The two paradigms are not dramatically different in terms of the images presented, differing only in the inclusion of cartoon eyes in the DFP condition. Nonetheless, this small difference was enough to elicit significantly different ERP activity. Hence, this study supports the studies cites above, and numerous others, that show that face processing is a very important component of human cognition. The results also show that people are very good at recognizing abstract representations of eyes. We did not assess more realistic images of eyes (such as photographs), but even cartoon images such as those presented here are immediately and effortlessly recognizable.

5 Conclusions

An online gaze-independent BCI system with the "dummy face with eyes only" paradigm was presented in this paper and compared to a "colored circle" paradigm. The online results demonstrate that this new approach with dummy faces is viable as stimulus in a gaze-independent BCI based on RSVP. In addition to outperforming the colored circle paradigm in terms of objective measures, the dummy faces approach was also superior in terms of subjective report.

Acknowledgments. This work was supported in part by the Grant National Natural Science Foundation of China, under Grant Numbers 61573142,61203127, 91420302, 61305028 and supported part by Shanghai Leading Academic Discipline Project, Project Number: B504. This work was also supported by the Fundamental Research Funds for the Central Universities (WG1414005, WH1314023 and WH1516018).

References

1. Wolpaw, J.R., Wolpaw, E.W.: Brain-Computer Interface: Principle and Practice. Oxford University Press, Oxford (2012)
2. Luck, S.T.: An Introduction to the Event-related Potential Technique (Cognitive Neuroscience). MIT Press, Cambridge (2005)
3. Birbaumer, N.: Brain–computer-interface research: coming of age. Clin. Neurophysiol. **117**, 479–483 (2006)
4. Liu, Y., Zhou, Z.T., Hu, D.W.: Gaze independent brain–computer speller with covert visual search tasks. Clin. Neurophysiol. **122**, 1127–1136 (2011)
5. Posner, M.I.: Orienting of attention: then and now. Q. J. Exp. Psychol. (Hove) **30**, 1–12 (2014)
6. Wolpaw, J.R., Birbaumer, N., McFarland, D.J., Pfurtscheller, G., Vaughan, T.M.: Brain-computer interfaces for communication and control. Clin. Neurophysiol. **113**, 767–791 (2002)
7. Treder, M.S., Blankertz, B.: (C)overt attention and visual speller design in an ERP-based brain-computer interface. Behav. Brain Funct. **6**, 28 (2010)
8. Brunner, P., Joshi, S., Briskin, S., Wolpaw, J.R., Bischof, H., Schalk, G.: Does the 'P300' speller depend on eye gaze. J. Neural Eng. **7**, 056013 (2010)

9. Acqualagna L., Blankertz B.: A gaze independent spelling based on rapid serial visual presentation. In: Proceedings of the IEEE EMBS, pp. 4560–4563 (2011)
10. Itier, R.J., Alain, C., Sedore, K., McIntosh, A.R.: Early face processing specificity: it's in the eyes. J. Cogn. Neurosci. **19**, 1815–1826 (2007)
11. Chen, L., Jin, J., Zhang, Y., Wang, X., Cichocki, A.: A survey of dummy face and human face stimuli used in BCI paradigm. J. Neurosci. Meth. **239**, 18–27 (2015)
12. Jin, J., Daly, I., Zhang, Y., Wang, X.Y., Cichocki, A.: An optimized ERP brain–computer interface based on facial expression changes. J. Neural Eng. **11**, 036004 (2014)
13. Kremláček, J., Kuba, M., Kubová, Z., Langrová, J.: Visual mismatch negativity elicited by magnocellular system activation. Vision. Res. **46**, 485–490 (2006)
14. Stefanics, G., Csukly, G., Komlósi, S., Czobor, P., Czigler, I.: Processing of unattended facial emotions: a visual mismatch negativity study. NeuroImage **59**, 3042–3049 (2012)
15. Hoffmann, U., Vesin, J.M., Ebrahimi, T., Diserens, K.: An efficient P300-based brain-computer interface for disabled subjects. J. Neurosci. Meth. **167**, 115–125 (2008)
16. Kimura, M., Katayama, J., Murohashi, H.: Attention switching function of memory-comparison-based change detection system in the visual modality. Int. J. Psychophysiol. **67**, 101–113 (2008)
17. Czigler, I.: Visual mismatch negativity and categorization. Brain Topogr. **27**, 590–598 (2014)
18. Jin, J., Allison, B.Z., Sellers, E.W., Brunner, C., Horki, P., Wang, X., Neuper, C.: An adaptive P300-based control system. J. Neural Eng. **8**, 036006 (2011)

A Kronecker Product Structured EEG Covariance Estimator for a Language Model Assisted-BCI

Paula Gonzalez-Navarro[1(✉)], Mohammad Moghadamfalahi[1],
Murat Akcakaya[2], and Deniz Erdogmus[1]

[1] Northeastern University, Boston, USA
gonzaleznavarro@ece.neu.edu
[2] University of Pittsburgh, Pittsburgh, USA

Abstract. Electroencephalography (EEG) recorded from multiple channels is typically used in many non-invasive brain computer interfaces (BCIs) for inference. Usually, EEG is assumed to be a Gaussian process with unknown mean and covariance, and the estimation of these parameters are required for BCI inference. However, relatively high dimensionality of the feature vectors extracted from the recorded EEG with respect to the number of supervised observations usually leads to a rank deficient covariance matrix estimator. In our typing BCI, RSVP Keyboard™, we solve this problem by applying regularization on the maximum likelihood covariance matrix estimators. Alternatively, in this manuscript we propose a Kronecker product structure for covariance matrices. Our underlying hypothesis is that the a structure imposed on the covariance matrices will improve the estimation accuracy and accordingly will result in typing performance improvements. Through an offline analysis we assess the classification accuracy of the proposed model. The results represent a significant improvement in classification accuracy compared to an RDA approach which does not assume any structure on the covariance.

Keywords: Structured covariances kronecker · Brain-Computer Interface (BCI) · Spatial temporal discriminant analysis · Event-Related Potential (ERP) · Multichannel Electroencephalogram (EEG)

1 Introduction

Non-invasive electroencephalography (EEG) based brain computer interfaces (BCIs) are designed as assistive technologies for people with severe speech and muscle impairments providing means for them to communicate with their caretakers and families [2]. Event relate potentials (ERPs) are commonly employed by the EEG-based BCIs to detect the user intend [1–3,5,7]. Donchin and Farewell demonstrated that ERPs can be used to design a letter by letter typing BCI [3]. The matrix based presentation paradigm used in their design is shown to be highly gaze dependent [10]. On the other hand, rapid serial visual presentation

© Springer International Publishing Switzerland 2016
D.D. Schmorrow and C.M. Fidopiastis (Eds.): AC 2016, Part I, LNAI 9743, pp. 35–45, 2016.
DOI: 10.1007/978-3-319-39955-3_4

(RSVP) paradigm is a gaze-independent alternative for matrix presentation paradigms. In RSVP, the symbols are rapidly presented as a time series on a prefixed location on the screen in a pseudo-random order [1,5,7].

RSVP Keyboard™ is a non-invasive EEG-based language-model-assisted BCI for typing which utilizes ERPs for intent detection. Inference module of the RSVP Keyboard™ probabilistically fuses the evidence extracted from the recorded multiple EEG channels with the probabilistic context information provided by a 6-gram language model [5–7]. This BCI system currently can employ both matrix-based presentation and RSVP paradigms. The EEG evidence is extracted using regularized discriminant analysis (RDA [6,7]). RDA is a generalization of the quadratic discriminant analysis (QDA) which applies regularization and shrinkage on the maximum likelihood class covariance matrix estimators to remedy rank deficiencies [4]. RSVP Keyboard™ utilizes RDA because the dimensionality of the extracted EEG feature vectors is relatively higher than the number of measurements collected for supervised learning.

Alternative to the RDA method, in this manuscript, we propose a Kronecker product structure for the covariance matrices. We show that modeling multichannel EEG using an auto-regressive moving average (ARMA) model under certain assumptions leads to a covariance matrix with a Kronecker product structure. In this structure the number of parameters is significantly lower than RDA. The maximum likelihood estimation of the proposed parametric model of covariance matrix along with regularization lead to significant improvement in classification performance. Our offline analysis shows that the median of the percentage of improvement for different subjects across different presentation paradigms is 1.111 %.

2   Inference in RSVP Keyboard™

RSVP Keyboard™ utilizes a visual presentation module to detect the user intent. The EEG collected during the visual stimulation is then employed in decision making procedure.

2.1   Visual Presentation

In letter by letter typing task we assume a dictionary set $\mathcal{D}$ of 26 letters in English alphabet, a space symbol "_" and a backspace symbol "<" as the set of all possible choices. Our system utilizes both matrix-based and rapid serial visual presentation paradigms. The different presentation paradigms are shown in Fig. 1a, b and c. Generally for all matrix-based presentation paradigms the dictionary members are arranged on a matrix shaped layout on the screen in gray color. In row and column presentation (RCP) paradigm the elements on each row or column of the matrix are assumed as a "trial" which are then flashed rapidly and in a pseudo-random order. One sequence for this presentation paradigm contains the presentation of all the rows and columns.

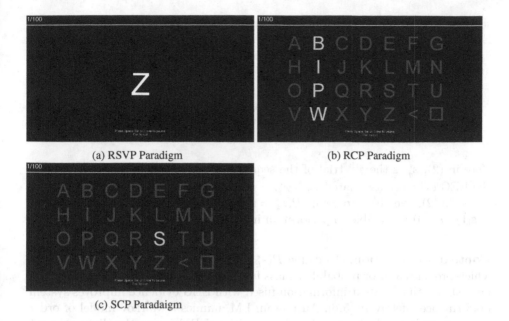

(a) RSVP Paradigm   (b) RCP Paradigm

(c) SCP Paradaigm

Fig. 1. Rapid serial visual and matrix-based presentation paradigms

After each sequence the system will attempt to make a decision however if a predefined confidence threshold is not satisfied the system will capture more EEG in response to more sequences to improve the decision confidence. Accordingly the set of sequences which lead to a decision is called an "epoch". Similarly, a trial in single character presentation (SCP) paradigm consists of only one element of dictionary and a sequence is defined as flashes of a subset of dictionary. For RSVP paradigm there exist no background matrix of characters but all the characters are presented on a prefixed location of the screen in a pseudo-random order and rapidly in time. In this presentation scheme each flashing letter is a trial and in each sequence a subset of dictionary is presented. The definition of epoch is the same among all presentation paradigms.

2.2   Decision Making

The decision making process in RSVP Keyboard^{TM} utilizes a maximum a posteriori (MAP) inference mechanism. During this procedure the context information from a language model (LM) is probabilistically fused with EEG evidence to produce a more accurate decision. The inference mechanism at epoch k and after observing sequence l is defined as follows:

$$\hat{s}_k^* = \arg \max_{s \in \mathcal{D}} P\left(s_k^* = s | \mathcal{E}^l; C\right) \tag{1}$$

where s_k^* is a random variable which represents the user intent in epoch k, $\hat{s}_k^*$ is the estimated user intent, $\mathcal{E}^l$ is the EEG evidences for all the observed l

sequences in epoch k. Assuming that conditioned on the unknown symbol, the EEG evidence and context information are independent from each other, and again conditioned on the unknown symbol all EEG evidence from different trials are independent, we can simplify Eq. (1) as:

$$\widehat{s_k^*} = \arg\max_{s \in \mathcal{D}} P(s_k^* = s|C) \prod_{\substack{i=1, \ldots, l \\ \{j \mid s \in \mathbf{s}_j^i\}}} \frac{p\left(e_j^i|1\right)}{p\left(e_j^i|0\right)} \tag{2}$$

Here in (2), $\mathbf{s}_j^i$ is the jth trial of the sequence i^{th} of epoch k and e_j^i represents the EEG evidence associated with s_j^i.

As in (2), one needs to define $P(s_k^* = s|C)$ and class conditional distributions $p(e|1)$, $p(e|0)$ to be able to perform an inference.

Context Information. To define $P(s_k^* = s|C)$ we utilize a letter n-gram LM which provides a prior probability mass function (PMF) over the dictionary. We have shown that context information fused with EEG evidence improves system performance effectively [5,6]. An n-gram LM, mimics a Markov model of order $n - 1$, trough which it estimates the conditional PMF over the dictionary set based on $n - 1$ previously typed letters. Let $C = \{s_m^*\}_{m=n-1, \ldots, 1}$, where s_m^* is the mth previously typed character, then

$$P(s|C) = P(s|\{s_m^*\}_{m=n-1, \ldots, 1}) = \frac{P(s, s_{n-1}^*, \cdots, s_1^*)}{P(s_{n-1}^*, \cdots, s_1^*)} \tag{3}$$

In our system, we use a 6-gram letter model, which is trained on the NY Times portion of the English Gigaword corpus [8].

Preprocessing and Feature Extraction. The class conditional distributions $p(e|1)$, $p(e|0)$ in RSVP Keyboard^{TM} are estimated over the EEG evidences. To extract the EEG evidence from the EEG time signals, we begin with applying a two step dimensionality reduction following a preprocessing of recorded EEG. We use g.USBAmp bio-signal amplifier with the sampling frequency of 256 Hz to acquire the data. A bandpass linear-phase finite impulse response (FIR) filter with bandpass of $[1.5, 42]$ Hz is then applied on the EEG data in order to improve the signal to noise ratio (SNR) and eliminate DC drifts. We down-sample the preprocessed data by order of 2. We concatenate the data from every channel in a time window of $[0, 500)$ ms, time locked to onset of ith trial, to form the feature vector $\mathbf{x}_i$ for that trial.

The supervised data required for estimating the class conditional distributions is recorded during "calibration" mode of the system [5]. Each calibration task of RSVP Keyboard^{TM} consists of 100 sequences. Before each sequence the user is presented with a target character which she/he is supposed to locate during that sequence. For RSVP and SCP paradigms the number of trials in each sequence is set to 10, and for RCP it is equal to number of all rows and columns in the matrix (for instance, here we are using a 4×7 matrix which leads to 11 trials in a sequence).

The labels for the feature vectors is assigned as 0 if the trial in a non-target, or 1 if the trial contains the target character. To increase the EEG ERP detection accuracy, we further quadratically project the feature vectors on to a space which maximizes the distance between two classes. In RSVPKeyobard^{TM} we use regularized discriminant analysis (RDA) which is a generalization of quadratic discriminant analysis (QDA) to perform this projection. In our system the dimensionality of feature vectors is relatively higher than the number of observation during a calibration session, hence we mainly utilize RDA to be able to estimate invertible covariance matrices. The maximum likelihood class conditional mean and covariance matrices are computed as follows:

$$\boldsymbol{\mu}_h = \frac{1}{N_h} \sum_{i=1}^{N} \mathbf{x}_i \delta(y_i, h)$$

$$\boldsymbol{\Sigma}_h = \frac{1}{N_h} \sum_{i=1}^{N} (\mathbf{x}_i - \boldsymbol{\mu}_h)(\mathbf{x}_i - \boldsymbol{\mu}_h)^T \delta(y_i, h)$$

(4)

where $y_i \in \{0,1\}$ is the label of $\mathbf{x}_i$, $h \in \{0,1\}$ is the class for which we are performing the estimation, N_h is the number of observations in class h and $N = N_0 + N_1$. RDA makes the estimated covariance matrices invertible by applying regularization and shrinkage.

$$\widehat{\boldsymbol{\Sigma}}_h(\lambda) = \frac{(1-\lambda)N_h \boldsymbol{\Sigma}_h + (\lambda) \sum_{h=0}^{1} N_h \boldsymbol{\Sigma}_h}{(1-\lambda)N_h + (\lambda) \sum_{k=0}^{1} N_h}$$

$$\widehat{\boldsymbol{\Sigma}}_h(\lambda, \gamma) = (1-\gamma)\widehat{\boldsymbol{\Sigma}}_h(\lambda) + (\gamma)\frac{1}{p} tr[\widehat{\boldsymbol{\Sigma}}_h(\lambda)]\mathbf{I}_p$$

(5)

Here, $\lambda, \gamma \in [0,1]$ are the shrinkage and regularization parameters, $tr[\cdot]$ is the trace operator and $\mathbf{I}_p$ is an identity matrix of size $p \times p$. RSVP Keyboard^{TM} optimizes the λ and γ for the maximum area under the receiver operating characteristics (ROC) curve (AUC) in a 10-fold cross validation framework. The RDA score for e_i, is then referred to as EEG evidence for trial $\mathbf{s}_i$.

$$e_i = \log \left(\frac{f_{\mathcal{N}}(\mathbf{x}_i; \boldsymbol{\mu}_1, \widehat{\boldsymbol{\Sigma}}_1(\lambda, \gamma))}{f_{\mathcal{N}}(\mathbf{x}_i; \boldsymbol{\mu}_0, \widehat{\boldsymbol{\Sigma}}_0(\lambda, \gamma))} \right)$$

(6)

where $f_{\mathcal{N}}(\mathbf{x}; \boldsymbol{\mu}, \boldsymbol{\Sigma})$ is the Gaussian probability density function with mean $\boldsymbol{\mu}$ and covariance $\boldsymbol{\Sigma}$.

Consequently we use these EEG evidences in kernel density estimation (KDE) framework to define class conditional distributions. In our system we use Silverman rule of thumb to define the kernel width for KDE [9].

3   Signal Modeling and Covariance Estimation

Currently in our system we employ RDA to estimate full-ranked class conditional covariance estimates. But for a non-structured maximum likelihood estimation of covariance matrix one needs to estimate many parameters (i.e. elements of covariance matrix). But due to lack of enough observation in a calibration session, this estimation might be prone to errors. We propose to use a Kronecker product structure for the covariance matrices. This structure reduces the number of the covariance parameters to be estimated using the assumption of stationarity in time and space. We show that defining an auto-regressive moving average (ARMA) (p,q) model for the multi-channel EEG recordings leads to Kronecker product structure under certain assumptions.

Define $\mathbf{v}[n]$ as the spatial feature vector of EEG recorded from N_{ch} EEG channels at time instant n:

$$\mathbf{v}[n] = \begin{bmatrix} v_1[n] \\ v_j[n] \\ \vdots \\ v_{N_{ch}}[n] \end{bmatrix}_{N_{ch} \times 1} \tag{7}$$

where $v_i[n]$ is the nth time sample recorded at channel i. Then define the feature vectors as:

$$\mathbf{x}[i] = \begin{bmatrix} \mathbf{v}[1] \\ \mathbf{v}[2] \\ \vdots \\ \mathbf{v}[N_t] \end{bmatrix}_{(N_{ch} N_t) \times 1} \tag{8}$$

where $\mathbf{v}[.]$ and accordingly $\mathbf{x}$ follows a multivariate Gaussian distribution and N_t is the number of time samples. We define an ARMA model for EEG signal as follows:

$$\mathbf{v}[n] = \sum_{k=1}^{p} A_k \mathbf{v}[n-k] + \sum_{j=0}^{q} b_j \mathbf{w}[n-j] \tag{9}$$

In (9), A_k represents the $N_{ch} \times N_{ch}$ signal weight matrix at lag k, b_j is an scalar weight for noise at lag j and $\mathbf{w}[n]$ represents multivariate wide sense stationary Gaussian noise for the nth time sample. Let us assume that the EEG signals among the channels is stationary. Then one can write (9) as:

$$\mathbf{v}[n] = \sum_{k=1}^{p} c_k \cdot \mathbf{v}[n-k] + \sum_{j=0}^{q} b_j \mathbf{w}[n-j] \tag{10}$$

in which c_k is an scalar weight of time for the signal at time lag k. Now lets further assume $p = 1$ and $b_j = 0 \; \forall j = 0 \ldots q$ then we can write:

$$\mathbf{v}_n = c_1 \cdot \mathbf{v}[n-1] \tag{11}$$

Then define:

1. Initial state $\mathbf{v}[0] \sim \mathcal{N}_{N_{ch}}(\boldsymbol{\mu}_{\mathbf{v}[0]}, \boldsymbol{\Sigma}_{\mathbf{v}}[0, 0])$
2. $E[\mathbf{v}[n]] = \boldsymbol{\mu}_{\mathbf{v}[n]}$
3. $\boldsymbol{\Sigma}_{\mathbf{v}}[m, n] = Cov[\mathbf{v}[m], \mathbf{v}[n]]$
$$= E[(\mathbf{v}[m] - \boldsymbol{\mu}_{\mathbf{v}[m]})(\mathbf{v}[n] - \boldsymbol{\mu}_{\mathbf{v}[n]})^T].$$

4. $\mathbf{x} = \begin{bmatrix} \mathbf{v}[1] \\ \mathbf{v}[2] \\ \vdots \\ \mathbf{v}[N_t] \end{bmatrix}_{(N_{ch}N_t) \times 1}$

Here note that based on the above definition we have $\boldsymbol{\Sigma}_{\mathbf{v}}[m, n] = \boldsymbol{\Sigma}_{\mathbf{v}}[n, m]$. Also we have:

$$\mathbf{v}[n] = (c_1)^n \cdot \mathbf{v}[0] \Rightarrow E[\mathbf{v}[n]] = (c_1)^n \cdot \boldsymbol{\mu}_{\mathbf{v}[0]} \qquad (12)$$

We further assume that the EEG signal is stationary in time. Lets assume $m < n$ hence we have:

$$\begin{aligned}
\boldsymbol{\Sigma}_{\mathbf{v}}[m, n] &= E\{\mathbf{v}[n]\mathbf{v}[m]^T\} - E\{\mathbf{v}[n]\}E\{\mathbf{v}[m]\}^T \\
&= c_1^{(n-m)} \cdot (E\{\mathbf{v}[m]\mathbf{v}[m]^T\} - \boldsymbol{\mu}_{\mathbf{v}[m]}\boldsymbol{\mu}_{\mathbf{v}[m]}^T) \\
&= c_1^{(n-m)} \cdot \boldsymbol{\Sigma}_{\mathbf{v}}[m, m] \\
&= c[|n - m|] \cdot \boldsymbol{\Sigma}_{\mathbf{v}}[0, 0] \\
&\text{where } c[|n - m|] = c_1^{(|n-m|)}
\end{aligned} \qquad (13)$$

According to definition of $\mathbf{x}$ one can define the covariance matrix of $\mathbf{x}$ as:

$$\boldsymbol{\Sigma}_{\mathbf{x}} = \begin{bmatrix} \boldsymbol{\Sigma}_{\mathbf{v}}[1, 1] & \cdots & \boldsymbol{\Sigma}_{\mathbf{v}}[1, N_t] \\ \boldsymbol{\Sigma}_{\mathbf{v}}[2, 1] & & \boldsymbol{\Sigma}_{\mathbf{v}}[2, N_t] \\ \vdots & & \vdots \\ \boldsymbol{\Sigma}_{\mathbf{v}}[N_t, 1] & \cdots & \boldsymbol{\Sigma}_{\mathbf{v}}[N_t, N_t] \end{bmatrix}$$

$$\qquad (14)$$

$$= \begin{bmatrix} c[0] & \cdots & c[N_t - 1] \\ c[1] & & c[N_t - 2] \\ \vdots & & \vdots \\ c[N_t - 1] & \cdots & c[0] \end{bmatrix} \otimes \boldsymbol{\Sigma}_{\mathbf{v}}[0, 0]$$

Finally, we assume the EEG signal is independent in time which means that $c[|n - m|] = 0$ for all $m \neq n$. Then we have:

$$\boldsymbol{\Sigma}_{\mathbf{x}} = c[0] \cdot \mathbf{I}_{N_t} \otimes \boldsymbol{\Sigma}_{\mathbf{v}}[0, 0] \qquad (15)$$

Here $\mathbf{I}_{N_t}$ is an $N_t \times N_t$ identity matrix.

Through a maximum likelihood framework we can estimate the parameter values of the structured covariance matrices. We specifically utilize a flipflop algorithm presented by Karl Werner in [11] for which we fix the time covariance matrix to identity and perform a one time estimation on channel covariance matrix.

4   Results

4.1   Participants

In this manuscript we utilized the calibration data collected from 9 healthy users who had consented to participate in our study according to the IRB-approved protocol (IRB130107) [5]. In our study, each user performed 12 calibration sessions for all possible combinations of 4 inter trial interval (ITI) values ($\{200; 150; 100; 85\}$ ms) and 3 presentation paradigms (RCP, SCP and RSVP). According to the International 10/20 configuration, data recorded from 16 EEG locations: Fp1, Fp2, F3, F4, Fz, Fc1, Fc2, Cz, P1, P2, C1, C2,Cp3, Cp4, P5 and P6.

4.2   Data Analysis and Results

We calculated the area under the receiver operating characteristics (ROC) curve (AUC) values, for every calibration data using a 10-fold cross validation. The goal of this analysis is to assess the changes in classification accuracy under the proposed signal model.

For each particular ITI and presentation paradigm (PP) combination, we compared the median of AUC values for RDA and the proposed model in Table 1, and also we show the number of participants who demonstrate improvement under the proposed model in Table 2. In Table 1 we can see an improvement for RSVP at ITI = 150 ms which is the optimal speed for this presentation paradigm [5]. Also, the proposed model seems to be most effective in RCP paradigm. However, we cannot observe any significant improvement for SCP at any ITI. As shown in Table 2 most of the population could benefit from the proposed model at every PP and ITI combination. Among all the users at every ITI and PP combinations, half of the AUC values fall bellow .811. We utilized this value to define a threshold for high AUCs and low AUCs. The Table 3 represents the median AUC values for regular RDA and proposed covariance estimation technique. As one can clearly see in this table the participants with low AUCs can benefit more from the new signal modeling scheme.

We also compute the number of participants who demonstrate a classification improvement regardless of particular ITI value and PP. We assumed a participant can benefit from this signal modeling scheme if the median of all 12 ITI and PP combination AUCs improves. The corresponding results are shown in Table 4.

Table 1. The median of changes in AUC for each PP and ITI combination among nine users

	RSVP	SCP	RCP
85 ms	2.867	−1.178	−0.383
100 ms	−2.089	0.956	2.156
150 ms	2.000	0.756	1.206
200 ms	−2.189	−1.633	3.022

Table 2. The number of participant for whom the proposed model improved the classification AUC, for each PP and ITI combination and among nine users

	RSVP	SCP	RCP
85 ms	5	6	7
100 ms	5	7	7
150 ms	4	4	6
200 ms	5	4	5

Table 3. Median of AUCs lower than 0.811 for the nine subjects when we use the signal modeling (SM) versus RDA for all PP and ITIs.

	RSVP		SCP		RCP	
Median	SM	RDA	SM	RDA	SM	RDA
85 ms	0.680	0.656	0.705	0.706	0.786	0.776
100 ms	0.722	0.698	0.788	0.754	0.781	0.754
150 ms	0.721	0.736	0.756	0.722	0.777	0.777
200 ms	0.725	0.736	0.790	0.780	0.795	0.786

Table 4. Improvement in median of AUCs among all 12 ITI and PP combination for each user.

US1	US2	US3	US4	US5	US6	US7	US8	US9
−0.402	1.54	1.269	−0.772	1.111	1.95	−0.181	2.750	−0.108

Table 4 shows that most of the population, 5 out of 9, demonstrate an improvement in classification AUC. Besides the amount of improvements is generally higher than 1 % while the performance degradation is less than 0.5 % for other users.

5   Discussions and Future Work

In this manuscript, we considered the EEG as a structured multivariate Gaussian data, and under certain assumptions, we modeled the covariance matrix of this signal to have a Kronecker product of a channel covariance matrix and an identity time covariance matrix. With this assumption on the covariance matrix, we reduced the number of parameters that are needed to be estimated. Correspondingly this decrease in the number of parameters to be estimated led to an increase in classification performance.

In this study at every presentation paradigm and inter trial interval combination, we compared the classification performances of two methods when the covariance matrix is estimated under the new structure versus the covariance is estimated without a specific structure using typical RDA. Results suggested that considering a structured EEG signal can significantly improve the ERP-detection specially when the RDA AUC is below 80 %. Future work will analyze and optimize additional structures such as Toeplitz or AR(p) structures for the covariance of the multichannel EEG signal.

Acknowledgment. This work is supported by NIH 2R01DC009834, NIDRR H133E140026, NSF CNS-1136027, IIS-1118061, IIS-1149570, CNS-1544895, SMA-0835976. For supplemental materials, please visit http://hdl.handle.net/2047/D20199232 for the CSL Collection in the Northeastern University Digital Repository System.

References

1. Acqualagna, L., Treder, M.S., Schreuder, M., Blankertz, B.: A novel brain-computer interface based on the rapid serial visual presentation paradigm. Proceed. EMBC **1**, 2686–2689 (2010)
2. Akcakaya, M., Peters, B., Moghadamfalahi, M., Mooney, A., Orhan, U., Oken, B., Erdogmus, D., Fried-Oken, M.: Noninvasive brain computer interfaces for augmentative and alternative communication. IEEE Rev. Biomed. Eng. **7**(1), 31–49 (2014)
3. Farwell, L.A., Donchin, E.: Talking off the top of your head: toward a mental prosthesis utilizing event-related brain potentials. Electroencephalogr. Clin. Neurophysiol. **70**(6), 510–523 (1988)
4. Friedman, J.H.: Regularized discriminant analysis. J. Am. Stat. Assoc. **84**(405), 165–175 (1989)
5. Moghadamfalahi, M., Orhan, U., Akcakaya, M., Nezamfar, H., Fried-Oken, M., Erdogmus, D.: Language-model assisted brain computer interface for typing: a comparison of matrix and rapid serial visual presentation. IEEE Trans. Neural Syst. Rehabil. Eng. **23**(5), 910–920 (2015)
6. Orhan, U., Erdogmus, D., Roark, B., Oken, B., Fried-Oken, M.: Offline analysis of context contribution to ERP-based typing BCI performance. J. Neural Eng. **10**(6), 066003 (2013)
7. Orhan, U., Hild, K.E., Erdogmus, D., Roark, B., Oken, B., Fried-Oken, M.: RSVP keyboard: an EEG based typing interface. In: International Conference on Acoustics, Speech and Signal Processing (ICASSP), pp. 645–648. IEEE (2012)
8. Roark, B., De Villiers, J., Gibbons, C., Fried-Oken, M.: Scanning methods and language modeling for binary switch typing. In: Proceedings of the NAACL HLT 2010 Workshop on Speech and Language Processing for Assistive Technologies, pp. 28–36. Association for Computational Linguistics (2010)

9. Silverman, B.W.: Density Estimation for Statistics and Data Analysis, vol. 26. CRC Press, Boca Raton (1986)
10. Treder, M.S., Blankertz, B.: Research (c)overt attention and visual speller design in an ERP-based brain-computer interface. Behav. Brain Funct. **6**, 28 (2010)
11. Werner, K., Jansson, M., Stoica, P.: On estimation of covariance matrices with kronecker product. Structure **56**(2), 478–491 (2008)

Poor BCI Performers Still Could Benefit from Motor Imagery Training

Alexander Kaplan[1,2,3(✉)], Anatoly Vasilyev[1,2], Sofya Liburkina[1,2],
and Lev Yakovlev[1,3]

[1] Lomonosov Moscow State University, Moscow, Russian Federation
akaplan@mail.ru, a.vasilyev@anvmail.com
[2] Pirogov Russian National Research Medical University, Moscow, Russian Federation
[3] Lobachevsky State University of Nizhni Novgorod, Nizhni Novgorod, Russian Federation

Abstract. Nowadays, there is a growing number of studies suggesting that coupled with the brain-computer interface (BCI) the motor imagery practice could be a helpful tool in neurorehabilitation therapy, but the actual neurophysiological correlates of such exercise are poorly understood. In this study we examined two of the most notable neurophysiological effects of motor imagery – the EEG mu-rhythm desynchronization and the increase in cortical excitability assessed with transcranial magnetic stimulation (TMS). We have found that subjects' BCI performance was highly correlated with mu-rhythm features and was not associated with the cortical excitability increase. Subjects with the lowest accuracy in BCI all had a statically significant excitability raise during motor imagery and did not differ from better performers. Our results suggest that poor BCI performers with weak EEG response still could benefit from the motor imagery training, and in that case cortex excitability level had to be considered for the control measurement.

Keywords: Motor imagery · Brain-computer interface · Transcranial magnetic stimulation · Classification accuracy · Electroencephalogram · Cortical excitability · Mu-rhythm · Neurorehabilitation

1 Introduction

Motor imagery (MI) is most commonly defined as a mental rehearsal or mental representation of person's own body parts' movement. MI is considered to be helpful as a training technique for neurorehabilitation of people with different motor disabilities [1, 2]. Professional athletes and musicians claim to use motor imagery, also referred as «mental practice» , to improve their performance as well [3].

Motor imagery is known to promote patterns of the event-related desynchronization (ERD), or suppression, of mu-rhythm found in EEG over the sensorimotor areas of the human cortex. These patterns could be identified in an ongoing EEG and decoded into commands for external devices providing direct communication channel between the brain and the outer world. Such a technique is called a brain-computer interface (or BCI) and was originally designed for the severely disabled patients with the limited

© Springer International Publishing Switzerland 2016
D.D. Schmorrow and C.M. Fidopiastis (Eds.): AC 2016, Part I, LNAI 9743, pp. 46–56, 2016.
DOI: 10.1007/978-3-319-39955-3_5

communication and motor capacities [4]. Recently, several new use cases for BCI are starting to emerge in both clinical and non-clinical application fields [5, 6].

It is believed that, in neurorehabilitation BCI approach promises an additional benefit for the motor imagery practice, because, firstly, it allows subject to learn the mental exercise by monitoring his or her own imagery quality, and secondly, promotes motivation for practice by creating an engaging feedback environment [7]. Moreover, detected MI could be translated into a command for a stimulating device (such as a functional electrical stimulation (FES) or an exoskeleton), which presumably complements the training by activating natural afferent pathways of sensorimotor system.

On the other hand, in order to work, MI-BCI requires a user to have a distinctive and consistent mu-rhythm response, which considerably varies among individuals, [8] and hence does not describe the motor imagery effort quality. Due to the weak or absent EEG response during MI, a substantial portion of the population is characterized as «BCI-illiterate» or «inefficient» indicating poor performance in a brain-computer interface circuit [9], and therefore those people are being eliminated from such activity. Although it is not clear to what extent BCI performance is determined by the user's capability to correctly perform motor imagery [10, 11], recent evidence suggests that individual neurophysiological [12] and anatomical [13] features play a significant role in MI-BCI aptitude. For training purposes, especially in a restricted and high-stakes clinical setting, it is important to establish whether the mu-rhythm reaction used in BCI happens to be a basic neurophysiological effect of MI (and therefore is connected with potential training efficiency) or rather mere manifestation of the motor-related mental activity with weak or absent relation to the target effect of training.

Another important neurophysiological effect of motor imagery is its ability to increase the excitability of primary motor cortex (M1) commonly assessed by the means of transcranial magnetic stimulation (TMS) [14]. Increasing cortex excitability, which translates into plasticity induction, is considered to be one of the most important goals of neurorehabilitation therapy and therefore appears to be a desirable effect of motor imagery practice. Nevertheless, very little research has been done to determine actual quantitative connection between excitability changes during motor imagery and other metrics such as BCI-performance and my-rhythm reaction. Takemi et al. in [15] have shown that the excitability and mu-rhythm desynchronization values are positively correlated within subjects on different trials, but it should be noted that, only subjects with noticeable ERD reaction participated in that study.

Considering the growing tendency to use BCI technology for motor imagery practice, it would be interesting to know whether high performance users are actually any different from the «BCI-illiterate» subjects in regard to MI-induced cortex excitability changes. Hence, the purpose of our research was to assess the connection between the user's BCI performance and the neurophysiological effects of motor imagery which are changes in EEG mu-rhythm amplitude and M1 cortex excitability.

2 Method

2.1 Subjects

18 healthy human subjects (6 females) participated in the experiment. There were no exclusion criteria other than neurological health. Hand dominance was assessed with the Edinburgh handedness questionnaire [16]: 15 of the subjects were right handed (score +0,875 ± 0,04), two – left handed (score −0,9 ± 0,00) and one – bimanual (score +0.1)). All of the participants gave their informed consent. The experimental procedure was approved by the Lomonosov Moscow State University Ethical Committee.

2.2 Sessions

Each subject participated in 5–8 motor imagery (BCI) sessions (experimental days) during the course of study. Some of the participants had previous MI-BCI-experience. Each BCI experimental session lasted 2–2.5 h. Last session comprised of the shortened BCI session protocol followed by the TMS measurement.

2.3 Motor Imagery Training

During regular sessions subjects were trained to perform kinesthetic motor imagery of sequential self-paced movements: II–V finger presses (flexion at metacarpophalangeal joint), II–V finger elevations (extension at metacarpophalangeal joint) and shoulder forward/backward circumduction (explained to subjects as «crawl stroke» from seated arm-down position). During motor imagery subjects were seated at a comfortable chair with their hands relaxed at armrests.

Subjects were asked to perform mental tasks on visual cues appearing on the LCD monitor in front of them. Icons with a depicted shoulder or fingers cued the specific motor imagery task and an abstract picture with lines and dots (or "visual scene") cued the visual attention task, during which the subject was asked to count elements of that picture. Visual attention and motor imagery cues were presented for 6–8 s in a semi-random sequence with 2–3 s intervals (blank grey background). During the feedback runs an empty horizontal rectangular frame was presented below the pictogram of the task cue. Subjects were asked to fill the frame (progress bar animation) as much as possible using the cued mental state.

2.4 Signal Acquisition and Processing

EEG recording was performed with 64 active electrodes system (ActiChamp, Brain Products GmbH, Germany) positioned according to the modified IFCN «10 %-system» [17]: A1, A2 positions were replaced with FT9 and FT10 accordingly, and electrodes in CP9 and CP10 positions (mastoids) were used as a reference. Impedance for all electrodes was kept below 20 kΩ. Signal was sampled at 500 Hz and bandpass-filtered in 0,05–49 Hz band.

EMG was recorded with two pairs of Ag/AgCl hat-shaped electrodes («ED6» , EasyCap GmbH, Germany) from extensor digitorum communis (EDC) and flexor digitorum superficialis (FDS) muscles. The skin under the electrodes was prepared with an abrasive paper and alcohol cotton swabs, so that the impedance could be kept within 1.5–3 kΩ interval (except for 2 subjects with 10–15 kΩ due to the skin condition). Signal was digitalized at 10 kHz using the NVX-52 amplifier (MKS, Zelenograd, Russia) and filtered in 5–3500 Hz band with the 4th-order Butterworth digital filter.

2.5 BCI Classification

BCI2000 software [18] with a custom classifier module was used for data recording and feedback environment. Offline calculations were performed in MATLAB. In order to classify the two mental tasks (MI and visual scene task), the 62-channel EEG signal was first bandpass filtered in 4–40 Hz, using a 4th-order Butterworth filter, and then spatially filtered using the Common Spatial Pattern (CSP) filter [19], calculated on the initial calibration run with same mental states. The CSP-filtered signal was analyzed in spectral domain using the short-time Fourier transform (FFT in 1 s windows with 90 % overlap), and then the extracted spectral power in the user-specific channel and frequency band was classified using naïve Bayes classifier with 10 Hz output sampling rate. The initial classifier was calculated on the 10-trial calibration run before feedback runs and it was subsequently updated (fully recalculated) using the most current data throughout the session. During the feedback runs classifier output was translated into the horizontal progress bar animation. Numerical value of filling percentage was displayed at the end of each 6 s-trial.

2.6 TMS Measurement

Single-pulse TMS was applied with a figure-of-eight shaped coil (outer diameter of each coil: 7 cm) connected to a Neuro MS/D magnetic stimulator («Neurosoft» , Ivanovo, Russia). Hotspot for the right FDS muscle was determined and TMS output was set to elicit 0.4-0.8 mV MEP during resting condition (~110–115 % of motor threshold). TMS measurement was divided into 5 runs. On each run subject performed two types of mental tasks – one of three motor imagery tasks (experimental condition) and a visual attention task (reference condition). During one run the visual attention stimulus was changed to a blank screen. Mental task cues were presented in the sequence of 3 (AAABB-BAAABBB…, 24 total) and during each of them TMS-pulse was delivered at random moment 2–5 s after the cue was displayed. 120 evoked responses were collected during TMS session in total (by condition: 36 – fingers flexion imagery, 12 – fingers extension imagery, 12 – shoulder circumduction imagery, 48 – visual attention state, 12 – blank screen). During TMS measurement online EMG-feedback was displayed at the right side of the screen as vertical bar with the real-time RMS (root-mean-square) value (300 ms window, 100 ms step). Participants were asked to find the hand position with minimal ongoing EMG amplitude and maintain the corresponding bar level constant during the whole run.

2.7 Data Analysis

For EEG patterns analysis only data from last two sessions were used. An average mu-rhythm ERD score was calculated as a percentage of the overlap between distribution of power spectra value of user-specific power band for two mental states – the motor imagery state and the visual attention state. The value was extracted from the peak ERD electrode location of the left hemisphere (typically, C3-position). In order to mitigate volume conduction effects and improve signal-to-noise ratio of individual electrodes, Surface Laplacian filter [20] was applied to the raw EEG signal.

BCI performance was evaluated for each subject on 100-trial (6 s/trial) sample with 50 trials per class (the motor imagery of right fingers flexion and the visual scene task). Classification accuracy was calculated as a percentage of correct classification time, which is the same as the average feedback score displayed for a subject.

Amplitude of motor-evoked potentials was measured peak to peak (between negative and positive phases of potential). Potentials with any signs of raised muscular activity during preceding 1000 ms interval were rejected by hand. MEPs in experimental condition (motor imagery) were normalized to mean amplitude of the reference condition («visual attention» or blank screen) on the same run.

3 Results

3.1 Classification Accuracy

BCI performance for all subjects was measured on 100-trial sample: 60 trials were extracted from the last session (same day as TMS-measurement) and 40 trials from the previous session. Each trial consisted of 6 s EEG recording, where subject was performing either a motor imagery of right fingers flexion or a «visual scene» task.

All of the participants achieved classification accuracy above chance level of 0.5 for two classes. Mean accuracy was 0.85, SD = 0.078, ranging from 0.68 to 0.96. Subjects

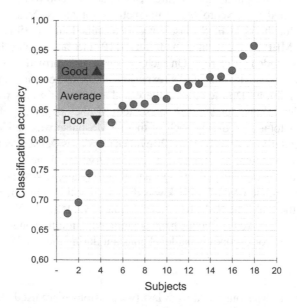

Fig. 1. Classification accuracy of all subjects measured on 100-trial sample

were assigned to one of the three categories according to their performance: poor (N = 5), average (N = 8) and good (N = 5) performers (Fig. 1).

3.2 Mu-rhythm Patterns

Mu-rhythm EEG patterns were evaluated for all the subjects using using the same 100-trial sample as for the classification accuracy measurements. Spectral changes in a subject-specific frequency band were calculated for the motor imagery state compared to the «visual scene» task that was used as a reference state. Raw EEG signal was filtered with Surface Laplacian and then spectral power values' distributions (FFT) were analyzed for both states for each channel and frequency. The distance between power values distributions was expressed as overlap percentage («ERD score») for each EEG channel. Subject's ERD score was chosen as the maximum single-electrode value at left sensorimotor area (electrodes FC5, FC3, FC1, C5, C3, C1, CP5, CP3, CP1).

A topographical representation of the average ERD score heatmap for all subjects is shown at Fig. 2 (right). Peak desynchronization was observed over C3-CP3 electrodes with symmetrical weaker activation over C4-CP4. For some of the subjects, frontal (electrodes F-Fc) desynchronization accompanied the reaction over sensorimotor cortex.

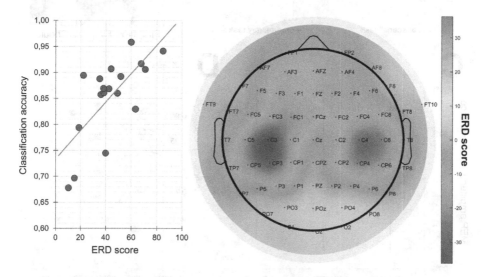

Fig. 2. Left – Correlation of ERD scores with BCI classification accuracy, each dot represents one subject, the solid line depicts linear regression. **Right** – Topographical representation of mean spectral changes during motor imagery (n = 18). Negative values (blue) represent decrease in mu-rhythm power (desynchronization) and positive values (orange) represent increase in mu-rhythm power (synchronization). (Color figure online)

Strong correlation (Pearson's r) of 0.71 (p < 0.05) was observed between classification accuracy and subject's ERD score (Fig. 2, left). Three of the subjects from the poor-performers group had the lowest ERD score below 20, indicating the absence of mu-rhythm reaction.

3.3   Cortex Excitability Measurement

Cortex excitability was assessed through TMS measurement performed at the end of the last experimental session of each subject. Motor evoked potentials (MEPs) were

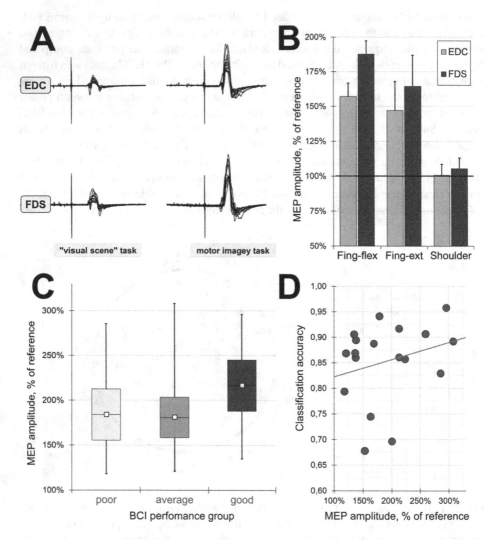

Fig. 3. **A** – Example of MEPs from FDS and EDC muscles during motor imagery and «visual scene» task acquired from one of subjects. **B** – Amplitude increase of MEPs in FDS and EDC muscles during three types of motor imagery for all subjects (n = 18). Mean values are shown with standard error indicated by whiskers, the solid line represents mean MEP amplitude in the reference condition. **C** – Amplitude increase of MEPs in FDS during motor imagery of fingers flexion imagery for subjects of three BCI performance groups. Square dots indicate mean values, boxes – standard error and «min-max» range is shown by whiskers. **D** – Correlation of MEPs amplitude increase with classification accuracy, each dot represents one subject, the solid line depicts linear regression.

collected in response to the suprathreshold transcranial magnetic stimulation of motor cortex (EDC muscle hotspot) during «visual scene» task and three of motor imagery states (fingers flexion, fingers extension, shoulder circumduction). Two of the muscles were monitored: extensor digitorum communis (EDC) and flexor digitorum superficialis (FDS). All MEPs were normalized to the mean values during the referential «visual scene» task, collected from the same muscle within the same recording sequence.

Motor imagery of both fingers movements resulted in a statistically significant (ANOVA, $p < 0.05$) MEPs amplitude increase (Fig. 3-B) in both muscles with mean values ranged from 157 % to 188 % of the referential state. Shoulder circumduction imagery didn't lead to statistically significant MEPs changes in either muscle.

Analysis of EDC MEPs during an imagery of the finger flexion revealed a significant variation between subjects. For all of the subjects the amplitude increase during imagery was statistically insignificant (Mann–Whitney U test, $p > 0.05$) and varied from 118 to 306 % of the referential state. MEPs increase did not correlate either with BCI classification accuracy (Pearson's $r = 0.27$) or with ERD score (Pearson's $r = 0.32$).

4   Discussion

4.1   BCI Performance

In the current research we have investigated only two-class BCI performance, whereas most of the research in this area is being concentrated on high-performance multiclass settings [21]. Our intention in that regard was to bring the experimental design of BCI training sessions closer to what is expected in clinical application: a simplified setting with fewer commands, short and regular training sessions.

In our research the group classification accuracy level was fairly high (85 %) compared to similar studies [22]. That happened because all of our subjects participated in at least five BCI training session, whereas in most of the other research performance was measured based on the single and often prolonged session using naïve subjects. Another reason for the increased accuracy is the use of a non-motor mental task with motor imagery. Previous research demonstrates that the choice of pairing mental states is of great importance for a good and consistent accuracy level [23].

4.2   Mu-rhythm Desynchronization

In this study for the majority of subjects we have observed patterns of desynchronization of bilateral structure, which is in accordance with our previous research [24] and backed up by several other studies [25, 26]. For the single motor imagery task recognition bilateral structure of the patterns allows to construct more robust spatial filter (CSP, [19]), which improves classification accuracy.

As was expected, mu-rhythm desynchronization magnitude was positively correlated with BCI-accuracy. That confirms our subjects used modulation of sensorimotor rhythms for BCI control. For patterns classification of subjects with a weak or absent ERD reaction (ERD score below 20) P-PO channels were dominant in the individual spatial filters indicating involvement of occipital alpha rhythm which is non-specific to the motor imagery task. Those subjects are most likely to be deemed as «BCI-illiterate» in regard of multiclass motor imagery setting, although in simplified our two-class BCI environment they yielded satisfactory results.

4.3 Cortical Excitability

When investigating cortical excitability changes, we have observed that motor imagery of fingers movement has led to statically significant increase in motor cortex excitability in both of the forearm muscles. We have not found clear EDC and FDS muscle differentiation in corresponding fingers movements – extension and flexion, often reported in similar studies [27]. In our opinion the main reason why it was happening is that it was quite hard to differentiate between the kinesthetic images of sequential upward and downward movements of fingers, since they share most of the perceived proprioceptive sensations. Indeed, as was expected, we observed no MEPs amplitude raise in forearm muscles for a shoulder movement, which is completely unrelated to fingers.

The MEPs amplitude increase was not correlated with either BCI accuracy or ERD reaction. Although subjects with the best BCI performance (and hence the strongest mu-rhythm ERD) tended to have higher increase in cortical excitability, statically significant difference was not observed.

Our results could be explained as a contribution of two reasons. First one relates to the properties of the measurements. Mu-rhythm power decreases during motor imagery. and thereby its modulation range is limited by the resting-state power value [12], which varies both in the general population and within subjects on different experimental days. That is why the subjects whose resting mu-rhythm power is closer to the noise level (undetectable amount) generally demonstrate poor BCI-performance. On the contrary, M1 excitability level increases during motor imagery and therefore has a greater measurable range.

The second explanation lies in the physiological nature of the measurements. Mu-rhythm appears to be an indicator of the general inhibitory input into the vast cortical areas, whereas M1 excitability reflects the state of the local neuron group corresponding to a discrete muscle. Based on prior knowledge, motor imagery should promote excitability of local cortical pathways involved in the imagined movement, but not necessarily alter the general inhibitory output of thalamocortical circuits.

Those explanations do not contradict with previous findings, published in [15, 28], since our conclusions address the intersubject level, while mentioned papers describe with-subject correlations. Taken together these results could be evidence that motor imagery involves several interconnected but separate sensorimotor pathways and different assessment strategies are needed for their exploration.

5   Conclusion

Our results suggest that if motor imagery practice is considered to be beneficial in regard to training discrete motor cortex pathways, poor BCI performance should not discourage users from mental exercises. EEG control should be accompanied by other cortex excitability measurements such as TMS to provide a more comprehensive estimate of physiological impact of the training.

Acknowledgements. This study was partially supported by funding from the Skolkovo Foundation (project #1110034) and from Russian Science Foundation (#15-19-20053). Authors also would like to acknowledge the work of Yuriy Nuzhdin responsible for software development used it this study for data acquisition and analysis.

References

1. Jackson, P.L., Lafleur, M.F., Malouin, F., Richards, C., Doyon, J.: Potential role of mental practice using motor imagery in neurologic rehabilitation. Arch. Phys. Med. Rehabil. **82**(8), 1133–1141 (2001)
2. Page, S.J., Levine, P., Leonard, A.: Mental practice in chronic stroke: results of a randomized, placebo-controlled trial. Stroke J. Cereb. Circ. **38**(4), 1293–1297 (2007)
3. Holmes, P., Calmels, C.: A neuroscientific review of imagery and observation use in sport. J. Mot. Behav. **40**(5), 433–445 (2008)
4. Wolpaw, J.R., Birbaumer, N., McFarland, D.J., Pfurtscheller, G., Vaughan, T.M.: Brain-computer interfaces for communication and control. Clin. Neurophysiol. Official J. Int. Fed. Clin. Neurophysiol. **113**(6), 767–791 (2002)
5. Kaplan, A., Shishkin, S., Ganin, I., Basyul, I., Zhigalov, A.: Adapting the P300-based brain–computer interface for gaming: a review. IEEE Trans. Comput. Intell. AI Games **5**(2), 141–149 (2013)
6. Rossini, P.M.: Noris Ferilli, M.A., Ferreri, F.: Cortical plasticity and brain computer interface. Eur. J. Phys. Rehabil. Med. **48**(2), 307–312 (2012)
7. Alonso-Valerdi, L.M., Salido-Ruiz, R.A., Ramirez-Mendoza, R.A.: Motor imagery based brain-computer interfaces: an emerging technology to rehabilitate motor deficits. Neuropsychologia **79**(Pt B), 354–363 (2015)
8. Grosse-Wentrup, M., Schölkopf, B.: A review of performance variations in SMR-based brain – computer interfaces (BCIs). In: Guger, C., Allison, B.Z., Edlinger, G. (eds.) Brain-Computer Interface Research, pp. 39–51. Springer, Heidelberg (2013)
9. Allison, B.Z., Neuper, C.: Could anyone use a BCI? In: Tan, D.S., Nijholt, A. (eds.) Brain-Computer Interfaces, pp. 35–54. Springer, London (2010)
10. Hammer, E.M., Halder, S., Blankertz, B., Sannelli, C., Dickhaus, T., Kleih, S., Muller, K.R., Kubler, A.: Psychological predictors of SMR-BCI performance. Biol. Psychol. **89**(1), 80–86 (2012)
11. Vuckovic, A., Osuagwu, B.A.: Using a motor imagery questionnaire to estimate the performance of a Brain-Computer Interface based on object oriented motor imagery. Clin. Neurophysiol. Official J. Int. Fed. Clin. Neurophysiol. **124**(8), 1586–1595 (2013)
12. Blankertz, B., Sannelli, C., Halder, S., Hammer, E.M., Kubler, A., Muller, K.R., Curio, G., Dickhaus, T.: Neurophysiological predictor of SMR-based BCI performance. NeuroImage **51**(4), 1303–1309 (2010)
13. Halder, S., Varkuti, B., Bogdan, M., Kubler, A., Rosenstiel, W., Sitaram, R., Birbaumer, N.: Prediction of brain-computer interface aptitude from individual brain structure. Front. Hum. Neurosci. **7**, 105 (2013)
14. Hashimoto, R., Rothwell, J.C.: Dynamic changes in corticospinal excitability during motor imagery. Exp. Brain Res. **125**(1), 75–81 (1999)

15. Takemi, M., Masakado, Y., Liu, M., Ushiba, J.: Event-related desynchronization reflects downregulation of intracortical inhibition in human primary motor cortex. J. Neurophysiol. **110**(5), 1158–1166 (2013)
16. Oldfield, R.C.: The assessment and analysis of handedness: the Edinburgh inventory. Neuropsychologia **9**(1), 97–113 (1971)
17. Nuwer, M.R., Comi, G., Emerson, R., Fuglsang-Frederiksen, A., Guerit, J.M., Hinrichs, H., Ikeda, A., Luccas, F.J., Rappelsburger, P.: IFCN standards for digital recording of clinical EEG. International federation of clinical neurophysiology. Electroencephalogr. Clin. Neurophysiol. **106**(3), 259–261 (1998)
18. Schalk, G., McFarland, D.J., Hinterberger, T., Birbaumer, N., Wolpaw, J.R.: BCI2000: a general-purpose brain-computer interface (BCI) system. IEEE Trans. Bio-Med. Eng. **51**(6), 1034–1043 (2004)
19. Ramoser, H., Muller-Gerking, J., Pfurtscheller, G.: Optimal spatial filtering of single trial EEG during imagined hand movement. IEEE Trans. Rehabil. Eng. Publ. IEEE Eng. Med. Biol. Soc. **8**(4), 441–446 (2000)
20. Perrin, F., Pernier, J., Bertrand, O., Echallier, J.F.: Spherical splines for scalp potential and current density mapping. Electroencephalogr. Clin. Neurophysiol. **72**(2), 184–187 (1989)
21. Wang, D., Miao, D., Blohm, G.: Multi-class motor imagery EEG decoding for brain-computer interfaces. Front. Neurosci. **6**, 151 (2012)
22. Guger, C., Edlinger, G., Harkam, W., Niedermayer, I., Pfurtscheller, G.: How many people are able to operate an EEG-based brain-computer interface (BCI)? IEEE Trans. Neural Syst. Rehabil. Eng. **11**(2), 145–147 (2003)
23. Friedrich, E.V., Neuper, C., Scherer, R.: Whatever works: a systematic user-centered training protocol to optimize brain-computer interfacing individually. PLoS One **8**(9), e76214 (2013)
24. Vasilyev, A.N., Liburkina, S.P., Kaplan, A.Y.: Lateralization of EEG patterns in humans during motor imagery of arm movements in the brain-computer interface (in Russian). Zh. Vyssh. Nerv. Deiat. **66** (2016)
25. Yuan, H., Liu, T., Szarkowski, R., Rios, C., Ashe, J., He, B.: Negative covariation between task-related responses in alpha/beta-band activity and BOLD in human sensorimotor cortex: an EEG and fMRI study of motor imagery and movements. NeuroImage **49**(3), 2596–2606 (2010)
26. Horenstein, C., Lowe, M.J., Koenig, K.A., Phillips, M.D.: Comparison of unilateral and bilateral complex finger tapping-related activation in premotor and primary motor cortex. Hum. Brain Mapp. **30**(4), 1397–1412 (2009)
27. Wright, D.J., Williams, J., Holmes, P.S.: Combined action observation and imagery facilitates corticospinal excitability. Front. Hum. Neurosci. **8**, 951 (2014)
28. Aono, K., Miyashita, S., Fujiwara, Y., Kodama, M., Hanayama, K., Masakado, Y., Ushiba, J.: Relationship between event-related desynchronization and cortical excitability in healthy subjects and stroke patients. Tokai J. Exp. Clin. Med. **38**(4), 123–128 (2013)

Predicting EEG Sample Size Required for Classification Calibration

Zijing Mao[1], Tzyy-Ping Jung[2], Chin-Teng Lin[3], and Yufei Huang[1]($\boxtimes$)

[1] Department of Electrical and Computer Engineering,
University of Texas, San Antonio, TX, USA
`mzj168@hotmail.com`, `yufei.huang@utsa.edu`
[2] Institute for Neural Computation,
University of California, San Diego, CA, USA
`jung@sccn.ucsd.edu`
[3] Brain Research Center, National Chiao Tung University,
Hsinchu, Taiwan
`ctlin@mail.nctu.edu.tw`

Abstract. This study considers an important problem of predicting required calibration sample size for electroencephalogram (EEG)-based classification in brain computer interaction (BCI). We propose an adaptive algorithm based on learning curve fitting to learn the relationship between sample size and classification performance for each individual subject. The algorithm can always provide the predicted result in advance of reaching the baseline performance with an average error of 17.4 %. By comparing the learning curve of different classifiers, the algorithm can also recommend the best classifier for a BCI application. The algorithm also learns a sample size upper bound from the prior datasets and uses it to detect subject outliers that potentially need excessive amount of calibration data. The algorithm is applied to three EEG-based BCI datasets to demonstrate its utility and efficacy. A Matlab package with GUI is also developed and available for downloading at https://github.com/ZijingMao/LearningCurveFittingForSampleSizePrediction. Since few algorithms are yet available to predict performance for BCIs, our algorithm will be an important tool for real-life BCI applications.

Keywords: Sample size prediction · Calibration · Brain computer interface · EEG · Rapid serial visual presentation · Driver's fatigue

1 Introduction

A brain computer interaction (BCI) system allows interactions between human and an external device through monitoring brain signals [1]. EEG-based BCIs have become increasingly popular in the past decade, finding real-life applications from controlling wheel chairs to monitoring human performance [2]. Most of the BCI systems require a calibration stage, where training samples are collected to build a classification model for event detection from brain signals. The current practice of BCIs relies on collecting an excessively large amount of calibration data to ensure that a robust classifier can be built. Such practice has become a bottleneck for the BCI applications in real-world

© Springer International Publishing Switzerland 2016
D.D. Schmorrow and C.M. Fidopiastis (Eds.): AC 2016, Part I, LNAI 9743, pp. 57–68, 2016.
DOI: 10.1007/978-3-319-39955-3_6

settings because such practice prolongs BCI training time and deteriorates user performance due to induced fatigue on users. Moreover, due to individual differences in brain responses, calibration needs to be adapted for each individual. Related efforts have been made to take advantage of machine learning (ML) algorithms such as active learning [3] and transfer learning [4, 5] by borrowing from existing data from the same or other subjects to reduce the calibration samples as much as possible. However, as long as there is a need for collecting calibration samples, determining an appropriate calibration sample size for each individual before the training is an important issue to be tackled. In fact, integrating sample size prediction together with transfer learning in the calibration stage should be a favorable practice.

Despite its importance, the problem for predicting calibration sample size for BCIs has not received much attention in the past. However, the problem of sample size estimation (SSE) [6] has been studied in many other fields for different purposes. The existing work stems mostly from three main types of methods. The first type is the power analysis for sample size calculation [7], a method that is widely applied in biostatistics, bioinformatics, and clinical research [7–9]. Power analysis requires information about effect size, significance level, and power of the underlying hypothesis testing to predict the sample size; sophisticated tools [9] have been developed for this analysis. However, power analysis concerns more on the statistical significance rather than the classification performance as in BCIs. The second type of methods treats SSE as an optimization problem and defines specific optimization functions to balance the cost and benefit of using a sample size [10]. However, these optimization-based SSE methods require knowledge to define cost and benefit in the same domain such that they can be compared and thus optimized; this knowledge is difficult to obtain in many applications including BCIs. For instance, while it is possible to assess the cost of collecting samples in BCIs in terms of money or time, it is nevertheless difficult to assess the benefit in performance improvement in terms of cost or time. The last type of methods is the learning curve fitting, which fits a regression model to the observed sample sizes and performances to capture the relationship between performance and sample size. Since 1936, learning-curve fitting has been studied and applied in many industrial fields [11]. One of the most widely used fitting model is the inverse power law [11], by the intuitive thought of more samples always improve the performance but improvements decay gradually. Because of its data-driven nature and ease of implementation, we apply it for the prediction of calibration sample sizes for BCIs.

We propose a novel adaptive algorithm for EEG calibration-sample-size prediction. The algorithm has several unique features tailored for BCI tasks. First, the algorithm utilizes the prior datasets commonly available in BCIs to suggest a baseline performance and to derive a population-wide sample size upper bound. Second, it adaptively fits the learning curve between performance and sample size for each individual and makes the prediction of calibration sample size when a satisfactory fitting confidence level is reached. Third, it also provides a way to identify subject outliers that potentially need excessive amount of calibration data. Fourthly, it can be used to select the best classifier for BCIs. We evaluated the algorithm and demonstrated its efficacy on three different BCI datasets. A Matlab package with GUI is also developed and released to facilitate the application of the proposed methods (https://github.com/ZijingMao/LearningCurveFittingForSampleSizePrediction).

The remainder of the paper is organized as follows. Section 2 discusses the proposed algorithm in details. Testing results are reported in Sect. 3. Conclusions are drawn in Sect. 4.

2   Materials and Methods

2.1   Experiments and Data

Data from three BCI experiments are used in this study to test the proposed algorithm. The experiments include two image Rapid Serial Visual Presentation (RSVP) [12] experiments and one simulated driving experiments for driver performance study. The RSVP experiments are Static Motion (D1) and the Cognitive Technology Threat Warning System (CT2WS or D2) [13, 14]. The static motion RSVP experiments include the presentations of color target images of enemy soldiers/combatants versus the background non-target images of village street scenes. The CT2WS experiment includes presentations of gray scale images, where target images include moving people and vehicle animations, whereas the non-targets are other types of animations such as plants or buildings. Each subject performed four sessions in static motion and only one session in CT2WS, where each session lasted for about 15 min. For both experiments, the images were presented at 2 Hz (one image presented every 500 ms) and brain signals were recorded with 64-channel Biosemi EEG systems at a sampling rate of 512 Hz. There were a total of 16 and 15 subjects in the static motion and CT2WS experiment, respectively. The simulated driving dataset (D3) includes EEG samples from 17 subjects, each performed a lane-keeping driving task in a virtual reality interactive driving platform with a 3-D highway scene [15]. Perturbations to the car were introduced into driving path every 8 to 12 s and driver's reaction time and the amount of the lane deviation was measured to assess the degree of driver's drowsiness. Each experiment lasted one and half hours during which EEG signals were measured from 30 electrodes. The reaction time (RT) is defined as the time between the onset of the lane perturbation and the moment when the subject starts steering the car. RT is used to define the drowsy or alert state of the driver. Particularly, when the reaction time is ≤ 0.7s, the driver is considered as alert, whereas when the reaction time is ≥ 2.1s, the driver is considered as drowsy.

2.2   Data Preprocessing

EEG data from three experiments were subject to the similar preprocessing steps. Particularly, the raw EEG data were first bandpass-filtered with a bandwidth ranging from 0.1–50 Hz in order to remove DC noise and electrical artifacts. Down-sampling was performed next to reduce the sampling rate from the original 512 Hz to 128 Hz, which is the maximum down-sampled frequency that does not produce aliasing at the high-passed frequency. Then, by following [16], one-second epochs of the EEG samples after each image onset were extracted for all the subjects to be used as data for calibration and prediction. In the end, about 13,500 epochs from Static Motion (~ 1000 epochs per subject) and about 10,400 epochs from CT2WS (~ 700 epochs per subject) were obtained. For the driving data, we used one-second epochs before the onsets of the perturbations as data for predicting the "drowsy" or "alert" state of the drivers. There is a total of 2,796 (764 drowsy and 2,032 alert) epochs from the 17 subjects. Because the sampling rate is 250 Hz, the dimension of one-second EEG epoch is $250 \times 30 = 7500$. Afterwards, normalization was applied to all the epochs. Each (channel × time) pair in the calibration set was normalized across epochs by z-score normalization. The test sets were then z-score normalized according to the calibration set mean and standard deviation. The goal for RSVP classification is to predict if the subject sees a target image based on the epoch data while for driving performance classification, the goal is to predict if the subject has a slow reaction time.

2.3 The Proposed Scheme for Calibration Sample Size Prediction

The goal of calibration sample size prediction is to suggest an appropriate sample size for calibrating the classification algorithm for a new subject. We consider a common scenario in BCIs, where the prior datasets collected from other subjects performing the same task are available and therefore a baseline performances P_B (e.g. $P_B = 0.9$ Area under ROC or AUC) for satisfactory event classification is learned. Intuitively, an appropriate sample size is the one needed for a classifier to reach the baseline performance, or the baseline sample size S_B as we will refer to next and we hope to predict S_B, denoted as $\widehat{S_B}$ for an individual by collecting only a small number of calibration samples from the subject. To this end, we propose an adaptive algorithm, where at the mth iteration, M new samples are collected and an intermedium prediction and its confidence are calculated using all the samples collected thus far. The final prediction is reached when the prediction confidence falls within a tolerate threshold (e.g. 95 % significance level). At the mth iteration, to make a prediction, a learning curve is first fitted to the performance of a classifier. A learning curve characterizes the classification performance (p_{Az}) as a function of calibration sample size s and as in [8], can be represented using an inverse power law (IPL) model [11]

$$p(s) = f(s; a, b, c) = a \times s^b + c, \tag{1}$$

where a, b and c, are the model parameters that represent the decay rate, learning rate, and bias, respectively. The goal of fitting is to estimate the parameters using the classification performances obtained at all m iterations. To this end, the non-linear least square method is applied in this work and a 95 % confidence interval $I(s)$ of the fitting for the sample size s is also reported. An illustration of this process is shown in Fig. 2. As can be seen, using the learning curve, the sample size s_A can be predicted from (1) by setting $p(s) = P_B$. Then, $I(s_A)$, the 95 % confidence interval at $s = s_A$, is compared with a predefined tolerance level T_s. We define T_s by calculating the ratio between curve fitting confidence interval bound and s_A. For example, if we set $T_s = 0.02$, it means the range of confidence interval is 2 % of s_A. If $I(s_A) < T_s$, then s_A is reported as the predicted baseline sample size; otherwise additional M samples will be collected and one additional iteration will be performed.

   For some subjects, S_B can be excessively large and it might not be prudent to collect such large samples given limited resources. To determine if S_B is too large, we resort to the prior datasets. Particularly, we bootstrap the dataset 100 times and for each boot-strapped data, we perform cross-validation to determine the baseline sample size S_B. Then, we counted the histogram of all the bootstrapped baseline sample sizes to generate the population-wide distribution of S_B. Based on this distribution, we esti-mated a population-wide sample size upper bound S_β, as $P(S_B > S_\beta) \leq 0.05$. Given that the prior dataset is large enough to capture the data distribution of the subject population, S_β can be interpreted as a sample size upper bound such that only 5 % of subjects require more samples to reach the baseline performance P_B. Therefore, the predicted baseline sample size $\widehat{S_B}$ for the subject of interest can be determined to be excessively large if $\widehat{S_B} > S_\beta$. In this case, we recommend $\widehat{S_B} = S_\beta$ if there is prior dataset for performing transfer learning. Otherwise, we suggest excluding this subject from this task. Taking together, we report $\widehat{S_B}$ as the predicted calibration sample size if $\widehat{S_B} < S_\beta$; otherwise, we suggest to collect S_β calibration samples and then apply transfer learning (TL) algorithms to improve the classification performance to P_B. The proce-dure of the algorithm is summarized as follows.

Initialize the baseline performance and sample size: P_B and S_β

Initialize sample size increment M and initial sample size s_c

Initialize the tolerance level

While $S_\beta > s_c$ **do**

- Obtain calibration performance $p_{Az}(s_c)$ based on s_c
- Based on all obtained p_{Az}s, fit learning curve $p(s)$
- Estimate the baseline sample size
- Estimate 95% CI, $I(s_A)$

  If $I(s_A) < T_s$ **do**

    - Predicted baseline sample size $\widehat{S_B} \leftarrow s_A$

    If $p_{Az}(s_c) > P_B$ **do**

      Break

    End if

  End if

- Current sample size $s_c \leftarrow s_c + M$

End while

If $\widehat{S_B} > S_\beta$ **or** $\widehat{S_B}$ does not exist **do**

- Set predicted baseline sample $\widehat{S_B} = S_\beta$; or exclude the current subject

Else

- Report predicted baseline sample $\widehat{S_B}$

End if

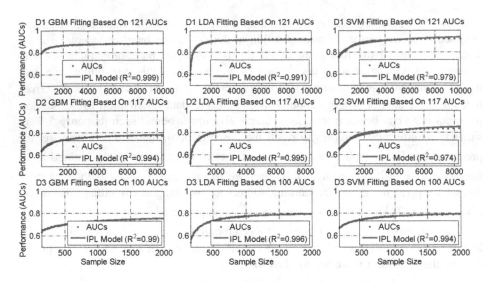

Fig. 1. Learning curve fitting of 3 datasets for 3 classification methods. The blue dots are AUCs obtained by calibration with an increasing size of EEG samples. These AUCs were obtained at sample sizes linear-spaced below 1,000 with a step size of 10 and log-spaced above 1,000 with a step size that amounts to 50 logarithmically even-spaced points between 10^3 and 10^4. (Color figure online)

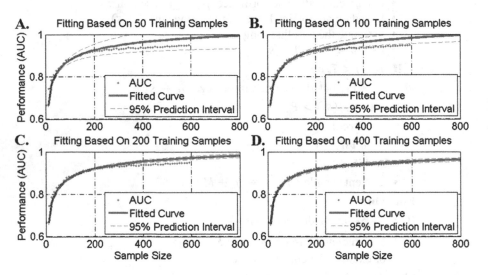

Fig. 2. An illustration of adaptive learning curve fitting. The blue dots are AUCs obtained by calibration with an increasing size of EEG samples. The figures show the fitting results of using different calibration sample sizes, where **A, B, C, D** used the 50, 100, 200, 400 calibration samples (which means using the first 5, 10, 20 and 40 blue dots) to fit the learning curve (red line) respectively. The data come from subject 1 of Static Motion RSVP (D1). (Color figure online)

We can also apply this algorithm to select the best classifier for the BCI task. Specifically, we predict the sample sizes for all candidate classifiers and the one that is associated with the smallest predicted sample size is selected.

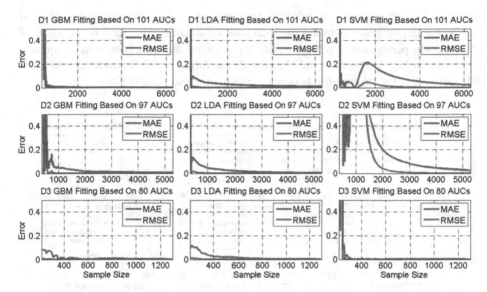

Fig. 3. Mean absolute error (MAE, blue line) and root mean squared error (RMSE, red line) as a function of calibration sample size. The horizontal axis is the sample size used for calibration and obtaining the baseline AUCs, and the vertical axis is the value of MAE and RMSE. (Color figure online)

3 Results

This section demonstrates the performance and utility of the proposed algorithm of calibration sample size prediction using 3 BCI datasets, as described in Sect. 2; and considered 3 classification algorithms including gradient boosting method (GBM) [17], linear discriminant analysis (LDA) [18] and support vector machines (SVM) [18]. As a result, we have nine different combinations for performance evaluation.

3.1 Learning Curve Fitting

We first examined the performance of learning curve fitting, where, for each dataset, we merged samples from all subjects and fitted the inverse power law model for each of the three classifiers, separately. Sample size increased from 300 to 10,000 in D1, from 300 to 8,500 in D2, and from 150 to 2,000 in D3, respectively and at a particular sample size, bootstrapping was performed to calculate the classification ROC of AUCs for each classifier. Figure 1 shows the results of nine fitted learning curves. We also calculated the R^2 statistic as a measurement of the goodness of fit (GoF). The R^2 is denoted by:

$$R^2 = \frac{\sum_n \left(f\left(s_n^{fit}; a, b, c \right) - p_n^{fit} \right)^2}{\sum_n \left(p_n^{fit} - \overline{p_{fit}} \right)^2}, \tag{2}$$

where s_n^{fit} and p_n^{fit} represent the nth fitting sample size and the corresponding ROC of AUCs, the denominator is called the total sum of squares, where $\overline{p_{fit}}$ is the mean of classification performance, and the numerator is called the regression sum of squares. As shown in Fig. 1, R^2 scores are high for all the fitting (> 97 %), indicating that the IPL can model the relationship between performance and sample size.

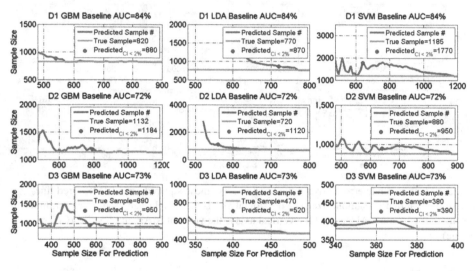

Fig. 4. Adaptive prediction of baseline sample size. The horizontal axis is the sample size used for calibration and obtaining a baseline AUCs. The vertical axis is the sample size predicted by learning curve in order to reach the baseline AUC. The green and red line indicates the true (S_B) and predicted ($\widehat{S_B}$) calibration sample size for the baseline AUC respectively. The blue dot represents the calibration sample size that can reach < 2 % of confidence interval for the learning curve fitting. (Color figure online)

Next, we examined the adaptive fitting of the learning curve and its ability to predict future performance as described above. Figure 2 shows an example of the adaptive fitting and prediction results for Subject 1 in static motion RSVP (D1). In Fig. 2A, the curve was fitted using first 5 AUC points (trained by 50 EEG samples). The predicted curve (red line) deviates slightly from the true AUCs after the 5th point (blue dots) and as expected, both deviations and prediction confidence intervals grow larger as we move further into a larger sample size. However, the true AUCs do fall in between the 95 % confidence interval (orange lines) consistently. As we increased the number of fitting points from 5 to 40 (trained by 50 to 400 EEG samples), the predicted curve became increasingly similar to the behavior of the true AUCs and at the same time the 95 % confidence interval grew much narrower (Fig. 2A–D). At 40 points, the

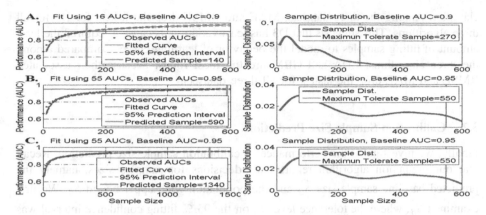

Fig. 5. Illustration of three scenarios that result in different sample size prediction. **A** and **B** are results from subject 1, D1, where the baseline AUCs P_B were set as 0.9 and 0.95, respectively. **C** shows the results from subject 2, D1 where $P_B = 0.95$. The blue dots are AUCs obtained by calibration with an increasing size of EEG samples. The red line is the fitted learning curve. The green vertical line is predicted sample size obtained from fitted learning curve in order to reach P_B. The figures in the right columns depict the distribution of calibration sample size estimated from the prior dataset in order to reach a given P_B. The blue line indicates the sample size distribution and the red line indicates the maximum tolerate sample size for calibration, calculated by the maximum 5 % of the sample size distribution. (Color figure online)

predicted curve closely resembled the true learning curve with very high confidence (Fig. 2D). To systematically evaluate the prediction, we use prediction mean absolute error (MAE) and root mean squared error (RMSE) for each dataset, as in [8], which are defined as

$$MAE = \frac{1}{N}\sum_n \left| f\left(s_n^{pred}; a, b, c\right) - p_n^{pred} \right|, \tag{3}$$

$$RMSE = \sqrt{\frac{1}{N}\sum_n \left(f\left(s_n^{Pred}; a, b, c\right) - p_n^{pred} \right)^2}, \tag{4}$$

where s_n^{Pred} and p_n^{Pred} are n^{th} sample size and corresponding AUC obtained by calibration with n EEG data samples. Figure 3 shows MAE and RMSE as a function of fitting sample size for all three datasets. For each dataset, AUCs associated with 20 largest sample sizes were retained and used for evaluating the prediction MAE and RMSE for learning curve fitted by an increasing sample size. Specifically, D1, D2 and D3 fitted the learning curve using calibration samples range from 300 to 6000, 300 to 5000 and 150 to 1300 with respect. As expected, both RMSE and MAE decrease and became very close to zero as the fitting sample size grows larger. In nearly all datasets, a mean error less than 0.1 can be reached after the sample size increased to 1,000, suggesting that the proposed adaptive prediction of learning curve is effective. The rate that RMSE or MAE drops is also an indication of data variation and robustness of classifier. Among the three datasets, MAE and RMSE drop the fastest for D3 for all three algorithms. This suggests that D3 has least variation, because it required the least amount of fitting samples to model the behavior of learning curve. Compared among the three algorithms, LDA and GBM are the most robust because their associated RMSE and MAE drop the fastest for all three datasets.

3.2   Calibration Sample Size Prediction

Finally, we investigated the performance of calibration sample size prediction. Recall that our prediction algorithm reports two decisions for samples sizes, namely the predicted baseline sample size $\widehat{S_B}$ and the population-wide upper bound S_β. We first examined $\widehat{S_B}$, where the tolerance level Ts on the 95 % fitting confidence interval was set to 2 %. For each dataset, 1,000 samples were randomly selected as the prior dataset, from which classification AUCs for each of the three classifiers were obtained. Then, the average AUCs of the three classifiers were used as the baseline performance P_B for each dataset. Figure 4 illustrates the trajectories of the adaptive prediction for all cases. Given a baseline performance, we gradually increased calibration data and updated learning curve coefficients. Once we reached a pre-set confidence level for the curve fitting, this algorithm would stop from obtaining new calibration data and provide a prediction of the calibration sample size that will be used in order to reach the baseline. For instance, it was predicted that for dataset D1, at the tolerance level 2 %, $\widehat{S_B}$ = 880 samples are needed for GBM to reach the baseline performance P_B = 0.84. In this case, the true sample size for P_B = 0.84 is 820 and therefore our algorithm predicted 30 more samples or a 7.5 % error. Setting a more stringent tolerance level can further reduce this error. Examining all nine cases, we can always observe convergence to the true calibration samples size as the sample size increases and the prediction result when compared with the baseline performance has an error of 17.4 % on average. More specifically, GBM has an average prediction error of 6.2 %, LDA has an error of 26.5 %, and SVM has an error of 20 %. Besides, it is observed that our algorithm usually overestimated the baseline sample size. In practice, an overestimation is preferred because an overestimated $\widehat{S_B}$ would always ensure that the baseline performance could be reached. As discussed previously, $\widehat{S_B}$ can be used to select classifier for BCI. In this case, LDA is selected for D1 and D2, whereas SVM is selected for D3. These selections are consistent with those based on the true baseline sample size, suggesting again that our prediction algorithm can correctly assess the relationship between sample size and classification performance.

Finally, we investigated the scenarios where we need to consider the population-wide upper bound S_β. Particularly, we used the dataset D1 to simulate three potential scenarios. For the first scenario, we set the baseline AUC P_B = 0.9. We used the randomly selected 1,000 samples to estimate the distribution of baseline sample size, from which we had S_β = 270 (Fig. 5A). Then, we focused on Subject 1 and determined that $\widehat{S_B}$ = 140. Since $\widehat{S_B} < S_\beta$, the calibration sample size was predicted to be 140 (Fig. 5A). In the second scenario, we increased the P_B = 0.95. Once again, we estimated the distribution of the baseline performance from the 1,000 prior data samples and $\widehat{S_B}$ for Subject 1. This time, we had $\widehat{S_B} = 550$ but predicted calibration sample $\widehat{S_B} = 590$ (Fig. 5B). Since $\widehat{S_B} > S_\beta$, we would suggest to collect 550 samples for calibration. However, notice that $\widehat{S_B}$ is only 40 samples more than S_β, therefore one might consider collecting the predicted 590 samples instead, if resources permit. In the third scenario, we still set $P_B = 0.95$ and therefore $S_\beta = 550$. However, we chose to predict the baseline sample size for Subject 2, where we had $\widehat{S_B} = 1,340$ (Fig. 5C). Since this time $\widehat{S_B} \gg S_\beta$, we would suggest to collect only 550 samples.

4 Conclusion and Future Work

This study proposed a new algorithm for predicting calibration sample size for EEG)-based classification in BCIs. The key component of the algorithm is an adaptive fitting of a learning curve. Instead of producing a single prediction, our algorithm outputs a predicted baseline sample size and a population-wide upper bound. Empirical results showed that our algorithm can correctly predict the behavior between classification performance and sample size. Providing two predicted sample sizes gives user more flexibility to reach a case-specific decision. In addition, the predicted sample size can be used to select an appropriate classifier for BCI.

Another important future direction is to investigate the integration of the sample size prediction methods with transfer learning to achieve reduced calibration data. There are two potential directions for this investigation. First, we can investigate progressive classifiers with TL and generate a learning curve for sample size prediction based on the results coming from these classifiers. Second, we can exploit TL when a subject with the predicted sample size much greater than our expected baseline calibration sample size. Specifically, we can design TL algorithms for the subject to improve the classification accuracy and also reduce calibration samples.

Acknowledgments. Research was sponsored in part by the Army Research Laboratory and was accomplished under Cooperative Agreement Number W911NF-10-2-0022. The views and conclusions contained in this document are those of the authors and should not be interpreted as representing the official policies, either expressed or implies, of the Army Research Laboratory or the U.S. Government. The U.S. Government is authorized to reproduce and distribute reprints for the Government purposes notwithstanding any copyright notation herein. This work received computational support from Computational System Biology Core at the University of Texas at San Antonio, funded by the National Institute on Minority Health and Health Disparities (G12MD007591) from the National Institutes of Health.

References

1. Wolpaw, J.R., Birbaumer, N., Heetderks, W.J., McFarland, D.J., Peckham, P.H., Schalk, G., et al.: Brain-computer interface technology: a review of the first international meeting. IEEE Trans. Rehabil. Eng. **8**, 164–173 (2000)

2. Bigdely-Shamlo, N., Vankov, A., Ramirez, R.R., Makeig, S.: Brain activity-based image classification from rapid serial visual presentation. IEEE Trans. Neural Syst. Rehabil. Eng. **16**, 432–441 (2008)
3. Wu, D., Lance, B.J., Parsons, T.D.: Collaborative filtering for brain-computer interaction using transfer learning and active class selection. PLoS ONE **8**, e56624 (2013)
4. Sun, S., Zhou, J.: A review of adaptive feature extraction and classification methods for EEG-based brain-computer interfaces. In: 2014 International Joint Conference on Neural Networks (IJCNN), pp. 1746–1753 (2014)
5. Panicker, R.C., Puthusserypady, S., Sun, Y.: Adaptation in P300 brain–computer interfaces: a two-classifier cotraining approach. IEEE Trans. Biomed. Eng. **57**, 2927–2935 (2010)
6. Eng, J.: Sample Size Estimation: How Many Individuals Should Be Studied? Radiology **227**, 309–313 (2003)
7. Suresh, K., Chandrashekara, S.: Sample size estimation and power analysis for clinical research studies. J. Hum. Reprod. Sci. **5**, 7 (2012)
8. Figueroa, R.L., Zeng-Treitler, Q., Kandula, S., Ngo, L.H.: Predicting sample size required for classification performance. BMC Med. Inform. Decis. Mak. **12**, 8 (2012)
9. Zodpey, S.P.: Sample size and power analysis in medical research. Indian J. Dermatol. Venereol. Leprology **70**, 123 (2004)
10. Meek, C., Thiesson, B., Heckerman, D.: The learning-curve sampling method applied to model-based clustering. J. Mach. Learn. Res. **2**, 397–418 (2002)
11. Cortes, C., Jackel, L.D., Solla, S.A., Vapnik, V., Denker, J.S.: Learning curves: asymptotic values and rate of convergence. Adv. Neural Inf. Process. Syst. **6**, 327–334 (1994)
12. Meng, J., Meriño, L.M., Shamlo, N.B., Makeig, S., Robbins, K., Huang, Y.: Characterization and robust classification of EEG signal from image RSVP events with independent time-frequency features. PLoS ONE **7**, e44464 (2012)
13. U.S. Department of the Army. Use of volunteers as subjects of research. AR 70–25 Washington DC. Government Printing Office (1990)
14. U.S Department of Defense Office of the Secretary of Defense, Code of federal regulations, protection of human subjects. 32 CFR 219, vol. 32 CFR 219 (1999)
15. Chuang, S.-W., Ko, L.-W., Lin, Y.-P., Huang, R.-S., Jung, T.-P., Lin, C.-T.: Co-modulatory spectral changes in independent brain processes are correlated with task performance. Neuroimage **62**, 1469–1477 (2012)
16. Sajda, P., Pohlmeyer, E., Wang, J., Parra, L.C., Christoforou, C., Dmochowski, J., et al.: In a blink of an eye and a switch of a transistor: cortically coupled computer vision. Proc. IEEE **98**, 462–478 (2010)
17. Friedman, J.H.: Stochastic gradient boosting. Comput. Stat. Data Anal. **38**, 367–378 (2002)
18. McLachlan, G.: Discriminant Analysis and Statistical Pattern Recognition, vol. 544. Wiley, New York (2004)

An SSVEP and Eye Tracking Hybrid BNCI: Potential Beyond Communication and Control

Paul McCullagh[1(✉)], Chris Brennan[1], Gaye Lightbody[1],
Leo Galway[1], Eileen Thompson[3], and Suzanne Martin[2]

[1] Computer Science Research Institute, Newtownabbey, UK
{pj.mccullagh,g.lightbody,l.galway}@ulster.ac.uk,
Brennan-C15@email.ulster.ac.uk
[2] Nursing & Health Research Institute, Ulster University, Jordanstown, UK
s.martin@ulster.ac.uk
[3] The Cedar Foundation, Malcolm Sinclair House, 31 Ulsterville Avenue,
Belfast BT9 7AS, UK
E.Thomson@cedar-foundation.org

Abstract. Brain-Neural Machine/Computer Interface (BNCI) has been used successfully as an assistive technology to restore communication, improve control and thus potentially enhance social inclusion. Recently BNCI technology and interfaces have evolved to become more usable, thereby allowing the recording of brain activity to become part of the wider self-quantification movement. A hybrid BNCI can provide a viable but alternative interface for Human Computer Interaction, which combines the inputs from BNCI and eye tracking. This hybrid approach has maintained information transfer rate but increased robustness and overall usability. The combination of two complementary technologies provides the possibility for investigating new ways of human enhancement and has the potential to open up new medical applications.

Keywords: Applications · BCI · Eye-tracking · Medical · SSVEP

1 Introduction

The quintessential application for Brain-Neural Machine/Computer Interface (BNCI) [1, 2] has been as an assistive technology for individuals suffering from neural dysfunction of such severity that other assistive technologies cannot offer appropriate functionality. Relevant conditions have included amyotrophic lateral sclerosis, cerebral palsy, stroke, or spinal cord injury [3]. BNCI aims to enable users to interact with a computer interface without the use of peripheral nerves and muscles, to restore communication, improve control and possibly enhance social inclusion [4]. Recently BNCI technology has evolved from complex research grade systems to more usable bespoke devices, thereby allowing the recording of Electroencephalographic (EEG) and neuronal activity to become part of the wider self-quantification movement. Swan states: *"Analyzing multiple QS (quantified self) data streams in real-time (for example, heart-rate variability, galvanic skin response, temperature, movement, and EEG activity) may likely be required for accurate assessment and intervention regarding biophysical state"* [5].

© Springer International Publishing Switzerland 2016
D.D. Schmorrow and C.M. Fidopiastis (Eds.): AC 2016, Part I, LNAI 9743, pp. 69–78, 2016.
DOI: 10.1007/978-3-319-39955-3_7

For non-invasive use this has led to a proliferation of cheaper, consumer devices, which can be easily donned and doffed, are more aesthetically pleasing, and use water-based or dry electrodes. Software development kits have become available to the non-specialist, thereby extending domain use into additional lifestyle applications, such as gaming [6] and brain training [7].

Part of the evolution of BNCI has been in the development of hybrid systems which go beyond pure EEG-based paradigms to those that accept multiple inputs from different modalities. Pfurtscheller *et al.* [8] provide an overview of hybrid Brain-Computer Interface (hBCI) systems, defining concepts and language which has strongly influenced research development in this area. They discuss different ways of combining Brain-Computer Interfaces, with the target of reducing errors, improving available selections, and creating a more usable and robust system. In this paper, we investigate a hBNCI approach, which influences the speed of operation of a graphical interface as measured by Information Transfer Rate (ITR). When an acceptable ITR has been reached, then the collaborative input modalities can be used to ensure more robust operation by reducing errors (paradoxically this may be at the expense of ITR, as damping may occur in the system). However, robustness of operation is a crucial factor for user acceptance, particularly for people with brain dysfunction. In addition, the collection of complementary BNCI and eye tracking data provides the potential for investigation beyond communication and control. Thus the application area for hBNCI can move beyond assistive technology, allowing the exploration of new applications, some of which can be in the medical domain.

2   Background and BNCI Users

Different experimental paradigms can be applied to generate the desired brain electrical activity, known as the electroencephalogram that facilitates the interaction with a chosen computer-based application. Prominent approaches include Event-Related Desynchronisation/Synchronisation (ERD/ERS), Steady State Visually Evoked Potentials (SSVEP), and the P300 oddball paradigm (with acoustic or visual stimulation). Each approach is hindered by its own set of limitations, such as time consuming training and recording, but many inhibiting issues are prevalent in all approaches, such as intra-subject variability, poor signal quality, and limited duration for wearing the technology. These issues have been limiting factors for wider exploitation of BNCI technology in the medical domain. EU FP7 funded projects such as BRAIN, BRAINABLE and Back Home aimed to bring BNCI technology out of the laboratory and into the homes of disabled users. This provided a significant stimulus for addressing communication and control. However, target users involved in the BRAIN study, for example, had cognitive challenges in addition to their physical disability. Furthermore, computer literacy also had an impact on the user acceptance of the technology [9]. In addition to usability issues, poorer BNCI performance was noted in the target user group of brain impaired people, as compared to the healthy control group, and the resulting SSVEP controlled system provided a less than acceptable level of accuracy [10] for the target user group.

3 Hybrid BNCI

There are technical reasons why it could be beneficial to combine different inputs for BNCI. As already highlighted, different modalities have their own merits and drawbacks, which are strongly aligned to the application and user variability. Amiri *et al.* [11] state: "Compared to other modalities for BCI approaches ..... SSVEP-based BCI system has the advantage of having higher accuracy and higher information transfer rate (ITR). In addition, short/no training time and fewer EEG channels are required." The BCI component is often used as a switch or selector, for example, see Pfurtscheller *et al.* [8]: ERD BCI (brain switch) with SSVEP (control of orthosis); ERD combined with SSVEP (joint selection); ERD combined with heart rate (joint selection); Eye gaze (selection) with ERD. In the example of a brain "switch" a control command is only allowed to be activated when a separate BCI control is active. Such a system mitigates the risk of false positives. In terms of "selection" it could be that the two inputs work collaboratively to make a more robust selection. Or, in the example of eye gaze with ERD, the initial selection is made using eye gaze but this decision is activated with ERD [12].

The prospect of combining a neural input with another mechanism such as eye gaze can address under performance issues of BNCI by people with brain dysfunction. Eye tracking-based control was investigated, producing a hybrid architecture, with the potential to overcome restrictions of speed and variability, thus providing a more robust operation [13, 14]. Eye-tracking technology has advanced significantly, producing low cost portable hardware components with open software interfaces mirroring the technical advances of BNCI. Consequently, an hBNCI system has been implemented to facilitate control of a computer interface and virtual domestic smart environment, as illustrated in Fig. 1.

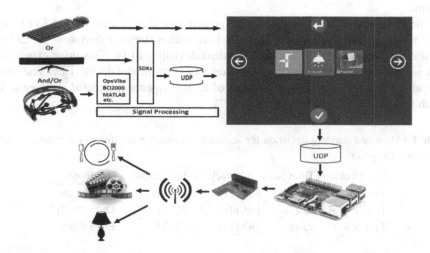

Fig. 1. Hybrid BNCI architecture showing input devices, signal processing options, user interface and actuation components

Users have the ability to open and close doors, control the television or indicate needs (need for drinking or eating) or emotions. Combining input modalities with biosignals that have different temporal properties presents a technical challenge in terms of both data fusion and apposite user interface development. However it can offer new opportunities beyond current BNCI.

An experiment was devised to test the robustness of the hybrid approach (albeit on a normal population). Twelve volunteers age 23–57 (8 male, 4 female) interacted with the user interface for three tasks: domotic control; multimedia playback and communication. Interaction was by 4-way choice (right, left, up, select). There were two conditions: eye-tracking only and eye tracking plus BNCI. The Eyetribe Tracker was used to record gaze (latency < 20 ms with an accuracy for 0.5–1 degree, with the subject located approximately 50 cm from the monitor). The Emotiv EPOC provided a BNCI component, using a teeth clench for select. This was chosen as the device comes pre-selected with a number of classified events (appropriate to the static electrode montage of this fixed device) as part of the Expressiv suite. Electronic communication between the eye-tracker/Emotiv headset and user interface is by User Datagram Protocol (UDP) packets, providing a flexible inter-process communication. These are generated/triggered asynchronously (by the participant) and managed by the user interface algorithm, with the slower EEG component acting as a confirmation of the less constrained eye-gaze. The packets are populated in real-time from the respective Eyetribe and Emotiv Application Programming Interfaces (APIs), allowing a responsive and controllable interface. Values for duration, accuracy, efficiency (defined in [15]), and ITR were computed (as defined by Gao et al. [16]). Tables 1 and 2 show the mean and standard deviation for user performance metrics: time, accuracy, efficiency and ITR for eye-tracking only and hybrid respectively. In Tasks 1 and 3 the ITRs are approximately constant but the accuracy and efficiency increase for the hBNCI. In Task 2 the metrics are maintained. Overall accuracy and efficiency are better for the hybrid system.

The ITRs of both configurations were greater than that of a previous SSVEP-only study which yielded a mean ITR of 15.23 bpm with a standard deviation of 7.9 bpm and a mean accuracy of 79 % with a standard deviation 14 %. This prior experiment used similar tasks with external stimulation LEDs, to modulate the EEG and assist navigation. However, crucially only 6 out of 23 participants completed all three tasks, which testified to its lack of robustness [17].

Table 1. Mean and standard deviation for accuracy, efficiency and information transfer rate for eye-tracker (N = 12)

Eye-Tracking	Time (sec)	Accuracy %	Efficiency %	ITR (bpm)
Task 1	42 (9)	88 (7)	80 (11)	40.98 (7.28)
Task 2	73 (7)	95 (4)	92 (7)	42.75 (3.65)
Task 3	25 (8)	83 (11)	73 (16)	39.75 (9.05)

Of course this hybrid is based on a low cost commercial headset. It has since been improved by incorporating an SSVEP component or components. The simplest configuration is to use an on-screen SSVEP stimulation as a switch for the eye tracker.

Table 2. Mean and standard deviation for accuracy, efficiency and information transfer rate for hybrid (N = 12)

Hybrid	Time (sec)	Accuracy %	Efficiency %	ITR (bpm)
Task 1	39 (6)	94 (6)	94 (8)	40.92 (6.12)
Task 2	77 (13)	95 (5)	94 (6)	39.49 (5.76)
Task 3	21 (2)	97 (7)	97 (7)	41.11 (5.36)

However, it is also possible to utilise four stimulation frequencies, allowing for the following navigation options: (i) SSVEP only; and (ii) SSVEP and eye tracking collaborative navigation. The key BNCI components are the quantification of the on-screen navigation and seamless integration with the user interface.

We utilised an intermediary data fusion module to synchronise multimodal interaction and issue a collective command, see Fig. 2. Firstly, the acquired brain signal is computed online for SSVEP signal detection and classification. Nuisance signals and noise are cancelled from the SSVEP response by applying the Minimum Energy Combination method and the best spatial filter for each subject at each frequency is determined automatically by the BCI. The detection of an SSVEP response in the user's EEG is based on power estimation, which occurs after spatial filtering and a statistical probability method has been applied. This combination enhances separation of the stimulus frequency component in the EEG [14]. When an appropriate SSVEP response is detected, the corresponding command is encapsulated within a UDP packet and forwarded for synchronisation in the data fusion module. At the same time, the eye tracking data is received by the data fusion module as a series of screen-based coordinates. The responsiveness of the eye tracker is dampened to prevent the coordinates

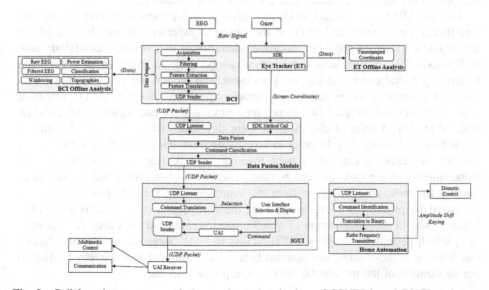

Fig. 2. Collaborative processes: fusion and synchronisation of SSVEP-based BNCI and eye tracker information and actuation events in the local environment.

buffering and to ensure screen-based coordinates coincide with the trajectory of a user gaze in real-time. If the coordinates do not match the SSVEP response then they are ignored until a matching response is detected. The BCI continuously processes the acquired signal so additional responses can be detected to provide supplementary commands or to rectify false positives. Both input modalities output data concurrently for the entirety of the trial. When both modalities are in agreement a command is classified and encapsulated in another UDP packet, which is transmitted to the graphical interface. At this stage, commands are translated into selections to actuate events in the local environment and provide feedback to the end user, completing the BCI cycle.

4 The Potential of hBNCI for Future Applications

We envisage hBNCI applications along two strands of development. The first will use widely accessible and affordable 'off the shelf' BNCI headsets (as demonstrated in the experiment above) with manufacturer supplied software interfaces and development kits. Such kits use dry- or water-based electrodes that can be worn with greater ease. Lifestyle applications include self-quantification for mindfulness or meditation [18], BNCI for HCI in gaming and leisure [19] as enhancement. The second category addresses medical applications using higher quality instrumentation, accessories and robust software with data stored in a standardised format; components that have also benefited from recent technical advances. Medically, BNCI has already been employed for stroke rehabilitation [20–22] and assessing disorders of consciousness [23, 24]. Better quality portable instrumentation can allow for free living assessment and a further example is ambulatory monitoring of EEG for detection of epilepsy or other neurophysiological abnormalities [25, 26] or in sleep studies [27].

For the hBNCI combining modalities (eye gaze for measuring compliance and identification of stimuli, and EEG for measuring engagement) it may be possible to investigate learning for people in classroom scenarios or to investigate conditions such as Dyslexia [28]. A significant contribution can be made in trying to understand the underlying neural cause and triggers associated with mental processing, communication and interaction issues defined as Autistic Spectrum Disorder (ASD). Friedrich *et al.* have successfully used BCI games for neurofeedback and treatment for children with ASD [29]. A suite of clinical tools were developed within the EU FP7 funded Michelangelo Project [30]. In order to investigate interaction of a child with ASD, a number of elements can be brought together: a task (e.g., an imitation game), engagement with the task (this can be determined from observation, video analysis or directly by measuring eye gaze from the computer and the effect of the task, as measured by physiological signals such as the electrocardiogram (ECG) and EEG). Figure 3 shows the visualisation of synchronized, aggregated data acquired during a task, which permitted therapists and clinicians to better ascertain, or identify, factors contributing to the onset of unwarranted behaviour during the task, thereby leading to personalization of the therapeutic intervention protocol in use.

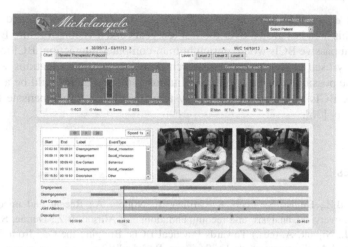

Fig. 3. Michelangelo project aggregated data visualisation on clinical user interface

The clinical tools also permitted further EEG analysis, which comprised off-line, artefact removal (using video playback to identify an appropriate resting state period), followed by event identification, such as eye contact during the task, during which the related EEG signal was processed via clustering techniques in order to identify areas of interest. The clinician is subsequently able to view the results from the analysis, select the appropriate number of synchrostates and visualize the corresponding brain activity for the event [31]. Consequently, such tools, which incorporate EEG as another physiological component, can potentially provide additional insights into both the treatment and understanding of the underlying conditions.

Subsequently, the hBNCI is potentially important for medical applications as it measures complementary biosignals: gaze which can infer attention and task engagement, for example, and brain activity can provide measures of processing of information by the brain. Hence (many) applications for which these components interact can be studied. Controlled psychophysiological studies such as the effect on the EEG of visual semantic content become possible (e.g. the brain's reaction to food for people with eating disorders [32], visual stimuli for people with addictions such as alcohol and smoking [33]). In addition, it is possible to correlate visual tasks with brain activity for basic research in areas such as monitoring smooth pursuit, saccades, motion onset visual evoked potential and quantification of nystagmus. This may allow further investigation of the vestibule-ocular reflex.

Recent technical advances leading to new lifestyle and novel medical application can extend the reach of BNCI from the specialist laboratory to the neurophysiology clinic and into the living room, thereby engaging a wide user cohort. Abdulkader *et al.* [34] provide an interesting review of BCI applications and the associated challenges. In reference to the medical domain they classify three streams: prevention, detection and diagnosis, and rehabilitation and restoration. For prevention they cite smoking, alcoholism and motion sickness; for detection and diagnosis they provide examples of tumor detection, brain disorders and sleep disorders; and for rehabilitation they provide examples of brain stoke, disability and psychological disorders.

Brunner *et al.* [35] provide an overview on how BCI research and European funding in this area has grown over the last ten years and a vision of future BCI. It was expected that passive BCIs would enrich human-computer interaction; BCI tools would be commonly used to support other research domains; and investigations would continue into the possibility of BCI for rehabilitation [36]; and there could be a shift from non-invasive BCIs to invasive BCIs for systems developed to compensate for movement disorders [36].

References

1. Allison, B.Z., Dunne, S., Leeb, R., Millan, J., Nijholt, A.: Recent and upcoming BCI progress: overview, analysis, and recommendations. In: Allison, B.Z., Dunne, S., Leeb, R., Millan, J., Nijholt, A. (eds.) Towards Practical BCIs: Bridging the Gap from Research to Real-World Applications, pp. 1–13. Springer, Berlin (2013)
2. Millán, J.D., Rupp, R., Müller-Putz, G.R., et al.: Combining brain-computer interfaces and assistive technologies: state-of-the-art and challenges. Front. Neurosci. **7**, 4 (2010)
3. Shih, J.J., Krusienski, D.J., Wolpaw, J.R.: Brain-computer interfaces in medicine. Mayo Clin. Proc. **87**(3), 268–279 (2012). doi:10.1016/j.mayocp.2011.12.008, Abdulkader, S.N., Atia, A., Mostafa, M.M.: Brain computer interfacing? applications and challenges. Egypt. Inf. J. **16**(2), 213–230 (2015). doi:10.1016/j.eij.2015.06.002
4. Wolpaw, J.R., Birbaumer, N., McFarland, D.J., Pfurtscheller, G., Vaughan, T.M.: Brain-computer interfaces for communication and control. Clin. Neurophysiol. **113**, 767–791 (2001). doi:10.1016/S1388-2457(02)00057-3
5. Swan, M.: The quantified self: fundamental disruption in big data science and biological discovery. Big Data **1**(2), 85–99 (2013). doi:10.1089/big.2012.0002. Mary Ann Liebert, Inc.
6. Coyle, D., Principe, J., Lotte, F., Nijholt, A.: Brain/neuronal - computer game interfaces and interaction. IEEE Trans. Comput. Intell. AI Games **5**(2), 77–81 (2013)
7. Lee, T.-S., Goh, S.J.A., Quek, S.Y., Phillips, R., Guan, C., et al.: A brain-computer interface based cognitive training system for healthy elderly: randomized control pilot study for usability and preliminary efficacy. PLoS ONE **8**(11), e79419 (2013). doi:10.1371/journal.pone.0079419
8. Pfurtscheller, G., Allison, B.Z., Brunner, C., Bauernfeind, G., Solis-Escalante, T., Scherer, R., Zander, T.O., Mueller-Putz, G., Neuper, C., Birbaumer, N.: The hybrid BCI. Front. Neurosci. **21**(4), 30 (2010)
9. Ware, M., Lightbody, G., McCullagh, P., Mulvenna, M., Martin, S., Thompson, E.: A method for assessing the usability of an on screen display for a brain–computer interface. Int. J. Comput. Healthcare **2**(1), 43–67 (2014). Inderscience
10. Mulvenna, M., Lightbody, G., Thomson, E., McCullagh, P., Ware, M., Martin, S.: Realistic expectations with brain computer interfaces. J. Assistive Technol. **6**(4), 233–244 (2012). doi:10.1108/17549451211285735
11. Amiri, S., Rabbi, A., Azinfar, L., Fazel-Rezai, R.: Review of P300, SSVEP, and hybrid P300/SSVEP brain-computer interface systems. In: Fazel-Rezai, (ed.) Brain-Computer Interface Systems - Recent Progress and Future Prospects (2013). ISBN 978-953-51-1134-4
12. Vilimek, R., Zander, T.O.: BC(eye): combining eye-gaze input with brain-computer interaction. In: Stephanidis, C. (ed.) UAHCI 2009, Part II. LNCS, vol. 5615, pp. 593–602. Springer, Heidelberg (2009)

13. Brennan, C.P., McCullagh, P.J., Galway, L., Lightbody, G.: Promoting autonomy in a smart home environment with a smarter interface. In: 37th Annual International Conference of the Engineering in Medicine and Biology Society (EMBC), pp. 5032–5035. IEEE (2105)
14. Galway, L., Brennan, C., McCullagh, P., Lightbody, G.: BCI and eye gaze: collaboration at the interface. In: Schmorrow, D.D., Fidopiastis, C.M. (eds.) AC 2015. LNCS, vol. 9183, pp. 199–210. Springer, Heidelberg (2015)
15. Volosyak, I., Cecotti, H., Valbuena, D., Gräser, A.: Evaluation of the Bremen SSVEP based BCI in real world conditions. In: 2009 IEEE International Conference on Rehabilitation Robotics, pp. 322–331. IEEE (2009)
16. Gao, S., Wang, Y., Gao, X., Hong, B.: Visual and auditory brain-computer interfaces. IEEE Trans. Biomed. Eng. 61(5), 1436–1447 (2014)
17. Brennan, C., McCullagh, P., Lightbody, G., Galway, L., Feuser, D., González, J.L., Martin, S.: Accessing tele-services using a hybrid bci approach. In: Rojas, I., Joya, G., Catala, A. (eds.) IWANN 2015. LNCS, vol. 9094, pp. 110–123. Springer, Heidelberg (2015)
18. Stinson, B., Arthur, D.: A novel EEG for alpha brain state training, neurobiofeedback and behavior change. Complement. Ther. Clin. Pract. 19(3), 114–118 (2013). doi:10.1016/j.ctcp. 2013.03.003
19. Plass-Oude Bos, D., Reuderink, B., van de Laar, B., Gürkök, H., Mühl, C., Poel, M., Nijholt, A., Heylen, D.: Brain-computer interfacing and games. In: Tan, D.S., Nijholt, A. (eds.) Brain-Computer Interfaces. Human-Computer Interaction Series. Springer-Verlag London Limited (2010). doi:10.1007/978-1-84996-272-8_10
20. Ortner, R., Irimia, D.C., Scharinger, J., Guger, C.: A motor imagery based brain-computer interface for stroke rehabilitation. Stud. Health Technol. Inform. 181, 319–323 (2012)
21. Xu, R., Jiang, N., Mrachacz-Kersting, N., Lin, C., Asin, G., Moreno, J., Pons, J., Dremstrup, K., Farina, D.: A closed-loop brain-computer interface triggering an active ankle-foot orthosis for inducing cortical neural plasticity. IEEE Trans. Biomed. Eng. 61, 2092–2101 (2014). 9294:1-1
22. Pichiorri, F., Morone, G., Petti, M., Toppi, J., Pisotta, I., Molinari, M., Paolucci, S., Inghilleri, M., Astolfi, L., Cincotti, F., Mattia, D.: Brain-computer interface boosts motor imagery practice during stroke recovery. Ann Neurol. 77(5), 851–865 (2015)
23. Lulé, D., Noirhomme, Q., Kleih, S.C., Chatelle, C., Halder, S., Demertzi, A., Bruno, M.-A., Gosseries, O., Vanhaudenhuyse, A., Schnakers, C., Thonnard, M., Soddu, A., Kübler, A., Laureys, S.: Probing command following in patients with disorders of consciousness using a brain-computer interface. Clin. Neurophysiol. 124, 101–106 (2013)
24. Risetti, M., Formisano, R., Toppi, J., Quitadamo, L.R., Bianchi, L., Astolfi, L., Cincotti, F., Mattia, D.: On ERPs detection in disorders of consciousness rehabilitation. Front. Hum. Neurosci. 20(7), 775 (2013)
25. Wolpaw, J., Wolpaw, E.W.: Brain-Computer Interfaces: Principles and Practice. Oxford University Press, USA (2012)
26. Huang, L., van Luijtelaar, G.: Brain computer interface for epilepsy treatment. In: Fazel-Rezai, R. (ed.) Brain-Computer Interface Systems - Recent Progress and Future Prospects (2013). ISBN 978-953-51-1134-4
27. Berka, C., Levendowski, D.J. et al.: EEG quantification of alertness: methods for early identification of individuals most susceptible to sleep deprivation. In: Caldwell, J.A., Wesensten, N.J. (eds.) Proceedings of the SPIE Defense and Security Symposium, Biomonitoring for Physiological and Cognitive Performance During Military Operations, vol. 5797, pp. 78–89 (2005)
28. Fadzal, C., Mansor, W., Khuan, L.: Review of brain computer interface application in diagnosing dyslexia. In: 2011 IEEE Control and System Graduate Research Colloquium (ICSGRC), pp. 124–128. IEEE (2011)

29. Friedrich, E.V.C., Suttie, N., Sivanathan, A., Lim, T., Louchart, S., Pineda, S.A.: Brain–computer interface game applications for combined neurofeedback and biofeedback treatment for children on the autism spectrum. Front. Neuroengineering 7, 21 (2013). doi:10.3389/fneng.2014.00021

30. Michelangelo Project. http://www.michelangelo-project.eu/en/. Accessed Feb 2016

31. Jamal, W., Das, S., Maharatna, K., Kuyucu, D.: Using brain connectivity measure of EEG synchrostates for discriminating typical and Autism Spectrum Disorder. In: 6th International IEEE/EMBS Conference on Neural Engineering, San Diego, pp. 1402–1405 (2013). doi:10.1109/NER.2013.6696205

32. Jáuregui-Lobera, I.: Electroencephalography in eating disorders. Neuropsychiatr. Dis. Treat. 8, 1–11 (2012). doi:10.2147/NDT.S27302

33. Lee Hong, N., McCullagh, P., Howard, R.: An electrocortical correlate of a history of alcohol abuse in criminal offenders. Psychol. Crime Law 7(14), 105–117 (2001). doi:10.1080/10683160108401790

34. Abdulkader, S.N., Atia, A., Mostafa, M.M.: Brain computer interfacing? applications and challenges. Egypt. Inf. J. 16(2), 213–230 (2015). doi:10.1016/j.eij.2015.06.002

35. Brunner, C., Birbaumer, N., Blankertz, B., Guger, C., Kübler, A., Mattia, D., Millán, J.D.R., Miralles, F., Nijholt, A., Opisso, E., Ramsey, N., Salomon, P., Müller-Putz, G.R.: BNCI Horizon 2020: towards a roadmap for the BCI community. Brain-Comput. Interfaces 2(1), 1–10 (2015)

36. Sellers, E.W., Vaughan, T.M., Wolpaw, J.R.: A brain-computer interface for long-term independent home use. Amyotrophic Lateral Sclerosis 11(5), 449–455 (2010)

Multi-Brain BCI: Characteristics and Social Interactions

Anton Nijholt[1,2(✉)] and Mannes Poel[1]

[1] University of Twente, Faculty EEMCS, Enschede, The Netherlands
a.nijholt@utwente.nl
[2] Imagineering Institute, Iskandar, Malaysia

Abstract. We investigate various forms of face-to-face and multiparty interactions in the context of potential brain-computer interface interactions (BCI). BCI has been employed in clinical applications but more recently also in domestic and game and entertainment applications. This paper focusses on multi-party game applications. That is, BCI game applications that allow multiple users and different BCI paradigms to get a cooperative or competitive task done. Our observations are quite preliminary and not yet supported by experimental research. Nevertheless we think we have put forward steps to structure future BCI game research and to make connections with neuro-scientific social interaction research.

Keywords: Brain-computer interfaces · Multi-brain computing · Hyper scanning · Affective computing · Neuroscience of social interaction · Games

1 Introduction

Human-Human Interaction (face-to-face interaction) and multi-party interaction are nowadays included in the research areas of Human-Computer Interaction (HCI). The assumption is that knowledge of how such interaction takes place can help to develop digital technology that can real-time support these interactions or to archive these interactions and later help to retrieve useful information from such recorded interactions. In both cases it is necessary that the digital technology is able to have a level of understanding of the interaction. Speech recognition and speech understanding are of course extremely useful when understanding verbal interactions. But not all human-human interactions and multi-party activity are speech only. Moreover, even in the case of speech, we need to understand the role of nonverbal speech (pauses, hesitations, prosody) and it is useful to know about accompanying facial expressions, gestures, and eye gaze behavior. In previous years we studied both global aspects of multi-party interaction [1] and synchrony of face-to-face interaction [2], including subtle aspects such as mimicry behavior [3, 4].

In recent years we have also seen that information that can be obtained from wearable physiological sensors is used to learn about its user. This information is used to inform a particular user about his or her performance during exercises and about health issues during longer periods of activity. We have not yet seen many research attempts that aim at investigating situations where users interact with each other and that physiological information

© Springer International Publishing Switzerland 2016
D.D. Schmorrow and C.M. Fidopiastis (Eds.): AC 2016, Part I, LNAI 9743, pp. 79–90, 2016.
DOI: 10.1007/978-3-319-39955-3_8

plays a role in the interaction. There is hardly any research that aims at detecting a user's cognitive or affective state - using other than visual and auditory cues - while interacting with others in a face-to-face or multi-party situation. There are exceptions, and interestingly, in the case of measuring brain activity (Brain-Computer Interfacing or BCI), they can often be found in many interactive interfaces and environments that have been designed by artists for mixed media performances [5–7].

BCI provides sensors and actuators with information about a user's affective and cognitive state. In addition a user can issue commands by manipulating his or her brain activity or by being receptive to sensorial stimuli that are caused by natural or artificially created events in the environment and then give feedback to the environment. Here we introduce research and trends in BCI and applications that assume multiple users at the same time. These applications will be looked upon in Sect. 2. It will be followed by a section (Sect. 3) with some global thoughts about cooperation and competition in general. A step towards distinguishing useful characteristics of cooperation and cooperation that can help in designing multi-brain applications is taken in Sect. 4. Section 5 connects BCI with research on neuroscience and social interaction. Some conclusions can be found in the final section.

2 Multi-Brain BCI: Applications and Characteristics

Interestingly, already in the 1970s artists looked at brain signals to be used for artistic and playful expression generated from simultaneously measured brain signals of more than one performer equipped with simple EEG devices. Ideas, examples, and applications are often related to being able to measure synchrony in brain activity of two or more subjects. More interest in such multi-brain processing emerged in the present century. In [8, 9] applications of research on multi-brain computing are mentioned and collected. Based on these papers we mention the following application areas:

- Joint decision making in environments requiring high accuracy and/or rapid reactions or feedback
- Joint/shared control and movement planning of vehicles or robots
- Assess team performance, stress-aware task allocation, rearrange tasks
- Characterization of group emotions, preferences, appreciations
- Social interaction research (two or more people)
- Arts, entertainment, games.

Not in all cases (almost) real-time use of measured brain activity is necessary. For example, in non-critical situations task allocation can be done while preparing a next task. Knowing about preferences and appreciations can help to design a next version of a product or interface. However, in this paper the focus is on real-time interactive use of the users' brain activities. Examples of multi-brain research in all of these applications areas can be found in the literature. For example, joint decision making during meetings and brain storm sessions and assessing team performance is a recurring theme in the research of Berka and colleagues [10]. Joint decision making and joint/shared control of (virtual) vehicles, robots and movement planning in critical situations has been addressed in [11, 12]. In this latter case we look at joint brain activity of event related or externally evoked potentials that are perceived by collaborating users at the same time (exogenous or sensory-driven neural activity), or the users' synchronized intentional manipulation of brain activity (endogenous activity). For example, for the latter case, joint imagery movement, in order to increase robustness and speed when performing a task in a critical situation.

When measuring group emotions and group preferences it is useful to distinguish between (1) small groups (two or more people) performing a particular task and interacting with each other, a usually (2) large group of people that attend a performance requiring audience participation, or an even (3) larger group of people that are addressed, not necessarily at the same time and in the same location, to evaluate a particular (multimedia) product [13]. In the first situation we are interested in understanding the group process and ways to improve it; this may concern decision making, but it can also concern less task-oriented issues such as social cohesion and empathy awareness; in that way it becomes part of social interaction research. In the second situation we are interested in having one or more persons' brain activity getting involved in creating or adapting a piece of life media art, maybe also in interaction with an artist/performer who is coordinating the joint life performance [14]. In the third situation we are interested in the statistics that can be obtained and from analysis we learn about preferences that help to improve the product. Measuring audience responses with BCI is less well known than with more traditional physiological sensors (heart rate and skin conductivity sensors), but with the more recently developed EEG wireless headsets with dry electrodes this will certainly change.

Finally, returning to the last bullet in the above list, multi-brain or multiparty BCI is researched in the context of (serious) games. Games usually assume more than one user. But of course, we can also have a user competing or collaborating with the game environment or its artificial agents. Whatever the situation, in game environments designers have the freedom to introduce problems, challenges, and unusual situations. Gamers can be guided into interaction situations where they have to collaborate, compete, cheat, conspire, and form alliances. In recent years these issues have also become part of BCI research. In artistic, game and entertainment applications artists and designers can introduce unexpected events, don't necessarily have to take care of efficiency issues and can introduce situations where gamers, performers, or audience members have to take unusual actions or unexpected partnerships. This makes BCI an interesting tool in games, entertainment, and performative arts, and, moreover, such applications can result into new research approaches from which new applications areas can follow.

3   Multi-Brain BCI: Thoughts on Competing, Collaborating

Here we are not interested in games of chance. We look at games that require skill and that include competition. Competition can be either among players or against the game system itself. When there are more players then players can cooperate in order to beat the system or to beat another team of players. The composition of teams can change during a game. A game can end when we have reached a particular goal defined by the game. However, it can also be the case that a game or our colleague players continue to offer us challenges and as long as we survive the game continues. We want to consider how BCI can be used in this context. That is, can we identify situations where brain activity of two or more players in the game can be integrated in order to perform a joint task, or can brain activity of two or more players be compared in order to determine who or which team performs a game task better than an opponent or an opposing team? It should be mentioned that although examples usually make references to videogames, there is no need to restrict ourselves to videogames. In fact, examples from traditional BCI research include the movement of artificial limbs and the navigation of wheel chairs. Actuator technology has become part of wearables, tangibles, and robots. Hence, games supported by BCI technology can be played in the real, physical world as well.

Competition and cooperation are issues we want to investigate. These are rather obvious issues in games, but also in many other situations. Whenever we have a situation where there are two or more people we can have agreement and disagreement about how to solve a problem. Some situations ask for cooperation, other situations ask for competition. The situations can be virtual: fighting, survival or achieving a high score in an entertaining videogame. But it can also be about performing with others in a serious game or a real-life situation: for example, a discussion or some other activity that requires verbal, nonverbal, or physical interaction. We already mentioned research aimed at evaluating a meeting participant's contribution to decision making in a small group meeting [10]. Obviously, this requires an analysis and comparison of his or her brain activity with the brain activity that can been measured from the other participants in the joint activity. More in general, we can have situations where we have multiple users and we can be interested, depending on the application, in the brain activity that is fastest available, the 'strongest' brain activity, the most consistent brain activity, the sum or the average of multiple users' brain activities. Obviously, it is also possible to consider mixtures of these possibilities and putting weights on the various possibilities.

Competition and cooperation are part of life performance art as well. Performative artists can create a piece of work that only becomes alive when audience members or museum visitors discover they can interact with the artistic installation. Performance art can also become alive when a performative artist has designed BCI audience involvement and real-time BCI audience interaction while he or she is performing. When an artistic or entertainment multimedia environment becomes accessible for the audience we can hope or expect that audience members cooperate and compete in order to make changes to the mixed media performance. In these applications multiple users wear a BCI device to give the artistic or game environment access to their affective state. Audio-visualized or other feedback from the artistic or entertainment application has impact on the user's or users' involvement and experience. Artists can design their BCI art with a focus on various ways of audience involvement. There can be a joint performance, but there can as well be a designed and implemented environment that allows and assumes feedback from audience members without further involvement of the artist or an environment that not only incorporates affective state information, but also expects explicit commands generated by one or more audience members. [7, 14].

There are many ways of cooperation and many ways of competition. For example, in a game environment gamers or teams of gamers can decide about their strategy and they make decisions about joint actions. However, not everyone in the team needs to agree. An opposing team will have the same problem. Full competition and full collaboration are extremes on a scale and these extremes and everything in between make it difficult to make decisions about how to use and compare brain activity to be detected from multiple users. In addition, competitors can decide to cooperate and when a certain sub goal has been achieved, start competing again. Especially in massively on-line role playing games we see situations where alliance forming occurs. In our view these games are not essentially different from many artistic BCI applications where a designer allows the audience to interact with his or her BCI installation or where the BCI artist performer accepts various forms of BCI audience involvement in the performance. See [15] for many of such examples in the artistic domain, in particular music performances.

At this moment a systematic review of such possible multi-brain applications needs more time and more effort than we can afford here. With 'more time' we certainly want to refer to the need of seeing more 'bottom-up' applications of BCI research where multiple users are involved. In recent road maps on BCI research [16] there is no or hardly any mentioning of BCI multi-brain research or applications. These road maps have been designed by traditional BCI researchers hardly being aware of applications for other than patients and disabled users.

4   Cooperation and Competition Using BCI: Interactions

It is possible to distinguish more simple examples of cooperation and competition in existing and potential multi-brain BCI applications. That is, artistic applications that don't involve complicated audience behavior or audience-performer interaction behavior. Or, as has been investigated more extensively, in multi-brain BCI game or training environments. And, of course, as mentioned before, we can be interested in neuro-marketing applications or applications where we want to analyze team performance and contributions of team members by measuring their brain activities. However, before attacking these problems, it is useful to consider more simple examples of cooperation and collaboration. From them we can learn about introducing BCI in games, in particular games that require more than one player.

4.1   Comparative and Interactive Games

Firstly, we can distinguish between comparative games and interaction games. As mentioned above, we are not interested in BCI applications of games of chance. We are interested in games where players have to use game playing skills and where BCI supports a players' game activity or even determines a player's game actions at a particular moment or being available to help in interpreting a user's or gamer's actions. In comparative games there is no game interaction between players. There is no interfering. A game is played and once having completed the game you can compare your score with the score of others. The game can be played in a social context, others can compete at the same time and your results can be compared in a competitive situation. But it is not the case that in any way your game actions change the state of the game in such a way that your opponent has to deal with an other than neutral situation. Hence, when two or more people compete in a game, it does not necessarily mean that one gamer's performance has impact on that of the other(s). It may even be the case that a gamer only becomes aware of the performance of another player when the game is ended or when he or she sees the score displayed in a ranking of others who have played the same game.

4.2   Turn Taking Without Control Interference and Without Game Interference

In a game on a pinball machine you can have both. You have a direct opponent and are in a battle to score more than this opponent with the balls you have. Maybe you can increase your efforts when you know about the score of your opponent. But there is no way you can leave the machine in a situation that is to your advantage. That is, making life for your direct opponent more difficult. And there is also a general ranking obtained from previously played games that shows how your performance compares with many others. 'Tilting' the machine is a possibility to cheat, but preventing, detecting, and punishing tilting are counter measures that have been introduced by the companies that sold such machines. Playing pinball using BCI (motor imagery) to detect whether the gamer intended to use the left or the right flipper has been discussed in [17]. There is not a continuous brain activity involved in the game. Gamers can compete by taking turns, and once a turn is taken brain activity can be used to control the flippers. Your score depends on your BCI skills, in this particular case, motor imagery.

4.3   Turn Taking Without Control Interference and with Discrete Game Interference

An example of a game with game interference is the Connect Four game. Here we have a vertical grid of 6×7 positions. Players take turn in putting coins on these positions by choosing a column to drop a coin. The game ends when a gamer has been able to connect four of his coins, either horizontally, vertically or diagonally. A BCI version of this game allows the users to choose a column to drop a coin using a P300 evoked response [18]. This changes the state of the game. Playing chess using BCI control of the moves is another example. Again, you make a move, your opponent waits until you finished and his or her move is usually dependent on the move you made. In both games this is different from the previous pinball example. There is competition and what a player does is very much dependent on what his opponent has done. But again, there is turn taking. And, each turn leads to a different situation that has to be assessed by the turn taking player. Actions can follow rules from a general strategy point of view. There may be conflicts between such a global view and what an opponent allows you to do. There is however, apart from frustrating your opponent by making moves he or she doesn't expect or like, an assessment of the game board situation and how it fits in your strategy to beat your opponent. At this moment there is no way of incorporating such thoughts in a BCI that helps you to improve your chess playing capabilities. Nevertheless, we can introduce BCI in chess playing, for example to move a piece from one position to the other. In [19], similar to the P300 Connect Four game and well known spelling applications, a chess player has to pay attention to his or her preferred move while being submitted to a display of possible moves. That is, the chess player uses P300 BCI control to select a start and a destination position among the 8×8 possible positions. In [20] imagery movement is used to tackle the same problem. These applications allow users without other communication possibilities than using their brains only, to play chess. Each player has to wait for the other player in order to make his move.

Although in these games BCI is used to play the game, we prefer not to call them BCI games. The reason is that the outcome of the game is not dependent on your BCI skills. You decide about the column (in the Connect Four game) or the chess move which you want to make. No BCI skills are needed for that. How the piece is moved is not in any way essential for the game. Whether you do that by physically picking up the piece, by clicking arrow keys on your keyboard, asking someone to do it for you or by, after having made the decision what move to make, having your brain activated in such a way that it becomes clear where a particular piece should move, does not help you to win. Obviously, we can go into 'subtleties' such as the efforts you have to make to have a piece moved from one position to the other on the chessboard goes at the expense of your thinking about what the right move should be. More interestingly is when we introduce time constraints. But then again, in real chess time constraints are meant to be constraints on the time you take about thinking about which next move to make, not about the time you need to make the next move. So, from the point of view of the original chess game, although this introduces an extra challenge, it leads to a different kind of game.

4.4 Turn Taking Without Control Interference and with Continuous Game Interference

In the examples mentioned above we have two different BCI paradigms. Motor imagery to decide between left and right in the pinball machine, P300 to decide among the columns of the Connect Four game, and P300 or motor imagery for deciding the position changes of a chess piece. It is not difficult to think of implementations of these games where other BCI paradigms, maybe taking more time, are used to make such decisions. In the examples a player can perform his or her action without having his action enhanced by other players (cooperation) or thwarted by other players (competition). Although there is turn taking, actions of players in a game can have real-time impact on the actions to be taken by an opponent, that is, by watching what the other player is doing during a turn, his or her opponent can prepare counter measures. For example, in a Pong game we have to look at the performance of our opponent and, in real-time, we have to move our bat up and down to anticipate the right position to return the ball. This example is quite different from the previous ones. We have real-time interaction between players. If we have the movement and speed controlled by BCI, then the players' BCI skills determine who is going to win. The players' actions – move the bat up and down - are fully determined by what is perceived on the screen. Evoked brain activity can be used to move the bat to the right position, but there is no need to compare brain activity of two opponents in this game. A version of this game using motor imagery to control the bats has been introduced in [21].

4.5 Continuous Control and Continuous Game Interference

As an example where brain activity of two (or more) players need to be compared in order to have a system to make a decision we can look at one of the first BCI games, the BrainBall game [22]. Two competing players are involved, their brain activities are measured and compared, and based upon this comparison a decision is made about the direction the ball should move. There are many more similar examples of such multi-brain applications in arts and games. In this BrainBall example we have to compare and 'subtract' brain activity information in order to determine who is the strongest. In other applications where users cooperate we have to 'add' brain activity information from different users in order to decide which way 'to go'. Which way 'to go' can be decided by the 'strength' of the brain activity of a group of people (a sum or an average). The brain activity involved can be about synchronized relaxation, event related potentials, evoked potentials, joint motor imagery or joint intentions to move, where the latter can be detected before physical or imagined movements. Various other examples have been discussed in [9]. They include (serious) game applications where two or more than two users participate in situations where their joint brain activity is measured and is used in game, entertainment or arts applications.

4.6 Multimodal, Multi-Brain, Hybrid, and Brain to Brain Fusion

One interesting issue in multimodal interaction research is how and when multimodal information that is obtained from a user has to be fused. Usually a distinction is made between fusion at the signal, the feature or the decision or application level [23–25]. Obviously, one of the 'modalities' can be brain waves and there are research examples where brain waves and gaze, brain waves and speech or brain waves and heart rate information is fused in order to get more complete information from a user. Modality switching in a BCI context is described in [26]. In multi-brain applications we usually have the situation that for all participants the same BCI marker contributes to the cooperative or competitive actions. This makes it possible to 'compare', to 'add' or 'subtract'. For example, in [12] we have users using motor imagery only and in [27–29] we have examples of multi-brain interaction using ERP only when performing a joint task. Earlier we have experimented with applications that require different BCI markers. For example, make a choice using SSVEP and then have the speed of an activity determined by the user's level of relaxation [30]. This is an example of sequential multimodality, rather than parallel multimodality [23].

In [31] the notion of hybrid BCIs was introduced to give a name to a BCI using two BCI paradigms or a BCI combined with another system. The authors didn't embed their observations in already existing multimodal and HCI research. Moreover, they required that "there must be at least one recordable brain signal that the user can intentionally modulate to effect goal-directed behavior" and that the user must obtain feedback. Clearly, this is not the way we have been looking at BCI in this paper and the way BCI has been incorporated in HCI research. We certainly accept multi-brain situations where users do not intentionally modulate their brain signals. They may be aware that there brain signals are recorded and, although not necessarily real-time, that is, no immediate feedback, may lead to changes in their interaction environment. Another example where we need to measure and integrate in parallel two BCI paradigms can be found in [32]. In this paper we have the standpoint that the cognitive or affective state of a BCI user has impact on brain waves that are evoked by external stimuli or by intended modulation, hence, detection of both is needed in order to improve the control that is intended by the user. The BCI system can compensate for the user's emotional state. More generally, we can think of multi-brain applications where more than one BCI paradigm is included or where multi-brain BCI is combined with, for example, multi-gaze, multi-gesture or multi-heart rate information. Audience participation based on merging heart rate and brain wave information is reported in [33].

Finally, we should mention brain-to-brain computing. Clearly, this involves two or more brains and, when looking at current research examples, it assumes cooperative BCI controlled interactions, where specific patterns of brain activity of one user are delivered, using transcranial magnetic stimulation, to a partner who can complete a particular task [34]. However, there is no attempt and also less reason to compare brain activity of the two participants in such an interaction.

5   Neuroscience and Social Interactions

In the previous sections our aim was to illustrate the various applications and characteristics of multi-brain computing for HCI purposes. In this decade the research area Neuroscience for Social Interaction (NSI) has drawn attention of many neuro-scientists. Clearly, when we talk about social interactions we assume interactions between two or more people. In this research area the notion of hyperscanning was introduced [35, 36]. Hyperscanning is the simultaneous scanning of multiple human brains in order to study brain patterns that emerge during multiparty interaction, for example, when having a conversation, when playing music or during game play. From a HCI point of view it is especially interesting to see how this field can contribute to the multi-brain and face-to-face interaction research topics related to cooperation and competition. How can this NSI research provide knowledge that helps us to interpret correctly commands or preferences issued or obtained from users while they cooperate or compete with others? NSI knowledge can also tell us about joint attention or other information related to performing a joint task that provides us not only with a context to interpret BCI signals, but also the possibility to make changes to the environment based on this information or alert the interactants to start a joint action or issue a multi-brain command. As examples we can mention the possibility to predict the next speaker in a multiparty interaction [37] or the detection of mimicry [38]. NSI helps us to obtain computational models of the interacting mind [39] and clearly, such models are helpful in interpreting minds that cooperate or are in competition.

6   Conclusions

This paper allowed us to discuss the need for a systematic approach to designing and evaluating multi-brain computing. It does not yet allow us to elaborate on the characteristics and parameters that need to be distinguished and introduced when attempting to model various forms of multi-brain interactions, let alone the embedding of multi-brain interactions in a natural multimodal interface and a multimedia display context. This needs further research. We are in need of research that embeds the issuing of cooperating or competing BCI commands in knowledge from the field of neuroscience for social interaction (NSI). Embedding means that we interpret BCI information that we plan to use, whether it is a user intended task control command or information that helps to adapt the environment to a situation that suits the aims of the game or task and the cognitive and affective state of the user. We think that the distinctions we made here can make us more aware of the issues that play a role and therefore help us to introduce a more systematic approach to designing multi-brain BCI applications in the future. Clearly, our observations are rather preliminary and require more elaboration in future research.

References

1. Jovanovic, N., op den Akker, R., Nijholt, A.: A corpus for studying addressing behavior in multi-party dialogues. J. Lang. Resour. Eval. **40**(1), 5–23 (2006)
2. Reidsma, D., Nijholt, A., Tschacher, W., Ramseyer, F.: Measuring multimodal synchrony for human-computer interaction. In: Sourin, A. (ed.) Proceedings CYBERWORLDS 2010, pp. 67–71. IEEE Computer Society Press, Singapore (2010)
3. Sun, X., Lichtenauer, J., Valstar, M., Nijholt, A., Pantic, M.: A multimodal database for mimicry analysis. In: D'Mello, S., Graesser, A., Schuller, B., Martin, J.-C. (eds.) ACII 2011, Part I. LNCS, vol. 6974, pp. 367–376. Springer, Heidelberg (2011)
4. Bilakhia, S., Petridisa, S., Nijholt, A., Pantic, M.: The MAHNOB mimicry database - a database of naturalistic human interactions. Pattern Recogn. Lett. **66**, 52–61 (2015)
5. Rosenboom, D. (ed.): Biofeedback and the Arts: Results of Early Experiments. A.R.C. Publications, Vancouver (1976)
6. Gürkök, H., Nijholt, A.: Brain-computer interfaces for arts. In: Affective Computing and Intelligent Interaction, pp. 827–831. IEEE Press, New York (2013)
7. Wadeson, A., Nijholt, A., Nam, C.S.: Artistic brain-computer interfaces: current state-of-art of control mechanisms. Brain-Comput. Interfaces **2**(2–3), 70–75 (2015)
8. Stoica, A.: MultiMind: multi-brain signal fusion to exceed the power of a single brain. In: Proceedings of the 3rd Conference on Emerging Security Technologies, pp. 94–98 (2012)
9. Nijholt, A.: Competing and collaborating brains: multi-brain computer interfacing. In: Hassanieu, A.E., Azar, A.T. (eds.) Brain-Computer Interfaces: Current Trends and Applications, pp. 313–335. Springer, Switzerland (2015)
10. Stevens, R, Galloway, T, Berka, C, Behneman A.: A neurophysiologic approach for studying team cognition. In: Proceedings of the Interservice/Industry Training, Simulation, and Education Conference (I/ITSEC), pp. 1–8 (2010)
11. Poli, R., Cinel, C., Matran-Fernandez, A., Sepulveda, F., Stoica, A.: Towards cooperative brain-computer interfaces for space navigation. In: Proceedings of the Intelligent User Interfaces (IUI 2013), pp. 149–159. ACM, New York (2013)
12. Wang, Y., Jung, T.-P.: A collaborative brain-computer interface for improving human performance. PLoS ONE **6**(5), 1–11 (2011)
13. Hasson, U., Landesman, O., Knappmeyer, B., Vallines, I., Rubin, N., Heeger, D.J.: Neurocinematics: the neuroscience of film. Projections **2**(1), 1–26 (2008)

14. Zioga, P., Chapman, P., Ma, M., Pollick, F.: A wireless future: performance art, interaction and the brain-computer interfaces. In: Proceedings of the ICLI 2014 - Interface: International Conference on Live Interfaces, pp. 220–230 (2014)
15. Mullen, T., et al.: MindMusic: playful and social installations at the interface between music and the brain. In: Nijholt, A. (ed.) More Playful User Interfaces, pp. 197–229. Springer, Singapore (2015)
16. Brunner, C., et al.: BNCI horizon 2020: towards a roadmap for the BCI community. Brain-Comput. Interfaces 2(1), 1–10 (2015)
17. Tangermann, M.W., Krauledat, M., Grzeska, K., Sagebaum, M., Vidaurre, C., Blankertz, B., Muller, K.R.: Playing Pinball with non-invasive BCI. In: Koller, D., Schuurmans, D., Bengio, Y., Bottou, L. (eds.) Advances in Neural Information Processing Systems 21 (NIPS 2008), pp. 1641–1648. Curran Associates, Red Hook (2008)
18. Maby, E., Perrin, M., Bertrand, O., Sanchez, G., Mattout, J.: BCI could make old two-player games even more fun: a proof of concept with "Connect Four". Adv. Hum.-Comput. Interact. 2012, 8 (2012)
19. Toersche, H.: Designing a brain-computer interface to chess. In: 7th Twente Student Conference on IT, pp. 1–9. University of Twente, Netherlands (2007)
20. Maruthappan, N., Iyengar, N., Sudip Patel, P.: Brain chess – playing chess using brain computer interface. In: ICBMG 2011 Workshop, IPCSIT, vol. 20, pp. 183–191. IACSIT Press, Singapore (2011)
21. Krepki, R., Blankertz, B., Curio, G., Müller, K.R.: The Berlin brain-computer interface (BBCI)—towards a new communication channel for online control in gaming applications. Multimed Tools Appl. 33(1), 73–90 (2007)
22. Hjelm, S.I., Browall, C.: Brainball: using brain activity for cool competition. In: Proceedings of the First Nordic Conference on Computer-Human Interaction (NordiCHI 2000), Stockholm, Sweden (2000)
23. Nigay, L., Coutaz, J.: A design space for multimodal systems: concurrent processing and data fusion. In: INTERACT 1993 and CHI 1993 Conference on Human Factors in Computing Systems (CHI 1993), pp. 172–178. ACM, New York (1993)
24. Bunt, H., Kipp, M., Maybury, M., Wahlster, W.: Fusion and coordination for multimodal interactive information presentation. In: Stock, O., Zancanaro, M. (eds.) Multimodal Intelligent Information Presentation, pp. 325–339. Springer, Berlin (2005)
25. Turk, M.: Multimodal interaction: a review. Pattern Recogn. Lett. 36, 189–195 (2014)
26. Gürkök, H., Hakvoort, G., Poel, M.: Modality switching and performance in a thought and speech controlled computer game. In: 13th International Conference on Multimodal Interfaces (ICMI 2011), pp. 41–48. ACM, New York (2011)
27. Kapeller, C., Ortner, R., Krausz, G., Bruckner, M., Allison, B.Z., Guger, C., Edlinger, G.: Toward multi-brain communication: collaborative spelling with a P300 BCI. In: Schmorrow, D.D., Fidopiastis, C.M. (eds.) AC 2014. LNCS, vol. 8534, pp. 47–54. Springer, Heidelberg (2014)
28. Cecotti, H., Rivet, B.: Subject combination and electrode selection in cooperative brain-computer interface based on event related potentials. Brain Sci. 2014(4), 335–355 (2014)
29. Stoica, A., Matran-Fernandez, A., Andreou, D., Poli, R., Cinel, C., Iwashita, Y., Padgett, C.: Multi-brain fusion and applications to intelligence analysis. In: SPIE 8756, Multisensor, Multisource Information Fusion: Architectures, Algorithms, and Applications, 87560N (2013)
30. Mühl, C., et al.: Bacteria hunt: evaluating multi-paradigm BCI interaction. J. Multimodal User Interfaces 4(1), 11–25 (2010)

31. Pfurtscheller, G., Allison, B.Z., Brunner, C., Bauernfeind, G., Solis-Escalante, T., Scherer, R., Zander, T.O., Mueller-Putz, G., Neuper, C., Birbaumer, N.: The hybrid BCI. Front Neurosci. **4**(30), 1–11 (2010)
32. Molina, G.G., Tsoneva, T., Nijholt, A.: Emotional brain-computer interfaces. Int. J. Auton. Adapt. Commun. Syst. **6**(1), 9–25 (2013)
33. Fan, Y.-Y., Sciotto, F.M.: BioSync: an informed participatory interface for audience dynamics and audiovisual content co-creation using mobile PPG and EEG. In: NIME 2013, KAIST, Daejeon, Korea (2013)
34. Stocco, A., Prat, C.S., Losey, D.M., Cronin, J.A., Wu, J., Abernethy, J.A., Rao, R.P.N.: Playing 20 questions with the mind: collaborative problem solving by humans using a brain-to-brain interface. PLoS ONE **10**(9), e0137303 (2015)
35. Babiloni, F., Cincotti, F., Mattia, D., Mattiocco, M., Fallani, D.V.F., Tocci, A., Bianchi, L., Marciani, M.G., Astolfi, L.: Hypermethods for EEG hyperscanning. In: Proceedings of the IEEE Engineering in Medicine and Biology Society (EMBC), vol. 1, pp. 3666–3669. New York, USA (2006)
36. Babiloni, F., Astolfi, L.: Social neuroscience and hyperscanning techniques: past, present and future. Neurosci. Biobehav. Rev. **44**, 76–93 (2014)
37. Dijkstra, K.V., Brunner, P., Gunduz, A., Coon, W., Ritaccio, A.L., Farquhar, J., Schalk, G.: Identifying the attended speaker using electrocorticographic (ECoG) signals. Brain-Comput. Interfaces **2**(4), 61–173 (2015)
38. Delaherche, E., Dumas, G., Nadel, J., Chetouani, M.: Automatic measure of imitation during social interaction: a behavioral and hyperscanning-EEG benchmark. Pattern Recogn. Lett. **66**, 118–126 (2015)
39. Mattout, J.: Brain-computer interfaces: a neuroscience paradigm of social interaction? A matter of perspective. Front. Hum. Neurosci. **6**, 114 (2012)

Comparing EEG Artifact Detection Methods for Real-World BCI

Michael W. Nonte[1]($\boxtimes$), William D. Hairston[2],
and Stephen M. Gordon[1]

[1] Scientific Research Department, DCS Corporation,
Alexandria, VA, USA
{mnonte,sgordon}@dcscorp.com
[2] US Army Research Laboratory,
Human Research and Engineering Directorate,
Aberdeen Proving Ground, Aberdeen, MD, USA
william.d.hairston4.civ@mail.mil

Abstract. One major challenge to the real-world use of brain-computer inter-face (BCI) technology is the decrease in classifier performance caused by degradations in electroencephalogram (EEG) signal quality due to artifacts from non-neural electrophysiological activity and the gross movement of sensors and other EEG hardware. These artifacts can contaminate or mask the neural signal and thus cause a decrease in the performance of BCI classifiers due to the system's diminished ability to extract relevant features. One strategy to combat this effect is to identify and remove artifact-contaminated segments of data. We compared four methods that utilize higher order statistics to detect and artifact data on their ability to improve BCI classifier performance. We evaluated these methods on two datasets: a motor movement task and a rapid serial visual presentation (RSVP) task. In addition to comparing artifact detection methods, we compared the improvement in BCI classifier performance gained by removing artifact data to the decrease in performance caused by diminishing the amount of data available for classifier training. We found that overall the use of abnormal spectra to detect artifacts resulted in the greatest improvement to BCI classifier performance.

Keywords: Brain-Computer Interface (BCI) · Electroencephalography (EEG) · Artifact detection

1 Introduction

One crucial aspect of any brain-computer interface (BCI) system is a pre-processing pipeline that removes or mitigates non-neural signal components. This requirement is especially important when electroencephalography (EEG) is used to record neural activity, as the amplitude of the measured neural signal is small relative to electro-physiological and environmental noise. Generally, any recorded signal component from a non-neural source that is equal or larger in amplitude to the target brain-derived components is referred to as an artifact. These include non-neural electrophysiological

D.D. Schmorrow and C.M. Fidopiastis (Eds.): AC 2016, Part I, LNAI 9743, pp. 91–101, 2016.
DOI: 10.1007/978-3-319-39955-3_9

activity as well as non-physiological sources of noise. Common physiological sources of artifacts include muscle activity, cardiac activity, eye blinks, and eye movement [1–3]. Non-physiological sources of artifacts include 50/60 Hz line noise, poor electrode contact, and cable sway [3]. Good BCI design attempts to control for and prevent artifacts, however, some artifacts such as eye blinks simply cannot be avoided, especially as research and BCI application moves out of confined settings and into more realistic, natural scenarios [4].

Artifacts can distort or mask the neurogenic signal in both the time and frequency domains [1]. BCI classifiers commonly extract time-amplitude or spectral features from EEG data to build a model distinguishing two or more different classes [5–9]. These classes may represent different behaviors, such as a left or right hand finger movement [5], or the neural responses to different stimuli, such as the presentation of a target or non-target image [6, 8]. The presence of artifacts can prevent a BCI classifier from building an accurate model, as the features extracted from contaminated training data may represent properties of the artifact rather than the underlying neural process. Additionally, the presence of artifacts in test data can cause misclassification even when the classification model is accurate. Thus it is beneficial to identify segments of data that are contaminated by artifact and remove them.

There exist multiple computationally efficient methods to identify segments of data contaminated by artifacts. These methods have typically been evaluated by computing a hit-rate using manually labeled artifact periods [2]. Using manually-labeled test data provides an evaluation criterion for a researcher looking to improve data quality for the sake of producing better statistical differentiation between experimental conditions or create a better visual representation of a neural process, but may not accurately inform the BCI developer about which artifact detection method will have the most positive impact on real-world BCI performance. For instance, it may be the case that the features used by a classifier are not affected by the presence of one or more types of artifacts, making the classifier resilient to their presence. Thus, the very definition of noise and artifact may be different to the BCI developer than it is for the researcher.

Additionally, the performance of a BCI classifier may actually decrease if the remaining data is insufficient to train an accurate model. That is, models can be overfit when data is too limited. There is a trade-off between improved performance due to the removal of artifact-contaminated data and a decrease in performance due to the reduction in the number of training samples; this tradeoff may differ depending on the BCI paradigm being used, the robustness of the classifier to noise, and the robustness of the classifier to a diminished training set.

In this work, we evaluate the ability of several popular artifact detection methods to improve the classification accuracy of common BCI classifiers. We compare these results to a case in which the training set size is held constant in order to distinguish the effects of removing artifact-contaminated data from that of reducing the size of the training set.

2 Background

2.1 BCI Classifiers

Three popular BCI classifiers were used for evaluation: common spatial patterns (CSP), hierarchical discriminant component analysis (HDCA), and xDAWN. CSP is designed for motor imagery and motor movement discrimination. CSP learns spatial filters to create components that maximize the ratio of variance between two task conditions, then uses the normalized log of variance of the component response as a feature for task discrimination [5, 9]. HDCA is a general-purpose classifier that is robust to temporal variability in the neural response. It divides data epochs into equal-sized, non-overlapping segments, trains a logistic regression classifier on each segment, then uses the output of each classifier to train a final logistic regression classifier that makes the final discrimination decision [6]. xDAWN was designed for oddball event detection and is commonly used for target detection in RSVP paradigms. It creates spatial filters to maximize the signal to signal plus noise ratio then trains a Bayesian linear discriminate analysis classifier on the resulting components [8].

2.2 Identifying Artifacts Using Signal Statistics and Spectral Power

One common method to deal with artifact-contaminated data is to simply remove it [1]. Prior to analysis, full datasets are commonly separated into equal-sized segments, called epochs, which are time-locked to events of interest. Delorme et al. [2] presented several methods using higher-order statistics, extreme values, and power spectral density to identify artifact-contaminated data. They showed that all of these methods were effective in identifying artifacts and that the detection of abnormal spectra was especially effective. We used four artifact detection methods presented in this work to rank the quality of data epochs: kurtosis, joint probability, extreme values, and abnormal spectra. Details of these methods can be found in [2, 10], but are paraphrased below.

Kurtosis. Kurtosis is a measure of the 'peakedness' of the probability distribution of a set of values. It is computed as the fourth standardized moment:

$$kurtosis(x) = \frac{E\{(x - \mu(x))^4\}}{(E\{(x - \mu(x))^2\})^2} \tag{1}$$

where x is the vector of data, $E\{\}$ is the expectation operator and μ is the mean of the data. The kurtosis of the normal distribution is 3. Kurtosis values much lower than 3 are indicative of data that is mostly concentrated above and below the mean, with few values near the mean. This may reflect a process that varies rapidly between two values, such as an AC artifact, or a sudden change in signal amplitude offset, such as a mechanical movement of the electrode or an ocular artifact [2]. Kurtosis values much higher than 3 are indicative of data that is mostly concentrated close to the mean. This reflects a process in which the majority of the values are the same, such as in the case of a disconnected electrode. Thus, data with an excessively large or small kurtosis may contain an artifact.

Joint Probability. Another method to utilize the distribution of values within an epoch to detect artifacts is joint probability. In a broad sense, it computes the likelihood of observing the distribution of values in an epoch, given the distribution of values in the entire dataset. A probability density function (D_e) is computed for each electrode (e) using the entire dataset. Within each epoch (i), the joint log probability of values is computed for each electrode using:

$$J_e(i) = -\log(\prod_{x \in A_i} p_{D_e}(x)) \tag{2}$$

where $p_{De}(x)$ is the probability of observing the value x given D_e over all data in channel e and A_i are the values in epoch i.

Extreme Values. Neurogenic EEG signals are typically smaller than 100 µV in amplitude [1]. Large deviations in signal amplitude are then most likely the result of non-neural signal contamination. Thus, segments of data containing values much larger in amplitude than the rest of the dataset may contain an artifact.

Abnormal Spectra. Clean EEG has a frequency range of 0.01 to 100 Hz and has a power spectral density (PSD) that falls off roughly proportional to increasing frequency [1]. Some artifact types have characteristic spectral properties that cause abnormal deviations from the typical EEG PSD. For example, muscle artifacts have a large power concentration between 20–60 Hz and eye-related artifacts have a large power concentration between 1–3 Hz [2]. Segments of data displaying large increases in power amplitude in these frequency ranges relative to the rest of the data may contain an artifact.

3   Methods

We evaluated our chosen artifact detection methods on their ability to improve BCI performance using two different BCI paradigms as exemplar cases. The first data set was a finger movement study in which subjects performed self-paced movement of the middle and index fingers of both hands. The second data set was a rapid serial visual presentation (RSVP) study in which subjects were asked to detect targets of interest within a stream of rapidly presented visual stimuli.

3.1   Participants

We used data from 14 of 18 participants in a rapid serial visual presentation (RSVP) experiment and from 11 of 12 subjects in a motor movement experiment. Datasets containing excessive artifacts were deemed inappropriate for the current study and excluded. The investigators obtained the approval of the Institutional Review Boards of the Army Research Laboratory's Human Research and Engineering Directorate and adhered to Army policies for the protection of human subjects [11, 12].

3.2   Stimuli and Procedure

Insurgent-Civilian RSVP. Subjects were seated in front of a computer monitor and presented simulated images from a desert metropolitan environment. Images were presented at a rate of 2 Hz. In each image, if a person holding a gun was present it was considered a target image; if no humans were present in the image it was considered a non-target image. Subjects were instructed to attend to the presented images and count the number of target images. A total of 110 target images and 1346 non-target images were presented to each subject. For more information regarding this study, see [13].

Finger-Tapping. Subjects performed self-paced finger tapping movements using the middle or index finger of either hand. The time at which the downward movement of the finger was completed was recorded using a force-detecting switch. Subjects were instructed to leave between 4 and 5 s between successive taps. In each two minute block, the subject was told which finger to tap. The finger being tapped was changed on each trial. Subjects completed a total of 32 blocks so that each finger was used in 8 blocks.

3.3   Physiological Recording

Insurgent-Civilian RSVP. EEG data were recorded at 1024 Hz from 64 scalp electrodes using a BioSemi ActiveII system (Amsterdam, Netherlands). Channels were referenced offline using the average potential measured at two electrodes placed over the left and right mastoids. The data was bandpass filtered 0.1–50 Hz to reduce signal drift and high frequency noise.

Finger-Tapping. EEG data were recorded at 1024 Hz from 256 scalp electrodes using a BioSemi ActiveII system (Amsterdam, Netherlands). Channels were referenced offline using the average potential measured at two electrodes placed over the left and right mastoids. The data was bandpass filtered 0.1–50 Hz to reduce signal drift and high frequency noise.

3.4   Rejecting Epochs Based on High-Order Statistics

BCI Classification. CSP and HDCA were used to discriminate left from right hand finger movements in the finger-tapping dataset. Finger-tapping data was resampled to 128 Hz and RSVP data was resampled to 256 Hz. None of the scalp electrode channels were removed in either dataset prior to analysis. Continuous data was segmented into epochs around the event of interest. The event of interest for the finger-tapping data was defined as the detection of the downward movement of a finger based on the switches. Finger-tapping data was epoched -500 ms to 1500 ms relative to the event for HDCA and 500 ms to 1500 ms relative to the event for CSP; these epoch windows were determined to be optimal for each classifier based on a preliminary parameter search. The event of interest for the RVSP dataset was the onset of the presentation of a target or non-target stimulus image. RSVP data was epoched 0 to 500 ms relative to the event for all classifiers.

Epoch Ranking. Joint probability, kurtosis, extreme values, and abnormal spectra methods were used to rank epoch quality. The joint probability was computed using the EEGLAB function jointprob.m [14]. Built-in MATLAB (MathWorks, Natick, MA) functions were used to compute kurtosis and extreme values. These measures were computed for each channel within each epoch and normalized within channel across all epochs. Epochs were then ranked based on the absolute value of their normalized value, with larger values indicating a higher likelihood of containing an artifact.

The power spectral density of each channel within epoch was computed using the MATLAB function pmtm.m which implements a slepian multi-taper method to estimate the power spectral density (PSD) for the epoch. The mean PSD within each channel across all epochs was subtracted from each channel PSD estimate. For each epoch, the maximum spectral power (in dB) was found in the 0-2 Hz range and the 20–40 Hz range; these correspond to the frequency range of typical eye and EMG artifacts, respectively [1]. These two values were treated as a vector and the L^2 norm was used as a derived value to rank the epoch quality.

Cross-Validation. A 20-by-5 cross validation procedure was used to estimate classifier performance. Epochs are first randomly assigned to one of five partitions. Four of the partitions are used to train the classifier then the predictive accuracy of the model is tested on the remaining partition. The partition that is held out as the test set is rotated until all five partitions have served as the test set exactly once. The data is then repartitioned and the same procedure carried out again; this is repeated 20 times.

Epoch Rejection. For each subject, rejection methods, and dataset, a baseline performance value (in AUC) was computed using the entire dataset. Next, each method was evaluated by removing set percentages of data based on the ranking variables described above. In each case the data was removed then the cross-validation scheme was rerun to obtain a new estimate of the classifier performance. The percentage of data removed was incremented until the decrease in performance caused by reducing the training data available outweighed the increase in performance caused by the removal of artifact-contaminated data. In this case, as the percentage of data removed increases, the size of the training set naturally decreases by default; we will call this the dynamic training set (DTS) case.

To observe the effect of removing artifact-contaminated data in the absence of changes in training set size, we repeated this process using a fixed testing and training set size. Based on the results of the DTS case, we selected a percentage of data removal where the effect of the reduced training set size seems to equally counteract the effect of removing artifact data. We constrain the size of the training (and test) sets based on the size of the training and test sets for this level of data removal. For example, if we have 100 epochs, select 50 % as our removal constraint, and use an 80/20 split for training and testing data, our training and test set sizes will be set at 40 (100*0.5*0.8) and 10 (100*0.5*0.2), respectively. In the baseline (no data removal) case, we would then select 40 epochs for the training set and 10 epochs for the test set from the pool of 100 epochs on each iteration of the outer fold of the cross-validation. When we begin removing artifact data, we first remove it from the pool of available epochs, and again select 40 epochs for the training set and 10 epochs for the test set. This ensures that any change in classifier performance is attributable to the removal of artifact contaminated data rather than a change in the size of the training set. We will refer to this case as the fixed training set (FTS) case.

4   Results

To compare the effect of different percentages of data removal, we performed a 3-way ANOVA test using percentage of data removed, artifact detection method, and subject as the three grouping variables. We compared conditions using the increase in AUC relative to the mean baseline (no data removed) AUC. A multiple comparisons test was then performed using the Tukey-Kramer method with an alpha value of 0.05 to determine which percentages of data removal caused a significant increase or decrease in AUC over baseline. Note that error bars in Figs. 1, 2, 3 and 4 represent minimal group separation distances as computed by the multiple comparisons test and not standard deviation because this gives a better depiction using a more relevant statistic.

4.1   Finger Tapping

HDCA. Figure 1 shows the results of the multiple comparisons test for HDCA classification performance on the finger-tapping data. In the DTS case, the detrimental effect of reducing the training set size clearly outweighs the improvement gained by removal of artifact-contaminated data. The joint-probability, kurtosis, and abnormal spectra methods of artifact detection all cause a decrease in performance relative to

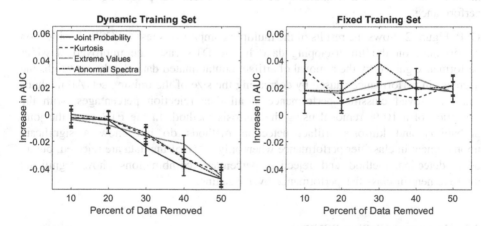

Fig. 1. Multiple comparisons for the effect of epoch rejection on HDCA performance in classifying right from left hand movements in a motor movement dataset. The effect of reducing the training set size significantly decreases AUC compared to baseline for all epoch rejection methods. In the dynamic training set (DTS) case, the size of the training and test sets decrease as the percentage of data removed increases. This decreases classifier performance and counteracts the positive effect of removing artifact data. In the fixed training set (FTS) case, the size of the training and test sets remain the same as the percentage of data removed increases. This control allows the effect of removing artifact data on classifier performance to be observed by itself.

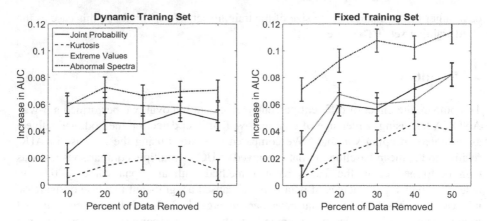

Fig. 2. Multiple comparisons for the effect of epoch rejection on CSP performance in classifying right from left hand movements in a motor movement dataset. The benefit of removing artifact contaminated data outweighs the detriment of decreasing the training set size.

baseline when 30 % or more of the data are rejected. The extreme values method of artifact detection performs even worse, showing a significant decrease in performance when 20 % or more of the data are rejected. In the FTS case, all rejection methods show an increase in classifier performance over baseline at all rejection percentage levels. Joint probability and extreme values show a weak upward trend in classifier performance, peaking at 40 % data removal, but the kurtosis and abnormal spectra methods do not show a relationship between data removal percentage and classifier performance.

CSP. Figure 2 shows the results of the multiple comparisons test for CSP classification performance on the finger-tapping data. In the DTS case, the improved classifier performance gained by the removal of artifact-contaminated data clearly outweighs the decrease in performance caused by decreasing the size of the training set. All methods cause improved classifier performance at all data rejection percentages, with the exception of a 10 % removal using the kurtosis method. In the FTS case, the joint probability and kurtosis artifact detection methods do not show a significant improvement in classifier performance when only 10 % of the data are rejected, but all other detection method and rejection percentage combinations show significant improvement in classifier performance over baseline.

4.2 Insurgent-Civilian RSVP

HDCA. Figure 3 shows the results of the multiple comparisons test for HDCA classification performance on the RSVP data. In the DTS case, the joint-probability and abnormal spectra artifact detection methods seem to overcome the decrease in performance due to decreased training set size. They show significant improvement over baseline at 25 % removal and above, and at 10 % removal and above, respectively. The kurtosis and extreme values methods do not cause a significant increase or decrease in

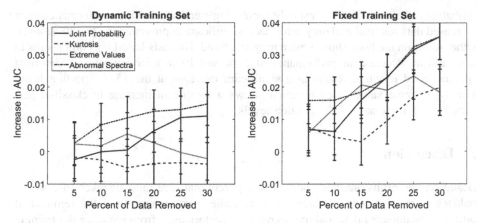

Fig. 3. Multiple comparisons for the effect of epoch rejection on HDCA performance in classifying target from non-target image presentations in an RSVP dataset.

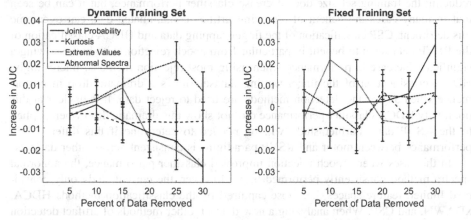

Fig. 4. Multiple comparisons for the effect of epoch rejection on xDAWN performance in classifying target from non-target image presentations in an RSVP dataset.

classifier performance. In the FTS case, all rejection methods show significant improvement over baseline. Performance improves over baseline for abnormal spectra at 5 % or greater data rejection, extreme values at 10 % or greater rejection, joint-probability at 15 % or greater rejection, and kurtosis at 20 % or greater rejection.

xDAWN. Figure 4 shows the results of the multiple comparisons test for xDAWN classification performance on the RSVP data. In the DTS case, the kurtosis method does not show a significant increase or decrease in performance. The joint-probability and extreme value methods show a significant decrease in classifier performance relative to baseline when 20 % or more of the data are removed. The abnormal spectra based rejection method shows a significant increase in performance from 20–25 % removal, but dips back below significance at the 30 % level. In the FTS case, the joint probability shows the only constantly increasing trend in classifier performance with increased data removal and only achieves a significant improvement at the 30 % level. Other rejection methods show a more irregular trend. Kurtosis-based rejection results in a significant decrease in performance at 5 % and 10 % rejection levels. Abnormal spectra based rejection results in a significant decrease at the 15 % rejection level. Finally, extreme value based rejection shows a significant increase in classifier performance at 10 % and 15 % rejection levels.

5 Discussion

Based on the results presented here, it is apparent that care must be taken to ensure a balance is met between the increase in classifier performance from the removal of artifact-contaminated data and the decrease in performance from reducing the training set size. In all cases other than RSVP classification with xDAWN, we see a clear difference in classifier performance between the fixed and dynamic training set cases, with the dynamic training set case consistently performing worse. This indicates that reducing the training set size does decrease classifier performance, but it can be seen that in many cases the benefit of removing artifact-contaminated data can overcome this detriment. CSP classification of the finger-tapping data and HDCA classification of the RSVP data seem to benefit in particular from epoch rejection with both showing a significant increase in performance when using most rejection methods. Interestingly, HDCA classification of the finger-tapping dataset shows a dramatic drop in performance when any of the detection methods are used to reject data. It is unclear at this point why HDCA classifier performance did not show this dramatic drop when applied to the RSVP data. Further study will be needed to determine if this difference in performance between motor and RSVP paradigms is consistent across other datasets.

In the cases where epoch rejection improved classifier performance, the abnormal spectra method consistently performed best. However, the current study only considered limited feature spaces, i.e. those captured by the classification methods HDCA, xDAWN, and CSP. When analyzing a new dataset, other methods of artifact detection should be considered, with the final selection tailored to the specific problem space. Based on our current results and the previous findings of Delorme et al. [2], we recommend the use of abnormal spectra as the starting point for improving BCI classifier performance.

In real-world BCI scenarios where the amount of training data is limited, careful consideration must be given as to how much data is rejected due to artifacts. The classifier-paradigm pairs studied here showed differences in their sensitivity to training set reduction and to artifact contamination. Further work must be done to develop an understanding of how to choose the best classifier for a paradigm, taking into consideration the amount of training data that will be available and the probability of artifact occurrence within that data.

Acknowledgements. This research was sponsored by the Army Research Laboratory and was accomplished under Cooperative Agreement Number W911NF-10-2-0022. The views and conclusions contained in this document are those of the authors and should not be interpreted as representing official policies, either expressed or implied, of the Army Research Laboratory or the U.S. Government. The U.S. Government is authorized to reproduce and distribute reprints for Government purposes notwithstanding any copyright notation herein.

References

1. Urigüen, J.A., Garcia-Zapirain, B.: EEG artifact removal—state-of-the-art and guidelines. J. Neural Eng. **12**(3), 031001 (2015)
2. Delorme, A., Sejnowski, T., Makeig, S.: Enhanced detection of artifacts in EEG data using higher-order statistics and independent component analysis. Neuroimage **34**(4), 1443–1449 (2007)
3. Lawhern, V., Slayback, D., Wu, D., Lance, B.J.: Efficient labeling of EEG signal artifacts using active learning. In: 2015 IEEE International Conference on Systems, Man, and Cybernetics (SMC), pp. 3217–3222. IEEE, October 2015
4. McDowell, K., Lin, C.T., Oie, K.S., Jung, T.P., Gordon, S., Whitaker, K.W., Hairston, W. D.: Real-world neuroimaging technologies. Access IEEE **1**, 131–149 (2013)
5. Müller-Gerking, J., Pfurtscheller, G., Flyvbjerg, H.: Designing optimal spatial filters for single-trial EEG classification in a movement task. Clin. Neurophysiol. **110**(5), 787–798 (1999)
6. Marathe, A.R., Ries, A.J., McDowell, K.: Sliding HDCA: single-trial EEG classification to overcome and quantify temporal variability. IEEE Trans. Neural Syst. Rehabil. Eng. **22**(2), 201–211 (2014)
7. Trejo, L.J., Rosipal, R., Matthews, B.: Brain-computer interfaces for 1-D and 2-D cursor control: designs using volitional control of the EEG spectrum or steady-state visual evoked potentials. IEEE Trans. Neural Syst. Rehabil. Eng. **14**(2), 225–229 (2006)
8. Rivet, B., Souloumiac, A., Attina, V., Gibert, G.: xDAWN algorithm to enhance evoked potentials: application to brain–computer interface. IEEE Trans. Biomed. Eng. **56**(8), 2035–2043 (2009)
9. Ramoser, H., Muller-Gerking, J., Pfurtscheller, G.: Optimal spatial filtering of single trial EEG during imagined hand movement. IEEE Trans. Rehabil. Eng. **8**(4), 441–446 (2000)
10. Delorme, A., Makeig, S., Sejnowski, T.: Automatic artifact rejection for EEG data using high-order statistics and independent component analysis. In: Proceedings of the 3rd International Workshop on ICA, vol. 457, p. 462, December 2001
11. Regulation, A.: 70–25: Use of Volunteers as Subjects of Research. US Dept of the Army, Washington, DC (1990)
12. US Department of Health and Human Services. "Code of federal regulations: Protection of human subjects" (2011)
13. Cecotti, H., Marathe, A.R., Ries, A.J.: Optimization of single-trial detection of event-related potentials through artificial trials. IEEE Trans. Biomed. Eng. **62**(9), 2170–2176 (2015)
14. Delorme, A., Makeig, S.: EEGLAB: an open source toolbox for analysis of single-trial EEG dynamics including independent component analysis. J. Neurosci. Methods **134**(1), 9–21 (2004)

Examining the Neural Correlates of Incidental Facial Emotion Encoding Within the Prefrontal Cortex Using Functional Near-Infrared Spectroscopy

Achala H. Rodrigo[1(✉)], Hasan Ayaz[2,3,4], and Anthony C. Ruocco[5]

[1] Department of Psychology, University of Toronto Scarborough, Toronto, Canada
achala.rodrigo@utoronto.ca
[2] School of Biomedical Engineering, Science and Health Systems, Drexel University,
Philadelphia, PA, USA
hasan.ayaz@drexel.edu
[3] Department of Family and Community Health, University of Pennsylvania,
Philadelphia, PA, USA
[4] Division of General Pediatrics, Children's Hospital of Philadelphia,
Philadelphia, PA, USA
[5] Mood and Anxiety Division, Centre for Addiction and Mental Health, Toronto, Canada
anthony.ruocco@utoronto.ca

Abstract. Previous neuroimaging research has implicated the prefrontal cortex (PFC) as a region of the brain that is vital for various aspects of emotion processing. The present study sought to examine the neural correlates of incidental facial emotion encoding, with regard to neutral and fearful faces, within the PFC. Thirty-nine healthy adults were presented briefly with neutral and fearful faces and the evoked hemodynamic oxygenation within the PFC was measured using 16-channel continuous-wave functional near-infrared spectroscopy. When viewing fearful as compared to neutral faces, participants demonstrated higher levels of activation within the right medial PFC. On the other hand, participants demonstrated lower levels of activation within the left medial PFC and left lateral PFC when viewing fearful faces, as compared to neutral faces. These findings are consistent with previous fMRI research, and suggest that fearful faces are linked to a neural response within the right medial PFC, whereas neutral faces appear to elicit a neural response within left medial and lateral areas of the PFC.

Keywords: fNIRS · Prefrontal cortex · Facial emotions · Incidental encoding

1 Introduction

1.1 Neural Correlates of Facial Emotion Processing

As human beings, the ability to recognize and appropriately respond to facial expressions of emotions is crucial for survival. Over the past few decades, neuroscientists have strived to better understand the neural mechanisms that underlie emotion recognition and processing [1]. Recent advances in neuroimaging techniques have made it possible to examine neural correlates of emotion processing more closely, and with improved

© Springer International Publishing Switzerland 2016
D.D. Schmorrow and C.M. Fidopiastis (Eds.): AC 2016, Part I, LNAI 9743, pp. 102–112, 2016.
DOI: 10.1007/978-3-319-39955-3_10

accuracy. In this vein, facial emotions have been a major focus of a significant body of research with potential applications ranging from the clinical domain to human computer applications [2–6].

Facial stimuli depicting emotions have been linked to activation in brain regions such as amygdala, basal ganglia, and occipito-temporal regions of the cortex [7, 8]. The prefrontal cortex (PFC) in particular, has been implicated as an important region that subserves facial emotion processing, perhaps in a regulatory capacity [9]. Accordingly, researchers have suggested that various sub-regions within the PFC may play distinct roles with regard to recognizing and regulating emotions [10, 11].

1.2 Functional Near-Infrared Spectroscopy

To date, neuroimaging techniques such as functional magnetic resonance imaging (fMRI) and positron emission tomography (PET), which assess localized brain activation by monitoring task-related hemodynamic responses, have been widely used. These traditional neuroimaging techniques, however, can be prohibitively costly. Furthermore, they require individuals to be immobile, thus are less feasible for real-world applications, or more ecologically valid investigations. Therefore, it is necessary to explore how novel neuroimaging techniques can be validated as practical and cost efficient alternatives. Functional near-infrared spectroscopy (fNIRS), an optical neuroimaging technique, is becoming increasingly popular as an economically feasible and a more versatile alternative to traditional neuroimaging techniques such as fMRI and PET.

fNIRS is a cost-effective and portable neuroimaging method that measures evoked relative changes in oxygenated (oxy-Hb) and deoxygenated hemoglobin (deoxy-Hb) in the cerebral cortex using light [12, 13]. More specifically, fNIRS utilizes near infrared light between the wavelengths of 700 nm to 900 nm that is introduced at the surface of the scalp. The backscattered light is then monitored to estimate the changes in concentration ratios of the main chromophores in the cortical tissue, namely oxy-Hb and deoxy-Hb [14]. This method of optical neuroimaging has been increasingly becoming popular among researchers, and it has been successfully deployed in various research contexts to examine neural activation reliably and at minimal cost [13, 15–17]. A main advantage that fNIRS provides, as compared to traditional neuroimaging techniques such as fMRI and PET, is its high portability. This makes fNIRS more versatile in its applications and highly accessible, allowing it to be deployed successfully in clinical applications and settings that promise higher levels of ecological validity [12, 18]. Previous studies have highlighted the potential utility of fNIRS in the context of examining the neural correlates of emotion perception [3, 19, 20], particularly within the PFC [21, 22]. Furthermore, a more recent study has also demonstrated the multimodal use of fNIRS, together with facial expression analysis [23].

1.3 Present Study

Gaining a clearer understanding of the neural correlates of facial emotion perception can have important implications for a variety of Neuroergonomic applications and brain computer interface settings [18, 24–26]. Such applications range from product usability studies at the design phase, to adaptive systems of complex man-machine interfaces. Further development in these areas are only possible if practical and real-time monitoring of localized brain activity can be achieved. Furthermore, because fNIRS can be miniaturized, battery operated, wireless, and ultra-portable, it is an ideal candidate for potential in-home use [27]. Therefore, it is important to further validate the utility of this novel technology, especially with regard to its sensitivity to neural correlates of facial emotion face perception.

In understanding the neural correlates of facial emotion perception, various levels of processing can be examined. At the lowest level of processing, exploring the incidental encoding of emotional faces can be an important step in identifying neural correlates of facial emotion processing. Specifically, it would be important to determine if a given neuroimaging technique, such as fNIRS, is adequately sensitive to detect changes that occur at this lowest level of facial emotion processing.

The present study sought to evaluate whether fNIRS can be used to reliably evaluate neural responses to incidental encoding of faces. More specifically, the neural correlates of incidental encoding of neutral and fearful faces within the PFC was explored.

2 Method

2.1 Sample

Thirty-nine healthy adults, recruited through the undergraduate research participant pool at the University of Toronto Scarborough and from the Greater Toronto Area, provided written informed consent to participate in the present study. This sample consisted of right handed participants (35 female), who were on average 28.46 years old ($SD = 12.09$). Upon completing informed consent, the participants also completed a screening that was used to rule out serious medical (i.e., severe head trauma) or psychological illness (i.e., major depressive disorder).

2.2 Incidental Facial Emotion Encoding Task

The incidental facial emotion encoding task consisted of a widely spaced event-related design, with 32 trials in total. The face stimuli consisted of 16 neutral and 16 fearful faces that were obtained from the 2D facial emotional stimuli database of the University of Pennsylvania's Brain Behavior Laboratory [28]. The faces were of diverse ethnic origins and were arranged in a quasi-random order. Half of the face stimuli in each emotion category consisted of female faces. During each trial, a face was presented to the participant for 250 ms on a black background, and was followed by a white crosshair fixation. Each trial had a duration of 20 s. The participants were asked to press a button with their right index finger if the face was male, and with the right middle finger if the face was female.

2.3 Neuroimaging Procedure

The participants were seated in a dimly lit room in front of a computer monitor and a keyboard. fNIR Imager 1000® (fNIR Devices, Potomac, MD), a 16-channel continuous wave fNIRS system, was used in the present study to examine neural activation. Measurements of raw light intensities were obtained at 500 ms intervals, with 1.25 cm of penetration into the cortical tissue within the PFC at 16 measurement locations [29]. Specifically, the imaging probe positioning on the forehead was aligned with electrode positions F7, FP1, FP2 and F8, based on the international 10–20 EEG system [30]. Thus, the fNIRS probe provided coverage over Brodmann areas 9, 10, 45 and 46. The fNIRS raw light intensities that were obtained during the experiment were first visually inspected to exclude problematic channels affected by noticeable motion artifacts, and then were subjected to signal processing algorithms. Specifically, high frequency noise, physiological and motion artifacts were systematically excluded using low pass finite impulse response and sliding window motion artifact rejection with the fNIRSoft® Software Package [13, 15, 31]. Activation segments of interest were demarcated by time synchronization markers. The study focused on oxy-Hb as the primary parameter of interest, and relative changes in oxy-Hb were estimated for each channel.

2.4 Statistical Analyses

Multilevel models, which nested the time-series of observations within participants, were estimated for each channel [32]. These models accounted for the possibility that the number of observations were unbalanced across participants. All models were conservatively estimated using an unstructured covariance matrix and the Satterthwaite method of estimating degrees of freedom [33]. The two emotion conditions were compared using contrast codes which examined the difference between fearful and neutral conditions (fearful coded as ½, and neutral coded as −½). Type I error in the analyses was controlled by using False Discovery Rate corrections for multiple comparisons [34, 35]. Data analyses were conducted using IBM SPSS Statistics Version 20.0 (IBM Corp. Released 2011. IBM SPSS Statistics for Windows, Version 20.0. Armonk, NY: IBM Corp.). Additionally, the time-series graphs for each channel were created for both conditions, also mapping a 95 % Confidence Interval (CI) for the purpose of further examining the differences in neural responses.

3   Results

3.1 Behavioral Results

Participants demonstrated equivalent reaction times during the fearful condition ($M = 710.17$ ms, $SD = 216.73$ ms), and the neutral condition ($M = 700.83$ ms, $SD = 216.79$ ms; $t(76) = -.13, p = .90, d = .04$). Participants also demonstrated similar accuracy across both fearful ($M = 85.2$ %, $SD = 10$ %) and neutral ($M = 89.9$ %, $SD = 14.04$ %) conditions ($t(76) = 1.85, p = .07, d = .39$).

3.2   Fearful vs. Neutral Activation

Significant main effects for the emotion condition was found across 10 of the 16 channels. More specifically, higher activation was found in channel 12 for the fearful condition as compared to the neutral condition ($b = .01$, $SE = .00$, $p < 0.01$), corresponding to a region within the right medial PFC. The fearful condition as compared to the neutral condition, on the other hand, was associated with lower activation in channels 1 to 9 ($b's < -.01$, $SE's = .00$, $p's < 0.01$), corresponding to a region encompassing the left medial and lateral regions of the PFC. These findings are depicted on a standard MRI template of the brain in Fig. 1, where blue and purple indicate lower activation (left PFC) and red and yellow indicate higher activation (right PFC).

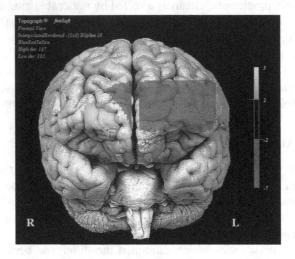

Fig. 1. Activation map depicting statistically significant activation differences across the PFC for the fearful vs. neutral activation contrast. (Color figure online)

3.3   Examining the Time-Series

The neural activation patterns observed across the duration of the trial for the neutral condition and the fearful condition are depicted in Fig. 2.

The neutral condition appeared to be linked to a pattern of activation within the PFC that was more lateral at first, which subsequently became more medial. More specifically, activation was initially seen in more lateral aspects of the right and left lateral PFC. Towards the end of the trial, however, the lateral activation appeared to subside, and was followed by increases in activation within the left medial PFC. In contrast to the neutral condition, the fearful condition appeared to elicit a pattern of activation within the PFC that was more medial at first, which subsequently became more laterally localized. More specifically, immediately following the face stimulus, activation was observed bilaterally in the PFC, in regions that were more medial as compared to the neutral condition. As the trial progressed, this pattern of activation was replaced with

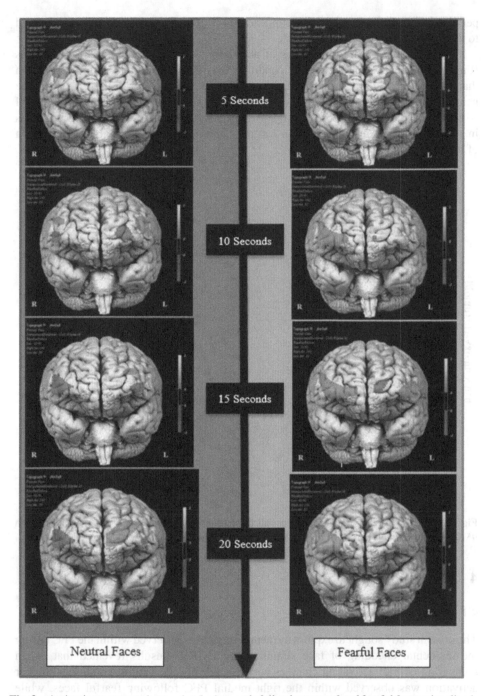

Fig. 2. Activation patterns observed at 5-s intervals following neutral and fearful faces, visualized on a standard MRI template of the brain. (Color figure online)

persistent bilateral activation, which appeared to be more laterally situated as compared to the initial response.

When comparing the time-series of activation for neutral and fearful conditions (Fig. 3), it appeared that the neutral condition may be linked to a pattern of activation that is focused on the left medial and lateral PFC. Specifically, in these regions, the neutral stimuli appeared to be followed by increases in activation, whereas the fearful stimuli appeared to demonstrate the opposite trend. A potential trend towards increases in activation for the fearful condition was only apparent within the right medial region of the PFC.

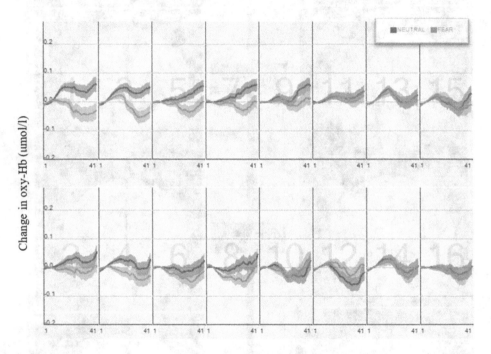

Fig. 3. The 20-s oxy-Hb time-series across all 16 channels for neutral and fearful conditions with 95 % confidence intervals (CI) shown as shaded areas around the grand mean. (Color figure online)

4   Discussion

4.1   Summary of Findings

The present study sought to explore the neural responses observed within the PFC during the incidental encoding of face stimuli using fNIRS. Results revealed that, when comparing overall activation changes between fearful and neutral conditions, higher activation was observed within the right medial PFC following fearful faces, while higher activation was observed within the left medial and lateral PFC following neutral faces. Exploring the time-series of activation revealed that the neutral condition appeared to be characterized by an initial lateral increase in activation followed by a later medial increase in activation. The fearful condition, on the other hand, appeared to be characterized by an initial increase in activation that appeared to be more medial, which was followed by increases in activation in more lateral regions of the PFC.

4.2 General Discussion

These findings appear to be in line with previous neuroimaging research. In a comprehensive meta-analysis of 105 fMRI studies, it was demonstrated that neutral face processing was linked to neural activation within an area encompassing the left medial PFC, while fearful face processing was linked to neural activation in an area encompassing the right medial PFC [8]. Results from the present study are consistent with these findings and show somewhat similar activation foci in response to neutral and fearful faces.

Results from the present study may also be consistent with the notion that the medial PFC may be an important region that subserves emotion regulation processes [10, 11], specifically in the context of perceiving threat. More specifically, it was demonstrated that the incidental encoding of fearful faces was immediately followed by a PFC response that was more medial, as compared to the neutral condition.

Importantly, the present study demonstrates that fNIRS can be deployed as an adequately sensitive neuroimaging tool that has the potential to reliably examine emotion related processes within the prefrontal cortex. This can have numerous important implications within the context of clinical applications, brain-computer interfacing and Neuro-ergonomics research overall. For example, the patterns of activation observed during the encoding of different facial emotions can potentially be used as biomarkers for studying emotion perception/regulation failure in clinical populations. Furthermore, assessment of emotion related processes directly from the brain can be utilized in usability studies during the design of products or adaptive systems, especially while users are engaged with them within in-home settings. Overall, being able to accurately and reliably identify neural responses to emotional stimuli can greatly aid in refining brain-computer interfaces, and user experience.

4.3 Limitations

It should be noted that the present study focused primarily on incidental encoding of static face stimuli, which may be associated with neural response patterns that are different from dynamic facial emotions that are encountered in real life [36]. It should also be important to consider the impact of variables such as gender, race, and age on the neural correlates of facial emotion processing. Although the present study attempted to control for these variables by including a quasi-random selection of stimuli, future research should aim to systematically address these questions with adequately powered studies.

4.4 Future Directions

The present study aimed to examine the feasibility of fNIRS in detecting emotion related processes within the PFC. Future research can further validate these findings by replicating these results in a larger sample, across more emotion categories and other types of emotion stimuli. Given the versatility of fNIRS, future studies should also examine the feasibility of using fNIRS in more ecologically valid, complex emotion processing tasks.

Acknowledgements. The authors would like to thank Stefano I. Di Domenico for his assistance with statistical analysis. The authors would also like to thank the research team at the Clinical Neurosciences Laboratory at the University of Toronto Scarborough for data collection and processing.

References

1. Phan, K.L., Wager, T., Taylor, S.F., Liberzon, I.: Functional neuroanatomy of emotion: a meta-analysis of emotion activation studies in PET and fMRI. Neuroimage **16**(2), 331–348 (2002)
2. Narumoto, J., Yamada, H., Iidaka, T., Sadato, N., Fukui, K., Itoh, H., Yonekura, Y.: Brain regions involved in verbal or non-verbal aspects of facial emotion recognition. Neuroreport **11**(11), 2571–2574 (2000)
3. Doi, H., Nishitani, S., Shinohara, K.: NIRS as a tool for assaying emotional function in the prefrontal cortex. Front. Hum. Neurosci. **7**, 770 (2013). doi:10.3389/fnhum.2013.00770
4. Liberati, G., Federici, S., Pasqualotto, E.: Extracting neurophysiological signals reflecting users' emotional and affective responses to BCI use: a systematic literature review. NeuroRehabilitation **37**, 341–358 (2015). doi:10.3233/NRE-151266
5. Ochsner, K.N., Silvers, J.A., Buhle, J.T.: Functional imaging studies of emotion regulation: a synthetic review and evolving model of the cognitive control of emotion. Ann. N. Y. Acad. Sci. **1251**, E1–E24 (2012). doi:10.1111/j.1749-6632.2012.06751.x
6. Etkin, A., Egner, T., Kalisch, R.: Emotional processing in anterior cingulate and medial prefrontal cortex. Trends Cogn. Sci. **15**(2), 85–93 (2011). doi:10.1016/j.tics.2010.11.004
7. Gorno-Tempini, M.L., Pradelli, S., Serafini, M., Pagnoni, G., Baraldi, P., Porro, C., Nichelli, P.: Explicit and incidental facial expression processing: an fMRI study. Neuroimage **14**(2), 465–473 (2001)
8. Fusar-Poli, P., Placentino, A., Carletti, F., Landi, P., Abbamonte, M.: Functional atlas of emotional faces processing: a voxel-based meta-analysis of 105 functional magnetic resonance imaging studies. J. Psychiatry Neurosci. JPN **34**(6), 418 (2009)
9. Wager, T.D., Barrett, L.F., Bliss-Moreau, E., Lindquist, K., Duncan, S., Kober, H., Mize, J.: The neuroimaging of emotion. Handb. Emot. **3**, 249–271 (2008)
10. Wager, T.D., Davidson, M.L., Hughes, B.L., Lindquist, M.A., Ochsner, K.N.: Prefrontal-subcortical pathways mediating successful emotion regulation. Neuron **59**(6), 1037–1050 (2008)
11. Kober, H., Barrett, L.F., Joseph, J., Bliss-Moreau, E., Lindquist, K., Wager, T.D.: Functional grouping and cortical–subcortical interactions in emotion: a meta-analysis of neuroimaging studies. Neuroimage **42**(2), 998–1031 (2008)
12. Irani, F., Platek, S.M., Bunce, S., Ruocco, A.C., Chute, D.: Functional near infrared spectroscopy (fNIRS): an emerging neuroimaging technology with important applications for the study of brain disorders. Clin. Neuropsychologist **21**(1), 9–37 (2007)

13. Ayaz, H., Shewokis, P.A., Bunce, S., Izzetoglu, K., Willems, B., Onaral, B.: Optical brain monitoring for operator training and mental workload assessment. Neuroimage **59**(1), 36–47 (2012). doi:10.1016/j.neuroimage.2011.06.023
14. Ayaz, H., Shewokis, P.A., Curtin, A., Izzetoglu, M., Izzetoglu, K., Onaral, B.: Using MazeSuite and functional near infrared spectroscopy to study learning in spa-tial navigation. J. Vis. Exp. **56**, e3443 (2014). doi:10.3791/3443
15. Rodrigo, A.H., Di Domenico, S.I., Ayaz, H., Gulrajani, S., Lam, J., Ruocco, A.C.: Differentiating functions of the lateral and medial prefrontal cortex in motor response inhibition. Neuroimage **85**, 423–431 (2014)
16. Ruocco, A.C., Rodrigo, A.H., Lam, J., Di Domenico, S.I., Graves, B., Ayaz, H.: A problem-solving task specialized for functional neuroimaging: validation of the Scarborough adaptation of the Tower of London (S-TOL) using near-infrared spectroscopy. Front. Hum. Neurosci. **8**, 185 (2013)
17. Di Domenico, S.I., Rodrigo, A.H., Ayaz, H., Fournier, M.A., Ruocco, A.C.: Decision-making conflict and the neural efficiency hypothesis of intelligence: a functional near-infrared spectroscopy investigation. NeuroImage **109**, 307–317 (2015)
18. Ayaz, H., Onaral, B., Izzetoglu, K., Shewokis, P.A., McKendrick, R., Parasuraman, R.: Continuous monitoring of brain dynamics with functional near infrared spectroscopy as a tool for neuroergonomic research: Empirical examples and a technological development. Front. Hum. Neurosci. **7**, 1–13 (2013). doi:10.3389/fnhum.2013.00871
19. Balconi, M., Molteni, E.: Past and future of near-infrared spectroscopy in studies of emotion and social neuroscience. J. Cogn. Psychol. **28**, 1–18 (2015). doi:10.1080/20445911.2015.1102919
20. Balters, S., Steinert, M.: Capturing emotion reactivity through physiology measurement as a foundation for affective engineering in engineering design science and engineering practices. J. Intell. Manuf. **28**, 1–18 (2015). doi:10.1007/s10845-015-1145-2
21. Heller, A.S., Johnstone, T., Peterson, M.J., Kolden, G.G., Kalin, N.H., Davidson, R.J.: Increased prefrontal cortex activity during negative emotion regulation as a predictor of depression symptom severity trajectory over 6 months. JAMA Psychiatry **70**(11), 1181–1189 (2013). doi:10.1001/jamapsychiatry.2013.2430
22. Ozawa, S., Matsuda, G., Hiraki, K.: Negative emotion modulates prefrontal cortex activity during a working memory task: A NIRS study. Front. Hum. Neurosci. **8**, 46 (2014). doi: 10.3389/fnhum.2014.00046
23. Sun, Y., Ayaz, H., Akansu, A.N.: Neural correlates of affective context in facial expression analysis: a simultaneous EEG-fNIRS study. In: Paper Presented at the 3rd IEEE GlobalSIP Conference, Symposium on Signal Processing Challenges in Human Brain Connectomics, Orlando, FL (2015)
24. Cowie, R., Douglas-Cowie, E., Tsapatsoulis, N., Votsis, G., Kollias, S., Fellenz, W., Taylor, J.G.: Emotion recognition in human-computer interaction. IEEE Signal Process. Mag. **18**(1), 32–80 (2001)
25. Parasuraman, R., Christensen, J., Grafton, S.: Neuroergonomics: the brain in action and at work. Neuroimage **59**(1), 1–3 (2012)
26. Parasuraman, R., Rizzo, M.: Neuroergonomics: The Brain at Work. Oxford University Press, New York (2007)
27. Zander, T.O., Kothe, C., Jatzev, S., Gaertner, M.: Enhancing human-computer interaction with input from active and passive brain-computer interfaces. In: Tan, D.S., Nijholt, A. (eds.) Brain-Computer Interfaces, pp. 181–199. Springer, London (2010)
28. Gur, R.C., Ragland, J.D., Moberg, P.J., Turner, T.H., Bilker, W.B., Kohler, C., Siegel, S.J., Gur, R.E.: Computerized neurocognitive scanning: I. Methodology and validation in healthy people. Neuropsychopharmacology **25**(5), 766–776 (2001)

29. Ayaz, H., Izzetoglu, M., Platek, S.M., Bunce, S., Izzetoglu, K., Pourrezaei, K., Onaral, B.: Registering fNIR data to brain surface image using MRI templates. In: Conference Proceedings of the IEEE Engineering in Medicine and Biology Society, pp. 2671–2674 (2006). doi:10.1109/IEMBS.2006.260835
30. Jasper, H.H.: Report of the committee on methods of clinical examination in electroencephalography. Electroencephalogr. Clin. Neurophysiol. **10**, 370–375 (1958)
31. Ayaz, H.: Functional near infrared spectroscopy based brain computer interface. (Ph.D. thesis), Drexel University, Philadelphia, PA (2010)
32. Bryk, A.S., Raudenbush, S.W.: Application of hierarchical linear models to assessing change. Psychol. Bull. **101**(1), 147 (1987)
33. Schluchter, M.D., Elashoff, J.T.: Small-sample adjustments to tests with unbalanced repeated measures assuming several covariance structures. J. Stat. Comput. Simul. **37**(1–2), 69–87 (1990)
34. Benjamini, Y., Drai, D., Elmer, G., Kafkafi, N., Golani, I.: Controlling the false discovery rate in behavior genetics research. Behav. Brain Res. **125**(1), 279–284 (2001)
35. Benjamini, Y., Hochberg, Y.: Controlling the false discovery rate: a practical and powerful approach to multiple testing. J. Roy. Stat. Soc.: Ser. B (Methodol.) **57**, 289–300 (1995)
36. Kilts, C.D., Egan, G., Gideon, D.A., Ely, T.D., Hoffman, J.M.: Dissociable neural pathways are involved in the recognition of emotion in static and dynamic facial expressions. Neuroimage **18**(1), 156–168 (2003)

Exploring the EEG Correlates of Neurocognitive Lapse with Robust Principal Component Analysis

Chun-Shu Wei[1,2,3], Yuan-Pin Lin[1], and Tzyy-Ping Jung[1,2,3(✉)]

[1] Swartz Center for Computational Neuroscience,
Institute for Neural Computation, Atlanta, USA
{cswei,yplin,jung}@sccn.ucsd.edu
[2] Institute of Engineering in Medicine, San Diego, USA
[3] Department of Bioengineering,
University of California San Diego, La Jolla, San Diego, CA, USA

Abstract. Recent developments of brain-computer interfaces (BCIs) for driving lapse detection based on electroencephalogram (EEG) have made much progress. This study aims to leverage these new developments and explore the use of robust principal component analysis (RPCA) to extract informative EEG features associated with neurocognitive lapses. Study results showed that the RPCA decomposition could separate lapse-related EEG dynamics from the task-irrelevant spontaneous background activity, leading to more robust neural correlates of neurocognitive lapse as compared to the original EEG signals. This study will shed light on the development of a robust lapse-detection BCI system in real-world environments.

Keywords: EEG · BCI · RPCA · Drowsiness · Lapse · Driving · Fatigue

1 Introduction

The neurocognitive lapse has been known as a critical safety issue in vehicle driving. Such momentary lapse causes approximate 1.9 million drivers to fatal car accidents with injury or death [1]. Technologies that enable instant lapse detection and feedback delivery to rectify drivers from the occurrence of lapse are thus urgently required. For the past two decades, the noninvasive brain-sensing technology, namely electroencephalogram (EEG), has been adopted for this purpose because of its high temporal resolution of brain signals allowing a prompt response to a neurocognitive lapse. For example, studies have shown strong EEG correlates of behavioral lapses, including power spectra [2–6] and autoregressive features [7, 8]. These EEG features could then be used to develop various on-line/off-line neuroergonomic systems for monitoring drowsiness, fatigue, and behavioral lapse in task performance [2, 3, 9–12]. It is believed that an effective computational approach that can further leverage EEG correlates of neurocognitive lapse is a crucial step for improving the practicability of BCI-based lapse detection system in real life, which is the main focus of this study.

© Springer International Publishing Switzerland 2016
D.D. Schmorrow and C.M. Fidopiastis (Eds.): AC 2016, Part I, LNAI 9743, pp. 113–120, 2016.
DOI: 10.1007/978-3-319-39955-3_11

Robust principal component analysis (RPCA) [13] has recently been shown to be able to separate task-relevant and sparse EEG dynamics from the spontaneous task-irrelevant background activity [14]. The study demonstrated that the RPCA could improve the characterization of emotion-related EEG patterns across different recording days, and in turn facilitate a more effective emotion-classification model. As such, the task-related EEG dynamics of interest could be extracted from the task-irrelevant spontaneous background activity using RPCA, and could alleviate the EEG variability across sessions [14]. Analogously, this study explores the applicability of the RPCA for assessing the EEG correlates of neurocognitive lapses during driving.

2   Materials and Methods

2.1   Experiment and EEG Recording

This proof-of-concept study employed an EEG dataset of eight subjects participating in a lane-keeping driving task (LKT) in which EEG data and human driving behavior were simultaneously recorded [15]. The experiments were conducted in a virtual-reality-based driving simulator. Each subject drove on a straight highway scene during the night with artificial lane-deviation events introduced every 6–10 s. In each lane-deviation event, the car would randomly drift toward to left or right, and the subject was instructed to steer the car back to the cruising position as soon as possible. The duration from the onset of lane-deviant to the onset of steering movement was defined as the reaction time (RT), which indexed the extent of neurocognitive lapse. Longer RT indicated poor driving performance at the given moment. The experiment started in early afternoon when afternoon slump often occurred and thus maximized the opportunity of collecting neurocognitive lapses. The entire session of LKT lasted about 90 min, which was long enough to collect sufficient data under both alertness and drowsiness.

The EEG data were recorded by a 32-channel Quik-Cap electrode system (Compumedics Neuroscan, Inc.). Thirty Ag/AgCl electrodes were deployed according to the modified international 10–20 system, and two reference electrodes were placed upon left and right mastoids. The EEG signals were sampled with 16-bit quantization and 500 Hz sampling rate.

2.2   Lapse Assessment

In this study, a lapse refers to momentary unresponsiveness to the lane-deviation event in the LKT, and its level was quantitatively estimated based on RT. This study empirically defined the RT as alertness if its value was below the 5th percentile of the RTs across entire session for each session. In order to calibrate the individual differences in the distributions of RT values, the RTs of each individual was further normalized into a range of 0 to 1, defined as follows [11, 12]:

$$LI = \max(0, (1 - e^{-(\tau - \tau_0)})/(1 + e^{-(\tau - \tau_0)})) \tag{1}$$

where LI is the normalized lapse index, τ is the RT for a lane-deviant event, and τ_0 is the RT of alert trials. That is, the higher LI value is, the more momentary lapse a subject is. This study used correlation analysis to investigate the relationship between the EEG dynamics and the changes of RT.

2.3 EEG Data Processing

The 30-channel EEG signals referenced to the arithmetic average of left and right mastoid were first submitted to a band-pass finite impulse response filter (2 to 30 Hz) to eliminate DC drift and high-frequency noise including 60 Hz powerline noise. Trials contaminated by artifacts or noise were manually inspected and removed. Next, the filtered 30-channel EEG data were down-sampled to 250 Hz for analysis.

Previous studies [2, 3] have reported significant EEG spectral correlates of RT in stereotype frequency bands, such as delta (2–5 Hz), theta (5–8 Hz), alpha (8–13 Hz), and beta (13–30 Hz) bands. This study thus examined the impact of RPCA processing on EEG spectral time series in the same EEG frequency bands. To assess the associations between EEG dynamics and cognitive lapses, this study first calculated the band power (logarithmic signal variance) of each channel within a 3-s window before the onsets of each lane-deviation events, and then correlated that with the corresponding RT values.

2.4 Robust Principal Component Analysis

The applicability of the RPCA [8] has been demonstrated in effectively separating emotion-relevant and sparse EEG dynamics from the spontaneous task-irrelevant background activity [9]. This study employed RPCA for assessing the EEG correlates of neurocognitive lapses during driving. The RPCA mathematically decomposes multi-channel EEG signals, $X \in R^{m \times n}$ (m: number of attributes, n: number of observations), into a sparse matrix, S, and a low-rank matrix, L, followed by $X = S + L$, which can be efficiently solved by a tractable convex optimization proposed in [13]:

$$\min_{S^+, L^+} \lambda \|S^+\|_1 + \|L^+\|_* \text{ subject to } X = S + L \tag{2}$$

where $\|\cdot\|_*$ denotes the matrix nuclear norm, *i.e.*, the sum of singular values, $\|\cdot\|_1$ denotes the L1 norm, *i.e.*, the sum of absolute values of matrix entries, S^+ is the optimized estimate of sparse component, L^+ is the optimized estimate of low-rank component, and λ is a positive regularizing parameter empirically defined as $\lambda = 1/\sqrt{max(m,n)}$ [13]. This study formed the input matrix (m: number of electrodes $\times$ number of time points in a 3-s epoch, n: number of epochs in a session) for each subject. The method of augmented Lagrange multipliers [16] was adopted to perform RPCA decomposition. After the RPCA decomposition, the correlation coefficients between the normalized RTs (the lapse index) and the EEG spectral features estimated separately from the original band-passed EEG signals, sparse component, and low-rank component were compared using a statistical assessment of Wilcoxon signed-rank test. This study hypothesized that the sparse components, S, would profitably extract lapse-related EEG dynamics, and therefore would be more correlated with the RTs, compared to the low-rank components, L, and the original EEG signals, X.

3   Results and Discussion

Figure 1 illustrates the time series of RT profiles before and after the proposed RT normalization in two representative subjects. The alert RT is set to 0.6 s to map the RT to the lapse index. When a RT value is close to the defined alert RT, the lapse index increases more linearly as RT increases, until it reaches to a plateau close to 1 as RT is 4 s or longer. This warping is based on an assumption that there is very little difference in the brain state between 4- and 10-second RT as the subject was unresponsive to lane-deviation events. As can be seen, before the RT normalization shown in Fig. 1(b), S1 seemed to retain alert across the entire session, while S2 frequently behaved with lapse after 10 min driving. However, the lapse index after the RT normalization exhibited realistic fluctuations of lapses for both S1 and S2 in a 90-min driving task as shown in Fig. 1(c).

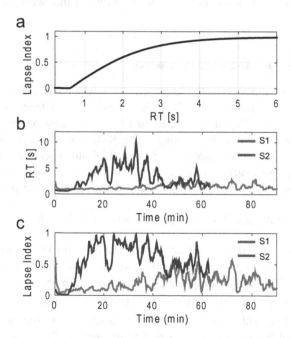

Fig. 1. Time series of RTs before and after RT normalization in two representative subjects. (a) the conversion from RT to the proposed lapse index with alert RT = 0.6 s. (b) the time series of original RTs in Subjects S1 and S2, and (c) the time series of the lapse index after RT normalization.

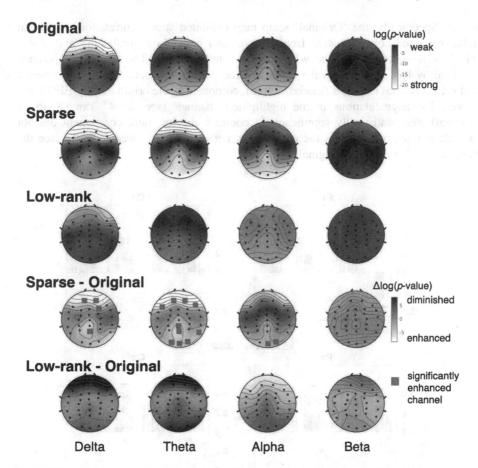

Fig. 2. The statistical significance of the correlations (log *p*-value) between RTs and band power using (from the top) the band-passed EEG signals (original), sparse components, and low-rank components at different scalp locations. The correlation intensity was estimated by logarithmic *p*-value from correlation analysis. Brightness in the gray-scaled topographies represents a strong correlation between the EEG band power and RTs. (the 4th row) Sparse - Original (the 5th row, Low-rank - Original) compares the significance of correlations between sparse (low-rank) and the original spectra. The red squares mark the channels with not only strong correlation (log(*p*)) < −11), but also significant increases from that of original EEG band power (*p* < 0.05). (Color figure online)

Figure 2 explores the statistical significance of the correlations (log *p*-value) between RTs and band power at different scalp locations using the (the 1st row) band-passed EEG signals, (the 2nd row) sparse components, and (the 3rd row) low-rank components. Brightness in gray-scaled topographies represents the correlation was statistically significant (a strong correlation) between the band power and RTs. The 4th (5th) row plots the differences of *p*-values between the 1st and the 2nd (3rd) rows. The red squares mark the channels whose correlations between the band power and RTs were significantly enhanced in terms of the *p*-value over using the original EEG band power. Specifically, the 'Original' scalp map exhibited strong correlations in frontal delta, moderate correlations in frontal theta, and parietal-occipital theta and alpha, which were somewhat in line with previous studies [2–4]. The sparse components obtained by RPCA enhanced the extents of the correlations between the EEG power and RTs at several channels (marked in red), compared to the original scalp-EEG band power. The augmentations in the highlighted channels (see the 4th raw, Sparse - Original) were statistically significant. In contrast, the low-rank component did not provide any improvement in the correlations between EEG power and RTs (see the bottom row, Low-rank – Original).

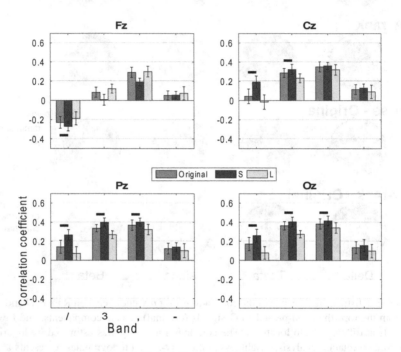

Fig. 3. The average correlation coefficients between band power and RTs at four representative scalp locations (Fz, Cz, Pz, and Oz) using the band-passed EEG signals (Original), sparse components (S), and low-rank components (L). Black bars indicate significant increase (either positive or negative) in correlation coefficient ($p < 0.05$) comparing S to Original.

Figure 3 plots the comparative correlation coefficients between band power and RTs using the band-passed EEG signals, sparse components, and low-rank components at four representative locations, including Fz, Cz, Pz, and Oz. The improvements of spectrum-RT correlation could be found by the enhancement in correlation coefficients between RTs and Fz delta, Cz delta and theta, Pz delta, theta, and alpha, and Oz delta, theta, and alpha power. In particular, the highest correlation could be obtained at Oz (alpha power) using the original band-passed EEG signal, where the sparse component further strengthened this correlation. Subtle discrepancy in statistical testing results could be found as compared to Fig. 2 due to the different measurements (logarithmic p-values and correlation coefficients) that were used in the statistical test. For instance, there is significant enhancement at F4 delta (see the red dot at delta, 1st column & 4th row in Fig. 2), but no significance at the nearby Fz delta. However, the correlation coefficient was significantly enhanced at Fz delta (see the top left of Fig. 3). Note that the sparse components generated features with higher correlations for most of the comparative conditions, which was consistent with the inference from the results shown in Fig. 2. The comparison of correlation coefficients suggests that sparse component can enhance the discriminative power of lapse-related EEG features.

The above findings evidently proved the posed hypothesis that the sparse EEG signals obtained by RPCA can profitably extract lapse-related EEG dynamics, and therefore carry more informative EEG spectral features accounting for behavioral lapses. In this preliminary proof-of-concept study, with such an improvement in feature extraction for EEG correlates of lapse, we believe that RPCA could boost the performance of a lapse detecting system.

While previous studies have applied independent component analysis (ICA) to extract highly informative EEG correlates of drowsiness [2, 9], a quantitative comparison between RPCA, ICA, and other related approaches on enhancing the quality of EEG features would be of interest to the researchers in this field and a natural next step of this study. Future work will also study to what extent the RPCA-enhanced EEG spectral correlates of neurocognitive lapse can improve the performance of lapse detection, which will increase the practicability of BCI-based lapse detection system in real life.

4 Conclusion

The present study empirically demonstrated the efficacy of RPCA for enhancing EEG correlates of neurocognitive lapse. Study results suggested that the RPCA could be used as a pre-processing step to extract the lapse-related EEG dynamics of interest from the spontaneous background activity, leading to a more robust lapse-detection BCI in real-world environments.

References

1. US National Sleep Foundation: 1.9 Million drivers have fatigue-related car crashes or near misses each year (2009). http://www.sleepfoundation.org/article/press-re-lease/19-million-drivers-have-fatigue-related-car-crashes-or-near-misses-each-year
2. Jung, T.P., Makeig, S., Stensmo, M., Sejnowski, T.J.: Estimating alertness from the EEG power spectrum. IEEE Trans. Biomed. Eng. 44, 60–69 (1997)
3. Lin, C.-T., Wu, R.-C., Liang, S.-F., Chao, W.-H., Chen, Y.-J., Jung, T.-P.: EEG-based drowsiness estimation for safety driving using independent component analysis. IEEE Trans. Circuits Syst. I: Regul. Pap. 52, 2726–2738 (2005)
4. Lal, S.K., Craig, A., Boord, P., Kirkup, L., Nguyen, H.: Development of an algorithm for an EEG-based driver fatigue countermeasure. J. Saf. Res. 34, 321–328 (2003)

5. Peiris, M.T.R., Jones, R.D., Davidson, P.R., Carroll, G.J., Bones, P.J.: Frequent lapses of responsiveness during an extended visuomotor tracking task in non-sleep-deprived subjects. J. Sleep Res. **15**, 291–300 (2006)
6. Davidson, P.R., Jones, R.D., Peiris, M., Davidson, T.R.: EEG-based lapse detection with high temporal resolution. IEEE Trans. Biomed. Eng. **54**, 832–839 (2007)
7. Rosipal, R., et al.: EEG-Based Drivers' drowsiness monitoring using a hierarchical gaussian mixture model. In: Schmorrow, D.D., Reeves, L.M. (eds.) HCII 2007 and FAC 2007. LNCS (LNAI), vol. 4565, pp. 294–303. Springer, Heidelberg (2007)
8. Zhao, C., Zheng, C., Zhao, M., Tu, Y., Liu, J.: Multivariate autoregressive models and kernel learning algorithms for classifying driving mental fatigue based on electroencephalographic. Expert Syst. Appl. **38**, 1859–1865 (2011)
9. Chuang, C.-H., Lai, P.-C., Ko, L.-W., Kuo, B.-C., Lin, C.-T.: Driver's cognitive state classification toward brain computer interface via using a generalized and supervised technology. In: The 2010 International Joint Conference on Neural Networks (IJCNN), pp. 1–7 (2010)
10. Wang, Y.-T., Huang, K.-C., Wei, C.-S., Huang, T.-Y., Ko, L.-W., Lin, C.-T., Cheng, C.-K., Jung, T.-P.: Developing an EEG-based on-line closed-loop lapse detection and mitigation system. Front Neurosci. **8**, 321 (2014)
11. Wei, C.-S., Wang, Y.-T., Lin, C.-T., Jung, T.-P.: Toward non-hair-bearing brain-computer interfaces for neurocognitive lapse detection. In: 2015 37th Annual International Conference of the IEEE Engineering in Medicine and Biology Society (EMBC), pp. 6638–6641 (2015)
12. Wei, C.-S., Lin, Y.-P., Bigdely-Shamlo, N., Wang, Y.-T., Lin, C.-T., Jung, T.-P.: Selective transfer learning for EEG-based drowsiness detection. In: 2015 IEEE International Conference on System, Man, and Cybernetics (SMC 2015), Hong Kong (2015)
13. Candès, E.J., Li, X., Ma, Y., Wright, J.: Robust principal component analysis? J. ACM. **58**, 11:1–11:37 (2011)
14. Jao, P.-K., Lin, Y.-P., Yang, Y.-H., Jung, T.-P.: Using robust principal component analysis to alleviate day-to-day variability in EEG based emotion classification. In: 2015 37th Annual International Conference of the IEEE Engineering in Medicine and Biology Society (EMBC), pp. 570–573 (2015)
15. Huang, R.-S., Jung, T.-P., Delorme, A., Makeig, S.: Tonic and phasic electroencephalographic dynamics during continuous compensatory tracking. NeuroImage. **39**, 1896–1909 (2008)
16. Lin, Z., Ganesh, A., Wright, J., Wu, L., Ma, Y.: Fast convex optimization algorithms for exact recovery of a corrupted low-rank matrix. In: Computational Advances in Multi-Sensor Adaptive Processing (CAMSAP) (2009)

Augmenting VR/AR Applications with EEG/EOG Monitoring and Oculo-Vestibular Recoupling

John K. Zao[1,2,4](✉), Tzyy-Ping Jung[1,2,6], Hung-Ming Chang[2,4],
Tchin-Tze Gan[2], Yu-Te Wang[1,6], Yuan-Pin Lin[6], Wen-Hao Liu[4],
Guang-Yu Zheng[4], Chin-Kuo Lin[3], Chia-Hung Lin[3], Yu-Yi Chien[5],
Fang-Cheng Lin[1,2,5], Yi-Pai Huang[1,2,5],
Sergio José Rodríguez Méndez[4], and Felipe A. Medeiros[1,7]

[1] NGoggle Inc., San Diego, CA, USA
{jzao,tjung,flin,yhuang,fmedeiros}@ngoggle.com,
ytwang@sccn.ucsd.edu
[2] Cerebra Technologies Co. Ltd., Hsinchu, Taiwan, ROC
{jerry.chang,gary.gan}@cerebratek.com
[3] Powerforce Tech. Co. Ltd., Hsinchu, Taiwan, ROC
{jimlin,carhome_lin}@powerforce.com.tw
[4] Department of Computer Science, National Chiao Tung University,
Hsinchu, Taiwan, ROC
{lwh0702,guanggyz,srodriguez}@pet.cs.nctu.edu.tw
[5] Department of Photonics, National Chiao Tung University,
Hsinchu, Taiwan, ROC
yuyichien2543.eo99g@g2.nctu.edu.tw
[6] Swartz Center for Computational Neuroscience, Institute for Neural
Computation, University of California at San Diego, La Jolla, CA, USA
{ytwang,yplin}@sccn.ucsd.edu
[7] Hamilton Glaucoma Center, Shiley Eye Institute, University of California at
San Diego, La Jolla, CA, USA

Abstract. Head-mounted virtual reality and augmented reality displays (a.k.a. VR/AR goggles) created a revolutionary multimedia genre that is seeking ever-broadening applications and novel natural human interfaces. Adding neuromonitoring and neurofeedback to this genre is expected to introduce a new dimension to user interaction with the cyber-world. This study presents the development of a Neuromonitoring VR/AR Goggle armed with electroencephalo-gram and electrooculogram sensors, programmable milli-Ampere current stimulators and wireless fog/cloud computing support. Beside of its potential use in mitigating cybersickness, this device may have potential applications in augmented cognition ranging from feedback-controlled perceptual training to on-line learning and virtual social interactions. A prototype of the device has been made from a Samsung Gear VR for S6. This study explains its technical design to ensure precision data sampling, synchronous event marking, real-time signal processing and big data cloud computing support. This study also demonstrates the effective-ness in measuring the event-related potentials during a visual oddball experiment.

© Springer International Publishing Switzerland 2016
D.D. Schmorrow and C.M. Fidopiastis (Eds.): AC 2016, Part I, LNAI 9743, pp. 121–131, 2016.
DOI: 10.1007/978-3-319-39955-3_12

Keywords: Virtual reality · Mixed reality · Augmented cognition ·
Cybersickness · Electroencephalography · Electrooculography ·
Oculo-vestibular recoupling

1 Introduction

Head-mounted 3D displays, encased in wearable eye goggles, adapted to users' head
and body movements, have succeeded in producing virtual reality (VR) and
mixed/augmented reality (MR/AR) images rivaling real-world sceneries in their
complexity and immensity. These devices can also produce images impossible or
unsafe to be captured in actual environments. Hence, AR/VR Goggles are having a
wide-range of emerging applications not only in entertainment but also in learning,
training, neurodiagnostics, psychotherapy and many other areas [1, 2]. Amidst the rapid
development of this new medium, natural user interfaces are urgently needed to
enhance interactions between its users and the virtual reality it creates. Motion and
gesture detection as well as gaze tracking are regarded as essential. Users' neuro-logical
responses are regarded by some visual artists as the necessary characterization of the
affective components of this new medium [3].

This study presents the development of a Neuromonitoring VR/AR Goggle armed
with multi-modal electrophysiological sensors, milli-Ampere current stimulators and
wireless IoT-cloud computing support. This system can capture and analyze electroencephalogram (EEG) and electrooculogram (EOG) in near real time to provide
users with brain state estimates as well as oculo-vestibular recoupling (OVR) feed-
backs. This goggle will have potential applications not merely in mitigating cybersickness [4] but also in enhancing users' sense of engagement in on-line learning and
virtual social interactions. Its EEG and EOG measurements can be used to evaluate
users' responses to different presentation forms [5] and to assess users' perception to
different syntactic elements in virtual reality [3].

The rest of this paper was divided into four sections: the potential use of EEG/ EOG
monitoring and OVR stimulation in VR/AR applications were reviewed in Sect. 2; the
architecture and functional components of the Neuromonitoring Goggle were introduced
in Sect. 3; the result of a pilot visual oddball experiment were discussed in Sect. 4; a
conclusion based on engineering tests and experiment results was given finally in Sect. 5.

2 Contribution of EEG/EOG and OVR to VR/AR Applications

EOG measured around the perimeters of subjects' eyes can be used to monitor the
dynamics of eye saccade and fixation. These features have long been exploited in
eye-based human-computer interfaces [6]. Recent studies showed that saccade durations and movement patterns can be used to estimate subjects' *attention levels* during
study sessions while fixation points and mean fixation durations can be used to assess
subjects' *accuracy of response* [7] in learning. In addition, the electromyogram
(EMG) captured from the same electrodes can be used to monitor eyelid movements.

Specifically, eye blink durations and intervals, eyelid closure delays and re-opening speeds are useful in estimating subjects' *fatigue levels* [8].

EEG data measured from the frontal, parietal and occipital regions of human brains are known to correlate with subjects' *cognitive* and *emotional states*. Spectral components in theta (4–7 Hz), alpha (8–12 Hz), and beta (13–30 Hz) bands have long been used to assess subjects' *attention* and *alertness* levels [9–11]. EEG generated by the Anterior Cingulate Cortex is known to be a biomarker of *rational cognitive functions* such as reward anticipation, decision making and empathy [12] while the differential asymmetric EEG measurements from 12 electrode pairs can accurately classify four emotional states: joy, anger, sadness, and pleasure while listening to music [13].

Cybersickness remains a "sore thumb" that may hinder the widespread use of VR technology [14]. Conflicting signals produced by users' oculomotor and vestibular systems is a main cause of this sickness. This Goggle enables *oculo-vestibular recoupling (OVR)* [4] by applying low-power transmastoidal direct-current or random-noise galvanic vestibular stimulation (GVS) [15] that are modulated based on in-situ EOG and 9-DOF motion measurements.

3   Development of Neuromonitoring VR/AR Goggle

The Neuromonitoring VR/AR Goggle Fig. 5(a) is a pervasive adaptive IoT platform that adds neuromonitoring and neurofeedback to VR/AR applications. As shown 1, the system consists of four components: a commercial *VR/AR Goggle*, a proprietary *Neuromonitor*, a smartphone/tablet *Operating Console* and an *IoT-Cloud Computing service* support. Bluetooth 4 communications among the Goggle, the Neuromonitor and the Console allow the system to be used completely untethered anytime anywhere. The WiFi-Internet connections of the Neuromonitor and the Goggle as IoT devices support Firmware-over-the-air (FOTA) programming, Linked Data mining and Cloud based machine learning. These capabilities enable rapid personalization as well as progressive refinement of brain state prediction models using transfer machine learning techniques (Fig. 1).

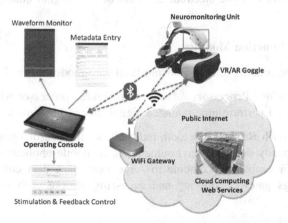

Fig. 1. System Architecture of Neuromonitoring VR/AR Goggle

VR/AR Goggle. Commercial products (current choice: Samsung Gear VR) were used to offer users with the immersive experience of virtual/augmented reality while monitoring their EEG/EOG signals and head movements using the Neuromonitor unit. Oculus Mobile SDK [16] and OpenGL ES 2.0 [17] were used to produce the VR/AR contents and augmentation. A distinct approach to use the Neuromonitoring Goggle is to embed special visual patterns and motion sequences into 3D/VR scenes and use these stimuli to evoke neuro-physiological/psychological responses. Potential applications in neurodiagnostics and perceptual learning can all take advantage of this immersive form of visual stimulation [Sect. 5].

Neuromonitor. This miniature device (3 cm $\times$ 4.5 cm $\times$ 1.5 cm in size excluding the Li battery) functions as an add-on to the VR/AR Goggle. The current prototype can capture six EEG channels Fig. 5(b) and two EOG/EMG channels Fig. 5(c) simultaneously at 500sps with micro-second timestamping synchronous to the Internet standard time. Its programmable current sources can inject 250 µA (rms) DC/AC/Gaussian random waveforms at 1000sps. Equipped with a multi-core embedded processor, a Bluetooth + Wi-Fi radio and a micro-SD storage, the device is well-positioned to serve as a wearable data hub for multi-modal electrophysiological signals.

Cloud Computing Support. The Neuromonitoring Goggle is merely an IoT frontend to a pervasive fog-cloud computing platform developed in the NCTU PET Lab [18]. A BCI Ontology [19] aligned with the W3C Semantic Sensor Network Ontology [20] was devised to capture the semantic structure of real-world brain-computer interactions. An on-line repository of BCI data conforming to Linked Data practice [21] was deployed and can be accessed via the CerebraWeb API [22]. This Cloud Computing platform can couple with smartphones or laptops connected to the Neuromonitor and recruit them to perform real-time signal processing and brain state prediction.

Operating Console. It is an Android mobile app that performs the "housekeeping" functions such as: remote control of Neuromonitor and VR visualization; real-time display of captured signals; management of the Linked Data repository. Aided with DC lead-off detection capability of the data acquisition unit, the real-time waveform display can alert the operator of loose electrode contacts or poor signal quality.

3.1   Hardware Function Modules

The Neuromonitor consists of the following hardware modules Fig. 2.

Embedded Dual-Core Processor. Advanced embedded processor with ample RAM can capture data and perform time-bounded signal processing simultaneously.

Wi-Fi and Bluetooth Radios. Bluetooth radio allows the neuromonitoring unit to be controlled in a locally deployed environment via a mobile application GUI. On the other hand, Wi-Fi enables the module to serve both as a data collection hub and Internet of Things gateway, offering and accessing various web services to other Internet nodes.

MicroSD Card. A 32 GB micro-SD on board allows the Neuromonitoring Goggle to store at least eight hours of recorded data.

Eight-Channel Biosensors. An eight-channel Biosensing frontend equipped with low-noise pre-amplifiers and a 24-bit sigma-delta analog-digital converter (ADC) is capable of synchronously collecting 2000 samples per second. Each channel is equipped with lead-off detection capability in order to check whether its electrodes have good contact with the subject scalp.

Two-Channel Programmable Current Sources. Two 256-step software programmable bi-directional current sources can optionally inject DC, AC or Gaussian random noisy currents with max. ± 1 mA amplitude or 250 μA rms value and [0.5 Hz, 50 Hz] band-width through four electrodes at Fz, Oz, left and right mastoids. These weak currents can offer sub-threshold galvanic vestibular stimulation (GVS) based on stochastic resonance as an attempt to recouple vestibular response with moving image perception. The authors are currently working with Martin J. McKeown's Pacific Parkinson's Research Center at the University of British Columbia to investigate its effectiveness in improving patients' motor control. We also tried to use similar approach to mitigate cybersickness. Given the known current waveforms, the current-induced artifacts can possibly be largely removed from the EEG/EOG signals using QR decomposition following by independent component analysis [23].

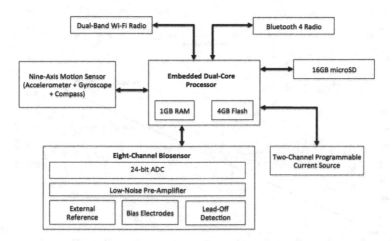

Fig. 2. Hardware functional modules of Neuromonitor

3.2 Software Functional Modules

The Neuromonitor operates not only with precise timing and real-time response; it also connects with other IoT frontends and fog/cloud servers through standard M2 M communication. Figure 3 illustrates its software functional modules.

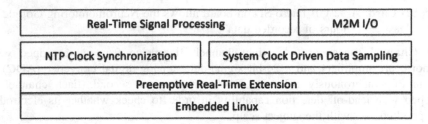

Fig. 3. Software functional modules of Neuromonitor

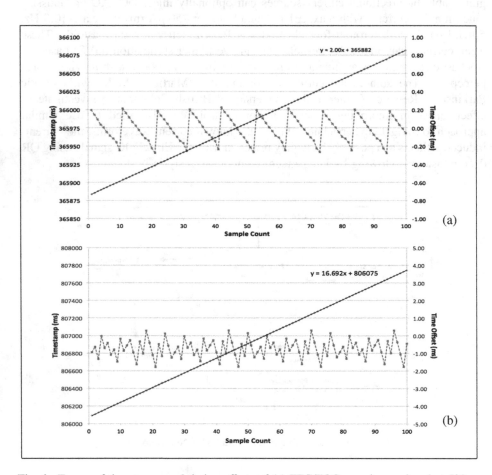

Fig. 4. Traces of timestamps and timing offsets of (a) EEG/EOG samples produced at 500sps and (b) visual stimuli frames at 60fps, both polled using 2048 Hz Linux System Clock.

Embedded Real-Time Linux Operating System. Neuromonitor employs standardized embedded Yocto Linux [24] with Preempt-RT extension to fulfill real time data processing and I/O requirements.

Machine-to-Machine Publish/Subscribe I/O. The Neuromonitor exchanges raw or processed data autonomously with other M2M devices using the MQTT Publish/Subscribe standard [25]. These demand-driven data transfers maintain the communication fabric of pervasive fog-cloud computing.

NTP Time Synchronization. With the use of Network Time Protocol (NTP), the VR/AR Goggle, the Neuromonitor and the Operating Console are all time-locked to the atomic clocks on the Internet with 1 μs resolution. All the components are synchronized to the same NTP server in order to maintain max. 1 ms timing offsets. The synchronized clocks are then used as the timing reference for all the timestamping of data samples and events.

Synchronous Multi-channel Data Sampling. The analog-to-digital converter (ADC) samples the eight-channel biosensor at 500sps while the data acquisition software driven by the Linux system clock polls the ADC at 2048sps. Figure 4(a) shows the time trace of 2 ms sampling intervals and the timing offsets within [−0.25 ms, +0.20 ms].

Synchronous Event Marking. Visual stimuli displayed on the VR/AR goggle are refreshed in 60fps while its timing is again sampled at 2048sps. Figure 4(b) shows the time trace of 16.692 ms frame intervals and the timing offsets within [−2 ms, +0.5 ms].

4 Pilot Experiments

A binocular visual oddball experiment preceded with open and closed-eye resting EEG recording was performed on subjects with normal or corrected to normal vision in order to evaluate the effectiveness of the Neuromonitoring Goggle in acquiring EEG signals as well as visual evoked responses in real-world environments.

Participants. Six healthy subjects (five male, one female; age: 21.2–58.3, median: 23.45, standard error: 5.81) participated in the oddball experiment, which was carried out at National Chiao Tung University (NCTU), Hsinchu, Taiwan. All subjects had previous experience with EEG recording. Informed consent was obtained from all of them. NCTU ethics committee has approved the study protocol and the procedures were carried in accordance with the approved protocol.

Method. The Neuromonitoring Goggle was worn by each subject in turn. A foam pad with EEG sensors was applied at the back of subject's head over the Goggle's back-pad to sooth the pressure. Small amount of electric-conductive gel was applied to the tip of the electrodes to improve conductivity. Four channels (Pz, Oz, O3, and O4) in the occipital region were used to record ERP signals.

Each subject went through first a resting EEG recording and then a visual oddball experiment with an approx. two-minute intermission. During the resting EEG recording, subjects were instructed to relax and keep their eyes open first and then closed without blinking for one minute each. During the oddball experiment, two white crosses (a crisscrossed one ▨ as the *target* and an up-right one ✚ as the *non-target*) were flashed with 100 ms duration over a black background in both eyes through the

Goggle. Subjects were asked to tap their figures at the desk when they saw the targets while remained inert when they saw the non-targets. The probability of target occurrence was set at 20 % while no two targets can directly follow each other. Target and non-target stimuli were presented in random order with randomized inter-stimulus intervals of 1400–2400 ms. These intervals are long enough to ensure no overlap between the event related potentials (ERPs) evoked by the visual stimuli and they are deliberately randomized to avoid habituation of neural responses. In order to reduce visual fatigue, targets and non-targets were grouped into a sequence of ten stimuli with a five-second rest period before each sequence. A small round dot appeared steady for four second in both eyes at the beginning of the rest period. During that time, the subjects were allowed to blink their eyes and relax briefly. Five of these sequences were composed into a session. Each subject was asked to go through ten sessions (again with two-minute intermissions in between) in order to accumulate a total of a hundred targets.

Results. Data collected from the first subject (#0) were discarded because the visual stimuli were set to low intensity. Among the remaining datasets, alpha waves were observed in all the resting EEG data recorded with the subjects' eyes closed. Figure 6 displays the $[\mu, \mu \pm 1\sigma]$ plot of the open-eye (blue) and closed-eye (red) EEG power spectral density (PSD) of subject #4 by applying multitaper analysis (NW = 4) onto

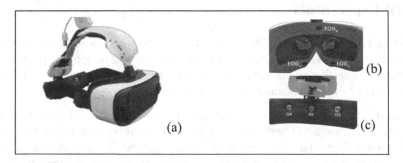

Fig. 5. Gear VR Neuromonitoring Goggle prototype (a) and EEG/EOG electrode placement (b) & (c)

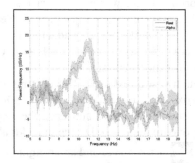

Fig. 6. Open and closed-eye EEG PSD of Subject #4 (Color figure online)

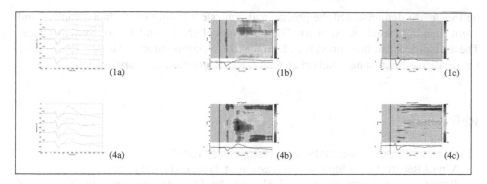

Fig. 7. Average ERP waveforms (a) and ERP maps of Oddball Target (b) and Non-target (c) responses of Subjects #1

five 50 % overlapped twenty-second segments of [1 Hz, 50 Hz] band-passed EEG data. A spectral peak of 17db appears clearly in the [8 Hz, 12 Hz] alpha band. Besides, both open/closed-eye PSDs diminished gradually with respect to the increase in frequency.

Synchronous averaging and ERP map construction [26] were applied to the event related potential (ERP) epochs collected from both the target and non-target events during the visual oddball experiment. Each epoch was taken from 200 ms before to 1200 ms after the onset of each target/non-target stimulus excluding the five-second rest periods. The first 200 ms of each epoch was taken as the baseline, the mean value of which was subtracted from the remaining samples. Moreover, The ERPs with amplitudes exceeding ±100 μV were removed from the dataset before further processing. Among the remaining five subjects, the average ERP waveforms of subjects 1 – 4 showed sharp target and non-target N2 pulses at all channels while the waveforms of Subject #5 seemed to show involuntary eye blinks in response to the stimuli. Only the ERPs of Subject #1 and #4 exhibited observable P3 pulses. Figure 7 displays the average ERP waveforms[1] as well as the target/non-target ERP maps of both subject #1 and #4. The ERP maps all showed clear P1 and N2 pulses in respond to the visual stimuli; however, the P3 pulses of subject #1 were smeared as he tapped his fingers while counting the target stimuli. It also seemed that the EEG signals captured from channel Pz were of better quality than those from Oz.

5 Conclusions

The detection of alpha waves in the open/closed-eye resting EEG and the P3 pulses in the ERPs evoked by the oddball target stimuli gave clear evidence that the Neuromonitoring Goggle is capable of capturing users' EEG signals and monitoring their brain responses towards visual stimulation. In addition, the engineering tests performed

---

[1] Each averaged ERP waveforms of channels Pz, Oz, O3 and O4 were shifted by −20 μV respectively in order to separate their traces.

on the device demonstrated the precise and consistent timing of its data sampling and event marking based on Network Timing Protocol (NTP) and Linux System Clock. These empirical results support the claim that the Neuromonitoring Goggle can be used for pervasive brain state monitoring with VR/AR goggle-based applications.

References

1. Stein, J.: Inside the box. TIME Mag. **186**(6), 30–39 (2015)
2. Virtual Reality: Grand Illusions. The Economist **416**(8953) (2015)
3. Brown, S.: Interactive Neurological Methods for Characterizing Syntactic Elements of Virtual Reality. Personal communication (2015)
4. Cevette, M.J., Stepanek, J., Cocco, D., Galea, A.M., Pradhan, G.N., Wagner, L.S., Oakley, S.R., Smith, B.E., Zapala, D.A., Brookler, K.H.: Oculo-vestibular recoupling using galvanic vestibular stimulation to mitigate simulator sickness. Aviat. Space Environ. Med. **83**(6), 549–555 (2012)
5. Yeh, K.H., She, H.C.: On-line synchronous scientific argumentation learning: nurturing students' argumentation ability and conceptual change in science context. Comput. Educ. **55**(2), 586–602 (2010)
6. Bulling, A., Gellersen, H.: Toward mobile eye-based human-computer interaction. IEEE Pervasive Comput. **9**(4), 8–12 (2010)
7. Chen, S.C., She, H.C., Chuang, M.H., Wu, J.Y., Tsai, J.L., Jung, T.P.: Eye movements predict students' computer-based assessment performance of physics concepts in different presentation modalities. Comput. Educ. **74**(1), 61–72 (2014)
8. Schleicher, R., Galley, N., Briest, S., Galley, L.: Blinks and saccades as indicators of fatigue in sleepiness warnings: looking tired? Ergonomics **51**(7), 982–1010 (2008)
9. Jung, T.P., Makeig, S., Stensmo, M., Sejnowski, T.J.: Estimating alertness from the EEG power spectrum. IEEE Trans. Biomed. Eng. **44**(1), 60–69 (1997)
10. Jap, B.T., Lal, S., Fischer, P., Bekiaris, E.: Using EEG spectral components to assess algorithms for detecting fatigue. Expert Syst. Appl. **36**(2), 2352–2359 (2009)
11. Wang, Y.T., Huang, K.C., Wei, C.S., Huang, T.Y., Ko, L.W., Lin, C.T., Cheng, C.K., Jung, T.P.: Developing an EEG-based on-line closed-loop lapse detection and mitigation system. Front. Neurosci. **8**, 321 (2014)
12. Decety, J., Jackson, P.L.: The functional architecture of human empathy. Behav. Cogn. Neurosci. Rev. **3**(2), 71–100 (2004)
13. Lin, Y.P., Wang, C.H., Jung, T.P., Wu, T.L., Jeng, S.K., Duann, J.R., Chen, J.H.: EEG-based emotion recognition in music listening. IEEE Trans. Biomed. Eng. **57**(7), 1798–1806 (2010)
14. LaViola Jr., J.J.: A discussion of cybersickness in virtual environments. ACM SIGCHI Bull. **32**(1), 47–56 (2000)
15. Kim, D.J., Yogendrakumar, V., Chiang, J., Ty, E., Wang, Z.J., McKeown, M.J.: Noisy galvanic vestibular stimulation modulates the amplitude of EEG synchrony patterns. PLoS One **8**(7), e69055 (2013)
16. Oculus Mobile SDK. Oculus. https://developer.oculus.com/documentation/mobilesdk/latest/. Accessed Mar 2016
17. OpenGL ES. Khronos Group. https://www.khronos.org/opengles/. Accessed 2016

18. Zao, J.K., Gan, T.T., You, C.K., Chung, C.E., Wang, Y.T., Méndez, S.J.R., Mullen, T., Yu, C., Kothe, C., Hsiao, C.T., Chu, S.L.: Pervasive brain monitoring and data sharing based on multi-tier distributed computing and linked data technology. Front. Hum. Neurosci. **8**, 370 (2014)
19. Rodríguez Méndez, S., Zao, J.K.: https://w3id.org/BCI-ontology. Accessed Mar 2016
20. Semantic Sensor Network Ontology. W3C. https://www.w3.org/2005/Incubator/ssn/ssnx/ssn. Accessed 2009–2011
21. Linked Data. http://linkeddata.org. Accessed 2009
22. CerebraWeb.net. NCTU Pervasive Embedded Technology (PET) Laboratory. http://cerebraweb.net. Accessed 2015
23. Kim, D.J., Yogendrakumar, V., Chiang, J., Ty, E., Wang, Z.J., McKeown, M.J.: Noisy galvanic vestibular stimulation modulates the amplitude of EEG synchrony patterns. PLoS One **8**(7), e69055 (2013)
24. Yocto Project. Linux Foundation Collaborative Project. https://www.yoctoproject.org/
25. Message Queuing Telemetry Transport. http://mqtt.org/. Accessed 1999
26. Makeig, S., Debener, S., Onton, J., Delorme, A.: Mining event-related brain dynamics. Trends Cogn. Sci. **8**(5), 204–210 (2004)

Electroencephalography and Brain Activity Measurement

Neural Correlates of Purchasing Decisions in an Ecologically Plausible Shopping Scenario with Mobile fNIR Technology

Murat Perit Çakır[1(✉)], Tuna Çakar[2], Yener Girişken[3,4], and Ari K. Demircioğlu[4]

[1] Graduate School of Informatics, Middle East Technical University, Ankara, Turkey
perit@metu.edu.tr
[2] Biostatistics and Medical Informatics, Acibadem University, Istanbul, Turkey
cakar.tuna@gmail.com
[3] Graduate School of Marketing Communications, Istanbul Bilgi University, Istanbul, Turkey
[4] ThinkNeuro Market Research Co., Istanbul, Turkey
{yener.girisken,ari.demircioglu}@thinkneuro.net

Abstract. In this paper we present our preliminary findings for the neural correlates of purchasing decisions made in a computerized setting as well as in an ecologically plausible supermarket environment. Participants who were randomly recruited from a database of typical customers maintained by a marketing consultancy company were given a specific budget and asked to make purchasing decisions for basic grocery items in two separate conditions. In the first condition, participants made their decisions in a computerized scenario, where in each trial a single product and its price were displayed for a fixed duration of time, and then the participants clicked on buttons to specify which products they wish to purchase. In the second experiment, participants made similar purchasing decisions while wandering around a custom-made grocery aisle with shelves including physical products. In both conditions participants' brain activities in their prefrontal cortices as well as their eye movements were recorded with a wireless fNIR device and a glass eye tracker respectively. In both conditions we observed higher mean oxygenation levels for the purchase decisions at the left dorso-medial prefrontal cortex. Despite the limited sample size, the oxygenation trends were similar in both purchasing situations. Our preliminary findings suggest that fNIR can effectively be employed to investigate neural correlates of purchasing behavior in ecological settings.

Keywords: Decision making · Neuroergonomics · Neuroeconomics · Optical brain imaging · Mobile fNIR

1   Introduction

Neuroeconomics has emerged as an interdisciplinary field to pursue the goal of developing a better understanding of the neurobiological factors that shape economic decisions [1]. In particular, neuroeconomics research seeks to further our understanding with regards to what variables are computed by the brain while humans are making different

© Springer International Publishing Switzerland 2016
D.D. Schmorrow and C.M. Fidopiastis (Eds.): AC 2016, Part I, LNAI 9743, pp. 135–146, 2016.
DOI: 10.1007/978-3-319-39955-3_13

kinds of decisions, and how those computations are implemented and constrained by underlying neurobiological processes, with the eventual goal of building biologically plausible models for human decision making [2]. Existing work in the field include decision making scenarios ranging from simple decision tasks such as choosing pizza over salad for lunch to decision making under uncertain, dynamically unfolding circumstances such as gambling tasks [3]. Although these studies include rather simplistic decision making scenarios due to the physical limitations imposed by brain imaging tools, they collectively identified important neural mechanisms underlying related cognitive and emotional processes such as reward evaluation, ambiguity/risk management and value comparison [4].

A number of brain imaging studies have focused on the role of the dopaminergic system in forming and updating expectations about rewards and value computation [4]. Monetary reward experience and evaluation processes have been found to activate several interconnected regions of this system, including the deep structures of the brain stem at ventral tegmental area (VTA) and the ventral striatum (vSTR), as well as the ventromedial prefrontal cortex (vmPFC) [5–7]. Especially the receipt of rewards were found to evoke activation in the vmPFC and the adjacent orbitofrontal cortex (OFC), which support the theory that these regions may be involved with computing the expected value of a reward [6]. Even activations observed at mPFC and striatum during passive viewing of products can be later used for predicting those consumer's choices involving those products [8]. In a recent study, Metereu and Dreher [9] found that the OFC/vmPFC region encodes a general unsigned anticipatory subjective value signal for both rewards and punishments.

Real world decision-making often involves uncertainty, which is another crucial factor that modulates the values attributed to choices. Imaging studies that involve uncertainties and risks in decision-making report activations in dorsolateral and lateral PFC, vmPFC, orbitofrontal cortex (OFC) and the anterior cingulate cortex (ACC) as well as subcortical regions including VTA, vSTR and amygdala [4, 10]. This distributed neural network is claimed to encode two components of a subjective value signal, namely expected value and risk probability [11]. The medial and lateral prefrontal cortex is claimed to play a role in integrating these two components [12]. The computations carried out in these regions are likely to be associated with subjective value signals, but not as robustly as the vmPFC/OFC regions. In particular, the dorso-lateral regions are argued to have a regulatory role on medial PFC during decision making scenarios [13]. However, the precise computational roles played by the dorso-medial and dorso-lateral areas remain to be an important issue in simple choice and reward processing paradigms in neuroeconomics [2].

Existing studies in neuroeconomics predominantly employ the fMRI method. Despite its superior spatial resolution, fMRI is an expensive and impractical neuroimaging technology for purchasing behavior studies in the field. In this paper, the functional near-infrared spectroscopy (fNIRS) method was employed to study purchasing behavior, which offers a low-cost, non-invasive and portable optical brain imaging

methodology. The aim of this study is to explore the plausibility of the fNIR methodology for neuroeconomics applications in the field, as well as to develop a neuro-phys-
iologically informed predictive models of purchasing behavior based on fNIR
measurements.

There are only a few fNIR studies published in the context of neuroeconomics.
Existing fNIR studies have identified activation patterns in the prefrontal cortex during
product selection [14], risk assessment [10], financial investment [15] and price prediction [16]. Mitsuda et al. [16] also proposed a support vector machine algorithm for
classifying price/product pairings that were tagged as expensive or inexpensive by the
participants with an accuracy of 70 %. The present study aims to contribute this line of
inquiry by investigating activation patterns in the PFC of consumers during a more
realistic, mundane purchasing scenario. In particular, we aimed to identify whether
positive and negative purchasing decisions differ in terms of the neural activity they
elicit in regions located at dorso-medial and dorso-lateral prefrontal cortex, and whether
we can observe a similar pattern when participants make purchasing decisions while
they walk around to freely inspect physical products located on a shelf.

The rest of the paper is organized as follows. The fNIR optical brain imaging technology and the experiment design are described in the next section. Next, we present
our main findings regarding activation patterns observed at the dmPFC and dlPFC
regions during purchasing decisions. The paper concludes with an overall discussion of
the results and pointers for future work.

2   Materials and Methods

2.1   Functional Near-Infrared Spectroscopy

fNIR is a neuroimaging modality that enables continuous, noninvasive, and portable
monitoring of changes in blood oxygenation and blood volume related to human brain
function. Neuronal activity is determined with respect to the changes in oxygenation
since variation in cerebral hemodynamics are related to functional brain activity through
a mechanism known as neurovascular coupling [17]. Over the last decade, studies in the
laboratory have established that fNIR spectroscopy provides a veridical measure of
oxygenation and blood flow in the brain [18]. fNIR is not only non-invasive, safe,
affordable and portable, it also provides a balance between temporal and spatial resolution which makes fNIR a viable option for in-the field neuroimaging.

fNIR technology uses specific wavelengths of light, introduced at the scalp, to enable
the non-invasive measurement of changes in the relative ratios of deoxygenated hemoglobin (deoxy-Hb or HbR) and oxygenated hemoglobin (oxy-Hb or HbO) in the capillary
beds during brain activity. Typically, an optical apparatus for fNIR Spectroscopy
consists of at least one near infra-red light source and a detector that receives light after
it has interacted with the tissue. Near-infrared light is known to diffuse through the intact
scalp and skull, which makes it suitable for tracing relative changes in the concentration
of specific chromophores in the neural tissue with non-invasive, spectroscopic methods
[19]. Whereas most biological tissue (including water) are relatively transparent to light
in the near infrared range between 700 to 900 nm, hemoglobin is a strong absorber of

light waves in this range of the spectrum. Within 700 to 900 nm, HbO and HbR are among the highest absorbers of infra-red light. This provides an optical window into neural tissue where one can approximate relative changes in the concentration of HbO and HbR based on how infra-red light is attenuated in neural tissue.

Photons that enter tissue undergo two different types of interaction: absorption and scattering [17]. Two chromophores, HbO and HbR, are strongly linked to tissue oxygenation and metabolism. The absorption spectra of HbO and HbR remain significantly different from each other allowing spectroscopic separation of these compounds to be possible by using only a few sample wavelengths. Once photons are introduced into the human head, they are either scattered by extra- and intracellular boundaries of different layers of the head (skin, skull, cerebrospinal fluid, brain, etc.) or absorbed mainly by HbO and HbR. A photo-detector placed on the skin surface at a certain distance from the light source can collect the photons that are scattered and thus have travelled along a "banana shaped path" from the source to the detector, which carry important information about the optical properties of the diffused neural tissue (Fig. 1). This raw light attenuation information is then converted into tissue oxygenation measures that quantify the relative changes in the presence of HbO and HbR within the banana shaped path by using a method called modified Beer Lambert law [20].

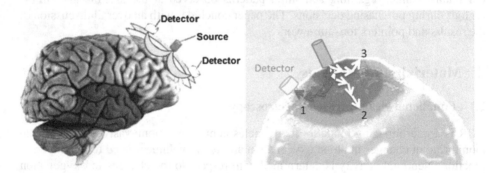

Fig. 1. The banana shaped path which includes the photons scattered back to the photo-detector (left). Representative paths (right), enumerated as 2 and 3 correspond to photons absorbed by the tissue and scattered out of the scalp without reaching the detector, respectively. (Color figure online)

2.2   Experiment Setup

Participants. 21 participants (10 female) in the age range 19–45 ($M = 32.15, SD = 7.42$) participated in this study. 12 participants (5 female) were randomly assigned to the computerized purchasing task that included photographs of several grocery items, whereas the remaining 9 participants (5 female) completed a similar task in front of a rack of shelves including real grocery items. Participants were selected randomly among volunteers reached via the consumer database of ThinkNeuro. All participants were right-handed and none of them had a history of psychiatric disorders. Participants were paid 25 Turkish Liras (TL) for their participation and 20 TL as a bonus in compensation for the items they selected to purchase during the experiment. The study was approved by the METU human subjects research ethics committee. Written informed consent was obtained prior to the experiment.

Experiment Design. The computerized purchasing task was comprised of 35 trials where participants were asked to make a purchasing decision for each individually displayed product based on the suggested price. In each block, the participants had 4 s for viewing a picture of the product, 4 s for viewing the picture and the price of the product, and 4 s to respond by pressing one of two buttons indicating a purchase or a pass, followed by a 8 s long fixation duration. Hence, each block lasted for 20 s, and the total duration of the experiment was about 12 min. The E-Prime software was used for the presentation of the experiment stimulus. The products consisted of snacks, beverages and cleaning supplies, which can be found in any local grocery stores (Fig. 2). The prices of the products were obtained from local groceries.

Fig. 2. An example product image used in the computerized purchasing task. The item was first displayed without the price tag (left), which is followed by the image with the price (right).

In the free shopping condition participants were given the same budget and asked to make their decisions by browsing through a rack of shelves including physical grocery items whose images were used during the computerized task (Fig. 3). In the first phase of the task, participants were asked to pick the selected item and place it in a shopping cart to indicate a purchasing decision. In the second phase of the experiment, experimenters asked each participant to find a specific item and put it on a desk. This search task was included in the experiment design as a control condition to compare against real purchasing decisions.

Participants in both conditions were informed that the experimenters would be able to provide them up to a total 40TL worth of the products that they selected. Subjects were also told that if they do not spend at least 40TL, they would receive only half of the unspent amount in an effort to reinforce buying behavior.

Fig. 3. A participant wearing the fNIR sensor as well as the ASL mobile eye tracker (left). A grocery store setup was used to investigate purchasing decisions in a more ecologically valid shopping scenario.

Materials, Apparatus and Software. While the participants were making purchasing decisions their eye movements were tracked with the help of an ASL mobile eye tracker, whereas the neural activity in their prefrontal cortex was monitored by a functional near-infrared spectroscopy (fNIR) system developed at Drexel University (Philadelphia, PA),

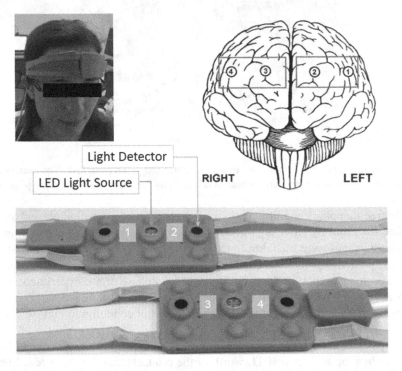

Fig. 4. The 4-channel split fNIR sensor (top, left), projection of the 4 measurement locations (optodes) on brain surface image (top, right), optodes identified on the split fNIR sensor (bottom). (Color figure online)

manufactured and supplied by fNIR Devices LLC (Potomac, MD; www.fnirdevices.com). The experimental setup consists of a flexible head-piece (sensor pad), a wireless control box for hardware management, and a computer that runs the COBI Studio software [21] for data acquisition. The filtering and conversion of raw fNIR signals into oxygenation measures were performed offline by using the fNIRsoft software [22]. Statistical tests on oxygenation measures were conducted with IBM SPSS v.23.

The fNIR sensor holds 2 light sources and 4 detectors (Fig. 4) to monitor oxygenation measures at 4 optodes located on the prefrontal cortex. The sensors have a source-detector separation of 2.5 cm, which allows for approximately 1.25 cm penetration depth to reach the cortical surface. This system can monitor changes in relative concentrations of HbO and HbR at a temporal resolution of 2 Hz. The locations of the regions on the cortical surface monitored by the sensor are displayed in Fig. 4, which correspond to Broadmann areas 9,10,44 and 45. These regions primarily include left/right dorsolateral prefrontal cortex (dlPFC) and left/right dorsomedial prefrontal cortex (dmPFC). Existing neuroimaging studies suggest that the prefrontal cortex has a special role in the processing of higher order cognitive functions such as working memory management, sequential processing of sensory and memory input, as well as response inhibition and decision making [23].

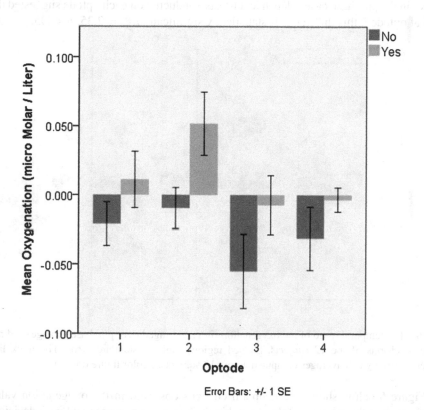

Fig. 5. The mean oxygenation values observed during purchase and pass decisions (Color figure online)

3   Results

In the computerized purchasing scenario, raw fNIR measures were obtained for buy/
pass decisions over a total of 35 grocery items. Raw fNIR data (4 optodes × 2 wavelengths) were low-pass filtered with a finite impulse response, linear phase filter with
order 20 and cut-off frequency of 0.1 Hz to attenuate the high frequency noise due to
respiration and cardiac cycle effects [24]. Saturated channels (if any), in which light
intensity at the detector was higher than the analog-to-digital converter limit were
excluded. Artifacts due to motion are detected and excluded by applying the sliding
windows motion artifact filter [25]. fNIR data epochs for the rest and task periods were
extracted from the continuous data using time synchronization markers. Blood oxygenation changes within each 4 optodes for the product, price and decision blocks were
calculated using the modified Beer-Lambert Law for task periods with respect to rest
periods at the beginning of each trial with the fNIRSoft software [22].

Firstly, mean oxygenation measures for each participant was computed over the
decisions they made for the 35 items during the experiment. Figure 5 below shows the
average oxygenation levels observed at each optode for purchase and pass decisions
made by the sample of 12 participants. Although the average oxygenation tends to be
higher in the purchase cases, dependent t-tests conducted on each optode suggested that
only at optode 2 this difference is statistically significant, $t(8) = 2.35, p < .05$.

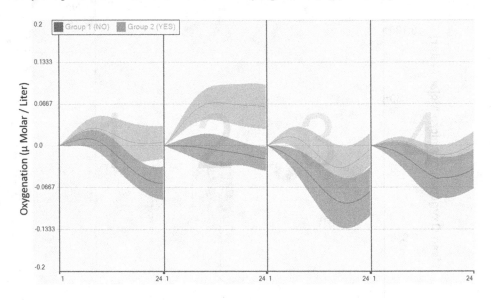

Fig. 6. The temporal trend of the oxygenation signal averaged over purchase (orange) and pass
(blue) decisions of the 12 subjects. Shaded regions indicate standard error. The thick lines
represent cell by cell averages computed across 12 subjects. (Color figure online)

Figure 6 below shows the temporal changes observed in the oxygenation values
averaged over the whole sample of 9 subjects during the purchase and pass decisions.

The shaded regions signify the standard error. The largest separation between purchase and pass cases is observed in optode 2, which is close to the left dmPFC region.

In the free shopping condition we focused on identifying how the oxygenation trend changed within 10 s long blocks that end at the moment when the subject placed the item in her/his shopping cart. We employed the same block structure for the latter half of the experiment where subjects simply searched for the items the experimenter asked him/her to find. Figure 7 compares the mean oxygenation values observed during purchase and search blocks. Dependent t-tests conducted for each optode indicated that the difference between purchase and search is significant at optode 1, $t(9) = 2.02, p < .05$ (one-tailed), and optode 2 $t(7) = 2.11, p < .05$ (one-tailed).

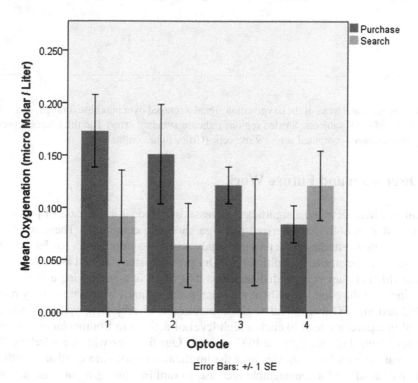

Fig. 7. The mean oxygenation values observed during purchase and search actions in the shopping condition. (Color figure online)

Figure 8 shows the time course of the oxygenation signals observed during purchase and search tasks averaged across 9 subjects. The purchase decisions tend to elicit higher levels of activity in the left dlPFC and left dmPFC.

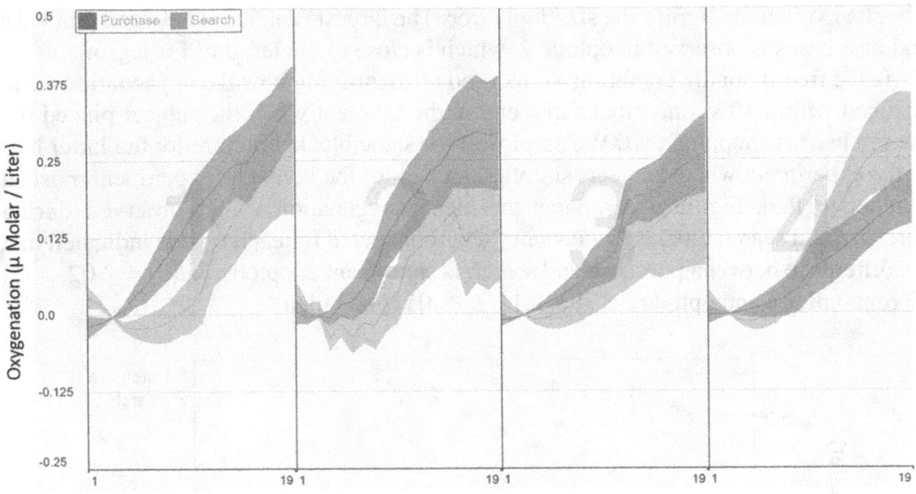

Fig. 8. The temporal trend of the oxygenation signal averaged over purchase (orange) and search (blue) tasks of the 9 subjects. Shaded regions indicate standard error. The thick lines represent cell by cell averages computed across 9 subjects. (Color figure online)

4   Discussion and Future Work

Overall, we have detected a significant increase in optode 2 in the case of purchasing decisions during both computerized and free shopping conditions. These results are consistent with the findings of a previous study where we employed a 16 channel fNIR sensor in the computerized condition [26]. Our previous study as well as the findings of existing fMRI studies suggest that decisions that result in a purchasing action significantly increase the neural activity at the frontopolar regions, which are closely related to OFC and vmPFC that modulate the computation of subjective values. Trials that resulted in a purchase tend to elicit a high level of activity in frontopolar as well as in the neighboring left and right dmPFC regions. Our findings with the wireless fNIR device that can monitor 4 optodes over the implicated regions are consistent with this trend. We also found a considerable increase in dmPFC during a purchase action as opposed to a pass or a search action. Finally, our results with the smaller split sensor suggest a stronger difference in the left hemisphere between purchase and no-purchase decisions.

In conclusion, this study demonstrated that fNIR can be used to monitor activations in the prefrontal cortex during purchasing decisions in the field. In the future, we aim to better exploit these suggestive statistical regularities to test the robustness of a predictive model of purchasing behavior in ecologically realistic settings. To that end, we plan to extend our sample size and incorporate eye movement metrics in an effort to build a multimodal model with reasonable predictive power for estimating the likelihood of a purchasing decision given the immediate neural and ocular trends.

Acknowledgments. The authors would like to thank Dr. Hasan Ayaz for his guidance and help during the analysis and processing of fNIR signals. This research and development project was supported by The Scientific and Research Council of Turkey, TUBITAK-1501 grant to ThinkNeuro (Project No: 3140565).

References

1. Politser, P.: Neuroeconomics: A Guide to the New Science of Making Choices. OUP, New York (2008)
2. Rangel, A., Clithero, J.: The computation of stimulus values in simple choice. In: Glimcher, P., Fehr, E. (eds.) Neuroeconomics: Decision Making and the Brain, 2nd edn, pp. 125–148. Academic Press, New York (2014)
3. Glimcher, P.W., Fehr, E. (eds.): Neuroeconomics: Decision making and the brain. Academic Press, New York (2014)
4. Smith, D.V., Huettel, S.A.: Decision neuroscience: neuroeconomics. Wiley Interdiscip. Rev. Cogn. Sci. **1**(6), 854–871 (2010)
5. Schultz, W.: Behavioral theories and the neurophysiology of reward. Annu. Rev. Psych. **57**, 87–115 (2006)
6. Knutson, B., Taylor, J., Kaufman, M., Peterson, R., Glover, G.: Distributed neural representation of expected value. J. Neurosci. **25**(19), 4806–4812 (2005)
7. Knutson, B., Rick, S., Wimmer, G.E., Prelec, D., Loewenstein, G.: Neural predictors of purchases. Neuron **53**, 147–156 (2007)
8. Levy, I., Lazzaro, S.C., Rutledge, R.B., Glimcher, P.W.: Choice from non-choice: predicting consumer preferences from blood oxygenation level-dependent signals obtained during passive viewing. J. Neurosci. **31**(1), 118–125 (2011)
9. Metereau, E., Dreher, J.C.: The medial orbitofrontal cortex encodes a general unsigned value signal during anticipation of both appetitive and aversive events. Cortex **63**, 42–54 (2015)
10. Holper, L., ten Brincke, R.H., Wolf, M., Murphy, R.O.: fNIRS derived hemodynamic signals and electrodermal responses in a sequential risk-taking task. Brain Res. **1557**, 141–154 (2014)
11. Ogawa, A., Onozaki, T., Mizuno, T., Asamizuya, T., Ueno, K., Cheng, K., Iriki, A.: Neural basis of economic bubble behavior. Neuroscience **265**, 37–47 (2014)
12. Tobler, P.N., Christopoulos, G., O'Doherty, J., Dolan, R.J., Schultz, W.: Risk-dependent reward value signal in human prefrontal cortex. PNAS **106**(17), 7185–7190 (2009)
13. McClure, S.M., Li, J., Tomlin, D., Cypert, K.S., Montague, L.M., Montague, P.R.: Neural correlates of behavioral preference for culturally familiar drinks. Neuron **44**(2), 379–387 (2004)
14. Kumagai, M.: Extraction of personal preferences implicitly using NIRS. In: Proceedings of IEEE SICE Annual Conference (SICE 2012), pp. 1351–1353 (2012)
15. Shimokawa, T., Misawa, T., Suzuki, K.: Neural representation of preference relationships. NeuroReport **19**, 1557–1561 (2008)
16. Mitsuda, Y., Goto, K., Misawa, T., Shimokawa, T.: Prefrontal cortex activation during evaluation of product price: a NIRS study. In: Proceedings of the Asia Pacific Industrial Engineering & Management Systems Conference (2012)
17. Obrig, H., Wenzel, R., Kohl, M., Horst, S., Wobst, P., Steinbrink, J., Villringer, A.: Near-infrared spectroscopy: does it function in functional activation studies of the adult brain? Int. J. Psychophysiol. **35**(2), 125–142 (2000)
18. Bunce, S.C., Izzetoglu, M., Izzetoglu, K., Onaral, B., Pourrezaei, K.: Functional near-infrared spectroscopy. IEEE Eng. Med. Biol. Mag. **25**(4), 54–62 (2006)

19. Jobsis, F.F.: Noninvasive, infrared monitoring of cerebral and myocardial oxygen sufficiency and circulatory parameters. Science **198**(4323), 1264–1267 (1977)
20. Cope, M., Delpy, D.T., Reynolds, E.O.R., Wray, S., Wyatt, J., Van der Zee, P.: Methods of quantitating cerebral near infrared spectroscopy data. In: Mochizuki, M., Honig, C.R., Koyama, T., Goldstick, T.K., Bruley, D.F. (eds.) Oxygen Transport to Tissue X, vol. 215, pp. 183–189. Springer, New York (1988)
21. Ayaz, H., Shewokis, P.A., Curtin, A., Izzetoglu, M., Izzetoglu, K., Onaral, B.: Using MazeSuite and functional near infrared spectroscopy to study learning in spatial navigation. J. Vis. Exp. (56), e3443 (2011). doi:10.3791/3443
22. Ayaz, H.: Functional Near Infrared Spectroscopy based Brain Computer Interface. Ph.D. Thesis, Drexel University, Philadelphia, PA (2010)
23. Izzetoglu, M., Izzetoglu, K., Bunce, S., Ayaz, H., Devaraj, A., Onaral, B., Pourrezaei, K.: Functional near-infrared neuroimaging. IEEE Trans. Neural Syst. Rehabil. Eng. **13**(2), 153–159 (2005)
24. Ayaz, H., Izzetoglu, M., Shewokis, P.A., Onaral, B.: Sliding-window motion artifact rejection for functional near-infrared spectroscopy. Conf. Proc. IEEE Eng. Med. Biol. Soc. **2010**, 6567–6570 (2010)
25. Ayaz, H., Shewokis, P.A., Bunce, S., Izzetoglu, K., Willems, B., Onaral, B.: Optical brain monitoring for operator training and mental workload assessment. Neuroimage **59**(1), 36–47 (2012)
26. Çakir, M.P., Çakar, T., Girişken, Y.: Neural Correlates of Purchasing Behavior in the Prefrontal Cortex: An Optical Brain Imaging Study. Paper presented at CogSci 2015, Annual Meeting of the Cognitive Science Society, Pasadena, CA, USA (2015)

Real-Time Monitoring of Cognitive Workload of Airline Pilots in a Flight Simulator with fNIR Optical Brain Imaging Technology

Murat Perit Çakır[1(✉)], Murat Vural[1,2], Süleyman Özgür Koç[2], and Ahmet Toktaş[2]

[1] Graduate School of Informatics, Middle East Technical University, Ankara, Turkey
perit@metu.edu.tr
[2] Turkish Aerospace Industries, Ankara, Turkey
{murat.vural,ozkoc,atoktas}@tai.com.tr

Abstract. Real-time monitoring of the flight crew's health status with ambient and body sensors have become an important concern to improve the safety and the efficiency of flight operations. In this paper we report our preliminary findings on a functional near-infrared spectroscopy (fNIR) based online algorithm developed for real-time monitoring of mental workload of an airline pilot. We developed a linear discriminant analysis (LDA) based classifier that aims to predict low, moderate and high mental workload states based on a set of features computed over a moving window of oxy- and deoxy-hemoglobin measures obtained from 16 locations distributed over the prefrontal cortex. In this paper we explore the predictive power of a model trained for a single pilot over a sample of eight pilots and discuss the technical challenges involved with real-time measurement of brain activity in a flight simulator environment that involves other infra-red sources.

Keywords: Mental workload estimation · Optical brain imaging · fNIR · Neuroergonomics · Linear discriminant analysis

1 Introduction

Flight-crew's cognitive and physical well-being is a critical factor on flight safety. International Civil Aviation Organization's (ICAO) statistics indicate that cognitive factors account for 26 % of the incidents and accidents in civilian flight operations [1]. Although modern avionics systems assist the flight crew in important ways to reduce their cognitive and physical load, piloting is still a cognitively demanding task where pilots' are expected to maintain a high level of situational awareness, actively monitor the flight instruments, engage in the planning of flight legs, communicate with the air traffic controller (ATC) and the co-pilot, perceive and remember instructions provided by the ATC, stay vigilant to anticipate and avoid possible issues etc. Such aspects of piloting typically put a significant burden on the attentional and working memory resources of the pilots, especially in the case of critical flight episodes such as take off and landing, as well as unexpected events such as emergencies and instrument failures.

© Springer International Publishing Switzerland 2016
D.D. Schmorrow and C.M. Fidopiastis (Eds.): AC 2016, Part I, LNAI 9743, pp. 147–158, 2016.
DOI: 10.1007/978-3-319-39955-3_14

Despite the critical importance of pilots' cognitive and physical well-being for the success of flight operations, there are currently no operational pilot health monitoring systems in today's airliner cockpits. Due to the technological advances in biomedical sensors, real-time monitoring of flight crew's health status with ambient and body sensors have become increasingly feasible. In the context of a European Union 7th Framework Programme for Research project, the Advanced Cockpit for the Reduction of Stress and Workload (ACROSS) consortium has been exploring the use of multiple sensors such as eye/body trackers, facial recognition software, heart rate sensors, and optical brain imaging sensors in real time for this purpose in an effort to improve the safety and the efficiency of flight operations.

Monitoring the level of mental workload is a critical component of such real-time flight-crew health monitoring applications. In the aviation domain, related studies have explored the use of various sensors such as electroencephalography (EEG), electrocardiogram (ECG), electromyogram (EMG), electrooculogram (EOG) and galvanic skin conductance (GSR) to relate measures such as brain activity, heart rate variability, eye blink frequency, pupil dilation, eye fixation, muscle contractions and electro-dermal activity with pilot's mental workload [2]. These studies reported that an increase in pilot's mental workload tends to be associated with an increase in heart-rate variability, an increase in the rate of respiration, a decrease in the rate and duration of eye blinks, and an increase in gaze fixation durations. However, the fact that such measures can be influenced by physical factors that are unrelated to mental workload makes it difficult to use a single physiological sensor for this purpose. For instance, changes in cockpit lighting or the illumination from flight displays may elicit similar changes at the ocular level, whereas heart variability and the rate of respiration may increase due to muscle fatigue rather than an increase in mental workload [3].

These challenges motivated the use of sensors such as EEG that can monitor brain activity directly in the cockpit. EEG monitors the changes in electric potentials due to neural activity via electrodes distributed over the scalp. EEG studies investigating the changes in the level of alertness and mental workload of pilots during simulated flight missions primarily focused on fluctuations in the power of EEG signals in the theta (4–8 Hz), alpha (8–12 Hz) and beta (12–18 Hz) bands [2]. For instance, decrease in vigilance and deterioration in performance are associated with increased EEG power spectra in the theta band together with a change in EEG alpha power, whereas slips in attention and drowsiness modulate alpha waves [4]. The main limitation of the EEG approach is the difficulties involved with sensor placement and ensuring good conductivity to ensure data quality, which makes it challenging to employ the EEG method in the cockpit.

Functional near-infrared spectroscopy (fNIR) provides an alternative approach for the real-time monitoring of brain activity in the cockpit. The optical nature of the fNIR method allows the design of portable, wearable and durable sensors that offer practical advantages particularly for neuroergonomic applications [5]. In a very recent application of fNIR on real-time mental workload assessment, Gateau et al. succeeded in distinguishing high versus low workload situations in a controlled flight simulator environment by using a support-vector machine algorithm [6]. Moreover, in the context of a task that progressively elicits more mental effort, Herff et al. demonstrated that single trial discrimination of workload can be accomplished with an accuracy up to 78 % with the help of a linear discriminant classifier [7]. These findings suggest that fNIR can be a viable option for real time monitoring of flight-crew's mental workload.

In this study we aim to build on this line of work by investigating the use of fNIR for real-time monitoring of pilot's mental workload during simulated flight scenarios. The study was conducted as part of the ACROSS project, which aims to bring together multiple remote and wearable sensors into a commercial grade flight simulator for synchronous monitoring of multiple measures related to the level of vigilance, drowsiness, emotional/physical well-being, mental workload and situational awareness of the flight crew in real-time. We developed a linear discriminant analysis (LDA) classifier to distinguish low, moderate and high levels of mental workload during realistic flight simulation scenarios. The flight scenarios were designed to elicit different levels of workload by incorporating regular flight operations such as take off, climb, en-route, approach, descend and landing episodes as well as unanticipated complications such as engine/instrument failure or executing a go-around. Our study differs from existing applications of fNIR in the aviation context in terms of the realism of the flight scenarios used, the number of workload levels considered, and the presence of other IR sources in the environment. We aimed to explore the potential of fNIR for real-time mental workload assessment in a realistic flight simulation environment.

The rest of the paper is organized as follows. The next section provides an overview of the optical brain imaging method employed in this study as well as a description of the data collection and processing stages. This is followed by a description of the LDA model, the training data and an evaluation of the model's predictions on other pilots' performance in the same environment. The paper concludes with a discussion of the findings and implications for future work.

2   Methodology

2.1   Functional Near-Infrared Spectroscopy

Functional near-infrared spectroscopy (fNIR) is a neuroimaging modality that enables continuous, noninvasive, and portable monitoring of changes in blood oxygenation and blood volume related to human brain function [8]. Neuronal activity is determined with respect to the changes in oxygenation since variation in cerebral hemodynamics are related to functional brain activity through a mechanism which is known as neurovascular coupling [9]. Over the last decade, studies in the laboratory have established that fNIR spectroscopy provides a veridical measure of oxygenation and blood flow in the brain [8, 9]. fNIR is not only non-invasive, safe, affordable and portable, it also provides a balance between temporal and spatial resolution which makes fNIR a viable option for *in-the field* neuroimaging.

Several neuro-imaging modalities such as fMRI, PET and fNIR are based on methods for monitoring the hemodynamic changes in the brain due to neuronal activity. Neurons require energy to get activated, which is supplied by the metabolization of glucose via astrocytes [10]. The metabolization process requires oxygen which is supplied by the hemoglobin molecules present in the capillary beds within the vascular system. When a group of neurons fire, they initially consume the oxygen present in their vicinity, which will produce an initial increase in the concentration of deoxy-hemoglobin (HbR) and a dip in the concentration of oxy-hemoglobin (HbO). In the order of 4–6 s, the vascular system responds to this local energy need by supplying more oxygenated blood towards that location, which increases the concentration of HbO and washes away the HbR. As the neural population returns back to its baseline activity level, the concentrations of HbR and HbO also come back to their baseline levels. The change in relative concentrations of HbR and HbO due to neuronal activity is called the hemodynamic response.

fNIR technology uses specific wavelengths of light, introduced at the scalp, to enable the non-invasive measurement of changes in the relative ratios of HbR and HbO in the capillary beds during brain activity. Typically, an optical apparatus for fNIR Spectroscopy consists of at least one near infra-red light source and a detector that receives light after it has interacted with the tissue. Near-infra red light is known to diffuse through the intact scalp and skull, which makes it suitable for tracing relative changes in the concentration of specific chromophores in the neural tissue with non-invasive, spectroscopic methods [11]. Whereas most biological tissue (including water) are relatively transparent to light in the near infrared range between 700 to 900 nm, hemoglobin is a strong absorber of light waves in this range of the spectrum. Figure 1 below shows the absorption characteristics of elements present in biological tissue. Within 700 to 900 nm, HbO and HbR are among the highest absorbers of infra-red light. Moreover, within this range, the absorption characteristics of these molecules criss-cross each other, which makes it possible to separate the two chromophores from each other. This provides an optical window into neural tissue where one can approximate relative changes in the concentration of HbO and HbR based on how infra-red light is attenuated in neural tissue.

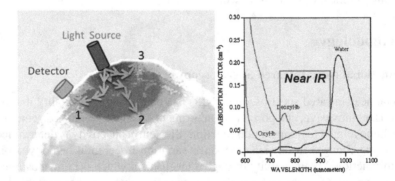

Fig. 1. The banana shaped path followed by the photons in the tissue (left). The optical window in which HbO and HbR have the strongest absorption characteristics in the IR range (right). (Color figure online)

Photons that enter tissue undergo two different types of interaction: absorption and scattering [9, 12]. Two chromophores, HbO and HbR, are strongly linked to tissue oxygenation and metabolism. The absorption spectra of HbO and HbR remain significantly different from each other allowing spectroscopic separation of these compounds to be possible by using only a few sample wavelengths. Once photons are introduced into the human head, they are either scattered by extra- and intracellular boundaries of different layers of the head (skin, skull, cerebrospinal fluid, brain, etc.) or absorbed mainly by HbO and HbR. If a photodetector is placed on the skin surface at a certain distance from the light source, it can collect the photons that are scattered and thus have travelled along a "banana shaped path" (Fig. 1) from the source to the detector, which carry important information about the optical properties of the diffused neural tissue. By using the Modified Beer Lambert Law, this information is converted into estimations of changes in relative concentrations of HbO and HbR [8].

2.2 Experiment Setup

Participants. Our sample include 8 pilots who have commercial/military flight hours in the range 3500–17000 h ($M = 10712$, $SD = 5057$). Pilots had normal or corrected to normal vision, and normal hearing. Participants did not report any history of psychiatric disorders. This study was approved by the Middle East Technical University Human Subjects Research Ethics Committee.

Materials, Apparatus and Software. The experiments were run at the premises of Thales Aviation (Cergy, France). In the context of the ACROSS project, several sensors including fNIR, SmartEye eye trackers, a Microsoft Kinect body tracker, a seat sensor and a heart rate sensor were installed on a Thales Airbus A320 simulator (Fig. 2). In this paper we focus only on the fNIR data collected in this setting. In order to shield the fNIR sensor from other infra-red sources such as the eye trackers and the Kinect body tracker, we used multiple layers of aluminium foil sawn inside a cloth cover that was installed over the fNIR sensor pad.

Fig. 2. A participant piloting the Thales Airbus 320 Simulator

While the pilots flew the scenarios the neural activity in their prefrontal cortex was monitored by a functional near-infrared spectroscopy (fNIR) system developed at Drexel University (Philadelphia, PA), manufactured and supplied by fNIR Devices LLC (Potomac, MD; www.fnirdevices.com). The real-time mental workload monitoring application consists of four modules; a flexible head-piece (sensor pad), a control box for hardware management, a computer that runs the COBI Studio software [12] for data acquisition, the DAQ Station module of fNIRSoft [13] for real-time low level processing of fNIR data, and a software application for real-time classification of mental workload level of the participant (Fig. 3).

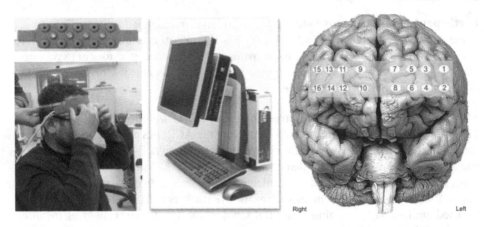

Fig. 3. The flexible sensor pad and its installation on the forehead (left), the fNIR data acquisition box (center), anatomical locations for the 16 optodes.

The fNIR sensor holds 4 light sources and 10 detectors, which obtains oxygenation measures at 16 optodes on the prefrontal cortex. The sensors have a source-detector separation of 2.5 cm, which allows for approximately 1.25 cm penetration depth to reach the cortical surface. This system can monitor changes in relative concentrations of HbO and HbR at a temporal resolution of 2 Hz. The locations of the regions on the cortical surface monitored by these two different sensors are displayed in Fig. 3, which correspond to Broadmann areas 9,10,44 and 45. Existing neuroimaging studies suggest that the prefrontal cortex has a special role in the processing of higher order cognitive functions such as working memory management, sequential processing of sensory and memory input, as well as response inhibition and decision making [8]. fNIR can monitor regions including left/right dorsolateral prefrontal cortex (dlPFC), left/right dorsomedial prefrontal cortex (dmPFC) and frontopolar cortex which are known to be associated with the abovementioned higher order cognitive processes.

In the scope of ACROSS project, the fNIR sensor is used to monitor the mental workload induced on pilot flying (PF) during the *aviate-navigate-communicate* tasks. The linkage between the mental workload monitoring and the fNIRS technology is based on the fact that the workload has direct relationship with the hemodynamic response and it can be measured by fNIRS technology.

Flight Scenarios. Pilots performed 4 flight scenarios during the experiment. The first scenario involved a free play task that took about an hour including sensor installation and demonstration of the flight simulator. After a rest period, the second scenario was run, which started in cruise mode and ended with normal workload landing. After the second scenario there was a lunch break. The third scenario also included cruise mode flight followed by a landing which was diverted to a different airport by the ATC, with the aim to increase the mental workload level. The final scenario simulated a high workload landing by having the ATC to initiate a sudden go-around due to late aircraft incursion on runway. During the climb an instrument failure (e.g. flap or engine failure) was initiated in order to further increase the mental workload level.

Data Processing. The fNIR sensor collects raw optical measures from 16 locations at 3 wavelengths (i.e. 730 nm, 805 nm, 850 nm) at 2 Hz. Raw optical signals are sampled in 60 s long blocks. A script executed by the DAQ station converts raw signals into HbO and HbR measures by using the Modified Beer Lambert Law by considering the first 10 s as a baseline. The script also computes the mean, standard deviation, slope, minimum, maximum and range values for HbO and HbR signals. The script streams the processed oxygenation measures to the mental workload classification application for every 5 s. The package sent by the script contains the oxygenation measures obtained for the last 60 s, together with a feature vector including mean, standard deviation, slope and range measures for HbO and HbR signals respectively. The features are fed into two discriminant functions to compute the distance between the feature vector and the centroids for mental workload categories. The application returns the closest centroid as the mental workload level estimate (Fig. 4).

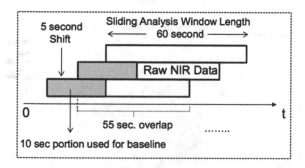

Fig. 4. The temporal progression of the employed sliding window method. Features used for mental workload estimation were sampled from a 60 s long window, which is updated every 5 s.

3 Mental Workload Estimation Model

3.1 Linear Discriminant Model

Discriminant analysis is a popularly used multivariate statistics method for the classification of neuroimaging signals [7]. The method is based on the eigenvalue decomposition of a high dimensional input space. Dimension reduction is accomplished by focusing on the discriminant functions that are a linear combination of several features, given a categorization as training input. The discriminant analysis method aims to find the most discriminating directions in the high dimensional vector space to achieve a comparable discriminating power among the existing data points.

Our LDA model uses 92 dimensional feature vectors to discriminate 3 different mental workload levels. The model is based on a single subject's fNIR data recorded during the simulated flight scenarios described above. The model parameters are estimated by using IBM SPSS v22. Due to high level of noise observed at optodes 8,10 and 16, the discriminant model was constructed on the remaining 13 optodes.

Prior to training, we prepared a training dataset by performing a qualitative analysis of the video files to judge the level of mental workload experienced by the subject during each of the three scenarios. Pilots' self-assessments of their mental workload which is collected after the experiment and the differences between the scenarios in terms of the presence of unexpected events such as failures are used as additional cues while manually marking the episodes for low, moderate and high mental workload. Once a mental workload assignment is made for each scenario, the annotated data is used for training a LDA model.

The discriminant analysis method computed 2 functions that significantly discriminate the three mental workload categories, where the first and second functions account for 73 % and 27 % of the total variability in the data. Wilk's lambda statistic suggest that these two functions significantly discriminate the three workload categories, $\chi^2(208) = 1047.32, p < .001$. The group centroids in the 2D space defined by discriminant functions 1 and 2 are plotted in Fig. 5. When the origin is taken as a reference, this plot suggests that function 1 distinguishes between lower (i.e. 0) versus higher (i.e. 1 and 2)

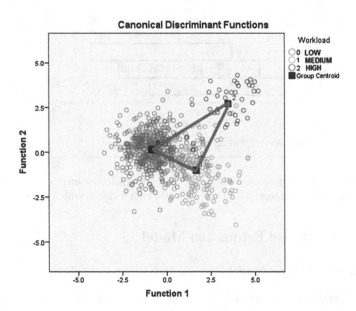

Fig. 5. The distribution of data points in the 2D space defined by the two LDA functions (Color figure online)

workload cases, whereas function 2 distinguishes high workload cases (i.e. 2) from lower workload cases (i.e. 0 and 1). Altogether, the functions predicts the mental workload categories with an accuracy of 91 %. Standardized LDA coefficients suggested that features obtained from optodes 1, 3, 5 on the left PFC and 13, 15 on the right PFC are the strongest contributors. Especially optodes 1, 3 and 13, 15 correspond to bilateral dorsolateral PFC region, which were also implicated in Gateu et al.'s [6] findings as strong contributors to mental workload estimation.

3.2 Model Evaluation

In order to evaluate the performance of the model, we sampled 69 episodes from the flight videos of 8 pilots that include routine flight episodes where we expect low mental workload as well as moments where events such as a flap or engine failure occurred that are expected to elicit higher levels of mental workload (Fig. 6). Table 1 summarizes the cross tabulation of predicted versus expected mental workload levels for the test cases. Of the 69 cases we analyzed, in 68.1 % of the cases there was a perfect match between the predicted and expected mental workload levels. The highest number of mismatches occurred when the model predicted a high MW case, whereas the expectation was low MW. As indicated under specific instances above, such cases happened due to fluctuations in the raw oxygenation measures due to excessive head motion or ambient noise in some of the optodes that contribute to the model and workload predictions.

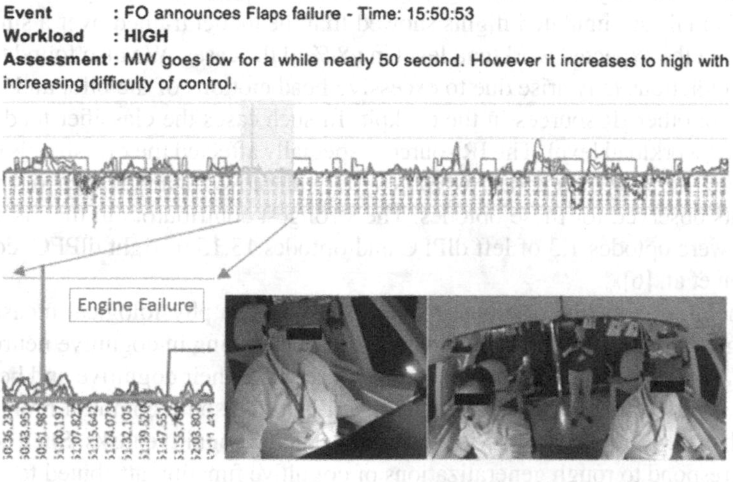

Event   : FO announces Flaps failure - Time: 15:50:53
Workload   : HIGH
Assessment : MW goes low for a while nearly 50 second. However it increases to high with increasing difficulty of control.

Fig. 6. One of 69 episodes sampled from the entire dataset. The sample episode shows the change in mental workload estimation from low to high following an engine failure alert.

Table 1. The distribution of predicted and expected mental workload levels

			Expected			Total
			0	1	2	
Predicted	0	Count	13	2	5	20
		%	18.8 %	2.9 %	7.2 %	29 %
	1	Count	0	5	0	5
		%	0 %	7.2 %	0 %	7.2 %
	2	Count	11	4	29	44
		%	15.9 %	5.8 %	42 %	63.8 %
Total		Count	24	11	34	69
		%	34.80 %	15.90 %	49.30 %	100 %

4   Discussion and Future Work

In this study we developed and evaluated a preliminary LDA based classifier that aim to predict low, moderate and high mental workload states of pilots in real-time based on a set of features computed over a moving window of HbO and HbR measures obtained from 16 locations distributed on the prefrontal cortex. The initial classifier was trained over a single pilot who ran through all three flight-scenarios with an accuracy of 92 %. This model was then used to predict the mental workload levels of the remaining 7 pilots in real-time while they were running the scenarios. A qualitative analysis of 69 events sampled from these simulated flights showed that the model trained over a single pilot could predict the expected workload level in 68 % of the cases. We also found that false positive predictions may arise due to excessive head motions of the pilot and the interference from other IR sources in the cockpit. In such cases the classifier tend to overestimate the workload level. The IR sources especially affected the raw signals obtained from the bottom row of optodes, which explains the lower standardized discriminant coefficients observed for these optodes. The strongest contributors to the discriminant functions were optodes 1,3 of left dlPFC and optodes 13,15 of right dlPFC, consistent with Gateu et al. [6].

In general, establishing a robust relationship between physiological measures and psychological states of subjects is a challenging undertaking in cognitive neuroscience research. Although each individual is unique in terms of their cognitive and behavioral attributes, years of neuroscience research has identified some common brain activity patterns that are valid across individuals during specific cognitive tasks. Such commonalities correspond to rough generalizations of cognitive function attributed to a number of anatomical areas. However, they may be useful for practical applications such as monitoring mental workload in real time. Findings in cognitive neuroscience and psychology have pointed out that attention is a scarce resource despite the immense computational power of the approximately 20 billion neurons inside the brain that can process information in parallel. When attention needs to be divided between multiple tasks or when the subject is confronted by a sudden, challenging problem, existing studies point out that there is an increased oxygen demand in prefrontal areas that are believed to be responsible for orchestrating the coordination between multiple neural resources distributed in the brain. Such novel forms of challenging stimulus that require conscious deliberation tend to activate a network of cortical areas known as the multiple demand system [14], which also includes areas in the bi-lateral prefrontal cortex that we relied on while developing a real-time mental workload assessment application. Although we still don't exactly know how the brain functions, such generalized findings in cognitive neuroscience based on imaging and lesion studies provide the necessary theoretical background that suggest the feasibility of an approach based on real-time monitoring of blood oxygenation in the cortex.

Although our mental workload estimation algorithm aims to capitalize on neural activation patterns that are assumed to be valid and consistent across participants, research on brain-computer interfaces (BCI) suggest that models that are customized for an individual provide more precise predictions about their intended behavior based on their brain activity. This is especially important in the BCI context, because subjects need to learn how to act with such novel interfaces, and there are important individual differences in how people acquire new skills. In our case, the information obtained from the brain is passively assessed without providing any feedback to the monitored participant. Moreover, we worked with expert pilots, so we did not focus on learning aspects or novice vs. expert contrasts. These factors allowed us to focus more on commonalities than individual differences while designing our mental workload estimations algorithm.

There are a number of issues to be addressed to improve the reliability of the mental workload estimate obtained via fNIR sensors. First of all, proper sensor placement and appropriate shielding of sensors from other IR sources is important for collecting useful information from the brain. Secondly, the model should be trained over a larger sample of subjects to construct a more robust, generalizable prediction model for workload assessment. Moreover, the algorithm design can be improved in several ways. A range of additional features such as skew, kurtosis, time to maximum for each sliding window could be used to better parametrize the distribution of the HbO and HbR signals. The effect of choosing different window size options on prediction accuracy should also be carefully studied. Filters that can be used to minimize the influence of head movements and saturated channels would also positively contribute to the prediction accuracy of the model. Finally, there are additional machine learning approaches such as deep learning networks, support vector machines and hidden markov models that can be exploited for better predictions. Some of these methods can even be fused with other sensors in the cockpit, such as the eye trackers, for improved accuracy.

Our discriminant function analysis showed that the strongest contributors to our workload assessment algorithm were optodes located in the left and right dorsolateral prefrontal cortex. Since these areas cover relatively a smaller part of the forehead, estimating mental workload with a smaller fNIR sensor seems to be feasible. The current device already supports a "split sensor", which can monitor 4 optodes located over left and right dorsolateral prefrontal cortex as well as left and right dorsomedial prefrontal cortex. Using a smaller sensor may improve crew acceptability as it is much more lightweight and easier to install. Moreover, the smaller size of the sensor also makes it relatively easier to shield from outside IR sources like eye-trackers or Kinect cameras. In the near future we expect to see further refinements in sensor design, which may allow us to use small patch like thin sensors wireless connected to the control box.

References

1. ICAO. Safety Report. International Civil Aviation Organization (2014). http://www.icao.int/safety/Documents/ICAO_2014%20Safety%20Report_final_02042014_web.pdf. Accessed 29 Feb 2016
2. Borghini, G., Astolfi, L., Vecchiato, G., Mattia, D., Babiloni, F.: Measuring neurophysiological signals in aircraft pilots and car drivers for the assessment of mental workload, fatigue and drowsiness. Neurosci. Biobehav. Rev. **44**, 58–75 (2014)
3. De Rivecourt, M., Kuperus, M.N., Post, W.J., Mulder, L.J.M.: Cardiovascular and eye activity measures as indices for momentary changes in mental effort during simulated flight. Ergonomics **51**(9), 1295–1319 (2008)
4. Dussault, C., Jouanin, J.C., Philippe, M., Guezennec, C.Y.: EEG and ECG changes during simulator operation reflect mental workload and vigilance. Aviat. Space Environ. Med. **76**, 344–351 (2005)
5. Ayaz, H., Onaral, B., Izzetoglu, K., Shewokis, P.A., McKendrick, R., Parasuraman, R.: Continuous monitoring of brain dynamics with functional near infrared spectroscopy as a tool for neuroergonomic research: empirical examples and a technological development. Front. Human Neurosci. **7**, 871 (2013)
6. Gateau, T., Durantin, G., Lancelot, F., Scannella, S., Dehais, F.: Real-time state estimation in a flight simulator using fNIRS. PLoS ONE **10**(3), e0121279 (2015)
7. Herff, C., Heger, D., Fortmann, O., Hennrich, J., Putze, F., Schultz, T.: Mental workload during n-back task-quantified in the prefrontal cortex using fNIRS. Front. Human Neurosci. **7**(1), 935–940 (2013)
8. Izzetoglu, M., Izzetoglu, K., Bunce, S., Ayaz, H., Devaraj, A., Onaral, B., Pourrezaei, K.: Functional near-infrared neuroimaging. IEEE Trans. Neural Syst. Rehabil. Eng. **13**(2), 153–159 (2005)
9. Obrig, H., Wenzel, R., Kohl, M., Horst, S., Wobst, P., Steinbrink, J., Villringer, A.: Near-infrared spectroscopy: does it function in functional activation studies of the adult brain? Int. J. Psychophysiol. **35**(2), 125–142 (2000)
10. Heeger, D.J., Ress, D.: What does fMRI tell us about neuronal activity? Nat. Rev. Neurosci. **3**(2), 142–151 (2002)
11. Wray, S., Cope, M., Delpy, D.T., Wyatt, J.S., Reynolds, E.O.R.: Characterization of the near infrared absorption spectra of cytochrome aa3 and haemoglobin for the non-invasive monitoring of cerebral oxygenation. Biochim. Biophys. Acta (BBA)-Bioenerg. **933**(1), 184–192 (1988)
12. Ayaz, H., Shewokis, P.A., Curtin, A., Izzetoglu, M., Izzetoglu, K., Onaral, B.: Using MazeSuite and functional near infrared spectroscopy to study learning in spatial navigation. J. Vis. Exp. **56**(3443), 10–3791 (2011)
13. Ayaz, H.: Functional Near Infrared Spectroscopy based Brain Computer Interface. Ph.D. Thesis, Drexel University, Philadelphia, PA (2010)
14. Duncan, J.: The multiple-demand (MD) system of the primate brain: mental programs for intelligent behaviour. Trends Cogn. Sci. **14**(4), 172–179 (2010)

Truthiness: Challenges Associated with Employing Machine Learning on Neurophysiological Sensor Data

Mark Costa[1,2(✉)] and Sarah Bratt[2]

[1] School of Information Studies, Syracuse University, Syracuse, USA
[2] M.I.N.D. Lab S.I. Newhouse School of Public Communications, Syracuse University, Syracuse, USA
{mrcosta,sebratt}@syr.edu

Abstract. The use of neurophysiological sensors in HCI research is increasing in use and sophistication, largely because such sensors offer the potential benefit of providing "ground truth" in studies, and also because they are expected to underpin future adaptive systems. Sensors have shown significant promise in the efforts to develop measurements to help determine users' mental and emotional states in real-time, allowing the system to use that information to adjust user experience.

Most of the sensors used generate a substantial amount of data, a high dimensionality and volume of data that requires analysis using powerful machine learning algorithms. However, in the process of developing machine learning algorithms to make sense of the data and subject's mental or emotional state under experimental conditions, researchers often rely on existing and imperfect measures to provide the "ground truth" needed to train the algorithms.

In this paper, we highlight the different ways in which researchers try to establish ground truth and the strengths and limitations of those approaches. The paper concludes with several suggestions and specific areas that require more discussion.

Keywords: Machine learning · Cognitive data · Method validity · fNIRS · Neurophysiological sensors

1 Introduction

The goal of using machine learning on data generated by neural sensors is to predict or identify a user's mental state in real-time. The roadmap to achieving that goal usually involves conducting controlled experiments, where subjects are exposed to a series of control and treatment conditions. Depending on the experimental setup, the subject's mental state under the treatment condition can be either identified through self-report measures, the nature of the task and its expected effect on mental state, or the subject's task performance. The labels are then used as predictor variables for machine learning

© Springer International Publishing Switzerland 2016
D.D. Schmorrow and C.M. Fidopiastis (Eds.): AC 2016, Part I, LNAI 9743, pp. 159–164, 2016.
DOI: 10.1007/978-3-319-39955-3_15

algorithms. Each of these approaches has drawbacks in terms of validity and reliability, which may lead us to train the algorithms on incorrectly labeled data (Hoskin 2012).

In an ideal world, the problems of mislabeled data would average out over large data sets – machine learning is successfully applied in many spaces where a high volume of data is available to train the models. However, in the applied neuroscience space the number of cases is usually very small and the dimensionality of the data is very large, which can easily lead to overfitted models. This is one of the reasons why developing models that work across subjects, experimental conditions, and/or treatments is very difficult.

To sum up the challenge in a single sentence, we are trying to build predictive models on unreliably tagged data under the curse of dimensionality.

There are valid reasons for undertaking this effort. First, these efforts will enable future systems that adapt to our mental, physical, and emotional state in real-time, helping us make better decisions, gain deeper insights, and solve bigger problems, from medical diagnoses to adaptive military technology (Gateau et al. 2015; Girouard 2010; Naseer and Hong 2015; Marx et al. 2015). Developing such systems will involve integrating voluminous data from multiple sensors, a task which machine learning is especially well-suited. This paper addresses one of the handful of challenges associated with building adaptive systems – identifying the ground truth to build upon when developing models and systems.

The remainder of the paper is structured as follows: first, a brief description of neurophysiological sensors is provided. Then, an overview of the approaches to labelling data for algorithm training purposes, and a discussion of the validity and reliability problems associated with the labeling approaches follows. The paper concludes with a discussion of potential solutions and directions for future research.

2 Generating Data

Neurophysiological sensors rely on different physical mechanisms to measure activity in the brain. For example, an EEG measures electrical activity generated by neurons firing within the brain, fNIRS measures blood flow to and from areas of the brain instigated by activation and deactivation of specific regions, and fMRI uses magnetic resonance imaging to track blood flow in a manner similar to fNIRS.

The main point to consider when thinking about labeling neurophysiological data for machine learning purposes is that the sensor generates one row of data every time it samples. For example, an fNIRS can be set to sample at 10 Hz, generating approximately 36,000 rows of data for a one hour experiment. For each row there may be some number of data points associated with the channels in the device, which we can call features. Supervised learning algorithms use those features and derivative features to build a model that predicts a label. Most algorithms perform this model creation and evaluation by passing over the data frequently, iteratively refining the weights given to each of the features until such a point that the algorithm has satisfied its optimization criteria. The labeling process involves estimating the subject's mental or emotional state at each of those points in time and assigning a category code (the label, or "class label") to that point in time or interval of time.

The labeling process results in at least a few error in the labeling process in the boundary regions between state shifts because identifying the exact point in time when a cognitive state changes in not currently possible. Furthermore, we argue in this paper that the labels in general are not entirely reliable due to limitations of the approaches available, and as a result, the trained models are not reliable. Using incorrectly labeled data to train a supervised algorithm would be analogous to teaching a child to add by giving her a set of addition problem examples with answers that were correct only some of the time, then expecting the child to know how to add when given a new set of problems.

Before going into detail justifying our argument, we start with a brief description of the approaches researchers have used to determine those labels and the justifications for making that choice (Fairclough and Gilleade 2014; Noah et al. 2015; Liu et al. 2015).

3 Approaches to Labeling Data

We identified three approaches to labeling the data – response based, task based, and task-performance based. Here we will refer to the label as "ground truth" – what the researcher believes to be the best approximation of the subject's mental or emotional state. Each approach has strengths and weaknesses, and none appears to be the superior approach.

3.1 Response-Based Labeling

Response based labeling uses the subject's subjective interpretation of their mental state as the ground truth. For example, researchers have used the self-assessment manikins (Bradley and Lang 1994; Balconi et al. 2015; Bandara et al. In press) and NASA TLX. Fundamentally, this boils down to asking the subject – were you upset, overloaded, angry, sad, etc. This requires a certain amount of self-awareness on the subjects, a fair degree of honesty (Paulhus and Vazire 2009), and a good recollection of how they felt over a period of time without succumbing to recency bias (Sackett and Larson Jr. 1990; Morrison et al. 2014).

Any one of the instruments listed above is considered well-validated *gross* measures of emotional or cognitive state. However, sensors sample anywhere between 1 and 1000 times per second, which means the subject's state needs to be accurately labeled for each of the intervals. For example, fNIRS focuses on the hemodynamics of the brain, and most devices sample somewhere in the vicinity of 10 Hz, tracking blood flow to regions that changes measurably within a 6–8 s window. Yet, we use a subject's best estimation of their mental state over a 16–30 s window, hoping that the most recent impression of their mental state does not prompt them to ignore the mode state. Researchers have noted repeatedly that self-reports do not have guaranteed accuracy, with some suggesting that a best practice is to triangulate their observations with other known, validated measures (Liu et al. 2015; Rusnock et al. 2015).

Response based labeling has certain advantages – it can be used to triangulate task-based labeling (see below), or to explore meaningful concepts that are tested using protocols that are known to reliably induce cognitive or emotional responses. An additional advantage of response based labeling is that it may also make it easier to connect the machine learning body of literature to other HCI literature that still relies heavily on self-report measures (Rek et al. 2013; Lottridge 2009; Olson and Kellogg 2014).

3.2 Task-Based Labeling

Task-based labeling involves using tasks that are known or expected to elicit certain mental or emotional states reliably (Ang et al. 2012; An et al. 2013). Task-based labeling is not reliable, even for well-established measures. For example, researchers developed and tested a game that was perceived to have multiple levels of difficulty and thus expected to provoke different levels of engagement. However, during their experiment, two subjects did not notice the difference in difficulty levels and seven did (Girouard et al. 2009). Any attempts to build models using fixed channels as inputs, where the channels are expected to map to specific areas of the brain, faces challenges as well. In some studies, handedness influences cerebral blood flow on certain tasks (Cuzzocreo et al. 2009). Finally, task-based labeling is built on the assumption that participants are engaged in the task.

Task-based labeling has certain advantages, with the most notable being that they avoid the limitations of response-based labeling of conditions. There are two additional benefits of task-based labeling – (1) it allows researchers to more accurately track expected changes in cognitive state because expected changes can be synced to changes in the task; and (2) researchers do not have to interrupt the flow of the experiment to ask the subject to rate his or her experience.

3.3 Performance-Based Labeling

Performance-based labeling involves establishing ground truth by measuring the subject's performance on a specific task. The general chain of assumptions appears to be that (a) the task relies on known cognitive processes, (b) performance on the task requires effort, and (c) performance is correlated with activation and failure is correlated with lack of activation. An example of performance-based labeling can be found in (James et al. 2010), where the researchers estimated cognitive burden generated by learning a visual-motor task by measuring the distance from the cursor to the target on the screen.

Performance-based labeling avoids the pitfalls of self-report measures in that they offer temporal granularity and do not require subjects to estimate their own state. They also avoid some of the limitations of task-based measures, most notably addressing the concern that subjects may or may not be engaged in the task. Performance-based labeling does not address limitations in terms of accurately localizing activation in individuals, although determining the subject's handedness appears to account for a large portion of behavioral lateralization (Lawlor-Savage and Goghari 2014).

4   Conclusion

In this paper we presented a provisional taxonomy for determining ground-truth of emotional or cognitive states in experiments involving the use of machine learning on neurophysiological data. Each approach has strengths and weaknesses, and researchers can either determine those limitations are within the limits of acceptability or employ triangulation procedures to improve their confidence in the measures. We are not arguing that researchers should always use triangulation (although it would be beneficial); instead, we would like to suggest starting a discussion on how it would be possible to estimate the upper boundary of accuracy for the algorithms based on the acknowledgement that the models were trained on data that had low n and was only partially accurate.

References

Ang, K.K., Yu, J., Guan, C.: Extracting and selecting discriminative features from high density NIRS-Based BCI for numerical cognition. In: The 2012 International Joint Conference on Neural Networks (IJCNN), pp. 1–6 (2012). doi:10.1109/IJCNN.2012.6252604

An, J., Lee, J., Ahn, C.: An efficient GP approach to recognizing cognitive tasks from fNIRS neural signals. Sci. China Inf. Sci. **56**(10), 1–7 (2013). doi:10.1007/s11432-013-5001-8

Balconi, M., Grippa, E., Vanutelli, M.E.: What hemodynamic (fNIRS), Electrophysiological (EEG) and autonomic integrated measures can tell us about emotional processing. Brain Cogn. **95**, 67–76 (2015). doi:10.1016/j.bandc.2015.02.001

Bandara, D., Song, S., Hirshfield, L., Velipasalar, S.: A more complete picture of emotion using electrocardiogram and electrodermal activity to complement cognitive data. In: HCI International 2016 Conference Proceedings. Springer, Toronto (In press)

Bradley, M.M., Lang, P.J.: Measuring emotion: the self-assessment manikin and the semantic differential. J. Behav. Ther. Exp. Psychiatry **25**(1), 49–59 (1994)

Cuzzocreo, J.L., Yassa, M.A., Verduzco, G., Honeycutt, N.A., Scott, D.J., Bassett, S.S.: Effect of handedness on fMRI activation in the medial temporal lobe during an auditory verbal memory task. Hum. Brain Mapp. **30**(4), 1271–1278 (2009). doi:10.1002/hbm.20596

Fairclough, S., Gilleade, K.: Advances in Physiological Computing. Springer Science & Business Media, New York (2014)

Gateau, T., Durantin, G., Lancelot, F., Scannella, S., Dehais, F.: Real-time state estimation in a flight simulator using fNIRS. PLoS ONE **10**(3), e0121279 (2015). doi:10.1371/journal.pone.0121279

Girouard, A., Solovey, E.T., Hirshfield, L.M., Chauncey, K., Sassaroli, A., Fantini, S., Jacob, R.J.: Distinguishing difficulty levels with non-invasive brain activity measurements. In: Gross, T., Gulliksen, J., Kotzé, P., Oestreicher, L., Palanque, P., Prates, R.O., Winckler, M. (eds.) INTERACT 2009. LNCS, vol. 5726, pp. 440–452. Springer, Heidelberg (2009)

Girouard, A.: Towards adaptive user interfaces using real time fNIRS. Tufts University, Medford, MA, USA (2010)

Hoskin, R.: The dangers of self-report. Sci. Brainwaves, 3 March 2012. http://www.sciencebrainwaves.com/the-dangers-of-self-report/

James, D.R., et al.: Cognitive burden estimation for visuomotor learning with fNIRS. In: Jiang, T., Navab, N., Pluim, J.P., Viergever, M.A. (eds.) MICCAI 2010, Part III. LNCS, vol. 6363, pp. 319–326. Springer, Heidelberg (2010)

Lawlor-Savage, L., Goghari, V.M.: Working memory training in schizophrenia and healthy populations. Behav. Sci. **4**(3), 301–319 (2014). doi:10.3390/bs4030301

Liu, N., Cui, X., Bryant, D.M., Glover, G.H., Reiss, A.L.: Inferring deep-brain activity from cortical activity using functional near-infrared spectroscopy. Biomed. Opt. Express. **6**(3), 1074–1089 (2015). doi:10.1364/BOE.6.001074

Lottridge, D.: Evaluating human computer interaction through self-rated emotion. In: Gross, T., Gulliksen, J., Kotzé, P., Oestreicher, L., Palanque, P., Prates, R.O., Winckler, M. (eds.) INTERACT 2009. LNCS, vol. 5727, pp. 860–863. Springer, Heidelberg (2009)

Marx, A.-M., Ehlis, A.-C., Furdea, A., Holtmann, M., Banaschewski, T., Brandeis, D., Rothenberger, A., et al.: Near-Infrared Spectroscopy (NIRS) neurofeedback as a treatment for children with Attention Deficit Hyperactivity Disorder (ADHD)—a pilot study. Front. Hum. Neurosci. **8**, 1038 (2015). doi:10.3389/fnhum.2014.01038

Morrison, A.B., Conway, A.R., Chein, J.M.: Primacy and recency effects as indices of the focus of attention. Front. Hum. Neurosci. **8** (2014). doi:10.3389/fnhum.2014.00006

Naseer, N., Hong, K.-S.: fNirs-based brain-computer interfaces: a review. Front. Hum. Neurosci. **9** (2015). doi:10.3389/fnhum.2015.00003

Noah, J.A., Ono, Y., Nomoto, Y., Shimada, S., Tachibana, A., Zhang, X., Bronner, S., Hirsch, J.: fMRI validation of fNIRS measurements during a naturalistic task. J.Visualized Exp. 100 (2015). doi:10.3791/52116

Olson, J.S., Kellogg, W.A.: Ways of Knowing in HCI. Springer Science & Business, New York (2014)

Paulhus, D.L., Vazire, S.: Thse self-report method. In: Robins, R.W., Chris Fraley, R., Krueger, R.F. (eds.) Handbook of Research Methods in Personality Psychology, pp. 224–239. Guilford Press, New York (2009)

Rek, M., Romero, N., van Boeijen, A.: Motivation to self-report: capturing user experiences in field studies. In: Collazos, C., Liborio, A., Rusu, C. (eds.) CLIHC 2013. LNCS, vol. 8278, pp. 111–114. Springer, Heidelberg (2013). doi:http://link.springer.com/chapter/10.1007/978-3-319-03068-5_19

Rusnock, C., Borghetti, B., McQuaid, I.: Objective-analytical measures of workload – the third pillar of workload triangulation? In: Schmorrow, D.D., Fidopiastis, C.M. (eds.) AC 2015. LNCS, vol. 9183, pp. 124–135. Springer, Heidelberg (2015)

Sackett, P.R, Larson Jr., J.R.: Research strategies and tactics in industrial and organizational psychology. Dunnette, M.D., Hough, L.M. (eds.) Handbook of Industrial and Organizational Psychology, vol. 1, 2nd edn. Consulting Psychologists Press, Palo Alto (1990)

Evaluation of Cognitive Control and Distraction Using Event-Related Potentials in Healthy Individuals and Patients with Multiple Sclerosis

Thomas J. Covey$^{(\boxtimes)}$, Janet L. Shucard, and David W. Shucard

Division of Cognitive and Behavioral Neurosciences, Department of Neurology,
Neuroscience Program, The Jacobs School of Medicine and Biomedical
Sciences, University at Buffalo, State University of New York, Buffalo, USA
{tjcovey, shucard, dshucard}@buffalo.edu

Abstract. Multiple Sclerosis (MS) is a disorder of the central nervous system that can result in cognitive dysfunction. Despite the prevalence of cognitive impairments in MS, few studies have directly examined dysfunction in the domain of cognitive control, which involves the monitoring of conflicting stimulus input and response options and the subsequent selection of an appropriate response (and inhibition of inappropriate responses). The present study examined event-related potential (ERP) indices of brain function in MS patients and healthy controls (HCs) for a Go/Nogo Flanker task of cognitive control. The task required participants to respond appropriately to a central target arrow stimulus that was flanked by non-target stimuli that were congruent, incongruent, or neutral with respect to the target. On some trials, a two-sided target arrow was presented, which required the inhibition of a response (Nogo). The Nogo stimulus also was surrounded by flankers (arrow primes or neutral). MS patients had slower reaction times during Go trials compared to HCs. Patients exhibited prolonged latencies for P1, frontal P2, N2, and P3 components compared to HCs. MS patients, compared to HCs, also had a more pronounced anteriorization for P3 amplitude during Nogo compared to Go trials, possibly indicating inhibitory dysfunction. Finally, decreased amplitude was also observed in MS patients compared to HCs for a positive-negative complex with very early latency onset, which may reflect dysfunction in early processing of the flanker stimuli. The findings indicate dysfunction at multiple stages of processing in MS patients during cognitive control.

Keywords: Cognitive control · Inhibition · Multiple sclerosis · ERPs

1 Introduction

Multiple Sclerosis (MS) is a neurodegenerative disorder that can result in demyelination, multi-focal lesions, and cortical atrophy [1–3]. Cognitive impairments are prevalent in MS in the domains of attention, working memory, learning, and executive functioning [4]. Brain structural abnormalities and atrophy in patients are predictive of deficits on tasks of cognitive performance [5–8]. Previous work examining cognitive

© Springer International Publishing Switzerland 2016
D.D. Schmorrow and C.M. Fidopiastis (Eds.): AC 2016, Part I, LNAI 9743, pp. 165–176, 2016.
DOI: 10.1007/978-3-319-39955-3_16

impairments in MS has covered a variety of cognitive domains; however, to date, few studies have specifically examined potential deficits in the domain of cognitive control in MS. Cognitive control involves the ability to monitor conflicting response options and the subsequent decision to respond (or inhibit a response) in a context-dependent manner. Selective attention to relevant information and the inhibition of distracting information are involved in this process. Given the profile of cognitive impairments commonly observed and the underlying neuropathology, it is plausible that MS patients may have deficits in cognitive control processes, particularly in inhibitory functioning.

Cognitive control has typically been studied using Go/Nogo type tasks (and also the Stop-Signal task, not discussed here). During a typical Go/Nogo task, participants are required to respond whenever they see a "Go" stimulus (e.g., a green circle) and withhold their response whenever they observe a "Nogo" stimulus (e.g., a red circle). Ongoing electroencephalographic (EEG) data can also be recorded while participants are completing the task, and event-related potential (ERP) measures of stimulus-specific brain processes can be derived. There has been extensive research on ERP measures obtained during Go/Nogo tasks. The P3 and N2 components, in particular, have been observed to be modulated by the demands of cognitive control tasks (for a review, see [9]). The P3 ERP component is a positivity that occurs at approximately 300–500 ms post-stimulus; the N2 component is a negativity observed at approximately 200–350 ms post-stimulus. A consistent finding has been that there is a more frontal-central scalp electrode maxima of P3 component amplitude for Nogo stimuli compared to Go stimuli, for which P3 has a more parietal maxima. This finding has been termed the "Nogo anteriorization" effect and is thought to be an index of response inhibition and/or evaluation of inhibitory processes. A typically frontal-central maximal N2 component has also been observed for Nogo stimuli, but the N2 has been posited to reflect conflict monitoring processes, and not necessarily response inhibition per se [9].

Flanker tasks have also been useful for studying processes that are related to cognitive control, such as selective attention and conflict monitoring. Flanker tasks typically involve the presentation of a central target arrow stimulus that is flanked by non-target arrow stimuli that are either directionally congruent (e.g., →→→→), or directionally incongruent (e.g., →←→). Congruent flankers result in faster responding (facilitation of attention), whereas prolonged response speeds are observed when the flankers are incongruent (increased distraction) [10, 11]. Several studies have examined ERPs during a Go/Nogo task with flanker stimuli [10, 11]. In these studies, Go trials had left or right target arrows that had congruent or incongruent flankers; Nogo stimuli also had flankers ("directional primes"). This work suggests that ERPs, including the N2 and P3 components, can potentially be modulated by flanker-target congruency, in addition to inhibitory control requirements. This methodology provides a useful means for examining cognitive control processes such as conflict monitoring and response inhibition while also being able to manipulate the level of distraction created by non-target flanker stimuli.

There have been only a few studies that have examined brain function in MS during Go/Nogo or flanker tasks. MS patients in a functional magnetic resonance imaging (fMRI) study [12] had greater activation of bilateral inferior frontal cortical regions compared to HCs for incongruent trials (incongruent > congruent contrast). In another study [13], participants were presented with congruent or incongruent target/flanker arrow stimuli. But on a small percentage of trials, the central target arrow turned red after a 150 ms delay, during which participants had to actively inhibit their response, if possible. The authors examined the error-related negativity (ERN), a negative component derived by averaging the EEG data for stop trials where there was an error of commission. The ERN was found to be significantly higher for MS patients compared to HCs. These studies suggest that MS patients may have disrupted brain function during flanker type tasks that require selective attention and inhibitory control.

In the present study, we used a Go/NoGo task that incorporated flanker stimuli to manipulate the level of conflict during the decision making process (Go/Nogo Flanker; adapted from [11]). This task allowed us to examine neural substrates of selective attention, inhibition, and distraction in HCs and MS patients. The task included congruent (facilitation), incongruent (increased distraction), and neutral stimulus types for Go trials; During Nogo trials, directional primes (increased distraction and response priming) or neutral flankers were also presented. Our primary goal was to assess differences in ERP components elicited during different task conditions between MS patients and HCs. We were particularly interested in whether there were differential effects for MS vs. HCs regarding P3 and N2 amplitude and latency during response inhibition (Nogo stimuli). Additional components reflecting different stages of processing were also examined.

2 Methods

2.1 Participants

Participant sample demographics can be found in Table 1. All individuals were tested as part of a larger study on cognitive training. Participants were administered the North American Adult Reading Test to estimate IQ (NAART; [14]). In the present manuscript, pre-training data for the Go/Nogo Flanker task are reported. One of two alternate versions of the task (both with equal difficulty) were semi-randomly administered to participants. Patients with clinically definite MS [15] were tested. The majority of MS patients had the relapsing remitting subtype (N = 10; relapsing progressive, N = 2, secondary progressive, N = 2, primary progressive, N = 1). Fifteen HC participants were semi-randomly selected, keeping demographic characteristics in mind, from a pool of 43 healthy individuals that had participated in the study, to achieve a sample size for the HC group that was similar to the MS group. The HC group participants were selected prior to and separate from any knowledge about behavioral performance and ERP measures and data viability (i.e. noise in the ERP). All participants were screened prior to testing, and excluded from the study if they had psychiatric, neurologic, or medical conditions (other than MS), history of head trauma, hearing problems, uncorrectable visual problems, or learning disorders. All participants provided informed consent and received compensation for participation. The study met the standards of the Internal Review Board of the State University of New York at Buffalo.

Table 1. Participant Demographics.

	Multiple sclerosis			Healthy controls		
	Mean	SD	N	Mean	SD	N
Age	34.73	8.34	15	27.40	4.58	15
Years of education	15.47	1.81	15	17.00	2.56	15
NAART est IQ	105.12	6.69	14	109.70	8.20	15
Years MS	11.53	8.06	15	–	–	–
Gender (% female)	73 %			73 %		

2.2 Go/Nogo Flanker Task

Participants were seated in front of a computer monitor that displayed the task stimuli and were given a four button response pad. Each trial was 2,050 ms long and began with a fixation cross. There was a 1,000 ms inter-stimulus interval. Participants were instructed to press the inner buttons on the response pad with their index fingers if a central target stimulus was a down arrow; press the outer buttons if the central target was an up arrow (equal number of up and down targets; these were Go trials, 70 % of all trials); or to withhold their response if the central target stimulus was a two-sided arrow (Nogo trials, 30 % of all trials). On each trial of the task, the central target arrow stimulus was surrounded by flanker stimuli, which preceded the onset of the target stimulus by 50 ms in order to induce a priming effect. Flanker stimuli then remained on the screen for the duration of target presentation (1,000 ms). See Fig. 1 for a depiction of the flanker/target combinations: For one third of the Go trials, the target and flanker pointed in the same direction (Go Congruent); for another third, the target and flanker pointed in opposite directions (Go Incongruent); and another third of the Go trials had flankers that were rectangles (Go Neutral). Up or down flankers were also presented for 2/3 of the NoGo trials (NoGo Prime trials). The other 1/3 of NoGos had rectangle flankers (NoGo Neutral). There were 250 total trials, and a short practice preceded the task block. Trial types were pseudo-randomly presented. Performance accuracy was recorded for all trials, and RT data were recorded for all Go trials. Measures examined in the present study include percent correct responses and correct response reaction time (RT) for Go Congruent, Go Incongruent, and Go Neutral trials; as well as accuracy and false alarms for Nogo Prime trials.

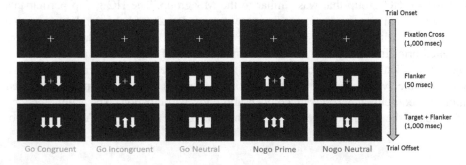

Fig. 1. Go/Nogo Flanker task

2.3   Event-Related Potential Analyses

Participants performed the task in a sound attenuated, dimly lit testing chamber while sitting in a comfortable chair. EEG recordings were obtained during the task using a 256 channel dense electrode array HydroCel Geodesic Sensor Net (Electrical Geodesics, Inc., Eugene OR) using a vertex reference. Impedances was generally kept below 60 kΩ. A bandpass filter of 0.1–100 Hz was applied during EEG recording and data were digitized at a sampling rate of 250 Hz. Data were then processed offline using Netstation version 4.4 (Electrical Geodesics, Inc., Eugene OR). A 25 Hz low pass filter was applied, then data were segmented into 1,100 ms epochs (200 ms prior to target onset, 900 ms post-target onset). Segment categories included Go Congruent, Go Incongruent, Go Neutral, Nogo Prime, and Nogo Neutral trial types. Following segmentation, automated artifact rejection algorithms were run and bad data were removed, as per previously described methods [16].

After automated artifact detection, each trial segment was then visually inspected. Segments that were not rejected using the automated algorithms but were observed to still contain artifact were then marked by the experimenter and rejected from subsequent averaging. Next, electrodes that were marked as bad either via the automated algorithms or by the experimenter were replaced by estimated data that were interpolated from other scalp locations. Data were then averaged for each trial category and re-referenced using the averaged reference derived from all scalp electrodes. Baseline correction was then applied to all averaged waveforms using the 150 ms time period prior to the onset of the flanker stimuli. Four participants were not included in ERP analyses due to excessive artifact resulting in a low trial count in the averaged waveforms. Thus, for all ERP analyses: HC, N = 14 and MS, N = 12. Nogo Neutral trials were not analyzed in the present study due to low trial counts. The average number of trials used to generate the averaged waveforms for the analysis in the present study, after all artifact rejection procedures is as follows: For MS, Go Congruent, M = 42.42, SD = 11.54; Go Incongruent, M = 41.17, SD = 10.55; Go Neutral, M = 42.00, SD = 12.34; Nogo Prime, M = 30.75, SD = 9.58; for HCs, Go Congruent, M = 43.86, SD = 10.54; Go Incongruent, M = 44.93, SD = 7.85; Go Neutral, M = 46.14, SD = 9.44; Nogo Prime M = 35.29, SD = 11.37.

ERPs at three midline clusters of electrodes (Fz, Cz, and Pz) were identified for statistical analyses, corresponding with the 10–20 electrode placement system. Analysis of the electrode clusters was conducted as described previously [16]. P1 and P3 components were observed at all clusters and analyzed accordingly (Fz, Cz, and Pz; see description in Results for additional detail regarding ERPs). P2 and N2 ERP components were observed primarily at Fz and analyses were restricted to this region. An early positive-negative complex at parietal leads (PN$_p$) was also observed prior to the onset of P1, so analysis for this complex was restricted to Pz. Based on the grand averages across all participants for each condition, windows for these components were applied to each individual participant's ERP data, and an automated algorithm was used to extract the peak amplitude and latency for each component for each subject. The ERP component windows were visually inspected prior to running the peak/latency extraction procedure to ensure that the correct ERP component was selected.

2.4   Statistical Analyses

Independent samples t-tests and chi-square tests were used to analyze demographic differences between groups. Behavioral and ERP data were analyzed using repeated measures ANOVAs. Greenhouse-Geisser corrected values were used in cases where sphericity was violated (noted as "gg corrected"). Partial eta squared (η_p^2) served as estimates of effect size for all ANOVAs. Independent samples t-tests were used to examine differences between groups when probing significant effects. Paired samples t-tests were used for all comparisons between conditions or leads. Alpha level was set at $p \leq .05$.

3   Results

3.1   Participant Demographics

MS patients and HCs did not significantly differ on IQ (estimated from NAART performance) or years of education. MS patients did, however, have a significantly higher mean age compared to HCs ($p = .006$). Chi-square analyses indicated that there were no significant differences between groups on gender proportion, left/right handedness, or ethnicity/race.

3.2   Go/Nogo Flanker Behavioral Performance

Behavioral data were analyzed for all subjects, regardless of their inclusion in the ERP analyses (N = 15 for both groups). Condition (Go Congruent, Go Incongruent, Go Neutral) X Group (MS, HC) repeated measures ANOVAs were used for Go accuracy and RT. For Go accuracy (% correct) there was a borderline Condition effect ($F(2, 56) = 2.765$, $p = .072$, $\eta_p^2 = .090$), but in general, accuracy was high across all conditions (around a mean of 95 % or greater). For Go RT, there was a significant Condition effect ($F(2, 56) = 63.324$, $p < .001$, $\eta_p^2 = .693$) and Group effect ($F(1, 28) = 6.266$, $p = .018$, $\eta_p^2 = .183$; see Fig. 2A). Post-hoc tests indicated a pattern for Go RT in which Incongruent > Neutral > Congruent ($p < .001$ for all comparisons). The Group effect was observed because MS patients had significantly slower RT compared to HCs, across all Go conditions. MS patients and HCs also did not differ on the number of errors of commission during Nogo Prime trials (false alarms).

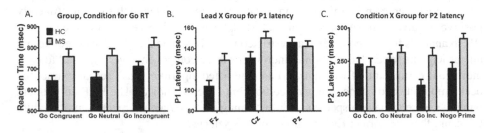

Fig. 2. Response speed and ERP latency effects.

3.3   Event-Related Potential Analyses

Figure 3 shows the grand averaged ERPs for midline electrodes. The P3 component was identified across all midline leads and conditions at approximately 300–600 ms post-target. The P1 component was also identified for all midline leads and conditions at approximately 80–180 ms post-target. The P1 and P3 components were analyzed across all midline clusters (Fz, Cz, Pz). Other components were more restricted to specific cluster leads. An N2 component was identified at frontal scalp sites at approximately 220–380 ms (analyses restricted to Fz). A positive frontal component was also identified at approximately 200–320 ms (P2 component, analyses restricted to Fz). There was also an early positivity and negativity observed at parietal leads, with the positivity peaking at approximately 30–40 ms post-target and a subsequent negatively peaking at approximately 60–80 ms (early parietal positive-negative complex, PN_p, analyses restricted to Pz). The PN_p component occurred prior to the onset of P1, and due to the early onset it may reflect early processing of the flanker stimulus and/or the flanker/target comparison. Condition (Go Congruent, Go Incongruent, Go Neutral, Nogo Prime) X Lead (Fz, Cz, Pz) X Group (MS, HC) ANOVAs were conducted for P1 and P3 amplitude and latency measures. Condition X Group ANOVAs were conducted for the frontal P2 and N2, and parietal PN_p measures.

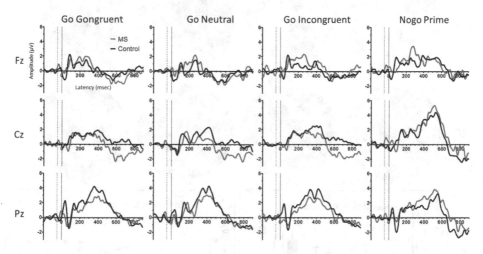

Fig. 3. Grand averaged ERPs for each trial type of the Go/Nogo Flanker task. The dashed line at −50 ms represents flanker onset. The solid line at 0 ms represents target onset. (Color figure online)

P3 Component. The P3 amplitude ANOVA yielded significant Condition X Group (F (3, 72) = 3.364, p = .034, gg corrected, η_p^2 = .123) and Condition X Lead (F(6, 144) = 7.419, p < .001, gg corrected, η_p^2 = .236) interactions. First we probed the Condition X Group interaction (see Fig. 4A and B). There were no statistically significant differences between the groups at any condition. However, it can be observed in the grand averages in Fig. 3, as well as the topographic maps in Fig. 4A that MS patients tended to have lower P3 Amplitude for Go trials, but higher P3 Amplitude for the Nogo Prime trials (especially at Cz and Pz), compared to HCs. For HCs, P3 amplitude was greater during Nogo Prime compared to Go Neutral and Congruent trials (p < .05 for both comparisons). For MS patients, the general pattern was that Nogo Prime > Go Incongruent > other Go conditions (p < .05 all comparisons). The Condition X Group interaction therefore appears to be driven by a larger relative difference between Nogo Prime and Go trial P3 amplitude in MS patients compared to HCs.

Next we probed the Condition X Lead effect (See Fig. 4A and C). For the Go Congruent and Go Neutral trials, P3 amplitude exhibited a pattern of Pz > Cz > Fz (parietal maxima, p ≤ .002 all comparisons). For Go Incongruent trials, P3 amplitude was lower at Fz compared to both Cz and Pz (p < .05 both comparisons). For Nogo Prime trials, P3 amplitude was greater at Cz compared to both Fz and Pz (p ≤ .019 both comparisons). In sum, the Condition X Lead effect for P3 amplitude appears to illustrate the typical Nogo anteriorization effect, wherein Nogo Prime trials exhibited a more anterior P3 amplitude compared to the Go trials.

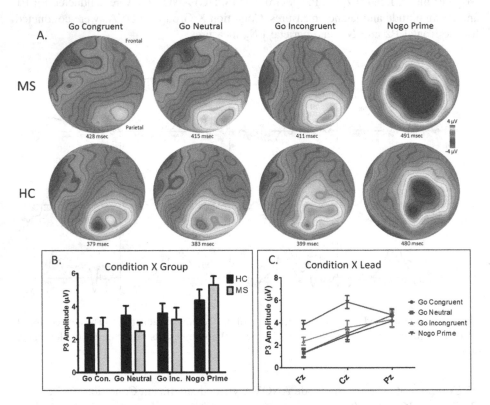

Fig. 4. (A) Topographic maps depict amplitude data above the canthomeatal line. The time point depicted is listed beneath each map (in msec) and corresponds to the group average for that condition. (B) and (C) depict mean and SEM for relevant P3 amplitude effects. (Color figure online)

The ANOVA for P3 latency revealed significant effects for Condition (F(3, 72) = 22.089, p < .001, η_p^2 = .479) and Group (F(1, 24) = 4.644, p = .041, ηp2 = .162). Post-hoc tests revealed that the Condition effect was driven by longer P3 latency for Nogo Prime compared to Go trials (p < .001 all comparisons). Longer P3 latency across conditions in MS patients compared to HCs accounts for the Group effect.

Frontal N2 Component. There were no significant main effects or interactions for the ANOVA for N2 amplitude. The N2 latency ANOVA revealed a significant Group effect (F(1, 24) = 9.486, p = .005, η_p^2 = .283), and a borderline Condition effect (F(3, 72) = 2.426, p = .073, η_p^2 = .092). The Group effect can be accounted for by longer N2 latencies in MS patients compared to HCs, irrespective of Condition (see Fig. 3).

P1 Component. The ANOVA for P1 amplitude yielded a significant Condition X Lead interaction (F(6, 144) = 2.595, p = .015, gg corrected, η_p^2 = .130). Post-hoc tests revealed that P1 amplitude at Fz was lower for Go Neutral compared to Go Congruent and Incongruent trials (p ≤ .008 for both comparisons); whereas P1 amplitude was greater for Go Neutral compared to Go Incongruent trials at Pz (p = .049, see Fig. 3). Notably, P1 amplitude was not different between groups.

For P1 latency, the ANOVA revealed a significant Lead X Group interaction (see Fig. 2B; F(2, 48) = 3.993, p = .025, η_p^2 = .143). There was a borderline Condition X Group interaction (F(3, 72) = 2.448, p = .071, η_p^2 = .093), and a significant effect for Condition (F(3, 72) = 5.228, p = .003, η_p^2 = .179). Probing the Lead X Group effect revealed that MS patients had longer P1 latency compared to HCs at Fz and Cz (p < .05 both comparisons), but not at Pz. Post-hoc tests for the Condition effect revealed that P1 latency was earlier for the Go Congruent trials compared to Go Neutral and Nogo Prime trials (p < .05). There was also a trend for earlier P1 latency for Go Incongruent compared to Go Neutral trials (p = .053).

Frontal P2 Component. For the P2 amplitude ANOVA, there was a significant Condition effect (F(3, 72) = 2.884, p = .042, η_p^2 = .107), but no effect or interaction involving the Group factor. The Condition effect was driven by greater overall P2 amplitude for the Nogo Prime trials compared to the other conditions (p < .05 all comparisons, see Fig. 3). The ANOVA for P2 latency revealed a significant Condition X Group interaction (see Fig. 2C; F(3, 72) = 4.544, p = .006, η_p^2 = .159). MS patients had longer frontal P2 latency compared to HCs for Go Incongruent and Nogo Prime trials (p ≤ .005 both comparisons, see Fig. 3), only. Thus, the interaction for P2 latency appears to be driven by prolonged latencies in MS patients compared to HCs for trials with distracting flankers.

Parietal Early Positive-Negative Complex (PN$_p$). The pronounced early parietal positivity and immediate subsequent negativity of the PN$_p$ appeared to be closely coupled in time, and we were therefore interested in examining this complex as a unit. We derived an amplitude measure for PN$_p$ by subtracting the negative peak amplitude from the positive peak amplitude of the complex for each subject, at each condition. The ANOVA for PN$_p$ yielded a significant Group effect (F(1, 24) = 5.087, p = .033, η_p^2 = .175, see Fig. 3), which can be accounted for by lower overall amplitude in MS patients compared to HCs.

4 Discussion

In the present study we examined ERPs obtained for a Go/Nogo Flanker task in MS patients and HCs. This task allowed for the assessment of conflict monitoring and response inhibition while also manipulating the level of distraction induced by the flanker stimuli. For Go trials, RT was enhanced by congruent flankers and delayed by incongruent flankers, across both groups. However, MS patients had delayed RT in general compared to HCs, across all Go trial types. The ERP results indicated disruptions at multiple stages of cognitive control in MS patients compared to HCs. MS patients exhibited (1) delays in ERP components reflecting early selective attention (longer P1 and frontal P2 latencies), (2) delayed latencies in components reflecting conflict monitoring (N2) and inhibitory control (P3), and (3) alterations in neural resources underlying inhibitory functioning, as evidenced by P3 amplitude effects. Reduced amplitude was also observed in MS patients for an ERP component complex with a very early onset that may reflect initial processing of the flanker stimuli (PN_p).

The Nogo P3 anteriorization effect was observed in both groups (Condition X Lead effect, Fig. 3A and C), consistent with the extant literature [9] and previous work that has used a Go/Nogo Flanker type task [10]. The P3 did not appear to be very strongly modulated by congruency of the Go flanker stimuli (but there were perhaps subtle differences for incongruent trials, see Fig. 4C). While this finding was true for both groups, MS patients exhibited a general attenuation of Go P3 amplitude and an enhancement of Nogo P3 amplitude compared to HCs (Condition X Group effect, see Figs. 3 and 4). Enhanced Nogo P3 amplitude in MS patients may reflect the need for additional recruitment of inhibitory resources to inhibit a response during Nogo trials. Attenuation of P3 amplitude during Go trials for MS patients may mean something different; it could potentially be an index of inefficient processing, altered resource allocation, or decreased resource recruitment, during response selection and stimulus/response evaluation. Further, P3 latency was also delayed in MS patients compared to HCs, across all conditions, indicating delayed central processing speed with respect to stimulus evaluation and/or inhibitory control.

N2 amplitude was not modulated as a function of trial type, nor was it different between groups, contrasting with some previous findings [10, 13, 18]. One possibility for this is that the flankers in our study, which occurred 50 ms prior to stimulus onset, engaged conflict monitoring processes (which are thought to be reflected by the N2 [9]) similarly across conditions. N2 latency, however, was prolonged in MS patients compared to HCs, which may reflect poorer efficiency and/or greater processing time to resolve conflict in MS.

Longer latencies were also observed in MS patients for several other ERP components. MS patients had longer P1 latency at frontal-central leads compared to HCs across all conditions of the task. While it is not typically examined in Go/Nogo paradigms, the P1 component is generally thought to reflect early selective attention and suppression of distracting information [17]. The delay in P1 latency in MS compared to HCs could possibly reflect delays in selective attention to the target stimulus and away from the flankers. The frontal P2 component had a longer latency in MS compared to HCs, but only for the Go Incongruent and Nogo Prime trials, which had the most distracting flanker stimuli. The delay in P2 latency in MS patient may therefore reflect delayed central processing speed under conditions for which there are incongruent or highly distracting non-target/flanker stimuli. This notion is also consistent with the belief that the P2 reflects selective attention and stimulus evaluation [17].

We identified an early positive-negative complex (PN_p) which emerged prior to the onset of the identified target related P1 component. The positive and negative components of this complex are clearly observed at parietal leads for the HCs, but they seem to be visibly attenuated in the MS group. This observation was confirmed with statistical analysis. This complex has not been examined previously in similar paradigms, but a positive-negative complex with similar timing can be observed in the grand averages reported in earlier studies that used a similar task [11, 18], although no analyses were conducted for these components. Given the timing of the PN_p, one could speculate that it may reflect very early processing of the flanker primes. It may be analogous to a P1-N1 complex, but in this case it may be associated with the flanker presentation, reflecting processing prior to the onset of the target-associated P1. Given the lack of prior research regarding this complex in this paradigm, this analysis should be regarded as exploratory. Further work is required to determine the nature of this complex and whether it may reflect legitimate dysfunction in MS. But it is nonetheless intriguing as a potential early marker of the dysfunction of priming processes in MS patients.

The present study was the first to examine a broad range of ERP components during a Go/Nogo Flanker task in MS patients. There were several limitations, including a relatively small sample size, age differences between groups, and the exploratory nature of some of the analyses (i.e., PN_p). The only previous study that examined ERPs in MS patients using a similar task focused the analysis on the error-related negativity (ERN) during "stop" trials [13]. The present study found that MS patients had longer RT compared to HCs during Go trials. Longer latencies were observed in MS patients for components that reflect early selective attention (P1, frontal P2), conflict monitoring processes (N2), and inhibitory processing/evaluation (P3). Frontal P2 latency delays in MS, in particular, may reflect delayed processing when the flankers are particularly distracting (Go Incongruent, Nogo Prime). Further, the Nogo P3 anteriorization effect was generally stronger in MS patients compared to HCs, likely reflecting a need to recruit additional neural resources to adequately perform the task and inhibit a response. The results demonstrate dysfunction in stimulus evaluation and in cognitive control processes in MS at multiple stages of processing.

Acknowledgements. This study was supported by pilot research grant PP2249 from the National Multiple Sclerosis Society and by a University at Buffalo Mark Diamond Research Fund Graduate Student Grant.

References

1. Cercignani, M., Iannucchi, G., Rocca, M.A., Comi, G., Horsfield, M.A., Filippi, M.: Pathologic damage in MS assessed by diffusion-weighted magnetization transfer MRI. Neurology **54**, 1139–1144 (2000)

2. Kutzelnigg, A., Lucchinetti, C.F., Stadelmann, C., Bruck, W., Rauschka, H., Bergmann, M., Shmidbauer, M., Parisi, J.E., Lassmann, H.: Cortical demyelination and diffuse white matter injury in multiple sclerosis. Brain **128**, 2705–2712 (2005)

3. Sanfilipo, M.P., Benedict, R.H.B., Sharma, J., Weinstock-Guttman, B., Backshi, R.: The relationship between whole brain volume and disability in multiple sclerosis: a comparison of normalized gray vs. white matter with misclassification correction. NeuroImage **26**, 1068–1077 (2005)

4. Chiaravalloti, N.D., DeLuca, J.: Cognitive impairment in multiple sclerosis. Lancet Neurol. **7**, 1139–1151 (2008)

5. Covey, T.J., Zivadinov, R., Shucard, J.L., Shucard, D.W.: Information processing speed, neural efficiency, and working memory performance in Multiple Sclerosis: Differential relationships with structural magnetic resonance imaging. J. Clin. Exp. Neuropsychol. **33**, 1129–1145 (2011)

6. Lazeron, R.H.C., Boringa, J.B., Schouten, M., Uitdehaag, B.M.J., Bergers, E., Lindeboom, J., Eikelenboom, M.J., Scheltens, P.H., Barkhof, F., Polman, C.H.: Brain atrophy and lesion load as explaining parameters for cognitive impairment in multiple sclerosis. Multiple Sclerosis **11**, 524–531 (2005)

7. Sacco, R., Bisecco, A., Corbo, D., Della Corte, M., d'Ambrosio, A., Docimo, R., Gallo, A., Esposito, F., Esposito, S., Cirillo, M., Lovorgna, L., Tedeschi, G., Bonavita, S.: Cognitive impairment and memory disorders in relapsing-remitting multiple sclerosis: the role of white matter, gray matter, and hippocampus. J. Neurol. **262**, 1691–1697 (2015)

8. Sanfilipo, M.P., Benedict, R.H.B., Weinstock-Gutmann, B., Bakshi, R.: Gray and white matter brain atrophy and neuropsychological impairment in multiple sclerosis. Neurology **66**, 685–692 (2006)

9. Huster, R.J., Enriquez-Geppert, S., Lavallee, C.F., Falkenstein, M., Herrmann, C.S.: Electroencephalography of response inhibition tasks: functional networks and cognitive contributions. Int. J. Psychophysiol. **87**, 217–233 (2013)

10. Groom, M.J., Cragg, L.: Differential modulation of the N2 and P3 event-related potentials by response conflict and inhibition. Brain Cogn. **97**, 1–9 (2015)

11. Kopp, B., Mattler, U., Goertz, R., Rist, F.: N2, P3 and the lateralized readiness potential in a nogo task involving selective response priming. Electroencephalogr. Clin. Neurophysiol. **99**, 19–27 (1996)

12. Shaurya Prakash, R., Erickson, K.I., Snook, E.M., Colcombe, S.J., Motl, R.W., Kramer, A.F.: Cortical recruitment during selective attention in multiple sclerosis: an fMRI investigation of individual differences. Neuropsychologia **46**, 2888–2895 (2008)

13. Lopez-Gongora, M., Escartin, A., Martinez-Horta, S., Fernandez-Bobadilla, R., Querol, L., Romero, S., Angel Mananas, M., Riba, J.: Neurophysiological evidence of compensatory brain mechanisms in early-stage multiple sclerosis. PLoS ONE **10**, e0136786 (2015)

14. Uttl, B.: North American adult reading test: age norms, reliability, and validity. J. Clin. Exp. Neuropsychol. **24**, 1123–1137 (2002)

15. Polman, C.H., Reingold, S.C., Banwell, B., Clanet, M., Cohen, J.A., Filippi, M., et al.: Diagnostic criteria for multiple sclerosis: 2010 revisions to the McDonald criteria. Ann. Neurol. **69**, 292–302 (2011)

16. Covey, T.J., Shucard, J.L., Violanti, J.M., Lee, J., Shucard, D.W.: The effects of exposure to traumatic stressors on inhibitory control in police officers: a dense electrode array study using a Go/NoGo continuous performance task. Int. J. Psychophysiol. **87**, 363–375 (2013)

17. Fonaryova Key, A.P., Dove, G.O., Maguire, M.J.: Linking brainwaves to the brain: an ERP primer. Dev. Neuropsychol. **27**, 183–215 (2005)

18. Kopp, B., Rist, F., Mattler, U.: N200 in the flanker task as a neurobehavioral tool for investigating executive control. Psychophysiology **33**, 282–294 (1996)

Auditory Alarm Misperception in the Cockpit: An EEG Study of Inattentional Deafness

Frédéric Dehais[✉], Raphaëlle N. Roy, Thibault Gateau,
and Sébastien Scannella

Human Factors and Neuroergonomics Department, ISAE, 10 av E. Belin,
31055 Toulouse Cedex 4, France
{frederic.dehais,raphaelle.roy,thibault.gateau,
sebastien.scannella}@isae.fr

Abstract. Missing auditory alarms is a critical safety issue in many domains such as aviation. To investigate this phenomenon, we designed a scenario involving three flying scenarios corresponding to three different level of difficulty along with an oddball paradigm in a motion flight simulator. This preliminary study was conducted with one pilot equipped with a 32-channel EEG. The results shown that manipulating the three levels of task difficulty led respectively to rates of 0, 37, and 54 % missed alarms. The EEG analyses revealed that this decrease in performance was associated with lower spectral power within the alpha band and reduced N100 component amplitude. This latter finding suggested the involvement of inattentional deafness mechanisms at an early stage of the auditory processing. Eventually, we implemented a processing chain to enhance the discriminability of ERPs for mental state monitoring purposes. The results indicated that this chain could be used in a quite ecological setting (i.e. three-axis motion flight simulator) as attested by the good results obtained for the oddball task, but also for more subtle mental states such as mental demand and stress level and the detection of target, that is to say the inattentional deafness phenomenon.

Keywords: Inattentional deafness · Stress · ERP · EEG · Alarm perception · Aviation · Passive brain computer interface

1 Introduction

Auditory alarms are used to alert the human operators of impeding off-nominal situations. These auditory warnings present several advantages as long as their detection doesn't produce head movement. For instance, they lead to faster responses than their visual counterpart. However, many studies and safety analyses reported the absence of response to these auditory alarms in several critical domains [3,9,20]. This inability to detect alarms may find several explanations. For instance, poor warning systems design are known to trigger spurious alarms thus leading to the so-called "Cry Wolf effect": the human operator consciously neglects such warnings especially under high workload settings [27].

© Springer International Publishing Switzerland 2016
D.D. Schmorrow and C.M. Fidopiastis (Eds.): AC 2016, Part I, LNAI 9743, pp. 177–187, 2016.
DOI: 10.1007/978-3-319-39955-3_17

Moreover, the design of the auditory signal itself may fail to capture attention due to its lack of salience or if it is too loud and distracting [21]. Another explanation is to consider the inattentional deafness hypothesis that states that unattended auditory stimuli may fail to reach awareness under high visual load conditions [19]. Since flying is a demanding task [4] that largely involves the processing of visual cues [5], the occurrence of unexpected auditory alarms could remain unnoticed [6,7].

This hypothesis is supported by a recent experiment that involves a simplified landing decision task based on the analysis of visual indicators under different load conditions while continuous electroencephalography (EEG) measurements were performed. During the task, a tone was presented, either a standard one, which participants were told to ignore, or a deviant one ("the alarm") which participants were told to overtly report. The analysis of the event related potentials (ERPs) showed that a drastic diminution of the late auditory component (P300) amplitude was concomitant with the occurrence of inattentional deafness [12]. However, the underlying concepts of scarce attentional resources may not be sufficient to fully account for the inattentional deafness phenomenon [16]. A complementary approach is to consider the existence of the visual dominance over hearing as demonstrated in several paradigms [26]. Reinforcement learning since childhood has probably lead the human beings to rely on visual information rather than on auditory ones. It is admitted that 80 % of the data to handle the flight safely are visual ones, thus leading the pilot to trust visual cues. Indeed, when visual information conflict with auditory ones, or when task demand is high, automatic gating mechanisms may take place and inhibit the processing of auditory information [17,18]. In order to verify this hypothesis, we recorded in a previous study electrophysiological measurements while participants supervised a simplified automated landing sequence by considering both visual and auditory signals. Our results revealed evidence of an early visual-to-auditory gating mechanism that occurs when visual parameters ("land") were contradictory to the auditory alarm ("go around"). This mechanism attenuates early auditory processing (N100) and could provide an alternative explanation to the inattentional deafness phenomenon in aeronautics [23].

In the present study, we intended to investigate auditory misperception with EEG in a motion flight simulator. The main objective of this study was to implement realistic experimental scenarios that could cause inattentional deafness under more ecological conditions than in previous work [12,23]. We therefore manipulated three different level of difficulty and test their effectiveness over the auditory signal detection. These three scenarios were tested on one pilot equipped with a 32-channel EEG. Eventually, in order to assess the feasibility of performing mental state estimation in the cockpit, we tested the use of machine learning algorithms on the collected data set.

2   Material and Method

2.1   Flight Simulator

We used the ISAE three-axis motion (roll, pitch, and height) flight simulator designed by the French Flight Test Center to conduct the experiment. It simulates a twin-engine aircraft flight model. The user interface is composed of a Primary Flight Display, a Navigation Display, and an upper Electronic Central Aircraft Monitoring Display page. The flight simulator is equipped with classical actuators such as the side-stick, the rudder, the throttle, the flaps levers and a complete autopilot to control the flight. Two stereophonic speakers, located under the displays on each side of the cabin, were used to broadcast continuous radio communications and the engine sound (70 dB), as well as to trigger the oddball sounds.

2.2   Scenarios

The participant performed three scenarios that differed from each other in the level of difficulty. In each of these scenarios, we used an oddball paradigm (stimulation with matlab psychtoolbox-3) with a total of 280 auditory stimuli: 70 targets (normalized pure tone, 1100 Hz at 88 dB) and 210 non-targets (normalized pure tone, 1000 Hz at 88 dB). The pilot used a Cedrus response pad, located below the throttle lever, to respond to auditory targets only, in each scenario (Figs. 1 and 2). The three scenarios lasted for about eight minutes each and were defined as follows:

- "Level 0" scenario: This was the reference scenario. In this experimental condition, the autopilot was engaged to level off the plane at a constant speed. The only task for the pilot was to respond to auditory target stimuli.
- "Level 1" scenario: This scenario consisted of performing a night manual approach and landing at Blagnac Airport (Toulouse, France) following the official procedure. The plane was initiated 30 nautical miles (NM) from Toulouse VOR DME (a radio beacon) at an altitude of 5000 ft. The pilot had to steer the aircraft to a heading of 210 degrees for 17 NM descending to an altitude of 3000 ft. He then had to steer 270 degrees until his radio-navigation beacon indicated a radial of 310 degrees. He eventually had to align to a heading of 144 degrees to capture the lateral axis of Toulouse Blagnac airport. In a distance of 5NM from Toulouse VOR DME, the pilot could initiate his descent to land safely on the landing ground.
- "Level 2" scenario: This scenario was identical to the previous one to the exception that we triggered a burning left-engine event at the beginning. A red light was flashing in the cockpit and we used a Bundle FOG 400 device to smoke out slightly the cabin every one minute. Moreover, this night landing was performed with no visibility. Eventually, the pilot was told that he had 8 min to perform this emergency landing.

Fig. 1. Participant in the motion flight simulator.

Fig. 2. Level 2 scenario, with smoke and red flashing warning. (Color figure online)

3   Participant and Protocol

The participant was a pilot (24 year old, 50 flight hours) from Institut Superieur
de l'Aeronautique et de l'Espace (ISAE) campus, recruited by local advertise-
ment and did not receive any payment for his participation. As a PPL pilot, he
reported normal or corrected-to-normal vision and normal audition. Once the
participant was told about the purpose of the experiment, he was sat in the
flight simulator, and the EEG was set. He then completed a 30 min training

session in which he performed manual approaches and landings. Eventually, he was then trained to perform the oddball task for five minutes. After the training, the experiment was started: the simulator motion was engaged to reproduce realistic flight sensations, and a continuous radio communication was also broadcasted to reproduce more ecological flight conditions.

3.1 Data Acquisition and Processing

A self-report of stress and mental demand level was collected using a visual analog scale (1 for very low, 7 for very high) after the experiment. Reaction times and accuracy for the detection of auditory alarms were collected using a Cedrus RB response-pad and stored in a matlab file.

EEG data were recorded continuously with a BioSemi EEG system (BioSemi©, Amsterdam) from 32 "active" (preamplified) Ag-AgCl scalp electrodes located according to the International 10/20 system, at a 512 Hz sampling rate and with a 0–104 Hz band-pass filter. The data were then re-referenced offline to the algebraic average of the left and right mastoids, down-sampled to 500 Hz, and filtered with a band-pass of 0.1–40 Hz. An independent component analysis using EEGlab[1] (13.4.4b version) was performed to isolate and reject eye blinks and movements. Data were later segmented into 1200 ms epochs starting 200 ms before the onset of each sound. Spectral power analyses were carried out on the continuous data in the 8–12Hz band, and ERPs were computed using EEGlab.

Moreover, in order to assess whether these EEG data could be used for mental state monitoring purposes, a preliminary test of machine learning techniques was performed on the data of this subject. The processing chain included a 100 Hz resampling and a baseline correction using the first 200 ms of each epoch. Next, a spatial filtering step that has been proven to work efficiently to enhance the discriminability of ERPs for mental state monitoring purposes [22]. Contrary to Roy and collaborators, only one filter was kept here. The filter that was selected had the higher associated eigenvalue. Lastly, the filtered signal (60 samples) was classified using a robust Linear Discriminant Analysis (LDA) (i.e. with a shrinkage estimation of the covariance matrices; [24]) and a random 10-fold cross-validation procedure to check the LDA performance. We evaluated the feasibility of discriminating between two signals:

- at the single-trial level;
- averaging two trials, when applicable.

Three analyses were performed:

- The first one was designed to allow the assessment of the performance of the processing chain that was originally designed for laboratory settings by Roy and collaborators [22]. This first test was performed on the ERP discrimination of targets (hits) and distractors in the level 0 scenario (test 1).

---

[1] www.sccn.ucsd.edu/eeglab.

Therefore, in this case the algorithm attempts to classify the **targets** vs. the **distractors**.

- The second test was performed on the binary estimation of the stress and mental demand using only the correctly detected targets for the level 0 and the level 1 scenarios (test 2). In this case, the algorithm attempts to classify the task demand, that is to say the **level 0** vs. the **level 2** conditions.
- The third test was performed on the binary estimation of the detection of targets in the level 2 scenario (test 3). Here, the algorithm attempts to classify the target **hits** vs. **misses**.

4   Results

4.1   Subjective and Behavioral Measurements

The Table 1 reports the participant's subjective ratings (stress, mental demand) for each scenario.

Table 1. Subjective rating

	Level 0	Level 1	Level 2
Stress	1	3	5.5
Mental demand	1	4	6.5

The analyses of the behavioral results revealed that the level of difficulty of the scenarios impacted the pilot's alarm detection rate. In the first scenario (level 0: level off flight) the pilot missed no alarm whereas he missed 38 % of them in the "level 1" condition (night landing). This rate increased in the third scenario ("level 2" condition: night landing with smoke in the cockpit) as the pilot misssed 58 % of alarms (Fig. 3).

4.2   Physiological Measurements

Scenario Load. The spectral analysis of the continuous EEG data showed a decrease of alpha power at parietal sites as a function of stress and mental demand (Fig. 4). More precisely, a decrease of the 10 Hz band was observed between "level 0" ($11.65 \mu V^2 / Hz$) and "level 1" ($9.5 \mu V^2 / Hz$). In addition, a larger decrease of the 10 Hz was observed between the "level 1" ($9.5 \mu V^2 / Hz$) and the "level 2" scenario ($3.5 \mu V^2 / Hz$).

Load × Sound Interaction. When looking at the interaction between the scenraio type and the sound type, we found that the sound-related N100 amplitude was affected differentially by the scenario depending on the sound type. Scalp topographies at 114 ms revealed a decrease of the fronto-central N100 amplitude for the more demanding scenario compared to the reference one for both the

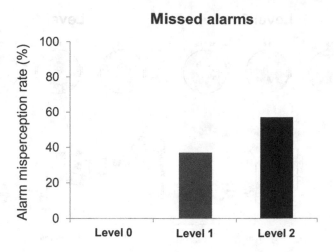

Fig. 3. Behavioral results of the participant.

standard sound and the alarm (Fig. 5). However, only the alarm-related N100 amplitude decreased in the "level 1" condition compared to the reference one. In addition, the N100 amplitude in the "level 0" scenario was larger for the alarm than for the standard sound while it was the opposite in the "level 1" scenario.

4.3   Deafness Classifier

The results obtained thanks to the passive BCI chain detailed in the Data acquisition and processing section are given in Table 2 for each mental state estimation procedure that was performed. For the first test, the attempt to classify the targets vs. the distractors in the level 0 condition, the best performance was obtained using the average of two trials, with 70 % of accuracy. This demonstrates that the chosen processing chain can work well in an ecological setting for a simple oddball task. As regards the more subtle mental state estimation tests, for both the workload level estimation and the detection estimation, the best performance is reached with a single trial, with respectively 61 % and 60 % of accuracy. Although far from perfect, these results show that it is possible to estimate detection and engagement in an ecological setting with performances above chance level.

5   Discussion

The main objective of this paper was to investigate inattentional deafness under realistic settings. We manipulated three levels of difficulty across the scenarios. In the reference scenario, the flying task was easy and not stressful as the pilot only had to respond to auditory alarms. In the second one, the task was more demanding and stressing as it involved a night approach and landing while responding to alarms. The last one was designed to be the most stressing and

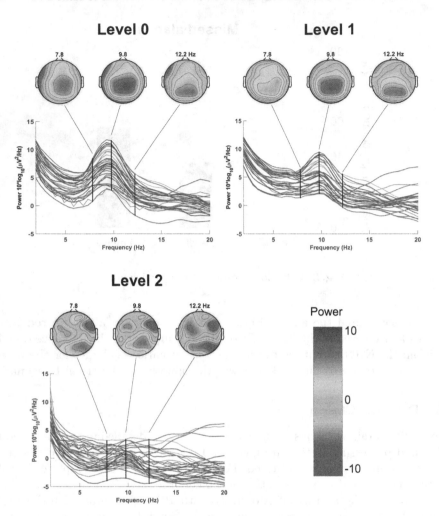

Fig. 4. Power spectral results on continuous EEG data for the three scenarios.

demanding as it involved a night approach and landing with a simulated engine failure (i.e. flashing warning and smoke in the cockpit). The participant's subjective results confirmed our assumptions as his rating indicated an increased level of stress and mental demand across the scenarios. As expected, the behavioral results revealed that the rate of missed alarms increased across these three scenarios (respectively of 0, 37, and 54 %). Consistently with these findings, the EEG frequency analysis revealed a decrease in spectral power within the alpha band across the three scenarios. Indeed, decrease in the this frequency band is associated with higher task demand [28] and stress situations [1]. Taken together our subjective, behavioral and electrophysiological results suggested that, when combined, increased task demand and stress were efficient to induce a high rate

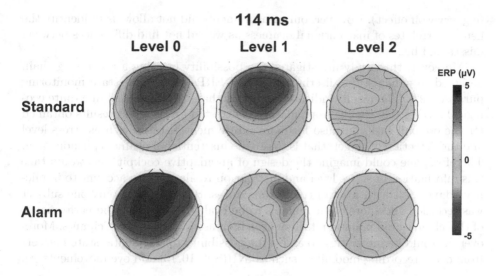

Fig. 5. Scalp topographies plotted at 114 ms post-stimulus onset.

Table 2. Mental State Estimation: average *(standard deviation)* performance for the 3 tests.

	Description		Algorithm performance	
Test	Classes	Condition	1 trial	2 trials
test 1	Targets vs Distractors	Level 0	60.60 *(2.68)*	**69.5 (3.56)**
test 2	Level 0 vs. Level 2	Hits	**61.42 (5.16)**	59.13 *(5.38)*
test 3	Hits vs. Misses	Level 2	**59.74 (5.96)**	58.14 *(2.48)*

of auditory misperception. They confirmed previous findings that increased task demand [11,12,16,23] and stress [7] impair attentional abilities. However, our experimental design did not allow us to disentangle the contribution of each of these factors to provoke this phenomenon.

The ERP analyses highlighted findings at the perceptual level with the N100 component. This ERP is the early electrophysiological signal of the stimulus processing in auditory primary cortices around 100 ms post-stimulus. In accordance with previous findings [15,25], the N100 amplitude was higher during the processing of the auditory alarm (low probability stimulus), than during the processing of the frequent sound in each conditions. More interestingly, the N100 amplitude was reduced as the level of difficulty increased, concomitantly with lower behavioral responses to the auditory alarm. It is well admitted that the N100 amplitude is an index of auditory-attention allocation [14]. This result may therefore suggest that an inattentional deafness phenomenon has occurred at the perceptual level (i.e. 100 ms). If this phenomenon had occurred at 300 ms (which was not the case) when the alarm reached awareness, one could have argued that it was a conscious and voluntary inhibition of the alarm (e.g. cry wolf effect). However, our measurements did not allow us to identify the neural correlates of inattentional deafness as we did not find differences between misses and hit.

Moreover, this study investigated the possibility of using a processing chain designed to enhance the discriminability of ERPs for mental state monitoring purposes [22]. The results indicated that this chain could be used in a quite ecological setting (i.e. the flight simulator) as attested by the good results obtained for the oddball task, but also for more subtle mental states such as stress level and the detection of target, that is to say the inattentional deafness phenomenon. Therefore, one could imagine the design of an adaptive cockpit that would take this information of stress level and inattention to alarms into account to implicitly adapt itself with a set of counter-measures. However, here only one subject was recorded and therefore it remains to be evaluated whether the performance of this chain would maintain itself or even increase for several participants. Moreover, it would be interesting to assess the possibility to use mental state markers from other recording modalities such as fNIRS [2,10,13] and eye movements [8].

Aknowledgement. This work was funded by Direction Generale de l'Armement ("Neuroergo" Project) and by the AXA Research Fund ("Neuroergonomics for flight Safety" Chair). We would like to express ou sincere gratitude to the members of the "Fondation ISAE" for their support.

References

1. Alonso, J., Romero, S., Ballester, M., Antonijoan, R., Mañanas, M.: Stress assessment based on eeg univariate features and functional connectivity measures. Physiol. Meas. **36**(7), 1351 (2015)
2. Ayaz, H., Shewokis, P.A., Bunce, S., Izzetoglu, K., Willems, B., Onaral, B.: Optical brain monitoring for operator training and mental workload assessment. Neuroimage **59**(1), 36–47 (2012)
3. Bliss, J.P.: Investigation of alarm-related accidents and incidents in aviation. Int. J. Aviat. Psychol. **13**(3), 249–268 (2003)
4. Causse, M., Péran, P., Dehais, F., Caravasso, C.F., Zeffiro, T., Sabatini, U., Pastor, J.: Affective decision making under uncertainty during a plausible aviation task: an fmri study. NeuroImage **71**, 19–29 (2013)
5. Dehais, F., Causse, M., Pastor, J.: Embedded eye tracker in a real aircraft: new perspectives on pilot/aircraft interaction monitoring. In: Proceedings from The 3rd International Conference on Research in Air Transportation. Federal Aviation Administration, Fairfax (2008)
6. Dehais, F., Causse, M., Régis, N., Menant, E., Labedan, P., Vachon, F., Tremblay, S.: Missing critical auditory alarms in aeronautics: evidence for inattentional deafness?. In: Proceedings of the Human Factors and Ergonomics Society Annual Meeting, vol. 56, pp. 1639–1643. Sage Publications (2012)
7. Dehais, F., Causse, M., Vachon, F., Régis, N., Menant, E., Tremblay, S.: Failure to detect critical auditory alerts in the cockpit evidence for inattentional deafness. Hum. Factors J. Hum. Factors Ergon. Soc. **56**(4), 631–644 (2014)
8. Dehais, F., Peysakhovich, V., Scannella, S., Fongue, J., Gateau, T.: Automation surprise in aviation: real-time solutions. In: Proceedings of the 33rd Annual ACM Conference on Human Factors in Computing Systems, pp. 2525–2534. ACM (2015)

9. Dehais, F., Tessier, C., Christophe, L., Reuzeau, F.: The perseveration syndrome in the pilot's activity: guidelines and cognitive countermeasures. In: Palanque, P., Vanderdonckt, J., Winckler, M. (eds.) HESSD 2009. LNCS, vol. 5962, pp. 68–80. Springer, Heidelberg (2010)
10. Gateau, T., Durantin, G., Lancelot, F., Scannella, S., Dehais, F.: Real-time state estimation in a flight simulator using fnirs. PloS one **10**(3), e0121279 (2015)
11. Giraudet, L., Imbert, J.P., Tremblay, S., Causse, M.: High rate of inattentional deafness in simulated air traffic control tasks. Procedia Manuf. **3**, 5169–5175 (2015)
12. Giraudet, L., St-Louis, M.E., Scannella, S., Causse, M.: P300 event-related potential as an indicator of inattentional deafness? PLoS one **10**(2), e0118556 (2015)
13. Hernandez-Meza, G., Slason, L., Ayaz, H., Craven, P., Oden, K., Izzetoglu, K.: Investigation of functional near infrared spectroscopy in evaluation of pilot expertise acquisition. In: Schmorrow, D.D., Fidopiastis, C.M. (eds.) AC 2015. LNCS, vol. 9183, pp. 232–243. Springer, Heidelberg (2015)
14. Hink, R.F., Van Voorhis, S., Hillyard, S., Smith, T.: The division of attention and the human auditory evoked potential. Neuropsychologia **15**(4), 597–605 (1977)
15. Kramer, A.F., Trejo, L.J., Humphrey, D.: Assessment of mental workload with task-irrelevant auditory probes. Biol. Psychol. **40**(1), 83–100 (1995)
16. Kreitz, C., Furley, P., Simons, D.J., Memmert, D.: Does working memory capacity predict cross-modally induced failures of awareness? Conscious. Cogn. **39**, 18–27 (2016)
17. Lebib, R., Papo, D., de Bode, S., Baudonnière, P.M.: Evidence of a visual-to-auditory cross-modal sensory gating phenomenon as reflected by the human p50 event-related brain potential modulation. Neurosci. Lett. **341**(3), 185–188 (2003)
18. Macaluso, E., Driver, J.: Multisensory spatial interactions: a window onto functional integration in the human brain. Trends Neurosci. **28**(5), 264–271 (2005)
19. Macdonald, J.S., Lavie, N.: Visual perceptual load induces inattentional deafness. Attention Percep. Psychophysics **73**(6), 1780–1789 (2011)
20. Meredith, C., Edworthy, J.: Are there too many alarms in the intensive care unit? an overview of the problems. J. Adv. Nurs. **21**(1), 15–20 (1995)
21. Peryer, G., Noyes, J., Pleydell-Pearce, K., Lieven, N.: Auditory alert characteristics: a survey of pilot views. Int. J. Aviat. Psychol. **15**(3), 233–250 (2005)
22. Roy, R.N., Bonnet, S., Charbonnier, S., Jallon, P., Campagne, A.: A comparison of erp spatial filtering methods for optimal mental workload estimation. In: Engineering in Medicine and Biology Society (EMBC), 2015 37th Annual International Conference of the IEEE, pp. 7254–7257. IEEE (2015)
23. Scannella, S., Causse, M., Chauveau, N., Pastor, J., Dehais, F.: Effects of the audiovisual conflict on auditory early processes. Int. J. Psychophysiol. **89**(1), 115–122 (2013)
24. Schäfer, J., Strimmer, K.: A shrinkage approach to large-scale covariance matrix estimationand implications for functional genomics. Stat. Appl. Genet. Mol. Biol. **4**(1), 1175–1189 (2005)
25. Singhal, A., Doerfling, P., Fowler, B.: Effects of a dual task on the n100–p200 complex and the early and late nd attention waveforms. Psychophysiology **39**(02), 236–245 (2002)
26. Sinnett, S., Spence, C., Soto-Faraco, S.: Visual dominance and attention: the colavita effect revisited. Percept. Psychophysics **69**(5), 673–686 (2007)
27. Wickens, C.D., Rice, S., Hutchins, S., Keller, M.D., Hughes, J., Clayton, K.: False alerts in the air traffic control traffic conflict alerting system: is there a "cry wolf" effect? Hum. Factors J. Hum. Factors Ergon. Soc. **51**, 446–462 (2009)
28. Wilson, G.F.: An analysis of mental workload in pilots during flight using multiple psychophysiological measures. Int. J. Aviat. Psychol. **12**(1), 3–18 (2002)

Multi-model Approach to Human Functional State Estimation

Kevin Durkee[1(✉)], Avinash Hiriyanna[1], Scott Pappada[1],
John Feeney[1], and Scott Galster[2]

[1] Aptima, Inc., Fairborn, USA
{kdurkee,ahiriyanna,spappada,jfeeney}@aptima.com
[2] Air Force Research Laboratory, Dayton, USA
scott.galster@us.af.mil

Abstract. With the growth and affordability of the wearable sensors market, there is increasing interest in leveraging physiological signals to measure human functional states. However, the desire to produce a reliable universal classifier of functional state assessment has proved to be elusive. In efforts to improve accuracy, we theorize the fusion of multiple models into a single estimate of human functional state could outperform a single model operating in isolation. In this paper, we explore the feasibility of this concept using a workload model development effort conducted for an Unmanned Aircraft System (UAS) task environment at the Air Force Research Laboratory (AFRL). Real-time workload classifiers were trained with single-model and multi-model approaches using physiological data inputs paired with and without contextual data inputs. Following the evaluation of each classifier using two model evaluation metrics, we conclude that a multi-model approach greatly improved the ability to reliably measure real-time cognitive workload in our UAS operations test case.

Keywords: Context · Human performance · Modeling and simulation · Physiological measurement · Workload · UAS · Cognitive states

1 Introduction

With the dramatic growth and affordability of the wearable sensors market in recent years, there is increasing interest throughout many work domains in leveraging human users' real-time physiological signals to measure functional states, such as workload, stress, and fatigue. In military defensive settings, the ability to monitor these states throughout a mission would be a valuable asset to optimize mission operations and warfighter workflow. As the complexity of military operations continues to increase, warfighters will become increasingly vulnerable to undesired cognitive states. Measuring cognitive states in relation to task and mission performance would provide the requisite data to detect if, and when, a warfighter has met his/her limits while diagnosing what intervention is best suited to sustaining good performance and obtaining the desired outcomes. By introducing this capability, assessments of operator states would become

© Springer International Publishing Switzerland 2016
D.D. Schmorrow and C.M. Fidopiastis (Eds.): AC 2016, Part I, LNAI 9743, pp. 188–197, 2016.
DOI: 10.1007/978-3-319-39955-3_18

integral system parameters about the mission to be proactively monitored and addressed before potential problems occur [1].

The ability to obtain real-time physiological data carries promise for providing such a capability to the warfighter. Physiological data have the substantial benefit of being an objective source of information that is theoretically available from any person working in any domain. The use of physiological data to classify a human operator's state has been extensively researched over the past few decades, frequently suggesting the existence of measurable indicators that are predictive of a particular state, or change in state [2, 3]. The majority of research has employed some combination of electroencephalography (EEG) [4], electrocardiography (ECG) [5], pupillometry [6], or galvanic skin response (GSR) [7]. For example, in the Air Force Multi Attribute Task Battery (AF_MATB) environment, Wilson and Russell (2003) introduced a novel application of artificial neural networks (ANNs) trained to each individual human performer for real-time mental workload classification using six channels of brain electrical activity, as well as eye, heart, and respiratory signals [2]. Wang et al. (2012) also employed the AF_MATB to introduce a novel hierarchical Bayesian technique that showed promise for cross-subject workload classification [3]. Although the majority of these and other studies have been laboratory based and often employ costly and/or invasive monitoring equipment, recent improvements in sensor reliability, level of invasiveness, set-up time, and cost have made the concept more compelling for high-fidelity work environments.

Assuming sensor limitations are eventually overcome, as current trends would suggest, several additional limiting factors still exist that have hindered progress in the area of human functional state assessment. Perhaps the most notable challenge is lack of consistent physiological indicators of a particular state or change in state. Most commonly these inconsistent patterns in physiological signals occur as a function of individual differences across people. However, this issue can also frequently occur across time (e.g., different days or times of day) for a specific individual person. These differences can be drastic; for instance, a highly reliable indicator of workload level for one person could provide no utility in assessing workload for another person, or vice versa. Prior research has often been forced to cater to this challenge by training a classifier on a per-person, per-day basis [2], or by including a given person's data in both the model training and model testing sets [3], neither of which is practical for implementing in real-world environments. Additionally, some individuals have few, or weak, discernible physiological indicators of a functional state, making it difficult to build a reliable model to classify a state of interest.

Over the past few years, we have made progress designing a universal machine learning based approach to pinpoint a human operator's state with high resolution (0-100 scale) and update frequency (second-by-second) with physiological-based assessment [8]. Our concept was further expanded to evaluate the added precision offered by integrating contextual data with physiological signals within a Functional State Estimation Engine (FuSE^2) [9]. The addition of contextual data in particular was shown to provide noteworthy improvements to the challenge of inconsistent and/or weak patterns in one's physiological signals. Although this comes at the cost of a model classifier being tied to a specific task environment, these results did not require the use of personalized models that were trained to a specific individual [9].

In spite of these improvements, the desire to produce a universal computational model for functional state assessment has proved to be difficult, and there remains significant room for innovation to solve this problem. For this reason, we have continued to investigate novel and supplementary strategies for more consistent model classifier results that would provide the necessary reliability for real-world utilization. One concept that has not been thoroughly explored in human functional state assessment is the convergence of multiple model classifiers into a single measurement of state. There is evidence in other related fields such as adaptive system development that basing decisions on a multi-model approach can outperform the same decisions being made from a single-model approach [10]. We theorize a similar approach would improve human state assessment given the many different ways that one's physiological data could be modeled, each having its own unique benefits and drawbacks. In addition, for situations in which no given model is able to accurately measure a human functional state, a multi-model approach can increase our confidence that the measurement challenges may lie in the data set itself (e.g., due to lack of distinguishable patterns), rather than a flaw in the use of machine learning and model development. This would necessarily shift the focus toward the need for more distinct and consistent sources of sensor data that can better indicate a person's functional state.

The objective of this work was to explore to what extent a multi-model approach can increase the accuracy of physiological-based cognitive state classifiers in a UAS task environment. In particular, our goal was to explore the multi-model approach from a bottom-up perspective by decomposing a cognitive state of interest into multiple subcomponents that are each individually modeled and subsequently fused together to build the construct. In the following sections we review a UAS study that was used to produce data for building real-time workload classifiers within the FuSE^2 system using both the single-model and multi-model approaches for comparative analysis. We also opted to examine the effects of adding two contextual data inputs– human computer interaction (HCI) rate and primary task performance – to investigate if the effect of using a multi-model approach remained present after the accuracy boost presented in our previous analysis [9]. Although FuSE^2 is capable of on-line supervised learning to adapt to an individual for improving model accuracy, we restrict the scope of this paper solely to cross-subject workload classification since a universal "plug and play" model that does not require per-subject training would be an ideal technological milestone.

2   Methods

2.1   Data Collection

Data were collected within a simulated UAS task environment – the Vigilant Spirit Control Station (VSCS) [11] – at the Human Universal Measurement and Assessment Network (HUMAN) Laboratory located at Wright-Patterson Air Force Base. We focused exclusively on cognitive workload for this study and the ensuing model development effort so as to constrain the problem space to a single human functional state that has wide applicability, particularly to UAS operations, and a large body of literature to draw from as needed. The UAS task simulation employed the VSCS operator interface

(Fig. 1) paired with a Multi-Modal Communication (MMC) tool for issuing communication requests [12] and a custom-built lights and gauges monitoring display. The primary task objective was to track a high value target (HVT) while keeping the HVT continuously positioned on the center of the UAS sensor crosshairs. Simultaneously, participants conducted two secondary tasks: (1) monitor the lights/gauges display and acknowledge each system event via button presses; and (2) verbally respond to each communication request via the MMC tool. Task difficulty was manipulated by modifying the HVT speed and motion complexity, the number of communication requests, and the number of light/gauge events in each five-minute trial. This task paradigm allowed for a gradual titration of task difficulty across 15 five-minute conditions ranging from easy to hard, which was intended to induce variations in workload and performance for each participant.

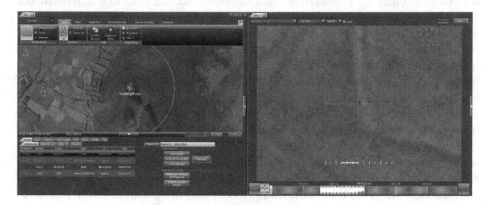

Fig. 1. The VSCS operator interface

There were 25 participants with each person completing one training session and one data collection session each. Dependent measures were threefold: (1) a suite of physiological metrics collected during each task condition consisting of six-channel EEG, ECG, off-body eye tracking, respiratory activity, electrodermal activity, and voice analysis features; (2) self-reported NASA Task Load Index (TLX) responses collected at the end of each trial [13]; and (3) system-based performance measures derived from Aptima, Inc.'s Performance Measurement Engine (PM Engine™) that utilized behavioral and situational data to estimate continuous performance for all three task requirements. NASA TLX responses and condition difficulties yielded a correlation of $r = 0.75$ across all subjects and $r = 0.89$ mean correlation within subjects, suggesting the manipulations were successful at inducing the intended variance in workload.

2.2 Model Development

Using the data collected from this study, a set of model-based classifiers was developed within the FuSE^2 system using machine learning techniques that train each classifier to output second-by-second workload estimates on a 0–100 scale. In accordance with the goals of this analysis, classifiers were trained for both the single-model and multi-model approach. The single-model approach was implemented in which the model inputs were trained directly to the composite NASA TLX response of total workload. In contrast, the multi-model approach was implemented in which a set of model inputs was trained to each of the six sub-scales of the NASA TLX provided by study participants. After the NASA TLX sub-scale models were trained as part of the multi-model approach, participants' sub-scale card sort data were used to weight each model's respective contribution in determining total workload. For both the single-model and multi-model approaches, this model training approach was done twice: once without contextual data as a model input, and once with contextual data as a model input.

Development of each model classifier adhered to the approach in Durkee et al. [8], in which we applied a noise injection algorithm to all NASA TLX responses under the assumption that workload does not remain perfectly static over time. This algorithm derives an estimate of "ground truth" on a second-by-second basis to which the model classifiers are subsequently trained. We refer to each series of ground truth estimates as the "desired model output" given each model classifier's attempt to find the best fit based on its feature inputs. Because it is impractical to obtain operator responses at very frequent intervals, this algorithm relies on a theoretically-grounded correlate of workload as the basis for injecting this noise. Although the same correlate was used for noise injection in the single-model approach as was done in our prior work [8, 9], the selected correlates for the sub-scale models in the multi-model approach varied. This was done because the six sub-scales that produce a NASA TLX value each have unique innate qualities that vary in different ways (e.g., mental demand varies based on mental activity, whereas physical demand varies based on physical activity). Hence, it was assumed the same correlate should not be used across these sub-scale models, and as such, careful consideration was given based on scientific theory supported with empirical literature.

Following the noise injection stage to produce desired model output values for training, a comprehensive training set was prepared containing all selected feature inputs and the desired model outputs. The training set included data from 19 of the 25 study participants, while the other six participants were randomly selected for model evaluation. A training process was initiated to derive model weights for each classifier based on minimizing error between the feature inputs and the desired model outputs. The selected physiological inputs for all model classifiers were three EEG channels (Fz, Pz, O2), ECG, and pupillometry; and, as previously mentioned, two versions of all models were created: one without context, and one with context.

2.3   Model Evaluation

After completing the model training process, the next objective was to produce test results in order to evaluate the accuracy of each workload classifier, particularly to assess how the multi-model approach impacted model accuracy relative to the single-model approach. Workload classifier results were produced through a batch playback of data collected from the six participants excluded from the training set. All six test participants completed the same 15 five-minute trials used to train the model classifiers, thus totaling 90 trials used for evaluation. The batch playback process simulated the production of real-time classifier results by outputting one workload estimate per second on a 0–100 scale for all models, totaling 300 values per model within each trial.

Model accuracy was analyzed via summary statistics in two ways: correlation and absolute difference between average model output and NASA TLX. In both cases, the summary statistics were used to assess how closely mean classifier output for each trial resembled its respective NASA TLX rating. A secondary objective was to assess the degree to which model accuracy changed as contextual data were included as model inputs alongside the physiological data inputs. A graphical plot is provided for each of the two model evaluation metrics along with discussion of observable trends. Each figure includes results on a per-participant basis across the two modeling approaches and both with/without context, for a total of four statistics per participant.

3   Results and Discussion

The two model evaluation metrics used in this analysis were: (1) correlation between average model output and NASA TLX; and (2) absolute difference between average model output and NASA TLX. For the correlation analysis, we believed it would be most suitable to derive a Pearson's correlation coefficient (r) on a per-person basis to better reflect how a given model tends to track any given person's cognitive workload across each trial. As such, the correlation coefficients for each of the six individual test participants and for all four workload classifications are illustrated in Fig. 2.

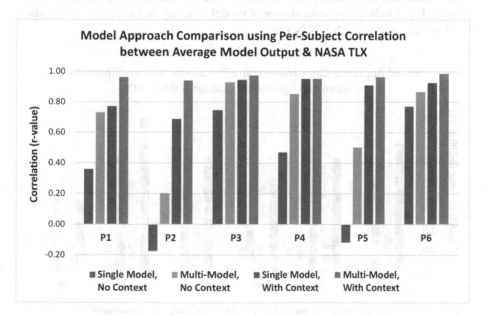

Fig. 2. Comparison of workload classification accuracy for six test participants using correlation between NASA TLX and average model output. (Color figure online)

The model approach with the highest correlations overall was the multi-model, with-context approach, which produced notably high correlations with $r = 0.94$ or higher for all six test participants. Perhaps the most noticeable finding in Fig. 2 is the consistent trend of improvement exhibited when shifting from a single-model approach to the multi-model approach, and similarly, from a no-context model to a with-context model. This trend occurs for all six test participants, albeit with varying degrees of improvement. This improvement is especially promising given the low correlations observed for participants P2 and P5 when using a single-model, no-context approach. The improvements in correlation were expected as a function of adding contextual data inputs. The effect of using a multi-model approach was less certain, though shifted in the hypothesized direction. From what can be observed in this small sample size, the magnitude of improvement for the multi-model approach was greater with the no-context models, as only minor improvements occurred for the with-context models. This may be due to the fact that with-context models already produced high correlations with a single-model approach. This finding may imply that for work environments in which contextual data inputs to workload classifiers are feasible, a multi-model approach might not be needed. However, if contextual data is not feasible as a model input, using a multi-model approach could produce substantial benefits.

The second model evaluation metric is the absolute difference between average model output and NASA TLX for each trial. This metric provides insight into each model's ability to produce workload classifications that accurately reflect the overall workload induced over the course of an entire trial. In contrast to Fig. 2, lower values shown in Fig. 3 indicate a greater degree of model accuracy by having a smaller difference from the desired NASA TLX value.

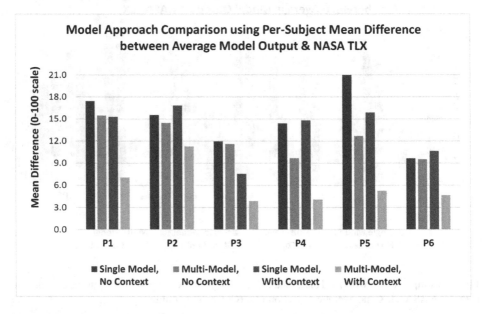

Fig. 3. Comparison of workload classification accuracy for six test participants using mean difference between NASA TLX and average model output. (Color figure online)

As shown in Fig. 3, the greatest accuracy (i.e., smallest difference from NASA TLX) was produced by the multi-model, with-context approach. On the 0-100 NASA TLX, this modeling approach resulted in a mean difference of less than 5.0 for four of the six test participants, with the other two participants having mean differences of 7.1 and 11.2 respectively. While this finding is generally consistent with the correlation statistics shown in Fig. 2, there are several additional key observations found in Fig. 3. Most notably, the magnitude of improvement using the multi-model approach is noticeably higher compared to the improvement provided by adding contextual data inputs. In five of the six test participants, shifting from a single-model, with-context approach to a multi-model, with-context approach reduced the mean difference by 50 % or greater. Further asserting the value provided with a multi-model approach is that a multi-model, no-context approach met or exceeded the single-model, with-context approach in five of the six test participants (P3 being the only exception).

4 Conclusions

In summary, we conclude that the utilization of a multi-model approach within our UAS task environment generally enhanced the FuSE^2 system's ability to accurately classify workload for 90 new trials across six test participants. This trend is observed for all six test participants across both model evaluation metrics (correlation & mean difference between NASA TLX and average model output) and occurs regardless of whether contextual data are included as model inputs. These results support our theory that relying on a single model classifier to produce consistently reliable estimates of human functional state presents risks, and that risk can effectively be mitigated through a diversified multi-model approach that is robust against the failure of any single model. We hypothesize the underlying cause of this potential improvement is due to the multitude of possible ways to process any given data set, and as such, each approach carries benefits and drawbacks that can never fully capture the entire picture in isolation. By blending a variety of approaches together, the complete picture can be more fully interpreted from multiple different angles and perspectives.

It is important to emphasize several key points to the multi-model approach that we believe influenced the promising results shown here. First, the human state assessments produced by the multi-model approach were driven bottom-up by the underlying NASA TLX sub-scale models. One potential drawback to the single-model approach is that workload, as the NASA TLX defines it, can be driven by different factors at different times, which may account for fewer discernible patterns to be discovered when focusing on the final aggregated NASA TLX value. We hypothesize that the FuSE^2 model classifiers were able to discover a more consistent pattern in the physiological and contextual training data sets by exposing the models to a more specific, low-level construct, as found in the NASA TLX sub-scales (namely, mental demand, physical demand, effort, frustration, temporal demand, and performance). Hence, it is possible that simply training a library of different models to the final aggregated NASA TLX value and fusing these results may not produce greater accuracy than a single-model approach. Another key point of emphasis is that each sub-scale model was trained using a different source of second-by-second noise that is theoretically most appropriate for each respective sub-scale construct. The mental demand sub-scale model, for example, used EEG data to drive this noise, whereas the physical demand sub-scale model used ECG data, as dictated by empirical research on these constructs.

Although these results are promising, future research is needed to more thoroughly investigate the multi-model approach with other human functional states and within different operator task environments. Additional research is also needed to investigate and compare the difference in model accuracy between the bottom-up developments of a human functional state classification approach (as was done in this analysis) versus training and fusing multiple models to assess the same construct. Next, further analysis must be done to assess the multi-model classifier approach on a second-by-second basis, rather than solely the aggregated classifier results across entire trials. Lastly, the present analysis and follow-on research needs should be performed with other combinations of physiological data features – in particular, non-EEG models that may also include blinks, saccades, and facial expressions, to name a few – that may be more appropriate for specific work environments of interest.

Acknowledgement. Distribution A: Approved for public release. 88ABW Cleared 01/25/2016; 88ABW-2016-0243. This material is based on work supported by AFRL under Contract FA8650-11-C-6236. Any opinions, findings, conclusions, or recommendations expressed in this material are those of the authors and do not necessarily reflect the views of AFRL.

References

1. Blackhurst, J., Gresham, J., Stone, M.: The quantified warrior: how DoD should lead human performance augmentation. Armed Forces J. **4**, 11 (2012)
2. Wilson, G.F., Russell, C.A.: Real-time assessment of mental workload using psychophysiological measures and artificial neural networks. Hum. Factors **45**(4), 635–644 (2003)
3. Wang, Z., Hope, R.M., Wang, Z., Ji, Q., Gray, W.: Cross-subject workload classification with a hierarchical bayes model. NeuroImage **59**(1), 64–69 (2012)
4. Gevins, A., Smith, M.E., Leong, H., McEvoy, L., Whitfield, S., Du, R., Rush, G.: Monitoring working memory load during computer-based tasks with EEG pattern recognition methods. Hum. Factors **40**, 79–91 (1998)
5. Hoover, A., Singh, A., Fishel-Brown, S., Muth, E.: Real-time detection of workload changes using heart rate variability. Biomed. Sig. Process. Control **7**, 333–341 (2012)
6. Just, M.A., Carpenter, P.A.: The intensity dimension of thought: Pupillometric indices of sentence processing. Can. J. Exp. Psychol. **47**(2), 310–339 (1993)
7. Setz, C., Arnrich, B., Schumm, J., La Marca, R., Troster, G.: Discriminating stress from cognitive load using a wearable EDA device. Technology **14**(2), 410–417 (2010)
8. Durkee, K., Geyer, A., Pappada, S., Ortiz, A., Galster, S.: Real-time workload assessment as a foundation for human performance augmentation. In: Schmorrow, D.D., Fidopiastis, C.M. (eds.) AC 2013. LNCS, vol. 8027, pp. 279–288. Springer, Heidelberg (2013)
9. Durkee, K., Pappada, S., Ortiz, A., Feeney, J., Galster, S.: Using context to optimize a functional state estimation engine in unmanned aircraft system operations. In: Schmorrow, D.D., Fidopiastis, C.M. (eds.) AC 2015. LNCS, vol. 9183, pp. 24–35. Springer, Heidelberg (2015)

10. Narendra, K.S., Balakrishnan, J.: Adaptive control using multiple models. IEEE Trans. Autom. Control **42**(2), 171–187 (1997)
11. Rowe, A.J., Liggett, K.K., Davis, J.E.: Vigilant spirit control station: a research testbed for multi-UAS supervisory control interfaces. In: Proceedings of the 15th International Symposium on Aviation Psychology, Dayton, OH (2009)
12. Finomore, V., Popik, D., Dallman, R., Stewart, J., Satterfield, K., Castle, C.: Demonstration of a network-centric communication management suite: multi-modal communication. In: Proceedings of the 55th Human Factors and Ergonomics Society Annual Meeting, HFES, Las Vegas (2011)
13. Hart, S.G., Staveland, L.E.: Development of NASA-TLX (Task Load Index): results of empirical and theoretical research. In: Peter, A.H., Najmedin, M. (eds.) Advances in Psychology, vol. 52, pp. 139–183. North-Holland, Amsterdam (2006)

Using fNIRS for Real-Time Cognitive Workload Assessment

Samuel W. Hincks[1](✉), Daniel Afergan[2], and Robert J.K. Jacob[1]

[1] Tufts University, Medford, MA 02145, USA
{shincks,jacob}@cs.tufts.edu
[2] Google Inc., Mountain View, CA 94043, USA
afergan@google.com

Abstract. In this paper, we evaluate the possibility of detecting continuous changes in the user's cognitive workload using functional near-infrared spectroscopy (fNIRS). We dissect the source of meaning in a large collection of n-backs and argue that the problem of controlling the content of a participant's mind poses a major problem for calibrating an algorithm using black box machine learning. We therefore suggest that the field simplify its task, and begin to focus on building algorithms that work on specialized subjects, before adapting these to a wider audience.

Keywords: fNIRS · Physiological interface · Implicit interface · Machine learning · Default mode network · Cognitive workload

1 Introduction

User interfaces typically deduce their user's intentions by measuring their physical gestures, within a tiny and agreed-upon space of device-dependent commands. Since the user produces each such input consciously, the mapping between physical gesture and digital effect should be transparent and immediate. Ongoing HCI research attempts to improve this bandwidth: to provide more information to the computer without posing an additional cognitive tax on the user. For example, whereas a conventional user interface (UI) is designed for a single prototypical user, a better UI recognizes differences among users, and can adapt its design appropriately.

But critical dimensions of the user vary from moment to moment. Humans, who like computers can be described with the metaphor of a continuously changing information processor, support multiple editions of themselves. Optimally, a user interface would characterize the user at each point in time. The goal of an *Implicit Interface* is to deduce the user's mood, intention, preference, and more general cognitive state from nonintentionally transmitted information. It then capitalizes on this information for the purpose of improved user experience in real time.

The design of an implicit or physiological interface can be divided into three parts:

- The *Measurement Component* dissects the user's cognitive processes into useful abstractions that can be inferred from behavioral or physiological data

© Springer International Publishing Switzerland 2016
D.D. Schmorrow and C.M. Fidopiastis (Eds.): AC 2016, Part I, LNAI 9743, pp. 198–208, 2016.
DOI: 10.1007/978-3-319-39955-3_19

- The *Data Mining Component* translates unorganized user data into accurate state predictions
- *The Design Component* crafts interfaces that adapt based on these predictions.

Work in implicit interfaces generally covers all three parts. This paper is motivated by the problem of building and calibrating a brain-computer interface based on functional near-infrared spectroscopy (fNIRS). We combine knowledge from cognitive and neuroscience with observations from single trial analysis to arrive at a set of recommendations. We first analyze a concrete implementation of an implicit interface using fNIRS, focusing on the possible improvements to the data mining components. The paper makes the following contributions:

- First, we reanalyze the data collected from a previous experiment [1] using machine learning.
- Second, to gauge the portability of this algorithm in a real-time cognitive workload prediction context, we examine the character of individual fNIRS trials.
- Third, we suggest a possible alternative method for inducing mental states involving controlled self-report and adaptively filtered fNIRS data
- Finally, we consider how thinking about psychological states in terms of task-positive and resting-networks may provide a more useful framework for interpreting fNIRS data.

2   Dynamic Difficulty Adjustment

2.1   Design Component

In [1], we identified a design problem. With j Unmanned Aerial Vehicles (UAVs) and k human monitors of these UAVs, what is the optimal distribution of the j UAVs among the k human monitors? The naive solution is to distribute workload equitably among the monitors (each one receiving j/k UAVs). However, each monitor has different cognitive endowment. In addition, their cognitive energy and capacity might fluctuate unpredictably over the course of an hour or a day. Equal distribution thus appears to be suboptimal. The UAV-monitor designer therefore poses a question to psychology: what cognitive abstractions can be characterized to elicit optimal user performance?

2.2   Cognitive Workload

We chose the cognitive workload or working memory state as cognitive abstraction. Working memory has fixed capacity and supports separate and somewhat parallelized buffers for different formats of data (spatial, verbal, episodic) [4]. It can be induced by the n-back task. In a visuospatial 1-back, the subject identifies whether or not a square on a grid matches what was seen in a previous iteration; in a visuospatial 2-back, the subject responds whether or not it matches the arrangement two iterations ago. Engagement of working memory activates the dorsolateral prefrontal cortex (dlPFC) [17]. It is a prime candidate for detection via EEG [9] as well as through peripheral physiological correlates such as changes pupillary response [5] and heart rate variability [14]. A useful physiological sensor for HCI has a likely entry-point into consumer grade electronics as well as a very specific physiological trace that is unlikely to be tricked by a user in motion in an unpredictable real world setting. For this reason, we focus on functional Near Infrared Spectroscopy (fNIRS).

2.3 Functional Near Infrared Spectroscopy

Given its relatively exterior neurobiological housing in the dlPFC, cognitive workload invites convenient detection using non-invasive light-based neuroimaging. fNIRS is a neuroimaging technique especially well-suited as a supplementary input device in a Brain-Computer Interface [1, 2, 11, 12, 15, 16]. A light source beams near infrared light that penetrates skin and bone; it is differentially absorbed by oxygenated and deoxy-genated hemoglobin in the neural bloodstream, so that a measurement of the photons returning to a nearby sensor can indicate the relative proportion of either quantity. Since inter-neuronal communication (the basic computational process of any mental activity) demands a continuous stream of oxygen, measurements of oxygen provides a rough barometer of the activity of the probed region. The depth of effective probing is limited (the distance between light source and detector approximates the maximum depth), but, especially compared to EEG, fNIRS provides spatially well-resolved information, meaning the signal fluctuates mostly in response to changes in biology of the underlying region. It requires little calibration; light sources and detectors need only to be placed flush on bare skin adjacent to the cranium; and the basic components of fNIRS can likely be miniaturized and integrated cheaply and seamlessly into consumer grade electronics such as head-mounted wearable computers in the future [8]. In fact, several labs are in the process of building and refining such a low-cost fNIRS [6].

2.4 Data Mining Component

Seeking to adaptively control task difficulty in a UAV-operation setting, we thus sought to continuously portray a user's cognitive workload using fNIRS. We used machine learning to translate successions of fNIRS data into discrete classifications of the user's state. We calibrated the machine learning algorithm on easy and hard versions of the n-back task. Specifically, subjects completed the easy 1-back task for 25 s, rested for 15 s, before completing the harder 3-back task. When complete, basic statistical features (mean and slope) were computed from the time series. These features, along with the associated class (1-back vs 3-back), were then fed into a support vector machine (SVM). Trained, the SVM could then theoretically estimate the probability that unseen 30 s time-series of fNIRS data pertained to a user experiencing either high workload or low cognitive workload.

2.5 Results

In the adaptive condition, the number of UAVs under the user's jurisdiction changed based on fNIRS-detected workload, and this significantly reduced the amount of user error compared to a non-adaptive condition with equivalent overall work.

3 Limitations with Machine Learning

Machine learning, which was also used previously [1, 2, 11, 12], has several advantages for detecting cognitive state. It leverages optimized function fitting methods, allowing it to find patterns which might elude a human observer utilizing classical statistical techniques. It has a built-in system for confirming that a state can be reliably induced and measured in a subject by cross-fold validation. It generalizes nicely for calibrating new algorithms: one need only replace the calibration task and corresponding labels. It assumes, rightly, that subjects have different brains and that probe placements differ slightly from one experiment to another. Finally, it doesn't require the designer of the algorithm to possess advanced neuroscientific expertise as the burden of discovering neural correlates of state is left to automated pattern discovery.

But it also has several disadvantages. The state of cognitive workload induced by the benchmark task may not match the state of cognitive workload in the ordinary course of the experiment. It might be that that the n-back induces only a very specific cognitive workload state with a neural profile that does not reflect the more general state which the system endeavors to measure. Similarly, the n-back may not enlist processing in the dorsolateral regions under measurement for a particular subject, in which case the more general state of workload may be detectable even though calibration task failed to enlist it. Most problematically, the real time user experience is not organized into neat serial trials with preceding baselines periods and clear starting points. A machine learning algorithm is calibrated on 30 s time segments only to be required to make predictions of a real task in continuous time. In the best case, where a user would transition from a baseline resting state into a thirty second experience of high cognitive workload, the time series would only align with the trials of the calibration period at that one point: 30 s after rest. In theory, every other prediction is doomed because of fundamental misalignment with the structure assumed during calibration.

The lack of reasonable ground truth for a state outside of the format of a well-controlled induction task makes it impossible to evaluate how well a machine learning based algorithm is actually performing. All that is known is that, in some percentage of experiments, some percentage of dependent variables are significantly superior in an adaptive condition that hinges on accurate real-time prediction.

4 Machine Learning Reanalysis

The approach of only examining average data and delegating large portions of the problem to black box machine learning may work, but it stymies progress towards a better algorithm, and needs to be supplemented with a calculated break down into exquisitely well-controlled individual trials. In this paper, we try to dissect the fNIRS workload signal. We begin by looking at the average case, before breaking the problem down to individual subjects, and ultimately individual trials.

In an exploratory re-analysis of the 27 subjects in [1], leave-one-trial-out analysis of each subject resulted in an average case performance of 66.6 %. In other words, when a machine learning algorithm was fed all but one of the fifteen 1-back trials and fifteen

3-back trials for any given subject, it correctly identified the excluded testing trial as belonging to either 1-back or 3-back with 66.6 % accuracy. Although several features, filters, and machine learning algorithms were tested, optimal performance involved Weka's SMO support vector machine [18] processing the mean, standard deviation, and slope-of-best-fit on the whole and second half of every channel. This combination has proven most useful in this and other experiments [15]. Curiously, optimal performance omitted data preprocessing techniques and filtering, possibly because respiratory signals such as heart rate variability, captured by the standard deviation feature, provide information to the calculation of workload. The fact that offline analysis advises against preprocessing and filtering further substantiates the problem of building an online algorithm from evaluation in an offline setting.

Classification accuracies ranged from 34.4 % to 89.2 %, with a standard deviation of 13.9 %. Five subjects had classification accuracies above 80 % (subjects 27, 25, 10, 8, 12). These subjects warrant further investigation.

In order to dissect the source of meaning in the data and get a better sense of the difficulty of the problem, we have selected the five best subjects (as measured through machine learning), and applied the following steps of preprocessing to their data. First, we have applied the Modified Beer Lambert Law to extract Hb and HbO. For simplification, we then merged values from neighboring sources on the forehead into single channels, before z-scoring the data, and applying a moving average algorithm, which sets each value to be the average of 16 readings (the device samples at 11.9 Hz) as well as a low pass filter at a cutoff of 0.5 Hz. Finally, we have anchored each trial at 0, setting each point in the 25 s trial to reflect the difference between it and the starting point.

In Fig. 1, we have added all trials into a common dataset and then merged these into one graph, where the dotted line reflects the average value and the thickness of the area chart reflects one standard deviation. Selecting among four possible graphs: either left or right prefrontal cortex and either Hb or HbO, we selected the most visually distinguishable graph. This graph agrees with the average case reported in the literature; that higher workload tends to signify an increase in oxygenation, especially in the left PFC [10]. It also shows how the change in oxygenation happens slowly, beginning some time after the trial begins.

In Fig. 2, we have applied the same selection procedure but for each individual subject. We show each individual trial to get a sense of the underlying variation. We note that for four out of five subjects the most visually distinguishable was on the left prefrontal cortex.

Each subject exhibits a visually apparent pattern with individual exceptions to that pattern. The key to designing an accurate algorithm is to figure out why certain trials break the trend. There are two plausible reasons:

A spontaneous and unrelated respiratory trend might be overwhelming a consistent neurological response.
The user might have lost focus or otherwise solved the problem under a different cognitive profile, thereby generating a different neurological response.

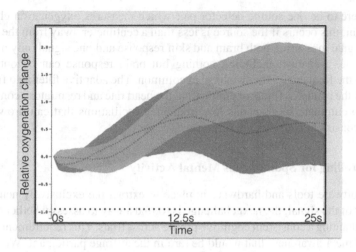

Fig. 1. Average left prefrontal cortex HbO activation for five subjects

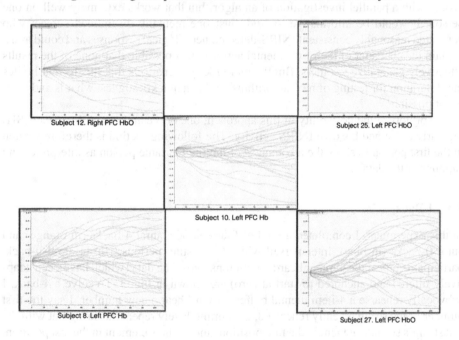

Fig. 2. Changes in Hb for five subjects

5 Towards a Better Algorithm

5.1 Adaptive Filtering

To mitigate the effect of spontaneous respiratory signals interfering with the true neurological response, it is possible to apply adaptive filtering [3, 19]. An adaptive filter requires there to be one source-detector pair which measures oxygenation changes in only the skin; this occurs if the source is less than a centimeter away from the detector. With one signal measuring both brain and skin response and one signal only measuring skin response, a channel including nothing but brain response can be obtained by subtracting the frequencies the two have in common. The adaptive filter also fulfills the purposes of the bandpass filters of eliminating the heart rate and respiratory components. It may also eliminate spontaneous low frequency oscillations that can drown out an otherwise consistent neurological response.

5.2   Controlling for Spontaneous Mental Activity

With the software tools and hardware in place to extract the exclusively neurological component of the signal, the next challenge is to find a way to assess whether or not the user is maintaining a consistent cognitive profile across trials. This requirement demands a degree of meta-awareness that would be rare in the average participant. We therefore combined our research that aims to build an algorithm that works moderately on many people with a parallel investigation of an algorithm that works extremely well on one person. It would be informative to study just one mentally disciplined subject who generated reasonably consistent fNIRS-detected neurological responses and could assist explain the character of their own mental activity. It is possible that none of the results effectively generalize to others. But the more likely scenario is that this format invites rapid iteration for testing of new algorithms, and can quickly suggest what is and what is not possible.

To prototype the possibility of this approach, one of the authors of this paper (SH) regularly examined his own fNIRS activity. The following section is therefore written in the first person to show the advantages of having the same person as interpreter and supplier of the data.

5.3   4-Back

In this experiment, I completed a total of fourteen 30 s aural 4-backs (in orange) and aural 0-backs (in blue), interspersed with 10 s resting periods. (In an aural n-back, participants repeat the number heard n iterations ago). The data (which have been adaptively filtered and anchored to start at zero) are shown in Fig. 3. To solve a 4-back, I subvocally rehearse a 4-item mental buffer. When I hear a new number, I say the first number of the string recently rehearsed, then immediately repeat the string but with the last string's second element in the first position, and the new element in the last position. As long as I keep escalating n, it is virtually impossible to solve the problem without granting the task the exclusive province of my attention. During a 0-back, I do not exert the same level of control over the activity of my mind. I complete the task, but occasionally my conscious mind is occupied by other thoughts or feelings.

What is especially interesting with fNIRS self-analysis is the possibility to dissect the trials which break an otherwise coherent pattern. The perfect self-analytical experiment is when you have a clear pattern, with exactly one exception. In this experiment, each condition has one exception. For the easy trials (when I was merely repeating

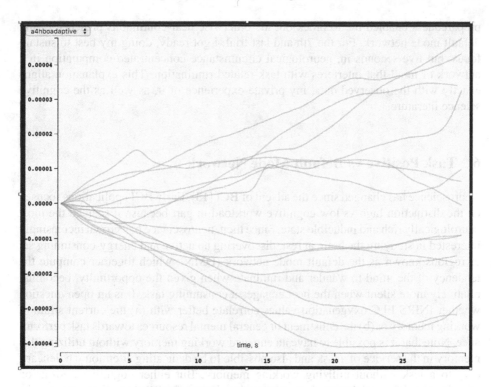

Fig. 3. Adaptively filtered change in HbO

numbers), one trial has the character of the 4-back trials. And for the 4-back trials, one trial has the character of the 0-back trials. The 4-back exception is especially interesting because it was the last trial in the series and I know exactly how it mentally unfolded. It was the last trial and I was getting tired. For the first five seconds, the trial unfolded like every other 4-back trial. I heard 0, then subvocally said zero. I heard 3; then subvocally said zero-three. I heard 5; then subvocally said zero-three-five. But then I heard six, and instead of adding it to a four-item buffer, I said aloud the first item in my buffer (zero), immediately noticed the mistake and then fumbled through the remainder trial unable to recover. Coincidentally, five seconds into the trial (approximately when I heard 5), there is a spike in the oxygenation levels in my left ventromedial prefrontal cortex.

There are three possible explanations for this. First, it could be entirely coincidental. I think this would be the wrong interpretation. The data is otherwise consistent, and the shift in oxygenation is a slope-value greater than anything observed in the dataset up until that point. Second, it is possible that I made the mistake, noticed the mistake, and the data reflects my frustration. But a subtle clue in the data dismisses this possible. The break in activation occurs two seconds *before* my noticing that I have failed the trial. That suggests the third possibility is true.

Five seconds into the trial, either a rhythmic biological force or a string of computational association, cemented computation in one of the nodes antithetical to proper focus. For 6/7 of the 4-back trials, a combination of task difficulty and mental preparedness enabled me to block out the otherwise near-continuous presence of my default mode network. For the 7th and last trial, I got ready, doing my best to sustain focus, but five seconds in, neurological circumstance concentrated computation in a network of mind that interferes with task-related rumination. This explanation aligns exactly with the observed data, my private experience of it, as well as the cognitive science literature.

6   Task Positive vs Default Mode Network

Neuroscience has changed since the advent of BCI [13]. Early BCI applications focused on the distinction high vs low cognitive workload in part because it seemed the most neurologically rich and inducible state. Since then, neuroscience has grown increasingly interested in studying the brain at rest, discovering an active and energy-consuming set of regions known as the default mode network (DMN), which together compute the tendency of the mind to wander and ruminate when given the opportunity, becoming relatively more silent when the host engages a consuming task. It is an open question whether fNIRS PFC oxygenation values correlate better with (a) the current strain of working memory or (b) the enlistment of general mental resources towards task performance. Note that it is possible to have an engaged working memory without utilizing this memory in the service of a task and also possible to be dedicating attention wholeheartedly to a task without utilizing working memory. But either cognitive abstraction explains the differentiability of an n-back signal from fNIRS data. Furthermore, the primary sensitivity of the fNIRS to (b) not (a) better fits the between subject variability of the signal.

With this more general portrayal of cognitive state, the failure to coerce a consistent cognitive state can easily be explained. In some cases, a 3-back requires the full enlistment of task-positive attention and the subject is both cognitively able and motivated to grant it. In other cases, because the task is too easy, too hard, or the subject is generally distracted, the subject is unable to enter a task-positive network. Similarly for the low workload induction: sometimes these trials are met with relative tranquility and other times a busily exploring default mode network.

Between participants, fMRI studies have shown that extroverts have a greater change in the fMRI signal in the dlPFC between three-backs and rest compared to introverts even though, behaviorally, they perform the same [7]. One explanation for this discrepancy is that introverts, being consistent self-monitors and relatively less capable to surrender attention to the external environment, fail to dislodge mild concurrent self-monitoring scripts as they complete n-backs. So while the cognitive processes in charge of their working memory remain their same, perhaps they fail to fully enter the task-positive network like the extroverts.

Task-related attention and cognitive workload overlap, but knowing them invites a different set of design considerations. The basic goal of any user interface is to facilitate task performance. Good user interfaces therefore mitigate distractibility and narrow their user's attention. Knowing the direction of the user's attention, internal or external, provides the basic measure governing the current effectiveness of a user interface: a broader and more useful piece of information than knowing the weight of their cognitive workload.

7 Conclusion

We suggest a return to simplicity in the design fNIRS-based cognitive state predictors. First, we recommend steering away from machine learning until the meaning of the data can be understood on a single trial basis. Second, we recommend adaptive filtering so that channels with exclusive brain activity can be examined. Third, we recommend perfecting an algorithm on only one or a handful of trained and disciplined subjects, before deciding how to train, calibrate, and deploy it on a random audience. Finally, we encourage future BCI studies, like contemporary neuroscience, begin to consider the relevance and usefulness of calibrating algorithms mind-wandering resting states.

References

1. Daniel, A., et al.: Dynamic difficulty using brain metrics of workload. In: Proceedings of the SIGCHI Conference on Human Factors in Computing Systems. ACM (2014)
2. Daniel, A., et al.: Brain-based target expansion. In: Proceedings of the 27th Annual ACM Symposium on User Interface Software and Technology. ACM (2014)
3. Aqil, M., et al.: Cortical brain imaging by adaptive filtering of NIRS signals. Neurosci. Lett. **514**(1), 35–41 (2012)
4. Baddeley, A.D., Hitch, G.: Working memory. Psychol. Learn. Motiv. **8**, 47–89 (1974)
5. Iqbal, S.T., Zheng, X.S., Bailey, B.P.: Task-evoked pupillary response to mental workload in human-computer interaction. In: CHI 2004 Extended Abstracts on Human Factors in Computing Systems. ACM (2004)
6. Si, J., Zhao, R., Zhang, Y., Zuo, N., Zhang, X., Jiang, T.: A portable fNIRS system with eight channels. In: SPIE BiOS, International Society for Optics and Photonics, 93051B–93051B (2015)
7. Kumari, V., Williams, S.C., Gray, J.A.: Personality predicts brain responses to cognitive demands. J. Neurosci. **24**(47), 10636–10641 (2004)
8. Ferrari, M., Quaresima, V.: A brief review on the history of human functional near-infrared spectroscopy (fNIRS) development and fields of application. Neuroimage **63**(2), 921–935 (2012)
9. Gevins, A., Smith, M.E.: Neurophysiological measures of cognitive workload during human-computer interaction. Theor. Issues Ergon. Sci. **4**(1–2), 113–131 (2003)
10. Herff, C., et al.: Mental workload during n-back task-quantified in the prefrontal cortex using fNIRS. Front. Hum. Neurosci. **7**(1), 935–940 (2013)
11. Peck, E., Afergan, D., Jacob, R.: Investigation of fNIRS brain sensing as input to information filtering systems. In: Proceedings of the 4th Augmented Human International Conference. ACM (2013)
12. Peck, E.M., et al.: Using fNIRS to measure mental workload in the real world. In: Fairclough, S.H., Gilleade, K. (eds.) Advances in Physiological Computing, pp. 117–139. Springer, London (2014)

13. Buckner, R.L., Andrews-Hanna, J.R., Schacter, D.L.: The brain's default network. Ann. N. Y. Acad. Sci. **1124**(1), 1–38 (2008)
14. Rowe, D.W., Sibert, J., Irwin, D.L.: Heart rate variability: indicator of user state as an aid to human-computer interaction. In: Proceedings of the SIGCHI Conference on Human Factors in Computing Systems. ACM Press/Addison-Wesley Publishing Co. (1998)
15. Solovey, E.T., et al.: Designing implicit interfaces for physiological computing: guidelines and lessons learned using fNIRS. ACM Trans. Comput.-Hum. Interact. (TOCHI) **21**(6), 35 (2015)
16. Solovey, E.T., et al.: Using fNIRS brain sensing in realistic HCI settings: experiments and guidelines. In: Proceedings of the 22nd Annual ACM Symposium on User Interface Software and Technology. ACM (2009)
17. Wager, T.D., Smith, E.E.: Neuroimaging studies of working memory. Cogn. Affect. Behav. Neurosci. **3**(4), 255–274 (2003)
18. Witten, I.H., et al.: Weka: practical machine learning tools and techniques with Java implementations, 17–81 (1999)
19. Zhang, Q., Strangman, G.E., Ganis, G.: Adaptive filtering to reduce global interference in non-invasive NIRS measures of brain activation: how well and when does it work? Neuroimage **45**(3), 788–794 (2009)

Modeling and Tracking Brain Nonstationarity in a Sustained Attention Task

Sheng-Hsiou Hsu$^{(\boxtimes)}$ and Tzyy-Ping Jung

Swartz Center for Computational Neuroscience,
Institute for Neural Computation,
University of California, San Diego, USA
{shh078, tpjung}@ucsd.edu

Abstract. In real-life situations, where humans optimize their behaviors to effectively interact with unknown and dynamic environments, their brain activities are inevitably nonstationary. Electroencephalogram (EEG), a widely used neuroimaging modality, has a high temporal resolution for characterizing the brain nonstationarity. However, quantitative measurements of EEG nonstationarity and its relations with human cognitive states and behaviors are still elusive. This study hypothesized that EEG nonstationarity could be modeled as changes of active sources decomposed by an Independent Component Analysis and proposed a model-based nonstationarity index (NSI) to quantitatively assess these changes. We tested the hypothesis and evaluated the NSI on EEG data collected from eight subjects performing a sustained attention task. Empirical results showed that values of the proposed NSI were significantly different when the subjects exhibited different levels of behavioral performance that inferred their brain states. The proposed approach is online-capable and can be used to track EEG nonstationarity in near real-time, which enables applications such as monitoring brain states during a cognitive task or predicting human behaviors in a brain-computer interface.

Keywords: Independent Component Analysis (ICA) · EEG · Nonstationarity

1 Introduction

In real-life situations, where humans organize and optimize their behaviors to deal with challenges in complex and ever-changing environments, their brain activities are inevitably nonstationary. Among a variety of biosignals, electroencephalography (EEG) has consistently exhibited neural correlates of human cognitions and has a high temporal resolution for characterizing the brain nonstationarity. However, more work is required to quantitatively measure the EEG nonstationarity and to investigate its relations with changes in human cognitive states and behaviors.

Previous EEG studies focused on time-frequency analyses of recordings from each scalp channel and found that changes of EEG band power correlated with brain states such as drowsiness levels [1, 2] under the assumptions that the number of underlying performance-related brain sources were fixed and their spatial locations were stationary.

© Springer International Publishing Switzerland 2016
D.D. Schmorrow and C.M. Fidopiastis (Eds.): AC 2016, Part I, LNAI 9743, pp. 209–217, 2016.
DOI: 10.1007/978-3-319-39955-3_20

On the contrary, this study assumed that as the brain changes between alertness and drowsiness states, the active brain sources might vary significantly.

Recent studies [3, 4] proposed a nonstationarity index (NSI) based on an adaptive Independent Component Analysis (ICA) method for detecting changes of co-activated brain sources or electrode displacements. Instead of using the NSI to evaluate errors of the adaptive ICA model, this study proposed to use the NSI to continuously and quantitatively assess deviations of brain activities from a fixed ICA model of a known brain state. In addition, we hypothesized that this concept could be applied to ICA models trained with EEG data from multiple brain states and the resultant NSIs could measure deviations of brain activities from the corresponding brain states and together may provide insights into brain nonstationarity. This study also modified the NSI used in [3, 4] to effectively measure model errors while ICA was applied to the new data and to reduce false alarms caused by artifacts. This study tested the hypothesis with EEG data collected from eight healthy volunteers performing a sustained-attention driving task [2, 5], where the subjects' brain states could be inferred by their behavioral performance.

2 Methods

2.1 Independent Component Analysis (ICA) Model

Standard ICA assumes a linear generative model, $x = As$, where x is N-by-T measurements (N: number of channels, T: number of time samples), s is unknown N-by-T source activities, and A is an unknown N-by-N mixing matrix. The blind separation of A and s can be solved by maximizing independence between sources, and the Infomax ICA [6] with natural gradient [7] has been used for efficient optimization with a general learning rule:

$$W \leftarrow W + \eta \left[I - f(y) \cdot y^T \right] W \tag{1}$$

where $y = Ws$, W is an "unmixing" matrix that ideally satisfies $WA = I$ such that $y = s$, I is an identify matrix, η is a learning rate, and f is a nonlinear function and is chosen differently across algorithms:

$$f(y) = \begin{cases} (1 - e^{-y})/(1 + e^{-y}), & \text{Infomax ICA} \\ \tanh(y) + y, & \text{Extended Infomax ICA} \end{cases}$$

The nonlinear functions defined above are for separating supergaussian sources, where most of sources in EEG data are supergaussian-distributed [3]. The learning in Eq. (1) stops when W converges, i.e. $\langle f \cdot y^T \rangle = I$, where $\langle \cdot \rangle$ represents an average over a block of data.

2.2   The Nonstationarity Index (NSI)

Recent studies [3, 4] have proposed that, instead of using $\langle f \cdot y^T \rangle$ as the ICA convergence criterion, this value could be a nonstationarity index that evaluates how well a model W fits new data. This index has been demonstrated to successfully detect abrupt electrode displacements [3] and changes of underlying sources [4] in simulated EEG data.

In this paper, instead of using the index to evaluate the performance of the adaptive ICA model described in [3, 4], we proposed to use the NSI to continuously and quantitatively assess deviations of brain activities from a fixed ICA model, W_0, of a known brain state. Specifically, we learned the model from a small amount of training data, applied the model to test data, x, in a sliding-window fashion, and computed a modified Nonstationarity Index (NSI):

$$NSI = \frac{\left\| \left\langle f_i \cdot y_j^T \right\rangle_{i \neq j} \right\|_F}{\| \langle y \cdot y^T \rangle \|_F} \qquad (2)$$

where $y = W_0 x$, $\left\langle f_i \cdot y_j^T \right\rangle_{i \neq j}$ represents off-diagonal elements of $\langle f \cdot y^T \rangle$, and $\| \cdot \|_F$ is the Frobenius norm. The numerator indicates the cross-talk errors of all sources in the model, W_0, when it fits the test data, removing the contributions of individual sources (diagonal elements); the denominator represents the covariance of the source activities and is applied to reduce false alarms of NSI caused by high-amplitude artifacts. A low NSI indicates that the model fits test data well and both training and test data are arising from the same set of brain sources. On the other hand, a high NSI represents the model fails to fit test data and thus the brain state has "shifted away" from that of the training data. The proposed NSI illustrates better empirical results and intuition compared to the NSI defined in [3, 4].

3   Materials

3.1   The Sustained Attention Task and EEG Data Processing

This study used the EEG data collected from eight subjects performing a sustained-attention driving task, which were analyzed and reported in [2]. During the task, the subjects were immersed in a driving simulator, where they were presented with lane-departure events and were instructed to steer the car back to the cruising position quickly. The duration from the onset of a lane-departure event to the onset of their responses was defined as reaction time (RT), which has been reported to be associated with alertness level or vigilance state [2, 8] The experiment lasted for 90 min such that various alertness levels were observed.

For each subject, 30-channel EEG data were recorded, band-pass filtered to 1–50 Hz, and down-sampled to 250 Hz. Bad channels in the recordings such as flat channels (due to poor contacts of electrodes) and poorly correlated channels (with single-channel isolated noises) were removed and interpolated using the PREP pipeline [9]. Furthermore, an online-capable artifact removal method, artifact subspace reconstruction (ASR) [10], was applied to reduce the effects of high-amplitude artifacts. These artifact-reduction methods facilitated the convergence of an ICA model.

3.2   EEG Analysis I: Relations Between NSI and RT Across Subjects

For each subject, the first 3-min EEG data were used to train an ICA model (W_0 in Eq. (1)) using the non-extended Infomax ICA implemented in EEGLAB [11]. It is worth noting that both the extended and non-extended Infomax ICA algorithms returned comparable results; we chose the one with less computational complexity. Principle Component Analysis (PCA) was applied before ICA to account for loss of data rank due to the removal of bad channels. The ICA model was then applied to the subsequent EEG data in a 30-s sliding window, and the NSI of the window was computed using Eq. (2) with $f(y) = (1 - e^{-y})/(1 + e^{-y})$.

The lane-departure trials were divided into three groups based on their RTs: short-RT (top 20 % trials with the shortest RT), moderate-RT (the top 20 % to 80 % trials), and long-RT (the bottom 20 % trials) groups according to [2]. Choosing the uneven numbers of trials in each group was because the RTs in the session were not normally distributed and the majority of trials had moderate RTs around one second. The NSI of each trial was defined as the NSI of the 30-s window right before the onset of the lane-departure event. Finally, the NSIs of all trials were z-scored within each session to remove inter-session variability, and three groups of trials were separately pooled across all subjects. For each pooled group of trials, its NSI's mean and standard error of mean were computed and two-sample unpaired t-test was performed to investigate the relations between the NSIs and the RTs.

3.3   EEG Analysis II: Comparisons of ICA Models and NSIs

To test the hypothesis that ICA models of different brain states and the resultant NSIs could measure deviations of brain activities from the corresponding brain states, we selected a typical subject who had significant fluctuations in RTs (local nonstationarity) through the session as an example. Under the assumption that behavioral performance (RT) reflects the subject's brain states (alertness vs. drowsiness states), we learned three ICA models based on 3-min data from different periods of the session: (a) an initial model using the first three minutes of the experiment (the black block in Fig. 1), (b) a drowsiness model using the data between minutes 15–18 (the red block in Fig. 1) where RTs were long, and (c) an alertness model using the data between minutes 40–43 (the green block in Fig. 1) where RTs were short. The same analysis (e.g. computation of NSI and grouping of trials) described in Sect. 3.2 was applied to the data from the subject except that no z-scoring of NSI and pooling of trials were needed for a single subject.

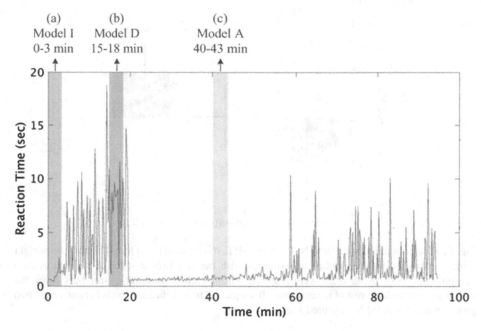

Fig. 1. The single-trial reaction times (RTs) over a 95-min experiment of a subject performing a lane-departure task. In the first 5 min of the session, the subject stayed alert and the RTs were short; from minutes 5 to 20, the subject had increased RTs that indicated drowsiness; from minutes 20 to 55, the subject performed very well again and went back to alertness state; from minute 55 to the end of the session, the subject had intermittent performance. Three 3-min blocks of data, on which ICA models were trained, were shown in the colored regions: Model I (Initial) 0–3 min, black; Model D (Drowsiness) 15–18 min, red; Model A (alertness) 40–43 min, green. (Color figure online)

4 Results

4.1 Relations Between NSIs and RTs Across Subjects

Figure 2 shows that the z-scored NSI of the short-RT trials were significantly lower than that of the moderate-RT trials, and the NSI of the moderate-RT trials were significantly lower than that of the long-RT trials. This result might have been due to the fact that the ICA model used to compute the NSI was trained with the first 3-min of the data where the subjects were fairly alert, evident from short RTs in response to lane-deviations within this period. The model therefore fitted the EEG data in alertness, and low NSI values were found for short-RT trials. In contrast, the model did not fit the EEG activities in drowsiness and resulted in high NSI values in long-RT trials. In sum, higher NSI value was associated with higher RT, suggesting that NSI could assess the deviations of current brain activities from the model trained with the data from the first three minutes of the experiment.

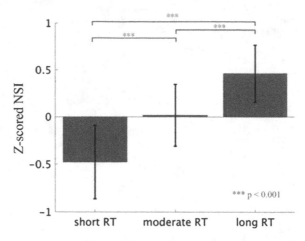

Fig. 2. The nonstationarity index (NSI) of short-RT, moderate-RT and long-RT trials from eight subjects using individual initial models (trained with the first three minutes of the data in each session). The NSIs of all trials were z-scored within each session. The error bars show the within-group standard error of mean across all subjects. The significance levels between each two groups were computed by unpaired t-tests.

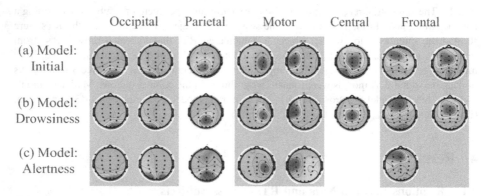

Fig. 3. Scalp maps of the select ICs from the three ICA models: (a) Model initial, (b) Model drowsiness, and (c) Model alertness. Occipital, parietal, motor, central, and frontal ICs were manually identified and grouped for comparisons.

4.2   Comparisons of ICA Models and NSIs

Figure 3 shows the validity and comparisons of the three ICA models as described in Sect. 3.3 (cf. Fig. 1). The models trained with 3-min of 30-channel EEG data ($250 \times 60 \times 3 = 45k$ samples) using the Infomax ICA were able to converge to ICs that were comparable and consistent with previous findings in [8]. Firstly, all three models successfully identified occipital, parietal, motor, central, and frontal components reported in [2, 8]. Secondly, we found appreciable differences between resultant component scalp maps obtained by the three ICA models trained with data from different brain states.

Figure 4 shows that both the initial model (Fig. 4a) and the alertness model (Fig. 4c) fitted the data of the short-RT trials well and resulted in lower NSI values than that of the moderate-RT trials; and the NSI values of the moderate-RT trials were significantly lower than that of the long-RT trials. On the other hand, the drowsiness model (Fig. 4b) fitted the data of the long-RT trials better and resulted in significantly lower NSI values than that of the moderate-RT and the short-RT trials.

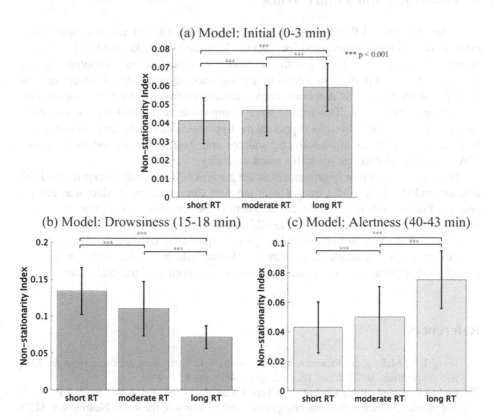

Fig. 4. The nonstationarity index of short-RT, moderate-RT and long-RT trials of the subject using three ICA models (shown in Fig. 1): (a) Initial model, (b) Drowsiness model, and (c) Alertness model. The error bars show the standard deviation within trials in each group.

In summary, the NSI of the drowsiness model was negatively correlated with RT while that of the alertness model was positively correlated with RT. Since the initial and the alertness model were trained with data from short-RT trials (corresponding to an alertness state), when the subject became drowsy, the brain activities have significantly changed from the data used to train the alertness model, leading to higher NSI values. In contrast, the drowsiness model was trained with the data from long-RT trials (corresponding to a drowsiness state), and thus higher NSI values were observed when the subject returned to alertness because the brain activities have significantly changed from the data used to train the drowsiness model.

Furthermore, the alertness model induced more significant differences in the NSIs between long-RT and short-RT trials than the initial model did, suggesting that training with data from shorter-RT trials could result in a more accurate model for the alertness state and a more effective NSI in tracking the corresponding nonstationarity.

5 Discussion and Future Work

Study results showed that the proposed ICA model-based NSI could quantitatively measure deviations of brain activities from the ICA model of a known brain state, e.g. alertness or drowsiness states, and the deviations or model errors correlated with the subjects' behavioral performance (RT) in the sustained-attention task. Furthermore, the NSIs based on multiple ICA models could all monitor the nonstationarity of the corresponding brain states. The results were comparable and consistent across eight subjects. These empirical results supported the hypothesis that brain nonstationarity can be modeled as changes of co-activated sources and their activities, and the proposed ICA model-based NSI can track this nonstationarity.

There is still room for improvement as the current NSI was still susceptible to EEG artifacts and the ICA model trained with the first three minutes of data was not yet optimal. Future work includes the development of new methods to improve the model performance and the robustness of the NSI to artifacts.

Finally, it is worth noting that the proposed approach is online-capable and can be used to track brain nonstationarity in near real-time, which enables many clinical and non-clinical applications that require continuous monitoring of the brain states.

References

1. Jung, T.P., Makeig, S., Stensmo, M., Sejnowski, T.J.: Estimating alertness from the EEG power spectrum. IEEE Trans. Biomed. Eng. **44**(1), 60–69 (1997)
2. Lin, C.T., Huang, K.C., Chao, C.F., Chen, J.A., Chiu, T.W., Ko, L.W., Jung, T.P.: Tonic and phasic EEG and behavioral changes induced by arousing feedback. Neuroimage **52**(2), 633–642 (2010)
3. Hsu, S.-H., Mullen, T., Jung, T.-P., Cauwenberghs, G.: Real-time adaptive EEG source separation using online recursive independent component analysis. IEEE Trans. Neural Syst. Rehabil. Eng. **24**(3), 309–319 (2015)
4. Hsu, S.H., Pion-Tonachini, L., Jung, T.P., Cauwenberghs, G.: Tracking non-stationary EEG sources using adaptive online recursive independent component analysis. In: Proceedings of the Annual International Conference of the IEEE Engineering in Medicine and Biology Society, EMBS, November 2015, pp. 4106–4109, August 2015
5. Huang, R.-S., Jung, T.-P., Makeig, S.: Event-related brain dynamics in continuous sustained-attention tasks. In: Schmorrow, D.D., Reeves, L.M. (eds.) HCII 2007 and FAC 2007. LNCS (LNAI), vol. 4565, pp. 65–74. Springer, Heidelberg (2007)
6. Bell, A.J., Sejnowski, T.J.: An information-maximization approach to blind separation and blind deconvolution. Neural Comput. **7**(6), 1129–1159 (1995)

7. Lee, T.-W., Girolami, M., Sejnowski, T.J.: Independent component analysis using an extended infomax algorithm for mixed subgaussian and supergaussian sources. Neural Comput. **11**(2), 417–441 (1999)
8. Chuang, C.H., Ko, L.W., Lin, Y.P., Jung, T.P., Lin, C.T.: Independent component ensemble of EEG for brain-computer interface. IEEE Trans. Neural Syst. Rehabil. Eng. **22**(2), 230–238 (2014)
9. Bigdely-Shamlo, N., Mullen, T., Kothe, C., Su, K.-M., Robbins, K.A.: The PREP pipeline: standardized preprocessing for large-scale EEG analysis. Front. Neuroinform. **9**, 16 (2015)
10. Mullen, T., Kothe, C., Chi, Y.M., Ojeda, A., Kerth, T., Makeig, S., Cauwenberghs, G., Jung, T.P.: Real-time modeling and 3D visualization of source dynamics and connectivity using wearable EEG. In: Proceedings of the Annual International Conference of the IEEE Engineering in Medicine and Biology Society, EMBS, pp. 2184–2187, January 2013
11. Delorme, A., Makeig, S.: EEGLAB: an open source toolbox for analysis of single-trial EEG dynamics including independent component analysis. J. Neurosci. Methods **134**(1), 9–21 (2004)

Linking Indices of Tonic Alertness: Resting-State Pupil Dilation and Cingulo-Opercular Neural Activity

Stefanie E. Kuchinsky[1,2($\boxtimes$)], Nick B. Pandža[1,3],
and Henk J. Haarmann[1]

[1] Center for Advanced Study of Language, University of Maryland,
College Park, MD, USA
{skuchins, npandza, hhaarman}@umd.edu
[2] Maryland Neuroimaging Center, University of Maryland,
College Park, MD, USA
[3] Program in Second Language Acquisition, University of Maryland,
College Park, MD, USA

Abstract. Maintaining alertness is critical to the successful performance of a variety of tasks, ranging from target detection to language comprehension. Previous studies have identified neural correlates of fluctuations in alertness, namely the cingulo-opercular network (CON) and the default mode network (DMN). The current study examined the extent to which pupil dilation, an autonomic physiological response, tracks variation in the CON and DMN in a functional neuroimaging and pupillometry resting-state session. The results revealed that increasing pupil dilation was associated with increasing CON activity and decreasing DMN activity, and that regions of these networks were functionally anti-correlated. Furthermore, individuals with better self-reported attention control abilities (i.e., more mindful of the present moment) exhibited a reduction in the trade-off between these systems. These results suggest that pupillometry provides a valuable proxy of activity in the neural systems that underlie alertness, which may be impacted by individual differences in mindfulness.

Keywords: Alertness · fMRI · Mindfulness · Pupillometry · Resting-state networks

1 Introduction

Successfully performing a long or tedious task depends on one's ability to maintain alertness. Also referred to as arousal, sustained attention, or vigilance (but contrasted with focused attention) [1], alertness is associated with broad sensitivity to changes in the environment or in one's internal state. Fluctuations in alertness are regulated by the widespread cortical release of norepinephrine via the locus coeruleus (LC) brainstem nucleus [2]. In particular, baseline LC activity is characterized by a relatively slow, tonic pattern of neural firing, which is linked to the intrinsic control of general arousal, that is, *tonic alertness* [3].

© Springer International Publishing Switzerland 2016
D.D. Schmorrow and C.M. Fidopiastis (Eds.): AC 2016, Part I, LNAI 9743, pp. 218–230, 2016.
DOI: 10.1007/978-3-319-39955-3_21

Cortical neural and physiological proxies of LC function have been investigated in order to circumvent the methodological challenges of recording LC brainstem activity in humans [4]. In particular, the LC has connections with the cingulo-opercular network (CON), which comprises the anterior cingulate cortex (ACC), bilateral anterior insulae/frontal opercula (AI/fO), and thalamus. The CON is engaged in challenging conditions [5], but more broadly, as individuals maintain alertness either at rest or during a task [6–8].

For example, in a recent functional magnetic resonance imaging (fMRI) study, participants performed a vigilance task in which they identified brief targets presented at unpredictable intervals [6]. Greater activity in the CON prior to stimulus presentation predicted better target detection. Interestingly, a vigilance benefit was also associated with reduced suppression of the default mode network (DMN). The DMN, whose core regions include the precuneus, bilateral angular gyri (AG), and the medial prefrontal cortex (mPFC), is canonically suppressed during task performance but upregulated at rest [9] or during mind wandering or self-reflection [10, 11]. Though DMN and CON activity are commonly anti-correlated across time [12, 13], research has shown that this relation varies across individuals [14] and following attention-based training programs (i.e., mindfulness meditation) [15, 16]. However, less is known about the extent to which CON-DMN connectivity is modulated by individual differences in the tendency to be aware of one's environment versus self-reflect, that is, their dispositional mindfulness [17].

Though there is mounting evidence that the balance between CON and DMN activity indexes tonic alertness, fMRI biomarkers are not feasible to collect for a variety of environments or individuals. Physiological measures of alertness may be more practical, such as pupil dilation, which is an autonomic, physiological response that varies with phasic and tonic changes in LC activity [18, 19]. Additionally, increasing pupil size has been associated with greater alertness in rats [20] and with noradrenergic drugs that increase arousal in humans [21].

Additional research is needed, however, to elucidate the extent to which pupil dilation can be used as a proxy of CON and DMN activity, or if it instead indexes a limited portion of the tonic alertness continuum (e.g., from attentive to inattentive). For example, one recent study has demonstrated that average pupil dilation across an fMRI resting-state scan, in which participants are given no explicit task, was correlated with activity in the LC and with regions of the ACC, right insula, and visual cortex [19]. These types of scans are sensitive to spontaneous fluctuations in neural activity across time (for example, as individuals naturally cycle through various states of alertness). This study suggests, then, that pupil dilation intrinsically varies with activity in attention-related regions. However, only positive correlations between dilation and neural activity were reported (increasing dilation with increasing activity) and only within a subset of CON regions. Given that the ACC and DMN are typically anti-correlated, we additionally predict that decreasing pupil dilation should be associated with greater DMN activity.

The current resting-state study aims to replicate and extend previous work by testing the extent to which (1) increasing pupil dilation is related to greater activity in regions of the CON, (2) decreasing dilation is related to greater activity in regions of the DMN, and (3) these areas function as coherent networks that are anti-correlated with one another. Finally, following research suggesting that individual differences in awareness of one's own attentional states modulates the relationship between CON and DMN activity [15, 16], we examined the extent to which (4) self-reported dispositional mindfulness altered functional connectivity between these networks.

2   Method

2.1   Participants

Twenty-three young adult participants were included in this study (an additional 15 were tested but had unusable pupillometry data, defined below). Participants were 18 to 30 years old ($M = 20.8$, $SD = 3.2$; 14 female), monolingual native American-English speakers, and right-handed (Edinburgh Handedness Inventory [22], $M = 84.6$, $SD = 11.6$, on a scale from -100 = maximally left handed to $+100$ = maximally right handed). All reported normal or corrected-to-normal visual acuity and hearing, no history of neurological or psychological disorders or events, no history of drug abuse, and no contraindications for MRI scanning, such as metal implants. They also indicated that they had no more than minimal meditation experience (e.g., breathing exercises during beginner-level yoga, but no mindfulness meditation exposure) and were not currently involved in cognition- or meditation-based training. Participants gave informed consent in compliance with the University of Maryland Institutional Review Board and the Declaration of Helsinki and were compensated for their participation.

2.2   Materials

Participants completed questionnaires regarding demographics, handedness, and mindfulness online using Qualtrics software (Provo, UT). The Five Facet Mindfulness Questionnaire (FFMQ) is a measure of individual differences in mindful disposition in daily life activities [23]. Participants self-report on a five-point Likert scale how true each of 39 statements are for them (e.g., "When I'm walking, I deliberately notice the sensations of my body moving"). A total mindfulness score was obtained by summing the responses (with appropriate items reverse scored): values could range from 39 (minimum) to 195 (maximum dispositional mindfulness).

2.3   Procedure

After providing informed consent, participants completed demographic and handedness questionnaires. In the MRI environment, structural and field-mapping scans were collected prior to the resting-state functional scans.

During the subsequent functional scans, physiological measurements were collected to control for potential individual differences that could confound our imaging results (i.e., respiration, heart rate). Respiration and heart rate were collected using a BIOPAC system that sampled at 1000 Hz (BIOPAC Systems, Inc., Goleta, CA, USA).

Pupil dilation was measured with an MR-compatible EyeLink 1000 Hz eye tracker (SR-Research, Ontario, Canada).

The resting-state scan lasted nine minutes and was collected prior to any experimental task to avoid potential carry-over effects that could influence network activity during the resting state [24]. For the duration of the scan, participants were instructed to fixate on five hash marks in the center of the screen (i.e., #####), which subtended four degrees of visual angle horizontally and one degree vertically. Such eyes-open, central fixation protocols have been shown to yield more robust and reliable patterns of resting-state connectivity, including for regions of the DMN and CON [25].

Following the scan session, participants filled out the FFMQ questionnaire, were debriefed, and compensated for their participation.

2.4 Analysis

Pupillometry. Pupil size values that the eye-tracker software detected as poor quality, occurring during a blink, a saccade, or a fixation that fell along the extreme edges of the screen (more than two-thirds of the screen width or height away from center), were removed and linearly interpolated. Participants for whom more than 50 % of the data required interpolation were removed from analyses [26]. Of the remaining 23 participants, on average 23.1 % ($SD = 16.8$ %) of trial time points were interpolated. Data were smoothed with a five-point moving average, down-sampled into 2200 ms bins to match the acquisition rate of the functional images (following previous research [19]), and z-score transformed. Finally, linear regression was used to estimate the extent to which the horizontal and vertical coordinates that described the gaze position predicted pupil size for each trial. The residualized variance, after accounting for the impact of gaze position on pupil, was entered into neuroimaging analyses. The average non-normalized pupil size for each individual was not correlated with the FFMQ scores, $r(21) = .16$, $p = .47$.

Neuroimaging. *Preprocessing.* Structural images were preprocessed using SPM8 (http://www.fil.ion.ucl.ac.uk/spm). The images were coregistered to Montreal Neurological Institute (MNI) space, skull-stripped (Brain Extraction Toolkit; [27]), segmented (using the New Segment tool), and the gray-matter segmented images were then normalized to a gray-matter standard-space MNI template.

Functional images were preprocessed using SPM8. Steps included: slice time correction, realignment and unwarping, coregistration to the MNI-aligned structural image, normalization to MNI space (using the warping parameters derived from structural preprocessing), and smoothing (8 mm kernel). The Linear Model of the Global Signal method [28] was then used to detrend the global mean signal fluctuations from the preprocessed images. Image volumes with significantly deviant signal (more than 2.5 standard deviations) relative to the global mean and with a significantly deviant number of voxels from their voxel-wise mean across the run were identified and modeled as two nuisance regressors in the first-level analysis [29]. Two motion nuisance regressors, representing 3D translational and rotational motion with respect to the onset of the scan, were calculated from the six realignment parameters generated in SPM via the Pythagorean Theorem [30, 31].

Correction for physiological noise was performed via RETROICOR [32] using Fourier expansions of different order for the estimated phases of the cardiac pulsation (2nd order) and respiration (2nd order). Corresponding confound regressors were created with the MATLAB PhysIO Toolbox [33] available as part of the TAPAS software collection (www.translationalneuromodeling.org/tapas). This yielded eight nuisance regressors for inclusion in first-level imaging statistics.

Statistics. A first-level analysis was performed to estimate the activity associated with the mean pupil dilation across the resting-state scan. The general linear model (GLM) contained a parameter that described the average pupil dilation (following preprocessing) during each TR and the censorship, motion, and physiological nuisance regressors described above. First-level GLMs were convolved with the SPM8 canonical HRF and high-pass filtered at 128 s. Contrasts were derived in the first-level analysis to examine the relative activation associated with increasing pupil dilation. Second-level GLMs were performed to examine the effects across participants.

The peak CON-related cluster resulting from the pupillometry analysis was used to define a seed region in a functional connectivity analysis. Activity across the timeseries was extracted for each participant from both the thresholded region of interest (ROI) and from a MNI gray matter mask (at least 20 % probability gray matter), which was included to control for overall fluctuations in neural activity. The two activity vectors were included as regressors in addition to the nuisance regressors in a first-level whole-brain analysis. Second-level statistics were performed to examine patterns of connectivity across individuals and their variation with individual differences in reported mindfulness (FFMQ score).

Thresholds for significance in imaging analyses were set at peak $p < .001$ uncorrected and cluster extent $p < .01$ uncorrected [34] unless otherwise noted. MNI coordinates of all of the significant clusters in each figure are listed in tables.

3   Results

3.1   Relationship Between Pupil Dilation and Resting-State Activity

We first tested the extent to which pupil dilation is sensitive to changes in activity in the CON and DMN across time (Fig. 1, Table 1). Consistent with previous research [19], increasing pupil dilation during a resting-state scan was associated with greater activity in regions of the CON, though in this study we observed more extensive pattern of activity (ACC extending into supplementary motor area, bilateral AI, thalamus), auditory cortex (bilateral superior temporal gyrus), and visual cortex (lingual gyrus, extending into the calcarine sulcus; Fig. 1, red).

Extending previous work, we also observed that decreasing pupil dilation was related to greater activity in the right temporo-parietal junction extending into the AG and in the right anterior temporal pole (Fig. 1, blue), which are both part of the dorsal medial subsystem of the DMN that has been associated with reflecting on the mental states of oneself or others (i.e., mentalizing) [35].

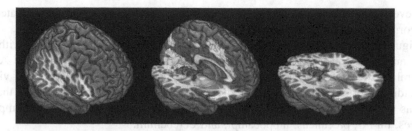

Fig. 1. Regions of the CON, visual and auditory cortex were upregulated with increasing pupil size (red). In contrast, decreasing pupil size was associated with activity in the right angular gyrus, a region of the DMN, and the right inferior temporal cortex (blue) (Color figure online).

Table 1. MNI coordinates of the regions that are engaged with increasing and decreasing pupil dilation during the resting-state session as shown in Fig. 1.

Pupil dilation	MNI coord.				Cluster size (voxels)
	x	y	z	t-score	
Increasing dilation					
Lingual gyrus	−5	−61	5	6.59	1363
Mid/anterior cingulate cortex	7	14	44	6.40	685
L anterior insula	−29	23	−1	6.25	507
R posterior cingulate cortex	7	−31	50	6.16	107
L mid/posterior cingulate cortex	−17	−37	38	5.93	140
L hippocampus	−14	−19	−7	5.60	139
L postcentral gyrus	−41	−16	41	5.57	116
R thalamus	7	−19	2	5.55	53
R precentral gyrus	40	−10	41	5.39	69
R superior temporal gyrus	49	−19	8	5.17	159
R cuneus	7	−82	38	4.91	82
R anterior insula	40	14	2	4.77	30
L postcentral gyrus	−23	−28	62	4.46	45
Decreasing dilation					
R temporo-parietal/angular gyrus	49	−70	14	5.00	44
R anterior temporal pole	52	20	−34	4.93	81

3.2   Functional Connectivity and Individual Differences in Mindfulness

To evaluate the extent to which the pupil-related regions from the previous analysis formed coherent neural networks, a functional connectivity analysis was performed. An ROI was defined as the thresholded peak CON-related cluster (i.e., the mid/anterior cingulate cortex cluster in Fig. 1/Table 1 with peak coordinate at [7, 14, 44]). The timeseries of this dorsal ACC ROI and, as a control, a gray matter mask were extracted for each participant across the resting-state scan. These regressors were entered into a first-level GLM for each participant to reveal the neural regions with a correlated or anti-correlated pattern of activation across time.

Figure 2A (red, Table 2) shows that the ACC was engaged in synchrony with the CON and with sensory cortices; functionally correlated regions included the ACC, bilateral AI/fO extending into middle frontal gyri, the thalamus, and regions of visual and auditory cortex. As predicted, activity in the ACC was anti-correlated with that of regions of the DMN (blue), including the bilateral angular gyri, inferior temporal cortices, mPFC, precuneus, hippocampi, and cerebellum.

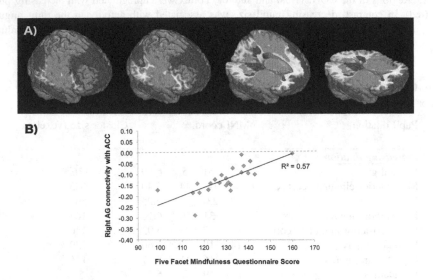

Fig. 2. (**A**) ACC activity is positively functionally correlated with activity in other CON regions, visual and auditory cortex (red) and anti-correlated with DMN regions (blue). More mindful individuals tended to exhibit a weaker anti-correlation between areas of the DMN and ACC (pink). (**B**) Extracted effect estimates (a.u.) clarify the relation between greater mindfulness (higher FFMQ score) and reduced anti-correlation of the ACC ROI and right AG shown in (A) (Color figure online).

FFMQ scores (M = 129.3, SD = 12.3) were entered as a regressor in a second-level GLM to investigate the extent to which the anti-correlation between ACC and DMN activity was modulated by individual differences in dispositional mindfulness. With increasing mindfulness, a weaker anti-correlation between the ACC and regions of the DMN, specifically in the right AG and the precuneus (Fig. 2A pink, Table 2), was observed. To clarify the direction of this result, the effect in the right AG cluster for each individual was plotted against their FFMQ score. Figure 2B depicts that while less mindful individuals exhibited a pattern of functional connectivity commonly reported in the literature (a strong, negative relation), mindful individuals tended to show little to no anti-correlation between the ACC and the right AG.

Table 2. Peak MNI coordinates of the regions that are functionally anti-/correlated with ACC activity across the resting-state session and that vary with individual differences in mindfulness (i.e., greater FFMQ score; see Fig. 2).

Functional connectivity	MNI coord.				Cluster size (voxels)
	x	y	z	t-score	
Positive					
Anterior cingulate cortex	−5	14	32	28.70	15838
L middle frontal gyrus	−35	44	26	8.37	294
R middle frontal gyrus	31	41	20	7.99	191
Calcarine sulcus	−14	−73	5	6.30	307
Negative					
R angular gyrus	40	−64	38	13.22	9905
R cerebellum	31	−85	−31	12.63	1587
L cerebellum	−2	−58	−52	9.92	119
Fornix	1	2	20	5.24	92
Greater FFMQ					
L precuneus	−14	−58	44	5.21	24*
R angular gyrus	43	−58	32	4.21	20**

*cluster extent $p = .062$, ** cluster extent $p = .085$

4 Discussion

The current study demonstrated a tight link between a physiological and a neural measure of tonic alertness. Supporting previous work [19], greater pupil dilation was associated with increasing neural activity within regions of the CON during the course of a resting-state session, in which participants simply fixated a screen for nine minutes. The CON has been described as a *salience network*, which integrates conflict monitoring, autonomic responses, and reward processing [36]. This system appears to facilitate the detection of salient stimuli that lead to rewarding behaviors, that is, an LC-driven pattern of scanning attention. The pupil-associated activity in this study may have been more extensive than previously reported for methodological reasons such as its enrollment of a larger, younger sample (i.e., 60 % more participants, mean age nine years younger, max age 18 years younger). Though research is needed to test the impact of such factors, aging has been shown to alter alertness and functional connectivity between the ACC and DMN even in middle-aged adults [37, 38].

Following studies showing that CON activity enhances sensory processing [39], we also observed that regions of primary and secondary auditory and visual cortices were associated with increasing pupil dilation in addition to the CON. However, the present study employed a resting-state design in which no stimuli were presented nor explicit task given, other than to fixate crosshairs in the center of a screen. The fixation symbols as well as scanner noise were consistent throughout the session. However with increasing alertness, participants may have become more aware of these environmental stimuli, which could explain the observed upregulation of sensory cortices. Though resting-state studies are informative about the systems underlying basic cognitive functions [40], future research should continue to explore the extent to which pupil dilation indexes alertness during explicit tasks (e.g., [19]). Indeed, the adaptive gain theory of LC function indicates that optimal task performance is associated with moderate levels of tonic alertness [2]. Very high levels of arousal, such as occur in periods of stress, may not be fully sampled in a resting-state study.

When not focused on the external environment, participants also likely engaged in mind wandering. The DMN is typically suppressed during active task processing, but relatively engaged during mind wandering and self-reflection [10, 11]. Extending previous research [19], we observed that decreasing dilation was associated with increasing engagement of the dorsal medial subsystem of the DMN. In particular, these regions are thought to interact with core regions of the DMN to support mentalizing [35]. Mentalizing involves ruminating on one's own or other people's mental states [41] and is thought to be a major component of mind wandering [42, 43]. Future research may more firmly establish the relationship between pupil dilation and activity in this DMN subsystem by probing the frequency and contents of mind wandering across a study.

To verify that the observed pupil-related regions were engaged as part of the CON and DMN networks, a functional connectivity analysis was performed using the pupil-related ACC region as a seed (along with a gray-matter control seed). In line with previous resting-state studies [12, 13], ACC activity was synchronously engaged with activity across the entire CON and anti-correlated with regions of the DMN. Thus, pupil dilation appears to track a range of alertness via its sensitivity to the trade-off between CON and DMN activity. By linking physiological and neural measures, our results suggest that pupillometry may provide an online measure of changes in alertness that is easier to collect and less costly than neuroimaging metrics.

Finally, we observed that the extent to which individuals had mindful dispositions altered the connectivity between the CON and DMN. Mindfulness refers to the ability to be aware in the present moment, non-judgmentally accepting one's thoughts and experiences [17]. In this study, individuals who scored higher on the FFMQ exhibited a weaker negative to null correlation. Though the CON and DMN are typically anti-correlated [12, 13], some research suggests that reading [44], autobiographical planning [45], vigilance tasks [6], or even awareness of mind wandering [10] may benefit from the coordinated activation of frontal attention and DMN networks. These studies hypothesized that the systems work together to regulate inner-directed thoughts or maintain internalized task goals in the face of shifting environmental stimuli. Extrapolating our results, one may expect a positive correlation with greater levels of dispositional mindfulness than sampled in the current study (Fig. 2B), such as may occur with mindfulness meditation training [46]. Indeed, a recent study showed increasing positive connectivity between frontal-attention and DMN regions following mindfulness meditation compared to a relaxation-only control [16]. Additionally, CON-DMN co-activations may be more readily observed in the context of explicit tasks, which impose greater demands on attentional processes. Studies currently underway will be analyzed to test these hypotheses.

The current study has implications for both basic and applied research. The ability to maintain tonic alertness is critical for performing many job-related activities accurately, quickly, and with minimal effort. For example, for government language professionals, detecting relevant information that occurs infrequently within text or spoken materials often requires substantial vigilance: individuals must be engaged in their primary task goal (reading/listening) while minimizing mind wandering. The ability to track fluctuations in alertness with pupillometry could lead to the development of real-time predictors of performance [47], thus improving our ability to select, train, and evaluate our workforce.

5   Conclusions

The current study demonstrated that variation in baseline pupil dilation tracks changes in the neural systems that underlie tonic alertness. In a simultaneous pupillometry and functional neuroimaging resting-state study, increasing dilation was associated with the engagement of the CON, while decreasing dilation was associated with greater DMN activity. A functional connectivity analysis revealed that these networks were anti-correlated, which was modulated by individual differences in self-reported mindful behavior in daily life. This work supports the feasibility of collecting online measures of tonic alertness and highlights that individual differences may modulate the neural systems that underlie it.

Acknowledgements. This material is based upon work supported, in whole or in part, with funding from the United States Government. Any opinions, findings and conclusions or recommendations expressed in this material are those of the author(s) and do not necessarily reflect the views of the University of Maryland, College Park and/or any agency or entity of the United States Government. We thank Jared Novick and Nina Hsu for their thoughtful discussion of this work as well as the study participants.

References

1. Oken, B.S., Salinsky, M.C., Elsas, S.M.: Vigilance, alertness, or sustained attention: physiological basis and measurement. Clin. Neurophysiol. **117**, 1885–1901 (2006)
2. Aston-Jones, G., Cohen, J.D.: An integrative theory of locus coeruleus-norepinephrine function: adaptive gain and optimal performance. Annu. Rev. Neurosci. **28**, 403–450 (2005)
3. Posner, M.I.: Measuring alertness. Ann. N. Y. Acad. Sci. **1129**, 193–199 (2008)
4. Eckert, M.A., Keren, N.I., Aston-Jones, G.: Looking Forward with the Locus Coeruleus (Commentary on Modafinil Shifts Human Locus Coeruleus to Low-Tonic, High-Phasic Activity During Functional MRI by Astafiev et al.). www.sciencemag.org/content/328/5976/309.1.short/reply#sci_el_13365
5. Vaden, K.I., Kuchinsky, S.E., Cute, S.L., Ahlstrom, J.B., Dubno, J.R., Eckert, M.A.: The cingulo-opercular network provides word-recognition benefit. J. Neurosci. **33**, 18979–18986 (2013)
6. Coste, C.P., Kleinschmidt, A.: Cingulo-opercular network activity maintains alertness. Neuroimage **128**, 264–272 (2016)
7. Sadaghiani, S., D'Esposito, M.: Functional characterization of the cingulo-opercular network in the maintenance of tonic alertness. Cereb. Cortex **25**, 2763–2773 (2015)
8. Kuchinsky, S.E., Vaden, K.I., Ahlstrom, J.B., Cute, S.L., Humes, L.E., Dubno, J.R., Eckert, M.A.: Task-related vigilance during word recognition in noise for older adults with hearing loss. Exp. Aging Res. **42**, 50–66 (2016)

9. Raichle, M.E., MacLeod, A.M., Snyder, A.Z., Powers, W.J., Gusnard, D.A., Shulman, G.L.: A default mode of brain function. Proc. Natl. Acad. Sci. **98**, 676–682 (2001)

10. Christoff, K., Gordon, A.M., Smallwood, J., Smith, R., Schooler, J.W.: Experience sampling during fMRI reveals default network and executive system contributions to mind wandering. Proc. Natl. Acad. Sci. **106**, 8719–8724 (2009)

11. Mittner, M., Boekel, W., Tucker, A.M., Turner, B.M., Heathcote, A., Forstmann, B.U.: When the brain takes a break: a model-based analysis of mind wandering. J. Neurosci. **34**, 16286–16295 (2014)

12. Fox, M.D., Snyder, A.Z., Vincent, J.L., Corbetta, M., Van Essen, D.C., Raichle, M.E.: The human brain is intrinsically organized into dynamic, anticorrelated functional networks. Proc. Natl. Acad. Sci. **102**, 9673–9678 (2005)

13. Damoiseaux, J.S., Rombouts, S.A.R.B., Barkhof, F., Scheltens, P., Stam, C.J., Smith, S.M., Beckmann, C.F.: Consistent resting-state networks. Proc. Natl. Acad. Sci. **103**, 13848–13853 (2006)

14. Chang, C., Glover, G.H.: Time-frequency dynamics of resting-state brain connectivity measured with fMRI. Neuroimage **50**, 81–98 (2010)

15. Kilpatrick, L.A., Suyenobu, B.Y., Smith, S.R., Bueller, J.A., Goodman, T., Creswell, J.D., Tillisch, K., Mayer, E.A., Naliboff, B.D.: Impact of mindfulness-based stress reduction training on intrinsic brain connectivity. Neuroimage **56**, 290–298 (2011)

16. Creswell, J.D., Taren, A.A., Lindsay, E.K., Greco, C.M., Gianaros, P.J., Fairgrieve, A., Marsland, A.L., Brown, K.W., Way, B.M., Rosen, R.K., Ferris, J.L.: Alterations in resting state functional connectivity link mindfulness meditation with reduced interleukin-6: a randomized controlled trial. Biol. Psychiatry. (in press)

17. Bishop, S.R., Lau, M., Shapiro, S., Carlson, L., Anderson, N.D., Carmody, J., Segal, Z.V., Abbey, S., Speca, M., Velting, D., Devins, G.: Mindfulness: a proposed operational definition. Clin. Psychol. Sci. Pract. **11**, 230–241 (2004)

18. Gilzenrat, M.S., Nieuwenhuis, S., Jepma, M., Cohen, J.D.: Pupil diameter tracks changes in control state predicted by the adaptive gain theory of locus coeruleus function. Cogn. Affect. Behav. Neurosci. **10**, 252–269 (2010)

19. Murphy, P.R., O'Connell, R.G., O'Sullivan, M., Robertson, I.H., Balsters, J.H.: Pupil diameter covaries with bold activity in human locus coeruleus. Hum. Brain Mapp. **35**, 4140–4154 (2014)

20. McGinley, M.J., David, S.V., McCormick, D.A.: Cortical membrane potential signature of optimal states for sensory signal detection. Neuron **87**, 179–192 (2015)

21. Phillips, M.A., Bitsios, P., Szabadi, E., Bradshaw, C.M.: Comparison of the antidepressants reboxetine, fluvoxamine and amitriptyline upon spontaneous pupillary fluctuations in healthy human volunteers. Psychopharmacology **149**, 72–76 (2000)

22. Oldfield, R.C.: The assessment and analysis of handedness: the Edinburgh inventory. Neuropsychologia **9**, 97–113 (1971)

23. Baer, R.A., Smith, G.T., Hopkins, J., Krietemeyer, J., Toney, L.: Using self-report assessment methods to explore facets of mindfulness. Assessment **13**, 27–45 (2006)

24. Pyka, M., Beckmann, C.F., Schöning, S., Hauke, S., Heider, D., Kugel, H., Arolt, V., Konrad, C.: Impact of working memory load on fMRI resting state pattern in subsequent resting phases. PLoS ONE **4**, e7198 (2009)

25. Patriat, R., Molloy, E.K., Meier, T.B., Kirk, G.R., Nair, V.A., Meyerand, M.E., Prabhakaran, V., Birn, R.M.: The effect of resting condition on resting-state fMRI reliability and consistency: a comparison between resting with eyes open, closed, and fixated. Neuroimage **78**, 463–473 (2013)

26. Siegle, G.J., Steinhauer, S.R., Stenger, V.A., Konecky, R., Carter, C.S.: Use of concurrent pupil dilation assessment to inform interpretation and analysis of fMRI data. Neuroimage **20**, 114–124 (2003)

27. Smith, S.M.: Fast robust automated brain extraction. Hum. Brain Mapp. **17**, 143–155 (2002)

28. Macey, P.M., Macey, K.E., Kumar, R., Harper, R.M.: A method for removal of global effects from fMRI time series. Neuroimage **22**, 360–366 (2004)

29. Vaden, K.I., Muftuler, L.T., Hickok, G.: Phonological repetition-suppression in bilateral superior temporal sulci. Neuroimage **49**, 1018–1023 (2010)

30. Kuchinsky, S.E., Vaden, K.I., Keren, N.I., Harris, K.C., Ahlstrom, J.B., Dubno, J.R., Eckert, M.A.: Word intelligibility and age predict visual cortex activity during word listening. Cereb. Cortex **22**, 1360–1371 (2012)

31. Wilke, M.: An alternative approach towards assessing and accounting for individual motion in fMRI timeseries. Neuroimage **59**, 2062–2072 (2012)

32. Glover, G.H., Li, T.Q., Ress, D.: Image-based method for retrospective correction of physiological motion effects in fMRI: RETROICOR. Magn. Reson. Med. **44**, 162–167 (2000)

33. Kasper, L., Marti, S., Vannesjö, S.J., Hutton, C., Dolan, R., Weiskopf, N., Stephan, K.E., Prüssmann, K.P.: Cardiac artefact correction for human brainstem fMRI at 7 Tesla. In: Proceedings of the Organization for Human Brain Mapping, p. 395. San Francisco, CA (2009)

34. Poline, J.B., Worsley, K.J., Evans, A.C., Friston, K.J.: Combining spatial extent and peak intensity to test for activations in functional imaging. Neuroimage **5**, 83–96 (1997)

35. Andrews-Hanna, J.R., Reidler, J.S., Sepulcre, J., Poulin, R., Buckner, R.L.: Functional-anatomic fractionation of the brain's default network. Neuron **65**, 550–562 (2010)

36. Seeley, W.W., Menon, V., Schatzberg, A.F., Keller, J., Glover, G.H., Kenna, H., Reiss, A. L., Greicius, M.D.: Dissociable intrinsic connectivity networks for salience processing and executive control. J. Neurosci. **27**, 2349–2356 (2007)

37. Carrier, J., Monk, T.H., Buysse, D.J., Kupfer, D.J.: Sleep and morningness-eveningness in the "middle" years of life (20–59 y). J. Sleep Res. **6**, 230–237 (1997)

38. Hampson, M., Tokoglu, F., Shen, X., Scheinost, D., Papademetris, X., Constable, R.T.: Intrinsic brain connectivity related to age in young and middle aged adults. PLoS ONE **7**, e44067 (2012)

39. Sadaghiani, S., Hesselmann, G., Kleinschmidt, A.: Distributed and antagonistic contributions of ongoing activity fluctuations to auditory stimulus detection. J. Neurosci. **29**, 13410–13417 (2009)

40. Buckner, R.L., Vincent, J.L.: Unrest at rest: default activity and spontaneous network correlations. Neuroimage **37**, 1091–1096 (2007)

41. Frith, C.D., Frith, U.: The neural basis of mentalizing. Neuron **50**, 531–534 (2006)

42. Buckner, R.L., Andrews-Hanna, J.R., Schacter, D.L.: The brain's default network: anatomy, function, and relevance to disease. Ann. N. Y. Acad. Sci. **1124**, 1–38 (2008)

43. Andrews-Hanna, J.R.: The brain's default network and its adaptive role in internal mentation. Neuroscientist **18**, 251–270 (2012)

44. Smallwood, J., Gorgolewski, K.J., Golchert, J., Ruby, F.J.M., Engen, H., Baird, B., Vinski, M.T., Schooler, J.W., Margulies, D.S.: The default modes of reading: modulation of posterior cingulate and medial prefrontal cortex connectivity associated with comprehension and task focus while reading. Front. Hum. Neurosci. **7**, 734 (2013)

45. Spreng, R.N., Stevens, W.D., Chamberlain, J.P., Gilmore, A.W., Schacter, D.L.: Default network activity, coupled with the frontoparietal control network, supports goal-directed cognition. Neuroimage **53**, 303–317 (2010)
46. Baer, R.A., Carmody, J., Hunsinger, M.: Weekly change in mindfulness and perceived stress in a mindfulness-based stress reduction program. J. Clin. Psychol. **68**, 755–765 (2012)
47. Marshall, S.P.: The index of cognitive activity: measuring cognitive workload. In: Human Factors and Power Plants, Proceedings of the 2002 IEEE 7th Conference on Human Factors Modeling, vol. 7, pp. 5–9. IEEE, Scottsdale, AZ (2002)

Evaluating Neural Correlates
of Constant-Therapy Neurorehabilitation
Task Battery: An fNIRS Pilot Study

Jesse Mark[1(✉)], Banu Onaral[1], and Hasan Ayaz[1,2,3]

[1] School of Biomedical Engineering, Science, and Health Systems,
Drexel University, Philadelphia, PA, USA
{jesse.alexander.mark,banu.onaral,
hasan.ayaz}@drexel.edu
[2] Department of Family and Community Health,
University of Pennsylvania, Philadelphia, PA, USA
[3] Division of General Pediatrics, Children's Hospital of Philadelphia,
Philadelphia, PA, USA

Abstract. The development of cognitive task battery applications for rehabilitation in telemedicine is a rapidly evolving field, with several tablet or web based programs already helping those suffering from working memory dysfunction or attention deficit disorders. However, there is little physiological evidence supporting a measurably significant change in brain function from using these programs. The present study sought to provide an initial assessment using the portable and wearable neuroimaging modality of functional near-infrared spectroscopy (fNIRS) that can be used in ambulatory and home settings and has the potential to add value in the assessment of clinical patients' recovery throughout their therapy.

Keywords: Functional near-infrared spectroscopy · fNIRS · Cognitive test battery · Neural rehabilitation · Telemedicine · Neuroergonomics

1 Introduction

Every year, there are over 600,000 cases of new or first strokes and over two million cases of traumatic brain injury in the United States alone [1, 2]. This constantly increasing group of patients require frequent neurorehabilitation therapy but may be unable to see clinicians as much as required. Taking into consideration recent technological developments such as low-cost tablet computers and cloud computing, the field of telemedicine has risen to meet the growing demand for available care at home settings [3]. Telemedicine applications allow for patients to perform clinician-mediated therapy and recover from the comfort of their own home, circumventing the need to travel to a specialized therapy clinic which often proves difficult due to various constraints. Moreover, the availability of telemedicine options has been shown to increase patient compliance [4] as well as be effective in treating apraxia of speech, motor control degradation in the arm, and other complications of stroke and injury [5, 6].

© Springer International Publishing Switzerland 2016
D.D. Schmorrow and C.M. Fidopiastis (Eds.): AC 2016, Part I, LNAI 9743, pp. 231–241, 2016.
DOI: 10.1007/978-3-319-39955-3_22

The importance of telemedicine also connects with the rapidly developing field of neuroergonomics. Neuroergonomics is the study of how the brain behaves in natural environments, in so-called ecological situations [7, 8]. Several studies have already proven the validity of this school of thought in areas ranging from air traffic control to interaction with virtual reality [9–11]. Recording the brain using a teletherapy application at home bypasses sterile lab environments and more closely simulates real-world use of the system.

Although computerized methods for cognitive rehabilitation designed for patients to use on demand are being continuously developed [12–14], most evidence of the efficacy of similar treatments is limited to behavioral or standardized psychological tests [15–17]. Moreover, these results are valid only for regimens developed by specialized clinicians, and studies have found that some commercial applications do not necessarily provide comparable results [18, 19]. These outline the need for controlled and independent assessment of the capabilities of cognitive rehabilitation tools and specifically neural correlates of the paradigms in use.

In this pilot study, we aimed to perform an initial assessment of select cognitive tasks in Constant Therapy (©2014 Constant Therapy, constanttherapy.com), an iPad-based cognitive rehabilitation app which is already in active use by clinicians and patients to augment traditional therapy. Constant Therapy provides over sixty tasks targeting various areas of cognition [20]. Two tasks targeting attention and working memory have been selected for the proof of concept experiment demonstrating that past studies related to cortical activation and task expertise are applicable to the tablet-based therapy paradigm [11]. We hypothesize that in line with earlier studies, there will be a quantifiable difference in the brain activation of healthy subjects when performing the same task at different difficulties [21]. This hypothesis was chosen for this pilot study to test if task-induced differences in brain activation could be detected in the Constant Therapy neurorehabilitation tool.

To test this hypothesis, we chose to use the portable and accessible neuroimaging modality of functional near-infrared spectroscopy (fNIRS). fNIRS is a safe, wearable and relatively low cost optical measuring system of neural activity related to cognitive state and workload [11, 22, 23]. Compared to the traditional neuroimaging systems such as electroencephalogram (EEG) and functional magnetic resonance imaging (fMRI), fNIRS has a balanced trade-off in spatial and temporal resolution, fast setup, silent operation, minimal restrictions, and a miniaturized, battery operated, and wearable sensor set that can be potentially used in a home setting, making it ideal for use with telemedicine brain monitoring in conjunction with therapy apps [24]. By including these physiological signals into the clinician's assessment of patient recovery, more effective therapy can be applied, which can therefore improve patient outcomes.

2 Method: Brain Activation Measurements During Tablet Therapy Application Use

2.1 Participants

Ten participants between the ages of 18 and 35 (five females, mean age = 23.2 ± 2.8 years) volunteered for this study. All confirmed that they met the eligibility requirements of being right-handed with vision correctable to 20/20, did not have a history of brain injury or psychological disorder, and were not on medication affecting brain activity. Prior to the study all participants signed consent forms approved by the Institutional Review Board of Drexel University.

2.2   Experimental Procedure

The experiment was performed in a single session lasting for approximately one hour. The sessions were held in a specially prepared subject room in our lab building free from distraction and outside interference (Fig. 1). Subjects were recorded using the fNIRS system as they performed the experimental protocol on a provided iPad 2 placed on a stand. The task application used for this experiment was Constant Therapy, a program that allows for clinicians to work with patients both directly and indirectly, and is notable for its ability to provide smart telemedicine even when subjects are at home. Each task was presented in randomized order and downloaded from the internet on the fly. The standard outcome measures of the program were in behavioral performance, the accuracy and latency of each trial.

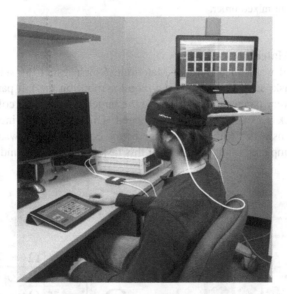

Fig. 1. Subject operating application on iPad with fNIRS headband attached. Data acquisition apparatus and program visible on table and stand beyond subject.

For the experiment, participants sat on a chair next to a desk with an iPad placed in a comfortable position before them, and were fitted with the fNIRS headband. Subjects were instructed to minimize head movement and only use their dominant (right) hands to interact with the iPad. The iPad was muted and screen brightness was set to maximum for consistency and clear view, and the iPad stand attached to the cover was set the same way for each subject. During the experiments the tablet screen was mirrored to a separate computer using Reflector 2 (©2016 Squirrels, LLC) and recorded using Microsoft Expression Encoder 4 (©2016 Microsoft Corporation).

The experiment was in two parts, one for each of the two tasks chosen, Symbol Matching and Pattern Recreation, as described below. Each of the tasks was given at two preselected difficulties, easy and hard, for a total of four block types throughout the experiment. In between blocks, subjects rested for 30 s to allow for their cortical oxygenation to return to resting levels, and a two-minute break was given in between the Symbol Matching and Pattern Recreation (Fig. 2). The exact order of blocks and whether Symbol or Pattern was presented first was balanced between subjects. The entire session took approximately 45 min.

Fig. 2. Sample timeline of experiment blocks showing order and timing. Difficulties are easy and hard presented in mixed order.

2.2.1 Symbol Matching Task

The first task used was called Symbol Matching, which tested the subject's attention (Fig. 3). In this task, subjects are shown a target symbol on the left part of the screen, and must select every panel exactly matching the target in shape and color, followed by hitting the "Check Answers" button to proceed. Clicking on an incorrect panel or hitting "Check Answers" without selecting every correct choice was considered an error. Subjects completed nine repetitions of this task in each block, and performed four

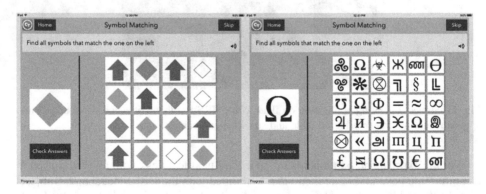

Fig. 3. Screenshots of easy and hard difficulties of Symbol Matching task

blocks of each difficulty for a total of eight blocks of Symbol Matching. Blocks were presented in a pseudo-random order.

2.2.2   Pattern Recreation Task

The second task used was Pattern Recreation, which tested the subject's working memory (Fig. 4). This task presents the user with a sequence of panels that flash one at a time, which the user must then recreate from memory. The number of panels in each trial varied from four to six depending on whether it was an easy or hard block. Hitting an incorrect panel or hitting one out of order was considered an error. If at any point the subject could not remember the remainder of the sequence, they were permitted to hit the "Repeat" button as many times as needed, which would then play back any remaining unpressed panels. Like before, subjects completed nine repetitions of each trial per block, and four blocks per difficulty for a total of eight. Blocks were again presented in a pseudo-random order.

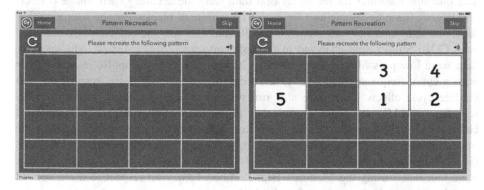

Fig. 4. Screenshots of instructional phase and in-progress step of Pattern Recreation task

2.3   Data Acquisition

We used a continuous wave fNIRS system (fNIR Devices LLC, fnirdevices.com) that was described previously in [11]. COBI Studio [22] software was used to acquire data from the headband and visualize and record light intensity at two wavelengths, 730 and 850 nm, at a rate of 2 Hz. The headband itself (Fig. 5) is a soft, flexible, and light-weight foam pad containing four LED light sources and ten near infrared light-sensitive detectors placed in a grid with a fixed 2.5 cm source detector distance, which combined to form a total of 16 distinct optodes (measurement areas). With the inclusion of ambient channels, 730 nm, and 850 nm, a total of 3 channels per optode, 48 channels data overall were collected. Time synchronization markers were used to align the signal with the start and end times of each block throughout the experiment session.

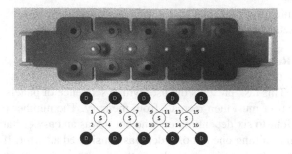

Fig. 5. fNIRS sensor pad and diagram of optode layout. Sensors (S), Detectors (D), and Optode numbers are as labelled.

2.4   Data Analysis

The outcome measures for the behavioral data were the accuracy (percentage correct) and latency (time to completion) for each trial within all blocks. For the neuroimaging data, raw light intensity measurements at 730 nm, 850 nm, and ambient light recorded with COBI Studio were analyzed in fnirSoft software [25]. First, raw light intensity data were low pass filtered with an order 20 Hamming finite impulse response filter with a cutoff frequency of 0.1 Hz to attenuate high frequency noise, respiration, and cardiac cycle effects. Data were also run through a sliding-window motion artifact rejection (SMAR) algorithm in order to eliminate motion artifacts and saturated channels [26]. Relevant blocks for each task were isolated and extracted using the manual markers. As the outcome measure, oxygenation that is oxygenated-hemoglobin (HbO) minus deoxygenated-hemoglobin (HbR) values for each of the sixteen optodes were calculated using the Modified Beer-Lambert Law with respect to a ten second local baseline at the beginning of each block.

For statistical analysis, a repeated measures linear mixed model analysis with Bonferroni correction was performed for both behavioral measures and average oxygenation changes for each block across difficulty conditions (alpha = 0.05).

3   Results

3.1   Behavioral Measures

The behavioral results of symbol matching task are shown in Fig. 6. As expected, both accuracy ($F_{1,451.2} = 9.87$, $p < 0.002$) and latency ($F_{1,438.5} = 920.53$, $p < 0.001$) were significantly different between easy and hard task conditions. Similar results were found for the pattern matching task which are shown in Fig. 7. Again, as expected, both accuracy ($F_{1,524.1} = 132.24$, $p < 0.001$) and latency ($F_{1,557.3} = 422.983$, $p < 0.001$) were significantly different across easy and hard conditions.

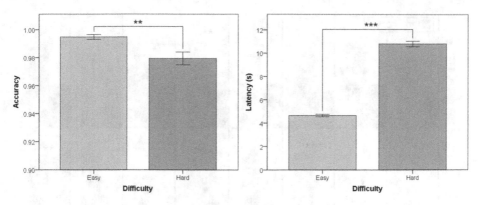

Fig. 6. Symbol Matching task behavioral results of accuracy (left) and latency (right) (**p < 0.002, ***p < 0.001). Error bars are the standard error of the mean (SEM).

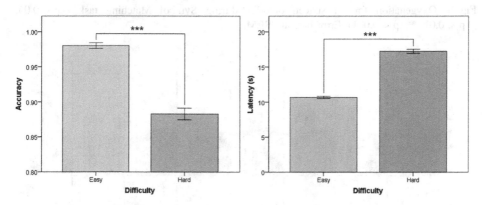

Fig. 7. Pattern Recreation task behavioral results of accuracy (left) and latency (right) (***p < 0.001). Error bars are SEM.

3.2 fNIRS Measures

Average oxygenation changes showed the high contrast between task conditions. As expected, the higher level of activity observed for difficult conditions indicated a higher level of effort for those conditions. Significant differences were found for all but one optode between Symbol Matching tasks (Fig. 8, Table 1), but only one optode was found to provide a significant difference in cortex oxygenation while subjects performed Pattern Matching (Fig. 9, Table 1).

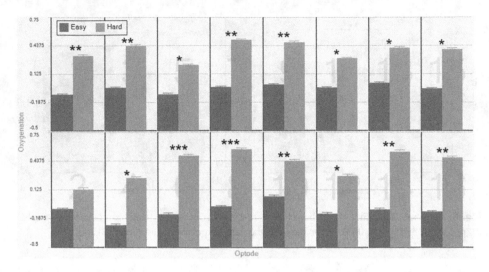

Fig. 8. Oxygenation for all sixteen optodes during Symbol Matching task (*p < 0.05, **p < 0.01, ***p < 0.001). Error bars are SEM.

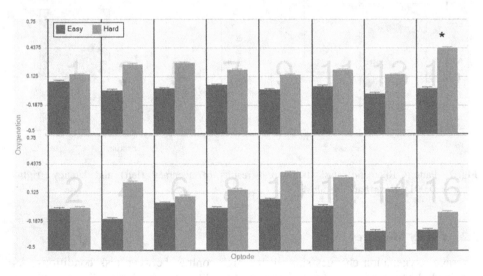

Fig. 9. Oxygenation for all sixteen optodes during Pattern Recreation task (*p < 0.05). Error bars are SEM.

Table 1 Mixed model statistical analysis results for Symbol and Pattern tasks

	Optode	1	2	3	4	5	6	7	8	9	10	11	12	13	14	15	16
Symbol	df_{num}, df_{den}	1,38.7	1,32.8	1,45.4	1,39.9	1,49	1,49.5	1,50.5	1,46.4	1,37	1,41.1	1,43.4	1,34.5	1,50.5	1,41.6	1,40.8	1,34.8
	F	8.65**	1.34	9.72**	5.02*	4.47*	15.65***	12.12**	20.45***	8.14**	10.35**	5.36*	4.38*	6.71*	9.76**	5.10*	9.81**
Pattern	df_{num}, df_{den}	1,50.7	1,45.6	1,59.1	1,59.4	1,64.6	1,54.3	1,59.6	1,56.3	1,60	1,53.5	1,63.5	1,53.2	1,59.1	1,59.3	1,55.9	1,58.3
	F	0.12	0.00	1.57	1.92	2.58	0.04	1.18	0.53	0.93	2.97	1.17	3.03	1.56	2.33	4.83*	0.40

4   Discussion

In this study, we aimed to perform an initial proof of concept neuroergonomic evaluation of a clinical teletherapy tool, Constant Therapy, using a wearable and safe fNIRS neuroimaging system. Anterior prefrontal cortex activity during performance of the two cognitive tasks (attention and working memory) yielded high contrast differences in oxygenation changes across the task conditions (easy vs. hard).

We found that healthy subjects performing the two selected tasks of a tablet-based therapy application performed statistically worse (lower accuracy and higher latency) on the hard difficulty as compared to the easy one. Moreover, using functional near-infrared spectroscopy of the prefrontal cortex we found measurable differences in the cortical oxygenation of the subjects performing these tasks, demonstrating that consistent neural correlates exist, and can be potentially applied to a wider population using this system. This agrees with previous studies done using fNIRS on cognitive workload while performing challenging tasks, and demonstrates that higher mental effort is correlated with higher brain activation [10, 11, 24, 27–29].

This pilot study was limited by the number of subjects, as well as the time constraints we allowed for each experimental session. Given longer sessions or multiple recordings taken over several days, we would likely see more significant contrast in both task conditions and the longitudinal plasticity differences. This was exacerbated by our limitation of only using two distinct tasks. We also had to limit the range of difficulties for each task, as it was necessary to keep the test engaging but not too challenging in order not to overload the subjects during repetitive performance [30]. In future studies, more of the wide variety of tasks available could be tested, which will provide a richer information base for use of fNIRS measurements in conjunction with Constant Therapy in the field.

This pilot study provided initial proof that fNIRS-based neuroimaging techniques could be used to assess brain function changes during performance of the tasks and also potentially assess the efficacy of cognitive therapy applications during actual clinical use. Although we controlled as many aspects of the procedure as possible for the pilot study, the program itself was unaltered from the commercially available version, and therefore demonstrates the ecological validity of our results. In addition, this was the first neuroimaging study applied specifically with the Constant Therapy rehabilitation application. The results encourage future studies that can focus on cross sectional and longitudinal designs, including clinical populations, to further assess the utility of fNIRS to add value to a clinician's ability to track and triage a patient's recovery using quantitative brain measures. Moreover, if brain measures are integrated into the task design's automated difficulty adjustment algorithms alongside the current smart analytics, they can improve the efficiency [31] and recovery speed as well as patients' compliance [32].

In summary, this study demonstrates that fNIRS is a good candidate to enhance design (usability) and/or clinical field use of cognitive rehabilitation systems.

Acknowledgements. The authors would like to thank Dr. Veera Anantha for his help with access to the Constant Therapy tasks.

References

1. http://www.cdc.gov/stroke/facts.htm
2. http://www.cdc.gov/traumaticbraininjury/get_the_facts.html
3. Oh, J.Y., Park, Y.T., Jo, E.C., Kim, S.M.: Current status and progress of telemedicine in Korea and other countries. Healthc. Inform. Res. **21**, 239–243 (2015)
4. Riegler, L.J., Neils-Strunjas, J., Boyce, S., Wade, S.L., Scheifele, P.M.: Cognitive intervention results in web-based videophone treatment adherence and improved cognitive scores. Med. Sci. Monit. **19**, 269–275 (2013)
5. Gaggioli, A., Meneghini, A., Morganti, F., Alcaniz, M., Riva, G.: A strategy for computer-assisted mental practice in stroke rehabilitation. Neurorehabil. Neural Repair **20**, 503–507 (2006)
6. Varley, R., Cowell, P.E., Dyson, L., Inglis, L., Roper, A., Whiteside, S.P.: Self-administered computer therapy for apraxia of speech: two-period randomized control trial with crossover. Stroke **47**, 822–828 (2016)
7. Parasuraman, R., Lee, J.D., Kirlik, A.: Neuroergonomics: Brain-Inspired Cognitive Engineering. Oxford University Press
8. Mehta, R.K., Parasuraman, R.: Neuroergonomics: a review of applications to physical and cognitive work. Front. Hum. Neurosci. **7**, 889 (2013)
9. Derosière, G., Mandrick, K., Dray, G., Ward, T.E., Perrey, S.: NIRS-measured prefrontal cortex activity in neuroergonomics: strengths and weaknesses. Front. Hum. Neurosci. **7**, 583 (2013)
10. Carrieri, M., Petracca, A., Lancia, S., Basso Moro, S., Brigadoi, S., Spezialetti, M., Ferrari, M., Placidi, G., Quaresima, V.: Prefrontal cortex activation upon a demanding virtual hand-controlled task: a new frontier for neuroergonomics. Front. Hum. Neurosci. **10**, 53 (2016)
11. Ayaz, H., Shewokis, P.A., Bunce, S., Izzetoglu, K., Willems, B., Onaral, B.: Optical brain monitoring for operator training and mental workload assessment. NeuroImage **59**, 36–47 (2012)
12. Kiran, S., Roches, C.D., Balachandran, I., Ascenso, E.: Development of an impairment-based individualized treatment workflow using an iPad-based software platform. Semin. Speech Lang. **35**, 038–050 (2014)
13. Des Roches, C.A., Balachandran, I., Ascenso, E.M., Tripodis, Y., Kiran, S.: Effectiveness of an impairment-based individualized rehabilitation program using an iPad-based software platform. Front. Hum. Neurosci. **8** (2015)
14. Dang, J., Zhang, J., Guo, Z., Lu, W., Cai, J., Shi, Z., Zhang, C.: A pilot study of iPad-assisted cognitive training for schizophrenia. Arch. Psychiatr. Nurs. **28**, 197–199 (2014)
15. Westerberg, H., Jacobaeus, H., Hirvikoski, T., Clevberger, P., Östensson, M.L., Bartfai, A., Klingberg, T.: Computerized working memory training after stroke–a pilot study. Brain Inj. **21**, 21–29 (2007)
16. Bogdanova, Y., Yee, M.K., Ho, V.T., Cicerone, K.D.: Computerized cognitive rehabilitation of attention and executive function in acquired brain injury: a systematic review. J. Head Trauma Rehabil. (2015). (Epub ahead of print)
17. Ayaz, H., Shewokis, P.A., Scull, L., Libon, D.J., Feldman, S., Eppig, J., Onaral, B., Heiman-Patterson, T.: Assessment of prefrontal cortex activity in amyotrophic lateral sclerosis patients with functional near infrared spectroscopy. J. Neurosci. Neuroeng. **3**, 41–51 (2014)

18. Melby-Lervag, M., Hulme, C.: Is working memory training effective? A meta-analytic review. Dev. Psychol. **49**, 270–291 (2013)
19. Smith, S.P., Stibric, M., Smithson, D.: Exploring the effectiveness of commercial and custom-built games for cognitive training. Comput. Hum. Behav. **29**, 2388–2393 (2013)
20. https://constanttherapy.com
21. Molteni, E., Contini, D., Caffini, M., Baselli, G., Spinelli, L., Cubeddu, R., Cerutti, S., Bianchi, A.M., Torricelli, A.: Load-dependent brain activation assessed by time-domain functional near-infrared spectroscopy during a working memory task with graded levels of difficulty. J. Biomed. Opt. **17**, 056005 (2012)
22. Ayaz, H., Shewokis, P.A., Curtin, A., Izzetoglu, M., Izzetoglu, K., Onaral, B.: Using mazesuite and functional near infrared spectroscopy to study learning in spatial navigation. J. Vis. Exp. **56**, 3443 (2011)
23. Fishburn, F.A., Norr, M.E., Medvedev, A.V., Vaidya, C.J.: Sensitivity of fNIRS to cognitive state and load. Front. Hum. Neurosci. **8**, 76 (2014)
24. Ayaz, H., Onaral, B., Izzetoglu, K., Shewokis, P.A., McKendrick, R., Parasuraman, R.: Continuous monitoring of brain dynamics with functional near infrared spectroscopy as a tool for neuroergonomic research: empirical examples and a technological development. Front. Hum. Neurosci. **7**, 871 (2013)
25. Ayaz, H.: Functional Near Infrared Spectroscopy Based Brain Computer Interface. Drexel University, Philadelphia, PA (2010)
26. Ayaz, H., Izzetoglu, M., Shewokis, P.A., Onaral, B.: Sliding-window motion artifact rejection for functional near-infrared spectroscopy. Conf. Proc. IEEE Eng. Med. Biol. Soc. **2010**, 6567–6570 (2010)
27. Ruocco, A.C., Rodrigo, A.H., Lam, J., Di Domenico, S.I., Graves, B., Ayaz, H.: A problem-solving task specialized for functional neuroimaging: validation of the Scarborough adaptation of the Tower of London (S-TOL) using near-infrared spectroscopy. Front. Hum. Neurosci. **8**, 185 (2014)
28. Hasan, A., Ben, W., Scott, B., Patricia, A.S., Kurtulus, I., Sehchang, H., Atul, R.D., Banu, O.: Cognitive workload assessment of air traffic controllers using optical brain imaging sensors. In: Advances in Understanding Human Performance, pp. 21–31. CRC Press (2010)
29. Gateau, T., Durantin, G., Lancelot, F., Scannella, S., Dehais, F.: Real-time state estimation in a flight simulator using fNIRS. PLoS One **10**, e0121279 (2015)
30. Durantin, G., Gagnon, J.F., Tremblay, S., Dehais, F.: Using near infrared spectroscopy and heart rate variability to detect mental overload. Behav. Brain Res. **259**, 16–23 (2014)
31. McKendrick, R., Ayaz, H., Olmstead, R., Parasuraman, R.: Enhancing dual-task performance with verbal and spatial working memory training: continuous monitoring of cerebral hemodynamics with NIRS. NeuroImage **85**(3), 1014–1026 (2014)
32. Yuksel, B.F., Oleson, K.B., Harrison, L., Peck, E.M., Afergan, D., Chang, R., Jacob, R.J.: Learn piano with BACh: an adaptive learning interface that adjusts task difficulty based on brain state. In: CHI 2016 (2016)

Overloaded and Biased? Using Augmented Cognition to Understand the Interaction Between Information Overload and Cognitive Biases

Randall K. Minas[1](✉) and Martha E. Crosby[2]

[1] Shidler College of Business, University of Hawaii at Manoa, 2404 Maile Way,
Honolulu, HI 96822, USA
rminas@hawaii.edu
[2] Department of Information and Computer Sciences, University of Hawaii at Manoa,
2550 Campus Road, Honolulu, HI 96822, USA
crosby@hawaii.edu

Abstract. Virtual teams are increasingly utilized in organizations, yet they often make poor decisions. Previous research has established that a primary cause of poor virtual team decision making is due to confirmation bias: team members focusing their cognitive resources on factual and normative information that supports pre-discussion preferences, rather than deeply considering information that challenges them. Building on this, the current study examines whether confirmation bias exists at varying levels of information load, establishing if confirmation bias is mediated by information overload. This study will utilize electroencephalography (EEG) and psychophysiology to examine changes in an individual's processing of information at three levels of information load. The individual will participate in a simulated team discussion on a decision-making task. These findings will elucidate whether virtual team members use confirmation bias as a heuristic problem solving approach in response to information overload or if confirmation bias is present in all virtual team interactions.

Keywords: Cognitive load and performance · Confirmation bias · Electroencephalography · Augmented cognition · Decision making · Virtual teams

1 Introduction

Virtual teams have been increasingly utilized in today's organizations over the past decade, and they are now commonplace in today's organizations [1, 2]. Virtual teams enable team members to be either spatially or temporally dispersed, yet able to readily communicate and solve problems [3]. Generally, virtual teams communicate via different forms of technology [4–7], including videoconferencing, email, online chat rooms, and instant messaging (IM). These different modes of communication vary in richness and synchronicity, providing flexibility in the way virtual teams communicate [8, 9]. These technologies enable certain process gains, such as the elimination of production blocking and increased anonymity [10]. However, despite these gains,

D.D. Schmorrow and C.M. Fidopiastis (Eds.): AC 2016, Part I, LNAI 9743, pp. 242–252, 2016.
DOI: 10.1007/978-3-319-39955-3_23

decades of research has shown that: virtual teams come to no better decisions than face-to-face teams and this problem exists at the level of individual information processing [11, 12].

Recently, a study used electroencephalography (EEG), electrodermal activity (EDA), and facial electromyography (EMG) to examine individual information processing in simulated virtual team interactions. While the individual was connected to the neurophysiological and psychophysiological equipment, they interacted with a simulator which they believed to be a real virtual team. The findings indicated that individuals processed information that conformed with their beliefs *before* the virtual team interaction differently than information that differed from individuals preferences before the virtual team interaction, indicating confirmation bias was present in the virtual team interaction [13]. The study, however, did not examine whether varying levels of information load led to confirmation bias, that is, the research was unable to answer if confirmation bias was a cause of information overload or a "default" bias individuals revert to during virtual team interactions.

This study examines whether increased information load in a virtual team is related to the presence of confirmation bias. In essence, we examine whether confirmation bias is a heuristic that individuals rely on once information processing becomes over-whelming. To examine this phenomenon, we will collect heart rate data, electrodermal response (EDR) and facial electromyography (EMG). We will also collect electroen-cephalography (EEG) data to examine changes in cognition that indicate confirmation bias as was done in [13]. This research will elucidate whether the confirmation bias reported in [13] is related to the individual's information load in a virtual team or is present even in low information load conditions. The findings will have implications for the design of collaborative technologies, specifically whether design should focus on alleviating confirmation bias or information overload.

2   Theoretical Background

2.1   Decision Making

The decision making process is a dynamic process involving multiple decision factors [14]. The pros and cons of each factor must be considered to reach an optimal decision [14]. Prior research has identified unique challenges in team decision making especially due to negotiating multiple opinions [15–17]. Other factors found to affect team deci-sion-making processes include cognitive processes [15, 18], cognitive anchors [15, 19], and the desire to stick to prior decisions [15, 20].

There are three distinct stages in the decision making process: the pre-decision stage, the decision stage, and the post-decision stage [14]. The scope of this study is limited to the first two. The pre-decision stage involves gathering information about the decision alternatives [14]. Teams are often formed because they have access to more information than any one decision maker acting alone [21]. Past research has shown that on average, teams make better decisions than individuals, even when they are comprised of team members with relatively homogenous backgrounds, perhaps because they are less likely to make major errors [22].

The net result is what Stasser [23] has called a "hidden profile" task. Each team member knows some baseline information that is known to all team members, which is often called "common information" [11]. Each team member also usually knows some "unique information" that is known only by them. This combination of information typically leads each team member to form initial pre-discussion preferences about the decision alternatives. Because these pre-discussion preferences are based on a mixture of common and unique information, it is not unusual for individual team members to develop different preferences prior to a team discussion.

During the decision stage, team members come together (face-to-face or virtually) to discuss the decision alternatives. During this process, they share the information they have, as well as their preferences for the different alternatives. Thus the information that team members contribute to and receive from the discussion can be organized into two distinct categories [24]. The first category is factual information about the decision alternatives. Factual information is devoid of opinion (although the choice of what factual information to contribute can be shaped by opinions) [25]. It simply states the facts and leaves the interpretation of those facts to the receiver. The second category is normative information about the preferences of the contributor. Normative information simply states which alternative(s) the contributor prefers, without providing underlying reasons [25].

Since most teams have a mix of common and unique information, it is not uncommon for team members to receive information they already know, as well as new information they do not know. This new information—information not considered in the pre-discussion stage—should be what a team member focuses on, because it is new and not yet considered [11]. Such new information received from other team members may support or challenge the pre-discussion preferences that a team member has developed. In theory, new information that challenges pre-discussion preferences is the most important and should receive the most attention because it has the greatest potential to change decisions [26–29]. However, prior research has shown that team decisions can be contaminated by information processing biases [14, 30, 31]. Virtual team decision making is also encumbered by these biases [13].

2.2 Confirmation Bias and Information Overload

One of the most common biases present in team discussions is confirmation bias. Confirmation bias is the tendency of people to ignore information that challenges their current decision preferences [32–34]. Thus not only do decision makers seek out selective information, but when they do uncover information that challenges their initial preferences, they resolve the cognitive dissonance by ignoring the contradictory information [32, 33, 35]. This can lead to the biased interpretation of new information they receive such that information that supports pre-discussion preferences is considered while information that challenges those preferences is ignored [32]. Thus the net effect of gathering new information, even unbiased information search that gathers new information that both supports and challenges existing decision preferences, is to reinforce the existing pre-discussion preferences, rather than helping decision makers find better solutions. This hurts decision quality if the initial decision preferences are incorrect [36].

Most of the research on bias in decision making has focused on individual decision making not, team decision making. One would hope that involving other people in the decision process, each of whom may bring their own—and potentially different—biases to the discussion, might overcome some of the selective information search and confirmation bias observed in individual decision making. Unfortunately, selective information search also has been observed in teams that meet face-to-face to make decisions [36]. Stasser and his colleagues have published many studies examining face-to-face decision making teams and have repeatedly found that teams engage in selective information search by focusing the discussion on common information known to all team members [23, 37–39]. Team members routinely choose not to share the unique information known only to them, and as a result, team decisions are often poor.

In [13] it is demonstrated through EEG that confirmation bias is present in virtual team discussions. However, the study did not examine whether the confirmation bias resulted from information overload experienced by the individual. Information overload describes the condition wherein there are more messages competing for attention than an individual is capable of processing [40]. This is of particular concern in the virtual team setting as virtual teams share more information than face-to-face teams [11]. Therefore, despite knowing that confirmation bias is present in a virtual team decision making, it is important to disentangle the underlying causes that result in confirmation bias being present. Extant research is conflicted on whether confirmation bias exists regardless of information load [41] or is a heuristic that we default to when we become overloaded (i.e., information load and confirmation bias interact) [42]. In essence, the question is whether information load increases the individual's tendency to rely on information they have already deemed to be true, at the expense of disregarding other conflicting information presented. Therefore, we hypothesize:

H1: An individual's processing of information will be affected by information load, such that an increase in information load results in an increase in the presence of confirmation bias.

3 Method

Our goal in this study is to understand how individual team members respond to new information they receive from other team members during a text-based ICT discussion in varying information load conditions. Therefore, the unit of analysis will be the individual, not the team. Given this focus, having real participants interact with each other and measuring the data at the individual level would introduce large error variance, because each team discussion is likely to be different. Therefore, we will use a simulator [see, 12, 43, 44] designed to look and act like a real Instant Messenger (IM) tool. The study participant can type comments in the simulator and see them contributed to the discussion. The simulator will present participants with a standardized script based off of a real-world virtual team discussion. In order not to bias the outcomes, participants were not informed that they were using a simulator until the end of the experimental session.

3.1 Participants

Participants will be undergraduate students from a state university who will receive course credit for their time. We aim to collect data on 40 subjects in a repeated measures design.

3.2 Task

We will use three hidden profile decision making tasks. In each task, we will ask the participants to select three of five fictitious student applicants to admit to the university. This task is based on one used extensively in prior research [e.g., 11, 45]. It has the advantage of being familiar to the participants, because each of them has successfully navigated the university entrance process and understands the task information (e.g., GPA, SAT). The version of the tasks we used are validated by the admissions office at the university where the experiment was conducted to ensure that the information it contained was appropriate.

Each task has two parts. First, the participant is given incomplete information about the five potential applicants and asked to make an initial decision of which three to admit. This corresponds to the pre-decision stage commonly encountered in decision making. Then the participant will be informed that they will work in a team with four other participants using a text-based discussion tool to discuss the information and reach a team decision that could be the same or different from their initial decisions. Participants will be informed that each team member has received incomplete information. Some common information is known to all team members but each team member had been given unique information that is known only to them, and that it was important to share this unique information and consider the new information contributed by others in order to reach a good decision.

The IM tool the participants will use is like most text-based discussion tools. The simulator will provide two onscreen windows. The top window displays the comments from "other team members" and the bottom window enabled the participants to type their comments (which were then displayed in the top window with the other comments). The participant was told that the other discussion participants were in different locations, and not with them in the research lab, because we were not collecting physiological data from them.

3.3 Treatments

There will be three treatments: a low, medium, and high information load condition. In the low information load condition, the virtual team discussion will move slowly, providing the participant with little information to process during the discussion. The high information load condition will move quickly providing the participant much information to process. The medium information load condition will contain a moderate amount of information for the subject to process. The way participants process the information in each condition will be compared to examine whether confirmation bias is present in each condition. The conditions will be counter-balanced across participants to control for any task order effects.

Independent Variable. The independent variable is the nature of the information contained in the simulator script displayed to the participants, with five levels explained below. The scripts were written to closely match the transcripts of discussions from student teams that had performed this task in prior experiments.

The script was designed to contain five types of information contained in target statements. The target statements contained factual information that supported the participant's pre-discussion decision preference and factual information that challenged the participant's pre-discussion decision preference (e.g., Don had one of the highest GPAs). We will record each participant's pre-discussion choice so we could cross check it against the target statements to ensure that preference supporting and preference challenging information was coded appropriately. Separate target statements will also contain normative information that supports the participant's pre-discussion decision preference and information that challenges it (e.g., I like Angela). Fifteen target statements contained irrelevant information designed to provide a baseline against which we could compare the other four types of information (e.g., I'm hungry). The irrelevant information was drawn from transcripts of teams that had performed this task in other experiments, so it commonly appears in team discussions of this type.

In the low, medium, and high information load treatments, we will vary the amount of the five types of target statements to increase information processing requirements on the participant.

Dependent Variables. Our dependent variables are cortical alpha wave activity, autonomic arousal, and emotional valence. These are operationalized using neurological and psychophysiological measures. EEG measures will be collected using a 14-channel headset (Emotiv Systems, San Francisco, CA, USA) with electrodes dispersed over the scalp along the 10–20 system [46] (see Fig. 1). The electrodes will make connection with the scalp surface via felt pads saturated in saline solution. The reference electrodes will be located at P3 and P4 over the inferior, posterior parietal lobule [46]. All other channels will be measured in relation to the electrical activity present at these locations, sampled at 128 Hz. Impedances will be verified and data collected using Emotiv Test-Bench Software Version 1.5.0.3, which will export it into comma-delimited format for subsequent analysis.

Autonomic arousal will be operationalized as skin conductance level measured with disposable electrodes filled with electrically neutral gel and adhered planar surface of the foot. A Biopac MP150 system will be used to collect the skin conductance data at 1000 Hz. Emotional valence will be operationalized as the relative activation of the corrugator supercilli muscle group (facial EMG). Corrugator EMG will be measured using a pair of mini (4 mm) reusable AG/AGCL electrodes filled with electrolyte gel placed above the subject's left eye after dead skin cells has been removed by a skin prep pad containing rubbing alcohol and pumice. The bipolar corrugator measures will be collected using the Biopac MP150 system with high pass filters set at 8 Hz. The full

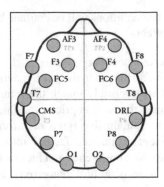

Fig. 1. Position of the electrodes on the EEG headset with labels along the 10–20 system

wave signal will be rectified and then contour integrated online at a time constant of 100 ms, and then sampled at 1000 Hz by the Biopac MP150 system.

Controls and Manipulation Checks. It is essential to ensure that participants perceive the simulator as a real team discussion. All participants will complete a post-session questionnaires that asked if they had noticed anything unusual about the team discussion. A variety of distractor questions (e.g., satisfaction with discussion, perceived effectiveness) will be included to better ensure that manipulation check question does not stand out. Participants that indicate they did not believe the simulated team discussions were not a real will be removed from the analysis.

Markers will be inserted by the researchers into the EEG data to indicate onset and end of the simulator's text discussion. A timestamp generated by the simulator program will be used to identify precisely when each statement is displayed. This timestamp marker for each target statement will then be matched to the EEG data.

3.4 Procedures

Participants will complete the experimental procedure individually after providing informed consent approved by the university's Institutional Review Board. The experiment will take place in an individual lab room. The entire research session will take about 90 min. The experiment will be controlled by E-Prime software.

Participants will be seated in a high back chair to minimize movement. They will be provided a standard keyboard and a mouse. The experimenter will then explain the procedure for attaching the physiological electrodes and fitting the EEG cap, answering any questions posed by the participant. After obtaining adequate impedance readings for the EDA, EMG and EEG measures, the protocol will continue with another brief handedness questionnaire.

Next the participant will receive information on the college admissions task and the pre-discussion information. They will be instructed that not only should they use this information to make their decision, but that they would be sharing the information they are given with the team. They will be given 3 min to read the information, which will be presented in the form of a data table. Then they must decide which three of five students they would choose to admit.

After making their pre-discussion decisions, the participant will be instructed on the nature of the discussion task. They will be told that the other discussion participants are located at various places across campus and not with them in the research lab because physiological data is not being collected from them. The participant will be told that they would participate in three different decision-making tasks. Each task will be a discussion that lasts for 12 min. The participant will be reminded that each team member received information known only to them. They will also be instructed that they should therefore share all the information they have and read all the information provided by other team members.

After the three virtual team decision making tasks are completed, the experimenter will remove the EEG cap and physiological sensors. The participant will then complete the post-experiment questionnaire. Finally, the participant will be debriefed, told of the deception, asked not to inform others of the deception, and thanked for their time.

3.5 Data Cleaning and Preparation

EEG data will be cleaned and analyzed using EEGLab [47]. One limitation of EEG is that cortical bioelectrical activity is extremely small in magnitude when compared to muscle movements across the head. Therefore, participant movement introduces artifacts of high-frequency and magnitude into the EEG data. These will be removed using two methods: EEGlab probability calculations and visual inspection. The EEGLab artifact rejection algorithm uses deviations in microvolts greater than three standard deviations from the mean to reject specific trials. However, additional artifacts are also apparent to the trained eye, so visual inspection of trials is essential in artifact removal [47].

In addition to trial-by-trial removal of artifacts, occasionally specific EEG channels must be rejected in an individual subject's data due to unacceptable impedance levels. This can be done in the current study using an automatic impedance detection feature of EEGLab.

Electrodermal and facial EMG data were aggregated to mean values per second using Biopac's Acqknowledge software. Change scores will be calculated by subtracting the physiological level at the onset of each target statement during the online discussion from each subsequent second across a 6-s window.

3.6 ICA Analysis of EEG Data

The first step of the EEG analysis will be an Independent Components Analysis (ICA) at the individual level. A common problem in neurophysiology research results from the collection of large amounts of data which, based upon the Central Limit Theorem, become normally distributed. However, the brain is comprised of discrete patches of cortex that are very active at some points in time and relatively non-active at others (i.e. – activity is not normally distributed across the scalp) [48]. ICA overcomes this problem by taking this Gaussian data and rotating it until it becomes non-Gaussian, thereby isolating independent components of activation. The ICAs are distributed patterns of activation across the 14-electrodes in the EEG system.

Initially, an EEGLab ICA performs a Principal Components Analysis (PCA). At each electrode site the program assesses which of the other electrode sites account for the most variance in the signal. Taking these weighted values it then relaxes the orthogonality constraint of PCA to isolate individual components of activation [48]. Each ICA component then represents a pattern of activation over the entire brain, not solely the activity present at a specific electrode. The number of independent components (ICs) depends on the number of electrodes in the dataset, as the algorithm is working in an N-dimensional space (where N is the number of electrodes). Most participants in the current study are expected to generate 14 distinct ICs, since our recording device has 14 electrodes.

Finally, using the K-means component of EEGlab the independent components at the individual level will be grouped into clusters containing similar components using procedures recommended by [49]. This procedure clusters similar ICs based upon their latency, frequency, amplitude, and scalp distribution [49]. Relevant clusters will be identified and a time-frequency decomposition will be performed to examine changes in event-related desynchronization of the alpha rhythm.

4   Potential Implications

This study seeks to elucidate whether confirmation bias and information load are mutually exclusive or mutually related. We examine cognitive and emotional changes present at the individual level in a virtual team interaction to understand how information load affects processing of different types of information. We believe the findings of this study have several implications for understanding virtual team interactions.

First, if we find that confirmation bias and information load interact, there are several areas of interest for design. Mainly, the question poised will be: How can we alleviate information load in a virtual team decision making setting? Exploring ways to design collaborative tools to reduce information load will also alleviate confirmation bias. Conversely, if we find that confirmation bias is unrelated to information load, the question poised would be: How do we design a collaborative tool to reduce confirmation bias? Both prospects will provide future directions for further research on this topic and give designers of collaborative tools insight into how to improve their software. Overall, the findings of this study will generate many avenues for future research on decision-making, collaboration and augmented cognition.

References

1. Zuboff, S.: In the Age of the Smart Machine: The Future of Work and Power. Basic Books Inc., New York (1984)
2. Chudoba, K.M., Wynn, E., Lu, M., Watson-Manheim, M.B.: How virtual are we? Measuring virtuality and understanding its impact in a global organization. Inf. Syst. J. **15**, 279–306 (2005)
3. O'Leary, M.B., Cummings, J.N.: The spatial, temporal, and configurational characteristics of geographic dispersion in teams. MIS Q. **31**, 433–452 (2007)

4. Bell, B.S., Kozlowski, S.W.J.: A typology of virtual teams. Group Organ. Manag. **27**, 14–49 (2002)
5. Duarte, D.L., Tennant-Snyder, N.: Mastering Virtual Teams: Strategies, Tools, and Techniques that Succeed. Jossey-Bass, San Francisco (1999)
6. Lipnack, J., Stamps, J.: Virtual Teams: Working Across Space, Time and Organizations. Wiley, New York (1997)
7. Townsend, A.M., DeMarie, S.M., Hendrickson, A.R.: Virtual teams: technology and the workplace of the future. Acad. Manag. Exec. (1993–2005) **12**, 17–29 (1998)
8. Daft, R.L., Lengel, R.H.: Organizational information requirements, media richness and structural design. Manag. Sci. **32**, 554–571 (1986)
9. Dennis, A.R., Fuller, R.M., Valacich, J.S.: Media, tasks, and communication processes: a theory of media synchronicity. MIS Q. **32**, 575–600 (2008)
10. Nunamaker, J.F., Dennis, A.R., Valacich, J.S., Vogel, D., George, J.F.: Electronic meeting systems. Commun. ACM **34**, 40–61 (1991)
11. Dennis, A.R.: Information exchange and use in group decision making: you can lead a group to information, but you can't make it think. MIS Q. **20**, 433–457 (1996)
12. Heninger, W.G., Dennis, A.R., Hilmer, K.M.: Research note: individual cognition and dual-task interference in group support systems. Inf. Syst. Res. **17**, 415–424 (2006)
13. Minas, R.K., Potter, R.F., Dennis, A.R., Bartelt, V., Bae, S.: Putting on the thinking cap: using NeuroIS to understand information processing biases in virtual teams. J. Manag. Inf. Syst. **30**, 49–82 (2014)
14. Zeleny, M.: Multiple Criteria Decision Making. McGraw-Hill, New York (1982)
15. Dean Jr., J.W., Sharfman, M.P.: Does decision process matter? A study of strategic decision-making effectiveness. Acad. Manag. J. **39**, 368–396 (1996)
16. Guzzo, R.A.: Group decision making and group effectiveness in organizations. In: P.S.G. Associates (ed.) Designing Effective Work Groups, pp. 34–71. Jossey-Bass, San Francisco (1986)
17. Hackman, J.R.: Groups That Work (and Those That Don't). Jossey-Bass, San Francisco (1991)
18. Bazerman, M.H.: Judgement in Managerial Decision Making. Wiley, New York (1990)
19. Tversky, A., Kahneman, D.: Judgment under uncertainty: heuristics and biases. Science **185**, 1124–1131 (1974)
20. Staw, B.M.: The escalation of commitment to a course of action. Acad. Manag. Rev. **6**, 577–587 (1981)
21. Hackman, J.R., Kaplan, R.E.: Interventions into group process: an approach to improving the effectiveness of groups. Decis. Sci. **5**, 459–480 (1974)
22. Kerr, N.L., Tindale, R.S.: Group performance and decision making. Annu. Rev. Psychol. **55**, 623–655 (2004)
23. Stasser, G., Stewart, D.: Discovery of hidden profiles by decision-making groups: solving a problem versus making a judgment. J. Pers. Soc. Psychol. **63**, 426–434 (1992)
24. Petty, R.E., Cacioppo, J.T., Schumann, D.: Central and peripheral routes to advertising effectiveness: the moderating role of involvement. J. Consum. Res. **10**, 135–146 (1983)
25. Kaplan, M.F., Miller, C.E.: Group decision making and normative versus informational influence: effects of type of issue and assigned decision rule. J. Pers. Soc. Psychol. **53**, 306–313 (1987)
26. Shoemaker, P.J.: Media Gatekeeping, 2nd edn. Longman, New York (1996)
27. Zajonc, R.B.: On the primacy of affect. Am. Psychol. **39**, 117–123 (1984)
28. Vinokur, A., Trope, Y., Burnstein, E.: A decision-making analysis of persuasive argumentation and the choice-shift effect. J. Exp. Soc. Psychol. **11**, 127–148 (1975)

29. Myers, D.G., Lamm, H.: The group polarization phenomenon. Psychol. Bull. **83**, 602–627 (1976)
30. Klayman, J.: Varieties of confirmation bias. In: Jerome Busemeyer, R.H., Douglas, L.M. (eds.) Psychology of Learning and Motivation, vol. 32, pp. 385–418. Academic Press, New York (1995)
31. McKenzie, C.: Increased sensitivity to differentially diagnostic answers using familiar materials: implications for confirmation bias. Mem. Cogn. **34**, 577–588 (2006)
32. Ask, K., Granhag, P.A.: Motivational sources of confirmation bias in criminal investigations: the need for cognitive closure. J. Invest. Psychol. Offender Profiling **2**, 43–63 (2005)
33. Koriat, A., Lichtenstein, S., Fischhoff, B.: Reasons for confidence. J. Exp. Psychol. Hum. Learn. Mem. **6**, 107–118 (1980)
34. Schulz-Hardt, S., Frey, D., Lüthgens, C., Moscovici, S.: Biased information search in group decision making. J. Pers. Soc. Psychol. **78**, 655–669 (2000)
35. Sloane, P.J., Williams, H.: Are "overpaid" workers really unhappy? A test of the theory of cognitive dissonance. Labour **10**, 3–16 (1996)
36. Jonas, E., Schulz-Hardt, S., Frey, D., Thelen, N.: Confirmation bias in sequential information search after preliminary decisions: an expansion of dissonance theoretical research on selective exposure to information. J. Pers. Soc. Psychol. **80**, 557–571 (2001)
37. Stasser, G., Titus, W.: Pooling of unshared information in group decision making: biased information sampling during discussion. J. Pers. Soc. Psychol. **48**, 1467–1478 (1985)
38. Stasser, G., Vaughan, S.I., Stewart, D.D.: Pooling unshared information: the benefits of knowing how access to information is distributed among group members. Organ. Behav. Hum. Decis. Process. **82**, 102–116 (2000)
39. Stewart, D.D., Stasser, G.: Expert role assignment and information sampling during collective recall and decision making. J. Pers. Soc. Psychol. **69**, 619–628 (1995)
40. Meadow, C.T., Yuan, W.: Measuring the impact of information: defining the concepts. Inf. Process. Manag. **33**, 697–714 (1997)
41. Arnott, D.: Cognitive biases and decision support systems development: a design science approach. Inf. Syst. J. **16**, 55–78 (2006)
42. Frey, D., Schulz-Hardt, S., Stahlberg, D.: Information seeking among individuals and groups and possible consequences for decision-making in business and politics. Underst. Group Behav. **2**, 211–225 (2013)
43. Garfield, M.J., Taylor, N.J., Dennis, A.R., Satzinger, J.W.: Research report: modifying paradigms - individual differences, creativity techniques, and exposure to ideas in group idea generation. Inf. Syst. Res. **12**, 322–333 (2001)
44. Hilmer, K.M., Dennis, A.R.: Stimulating thinking: cultivating better decisions with groupware through categorization. J. Manag. Inf. Syst. **17**, 93–114 (2000)
45. Robert, L.P., Dennis, A.R.: Paradox of richness: a cognitive model of media choice. IEEE Trans. Prof. Commun. **48**, 10–21 (2005)
46. Herwig, U., Satrapi, P., Schönfeldt-Lecuona, C.: Using the international 10–20 EEG system for positioning of transcranial magnetic stimulation. Brain Topogr. **16**, 95–99 (2003)
47. Delorme, A., Makeig, S.: EEGLAB: an open source toolbox for analysis of single-trial EEG dynamics including independent component analysis. J. Neurosci. Methods **134**, 9–21 (2004)
48. Onton, J., Makeig, S.: Information-based modeling of event-related brain dynamics. In: Christa, N., Wolfgang, K. (eds.) Progress in Brain Research, vol. 159, pp. 99–120. Elsevier, Amsterdam (2006)
49. Delorme, A., Makeig, S.: EEGLAB Wikitutorial, May 2012. http://sccn.ucsd.edu/wiki/PDF:EEGLAB_Wiki_Tutorial

Session-to-Session Transfer in Detecting Steady-State Visual Evoked Potentials with Individual Training Data

Masaki Nakanishi[1(✉)], Yijun Wang[1,2], and Tzyy-Ping Jung[1]

[1] Swartz Center for Computational Neuroscience, Institute for Neural Computation, University of California San Diego, La Jolla, CA, USA
{masaki, jung}@sccn.ucsd.edu
[2] State Key Laboratory on Integrated Optoelectronics, Institute of Semiconductors, Chinese Academy of Science, Beijing, China
wangyj@semi.ac.cn

Abstract. The information transfer rate (ITR) of steady-state visual evoked potential (SSVEP)-based brain-computer interfaces (BCIs) has been significantly improved in the past few years. Recent studies have demonstrated the efficacy of advanced signal processing methods, which incorporate preliminarily recorded individual training data in SSVEP detection. However, conducting experiments for collecting training data from each individual is cumbersome because it is time-consuming and may cause visual fatigue. To simplify the training procedure, this study employs a session-to-session transfer method, which uses transfer templates obtained from datasets collected from the same subjects on a different day. The proposed approach was evaluated with a 40-class SSVEP dataset from eight subjects, each participated in two sessions on two different days. Study results showed that the proposed transfer method achieved significantly higher performance than conventional method based on canonical correlation analysis (CCA). In addition, by employing online adaptation, the proposed method reached high performance that is comparable with the most efficient approach in previous studies. These results indicate the feasibility of a high-performance SSVEP-based BCI with no or little training.

Keywords: Brain-computer interfaces (BCI) · Canonical correlation analysis (CCA) · Electroencephalogram (EEG) · Steady-state visual evoked potentials (SSVEP) · Transfer learning

1 Introduction

Steady-state visual evoked potentials (SSVEPs) are the brain's electrical responses to flickering visual stimuli. SSVEPs have been widely used in electroencephalogram (EEG)-based brain-computer interface (BCI) systems due to the advantage of high information transfer rate (ITR) [1, 2]. In SSVEP-based BCIs, users are required to gaze at one of multiple visual stimuli tagged with different stimulation properties such as frequencies and/or phases [1]. A target visual stimulus can be identified through analyzing the elicited SSVEPs using target identification methods. In this way, an SSVEP-based BCI can translate intentional brain activities into commands to control external devices.

© Springer International Publishing Switzerland 2016
D.D. Schmorrow and C.M. Fidopiastis (Eds.): AC 2016, Part I, LNAI 9743, pp. 253–260, 2016.
DOI: 10.1007/978-3-319-39955-3_24

Performance of SSVEP-based BCIs can be attributed to several factors including stimulus presentation, multiple target coding, and target identification algorithm [3]. In recent studies, advanced stimulus presentation and target coding methods significantly increased the number of stimuli that can be presented on a computer monitor [3–6]. For instance, 32-target and 40-target spellers that employed hybrid frequency and phase coding were designed [3, 6, 7]. The target identification method also plays an important role in improving the performance of SSVEP-based BCIs. Recent advances in signal processing methods, which incorporate individual training data, have been proposed to improve the performance of SSVEP detection [8]. Although these methods achieved better performance than conventional training-free methods, the training procedure can be time consuming and may cause visual fatigue because multiple trials have to be recorded before online operation.

To address this issue, Yuan et al. employed a transfer-learning approach, which transfers SSVEP templates from existing subjects to a new subject, and demonstrated the effectiveness of the method to improve the target identification accuracy compared with other training-free approaches [9]. However, since it is known that there is individual difference in anatomical shape and extent of area V1, where the source of SSVEPs is located at [10, 11], the performance improvement of transferring SSVEP data from different subjects might be limited. Therefore, this study employs a session-to-session transfer method (i.e., training data collected from the same subjects on a different day) to reduce training time and investigated the performance of the proposed approach in terms of the classification accuracy and ITRs.

2   Material and Method

2.1   Experimental Design

EEG data were recorded in a simulated online BCI experiment. 40 visual stimuli were presented on a 23.6-in. liquid-crystal display screen with a resolution of $1{,}920 \times 1{,}080$ pixels and a refresh rate of 60 Hz. The stimuli were arranged in a 5×8 matrix, and tagged with 40 different frequencies (8.0 Hz to 15.8 Hz with an interval of 0.2 Hz) with 4 different phases $(0, 0.5\pi, \pi, 1.5\pi)$. The stimulation frequencies and phases were generated using the joint frequency-phase modulation (JFPM) method [7].

Eight healthy subjects with normal or corrected-to-normal vision participated in this study. Each subject performed the experiment on two different days. All subjects read and signed an informed consent form before participating in the experiment. The subjects sat in a comfortable chair positioned approximately 70 cm from a computer monitor, and gazed at one of the visual stimuli. From each subject, six 5 s-long data and fifteen 1 s-long data of SSVEPs for each visual stimulus were recorded in two experiments conducted on different days. The intervals of two experiment days differed across individuals. After stimulus offset, the screen was blank for 0.5 s before the next trial began. EEG data were acquired using a Synamps2 system (Neuroscan, Inc.) at a sampling rate of 1,000 Hz. Nine electrodes placed over the parietal and occipital areas (Pz, PO5, PO3, POz, PO4, PO6, O1, Oz, and O2) were used to measure SSVEPs.

2.2   Target Identification

This study employed the canonical correlation analysis (CCA) based target identification algorithm with individual calibration templates and transferred templates from a different day [8, 9]. The online transferred template-based CCA proposed by Yuan et al., which updates the transferred templates adaptively in online operation, was also tested in this study [9]. In addition, we tested the standard CCA, which is an unsupervised approach, as a comparative method. In all methods, filter bank analysis was applied [12].

Standard CCA. CCA has been widely used to detect the frequency of SSVEPs [13, 14]. In the CCA-based SSVEP detection method, canonical correlation between multichannel EEG signals $X \in \mathbb{R}^{N_c \times N_s}$ and sine-cosine reference signals $Y \in \mathbb{R}^{2N_h \times N_s}$ are calculated as:

$$\rho(X, Y) = \max_{w_x, w_y} \frac{E\left[w_x^T X Y^T w_y\right]}{\sqrt{E\left[w_x^T X X^T w_x\right] \cdot E\left[w_y^T Y Y^T w_y\right]}} \qquad (1)$$

Here, N_c, N_s and N_h denote the number of channels, the number of sampling points, and the number of harmonics being considered, respectively. The maximum of ρ with respect to w_x and w_y is the maximum canonical correlation. The reference signal Y_{f_n} corresponding to the stimulus frequency f_n are defined as:

$$Y_{f_n} = \begin{bmatrix} \sin(2\pi f_n t) \\ \cos(2\pi f_n t) \\ \vdots \\ \sin(2\pi N_h f_n t) \\ \cos(2\pi N_h f_n t) \end{bmatrix}, t = [1, 2, \ldots, N_s] \cdot \frac{1}{f_s}. \qquad (2)$$

Where, f_s is the sampling frequency. The frequency of the reference signals with maximal correlation was selected as the frequency of the SSVEPs.

CCA with Individual Training Data. Our recent studies proposed an extended CCA-based method which incorporates individual training data [3, 8, 15]. This method exploits important signal characteristics from existing training data for improving the target identification. In this method, a spatial filter $w_{\widehat{xy}}$ that maximizes the signal-to-noise ratio (SNR) of training set $\widehat{X}_n$ for n-th target was first obtained by performing CCA with $\widehat{X}_n$ and Y_{f_n}. Also, a spatial filter w_{xy} that maximizes the SNR of test EEG data X was obtained by performing CCA with X and Y_{f_n}. After that, Pearson's correlation coefficients between test data X and training data $\widehat{X}_n$ projected onto these two spatial filters and CCA with test data X and reference signal Y_{f_n} were calculated as:

$$\boldsymbol{r}_n = \begin{bmatrix} r_{n,1} \\ r_{n,2} \\ r_{n,3} \end{bmatrix} = \begin{bmatrix} r\left(\boldsymbol{X}^T \boldsymbol{w}_{\widehat{xy}}, \widehat{\boldsymbol{X}}_n^T \boldsymbol{w}_{\widehat{xy}}\right) \\ r\left(\boldsymbol{X}^T \boldsymbol{w}_{xy}, \widehat{\boldsymbol{X}}_n^T \boldsymbol{w}_{xy}\right) \\ r(\boldsymbol{X}^T \boldsymbol{w}_x, \boldsymbol{Y}_{f_n}^T \boldsymbol{w}_y) \end{bmatrix}. \tag{3}$$

Where, $r(a, b)$ indicates the Pearson's correlation analysis between two one-dimensional signals a and b. The following ensemble classifier can be used as the final feature in target identification:

$$\rho_n = \sum_{i=1}^3 \text{sign}(r_{n,i}) \cdot r_{n,i}^2. \tag{4}$$

The template $\widehat{X}_n$ that maximizes the weighted correlation value ρ_n is selected as the reference signal corresponding to the target. In this study, two training datasets were used to make separate templates to evaluate the intra-day and inter-day variability in the SSVEP detection. These methods are termed individual template-based CCA (it-CCA) and transfer template-based CCA (tt-CCA), respectively [9].

Online transfer-template CCA (ott-CCA). In this study, the online tt-CCA (ott-CCA) proposed by Yuan et al. was also tested to investigate the efficacy of online adaptation in session-to-session transfer SSVEP detection [9]. The ott-CCA updates the transferred templates in online operation as follows: (1) Calculate the difference between the first and second largest feature value ρ_n among all candidate targets, (2) If the difference is higher than a pre-defined threshold *thr*, update the template via Eq. (5).

$$\widehat{X}_n^{\text{new}} = \frac{1}{m_n^{\text{new}}} \left(m_n^{\text{old}} \widehat{X}_n^{\text{old}} + X \right) \tag{5}$$

where $\widehat{X}_n^{\text{old}}$ and $\widehat{X}_n^{\text{new}}$ are old and new templates for n-th target. m_n^{old} is the number of the trials that have been used to get the averaged template and $m_n^{\text{new}} = m_n^{\text{old}} + 1$. According to the previous study [9], the threshold *thr* was set to 0.1.

Performance Evaluation. In this study, the performance of aforementioned methods was tested with the test dataset, which consisted of nine (the seventh to fifteenth) trials from day 2. To evaluate the performance of session-to-session transfer learning approaches, we prepared two separate templates from first six trials from day 2 for it-CCA, and all six trials from day 1 for tt-CCA.

The performance was evaluated by the target identification accuracy and information transfer rate (ITR) calculated as [16]:

$$ITR = \left(\log_2 N_f + P \log_2 P + (1 - P) \log_2 \left[\frac{1 - P}{N_f - 1} \right] \right) \times \left(\frac{60}{T} \right) \tag{6}$$

where N_f is the number of visual stimulus (i.e., $N_f = 40$ in this study), P is the target identification accuracy, and T (seconds/selection) is the average time for a selection. This study calculated the performance with different T (Target gazing time: 0.1 s to 1.0 s with an interval of 0.1 s; Gaze shifting time: 1.0 s).

3 Results

Figure 1 shows the averaged accuracy of target identification and the ITR across subjects with different data lengths. In general, template-based CCA methods outperformed the filter bank CCA (FBCCA) regardless of the data length. One-way repeated measure analysis of variance (ANOVA) showed there was significant difference in the target identification accuracy between four methods under all data length ($p < 0.05$). Although the performance of tt-CCA was lower than that of it-CCA, tt-CCA significantly improved the performance over FBCCA. With longer data length (e.g., >0.6 s), ott-CCA significantly improved the accuracy over tt-CCA (ott-CCA vs. tt-CCA; 0.6 s: 82.50 ± 4.42 % vs. 78.54 ± 4.20 %, $p < 0.05$, 0.7 s: 89.97 ± 3.02 % vs. 85.59 ± 3.42 %, $p < 0.05$, 0.8 s: 93.30 ± 2.42 % vs. 90.56 ± 2.89 %, $p < 0.05$, 0.9 s: 94.79 ± 1.77 % vs. 92.43 ± 2.50 %, $p = 0.05$, 1.0 s: 95.03 ± 2.02 % vs. 92.85 ± 2.35 %, $p < 0.05$). Although there was significant difference in the accuracy between ott-CCA and it-CCA, ott-CCA achieved comparable accuracy to it-CCA (ott-CCA vs. it-CCA; 0.9 s: 94.79 ± 1.77 % vs. 96.32 ± 1.67 %, $p < 0.05$, 1.0 s: 95.03 ± 2.02 % vs. 96.88 ± 1.41 %, $p < 0.05$). The difference of ITRs between these methods was consistent with that of the accuracy. The data length corresponding to the highest ITR was different for each method (FBCCA: 1.0 s, 92.451 ± 5.26 bits/min, it-CCA: 0.7 s, 164.38 ± 8.93 bits/min, tt-CCA: 0.8 s, 147.16 ± 7.68 bits/min, ott-CCA: 0.8 s, 155.10 ± 6.84 bits/min).

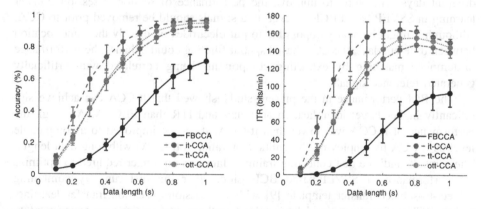

Fig. 1. Averaged accuracy of target identification and ITRs across subjects with different data lengths. The error bars indicate standard errors.

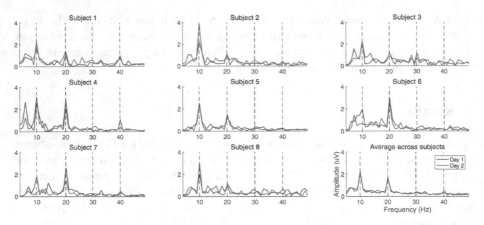

Fig. 2. Amplitude spectra of SSVEP signals at 10 Hz recorded from different days for each subject. The dash lines indicate the fundamental and harmonic frequencies (Color figure online).

4 Discussions

To compare the difference of SSVEP characteristics recorded from different days, the amplitude spectra of SSVEPs were calculated by the fast Fourier transform (FFT). Figure 2 depicts examples of the amplitude spectra of single-channel SSVEPs at 10 Hz for all eight subjects and the average spectrum. The spectra show that the fundamental and harmonics frequency components have higher amplitude than the background EEG signals. Interestingly, in two out of eight subjects (Subjects 6 and 7), the amplitude at the second harmonic frequency was higher than that at the fundamental frequency on both days. Despite of this consistency in the fundamental and harmonic components in response to flickering visual stimuli, background EEG signals are different between different days. Therefore, to improve the performance of session-to-session transfer learning in SSVEP-based BCIs, background signals should be removed prior to CCA. Although it might be nearly impossible to put electrodes on exactly the same location between different days, the CCA-based spatial filtering could enhance the performance of template matching by extracting components being correlated with artificially generated reference signals.

The BCI performance in the present study showed that tt-CCA can achieve significantly higher target identification accuracy and ITR than FBCCA. Although the performance of tt-CCA was lower than it-CCA, it can be improved to a comparable level as it-CCA by employing the online adaptation (ott-CCA) with long data length. These results indicate that collecting training data was no longer required to optimize the performance of SSVEP-based BCIs since after the first run. By combining subject-to-subject transfer template [9] with the session-to-session transfer learning, higher BCI performance could be obtained without any preliminary experiment to record training data.

5 Conclusion

This study showed that a session-to-session transfer method could facilitate the training procedure in an SSVEP-based BCI using individual calibration data. In addition, the adaptive approach can further optimize individual templates while users are operating the system. These findings suggest that session-to-session transfer is efficient for implementing a high-speed SSVEP-based BCI system with zero training.

Acknowledgement. This research was supported in part by a gift fund from Swartz Foundation, by Army Research Laboratory (W911NF-10-2-0022), DARPA (US-DID11PC20183), and UC Proof of Concept Grant Award (269228).

References

1. Wang, Y., Gao, X., Hong, B., Jia, C., Gao, S.: Brain-computer interfaces based on visual evoked potentials: feasibility of practical system design. IEEE Eng. Med. Biol. Mag. **27**(5), 64–71 (2008)
2. Gao, S., Wang, Y., Gao, S., Hong, B.: Visual and auditory brain-computer interfaces. IEEE Trans. Biomed. Eng. **61**(5), 1436–1447 (2014)
3. Nakanishi, M., Wang, Y., Wang, Y.T., Mitsukura, Y., Jung, T.P.: A high-speed brain speller using steady-state visual evoked potentials. Int. J. Neural Syst. **24**(6), 1450019 (2014)
4. Wang, Y., Wang, Y.T., Jung, T.P.: Visual stimulus design for high-rate SSVEP. Electron. Lett. **46**(15), 1057–1058 (2010)
5. Nakanishi, M., Wang, Y., Wang, Y.T., Mitsukura, Y., Jung, T.P.: Generating visual flickers for eliciting robust steady-state visual evoked potentials at flexible frequencies using monitor refresh rate. PLoS ONE **9**(6), e99235 (2014)
6. Chen, X., Chen, Z., Gao, S., Gao, X.: A high-ITR SSVEP based BCI speller. Brain-Comp. Interfaces **1**(3–4), 181–191 (2014)
7. Chen, X., Wang, Y., Nakanishi, M., Gao, X., Jung, T.P., Gao, S.: High-speed spelling with a noninvasive brain-computer interface. Proc. Natl. Acad. Sci. U. S. A. **112**(44), E6058–E6067 (2015)
8. Nakanishi, M., Wang, Y., Wang, Y.T., Jung, T.P.: A comparison study of canonical correlation analysis based methods for detecting steady-state visual evoked potentials. PLoS ONE **10**(10), e140703 (2015)
9. Yuan, P., Chen, X., Wang, Y., Gao, X., Gao, S.: Enhancing performances of SSVEP-based brain-computer interfaces via exploiting inter-subject information. J. Neural Eng. **12**, 046006 (2015)
10. Brindley, G.: The variability of the human striate cortex. J. Physiol. **225**, 1–3 (1972)
11. Stensaas, S., Eddington, D., Dobelle, W.: The topography and variability of the primary visual cortex in man. J. Neurosurg. **40**, 747–755 (1974)
12. Chen, X., Wang, Y., Gao, S., Jung, T.P., Gao, X.: Filter bank canonical correlation analysis for implementing a high-speed SSVEP-based brain-computer interface. J. Neural Eng. **12**, 046008 (2015)
13. Lin, Z., Zhang, C., Wu, W., Gao, X.: Frequency recognition based on canonical correlation analysis for SSVEP-based BCIs. IEEE Trans. Biomed. Eng. **52**, 1172–1176 (2007)

14. Bin, G., Gao, X., Yan, Z., Hong, B., Goa, S.: An online multi-channel SSVEP-based brain-computer interface using a canonical correlation analysis method. J. Neural Eng. **6**, 046002 (2009)
15. Wang, Y., Nakanishi, M., Wang, Y.T., Jung, T.P.: Enhancing detection of steady-state visual evoked potentials using individual training data. In: 36th Annual International Conference of the IEEE Engineering in Medicine and Biology Society, pp. 3037–3040. Chicago, IL (2014)
16. Cheng, M., Gao, X., Gao, S., Xu, D.: Design and implementation of a brain-computer interface with high transfer rate. IEEE Trans. Biomed. Eng. **49**(10), 1181–1186 (2002)

Paired Associative Stimulation with Brain-Computer Interfaces: A New Paradigm for Stroke Rehabilitation

Nikolaus Sabathiel[1(✉)], Danut C. Irimia[1], Brendan Z. Allison[1], Christoph Guger[1,2], and Günter Edlinger[1,2]

[1] Guger Technologies OG, Herbersteinstrasse 60, 8020 Graz, Austria
{sabathiel,irimia,allison,guger,edlinger}@gtec.at
[2] g.tec Medical Engineering GmbH, Sierningstrasse 14, 4521 Schiedlberg, Austria

Abstract. In conventional rehabilitation therapy to help persons with stroke recover movement, there is no objective way to evaluate each patient's motor imagery. Thus, patients may receive rewarding feedback even when they are not complying with the task instructions to imagine specific movements. Paired associative stimulation (PAS) uses brain-computer interface (BCI) technology to evaluate movement imagery in real-time, and use this information to control feedback presented to the patient. We introduce this approach and the RecoveriX system, a hardware and software platform for PAS. We then present initial results from two stroke patients who used RecoveriX, followed by future directions.

Keywords: Paired associative stimulation (PAS) · Brain-computer interface (BCI) · Motor imagery · Stroke · Rehabilitation

1 Introduction

Until a few years ago, the brain-computer interface (BCI) research community was strongly focused on providing communication for persons with severe motor disabilities who could not reliably communicate otherwise. Many such BCIs relied on motor imagery (MI) [1, 2, 11, 14]. While these efforts have met with some success, they have yielded little benefit to people outside of this relatively small patient group. Recent scientific and commentary articles have presented new directions with BCI technology, including new goals with new patient groups.

One of the most promising new directions entails using BCIs based on MI to provide new options for stroke patients [3–9, 12, 13]. Rather than providing communication, the MI is used to introduce closed-loop feedback within conventional motor rehabilitation therapy. This approach is called paired associative stimulation (PAS) because it pairs each user's motor imagery with stimulation and feedback, such as activation of a functional electrical stimulator (FES), avatar movement, and/or auditory feedback indicating successful task completion.

PAS is a crucial element of the feedback cycle because of Hebbian learning, which is widely recognized as a fundamental principle of learning. Hebbian learning states

© Springer International Publishing Switzerland 2016
D.D. Schmorrow and C.M. Fidopiastis (Eds.): AC 2016, Part I, LNAI 9743, pp. 261–272, 2016.
DOI: 10.1007/978-3-319-39955-3_25

that neural connections are strengthened only when the presynaptic and postsynaptic neurons are both active. Conventional rehabilitation therapy is unpaired, because feedback often occurs when users are not performing the required MI. Users would thus receive rewarding feedback even though they are not producing the necessary MI and concordant neural activation [11]. This is a major reason why conventional movement rehabilitation therapy tends to produce, at best, moderate improvement during the acute phase. Improvement after the acute phase is even rarer.

Figure 1 illustrates the concept underlying RecoveriX, a complete hardware and software platform that can record, analyze, and utilize EEG activity in real-time to "close the loop" in stroke rehabilitation. The user (top left) imagines or performs specific movements, such as wrist dorsiflexion. The resulting EEG activity is detected through electrodes positioned in an electrode cap, then sent to an amplifier. In this figure, the amplification occurs through a small purple box on the back of the cap, and the resulting EEG signals are then transmitted wirelessly to a laptop. The laptop manages data analysis and presentation of feedback.

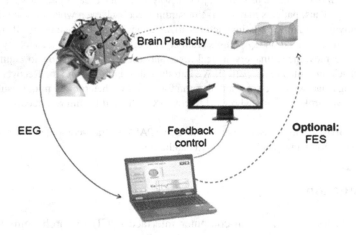

Fig. 1. A schematic illustration of the conceptual approach used in RecoveriX.

Like conventional therapy, RecoveriX users are instructed to imagine motor activity and receive feedback (specifically, through an avatar and FES). Unlike conventional therapy, RecoveriX users also wear an EEG cap that monitors MI that influences the feedback. The key element of PAS is the real-time connection between brain activity and feedback. In Fig. 1, this feedback is provided through an FES and a third-person view of an avatar's hands. The feedback only occurs when the user imagines movement. Thus, unlike conventional therapy, the feedback is always paired with brain activity.

This paper presents further details about our system, experimental procedures, and other methods, results from two patients, and future directions. Many of our future directions will be addressed within the new RecoveriX project, an SME Instrument active from 2016–2018. Since PAS is a new research direction, and RecoveriX is the first system to implement it, we currently have only initial results available.

2   Methods

2.1   Subjects

We present data from two subjects, both of whom signed a consent form. Subject 1 is a right-handed man, born in 1953, who suffered a stroke in 2014 that left him with some difficulty moving his right hand. Shortly after his stroke, he participated in 24 RecoveriX training sessions. Subject 2 is a right-handed woman, born in 1974, who had a stroke in 2010. After her stroke, her left hand was completely paralyzed. For two years, she participated in conventional therapy, which produced no improvement. In 2014, she participated in 10 RecoveriX training sessions.

Both patients were recorded in an open room at the Rehabilitation Hospital of Iasi. The patients were not placed in an anechoic chamber to reduce noise that might affect the EEG, and none of the equipment was placed in a shielded area.

2.2   Data Acquisition

Data were recorded from a 45 channel electrode cap using g.Ladybird active electrodes (Fig. 2). We recorded from electrode sites overlying the sensorimotor area. The ground electrode was placed on the forehead and the reference on the right ear lobe. Data were transmitted via cables to a g.HIamp, which then relayed the data to a laptop that was running the RecoveriX software.

The method of CSP yields a set of spatial filters that are designed to minimize the variance of one class while maximizing it for the other class. Given N channels of EEG for each left and right trial, the CSP method provides an $N \times N$ projection matrix. This matrix is a set of subject-dependent spatial patterns, which reflect the specific activation of cortical areas during hand movement imagination. With the projection matrix W, the decomposition of a trial X is described by

$$Z = WX \tag{1}$$

This transformation projects the variance of X onto the rows of Z and results in N new time series. The columns of W^{-1} are a set of CSPs and can be considered as time-invariant EEG source distributions. Due to the definition of W, the variance for a left hand movement imagination is largest in the first row of Z and decreases in each subsequent row. The opposite occurs for a trial with right hand motor imagery. To classify the left and right trials, the variances have to be extracted as reliable features of the newly designed N time series. However, it is not necessary to calculate the variances of all N time series. The method provides a dimensionality reduction of the EEG. Mueller-Gerking et al. [15] showed that the optimal number of CSPs is four. Based on their results, after building the projection matrix W from an artifact corrected training set X_T, only the first and last two rows (p = 4) of W are used to process new input data X. Then the variance (VAR_p) of the resulting four time series is calculated for a time window T. These values are normalized and log transformed according to the formula:

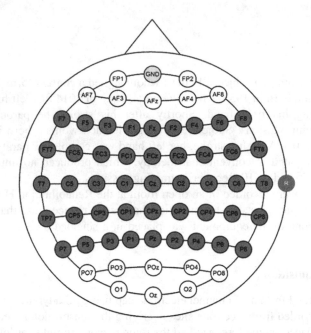

Fig. 2. The electrode montage, with sites used shown in red (Color figure online).

$$f_p = \log_{10}\left(\frac{VAR_p}{\sum_{P=1}^{4} VAR_p}\right) \tag{2}$$

Where f_p (p = 1.4) are the normalized feature vectors and VAR_p is the variance of the p-th spatially filtered signal. These four features can be classified with a linear discriminant analysis (LDA) classifier.

2.3   Stimuli and Procedure

After informed consent and being prepared for EEG recording, each patient was seated in a comfortable chair, about one meter in front of a monitor that presented cues and feedback (see Fig. 3). FES pads were placed over the dorsal side of the forearm with the affected hand. Figure 3 shows Patient 1, who had FES pads over the right forearm. Each trial began with a cue presented on a monitor in the form of a red arrow pointing to the left or right, which instructed the subject to imagine left or right hand movement. After a delay of 0.5 s, the user began to receive two types of feedback. First, a blue bar extended to the left or right, indicating both the direction and magnitude of the motor imagery. Second, the FES would activate if the user was imagining movement in the affected hand. This FES was sufficiently strong to cause movement in the affected hand. Feedback continued for 4 s, after which the screen went blank and any FES activation ended. There was a 2 s break before the next trial began (Fig. 4).

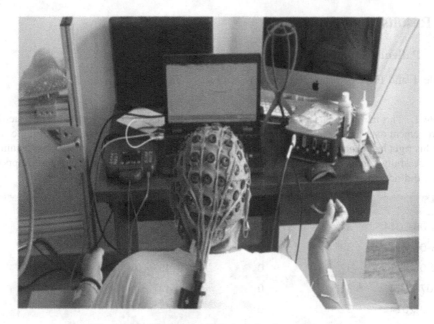

Fig. 3. A photograph of Patient 1 using the system.

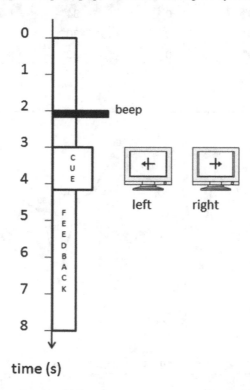

Fig. 4. Timing within one trial. A fixation cross appears when the trial begins A short beep cues the user after two seconds. One second later, a visual cue is presented. From 4.25 s until the end of the trial (8 s), online feedback is presented.

3 Results

3.1 Patient 1

Table 1 and Figs. 5, 6 and 7 present results from Patient 1.

Table 1. This table presents results from the 9-HPT with Patient 1. These results indicate steady improvement over about three months. At the end of training, the subject could perform the test with his right hand about as well as his unaffected left hand. The times indicate the time required to successfully complete the task. "Falls" reflects the number of times that a peg was dropped, which did not occur with either hand.

Date:	Left hand	Falls	Right hand	Falls
24-06-2014	31"	0	1'5"	0
26-06-2014	32"	0	54"	0
29-06-2014	32"	0	45"	0
2-07-2014	31"	0	42"	0
6-09-2014	31"	0	42"	0
9-09-2014	29"	0	38"	0
12-09-2014	29"	0	34"	0
15-09-2014	29"	0	30"	0
11-01-2015	29"	0	30"	0

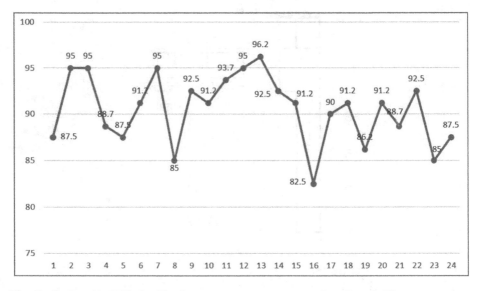

Fig. 5. Patient 1's BCI classification accuracy across twenty four RecoveriX usage sessions. Chance accuracy was 50%.

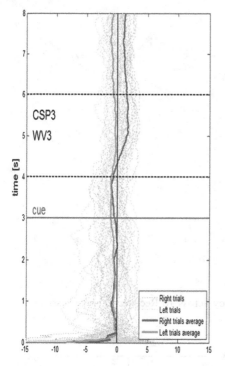

Fig. 6. Patient 1's LDA values in session 1 (Color figure online).

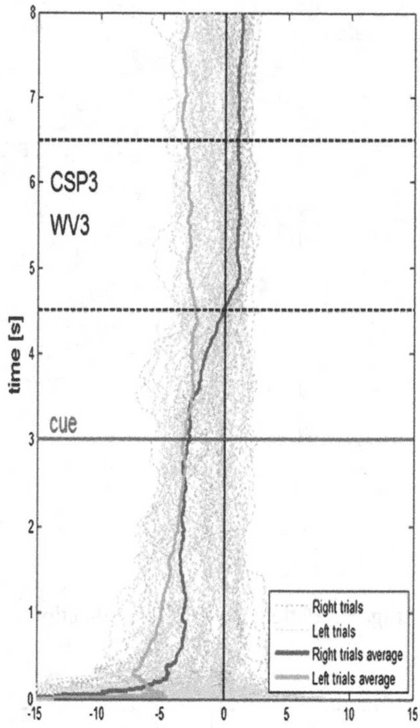

Fig. 7. Patient 1's LDA values in session 24 (Color figure online).

3.2 Patient 2

We did not attempt the 9-HPT with Patient 2, because her left hand movement impairment was too severe. However, Fig. 8 below shows that she regained limited left hand control after only ten training sessions.

Fig. 8. Three images showing Patient 2 performing left wrist dorsiflexion.

Figure 9 presents BCI classification accuracy across Patient 2's ten sessions of BCI use. Since she was effectively participating in a two-choice task, accuracy in the first two sessions is only slightly better than chance accuracy of 50%. The remaining eight sessions exhibit a substantial, though not monotonic, improvement (Figs. 9, 10 and 11).

268   N. Sabathiel et al.

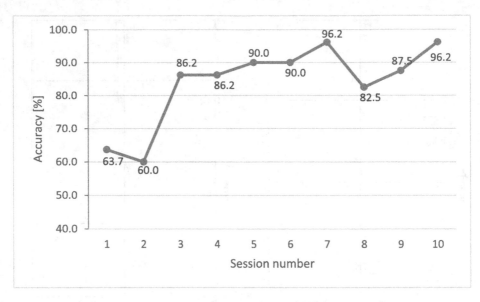

Fig. 9. Patient 2's BCI classification accuracy across 10 RecoveriX usage sessions.

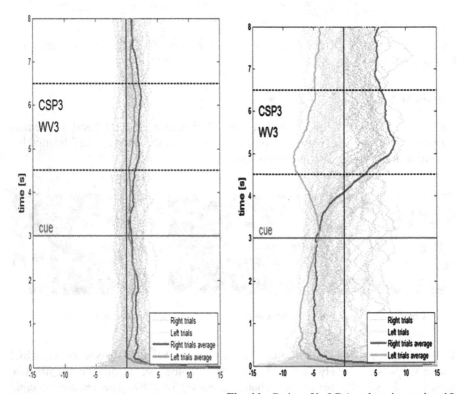

Fig. 10. Patient 2's LDA values in session 1 (Color figure online).

Fig. 11. Patient 2's LDA values in session 10 (Color figure online).

4 Discussion

4.1 Discussion of Results

Our results include both electrophysiological and behavioral analyses, including BCI accuracy, scalp maps, and performance on standardized tests such as the Nine-Hole Peg Test (9-HPT). These results support our view that RecoveriX can effectively incorporate EEG activity within a closed loop neurofeedback paradigm, and lead to improved functional outcomes. Notably, we present promising results even during the post-acute stage, after conventional therapy was ineffective.

4.2 Future Directions

We emphasize that these are still preliminary results. We do not have a direct comparison between conventional and PAS therapy. This is a major future direction that is clearly needed, and is currently our highest research priority, but is well beyond the scope of this preliminary report. Patient 2 did regain limited movement with RecoveriX after conventional therapy was unsuccessful, but this is only one result without a properly controlled experiment. This paper also validates the RecoveriX approach from a technical perspective by demonstrating that, at least with the two patients using the prototype system presented here, our system can function in real-world settings.

Another future direction involves improved immersive software to present feedback and maximize users' engagement. The patients described above saw feedback in the form of a blue bar, which has been used in many MI BCI studies but it graphically simple. We are exploring more advanced environments, such as different views of an avatar whose movements attempt to mimic the movements that the user imagines. In addition to providing feedback, these avatars could also help instruct users regarding which movements to perform. Figure 12 presents three examples of avatar feedback for different types of movements.

Fig. 12. Examples of immersive environments with avatars to provide instructions and visual feedback. Left: imagine left wrist dorsiflexion; Middle: a different view for imagining left elbow flexion; Right: imagine knee extension.

Figure 12 also reflects our effort to expand the movements that RecoveriX can detect and support. The work presented here only addressed wrist and grasp function. In future work, we hope to support a broader range of movement types, including more upper-limb activities and lower limb movements. This will allow us to help a broader range of patients who are seeking rehabilitation for different areas impaired by stroke. This effort partly leverages our activity in the EU-funded BETTER project, which explored BCIs for lower-limb and gait rehabilitation.

We are also exploring improved hardware. The patients presented here used a 16 channel wired electrode cap with gel electrodes. However, we recently developed a wireless version with a smaller montage focused over motor areas. This system (see Figs. 1 and 8) has a much smaller amplifier that is weighs only 70 g, and should be more practical in field settings. Furthermore, based on analyses with 16 channel data, we identified the most useful electrode sites for PAS. Figure 13 presents the new montage that we plan to use for future research.

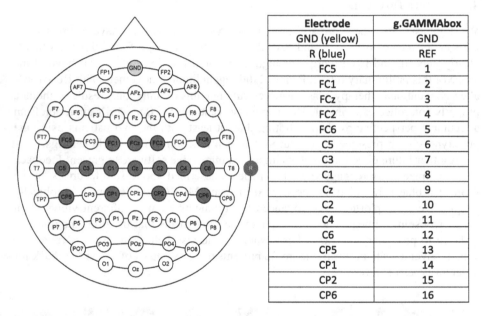

Electrode	g.GAMMAbox
GND (yellow)	GND
R (blue)	REF
FC5	1
FC1	2
FCz	3
FC2	4
FC6	5
C5	6
C3	7
C1	8
Cz	9
C2	10
C4	11
C6	12
CP5	13
CP1	14
CP2	15
CP6	16

Fig. 13. The new montage that we plan to use for future research. The electrode sites are centered around C3, C4 and Cz. All electrodes are placed near the sensorimotor cortex (Color figure online).

Another future direction involves incorporation of other signals to complement EEG activity. EMG (electromyogram) measures and position sensors are of obvious value, and other signals such as heart rate and eye activity could help identify (at least) if users are confused, frustrated, or overloaded. This idea leverages the "hybrid" BCI concept [10], essentially creating a system called a brain-neuronal computer interface (BNCI) that could be more informative than EEG alone [11, 12].

Finally, beyond influencing the PAS feedback loop, real-time detection of MI could be helpful for assessing compliance. Physiotherapists recognize that patients often do not comply with task instructions. Noncompliance may occur because patients are unmotivated, inattentive, unable to maintain the required MI throughout the trial, uncomfortable with the advanced technologies in rehabilitation, or misunderstand task instructions. BCI research has also shown that differences in task instructions can affect BCI classification accuracy [14]. By determining when users are performing the correct MI, and assessing the intensity of this MI, RecoveriX and other tools could help patients and therapist recognize noncompliance. Therapists could then take corrective measures such as providing revised instructions, counseling patients to improve motivation, and/or modifying the task and feedback environment.

References

1. Guger, C., Edlinger, G., Harkam, W., Niedermayer, I., Pfurtscheller, G.: How many people are able to operate an EEG-based brain-computer interface (BCI)? IEEE Trans. Neural Syst. Rehabil. Eng. **11**(2), 145–147 (2003)
2. Wolpaw, J.R., Winter Wolpaw, E. (eds.): Brain-Computer Interfaces: Principles and Practice. Oxford University Press, Oxford (2012)
3. Silvoni, S., Ramos-Murguialday, A., Cavinato, M., Volpato, C., Cisotto, G., Turolla, A., Piccione, F., Birbaumer, N.: Brain computer interface in stroke: a review of progress. Clin. EEG Neurosci. **42**(4), 245–252 (2011)
4. Mattia, D., Pichiorri, F., Molinari, M., Rupp, R.: Brain-computer interface for hand motor function restoration and rehabilitation. In: Allison, B.Z., Dunne, S., Leeb, R., Nijholt, A. (eds.) Towards Practical Brain-Computer Interfaces, pp. 131–154. Springer, Berlin (2012)
5. Xu, R., Jiang, N., Mrachacz-Kersting, N., Lin, C., Asin, G., Moreno, J., Pons, J., Dremstrup, K., Farina, D.: A closed-loop brain-computer interface triggering an active ankle-foot orthosis for inducing cortical neural plasticity. IEEE Trans. Biomed. Eng. **9294**, 1 (2014)
6. Belda-Lois, J.M., Mena-del Horno, S., Bermejo-Bosch, I., Moreno, J.C., Pons, J.L., Farina, D., Iosa, M., Tamburella, F., Ramos Murguialday, A., Caria, A., Solis-Escalante, T., Brunner, C., Rea, M.: Rehabilitation of gait after stroke: a review towards a top-down approach. J. Neuroeng. Rehabil. **8**, 66 (2011)
7. Ortner, R., Irimia, D.C., Scharinger, J., Guger, C.: A motor imagery based brain-computer interface for stroke rehabilitation. Stud. Health Technol. Inform. **181**, 319–323 (2012)
8. Ang, K.K., Guan, C., Phua, K.S., Wang, C., Zhou, L., Tang, K.Y., et al.: Brain-computer interface-based robotic end effector system for wrist and hand rehabilitation: results of a three-armed randomized controlled trial for chronic stroke. Front. Neuroeng. **7**, 30–31 (2014)
9. Ortner, R., Ram, D., Kollreider, A., Pitsch, H., Wojtowicz, J., Edlinger, G.: Human-computer confluence for rehabilitation purposes after stroke. In: Shumaker, R. (ed.) VAMR 2013, Part II. LNCS, vol. 8022, pp. 74–82. Springer, Heidelberg (2013)
10. Pfurtscheller, G., Allison, B.Z., Brunner, C., Bauernfeind, G., Solis-Escalante, T., Scherer, R., Zander, T.O., Mueller-Putz, G., Neuper, C., Birbaumer, N.: The hybrid BCI. Front. Neurosci. **21**(4), 30 (2010)
11. Neuper, C., Allison, B.Z.: The B of BCIs: neurofeedback principles and how they can yield clearer brain signals. In: Actis, R., Galmonte, A. (eds.) Different Psychological Perspectives on Cognitive Processes: Current Research Trends in Alps-Adria Region, pp. 133–153. Cambridge University Press, Cambridge (2014)

12. Brunner, C., Birbaumer, N., Blankertz, B., Guger, C., Kübler, A., Mattia, D., Millán, J.D.R., Miralles, F., Nijholt, A., Opisso, E., Ramsey, N., Salomon, P., Müller-Putz, G.R.: BNCI Horizon 2020: towards a roadmap for the BCI community. Brain Comput. Interfaces 2(1), 1–10 (2015)
13. Allison, B.Z., Dunne, S., Leeb, R., Millan, J., Nijholt, A.: Recent and upcoming BCI progress: overview, analysis, and recommendations. In: Allison, B.Z., Dunne, S., Leeb, R., Millan, J., Nijholt, A. (eds.) Towards Practical BCIs: Bridging the Gap from Research to Real-World Applications, pp. 1–13. Springer, Berlin (2013)
14. Neuper, C., Scherer, R., Reiner, M., Pfurtscheller, G.: Imagery of motor actions: differential effects of kinesthetic and visual-motor mode of imagery in single-trial EEG. Brain Res. Cogn. Brain Res. 25(3), 668–677 (2005). Epub 19 October 2005
15. Müller-Gerking, J., Pfurtscheller, G., Flyvbjerg, H.: Designing optimal spatial filters for single-trial EEG classification in a movement task. Clin. Neurophysiol. 110(5), 787–798 (1999)

Single Trial Variability of Event-Related Brain Potentials as an Index of Neural Efficiency During Working Memory

David W. Shucard[✉], Thomas J. Covey, and Janet L. Shucard

Division of Cognitive and Behavioral Neurosciences, Department of Neurology,
Neuroscience Program, The Jacobs School of Medicine and Biomedical Sciences,
University at Buffalo, The State University of New York, Buffalo, USA
{dshucard,tjcovey,shucard}@buffalo.edu

Abstract. Event-related brain potentials (ERPs) to a particular stimulus are extracted from the continuous electroencephalogram (EEG) through signal averaging techniques. The most extensively studied ERP component, P300 (P3, or P3b), occurs at approximately 300–800 ms post-stimulus. P3 amplitude and latency are markers of the attentional/cognitive resources devoted to the task and the timing (within msecs) of central processing speed of an individual's cognitive response to a stimulus, respectively. Variability in the timing and amplitude of components in the single EEG trials that contribute to the averaged ERP has been of particular interest to our laboratory because it may provide an index of central information processing efficiency. Examination of single trial variability (STV) can provide a level of analysis beyond traditional ERP measures and offers a unique marker of the functional integrity of neural pathways. In the present study we examined ERP STV as it relates to WM demand or load during a visual n-back task in normal adult participants. Performance measures and the scalp-recorded EEG were obtained during the n-back task. Frontal and parietal scalp averaged ERPs were derived from the EEG time-locked to the stimuli. The mean and variability (SD) of the peak amplitude and latency were then obtained from the single trial data for each participant and condition. Results showed that as WM load increased, behavioral measures of processing speed slowed, behavioral efficiency decreased, and the number of correct responses decreased. Correlations for both latency and amplitude between the P3 component derived from the averaged ERP and the P3 component derived from the single trials were generally high, indicating that the P3s for individual trials identified by our STV procedure were representative of the P3s in the averaged ERP obtained by standard signal averaging procedures. P3 STV analyses also showed differential effects between frontal and parietal scalp sites for both amplitude and latency variability that were related to WM load. Both frontal P3 latency STV and amplitude increased as WM load increased, indicating decreased neural efficiency associated with an increase in WM load. Single trial ERP variability measures may provide potential physiological markers of the neural efficiency of brain processes engaged in cognitive functions, such as working memory.

Keywords: Working memory · ERP · Single trial variability

© Springer International Publishing Switzerland 2016
D.D. Schmorrow and C.M. Fidopiastis (Eds.): AC 2016, Part I, LNAI 9743, pp. 273–283, 2016.
DOI: 10.1007/978-3-319-39955-3_26

1   Introduction

1.1   Electrophysiological (Event-Related Potentials, ERPS)

Event-related brain potentials (ERPs) to a particular stimulus (e.g., letters that are designated as "targets") are extracted from the continuous electroencephalogram (EEG) through signal averaging techniques. The most extensively studied ERP component, P300 (P3, or P3b), occurs approximately 300 to 800 ms post-stimulus, and its latency and amplitude are influenced by cognitive factors such as the ability to detect a target and the salience of the target to the subject [see for review 1, 2]. The P3 amplitude and latency are markers of the attentional resources devoted to the task and the timing (central processing speed) of a subject's cognitive response to a stimulus, respectively. To this end, the P3 component is ideal for studying the physiological correlates of attention in both normal and clinical populations, when difficulties in attention, speed of information processing, and working memory may be present.

1.2   The ERP and Working Memory

Working memory (WM), or the ability to maintain and manipulate information briefly in time, is key to higher cognitive functioning such as language, planning, and problem solving [see for example, 3]. Working memory is conceptualized as a network of distributed systems invoking higher order attentional demands required for holding and manipulating information in one's mind for a relatively short period of time. Working memory has been divided into two processes: Executive control (responsible for the encoding, manipulation, and retrieval of information) and maintenance (keeping information available during a period of time). These working memory processes, mainly through fMRI studies, have been associated with specific brain structures: The prefrontal cortex (responsible for executive control processes and some role in active maintenance), and the posterior areas including the parietal cortex (responsible for active maintenance) [4–7] are two of the primary brain areas involved in WM. Druzgal and D'Esposito [8] found that during encoding and delay (maintenance) periods, prefrontal activation increased with memory load. We found significant WM deficits in patients with Systemic Lupus Erythematosus (SLE) that increased with WM load [e.g., 9].

Although imaging techniques lend themselves well to the identification of the anatomical components of WM, for example, the temporal sequence of events is best studied using ERPs. ERPs provide high temporal resolution (in milliseconds), indices of resources allocated to the task, and scalp topographical representations. It is possible to obtain a precise measure of the timing of activity induced by frontal cortical networks activated during cognitive processes such as the different components of WM. A study by McEvoy et al. [10] measured ERPs to a verbal and spatial n-back task and found that increasing the WM demands (or load) resulted in attenuation of P3 amplitude at the parietal site. Additionally, the correct "matches" produced greater amplitude P3 than nonmatching stimuli. They suggested that their findings can be interpreted in terms of the amount of neural resources allocated to the task. A number of other studies reported similar findings of a posterior P3 amplitude decrease as WM load increased, as well as a frontal P3 amplitude increase as a function of increased load [11, 12]. Research in our laboratory suggested that there is a balance between frontal and parietal brain regions related to the allocation of attentional resources and WM load, measurable by ERP P3 amplitude [13].

1.3 Single Trial Variability

Recently, there has been increased interest in intra-individual variability in both the behavioral and neuroscience literature [14, 15]. Intra-individual variability is considered to play a significant role in information processing capacity in the individual. For example, Bielak et al. reported that intra-individual variability of reaction time (RT) predicted cognitive outcomes five years later. Measures of intra-individual variability are of interest because they provide an index of central processing efficiency. Previously, we have used measures of single trial ERP latency variability to study mechanisms underlying ERP average amplitude changes in animals [see for example, 16, 17]. The amount of variability in ERP peak latency across single trials has an effect on the averaged ERP response such that increased STV can decrease the averaged peak amplitude and increase its latency. Such information about the single trials that comprise the ERP average can provide another level of analysis of ERP data besides traditionally used measures of ERP component amplitude and latency described above. In the present study, analysis of STV of the P3 response offered further insight into possible mechanisms responsible for the P3 amplitude and latency differences seen during different cognitive conditions and more importantly, STV could provide a functional marker of the integrity of neural pathways related to cognitive processes in different clinical populations that have cognitive dysfunction such as Multiple Sclerosis. For example, white matter integrity might be compromised in certain patients, leading to greater STV and, in turn, deficits in processing speed and WM.

Thus, variability in the timing and amplitude of ERP components in the single EEG trials that contribute to the averaged ERP could serve as an index of central processing efficiency and has the potential to provide unique information about the recruitment of brain resources for complex cognitive processes such as WM. Note that the distributions of a single trial ERP component illustrated in Fig. 1 could also potentially be independent of the average of the ERP component. In the figure to the left, there is a longer mean latency for Condition 2 and no difference in STV between Condition 1 and 2. In the middle figure, the mean latencies are identical between Conditions even though there is a broader distribution of single trials for Condition 2. In the figure on the right, there is longer mean latency and greater STV for Condition 2 than Condition 1. Thus, the average ERP latency/amplitude could be independent of or dependent on the STV. The relationship between the average and the single trials, we believe is important to determine because it could provide information about the efficiency of the system. For example, the relationship between single trials and the average may look like the figure on the right in patients with white matter damage or demyelinating processes.

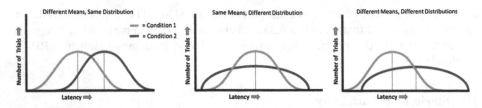

Fig. 1. Hypothetical frequency distribution of single trials for the latency of the P3 ERP component. (Color figure online)

Using a program developed in our laboratory, we examined ERP P3 STV (both amplitude and latency) as it relates to WM load during a visual n-back task in normal adult participants. We predicted that STV of P3 amplitude and latency would increase as a function of the load placed on WM, reflecting increased variability in central processing due to increased demands on WM.

2 Methods

Participant Characteristics: Twenty healthy controls were tested [age in years, mean = 45.7, SD = 9.33; 65 % female; years of education, mean = 14.2, SD = 1.77; estimated IQ (National Adult Reading Test, NART), mean = 108, SD = 8.07]. This study was approved by an internal Institutional Review Board of the State University of New York at Buffalo and written informed consent was obtained from all participants.

Visual n-back Paradigm: The visual n-back working memory task, illustrated in Fig. 2, was used to test processing speed and WM. The n-back is a data rich task that allowed us to obtain behavioral and electrophysiological data simultaneously while manipulating WM load. The behavioral data derived from the n-back task included information processing speed (as measured by RT to both match and non-match stimuli) and accuracy of the response. ERP data were obtained under the three WM load conditions of increasing difficulty (n-back conditions, 0-, 1-, 2-back, consecutively). The n-back task requires attention to visual stimuli and the ability to remember and determine the presence of a particular target stimulus. For the 0-back condition, participants were asked to identify a target letter "X" in a sequence of letters presented one at a time on a computer screen. For the 1-back condition, participants determined whether or not each letter matched the previously presented letter (one back). For the 2-back condition, participants determined whether or not each letter matched the letter two letters back. There were 150 trials in each condition. Stimulus duration was 400 ms with a 2 s inter-stimulus interval. Eleven letters of the alphabet were used as stimuli. Participants were required to respond via button presses to all trials (match and non-match).

ERP Analysis: Continuous EEG was recorded during the n-back procedure using a Neuroscan EEG data acquisition and analysis system. Data were recorded from 14 scalp sites with a linked ears reference and forehead ground. Data were filtered during acquisition with a bandpass of 0.1–100 Hz and digitized at a sampling rate of 250 Hz.

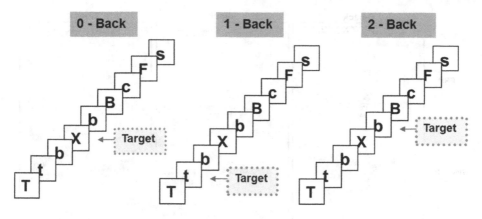

Fig. 2. Diagram of the visual n-back task

EEG data were segmented epochs with 300 ms pre-stimulus and 1600 ms post-stimulus. A 0.1–25 Hz filter was applied with 24 dB octave roll off, and automated artifact rejection procedures were conducted. Averaged ERPs were obtained for each participant for each condition. Because of the theoretical significance of the frontal-parietal network in WM function, we focused our averaged and STV P3 analyses on frontal and parietal midline scalp leads: Fz and Pz, for 0-, 1-, and 2-back conditions.

Single Trial Variability Analysis: Grand averaged ERPs for each condition/lead served as templates for the determination of a window surrounding the P3 component. Figure 3 presents a single trial analysis for an individual participant and the averaged ERP resulting from single EEG trials. The window width was defined by taking the average distance (in msec) from the N2 (negative ERP component occurring before the P3) to the P3 component for each of the grand averaged ERPs. An algorithm written in MATLAB selected the P3 for each trial by determining the region in the window of the single trial that most strongly correlated (point by point) with the template ERP P3 component. Single trial amplitudes that were below −25 μV or above 70 μV were excluded from the STV analyses. Non-baseline corrected data were used. Figure 3 also illustrates the distribution of P3 latencies and amplitudes across trials for a participant as determined by the STV analysis. Note the variability of peak latencies and amplitudes across trials.

The averaged ERP at Fz for each n-back condition is presented across the top of the figure. Just below the averages is an overlay of the individual trials that make up each averaged ERP (single trial EEG). The bottom two rows of the figure are graphic illustrations of the variability of the P3 response detected by the program. Note that STV of latency increases as WM load increases from the 0-back to the 2-back.

Statistical Analyses: Pearson correlations were used to assess the relationships between various measures. Repeated measures ANOVA were used to evaluate condition and lead effects. Post hoc testing was conducted using paired t-tests. Significance was set at p ≤ .05.

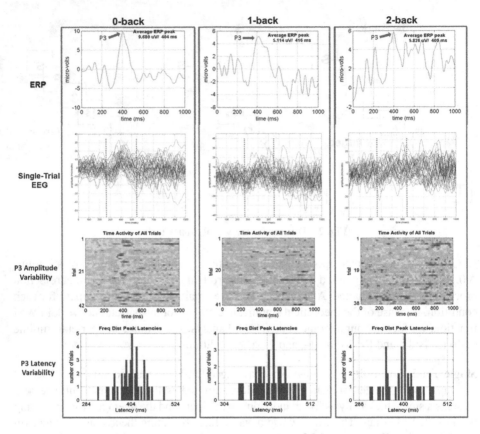

Fig. 3. Averaged ERPs and single trial data from one electrode for one participant

3 Results

Reliability of the Measure: Table 1 below presents the relationships obtained between the ERP template and the single trial P3 components identified for the frontal and parietal scalp leads across all participants, within the pre-defined component window. Note that the coefficients were all good accounting for about 50 % of the variance [e.g., $(0.76^2) = .58$]. These findings indicate that the template selected from the participant's averaged ERP was successfully used to identify the P3 component in the single trials for most participants.

In addition to the relationship between the template window derived for the P3 component and the P3 identified in the single trials, we examined the relationship between the participant's P3 amplitude and latency derived from the single trial analysis, averaged across the individually selected trials, and the P3 amplitude and latency obtained via standard signal averaging (component selected following averaging). Tables 2 and 3 present these data. Note that the correlation coefficients are generally high for both amplitude and latency, however there appears to be weaker relationships between the derived and standard latencies than with amplitude, particularly for the parietal lead during the condition with the highest WM load (2-back).

Table 1. Correlation coefficients between the P3 template and the single trial P3 response

	Mean	St. Dev.	Min	Max
Fz 0-back	0.76	0.04	0.67	0.82
Pz 0-back	0.74	0.06	0.55	0.81
Fz 1-back	0.73	0.04	0.66	0.79
Pz 1-back	0.70	0.05	0.65	0.80
Fz 2-back	0.72	0.05	0.60	0.79
Pz 2-back	0.71	0.04	0.65	0.77

Table 2. Correlations between ERP P3 amplitudes derived from single trial analysis and those from the averaged ERP

Derived avg P3 amplitude	Event-related potential P3 amplitude					
	Fz 0-back	Pz 0-back	Fz 1-back	Pz 1-back	Fz 2-back	Pz 2-back
Fz 0-back	.942***	-	-	-	-	-
Pz 0-back	-	.942***	-	-	-	-
Fz 1-back	-	-	.940***	-	-	-
Pz 1-back	-	-	-	.952***	-	-
Fz 2-back	-	-	-	-	.905***	-
Pz 2-back	-	-	-	-	-	.949***

*** = $p < .001$
** = $p < .01$

Table 3. Correlations between ERP P3 latencies derived from the single trial analysis and those obtained from the averaged ERP

Derived avg P3 latency	Event-related potential P3 latency					
	Fz 0-back	Pz 0-back	Fz 1-back	Pz 1-back	Fz 2-back	Pz 2-back
Fz 0-back	.957***	-	-	-	-	-
Pz 0-back	-	.776***	-	-	-	-
Fz 1-back	-	-	.955***	-	-	-
Pz 1-back	-	-	-	.956***	-	-
Fz 2-back	-	-	-	-	.872***	-
Pz 2-back	-	-	-	-	-	.567***

*** = $p < .001$
** = $p < .01$

Behavioral Effects: In that the focus of this study was on the STV measure, the performance effects will only be summarized here. Accuracy (correct matches), information processing speed (Reaction Time, RT), and behavioral efficiency (Standard

deviation of RT), all were related to WM load. That is, as WM load increased, performance decreased (ANOVA yielded significant Condition effects for each of these measures). Accuracy decreased particularly between the 1 and 2-back conditions. Reaction
time and standard deviation of RT increased from the 0 to 1 to 2 back conditions.

ERP Findings: A Condition × Lead ANOVA for P3 latency failed to yield any significant effects, although P3 latency at the Pz scalp site was generally longer across all
three n-back conditions. A Condition × Lead ANOVA for P3 amplitude yielded a
significant interaction (Condition × Lead, $F = 4.25$, $p = .025$). The findings indicate that
P3 amplitude was highest for Pz at the 0-back condition and decreased as a function of
WM load. The P3 amplitude for Fz was lower than Pz but did not show a significant
decrement from the 1- to 2-back condition. Figures 4 and 5 illustrate these results.

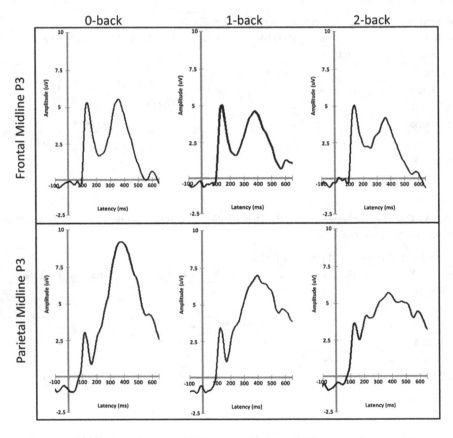

Fig. 4. Grand averaged ERPs to the 0-, 1-, and 2-back conditions

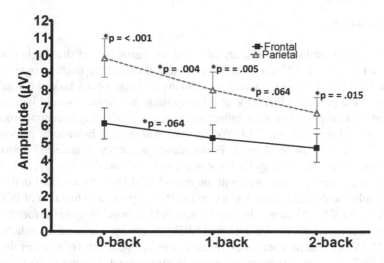

Fig. 5. Condition × Lead effect for P3 ERP amplitude

Single Trial Variability Findings: Separate Condition × Lead ANOVAs with STV as the dependent measure for ERP latency and amplitude yielded significant Condition and Lead effects for latency (F = 7.40, P = .005; F = 8.36, P = .009, respectively) and a significant Condition × Lead interaction for Amplitude (F = 4.80, p = .015). Figure 6a–c illustrate these findings. As can be seen from Fig. 6B and C, P3 latency variability across trials was greatest during the 1- and 2-back conditions compared to the 0-back. The 2-back condition had greater latency STV than either the 0- or 1-back. In regards to lead, STV was greatest at the parietal scalp site compared to the frontal site. As seen in Fig. 6A, the pattern of amplitude variability across n-back conditions differed between Fz and Pz scalp sites. Importantly, frontal P3 STV for amplitude markedly increased from the 1- to the 2-back condition. The parietal P3 did not show this effect.

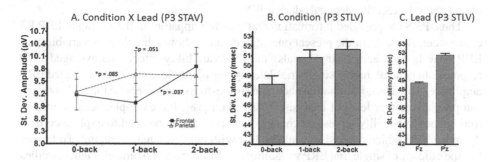

Fig. 6. STAV = single trial amplitude variability; STLV = single trial latency variability.

4   Discussion

In this study we examined the efficacy of using the variability of the single trials that comprise an average ERP as a biomarker of neural efficiency during cognition. We examined P3 STV as it relates to WM load during a visual n-back task in normal adult participants. We predicted that STV of P3 amplitude and latency would increase as a function of the load placed on WM, reflecting increased variability in central processing due to increased demands on WM. We showed that n-back behavioral performance varied as a function of WM load. Performance accuracy decreased, information processing speed as measured by RT became slower, and variability of RT, a behavioral index of neural efficiency increased with increased WM load. As reported in the literature, P3 amplitude decreased, particularly at the Pz scalp site as a function of WM load. Interestingly, STV for P3 latency increased with WM demand, despite the fact that there were no condition effects for the averaged ERP P3 latency. This finding indicates that increased STV of P3 latency across trials may occur independently of whether the signal averaged ERP P3 latency measure changes. With minimal demand on WM (0-back) STV for P3 amplitude at Fz and Pz was similar. At moderate WM demand (1-back), there was a subtle (albeit, not significant) increase in STV of P3 at Pz. With high WM demand (2-back), STV of P3 at Fz significantly increased from that seen in the 1-back condition. These STV amplitude findings could indicate differential recruitment of frontal and parietal resources during different levels of WM engagement. During moderate WM demand, increased variability at Pz could reflect engagement of posterior maintenance processes. During the 2-back, there is likely increased recruitment of neuronal resources associated with the frontal cortex due to the need for more executive or top down control, necessitated by increased task demand. Increased STV amplitude of P3 at Fz may reflect recruitment of these frontal resources. Placed within the context of the literature that relates frontal and parietal regions to executive and maintenance aspects of WM, respectively, the results are consistent with the possibility that Pz P3 amplitude variability may reflect maintenance, whereas Fz P3 amplitude variability may reflect central executive demands during WM.

Thus, P3 STV provided information that was not apparent in the averaged ERP P3 component. Aside from the present one, studies have shown that there is variability in ERP peak latency across single trials, and this variability affects the averaged ERP response. In general, higher single-trial-latency variability leads to lower averaged ERP amplitude [16]. Thus, information about the single-trials that comprise the ERP average can provide another level of analysis of ERP data [18]. For example, because trial-to-trial latency variability represents change over time, it can be used to explore cortical dynamics [19] which otherwise would be lost with conventional averaging. To further test the efficacy of single trial ERP variability as a biomarker of neural efficiency, studies should be conducted in which ERP measures are linked with MRI measures of microscopic damage such as demyelinating processes in neural networks involved in cognition. Such structure-function studies will help clarify the functional significance of the variability of single trials that comprise the averaged ERP.

Acknowledgements. Partial support for this research was provided by a grant from the National Multiple Sclerosis Society and the Jog for the Jake Foundation.

References

1. Polich, J.: Updating P300: an integrative theory of P3a and P3b. Clin. Neurophysiol. **118**, 2128–2148 (2007)
2. Kok, A.: On the utility of P3 amplitude as a measure of processing capacity. Psychophysiology **38**, 557–577 (2001)
3. Baddeley, A.: Working memory: looking back and looking forward. Nat. Rev. Neurosci. **4**, 829–839 (2003)
4. Carlson, S., Martinkauppi, S., Rama, S., Salli, P., Korvenoja, E., Aronen, H.J.: Distribution of cortical activation during visuospatial n-back tasks as revealed by functional magnetic resonance imaging. Cereb. Cortex **8**(8), 743–752 (1998)
5. Cohen, J.D., Braver, W.M., Nystrom, T.S., Noll, L.E., Jonides, D.C., Smith, J.: Temporal dynamics of brain activation during a working memory task. Nature **386**, 604–607 (1997)
6. Fuster, J.M.: Frontal lobes. Curr. Opin. Neurobiol. **3**, 160–165 (1993)
7. Gathercole, S.E.: Neuropsychology and working memory. Neuropsychology **8**, 494–505 (1994)
8. Druzgal, T.J., D'Esposito, M.: Dissecting contributions of prefrontal cortex and fusiform face area to face working memory. J. Cogn. Neurosci. **15**, 771–784 (2003)
9. Shucard, J.L., Lee, W.H., Safford, A., Shucard, D.W.: The relationship between processing speed and working memory demand in systemic lupus erythematosus: evidence from a visual n-back task. Neuropsychology **24**, 45–52 (2011)
10. McEvoy, L.K., Smith, M.E., Gevins, A.: Dynamic cortical networks of verbal and spatial working memory: effects of memory load and task practice. Cereb. Cortex **8**, 563–574 (1998)
11. Watter, S., Geffen, G.M., Geffen, L.B.: The n-back as a duel-talk: P300 morphology under divided attention. Psychophysiology **46**, 307–311 (2001)
12. Wintink, A.J., Segalowitz, S.J., Cudmore, L.J.: Task complexity and habituation effects on frontal P300 topography. Brain Cogn. **46**, 307–311 (2001)
13. Shucard, J.L., Tekok-Kilic, A., Shiels, K., Shucard, D.W.: Stage and load effects on ERP topography during verbal and spatial working memory. Brain Res. **1254**, 49–62 (2009)
14. Bielak, A.A.M., Hultsch, D.F., Strauss, E., McDonald, S.W.S., Hunter, M.A.: Intraindividual variability in reaction time predicts cognitive outcomes five years later. Neuropsychology **24**, 731–741 (2010)
15. Mohr, P.N.C., Nagel, I.E.: Variability in brain activity as an individual difference measure in neuroscience. J. Neurosci. **30**, 7755–7757 (2010)
16. Specht, C.M., Shucard, D.W.: Single-trial latency variability does not contribute to fast habituation of the long-latency averaged auditory evoked potential in the albino rat. Electroencephalogr. Clin. Neurophysiol. **100**, 462–471 (1996)
17. Shucard, D.W., Santa Maria, M.P., Specht, M.C., Podkulski, M.: Single-trial latency variability of auditory evoked potentials may indicate immediate memory in the albino rat. Int. J. Psychophysiol. **47**, 229–241 (2003)
18. Usal, A., Segalowitz, S.J.: Sources of P300 attenuation after head injury: single trial amplitude, latency jitter, and EEG power. Psychophysiology **32**, 249–256 (1995)
19. Delorme, A., Makeig, S., Fabre-Thorpe, M., Sejnowski, T.: From single trial EEG to brain area dynamics. Neurocomputing **44–46**, 1057–1064 (2002)

Cognitive Modelling and Physiological Measuring

A More Complete Picture of Emotion Using Electrocardiogram and Electrodermal Activity to Complement Cognitive Data

Danushka Bandara[1,2(✉)], Stephen Song[2], Leanne Hirshfield[2], and Senem Velipasalar[1]

[1] Department of Electrical Engineering and Computer Science,
Syracuse University, Syracuse, NY, USA
dsbandar@syr.edu
[2] M.I.N.D. Lab, S.I. Newhouse School of Public Communications,
Syracuse University, Syracuse, NY, USA

Abstract. We describe a method of achieving emotion classification using ECG and EDA data. There have been many studies conducted on usage of heart rate and EDA data to quantify the arousal level of a user [1–3]. Researchers have identified a connection between a person's ECG data and the positivity or negativity of their emotional state [4]. The goal of this work is to extend this idea to human computer interaction domain. We will explore whether the valence/arousal level of a subject's response to computer based stimuli is predictable using ECG and EDA, and whether or not that information can complement recordings of participants' cognitive data to form a more accurate depiction of emotional state. The experiment consists of presenting three types of stimuli, both interactive and noninteractive, to 9 subjects and recording their physiological response via ECG and EDA data as well as fNIRS device. The stimuli were selected from validated methods of inducing emotion including DEAP dataset [5], Multi Attribute Task Battery [6] and Tetris video game [7]. The participants' responses were captured using Self-Assessment Manikin [8] surveys which were used as the ground truth labels. The resulting data was analyzed using Machine Learning. The results provide new avenues of research in combining physiological data to classify emotion.

Keywords: Electrocardiography · Electrodermal activity · fNIRS · Valence · Arousal · Human computer interaction

1 Background and Literature Review

1.1 Nature of Emotion and Connection to Physiological Measures

Emotion is a complex phenomenon, often difficult for humans, not to mention machines, to recognize and respond appropriately [9, 10]. "Valence and arousal" [11] are two dimensions widely used and validated in neuro-physiological research. Arousal is conceptualized as "a unitary force that intensifies motivated behavior [20]." As superordinate dimensions of emotion, arousal is a dimension of emotion that maps

© Springer International Publishing Switzerland 2016
D.D. Schmorrow and C.M. Fidopiastis (Eds.): AC 2016, Part I, LNAI 9743, pp. 287–298, 2016.
DOI: 10.1007/978-3-319-39955-3_27

intensity, while the dimension of the emotion being pleasant versus unpleasant (i.e., the direction of emotion) is dedicated to valence [17]. Russell's circumplex model of affect is arguably the most popular model depicting the arousal and valence dimensions and their relation to emotional state [39]. Research states that most people's neutral (baseline) state is located near point (0, 0) in Russell's model [39] (Fig. 1).

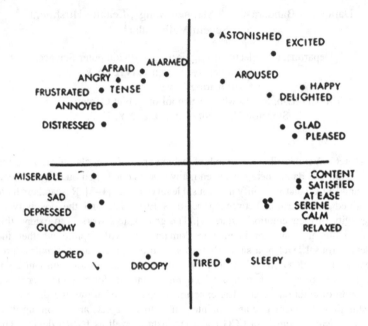

Fig. 1. Russel's circumplex model of emotion

This study considers valence and arousal as having "Low" and "High" states without concerning ourselves with the granular details of Russel's model. Therefore we will try to classify between high and low valence, and high and low arousal.

The most common 'measures' of emotion are done using self-report surveys, such as the Self-Assessment Manikin (SAM) or the Positive and Negative Affect Scale (PANAS) survey instruments [12]. The SAM uses a non-verbal pictorial assessment technique that directly measures the pleasure, arousal, and dominance associated with a person's affective reaction to a wide variety of stimuli. In this work we will focus on each of these factors as it relates to the physiological readings.

1.2   Physiological Manifestations of Emotion

Electrodermal Activity on Emotion. Arousal can be measured as difference in skin conductance, as a result of increased activity in eccrine sweat glands on palm or sole [17]. The activity of eccrine glands is thought to be related to both central and peripheral nervous system. A meta-analysis on a series of studies found that brain regions that are thought to be involved in generating emotional response are also involved in eccrine glands activity [21]. Also, eccrine glands is innervated by the sympathetic branch of autonomic nervous system in peripheral nervous system. Thus, higher activity in skin conductance is thought as an index of higher arousal.

The relationship between body and brain is thought to be interactive and influence each other [9]. This embodiment view of body and mind in human emotion found that brain activity is influenced by afferent and efferent signals from the body [13, 14]. Under this perspective, arousal is related to sympathetic activation in the autonomic branch of the peripheral nervous system, which is observed in skin conductance and heart rate [1, 15, 16]. In this experiment, Skin Conductance was measured in a form of Electrodermal activity (EDA) and heart rate was measured as electrocardiogram (ECG).

The connection between heart rate and cognition has been studied in literature [17]. There have been a multitude of studies that attempt to translate the arousal aspect of emotion to EDA [18, 19]. There have been limitations in using ECG data to detect arousal due to the confounding effect of arousal and attention involved in heart rate [1, 2, 16]. By using machine learning technique, this study intends to seek if we can singulate an index for arousal from ECG by combining it with EDA.

Heart Rate on Emotion. Heart Rate is also known to be related to emotional response on stimuli [1]. However, a confounding effect in heart rate makes it complicated to use it as an index for arousal, such that sympathetic nervous system activation is associated with arousal and faster heartbeat while parasympathetic nervous system activation that is associated with cognitive effort usually takes place as well for stimuli [17]. Although majority of studies [1, 3, 5, 9, 17] focused on the relationship between heart rate and arousal or attention, a more recent study found that the height of R-wave was lower when the stimuli had more arousal potential [22]. This finding suggests that analyzing other artifacts of the PQRST waveform in ECG may reveal direct relationships between ECG artifacts and arousal.

1.3   Machine Learning Efforts on ECG, EDA Data

ECG and EDA data are interesting as physiological responses despite being single channel time series data, there is a variety of features that can be derived from them (SCR, SCL, Heart Rate, Heart Rate Variability). They also represent correlations with emotional and neuronal activity as mentioned above. Methods such as sliding window, time shifting/warping [22] and symbolic representations [23] are used in analysis of time series data. Selvaraj et al. [30] used Bayesian classifier, Regression tree, k-Nearest Neighbor and fuzzy k-Nearest Neighbor on ECG data to classify emotional state. As discussed earlier, One of the most sensitive markers for emotional arousal is Electrodermal Activity (EDA). EDA reflects the amount of sweat secretion from sweat glands triggered by emotional stimulation. To equally assess both the quality of an emotion and its intensity, it is worth combining cognitive data with skin conductance measures to obtain higher accuracy than the individual measures. There have been research into combining EEG data with ECG data in literature [31]. Even combining

EEG with other physiological sensors such as Eye Tracking [32] and Electromyography (EMG) [33]. However there is limited literature on combining fNIRS and GSR data [34]. This work incorporates cognitive data from fNIRS and ECG data along with EDA to obtain higher Emotion classification accuracy.

1.4 Functional Near Infrared Spectroscopy

The fNIRS device uses light sources in the wavelength range (690–830 nm) that are pulsed into the brain (Fig. 2).

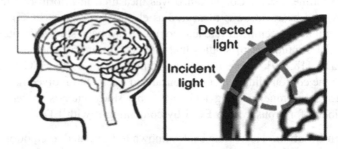

Fig. 2. Light is pulsed into the cortex, and detectors measure the light reflected back out of the cortex.

Deoxygenated hemoglobin (Hb) and oxygenated hemoglobin (HbO) are the main absorbers of near-infrared light in tissues during hemodynamic and metabolic changes associated with neural activity in the brain [40]. These changes can be detected by measuring the diffusively reflected light that has probed the brain cortex [40, 41].

fNIRS has been used to classify various cognitive states while computer users complete tasks under normal working conditions [35]. It has also recently been successfully used to classify emotional state of the user [36] and, as noted above, one purpose of the current study is to complement the utility of fNIRS measurements in the classification of emotion.

2   Experiment

2.1   Stimuli Selection

Music Video Segments. A subset of music video segments from the Database for Emotional Analysis using Physiological Signals (DEAP) mentioned previously [6] **were selected as stimuli to elicit participant emotions.** The DEAP research team selected the videos using a semi-automated method of user-tagged videos and subjectively rejected videos where the tag was not reflective of the emotion induced (e.g. a "happy songs about sad topics") [6]. The original DEAP dataset stimulus materials consisted of 40 music videos that had been found to induce consistent self-report scores in the outer boundaries of the four quadrants of the circumplex model.

Multi Attribute Task Battery (MATB). Psychology and neuroscience showed that emotions are connected to high-level reasoning; they are tightly linked to decision-making processes [38]. Also researchers have found connections between workload and emotion [37]. Therefore the different levels of workload are expected to elicit different emotional response. The Multi-Attribute Task (MAT) Battery provides a benchmark set of tasks for use in a wide range of laboratory studies of operator workload. The battery also provides a high degree of experimenter control and freedom to use diverse test subjects [28]. In this experiment, the MATB sessions were customized into 3 different workload levels (Low, Medium, High) in order to elicit different levels of workload in the user. This was achieved by presenting different frequencies of tasks to the user.

Tetris. The Tetris version [29] was customized to elicit different difficulty levels similar to MATB above. The difficulty levels were changed by adjusting the time between steps in Tetris

200 ms between Tetris steps-hard
300 ms between Tetris steps-medium
400 ms between Tetris steps-easy

2.2   Equipment Setup

Electrocardiogram (ECG) electrodermal activity (EDA) and was measured using Biopac MP150 system. The sample rate was set up as 1000 kHz using AcqKnowledge 4.2 software. For ECG, Mason-Likar lead placement was employed [24] (Fig. 3).

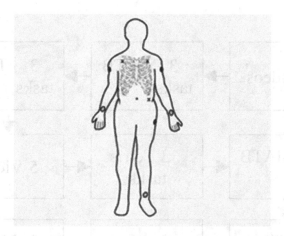

Fig. 3. Application of Mason-Likar lead placement for ECG (marked as x) [25]

fNIRS was setup to take concurrent measurements of cognitive data. The equipment used was a Hitachi ETG-4000 with 3X11 probe configuration (Fig. 4).

Fig. 4. Equipment setup on participant

2.3   Protocol

9 college age subjects took part in this experiment. 6 were men and 3 were women.

The subjects were provided instructions on how to do the different activities. Then they ran through a demo of each task to get familiar. After that, the ECG and EDA electrodes were placed on their body. And the fNIRS was placed on their head. Next the subject was presented with the tasks in a pseudo randomized block design (Fig. 5).

Before each stimuli, the subject was presented with a REST screen for 30 s. This was to get the subject to baseline level before the start of stimulus. Each task was one minute long.

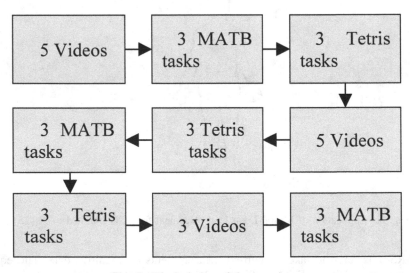

Fig. 5. Block design of the experiment

2.4 Post Task Surveys

Subjects were given a survey after each task to gage their perceived Arousal, Valence, Dominance, Liking and workload levels (Fig. 6).

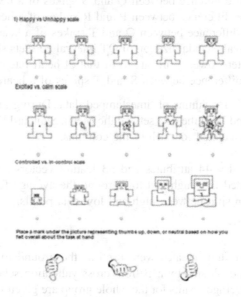

Fig. 6. Post task survey presented to participants

2.5 Data Analysis

Preprocessing. The raw data for ECG signal was presented in millivolt (mV), and EDA was in micro Siemens. By using 'ECG interval extraction' function in *AcqKnowledge 4.2*, PQRST waveform was analyzed into variables: RR interval, heart rate, R height, P height, QRS interval, PRQ interval, QT interval, corrected QT interval, and ST interval (Fig. 7).

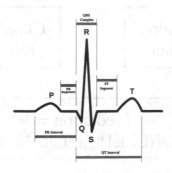

Fig. 7. Heart rate waveform [42]

- RR interval: Time difference between R spikes of each heartbeat
- Heart Rate: Number of heartbeats in a minute
- R height: The height if R spike artifact
- P Height: The height if P spike artifact
- QRS interval: time difference between Q and S spikes of a heartbeat
- PRQ interval: time difference between P and R spikes of a heartbeat
- QT interval: time difference between Q and T spikes of a heartbeat
- corrected QT interval: standardization of QT interval corrects shortened/lengthened QT interval in faster/slower heart rate to fit that of heart rate of 60
- ST interval: time difference between S and T spikes of a heartbeat

The data set contains 11 columns of timestamped data. During preprocessing, the 33 trials data was extracted from the data set and the Mean, Standard Deviation, Maximum and Minimum was calculated for each of the columns.

This resulted in 11 * 4 = 44 attributes and 33 feature vectors for each subject. The survey data was divided into high and low around the average for each person. This was to ensure an even split between high and low data points.

Machine Learning.

ECG Data. The labels thus created were used as the ground truth and fed into the classifier. Which was evaluated by a 10 fold cross validation scheme. The results for each individual and average results for the whole group are given in the results section.

Fusion of ECG and fNIRS Data. The fusion of ECG and fNIRS data was done using a simple label weighting method. The labels obtained by each classifier were combined linearly to get final labels. The weighting of the classifications has only two possibilities.

Case 1: Weight assigned to ECG data prediction < Weight assigned to fNIRS data prediction.

Case 2: Weight assigned to fNIRS data prediction < Weight assigned to ECG data prediction (Fig. 8).

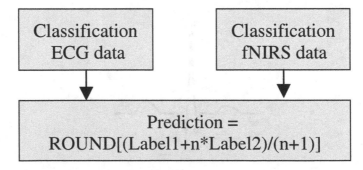

Fig. 8. Fusion of ECG and fNIRS classifiers

This prediction was compared with the binary survey label to get the accuracy of prediction.

3 Results

3.1 Valence Classification Using ECG Data

See Table 1.

Table 1. ECG classification accuracy for valence

Subject	Naïve Bayes	SVM	Bagging of 10 SVM classifiers
Average accuracy	58 %	70 %	62 %

3.2 Arousal Classification Using ECG Data

See Table 2.

Table 2. ECG classification accuracy for arousal

Subject	Naïve Bayes	SVM	Bagging of 10 SVM classifiers
Average accuracy	61 %	60 %	63 %

3.3 Results from Combination of Cognitive and ECG/EDA Data

Case1: Weight assigned to ECG data prediction < Weight assigned to fNIRS data prediction.

Classification accuracy of combined ECG and fNIRS data using Naive Bayes classifier = 85.85 %.

Classification accuracy of combined ECG and fNIRS data using SVM classifier = 66 %.

Case 2: Weight assigned to fNIRS data prediction < Weight assigned to ECG data prediction.

Classification accuracy of combined ECG and fNIRS data using Naive Bayes classifier.

Accuracy = 93.93 %.

Classification accuracy of combined ECG and fNIRS data using SVM classifier = 61.27 %.

The Naive Bayes classifier gave higher accuracy when combining ECG and fNIRS data whereas SVM accuracy was unchanged.

4 Conclusion

The results show that the combination of Electrocardiogram/Electrodermal Activity and cognitive data (fNIRS) provides higher accuracy than Electrocardiogram/Electrodermal Activity alone. A further explication of this work would be to apply it to a larger data set as well as cross subject data. However this work does emphasize the need for more research into fusion of physiological data to boost the accuracy levels.

References

1. Lang, A.: Involuntary attention and physiological arousal evoked by structural features and emotional content in TV commercials. Commun. Res. 17(3), 275–299 (1990). doi:10.1177/009365090017003001
2. Zillmann, D.: Excitation transfer in communication-mediated aggressive behavior. J. Exp. Soc. Psychol. 7(4), 419–434 (1971). http://dx.doi.org/10.1016/0022-1031(71)90075-8
3. Bradley, M.M., Codispoti, M., Cuthbert, B.N., Lang, P.J.: Emotion and motivation I: defensive and appetitive reactions in picture processing. Emotion 1(3), 276–298 (2001). doi:10.1037/1528-3542.1.3.276
4. Brosschot, J.F., Thayer, J.F.: Heart rate response is longer after negative emotions than after positive emotions. Int. J. Psychophysiol. 50(3), 181–187 (2003)
5. Kim, K.H., Bang, S.W., Kim, S.R.: Emotion recognition system using short-term monitoring of physiological signals. Med. Biol. Eng. Comput. 42(3), 419–427 (2004)
6. Koelstra, S., Muhl, C., Soleymani, M., Jong-Seok Lee, A., Yazdani, T., Ebrahimi, T., Pun, A.Nijholt, Patras, I.: DEAP: a database for emotion analysis; using physiological signals. IEEE Trans. Affect. Comput. 3(1), 18–31 (2012). doi:10.1109/T-AFFC.2011.15
7. Comstock, J.R., Arnegard, R.J.: The Multi-attribute Task Battery for Human Operator Workload and Strategic Behavior Research. National Aeronautics and Space Administration, Langley Research Center, Hampton (1992)
8. Chanel, G., Rebetez, C., Bétrancourt, M., Pun, T.: Emotion assessment from physiological signals for adaptation of game difficulty. IEEE Trans. Syst. Man Cybern. Part A Syst. Hum. 41(6), 1052–1063 (2011)
9. Bradley, M.M., Lang, P.J.: Measuring emotion: the self-assessment manikin and the semantic differential. J. Behav. Ther. Exp. Psychiatry 25(1), 49–59 (1994)
10. Plutchik, R.: The nature of emotions human emotions have deep evolutionary roots, a fact that may explain their complexity and provide tools for clinical practice. Am. Sci. 89(4), 344–350 (2001)
11. Scherer, K.R.: What are emotions? And how can they be measured? Soc. Sci. Inf. 44(4), 695–729 (2005)
12. Russell, J.A.: A circumplex model of affect. J. Pers. Soc. Psychol. 39(6), 1161–1178 (1980)
13. Barrett, L.F., Lindquist, K.A.: The embodiment of emotion. In: Semin, G.R., Smith, E.R. (eds.) Embodied Grounding: Social, Cognitive, Affective, and Neuroscientific Approaches, pp. 237–262. Cambridge University Press, New York (2008)
14. Andreassi, J.L.: Psychophysiology: Human Behavior and Physiological Response. Psychology Press, New York (2013)
15. Lane, R.D., McRae, K., Reiman, E.M., Chen, K., Ahern, G.L., Thayer, J.F.: Neural correlates of heart rate variability during emotion. NeuroImage 44(1), 213–222 (2009)

16. Boucsein, W.: Electrodermal Activity. Springer Science & Business Media, New York (2012)
17. Potter, R.F., Bolls, P.D.: Psychophysiological Measurement and Meaning: Cognitive and Emotional Processing of Media. Routledge, New York (2012)
18. Shi, Y., Ruiz, N., Taib, R., Choi, E., Chen, F.: Galvanic skin response (GSR) as an index of cognitive load. In: CHI 2007 Extended Abstracts on Human Factors in Computing Systems, pp. 2651–2656. ACM, April 2007
19. Westerink, J.H., Van Den Broek, E.L., Schut, M.H., Van Herk, J., Tuinenbreijer, K.: Computing emotion awareness through galvanic skin response and facial electromyography. In: Westerink, J.H.D.M., Ouwerkerk, M., Overbeek, T.J.M., Frank Pasveer, W., de Ruyter, B. (eds.) Probing Experience, pp. 149–162. Springer, Netherlands (2008)
20. Zillmann, D.: Television Viewing and Arousal Television and Social Behavior. U.S. Government Printing Office, Washington (1981)
21. Kober, H., Barrett, L.F., Joseph, J., Bliss-Moreau, E., Lindquist, K., Wager, T.D.: Functional grouping and cortical–subcortical interactions in emotion: a meta-analysis of neuroimaging studies. NeuroImage 42(2), 998–1031 (2008). doi:10.1016/j.neuroimage.2008.03.059
22. Dousty, M., Daneshvar, S., Haghjoo, M.: The effects of sedative music, arousal music, and silence on electrocardiography signals. J. Electrocardiol. 44(3), 396.e391–396.e396 (2011). http://dx.doi.org/10.1016/j.jelectrocard.2011.01.005
23. AcqKnowledge [Computer Software] (2014). http://www.biopac.com/
24. Farrell, R.M., Syed, A., Syed, A., Gutterman, D.D.: Effects of limb electrode placement on the 12- and 16-lead electrocardiogram. J. Electrocardiol. 41(6), 536–545 (2008). http://search.proquest.com/docview/216204094?accountid=14214
25. Electrode placement [Online image] (2014). http://advancedparamedicine.ca/posts/limb-leads. Accessed 10 Feb 2016
26. Berndt, D.J., Clifford, J.: Using dynamic time warping to find patterns in time series. In: KDD workshop, vol. 10, no. 16, pp. 359–370, July 1994
27. Lin, J., Keogh, E., Lonardi, S., Chiu, B.: A symbolic representation of time series, with implications for streaming algorithms. In: Proceedings of the 8th ACM SIGMOD Workshop on Research Issues in Data Mining and Knowledge Discovery, pp. 2–11. ACM, June 2003
28. Comstock Jr., J.R., Arnegard, R.J.: The multi-attribute task battery for human operator workload and strategic behavior research (1992)
29. McIntyre, R.C.: TetrisCSharp. Computer software (2011)
30. Selvaraj, J., Murugappan, M., Wan, K., Yaacob, S.: Classification of emotional states from electrocardiogram signals: a non-linear approach based on hurst. Biomed. Eng. Online 12, 44 (2013)
31. Schmidt, L.A., Trainor, L.J., Santesso, D.L.: Development of frontal electroencephalogram (EEG) and heart rate (ECG) responses to affective musical stimuli during the first 12 months of post-natal life. Brain Cogn. 52(1), 27–32 (2003)
32. Zheng, W.L., Dong, B.N., Lu, B.L.: Multimodal emotion recognition using EEG and eye tracking data. In: 2014 36th Annual International Conference of the IEEE Engineering in Medicine and Biology Society (EMBC), pp. 5040–5043. IEEE, August 2014
33. Wexler, B.E., Warrenburg, S., Schwartz, G.E., Janer, L.D.: EEG and EMG responses to emotion-evoking stimuli processed without conscious awareness. Neuropsychologia 30(12), 1065–1079 (1992)
34. Hirshfield, L.M., Bobko, P., Barelka, A., Hirshfield, S.H., Farrington, M.T., Gulbronson, S., Paverman, D.: Using noninvasive brain measurement to explore the psychological effects of computer malfunctions on users during human-computer interactions. Adv. Hum. Comput. Interact. 2014, 2 (2014)

35. Hirshfield, L., Costa, M., Bandara, D., Bratt, S.: Measuring situational awareness aptitude using functional near-infrared spectroscopy. In: Schmorrow, D.D., Fidopiastis, C.M. (eds.) AC 2015. LNCS, vol. 9183, pp. 244–255. Springer, Heidelberg (2015)
36. Bandara, D.S.: Emotion-Reading: Affective Analysis Using fNIRS. https://arxiv.org/submit/1490836/view. Accessed 24 Feb 2016
37. Myrtek, M., Deutschmann-Janicke, E., Strohmaier, H., Zimmermann, W., Lawerenz, S., Brügner, G., Müller, W.: Physical, mental, emotional, and subjective workload components in train drivers. Ergonomics 37(7), 1195–1203 (1994)
38. Marg, E.: DESCARTES' ERROR: emotion, reason, and the human brain. Optom. Vis. Sci. 72(11), 847–848 (1995)
39. Russell, J.A.: A circumplex model of affect. J. Pers. Soc. Psychol. 39, 1161–1178 (1980)
40. Chance, B., Zhuang, Z., UnAh, C., Alter, C., Lipton, L.: Cognition-activated low-frequency modulation of light absorption in human brain. Proc. Natl. Acad. Sci. 90(8), 3770–3774 (1993)
41. Izzetoglu, K., Bunce, S., Onaral, B., Pourrezaei, K., Chance, B.: Functional optical brain imaging using near-infrared during cognitive tasks. Int. J. Hum. Comput. Interact. 17(2), 211–227 (2004)
42. Atkielski, A.: Schematic diagram of normal sinus rhythm for a human heart as seen on ECG. Digital image. Sinus rhythm labels. Wikimedia commons (2007)

Real-Time Fatigue Monitoring
with Computational Cognitive Models

Leslie M. Blaha[1]([✉]), Christopher R. Fisher[1]([✉]), Matthew M. Walsh[2],
Bella Z. Veksler[1], and Glenn Gunzelmann[1]

[1] Air Force Research Laboratory, Wright-Patterson AFB, OH, USA
{leslie.blaha,christopher.fisher.27.ctr,glenn.gunzelmann}@us.af.mil,
bellav717@gmail.com
[2] Tier1 Performance Solutions, Covington, KY, USA
mmw188@gmail.com

Abstract. Real-time monitoring with cognitive models offers the unique
ability to both predict performance decrements from behavioral data and
identify the responsible cognitive mechanisms for targeted interventions.
However, their potential has not been realized because current parameter updating methods are prohibitively slow. We present a paradigm
that enables real-time monitoring using cognitive models and demonstrate its implementation with a fatigue-sensitive task. In this demonstration, an operator workstation, a cognitive model, and a monitoring
station are networked such that task performance data are sent to a central server that estimates model parameters and generates model-based
performance metrics. These are sent to a monitoring station where they
are summarized graphically together with model fit diagnostics. This
constitutes an infrastructure that can be leveraged for future predictive
adaptive system designs.

Keywords: Cognitive augmentation · Real-time monitoring · Parameter estimation · Fatigue · ACT-R · Computational cognitive models

1 Introduction

We envision a future wherein computational cognitive models are employed in
real time to monitor and predict operator performance [9]. It is widely acknowl-
edged that cognitive moderators, like fatigue, stress, and task load, can negatively impact performance (e.g., [7]). Naïve approaches to mitigating these moderators involve simple observations, whereby an intervention is administered,
usually by a human observer, after a performance decrement is detected. This
method suffers from two critical shortcomings. The first is that simple observation is not predictive. An intervention is administered only after performance is
already deteriorating and, in some sense, after it is too late. Consequently, poor
performance is inevitable. A second shortcoming is that simple observation is
purely descriptive, not prescriptive. An intervention—such as resting, altering
the task, or recommending a new task strategy—cannot be prescribed because

© Springer International Publishing Switzerland 2016
D.D. Schmorrow and C.M. Fidopiastis (Eds.): AC 2016, Part I, LNAI 9743, pp. 299–310, 2016.
DOI: 10.1007/978-3-319-39955-3_28

the reason for performance decrements is unknown. Without recognizing the source of the performance decrement, there is little basis for selecting appropriate cognitive augmentations. A theoretically grounded method is needed for monitoring the human cognitive system so that performance decrements can be predicted and mitigated through appropriate, targeted interventions.

We propose using cognitive models to assess cognitive states in real time. As mathematical and computational instantiations of cognitive theories, cognitive models offer the ability to make inferences about the processes underlying task performance and how those processes respond to cognitive moderators. Changes in key model parameters representing affected cognitive mechanisms reflect fluctuations in moderating factors. When the cognitive mechanisms are captured in this way, performance decrements can be understood, predicted, and mitigated through theoretically-informed interventions. However, heretofore, the explanatory power of cognitive models has been limited to post-task assessment because computationally intensive simulation is required to fit a model to data. This process can require hours or even days to complete.

In this paper, we present a novel paradigm enabling real-time cognitive modeling for performance monitoring and demonstrate its application to real-time fatigue monitoring with a model specified in the cognitive architecture Adaptive Control of Thought–Rational (ACT-R) [1]. Our demonstration consists of an operator workstation recording someone's behavior, a server implementing real-time parameter estimation, and a (possibly remote) monitoring station summarizing performance metrics. This three-part architecture leveraging networked computational resources is one possible design enabling remote, portable cognitive model-based performance monitoring.

2 Parameter Estimation

2.1 Standard Methods

A variety of methods are currently available for estimating model parameters [14]. These methods include grid search, gradient descent optimization algorithms (e.g., simplex algorithm, simulated annealing), and various algorithms inspired by biological evolution. One commonality underlying these methods is a trade-off between speed and accuracy. Higher estimation accuracy can be achieved by searching more of the parameter space, but this is costly as it requires more time and computational resources. Even with the benefit of parallel computing, these methods are prohibitively slow and offer limited scalability to complex models. This computational bottleneck has two primary causes: (1) simulations are computationally intensive, and (2) similar areas of the parameter space may be searched repeatedly. The resulting speed-accuracy trade-off is at odds with a fundamental requirement of real-time monitoring: parameter estimation must be fast *and* accurate, not a compromise between the two. This problem is further exacerbated by the need to continually update parameters as new data become available. Thus, the major challenge for real-time monitoring

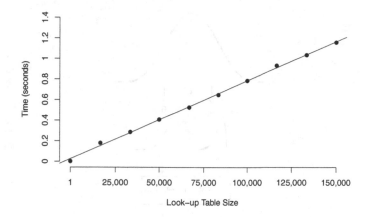

Fig. 1. Total parameter estimation time in the PDLT method as a function of look-up table size. Each data point represents the mean of 50 look-up repetitions.

with cognitive models is minimizing the parameter estimation speed-accuracy trade-off.

2.2 Pre-computed Distributed Look-Up Table

Our approach eliminates the aforementioned bottleneck through the use of pre-computation and distributed computing, resulting in efficient parameter estimation suitable for simulation-based models. In our method, incoming data from the experiment are compared to model predictions stored in a distributed look-up table with the aid of distributed computing. The parameters corresponding to the best matching predictions are selected as the best-fitting parameters. Accordingly, we termed this method the Pre-computed Distributed Look-up Table (PDLT) method. As shown in Fig. 1, the PDLT method is fast and exhibits a linear increase in computing time as the look-up table size increases. For the relatively simple, 4-parameter model used herein (described below), the PDLT consisted of 150,000 values, and PDLT search required little more than 1 s to complete. By contrast, parameter estimation for the same model using a simplex algorithm implemented on the same hardware can take 1 to 40 min, depending on several factors, including the numbers of starting points, iterations, simulations per evaluation, the speed of the model (complexity), and the model parameter values which scale to the predicted reaction times. The PDLT method has the additional advantage that it easily scales up to slower, more complex models: after the PDLT is constructed, the look-up process is invariant to the time required to simulate the model.

The PDLT method involves three steps, illustrated in Fig. 2:

1. **Define the distribution of parameters, Θ.** The first step is to define a distribution over the allowable parameter space, Θ, from which parameter combinations, θ, are sampled. The distribution's dimensionality reflects the

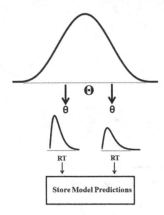

Fig. 2. A diagram of the PDLT method. For simplicity of this drawing, Θ is a uni-dimensional space, depicted by the Gaussian distribution. Individual samples $\theta \in \Theta$ make predictions for reaction time (RT) distributions.

number of parameters in the model; the shape and range of the distribution encodes which combinations of parameters are likely to be consistent with human behavior. Information from relevant psychological theory and empirical parameter estimates from prior studies are used to inform the construction of this distribution.

2. **Simulate predictions for each parameter combination, θ.** The second step is to simulate model predictions for each parameter combination, θ, and to summarize the predictions with a statistic. As shown in Fig. 2, the model we use for this demonstration generates reaction time (RT) distributions, but other models might generate different behavioral outputs. Other possible statistics include proportions, means, quantiles, or kernel density functions. What is important is that the statistic is a sufficient estimator, which means that the statistic contains all of the information for parameter estimation available in the raw data. The fit of the model is assessed by comparing the statistic computed from the model prediction to the corresponding statistic computed from the empirical data by means of root mean squared error (RMSE) or maximum likelihood.

3. **Store data in the look-up table.** The final step is to store the parameter combinations, θ, and corresponding predictions in a distributed array. Once the distributed array is constructed, it can be saved and re-used for future applications of the same model.

3   Real Time Fatigue Monitoring

Now that we have outlined the PDLT method for real-time parameter estimation, we describe its application for real-time fatigue monitoring. Figure 3 provides a generic schematic of the information flow in our demonstration. Data flows from the left to the right through networked computational resources. Beginning on the left, an operator executes a task at a workstation. Data are continuously transferred from the workstation to a central server, where the PDLT method updates model parameters after every new data point arrives. The server consists of a cluster of computers that perform the PDLT method and generate empirical and model-based performance metrics. Finally, the metrics and model output are transferred to a monitoring station where a human supervisor can observe performance through a summary dashboard. The dashed arrow connecting the server to the operator workstation represents potential for additional cognitive augmentation/intervention. When the model predicts performance decrements, it could, in principle, send feedback to the user or communicate to software designed to mitigate fatigue in affected cognitive systems (e.g., motor or visual modules). In the following sections, we describe a fatigue-sensitive task and corresponding ACT-R model, as well as the fatigue monitoring metrics and components of a supervisory dashboard.

3.1 Psychomotor Vigilance Task

We demonstrate real-time fatigue monitoring with the psychomotor vigilance task (PVT) [6]. The PVT is a simple detection task sensitive to fatigue due to sleep deprivation, circadian rhythm variations, and extended time on task [2]. Within each trial, operators wait a random inter-stimulus interval (ISI) of 2–10 s for a visual cue to appear on a computer screen or display device. Once the cue is detected, operators respond by keystroke as quickly as possible. After a response is submitted, RT feedback is displayed for one second, and then a new trial begins. Performance on the PVT exhibits predictable changes as operator fatigue increases. First, the RTs get slower, resulting in an RT distribution with a longer right tail. Second, the number of lapses (missed responses or RTs > 500 ms) and false starts (responses before stimulus onset or RTs < 150 ms) both

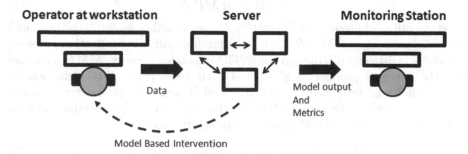

Fig. 3. A diagram of the real-time fatigue monitoring demonstration. The operator on the left performs the PVT task at a computer workstation, while a separate individual monitors performance from a remote monitoring station (right-hand side). The two individuals need only be networked to the central server. The dashed line back to the operator represents possible feedback or intervention strategies not implemented in the current demo.

increase. The PVT is typically run in 10 min intervals; shorter versions of the PVT (5 min and sometimes as little as 2 min) have also been demonstrated to show sensitivity to fatigue during sleep deprivation [13]. However, fatigue effects are not confined to instances in which subjects are sleep deprived. After 35 min of performing the PVT, performance decrements can be as pronounced as those found in operators who were awake for 29 h [15].

3.2   ACT-R Fatigue Model

Gunzelmann and colleagues [8] developed a model in the ACT-R cognitive architecture to capture performance in the PVT under different degrees of fatigue. ACT-R is a cognitive architecture or computational framework for instantiating comprehensive theories of cognition [1]. The ACT-R cognitive architecture contains a set of information-processing modules, each specializing in a specific mechanism, such as vision, declarative memory, or motor execution. Each of these modules is connected to a centralized procedural module that selects and regulates the internal actions of the architecture. Decision making behaviors emerge over a sequence of production cycles. A production cycle begins when the internal state of the cognitive architecture and environment are compared to the production rule selection criteria. Much like an if–then statement, a production rule is enacted when the conditions of the architecture or environment match its criteria. After a production rule is enacted, a new state is realized, marking the beginning of the next production cycle.

The ACT-R model of PVT performance is based on three productions [8,16]: (1) wait, (2) attend, and (3) respond. The model decomposes the process into four primary parameters: Utility U_S, Threshold U_T, fatigue decrement FP_{dec}, and *cycle time*. On each production cycle, one of the three productions is selected stochastically based on its match with the state of both the environment and the cognitive architecture. The match is formalized with the following utility function:

$$U_{ij} = U_S(U_i - MMP_{ij}) + \epsilon. \tag{1}$$

U_{ij} is the utility of production i in state j, U_S is the utility scalar, U_i is the stored utility for production i, MMP_{ij} is the mismatch penalty for production i in state j, and ϵ is logistically distributed noise. The mismatch penalty, MMP_{ij}, ensures that the incorrect production is selected with a low probability. Behaviorally, this manifests as infrequent false starts and lapses. The parameters U_S and U_T jointly determine the production selection probability. The production with highest utility is selected and enacted if its utility exceeds U_T:

$$\text{Production} = max(U_{ij}) \text{ if } max(U_{ij}) > U_T. \tag{2}$$

The difference between U_S and U_T, denoted as *Diff*, is an important indicator of fatigue. As *Diff* decreases, the selection of production rules becomes more stochastic. This increases false starts and lapses in the model's behavior. When none of the production utilities exceed U_T, a microlapse occurs. On the subsequent production cycle, U_S is decremented according to the parameter

FP_{dec}: $U_S = U_S \cdot FP_{dec}$. The likelihood of microlapses increases in subsequent production cycles and can eventually culminate in a behavioral lapse. The parameter *cycle time* governs the duration of production selection at the beginning of each production cycle. The production cycles' summed durations result in the observed RT.

In creating the PDLT, we used maximum likelihood estimation to find the best fitting parameters for a given set of data. This entails adjusting the parameters until the probability of the data given the model is maximized. Because no analytic solution for the likelihood function exists for this ACT-R model, we approximated the underlying distribution with a kernel density function. This method fits a smooth function to a distribution of simulated data. The kernel density estimator interpolates the probability density of a target RT by weighting simulated RTs as a decreasing function of distance from the target value. Goodness-of-fit was assessed with the log likelihood fit statistic, formed by summing the natural log of the predicted probabilities across all responses.

3.3 Software and Hardware

Communication between the operator workstation, server, and monitoring station was mediated through websockets. We implemented the PDLT method in Julia, a fast, high-level scientific programming language freely available through an MIT license [3]. The PVT and dashboard were programmed in JavaScript to maximize portability, and the plots were generated with the D3 library [5]. The server implementing the PDLT consisted of four Mac Pro desktop computers consisting of sixteen 3 GHz cores and 32 GB RAM.

3.4 ACT-R PVT Model PDLT

1. **Define the distribution of parameters, Θ.** We used multivariate Gaussian distributions based on parameters from individuals who were well-rested and sleep-deprived for 72 h [16]. The multivariate Gaussian distribution ensures efficient sampling of the parameter space by taking into account the central tendency and covariance structure within the empirical distribution of parameters.
2. **Simulate predictions for each parameter combination, θ.** We sampled 150,000 parameter combinations to achieve a high degree of accuracy while also maintaining speeds necessary for trial-by-trial updating of the model. Half of the 150,000 parameters were sampled from a parameter distribution representing well-rested individuals, and the remaining half were sampled from a parameter distribution representing sleep-deprived individuals.
3. **Store data in the look-up table.** Consistent with Fig. 1, the PDLT for 150,000 parameters requires 1.2 s to search, which fits within the minimum 2 s ISI window for the PVT task.

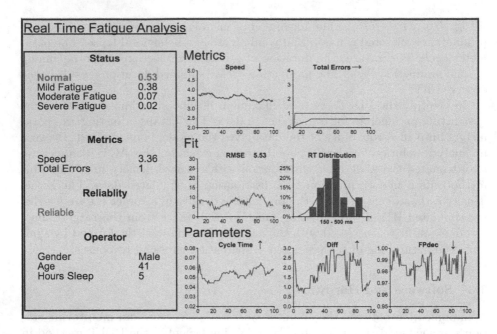

Fig. 4. PVT Metrics Dashboard. The data contained herein include 100 PVT trials. Human performance is plotted in blue, and model data are plotted in red. X-axes are the number of trials in all plots, except for the RT Distribution whose axis is RT. Arrows within each plot title indicate whether the last 10 values are on an increasing (↑), decreasing (↓) or stable trend (→). (Color figure online)

3.5 Performance Monitoring Dashboard

As a demonstration, we selected 100 trials from one participant who completed an extended PVT session [15] and sequentially fed this data into the fatigue monitoring system. Trial-by-trial, the ACT-R PVT model was fit to the data, and the dashboard received updated metrics and model output. The metrics and model outputs were computed from a 20-trial moving window. A screen shot of the dashboard is shown in Fig. 4, illustrating the data after the entire 100-trial session was completed. Information streamed into the dashboard is broken down into three categories explained in further detail below. In addition to three types of data about the operator and model, a key to the dashboard is presenting principled inferences about the operator state and model reliability for rapid assessment. Herein, we propose an initial set of heuristics for fatigue monitoring, which are summarized in the right-hand panel.

Operator Performance Metrics. PVT performance can be tracked by diagnostic metrics sensitive to the effects of fatigue, which are reviewed by Basner and colleagues [2]. While a number of metrics have been proposed, they are all variations on response speed, number of lapses, and number of false starts.

According to Basner et al., the two metrics most sensitive to acute total sleep deprivation are (1) the total errors, defined as the number of lapses and false starts together, and (2) speed, defined as mean(1/RT). The latter is also sensitive to chronic sleep restriction. While we include these in our dashboard, ultimately, the choice of metrics is left to individual applications and operator needs.

The top Metrics row shows the response speed, mean(1/RT), in the left plot. Operator RTs are blue, and model RTs are red. In this example, the two sets of data are nearly identical after 30 trials. The down arrow indicates that speed is on a decreasing trend after 100 trials. The right plot, Total Errors, tracks both the number of lapses (solid lines) and the number of false starts (dashed lines). Note that in this data set, there were no false starts, so that line is on the 0 value. The human data (blue) produces a step function when an error occurs; the model (red) is more graded as it represents the expected number of errors over time. The flat arrow shows a steady trend in the human performance after 100 trials.

Model Fit. The validity of the model assessment depends critically upon the fit of the model to the data. A large discrepancy between the data and model prediction will lead to invalid inferences. Accordingly, Fig. 4 displays two fit assessment plots in the middle row. The left plot tracks RMSE as a function of trial. Although maximizing the log likelihood has desirable statistical properties [4], it has poor interpretability due to log-scaling. To improve interpretability, the dashboard displays RMSE between the empirical and predicted RT quantiles. The quantiles correspond to the $10^{th}, 20^{th}, \ldots, 90^{th}$ percentiles, excluding any false start RTs to reduce volatility. One attractive property of the RMSE is its intuitive scaling: RMSE represents the standard deviation between observed and predicted values in milliseconds. A large value for RMSE could indicate either that the model is not valid for the task or that the parameter space was not properly sampled when constructing the PDLT. Should an application of the PDLT technique find unacceptably large RMSE values, *post hoc* model analysis is recommended to determine which of these possibilities resulted in a misfit and to improve the PDLT as needed.

The RT Distribution plot illustrates the histogram of operator RTs (blue) with the best-fitting model prediction overlaid in red. Only valid RTs are shown, in the range of 150–500 ms, excluding false starts and lapses. This provides a fast visual assessment of the similarity in the two distributions in a way that would highlight any strong differences in central tendency or shape.

Model Parameters. In the bottom row of Fig. 4, the dashboard tracks the history of values for *cycle time*, *Diff*, and FP_{dec} throughout the task. We opted to track these particular parameters because *Diff* is the most sensitive indicator of fatigue; *cycle time*, although invariant to fatigue, is an indicator of individual differences in baseline speed, and lower values of FP_{dec} correspond to an increased likelihood of micro-lapses.

Summary Panel. In time critical situations, integrating and interpreting the data may require more time than is available. For this reason, the dashboard provides a summary panel (left side) displaying the most pertinent information to facilitate rapid fatigue assessment. Starting from the top, the summary panel includes a status indicator, highlighting the operator's most likely level of fatigue in red (detailed below). Next, the summary panel displays the current state of the performance metrics. A reliability indicator located below the metrics provides a binary classification of the quality of model fit. Here, "Reliable" is a green font if RMSE < 15 ms, and "Unreliable" is a red font when RMSE ≥ 15 ms.[1] Finally, the summary panel includes demographic information about the operator, which can be useful when monitoring multiple operators.

The status indicator is designed to distill the available data into one of $N_s = 4$ ordinal fatigue categories: normal, mild fatigue, moderate fatigue, and severe fatigue. We used a Bayesian classifier to categorize performance into ordinal fatigue categories according to the composite parameter *Diff*, which is the strongest indicator of fatigue in the ACT-R model. Our rationale is that model fitting serves as a data reduction method that maps a full distribution of behaviors—including the aforementioned fatigue metrics—onto a small set of meaningful parameters. Because parameters associated with similar levels of fatigue tend to cluster together, they can be further distilled into categories. The intuition behind our application of the Bayesian classifier is that it measures the degree to which an estimated value of *Diff* is consistent with various categories whose underlying dimensions are graded and partially overlapping. Thus, the results of the Bayesian classifier should be interpreted as a category probability rather than a posterior probability of the ACT-R model. Formally, the Bayesian classifier is defined as:

$$\Pr(S_i|\hat{\omega}_t) = \frac{Pr(\hat{\omega}_t|S_i)Pr(S_i)}{\sum_{i=1}^{N_s} Pr(\hat{\omega}_t|S_i)Pr(S_i)}, \tag{3}$$

where S_i is fatigue category i, and $\hat{\omega}_t$ is the maximum likelihood estimate of *Diff* on trial t. The likelihood of the $\hat{\omega}_t$ given category S_i is defined as:

$$\Pr(\hat{\omega}_t|S_i) = \phi(\hat{\omega}_t; \mu_i, \sigma_i) \tag{4}$$

where ϕ is the Gaussian distribution probability density function, μ_i is the mean, and σ_i is the standard deviation. We eliminate the influence of the prior probabilities $Pr(S_i)$ by setting them equal to $\frac{1}{4}$.[2] Each category of fatigue is represented as a Gaussian model corresponding to a distribution of parameters that typify a given level of fatigue. The distributions of *Diff* were formed from the 35 min PVT study using the 17 individuals who exhibited time-on-task fatigue [15]. Fatigue

---

[1] It is important to note that this threshold is intended as a rough guideline for assessing this model fit for the PVT specifically. For PDLT-based monitoring with other models or tasks, RSME thresholds should be appropriately assessed and tailored.

[2] Updating priors in this context is problematic because parameters are estimated from overlapping windows of data, resulting in non-independence.

categories were defined by the *Diff* values taken from four equally spaced time intervals over the 35 min PVT session, reflecting increasing levels of fatigue. Note that the categories are intended to be a rough guideline for decision making.

4   Conclusion and Outlook

Until now, using cognitive models for real-time monitoring has been hampered by practical limitations. These are the result of computationally intensive simulations required for parameter estimation, far exceeding the time available during task execution. Leveraging the PDLT method, we achieve real-time fatigue monitoring with the PVT, a proof-of-concept demonstration that performance can be remotely monitored with cognitive models in real time. We lay the foundation for real-time adaptive systems which rely on cognitive models to aid in recommending interventions designed to mitigate performance decrements by targeting appropriate cognitive mechanisms.

Our real-time fatigue monitoring paradigm can be expanded in several ways. First, we must integrate additional fatigue contributors like sleep history, consistent with fatigue risk management strategies [10–12]. This is particularly important for refining the ordinal fatigue categories. Parameter values derived from various levels of sleep deprivation should augment the time-on-task parameters for more robust categories reflecting the interaction of chronic sleep deprivation and acute fatigue. Additionally, we are currently extending the paradigm from performance monitoring to performance prediction. This entails a dynamic model in which key parameters are functions of time to capture increasing fatigue [15]. There are several benefits with this approach over the current moving window, such as stabilizing parameter estimates, eliminating correlated errors via conditional independence, and predicting performance decrements on future trials.

The PDLT method is agnostic to the specific model or application domain. Thus, if validated models are available, cognitive model-based monitoring can be implemented to capture and mitigate the effects of other moderators. For example, we might monitor task load impacts during dynamic multitasking, requiring multiple cognitive systems and multiple candidate sources of overload. Slow response speeds, for example, might be caused by missed information, sensory overload, or overtaxed memory retrieval. Internal states of the cognitive model will provide critical insights about the source of observed performance decrements. Values like number of items in a buffer or proportion of executed productions provide a novel set of metrics for the otherwise unobservable internal state of the operator. Thus, PDLT might be extended to store those internal states as well as the predicted behaviors for even deeper insights into cognitive states. Importantly, the PDLT, once established, can be accessed simultaneously for multiple observers, granting a single supervisor the ability to monitor multiple individuals simultaneously. Thus, the PDLT method brings us closer to a radically different future of cognitive model-based monitoring and performance enhancement.

Acknowledgments. We thank Brad Reynolds for software programming assistance. The views expressed in this paper are those of the authors and do not reflect the official policy or position of the Department of Defense or the U.S. Government. This research was supported by a 711th Human Performance Wing Chief Scientist Seedling grant to G.G. and L.M.B.

References

1. Anderson, J.R.: How Can the Human Mind Occur in the Physical Universe? Oxford University Press, New York (2007)
2. Basner, M., Dinges, D.F.: Maximizing sensitivity of the psychomotor vigilance test (PVT) to sleep loss. Sleep **34**(5), 581–591 (2011)
3. Bezanson, J., Edelman, A., Karpinski, S., Shah, V.B.: Julia: a fresh approach to numerical computation (2014). arXiv preprint arXiv:1411.1607
4. Van den Bos, A.: Parameter Estimation for Scientists and Engineers. Wiley, New York (2007)
5. Bostock, M., Ogievetsky, V., Heer, J.: D^3 data-driven documents. IEEE Trans. Vis. Comput. Graph. **17**(12), 2301–2309 (2011)
6. Dinges, D.F., Powell, J.W.: Microcomputer analyses of performance on a portable, simple visual RT task during sustained operations. Behav. Res. Methods Instrum. Comput. **17**(6), 652–655 (1985)
7. Gluck, K.A., Gunzelmann, G.: Computational process modeling and cognitive stressors: background and prospects for application in cognitive. In: The Oxford Handbook of Cognitive Engineering, p. 424 (2013)
8. Gunzelmann, G., Gross, J.B., Gluck, K.A., Dinges, D.F.: Sleep deprivation and sustained attention performance: integrating mathematical and cognitive modeling. Cogn. Sci. **33**(5), 880–910 (2009)
9. Gunzelmann, G., Veksler, B.Z., Walsh, M.M., Gluck, K.A.: Understanding and predicting the cognitive effects of sleep loss through simulation. Trans. Issues Psychol. Sci. **1**(1), 106 (2015)
10. Hobbs, A., Avers, K.B., Hiles, J.J.: Fatigue risk management in aviation maintenance: current best practices and potential future countermeasures. Technical report, DTIC Document (2011)
11. Hursh, S.R., Redmond, D.P., Johnson, M.L., Thorne, D.R., Belenky, G., Balkin, T.J., Storm, W.F., Miller, J.C., Eddy, D.R.: Fatigue models for applied research in warfighting. Aviat. Space Environ. Med. **75**(Supplement 1), A44–A53 (2004)
12. Lerman, S.E., Eskin, E., Flower, D.J., George, E.C., Gerson, B., Hartenbaum, N., Hursh, S.R., Moore-Ede, M., et al.: Fatigue risk management in the workplace. J. Occup. Environ. Med. **54**(2), 231–258 (2012)
13. Loh, S., Lamond, N., Dorrian, J., Roach, G., Dawson, D.: The validity of psychomotor vigilance tasks of less than 10 min duration. Behav. Res. Methods **36**(2), 339–346 (2004)
14. Rangaiah, G.P.: Stochastic Global Optimization: Techniques and Applications in Chemical Engineering, vol. 2. World Scientific, Singapore (2010)
15. Veksler, B., Gunzelmann, G.: Functional equivalence of sleep loss and time on task effects in sustained attention (Under Review)
16. Walsh, M.M., Gunzelmann, G., Van Dongen, H.P.: Comparing accounts of psychomotor vigilance impairment due to sleep loss. In: Annual Meeting of the Cognitive Science Society, Pasadena, California, pp. 877–882 (2015)

Introduction to Real-Time State Assessment

Brett J. Borghetti[✉] and Christina F. Rusnock

Air Force Institute of Technology, Wright-Patterson AFB, Dayton, OH, USA
{brett.borghetti,christina.rusnock}@afit.edu

Abstract. Real-Time State Assessment (RTSA) is the act of continuously monitoring an individual in order to estimate the human's current state. Examples of
real time state assessment include estimating workload, fatigue, stress, and attention from physiological measures such as Electroencephalogram (EEG) or eye-
tracking inputs. When estimated in real-time, the state of the human can aid
dynamic task allocation systems in determining when to intervene and what
course of action should be taken to mitigate potential problems or to improve
system performance. In this paper we provide an introduction to the field of RTSA
study, including an overview of modeling techniques and assessment methods.
RTSA's challenges are discussed, and recent work in the area is reviewed.

Keywords: Real-time · State assessment · Modeling · Human performance
modeling · Neuroergonomics · Dynamic task allocation

1 Introduction

Real-Time State Assessment (RTSA) is the act of continuously estimating a human's
current state while the individual is performing activities. There are many attributes
which comprise the human's state, but the attributes which are important for state-based
estimation will vary depending on the activity the human is performing. For example,
some tasks require mental activity. For such tasks, mental workload is the state, and it
is comprised of two attributes: an individual's cognitive capacity and the mental
demands of the task. Most human state attributes are not directly measurable. Because
attributes are not directly measurable, they must be estimated, using inference or
modeling techniques to derive the attributes from other measurable characteristics such
as task performance, or physiologically-sensed brain and body activity. Throughout the
rest of this paper, human state and state attributes that comprise a state will be used
interchangeably.

1.1 Facets of RTSA

RTSA is characterized by several themes:

- State Assessment: determining what the operator is *experiencing*. Operator states are
  a level of abstraction higher than direct measurements like heart rate.
- Non-invasive Sensing: the act of measuring and collecting *quantitative* data with
  minimal disruption to the operator's ability to accomplish the task.

© Springer International Publishing Switzerland 2016
D.D. Schmorrow and C.M. Fidopiastis (Eds.): AC 2016, Part I, LNAI 9743, pp. 311–321, 2016.
DOI: 10.1007/978-3-319-39955-3_29

- Model-Based: (complex) *computational models* are used to transform sensed-data to state estimates. These models are mathematical rather than associative. They may be closed-form or simulation-based.
- Real-Time: the state estimation is accomplished *continuously*, and with *minimal latency* between sensing and state estimation.

Some example operator state attributes include experienced workload or workload categorization, stress, fatigue, and attention.

1.2 Motivation

Operator real-time state assessment provides several opportunities that would otherwise be inaccessible, such as dynamic task allocation, computer augmentation, and adjustable autonomy.

Task allocation is the act of determining which tasks to load on which processing units. In the context of human-machine teams, the system could use information about the environment, task, and operator state in order to determine which entity (human or machine) to assign a task to. Optimal task allocation is a computationally complex process, even when all of the tasks and available task-doers are known a priori. When tasks are arriving throughout an event, or actions create new tasks, allocation becomes even more challenging. Dynamic task allocation is, perhaps, the most challenging because it could entail reallocating tasks or portions of tasks before completion. Awareness of operator state can help filter the available options for task (re)assignment, and can enable the allocator to know when a human may need help completing a task. A key facet of the dynamic task allocation decision is knowledge of the human operator's level of workload, and thus remaining available capacity.

Computer assistance can also be improved with information about the operator's state. Without knowledge of operator state, the human may be provided with computer assistance when they don't need it, or they mail fail to receive it when it would be beneficial. With knowledge of operator state, computers can determine the need for and type of assistance to provide for the operator.

2 Selecting and Fitting Computational Models

One of the characteristics of RTSA is its use of computational models. Computational models use logic and formulas to accept inputs and parameters and produce outputs. These inputs and outputs are jointly referred to as observed data. The parameters are components of the model which are used to tune the model to make it fit the observed data well.

Computational models differ from other types of social-science models such as concept (box-and-arrow) models, flow charts, or process diagrams which often only describe interrelationships or flow, but cannot be used to make numerical or categorical estimations – a requirement for operator state assessment. Computational models have clearly defined inputs and output which may be categorical, interval, or cardinal.

Additionally, computational models may be deterministic or stochastic, as well as closed-form or iterative. Given a fixed set of input values, deterministic models produce the same output every time, while stochastic models may have variance in their output. Closed-form models use mathematical formulas which produce an answer directly from the inputs. Iterative models may search, or attempt to converge on an output value which maximizes some mathematical formula. Often, iterative models provide approximate solutions.

Another facet of building computational models is to fit the model to the phenomenon it is modeling. Many types of models have parameters (coefficients, constraints, thresholds) by which the model can be tuned to fit the data. There are two general philosophies to model fitting: (1) learn relationships from the data, or (2) adjust the parameters of a pre-defined relationship to best fit the data.

Supervised machine learning (also known as statistical machine learning) is the term describing training models to learn relationships directly from data. First, a machine learning model type such as a linear regression, random forest, support vector machine, or neural network is selected, based on properties of the domain being modeled. Next, a dataset of desired model inputs and outputs is partitioned into a training set and a testing set. During training, the model-fitting algorithm tunes the internals of the model to minimize error on the predicted variable. The test dataset is input into the model to measure performance and quality of fit – this enables determination of whether the model can perform its intended function in determining operator state. A desirable property of the machine learning approach is that one doesn't have to know the inner properties of a process in order to use the approach – thus it is good for working with operator state assessment aspects for which there has been little theoretical work accomplished. For more details on supervised machine learning, see James [1].

An alternate approach attempts to fit parameters of pre-defined theory-inspired models to the desired data. These models have a-priori well defined sets of relationships between inputs and outputs and the fitting process usually focuses on optimal parameter search. One well-known method of parameterization is Maximum Likelihood Estimation - to choose the set of parameters which maximizes the likelihood that the observed data came from the model with that set of parameters. A desirable feature of this approach is that the models are more robust to data noise than machine learning models.

3 Using Computational Models

Two key reasons to use computational models in real-time state assessment are to (1) estimate an aspect of the operator's state, and (2) to determine the characteristics of the situation which affect the dynamics of the operator's state. The first reason is often referred to as estimation, and the second reason is known as inference.

3.1 Estimation

Estimation is determining the operator state from evidence, often from physiological measurements or behavior in the task environment. In machine learning models, the observed physiological measurements are input into a trained model, and the model outputs a nominal class or a numerical value representing the state characteristic of interest. Example inputs include using electroencephalography (EEG) or electrocardiogram (ECG) data to predict alertness & drowsiness [2–5], or operator stress and workload [6–9]. Cognitive models can also be used to estimate operator state [10].

Estimation can be used in three ways, depending on whether the researcher desires to use past, present, or future model-generated estimations. Estimations of past events can be used to develop explanations for what occurred in a previous operator situation. Past estimations can also provide a comparison for calibration of either the model or the task environment or both. Perhaps the most common use of estimation is for controlling some aspect of the task in the present. For example, suppose that a model using EEG as input had estimated that workload was increasing for the operator. Then a system that controls the level of autonomy could automatically increase the assistance provided to the operator [11, 12]. Future estimates – known as predictions – can also be used for system design purposes [13].

3.2   Inference

When working with models, inference is determining how changes in the input features impact the output [1]. For example, suppose that for a specific operator task, researchers collected EEG data for a set of numerical workload levels. If the researchers fit a machine learning model which accepted EEG data as input and produced a numerical value for workload as output, they could use it to explore the relationship between these variables. By exploring how variance in the input values affect the numerical output, the researchers could determine which EEG frequency bands, or combinations of bands, are associated with increased or decreased workload. In this way, the researchers could develop and test hypotheses regarding which portions of the brain and which types of neural activities were occurring during various levels of workload.

3.3   Considerations for Continuous and Time Series Evaluation

In the previous sections, the primary focus of real-time state assessment has been to model the relationship between physiologically-sensed information and some state characteristic of the human operator. The techniques presented so far presume independence of samples over time. In independent-samples models, the current state is independent of previous states. However, it is likely that physiological states are not independent of previous states. Thus, additional modeling methods such as Bayesian cognitive modeling should be considered. Bayesian techniques allow for the representation of the prior state which is updated with new evidence using Bayes' Law, providing support for dynamic models which consider prior states. An example Bayesian technique for dynamic modeling of state transitions over time is the Hidden Markov Model (HMM) [14]. For example, Fan and Yen [15] use HMMs to model human cognitive loads in members of a team. Each model tracks a team member (partner) and attempts to "predict its human partner's instantaneous cognitive load status" over time. Unfortunately, due to their additional complexity and required parameters, HMMs generally require more data than their stateless counterparts.

4 Assessing Computational Models

When developing models, one of the most important activities is to determine their readiness for their intended use. In this section we address quantitative measurement of the performance of models during estimation. We focus on the two main types of models: those that output real-valued numerical estimations and those that estimate one of a set of nominal categories.

For real-valued numerical estimations, there are several measures of assessment, including R-squared and its derivatives, as well as Root Mean Squared Error (RMSE). Nominal category estimation accuracy can be evaluated using confusion matrices and classification accuracy. For two-class estimations, additional assessment techniques include specificity (also known as false positive rate) and sensitivity (also known as true positive rate). Related assessments such as precision and recall can be presented in a single value, the F_1-score, to allow quick comparisons between models. When a model can be tuned through various combinations of true positive rate and false positive rate, another technique available is to generate a Receiver Operator Characteristic curve as well as its associated Area Under the Curve (AUC).

Before discussing each of these performance measures in more detail we must first illuminate an important rule for evaluation. When quantifying model performance ensure that the data used to evaluate the quality of the model was never used to build or tune the model. This is important because if data is used to fit a model, the model will often fit too well, actually encoding the idiosyncrasies of the data used to fit it, thus providing an overestimate of actual quality of the model fit. This phenomenon is called overfitting, and can lead to models which will not perform well when operating on previously unseen input data. Thus it is important that when evaluating the performance of a model, to hold out a set of data solely for evaluation.

4.1 R-Squared

R-squared is a simple measure of the amount of variance explained by the model as depicted in Eq. 1.

$$1 - \frac{RSS}{TSS} \tag{1}$$

RSS is the residual sum of squared errors (the sum of squared errors that reside between the true values and the values the model estimates) and TSS is the total sum of squared errors (the sum of squared differences between the true values and the mean of the true values). R-squared resides between 0 and 1 with values closer to one representing models that better explain the relationship between input and output, and values closer to 0 representing little of the relationship.

4.2 Root Mean Squared Error

Root Mean Squared Error (RMSE) is the square root of the sum of the error terms on the test-set predictions, as depicted in Eq. 2.

$$\sqrt{\sum_n (y_i - \hat{y}_i)} \tag{2}$$

One of the benefits of RMSE is that it provides an estimate of average numerical error of estimation in the same units as the original estimates.

4.3 Confusion Matrices and Classification Accuracy

When a model produces an estimate of the nominal category membership to which an observation belongs, a different measure of the quality of estimation is required. Confusion matrices provide a complete numerical categorization of the estimated and actual classes an observation belongs to. A confusion matrix lists the estimated category in rows and the true category in columns – as shown in (Table 1). At the intersection of a row and column is the number of observations in the estimated category for that row that are actually categorized for that column. Since the labeling of the rows and columns is identical, the quantity of counts along the top-left-to-bottom-right diagonal of the matrix represents correct estimations, and the quantities off of this diagonal represent errors. In this example there are 36 correct estimations and 18 incorrect estimations. In this example, we also see that while there were equal numbers of each category, the model estimated more of the members as category A than any of the other categories. Because it provides detailed information about how each type of category was classified, a confusion matrix can help diagnose particular problems with model biases.

Table 1. Example confusion matrix

		True Category			
		A	B	C	Total
Estimated Category	A	15	3	5	23
	B	1	12	4	17
	C	2	3	9	14
	Total	18	18	18	54

Classification accuracy can be quickly computed from the confusion matrix: it is the sum of the quantities on the diagonal divided by the total number of observations. In the example, there are 36 correctly classified observations out of 54 total observations, achieving 66.7 % accuracy.

4.4 Specificity, Sensitivity, Precision and F_1-Score

When working with two-category classification models, one can compute additional measures of model performance. Often, these categories are referred to as positive and negative. In medical parlance, the positive category is generally the abnormal category, (disease) and the negative category is the normal category (normal health). If one of the classes is considered positive (operator experiencing abnormal workload) and the other negative (operator experiencing normal workload), then the sensitivity (true positive rate; recall), and specificity (false positive rate; type-1 error), true negative rate and false negative rate can be computed. Sensitivity (correctly categorized positives divided by total actual positives) describes the rate at which the undesired condition is correctly identified, while Specificity (false positives divided by total actual negatives) describes the rate at which the normal category is falsely categorized as abnormal. Precision (true positives divided by predicted positives) characterizes the ability of the model to estimate positives correctly. Precision and recall (sensitivity) are independent, but a particular pair of precision and recall values can be converted into a single numerical value for comparison with other models: the F_1-score, as shown in Eq. 3.

$$F_1 = 2 \cdot \left(\frac{precision \cdot recall}{precision + recall} \right).$$ (3)

4.5 Receiver Operator Characteristic Curves

Often, models have tunable parameters, enabling them to set priorities for more positives to be correctly estimated at the expense of incorrectly categorizing negatives as positives. By sweeping the tunable parameters over their range, a set of characteristic data point tuples (true positive rate, false positive rate) can be collected – one for each setting. If these data points are assembled in a single plot such that the false positive rate (FPR) value is on the x-axis and the true positive rate (TPR) is on the y-axis, the result is a Receiver Operator Characteristic (ROC) curve. An optimal model is one in which the TPR is 100 % without any false positives. This model would have an elbow-shaped ROC which runs from (0,0) to (0,1) to (1,1). Assuming an equal number of positives and negatives, a model which was no-better than a random guess would have a ROC which coincides with the diagonal line from (0,0) to (1,1). Most model qualities are somewhere between these two extremes; most ROCs for such models lie between these two curves. Once a ROC curve is generated for a model, the area under the curve (AUC) can be computed. A perfect model will have an AUC of 1 while a random model will have an AUC of 0.5. Most models will have AUCs residing between 0.5 and 1, and these allow models to be quickly compared. Figure 1 shows an example ROC curve, as well as the point with the best F_1 score and the point with the best accuracy.

These assessment techniques and characteristics provide a brief introduction to the field of assessing human state assessment models. For more assessment techniques, see James et al. [1].

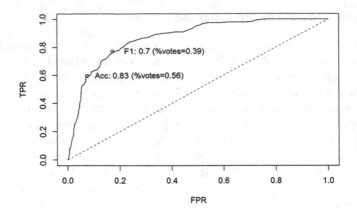

Fig. 1. Receiver operator characteristic curve for high/low workload classification (Area under curve = 0.87) [7]

5   Challenges for RTSA

Real-time state assessment is marked by a number of challenges. Some challenges stem from the nature of the domain: trying to characterize the internal state of a human operator from external observations. Other challenges are caused by the dynamic situations that unfold in real operations. Still other challenges are caused when trying to generalize research for use in situations where individual differences between subjects are unknown.

Because the research task involves humans, developing and testing RTSA models is potentially more arduous than developing and testing components or software. Perhaps the largest resource expenditure for human research will be time. When executing a task, if the researcher desires to understand the relationship between physiologically-sensed data and human state, the researcher must first train the human on the task until the human achieves steady state, thus entailing costly training time. Conversely, if the researcher is looking to explore how human's state changes as the human is learning a task, the researcher only has one opportunity per individual to measure the learning-induced state. One opportunity per person means many people may be required to achieve the desired effect size.

If the researcher wishes to explore human response to rare anomalous events in the context of normal, frequent events, the researcher needs to make those events be truly rare and believably infrequent – requiring extra time in the experiment where humans are exposed to a large number of normal events. Exploring human operator response to automation has a similar problem in requiring lengthy human trials. Because automation generally provides a dynamic response to the human behavior in the experiment, there could be many sequences of interaction which need to be explored.

When trying to generalize research findings, individual differences, task differences, and the research environment play a role. Individual differences may require models be tuned individually for each person: models which make excellent state estimates on one person may not work well on others. Ideally researchers would like to find invariant relationships which hold true in many situations - such as relationships between brain signals and operator overload. However, if the tasks are different enough, at some point, the relationship is likely to not hold. Smith et al., studies cross-task and cross-subject applicability, presenting a deeper exploration in [9]. Furthermore, if the original research was accomplished in one setting (such as a lab), the operator may not experience state transitions in the same way in a different setting (such as an aircraft cockpit). Stressors in the new environment which were not present in the research environment could easily change the relationship and cause the model to estimate state poorly.

6   Examples from the Community

Groundbreaking research to tackle these challenges continues. Hsu and Jung address the challenge of brain nonstationarity during a sustained attention driving task [16]. They propose a novel nonstationarity index (NSI) to evaluate these changes. Derived using independent component analysis (ICA) on EEG data, NSI indicates deviations in brain states over time. Their NSI shows significant differences between early (alert) phases of driving, and later (reduced-alertness) phases in the sustained attention task, finding that higher NSI values were associated with longer reaction time. Because NSI computation is relatively lightweight and is online-capable, NSI can be used as an indicator of alertness in real-time.

In another study, Du and Kim use eye tracking metrics to estimate performance on a human-in-the-loop tracking task [17]. Their task environment required participants to defend a ship which was potentially being attacked from the air. The subject's role was to identify unknown air tracks as type of aircraft and whether the aircraft was friendly or hostile: their performance was scored based on accuracy of their identification. Additionally, to capture their experienced workload difficulty, subjects were given a NASA-TLX workload survey [18] at the end of each trial. Subjects were broken into three groups based on their accuracy in the task (high, medium, low) and their eye-tracking metrics evaluated. While the average eye-tracking fixation times did not appear to be correlated with performance, human performance was statistically significantly inversely related to experienced workload, mirroring the findings of many other studies.

As discussed in the section on challenges to RTSA, individual differences make defining a single generalizable model which makes good state estimations across many individuals difficult. Yet separate individual-tuned models are often time-and-resource-intensive to parameterize. To address these difficulties, Blaha et al., explore a novel paradigm for updating computational cognitive model parameters in real-time using measures of human performance in a fatigue-sensitive psychomotor vigilance task (PVT) [19]. During the task, subjects are asked to respond by keystroke as quickly as possible after an on-screen cue is presented. Response time is gathered as the subject experiences fatigue (indicated by longer response times and false starts). An Adaptive Control of Thought-Rational (ACT-R) cognitive model is developed to model the behavior of the subject under fatigue: parameters are fit using maximum likelihood estimate (MLE) which adjusts the parameters until the probability of the subject data given the model is maximized. To minimize computation time, a pre-computed distributed lookup table (PDLT) is used to encode model output from a 4-parameter model. Using this lookup table is the key which enables real-time operation – a lookup in the table requires little more than a second, while parameter estimation implemented on the same hardware would take 20–40 min – a speed improvement of at least 600×. Another benefit of the lookup table is that the lookup time is invariant to the time required to estimate the parameters through simulation – which is important if the researcher wishes to employ more complex models in real-time.

7   Recommendations

While some progress has been made in real-time state assessment, more remains before the research is ready for ubiquitous use. Our recommended areas of improvement include: (1) improving sensed-data quality; (2) employ stateful model representations; (3) create human-readable state visualizations; (4) combine human state and environment state assessment.

Sensed data, especially physiologically-collected data such as EEG signals, are prone to artifacts. Some physical artifacts caused by muscle movements have mature removal techniques [20–22], but there are also cognitive artifacts which occur when the individual is performing other mental activities beyond the task at hand. Removing cognitive artifacts may require alternative approaches such as difference analysis with cognitive models.

As discussed in Sect. 3.3, stateful models which keep track of the change in state over time may be better suited for modeling operator state than those which assume that the human state at each moment in time is independent from previous and future moments.

While much research focuses on using state estimates for machine decisionmaking (e.g. dynamic task allocation; adaptive automation), human readable state representations have largely been ignored. Ad-hoc output representations are used largely for debugging and model-tuning processes. If common visual interface elements were available for state representation and expression, not only would these activities become easier, but so would the role of a team supervisor who could make informed decisions which consider the state of his workforce.

Human state assessment is certainly important, yet it is only part of the picture of an integrated human-machine team. Combining human state information with machine and environment state can yield a better overall picture of the team's condition. Armed with a better picture of the overall situation, decisionmaking entities should be able to make decisions which improve overall team performance.

Acknowledgements. The views in this article are those of the authors and do not necessarily reflect the official policy or position of the Department of the Air Force, Department of Defense nor the U.S. Government.

References

1. James, G., et al.: An Introduction to Statistical Learning with Applications in R, 1st edn. Springer, New York (2013)
2. Lin, C.-T., et al.: Development of wireless brain computer interface with embedded multitask scheduling and its application on real-time driver's drowsiness detection and warning. IEEE Trans. Biomed. Eng. **55**(5), 1582–1591 (2008)
3. Ganesan, S., et al.: Real-Time non linear bio-signals detection using fuzzy logic for wireless brain computer interface. Ijcns.Com, vol. 2 (2010)
4. Byrne, E.A., Parasuraman, R.: Psychophysiology and adaptive automation. Biol. Psychol. **42**(3), 249–268 (1996)
5. Jung, T.P., et al.: Estimating alertness from the EEG power spectrum. IEEE Trans. Biomed. Eng. **44**, 60–69 (1997)
6. Poythress, M., et al.: Correlation between expected workload and EEG indices of cognitive workload and task engagement. Found. Augment. Cogn. **1**, 32–44 (2006)
7. Giametta, J.J., Borghetti, B.J.: EEG-based secondary task detection in a multiple objective operational environment. In: Proceedings of the 14th International Conference on Machine Learning and Applications (ICMLA) (2015)
8. Gevins, A., Smith, M.E.: Neurophysiological measures of cognitive workload during human-computer interaction. Theor. Issues Ergon. Sci. **4**(1–2), 113–131 (2003)
9. Smith, A.M., et al.: Improving model cross-applicability for operator workload estimation. Proc. Hum. Factors Ergon. Soc. Annu. Meet. **59**(1), 681–685 (2015)
10. Jo, S., et al.: Quantitative prediction of mental workload with the ACT-R cognitive architecture. Int. J. Ind. Ergon. **42**(4), 359–370 (2012)
11. Fairclough, S.H.: Fundamentals of physiological computing. Interact. Comput. **21**(1–2), 133–145 (2009)
12. Prinzel, L.J., et al.: Effects of a psychophysiological system for adaptive automation on performance, workload, and the event-related potential P300 component. Hum. Factors **45**(4), 601–613 (2003)
13. Parasuraman, R.: Neuroergonomics: research and practice. Theor. Issues Ergon. Sci. **4**(1–2), 5–20 (2003)
14. Russell, S.J., Norvig, P.: Artificial Intelligence: A Modern Approach, 3rd edn. Pearson, London (2009)
15. Fan, X., Yen, J.: Modeling cognitive loads for evolving shared mental models in human-agent collaboration. IEEE Trans. Syst. Man Cybern. B Cybern. **41**(2), 354–367 (2011)
16. Hsu, S.-H., Jung, T.-P.: Modeling and tracking brain nonstationarity in a sustained attention task. In: Human-Computer Interaction International (2016)
17. Du, W., Kim, J.H.: Performance-based eye-tracking analysis in a dynamic monitoring task. In: Human Computer Interaction International (2016)
18. Hart, S.G., Staveland, L.E.: Development of NASA-TLX (Task Load Index): results of empirical and theoretical research. Adv. Psychol. **52**(C), 139–183 (1988)
19. Blaha, L.M., et al.: Real-time fatigue monitoring with computational cognitive models. In: Human Computer Interaction International (2016)
20. Klass, D.W.: The continuing challenge of artifacts in the EEG. Am. J. EEG Technol. **35**, 239–269 (1995)
21. Jung, T.P., et al.: Removing electroencephalographic artifacts by blind source separation. Psychophysiology **37**(2), 163–178 (2000)
22. Fatourechi, M., et al.: EMG and EOG artifacts in brain computer interface systems: a survey. Clin. Neurophysiol. **118**(3), 480–494 (2007)

User Abilities in Detecting Vibrotactile Signals on the Feet Under Varying Attention Loads

Alison Gibson[1,2(✉)], Andrea Webb[2], and Leia Stirling[1]

[1] Massachusetts Institute of Technology, Cambridge, MA 02139, USA
aegibson@mit.edu
[2] Draper Laboratory, Cambridge, MA 02139, USA

Abstract. The future of human space exploration will involve extra-vehicular activities (EVA) on foreign planetary surfaces (i.e. Mars), an activity that will have significantly different characteristics than the common exploration scenarios on Earth. The required use of a bulky, pressurized EVA suit perceptually disconnects human explorers from the hostile foreign environment, increasing the navigation workload and risk of collision associated with traversing through unfamiliar, rocky terrain. To assist the explorer in such tasks, multi-modal information presentation devices are being designed and evaluated. One application is to assist astronauts in ground obstacle avoidance via tactile channels of the feet. Before utilizing these signals as a form of information presentation, it is necessary to first characterize the tactile perception capabilities of the feet for selected vibration location and signal types, in particular during distracted attention states. The perception of tactile signals must be robust under various cognitive loads as the user will be involved in multiple tasks. The current study consisted of participants completing a vibrotactile detection study, with independent variables of attention state, vibration location and vibration signal type. Tactile cues were provided using haptic motor vibrations at six different locations on each foot for four different vibration levels (High, Low, Increasing and Decreasing), resulting in 24 unique vibrations per foot. Each treatment was repeated six times per attention state and vibrations were presented randomly within a time window of 2–7 s. After each trial, participants indicated the location and level of the vibration perceived. Accuracy of response was analyzed across conditions and results provide implications for the presentation of tactile information on the feet under varying attention states.

Keywords: Haptics · Vibrotactile display · Foot perception · Attention

1 Introduction

Manned missions to Mars and the Moon will involve space and surface operations that impose much higher risk and workload on astronauts than similar activities on Earth. The most complex of these operations are those involving

© Springer International Publishing Switzerland 2016
D.D. Schmorrow and C.M. Fidopiastis (Eds.): AC 2016, Part I, LNAI 9743, pp. 322–331, 2016.
DOI: 10.1007/978-3-319-39955-3_30

Extra-Vehicular Activity (EVA), which occurs when astronauts exit the protective environment of the spacecraft and enter the vacuum of space or a thin atmosphere of another planet while wearing a bulky spacesuit. These activities become challenging due to restricted visual cues, the absence of auditory information, and the restrictions placed on somatosensory and proprioceptive feedback from altered gravity and the pressurized suit [1].

Surface EVA operations will include assembly and construction of structures, geologic exploration and protective shelter excavation [2]. Such activities come with inherent risk of injury or damage to life-support equipment (i.e. the suit) since trips and falls are likely to occur on unfamiliar, rocky terrain. Due to the physical nature of these tasks in combination with restricted time, resources, and perceptual capabilities of crewmembers, there is a critical need to design multimodal interfaces for optimizing task performance and minimizing risks in such conditions [2]. Of particular interest is an information presentation device that can aid in obstacle avoidance during surface exploration and way-finding [3]. To assist astronauts in safely navigating to another crewmember, shelter or rover while traversing through rugged terrain, multi-modal information presentation devices are being designed and evaluated [3]. While there is a large body of research across different applications that is integrating information via auditory and visual channels, tactile channels for information mapping has not been thoroughly characterized yet, and could be of great use in intuitively conveying alerts about surface features, inclination, and obstacles in a path. Srikulwong and Oneill [4] highlighted demonstrations of tactile displays that can aid in navigation, target detection, and overall situation awareness in operational settings.

Since haptic technologies are relatively new and their applications in mapping information to human feet in particular are not well studied, it isn't clear what set of magnitudes, frequencies, or locations would be best when using vibrotactile signals to convey information. Compared to visual and auditory channels, the perception thresholds and cognitive interactions for tactile signals are less understood [5]. Vibrotactile displays for alerts, bodypart orientation, and directional navigation tasks have been implemented successfully on the arms [6–10], shoulder [11], waist [12–16] and through a body suit [17], but there have been very few applications utilizing the feet. One study successfully demonstrated the ability of a sandal-like vibration interface to promote and maintain a specific walking pace [18] and another used vibrating toe rings to signal direction changes while walking towards a preset destination [19], but none thus far have used tactile signals on the feet for aiding in obstacle avoidance while walking through rough and unknown terrain. Previous vibrotactile navigation studies have used haptic signals to command direction changes (right/left) or inform approximate distances to a destination, but none have tried to convey information about small obstacles directly in one's walking path (e.g. a rock that needs to be stepped over or moved around), which may require increased information presentation on this sensory channel.

Before vibrotactile signals can be implemented in a multi-modal navigational aid, it is necessary to first understand the tactile perception capabilities of the feet for the locations and signal types under consideration, in particular during states of divided attention. The detection of the perceived tactile signal must be robust enough to withstand various cognitive loads since the practical use of such an interface would undoubtedly occur while the user is multi-tasking. Load theory [20–22] suggests that perceptual and cognitive demands (or loads) have a limited capacity beyond which selective attention can fail, negatively affecting sensory perception or cognitive performance. Fitousi and Wenger [23] emphasize that research attributes selective attention and performance failures to such mental capacity limitations. In the case of an astronaut under high cognitive load from multi-tasking, it's therefore imperative that the vibrotactile stimuli carrying critical information be stimulating enough to be perceived during narrowed attentional focus.

The sensory systems of the feet enable sufficient vibrotactile perception using off-the-shelf tactors [24]. To better understand how to incorporate tactile signals for robust signal detection in the assistive device of interest, the current study examined four types of vibrations at six different locations per foot under varying attention loads. Independent variables consisted of vibration signal type (High, Low, Increase, Decrease), location (1–6), attention state (Focused or Distracted), foot (Right or Left) and order of attention condition assignment. The dependent variables were perceived location accuracy (ability to detect vibration at a specific location), and perceived vibration type accuracy (ability to detect the type of vibration signal). It was hypothesized that attentional load would negatively affect perception accuracy, and that certain locations and vibration types may be more detectable than others.

2 Methods

2.1 Participants

The participants consisted of ten healthy adults (3 females, 7 males) between the ages of 19 and 27 (M = 23.3, SD = 2.4). The experimental protocol was approved by the MIT Committee on the Use of Humans as Experimental Subjects (COUHES) and all participants provided written consent. Participants were excluded from the study if they reported irregularity or abnormalities with tactile perception on the feet or any injuries to the lower extremities. Participants were mostly right-handed (8 of 10), while one was left-handed and one was ambidextrous.

2.2 Materials

A custom haptic display was developed that applied four kinds of vibrations at six locations on each foot: one on the tip of the big toe, three on the lateral side, one on the back of the heel, and one in the center of the medial side of the foot (Fig. 1). Vibrations were created by small haptic motors (Vibrating Mini Motor Disc, Adafruit, New York City, NY) of 10 mm diameter and 2.7 mm thickness. All vibrations were 1.5 s in duration and consisted of one of the four vibration levels at an amplitude of roughly 0.8–1.2 g: High (11000 RPM), Low (2750 RPM), Increase and Decrease. The Increase vibration level went from the Low level to the High level and the Decrease vibration level did the opposite. The haptic motors were each controlled by an individual driver board (DRV2605, Texas Instruments, Dallas, TX) that received input in the form of a Pulse Width Modulation (PWM) signal from a microcontroller (Arduino UNO, Arduino, Massimo, Italy). The High vibration level had a 100 % duty cyle at 5 V while the Low vibration level had a 25 % duty cycle at 5V. The haptic motors were placed on participants' feet with double-sided tape and reinforced with athletic wrap for the duration of the experiment. Participants used a custom graphical user interface (GUI) that commanded the motors via serial ports and recorded participant responses for each trial.

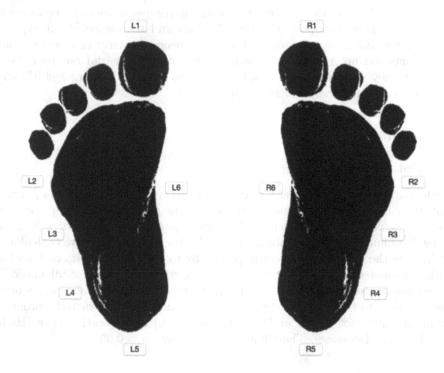

Fig. 1. Diagram of vibration motor locations from experiment GUI.

2.3 Experimental Protocol

Participants completed the experiment while in a focused state of attention (Focused condition) and in a distracted state of attention (Distracted condition), where the order of these conditions were counterbalanced (i.e. participants completed the trials for one or the other first). During the Focused trials, participants were instructed to focus on their feet and pay close attention to the vibration sensations. For the Distracted trials, participants were presented a random number between 0 and 100 at the beginning of each trial and instructed to count up from that number in increments of three until they felt the vibration. Four different vibration levels for six different locations per foot results in 48 unique vibration combinations, and participants experienced each combination for six trials during each attention condition, totaling to 576 trials overall. The 288 trials for each attention condition (Focused or Divided) were randomized in a pre-determined order. The numbers used in the Divided trials were the same for all participants to maintain the total difficulty of each trial (e.g. some numbers may be harder to count up from). To ensure that participants could not predict when the vibration would occur during each trial, each vibration took place at a random point in time between 2–7 s after pressing the "Next Trial" button on the GUI. Once a vibration was felt, participants selected the location on the foot where they perceived the vibration and then selected the type of vibration felt. Each response was recorded and deemed correct or incorrect, but participants did not receive this feedback. If a participant did not perceive a vibration, they were instructed to select a button labeled "I didn't feel it", and that trial's response was recorded as undetected.

3   Results

3.1   Data Analysis

The location responses were used to calculate perceived location accuracy scores while the vibration type responses were used to calculate perceived type accuracy scores. As a result, each participant had two separate accuracy scores for each of the 48 unique vibration combinations. In both cases, accuracy was calculated by dividing the number of correct responses by total trials for that combination (six). An undetected trial counted as an incorrect response in these calculations. A repeated-measures ANOVA was performed on each of the two accuracy scores, where main effects included attention state (Focused or Distracted), order of attention state, foot (Right or Left), location (1–6) and vibration type (High, Low, Increase, Decrease). The Significance level was $\alpha = 0.05$.

3.2   Perceived Location Accuracy

Results showed no statistically significant effects on perceived location accuracy ($p > 0.05$ for all main effects and interactions). Participants performed well in discriminating the locations where vibrations occurred (Fig. 2). The most common errors were confusing location 3 with neighboring locations or not detecting vibrations at location 3 (specifically during Low vibrations); although, these errors were highly subject dependent, which explains the large standard error.

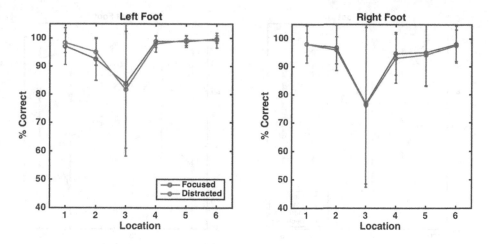

Fig. 2. Average perceived location accuracy and standard error for each foot and attention state.

3.3 Perceived Type Accuracy

Results showed significant main effects of Attention, Type, and several interactions between Location, Type and Foot (Table 1). Participants had higher average accuracy in discriminating vibration type during Focused trials (M = 79.82 %, SE = 3.35 %) compared to Distracted trials (M = 70.76 %, SE = 4.47 %). Accuracy was lower for dynamic vibrations (Increase and Decrease) compared to the static vibrations (High and Low), yet these differences are less consistent across locations on the Right foot (Fig. 3).

Table 1. Significant within-subjects effects for perceived vibration type accuracy.

Effect	F	Sig.
Attention	6.14	.038
Type	6.02	.004
Foot*Location	5.66	.002
Location*Type	2.58	.002
Foot*Type	3.67	.026
Foot*Location*Type	2.11	.028

3.4 Undetected Vibrations

Vibrations at certain locations were undetected and occurred mostly during the Low vibration types (Table 2). In addition, the undetected responses were

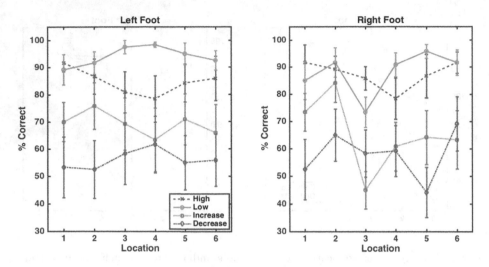

Fig. 3. Perceived vibration type accuracy mean and standard error for each location, type and foot (here both attention states are pooled).

unevenly distributed across participants. It is important to take these data into consideration while examining the statistical interactions between Type, Location and Foot.

Table 2. Percentages of undetected vibrations across all trials and participants. All dashed cells and cells not shown have zero undetected responses for those trials.

		Focused					Distracted		
		R3	R5	L1	L2	L5	R3	R5	L2
Type	High	-	-	1.7%	-	-	-	-	-
	Low	21.7%	1.7%	-	6.7%	-	20%	3.3%	5%
	Increase	-	-	-	-	-	-	-	-
	Decrease	-	-	-	-	1.7%	-	-	-

4   Discussion and Conclusions

The current study examined the effect of attention load, foot, location and vibration type on haptic foot perception. It was hypothesized that distracted attention states would decrease perception accuracy due to limited attentional resources, and that certain vibrations types would be easier to detect than others. The experimental data support a decrease in perceived vibration type accuracy due to attentional state, and show that distinct locations and vibration types could be more accurately perceived than others. The data also provides insight on location and vibration type perception. Overall, these results provide useful implications for vibrotactile interface design for the feet.

Results show that tactile perception is degraded during distracted states of attention. This has implications when designing interfaces that map critical information to sensory signals. Detection of time critical signals must be robust enough to eliminate ambiguity and human-device incompatibility risks. While attention state affected perceived vibration type accuracy in the current study, it did not significantly affect perceived location accuracy. Therefore, when designing haptic information presentation devices, it may be more reliable to use location to convey critical information while other details in the signal can provide additional sub-critical information.

With average perceived location accuracy scores close to 100 % for most foot locations, vibrations at these locations are promising for applications in tactile displays. Although, limitations exist with the locations on the lateral side of the foot. For certain individuals, sensation in this area may not have fine enough location resolution, and the lateral longitudinal arch (Location 3) may be the least sensitive, as a few participants often confused it with neighboring Locations 2 or 4 on both feet. The subject-specificity of haptic thresholds on other foot locations has been observed in previous research [25]. It's also important to consider that Low vibration types at this location on the Right foot were undetected quite often by most participants, which contributes to the lower average perceived location accuracy for Location 3 on the Right foot. Going forward, it may be favorable to only include one or two locations on the lateral side of the foot for vibrotactile inputs (i.e. Locations 2 and/or 4).

User abilities in perceived vibration type accuracy vary greatly by type, foot and location (Fig. 3). Participants reported occasional difficulty in detecting the difference between High vibrations and the dynamic vibrations (Increase and Decrease), which is observed in their trial responses. Participants stated that they usually selected High during these moments of confusion, which is consistent with lower accuracy for dynamic vibrations, with Decrease types being the hardest to distinguish. Participants reported that when a vibration started at the High level and then decreased, it was harder to detect this change than in the case for an increasing vibration, which could be due to the cutaneous sensation of the High level overpowering the proceeding lower levels. These results suggest that decreasing vibration signals are not adequately detectable and should not be used for critical information presentation. It is hypothesized that if the Decrease type was removed from the current study, perceived type accuracy for High vibrations may have been higher than those for Low vibrations, especially since High levels were rarely undetected. Regarding the Increase vibration type, distinguishing these from High types may be easier than is the case for Decrease types, but there is still insufficient evidence that it's reliable enough to convey critical information in a haptic interface application.

Vibrations were rarely undetected except for those of type Low at Location 3 on the Right foot, which had an unusually high occurrence (about 20 % of all R3-Low trials). It is unclear why the undetected signals are only for the Right foot. The vast majority of participants were right-handed, so it is possible that the lateral side of the dominant foot is less sensitive and has a higher tactile detection threshold, but this is just speculation. This phenomenon could also be device related (e.g. the motor at this location malfunctioned during certain Low vibrations), but is unlikely since there were not detection issues with other vibration types at this location. The Low, Increase, and Decrease vibration types on the Right foot appear to have more variability in perceived accuracy type across locations, suggesting that the perception capabilities of the Right and Left feet do differ in some ways.

Overall, results demonstrate that the haptic perception capabilities of the feet for selected locations and vibration types is sufficient for use in a vibrotactile interface. High and Low vibrations are successfully perceived at most of the locations studied, and will be implemented in future studies. Careful consideration should be taken when utilizing quickly increasing/decreasing vibrations or locations on the lateral side of the foot. Most importantly, signal perception should be robust enough to withstand attentional loading, so haptic signal location should convey the critical information while the more subtle signal properties can supplement with less critical information. Future work should examine alternate dynamic patterns, such as pulsing vibrations, as well as examine how tactile foot perception is affected by body motion (i.e. walking or running). The results of the current study will guide design of a multi-modal device for obstacle avoidance, where sensory reinforcement via visual channels may be incorporated.

While the current application of interest involves a wearable interface for obstacle avoidance, the growing range of computing devices, computational power and input/output capabilities opens doors for numerous other applications in human-computer interaction [5]. The integration of haptic communications in technology presents novel applications in teaching/training, telerobotics, entertainment and gaming [26].

References

1. NASA. Std-3000. man systems integration standards. National Aeronautics andSpace Administration, Houston, USA (1995)
2. Godfroy, M., Wenzel, E.M.: Human dimensions in multimodal wearable virtual simulators for extra vehicular activities. In: Proceedings of the NATO Workshop on Human Dimensions in Embedded Virtual Simulation, Orlando, FL (2009)
3. Holden, K., Ezer, N., Vos, G.: Evidence report: risk of inadequate human-computer interaction. NASA Human Research Program: Space Human Factors and Habitability (2013)
4. Srikulwong, M., O'Neill, E.: A comparative study of tactile representation techniques for landmarks on a wearable device. In: Proceedings of the SIGCHI Conference on Human Factors in Computing Systems, pp. 2029–2038. ACM (2011)
5. Sebe, N., Jaimes, A.: Multimodal human-computer interaction: a survey. Comput. Vis. Image Underst. **108**, 116–134 (2007)
6. Scheggi, S., Morbidi, F., Prattichizzo, D.: Human-robot formation control via visual and vibrotactile haptic feedback. IEEE Trans. Haptics **7**(4), 499–511 (2014)
7. Sergi, F., Accoto, D., Campolo, D., Guglielmelli, E.: Forearm orientation guidance with a vibrotactile feedback bracelet: on the directionality of tactile motor communication. In: 2008 2nd IEEE RAS & EMBS International Conference on Biomedical Robotics and Biomechatronics, BioRob 2008, pp. 433–438. IEEE (2008)

8. Matscheko, M., Ferscha, A., Riener, A., Lehner, M.: Tactor placement in wrist worn wearables. In: 2010 International Symposium on Wearable Computers (ISWC), pp. 1–8. IEEE (2010)

9. Guo, W., Ni, W., Chen, I., Ding, Z.Q., Yeo, S.H., et al.: Intuitive vibro-tactile feedback for human body movement guidance. In: 2009 IEEE International Conference on Robotics and Biomimetics (ROBIO), pp. 135–140. IEEE (2009)

10. Stanley, A.A., Kuchenbecker, K.J.: Evaluation of tactile feedback methods for wrist rotation guidance. IEEE Trans. Haptics 5(3), 240–251 (2012)

11. Bosman, S., Groenendaal, B., Findlater, J.-W., Visser, T., de Graaf, M., Markopoulos, P.: GentleGuide: an exploration of haptic output for indoors pedestrian guidance. In: Chittaro, L. (ed.) Mobile HCI 2003. LNCS, vol. 2795, pp. 358–362. Springer, Heidelberg (2003)

12. Van Erp, J.B.F., Van Veen, H.A.H.C., Jansen, C., Dobbins, T.: Waypoint navigation with a vibrotactile waist belt. ACM Trans. Appl. Percept. (TAP) 2(2), 106–117 (2005)

13. Tsukada, K., Yasumura, M.: ActiveBelt: belt-type wearable tactile display for directional navigation. In: Mynatt, E.D., Siio, I. (eds.) UbiComp 2004. LNCS, vol. 3205, pp. 384–399. Springer, Heidelberg (2004)

14. Srikulwong, M., O'Neill, E.: Wearable tactile display of directions for pedestrian navigation: comparative lab and field evaluations. In: 2013 World Haptics Conference (WHC), pp. 503–508. IEEE (2013)

15. Flores, G., Kurniawan, S., Manduchi, R., Martinson, E., Morales, L.M., Sisbot, E.A.: Vibrotactile guidance for wayfinding of blind walkers. IEEE Trans. Haptics 8(3), 306–317 (2015)

16. Lee, B.-C., Martin, B.J., Sienko, K.H.: Comparison of non-volitional postural responses induced by two types of torso based vibrotactile stimulations. In: 2012 IEEE Haptics Symposium (HAPTICS), pp. 195–198. IEEE (2012)

17. Lieberman, J., Breazeal, C.: TIKL: development of a wearable vibrotactile feedback suit for improved human motor learning. IEEE Trans. Robot. 23(5), 919–926 (2007)

18. Watanabe, J., Ando, H.: Pace-sync shoes: intuitive walking-pace guidance based on cyclic vibro-tactile stimulation for the foot. Virtual Reality 14(3), 213–219 (2010)

19. IDEO. Technojewelry for ideo (2001). https://www.ideo.com/work/technojewelry

20. Lavie, N.: Distracted and confused?: selective attention under load. Trends Cogn. Sci. 9(2), 75–82 (2005)

21. Lavie, N.: Perceptual load as a necessary condition for selective attention. J. Exp. Psychol. Hum. Percept. Perform. 21(3), 451 (1995)

22. Lavie, N.: Selective attention, cognitive control: dissociating attentional functions through different types of load. Attention Perform. XVIII, 175–194 (2000)

23. Fitousi, D., Wenger, M.J.: Processing capacity under perceptual and cognitive load: a closer look at load theory. J. Exp. Psychol. Hum. Percept. Perform. 37(3), 781 (2011)

24. Trulsson, M.: Mechanoreceptive afferents in the human sural nerve. Exp. Brain Res. 137(1), 111–116 (2001)

25. Priplata, A., Niemi, J., Salen, M., Harry, J., Lipsitz, L.A., Collins, J.J.: Noise-enhanced human balance control. Phys. Rev. Lett. 89(23), 238101 (2002)

26. Steinbach, E., Hirche, S., Ernst, M., Brandi, F., Chaudhari, R., Kammerl, J., Vittorias, I.: Haptic communications. Proc. IEEE 100, 937–955 (2012)

Estimate Emotion Method to Use Biological, Symbolic Information Preliminary Experiment

Yuhei Ikeda, Yoshiko Okada[✉], and Midori Sugaya[✉]

College of Engineering, Shibaura Institute of Technology, Tokyo, Japan
doly@shibara-it.ac.jp

Abstract. Imagine the day that a robot would comfort you when you feel sad. To achieve the ability to estimate emotion and feeling, a lot of work has been done in the field of artificial intelligence [1] and robot engineering that focuses on human robot communications, especially where it applies to therapy [2, 3]. Generally, estimating emotions of people is based on expressed information such as facial expression, eye-gazing direction and behaviors that are observable by the robot [4–6]. However, sometimes this information would not be suitable, as some people do not express themselves with observable information. In this case, it is difficult to estimate the emotion even if the analysis technologies are sophisticated. The main idea of our proposal is to use biological information for estimating the actual emotion of people. The preliminary experiments show that our suggested method will outperform the traditional method, for the people who cannot expressed emotion directly.

Keywords: Estimate emotion · Robotics application · Biological information · Estimation · Feeling

1 Introduction

Estimation of emotion is one of the major interests amongst robotics interaction development researchers. Extensive research has been carried out towards this end, especially focused on extracting the rules and features of expressions such as user's eye-gaze direction [4], head position, facial and mouth expression [5] and behaviors [6]. These approaches use observable symbols that people can sense with senses (sight, hearing, touch, etc.) to estimate emotion. However, the limitation of these approaches is that it is difficult to apply them when facial expressions or words and emotion differ from the norm. For example, people can fake a smile when feeling angry inside. In psychology, researchers consider that emotions are sometimes not expressed, and information that is expressed - such as facial expressions, voices and emotion - can differ from the true emotion. This has been widely recognized in psychology [7]. Our research is based on this understanding and aims to understand true feelings. To estimate emotion we use biological information such as brain waves and heart rate. We intend to measure the human conditions such as being excited [8], stressed [9], concentrating [10], and relaxing [11]. In particular, for emotion, based on the Circumflex Model of Russell [12], by using biometric information, various studies have performed human emotion estimation, and reported that certain evaluations can be made [10].

© Springer International Publishing Switzerland 2016
D.D. Schmorrow and C.M. Fidopiastis (Eds.): AC 2016, Part I, LNAI 9743, pp. 332–340, 2016.
DOI: 10.1007/978-3-319-39955-3_31

However, in those studies, the engineering implementation methods and algorithms have not been sufficiently presented.

The purpose of this study is to present an algorithm for the psychology model to separate the symbols and feelings, to estimate emotion with the biological information from the proposed method, and to complement it with brain waves and heart rate. The implemented system and planned experiments are intended to provide an algorithm and evaluation method for the accuracy of emotion estimate. Since the evaluation is the result of the limited method presented in this research, it is necessary to experiment by increasing the number of subjects in the future.

Structure of this paper is as follows: In Sect. 2, we propose the emotion estimate method; in Sect. 3, we propose the experiment and evaluation, and in Sect. 4, we conclude.

2 Estimation Method with Biological Information

2.1 Issues and Objectives

As we described in the introduction, we embody the technique that estimates emotion by using biological information. Firstly, we try to separate an emotion into information that is expressed externally, and interior information, in accordance with the psychological classification [7]. The expressed information, we call symbolic information that people use in communication such as words, voice and facial expression. On the other hand, the interior information we call emotional information that is internal. Without taking into account physiological phenomena such as breathing, pulse and blood pressure, it can be difficult to understand the state of the person. These biological signals have been used in areas such polygraph testing [13]. This is something that detects a number of physiological phenomena such as electrical and physical signals like breathing, pulse, blood pressure, etc. However, there has not been enough research on estimating emotion through using direct biological information from the person.

The purpose of this research is based on the separation of the symbolic and emotional in psychology, and an object is to present an algorithm using biometric information such as brain wave and heart rate speculation emotions. With this proposed method, we will achieve an accurate estimation by integrating symbolic and biological information. As a first step, we outline the proposed method to estimate emotion with the facial expression analysis technology.

2.2 Proposed Method

Firstly, we define the symbolic information and emotional information. Symbolic information is defined as that which can be easily read by the five senses.

On the other hand, emotional information is defined as that which people can hardly read by using the five senses. (Table 1) Symbolic information is standing on the premise that language and culture are shared and you can read signs of emotion to some extent from such words and expressions. Also, with the emotional information, it does not matter whether you know the person or not.

Table 1. The definition of emotion and symbol

	Definition	Information used in estimation
Symbol	Easy-to-read information on an objective	Facial expressions, language, voice, etc.
Emotion	Difficult information read to objectively	Heart rate, brain waves, heart rate, etc.

We describe a method of emotional decision-making. Emotion is a vague concept, and is interpreted differently by different people. Russell showed Russell's Circumflex Model that was structured for emotion. In this research, for the classification of the emotion, the data obtained by the brain wave and pulse, and mapped onto a two-dimensional plane, allowing for the identification of emotion. This method has already been presented in the research of Sakamatsu [14], Yamamoto [15], Hayashi et al. [16], Yamamoto et al. saw that being relaxed or tense will appear due to a change in emotional information by communicating with the autonomic nervous system, and proposed an analysis technique that measures according to the model. In this paper we show that excitement and tension increases the heart rate, and skin temperature rises due to the contraction of the blood vessels. On the other hand, it has been shown that parasympathetic acting upon relaxation reduces heart rate, and dilates blood vessels. In addition, Sakamatsu shows the state of the autonomic nervous system corresponding to the degree of concentration by Russell's Circumflex attention and meditation by brain wave a portion corresponding to the awakening degree of the model in the vertical axis.

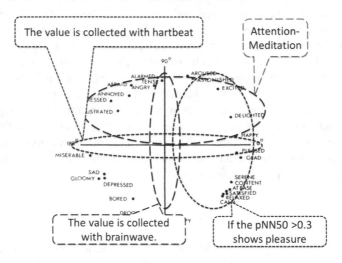

Fig. 1. Russell's circumflex model [12]

Furthermore, in physiology, it is known that when emotional behavior occurs, the activity of the sympathetic nerve is enhanced, so we thought it would be possible to estimate emotions such as excitement, sadness and anxiety. Therefore, we thought that it applies to the horizontal axis of Russell's Circumflex Model. The circular ring model that associates the two values is shown in Fig. 1. The estimation of emotion using this model have already been proposed by Sakamatsu [14]. In our research, the same value as Sakamatsu's Y-axis of Russell's Circumflex Model was assumed as the brain wave. The value is obtained with a brain wave headband [17] that the algorithm is provided as a value of attention and meditation from zero to 100. On the other hand, the pulse is known to increase with growing activity of the sympathetic nervous system in the event of emotional behavior from a physiological point of view. It is also believed to be capable of measuring emotions such as excitement, sadness and anxiety. Skamatsu's research also uses pulse as value of X-axis in Russell's Circumflex Model. They use the value at the pulse over a one minute interval [14]. In this research, we used pNN50. The measurement time and interval of pNN50 is shorter than the one minutes, and it is widely used in the measure of heart rate variability (HRV) [18]. As described above, the data processing emotion estimate using biometric information in this research is organized as follows.

(1) Calculate pulse calculated from pNN50 from the sensor.

(2) Calculate the degree of awakening by the value obtained by the operation of the brain waves.

(3) The value of (1) and (2) carry out the emotion estimate.

2.3 How to Apply Heart Rate and Brain Wave for the Method

The determination of pleasant - unpleasant uses the pulse using a pNN50 [18]. Determination of pNN50 is as follows:

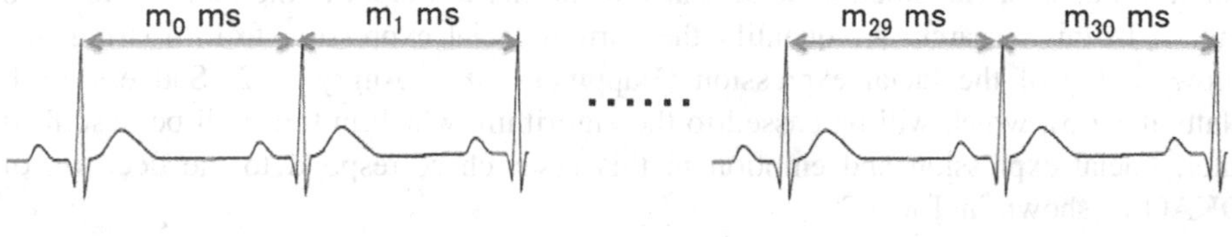

Fig. 2. pNN50, Pulse interval

m0 ~ m30 of Fig. 2 shows a pulse interval. The difference between the adjacent pulse interval is Diff. Then, ask the 30 pieces of pulse interval Diff like $DDiff_0 = |Hbt_1 - Hbt_0|$, $DDiff_1 = |Hbt_2 - Hbt_1|$, ... $DiffD_{30} = |Hbt_{30} - Hbt_{29}|$. After that, the 30 pieces of 50 ms or more of the ratio of the Diff of the Diff calculated (the number of the number / Diff of 50 ms or more of Diff), the value of the ratio and pNN50 [18]. This value is determined to be pleasant higher has become an index of Pleasant - discomfort. In order to deal with the value of the pNN50 as the value of the X-axis of Russell's Circumflex Model, we decided on a reference point. We have a value that becomes the point of origin 0.3. Because the standard value of pNN50 is 0.3 [19]. Originally, if the focus is on real-time, the accuracy is reduced, or to guarantee accuracy, real-time is reduced. It is trade-off requirement. In this research, we use pNN50, satisfying the real-time requirement without reducing accuracy.

Brain wave sensors used in this research implemented an algorithm that calculates the attention and meditation at a level from zero to 100. In this research, the value of the Y-axis of the Russell's Circumflex Model is "Attention-meditation" ([14] reference). This value is referred to as an awakening degree. Awakening degree is −100 (attention: 0, meditation: 100) ∼ 100 (attention: 100, meditation: 0) takes a value in. In Russell's Circumflex Model, an awakening degree at the origin or zero means attention = meditation.

Based on the calculation of biological information such as heart rate and brainwave, we apply Russell's Model to estimate the emotion. Using these parameters, we determine that the "joy emotion" in the case that awakening degree is 0 or more and pNN50 is 0.3 or more.

3 Preliminary Experiment

3.1 Compared Method

In this research, in order to know the effect of our approach, we compare the two methods that use biometric information for estimating emotion, and use only the symbolic information. In this research, we use an existing determination algorithm, because analysis of symbolic information is not the purpose of this research. Facial expressions are the symbols to be estimated on the subjects because it is easier to detect than other symbolic information, such as voice and gestures. The detection of the facial expression is done using Omron's OKAO VISION [20] (Fig. 5). OKAO VISION recognizes the face of the person as shown in Fig. 6 in the camera of the face recognition function. Next, it reads five types of facial expressions (Surprise, Anger, Natural, Sadness, Happiness). Next, it has the ability to output in the log, as shown in Fig. 7. In this research, we quantify the current facial expression from a string that shows a log of the facial expression (Happiness → 5, Angry → 2, Sadness → 4, Natural → 3), which will be passed to the algorithm, which in turn will be described later. Facial expression and emotion in this research correspond to the decision of OKAO as shown in Table 2.

Table 2. Correspondence of the judgment in the actual emotion and the determination with the parameter

Decision of OKAO	Happiness	Angry	Sadness	Natural
Decision of emotion	Joy	Angry	Sad	Comfort
Numeric value to pass	5	2	4	3

The value of the passed facial expression from OKAO VISION determines the Emotion in the "facial expression determination algorithm". It should be noted that this algorithm is to take only the facial expression of "joy". This algorithm determines that the "joy facial expression" in the event that the value of the facial expression is 5.

3.2 Experimental Method and Evaluation

We carried out the proposed method to test the validity of the estimation of emotion method using the symbolic/emotional model. Note that the subject was to be treated only for the emotion of "joy" in this experiment. Brain waves were detected by a Neuro sky's Mindwave Mobile [17]. An Arduino heartbeat sensor [21] from the Tokyo devices company detected the pulse. As an evaluation index, Mean of Absolute Error (*MAE*) was adopted to use the broadest value as an index to measure the accuracy. We compared the *MAE* f symbolic information using the pulse and heart rate and biological information using facial expression. The formula for the *MAE* is as follows.

$$\text{Joy}_{\text{MAE}} = \left| \frac{\text{Number of determinate emotion while watching the video}}{\text{Number of determinate emotion while watching the video}} \right. \\ \left. - \frac{\text{Number determined that the "joy"}}{\text{Number of determinate emotion while watching the video}} \right|$$

3.3 Procedure

The participants were two people (a 21 and a 23-year-old man). The experiment was carried out in the laboratory and, in order to realize the goals of the robot study, we implemented the reaction operation on the robot too. Robot was used to switch sciences company of Rapiro [22]. Determination of the reaction operation compares the emotion determined by expression and biological information. If they were different, the robot swung its hands and face to the side as if to deny. On the other hand, if they were the same, the robot raised one hand as to rejoice together.

The experimental procedure is as follows:

(1) In order to evoke the emotional of "joy", the subject searches for an interesting video [16];

(2) the subject watches the video;

(3) facial expressions and biometric information is detected by the sensors;

(4) facial expression determination as to whether emotions based on the value calculated from the camera is "joy". Biometric information determined whether the emotional of "joy" on the basis of the "emotional decision algorithm" (Fig. 3).

Fig. 3. Situation of the experiment

(5) comparison of the emotional of facial expression and biological information, and the robot operation.

※ 3–5 are repeated each second between the videos.

3.4 Result of the First Experiment

When participant A watched the video, his facial expression was "joy" for the whole time during the video playback, therefore, the value of the *MAE* became 0. However, when using the biological information, *MAE* increased to 28. We considered that showed the result that the facial expression has a higher accuracy because participant A has the attribute of rich facial expression (Table 3).

Table 3. Result of the first experiment

	Facial expression (*MAE*)	Biological information _(*MAE*)
Participant A	0	28
Participant B	100	25
Average of A, B	50	26.5

On the other hand, participant B had no detection of "joy of facial expression" so *MAE* had the very high value of 100. However, participant B in the case of biological information has the detection of "joy" a lot of time, with a *MAE* value of 25, and accuracy is increased significantly compared with the case of facial expression. Participant B had the attribute of not being expressive. As a result, the average of *MAE* of all participants is facial expression 50, and the biological information was 26. In the emotion estimation of "joy", biological information is better than symbolic information.

3.5   Issues and Improvement

In the first experiment, the number of participants is too few for understanding its effectiveness. Therefore, to establish the significance of the proposed method, an experiment was conducted with 11 participants. In addition, the next experiment added to the determination of the "comfort of emotional". The experimental procedure is generally the same as in the first experiment, but there are some changes. First, a video was to be searched for "relaxing." [16] to the participants. In addition, it added the operation of resting for 2 min between video views to stabilize the value of the biological information between (1) and (2).

Table 4. nd experiment result (the video such as drawn, interesting)

	Facial expression (Joy)	Biological information (Joy)
Participant 1	100	38
Participant 3	100	75
Participant 10	85	60
Average of participants	95	57.6

3.6   Result of the 2nd Experiment

The experimental results are shown in Tables 4 and 5. The participants choose to search for a comforting video or search for a pleasurable video. Three of the 11 participants chose to search for a pleasurable video and eight of the participants chose the comfort option. If the average *MAE* is taken using the symbolic information, the joy of the video is 95, the comfort of video was 89.7. If the average of *MAE* in the case of

Table 5. nd experiment result (Relaxing the video)

	Facial expression (Comfort)	Biological information (Comfort)
Participant 2	100	48
Participant 4	100	24
Participant 5	38	34
Participant 7	97	23
Participant 8	100	42
Participant 11	83	82
Participant 12	100	38
Participant 13	100	28
Average of participants	89.7	39.8

estimates the emotion in the biological information, joy of the video is 57.6, comfort of video has become 39.8. From this result, the biological information and the facial expression of both of *MAE* of emotion of "easy" was lower. So, the accuracy of the emotion of the "easy" was higher. In addition, there was a difference of out-friendliness of the emotion by between personalities and there are differences in accuracy by the number of participants were suggested.

However, the overall value of *MAE* was higher compared with the experiment 1; the emotion estimation accuracy has decreased.

4   Conclusion

In this research, we present a method of determining emotion using biological information in the emotion estimation. The results of first experiment lead to the 2nd experiment but from the result of 2nd experiment, there is a problem that further accuracy has deteriorated. In future, we will develop improvements, and we hope to continue working on the problems one by one, in order to solve them.

Acknowledgement. We would like to thank Tateishi Science Foundation, and MEXT/JSPS KAKENHI Grant 15K00105 for a grant that made it possible to complete this study.

References

1. Muehlhauser, L., Helm, L.: Intelligence explosion and machine ethics. In: Eden, A.H., Moor, J.H., Søraker, J.H., Steinhart, E. (eds.) Singularity Hypotheses: A Scientific and Philosophical Assessment, pp. 101–126. Springer, Heidelberg (2012)
2. Weingartz, Sarah: Robotising Dementia Care? A Qualitative Analysis on Technological Mediations of a Therapeutic Robot Entering the Lifeworld of Danish Nursing Homes. MA European Studies of Science, Society and Technology (ESST), Cambridge (2011)
3. Ekman, P.: Universals and cultural differences in facial expressions of emotions. In: Cole, J. (Ed.) Nebraska Symposium on Motivation, pp. 207–282 (1972)
4. Traver, V., Javier, D.E.L., Pobil, A.P., Pérez-Francisco, M.: Making service robots human-safe. In: Proceedings of 2000 IEEE/RSJ International Conference on Intelligent Robots and Systems, 2000 (IROS 2000), pp. 696–701. IEEE (2000)

5. Song, W.-K., et al.: Visual servoing for a user's mouth with effective intention reading in a wheelchair-based robotic arm. In: IEEE International Conference on Robotics and Automation, Proceedings 2001 ICRA, pp. 3662–3667. IEEE (2001)
6. Ono, K., Miyamichi, J., Yamaguchi, T.: Intelligent robot system using "model of knowledge, emotion and intention" and "information sharing architecture". In: Proceedings of 2001 IEEE International Symposium on Computational Intelligence in Robotics and Automation, pp. 498–501. IEEE (2001)
7. Hiraki, N.: Zibun no kimochi wo kichinto<Tsutaeru>gizyutsu (Techniques to communicate properly my feelings). PHPKenkyuzyo (2007)
8. Ohkura, M., et al.: Measurement of "wakuwaku" feeling generated by interactive systems using biological signals. In: Proceedings of KANSEI Engineering and Emotion Research International Conference, pp. 2293–2301 (2010)
9. Minamitani, H.: Fatigue and stress. J. Soc. Biomechanisms 21(2), 58–64 (1997)
10. Navalyal, G.U., Gavas, R.D.: A dynamic attention assessment and enhancement tool using computer graphics. Hum.-Cent. Comput. Inf. Sci. 4(1), 1–7 (2014)
11. Chu, K.-Y., Wong, C.Y.: Player's attention and meditation level of input devices on mobile gaming. In: IEEE 2014 3rd International Conference on User Science and Engineering (i-user), pp. 13–17 (2014)
12. Russell, James A.: A circumplex model of affect. J. Pers. Soc. Psychol. 39(6), 1161–1178 (1980)
13. Grimm, M., et al.: Primitives-based evaluation and estimation of emotions in speech. Speech Commun. 49(10), 787–800 (2007)
14. Sakamatsu, H., et al.: Proposal of self-feedback interface by MMD model based on detecting emotions using biosensors. In: 2015 Information Processing Society of Japan, pp. 602–605 (2015)
15. Kawazoe, J., Mizuki, Y.Y.T., Tokuda, T.Y.K.T.H.: momo!: Mood modeling and visualization based on vital information. In: IPSJ ubiquitous computing system (UBI), pp. 79–86 (2007)
16. Hayashi, M., Miyashita, H., Okada, K.: A mapping method for KANSEI information utilizing physiological information in virtual reality space. In: Groupware and Network Services (GN), pp. 25–30 (2008)
17. MindWave (2015). http://store.neurosky.com/pages/mindwave
18. Mietus, J.E., et al.: The pNNx files: re-examining a widely used heart rate variability measure. Heart 88(4), 378–380 (2002)
19. Moscato, F., et al.: Continuous monitoring of cardiac rhythms in left ventricular assist device patients. Artif. Organs 38(3), 191–198 (2014)
20. Image Sensing Technology | Products | OMRON Electronic Components Web (2015). https://www.omron.com/ecb/products/mobile/
21. Arduino Heartbeat sensor Shield Kit A.P. Shield 05_Tokyodevices (2015). https://tokyodevices.jp/items/3
22. RAPIRO: official site (2015). http://www.rapiro.com/ja/

Job Analysis and Cognitive Task Analysis in National Security Environments

Robert Kittinger[✉], Liza Kittinger, and Glory E. Avina

Sandia National Laboratories, Albuquerque, NM, USA
rskitti@sandia.gov

Abstract. The critical cyber-infrastructure of the United States is under a constant barrage of attacks. Adversaries (foreign and domestic) attack the nation's systems in order to test their design and limits; to steal information (spy); to damage the system; and embed malware which can be deployed at a later time. The ability of the United States' military and federal civilian departments to detect, delay, and respond to these attacks is essential to our national security. Identifying the best personnel to place in these critical occupations requires understanding the knowledge, skills, abilities and other factors (KSAOs) necessary to successfully complete important job tasks. It is also beneficial to understand the cognitive aspects of the job and when cognitive load is too high; when cognitive fatigue is setting in; and how these affect job performance. These factors are identified and measured by Industrial-Organizational (I-O) psychologists using the methods of job analysis and cognitive task analysis.

Keywords: Job analysis · Cognitive task analysis · Work analysis · Cybersecurity · Cyber defenders · National security · NASA-TLX

1 The Challenge of Person-Job Fit

It could be argued that nearly anyone can do any job with enough training, but there are advantages to putting the most qualified people in job positions from the start and serious disadvantages to having non-experienced applicants performing jobs they are not qualified for. It is both comical and accurate, to say that no one should have to hear the first author of this paper play Johann Sebastian Bach's *Ascension Oratorio* on the piano. The author has no experience, knowledge, skills, abilities, or other characteristics (KSAOs) to support this effort. For this reason, some jobs have very specific criteria that, if identified and used in selection, can save organizations money, can minimize turnover and training costs, and lower on-the-job injury rates [1]. Placing the most-qualified people in the best-fit jobs can also boost employee morale, team performance, and corporate knowledge retention (minimizing "brain drain" caused by attrition) [2]. In addition to KSAOs, some job criteria are even legally deemed necessary for a given job - these are BFOQs (bona fide occupational qualifications). For example, a city may require a firefighter to be able to carry a simulated-human weighing 150 lbs for a distance of 100 feet to prepare them for real world scenarios that have life-or-death consequences [3, 4]. This example demonstrates that BFOQs are required and considered necessary for the normal operations of the position.

© Springer International Publishing Switzerland 2016
D.D. Schmorrow and C.M. Fidopiastis (Eds.): AC 2016, Part I, LNAI 9743, pp. 341–347, 2016.
DOI: 10.1007/978-3-319-39955-3_32

1.1   The Challenge for Cyber Defenders

There is a new cold war emerging: the persistence escalation of cyber warfare. As cyber technologies continue to evolve, foreign policy has been slow to react; the cost barrier to entry has been lowered; the lines between nation states, paramilitary groups, and common hackers have blurred; the value of information has gone up; and the origins of attacks have been obscured - hindering the ability to place blame during diplomatic negotiations. For all of these reasons, the job being executed by our country's cyber defenders is of great importance and having the best cyber defenders in those jobs is imperative.

1.2   The Challenge for the Decision Maker

Whether it is through the military, national laboratories, private sector organizations, or other organizations, it is critical to have highly qualified cyber defenders on board to protect internal networks. This critical need must be recognized by the organization's management and hinges on a human's choice. When a job is posted and ten resumes arrive, how is the best job candidate selected? How does the selection team discriminate between candidates which are experts and those which are novices? These questions become harder when applicants resumes contain similar certifications (e.g., ISACA Certified Information Security Manager [CISM], CompTIA Advanced Security Practitioner [CASP], International Information Systems Security Certification Consortium [ISC2], Certified Information Systems Security Professional [CISSP], Global Information Assurance Certification [GIAC]), and similar experience with tools (e.g., EnCase Enterprise, SANS Investigative Forensic Toolkit [SIFT], Splunk, Sandia Cyber Omni Tracker [SCOT]). When applicants all look the same, what should the hiring decision be based on? Should it be their personality during the job interview; their college grade point average (GPA); or the perceived pedigree of their college? This hiring challenge extends beyond cyber defenders and is generally faced by people in almost every organization, every day, for one job position or another.

If the job is important to the organization and it is a resource-constrained organization that cannot hire all of the job candidates, it is in the best interest of the company to have a trained work analyst, such as an Industrial-Organizational Psychologist (I-O psychologist), conduct a job analysis. If the job you are hiring for requires many mental tasks (e.g., logic reasoning, creativity, memorization, decision making), having that expert conduct a cognitive task analysis (CTA) is also advisable. Utilizing a job analysis and/or CTA are important because they can identify the most important parts of the job, and which factors will be most predictive of future job performance.

2   Job Analysis and Cognitive Task Analysis

Job analysis and CTA are the scientific methods for systematically breaking jobs down into their component parts (observable tasks and unobservable tasks, respectively) and analyzing the relative importance of those tasks [5]. The following sections describe each of these methodologies in further detail.

2.1   Job Analysis

Job analysis (aka work analysis) in its simplest form is the systematic decomposition of a job into individual job tasks. The U.S. Department of Labor's O*Net website is a valuable resource and starting point for many job analyses (www.onetonline.org). Although basic job analysis only identifies the job tasks, the majority of job analyses go beyond this and collect additional data based on the needs and resources of the project.

The most common data to collect during a job analysis are:

1. knowledge, skills, abilities, and other factors (KSAOs) needed in order to success-fully perform the job
2. related subtasks when tasks can be broken down further
3. the equipment, machines, tools and technology (EMTTs) utilized by employee to successfully perform the job
4. related organizational competencies such as leadership and dutifulness
5. various task ratings (difficulty, importance, frequency, complexity, or criticality).

The additional data to be collected is determined by the need of the project and the resource limitations. The person conducting the job analysis should always ask, "What mission is this job analysis supporting?"; "What deliverables are needed to support that mission?" and "What resources do I have access to?"

The quality of the job analysis is highly linked to the resources available. Organizational management should ask themselves if a trained work analyst (I-O psychologist, human factors analyst, etc.) should be hired to do the work needed to build an effective workforce. If it is a national or geographically distributed organization, it is also vital to have a representative sample of Subject Matter Experts (SMEs) from multiple sites/states. Will the person conducting the job analysis be given access to six SMEs, 12 SMEs, or none at all? Will they conduct a two-hour, full day, or even a week-long job analysis workshop with the SMEs? If, a job analyst is not allowed to pull the workers away from their job tasks for a job analysis workshop, how long will they be allowed to shadow the workers to observe their work and ask questions while they are doing the work? If no SMEs are available to provide job task ratings, how much time will be allotted to collect ratings from incumbents and how many incumbents will the job analyst have access to? Will there be time to train the job task raters on how to accurately provide task ratings (i.e., difficulty, importance, frequency, duration, and criticality)? These are a few of the most critical resource-related questions to ask, though many others exist as well (e.g., Is there an available training room to use? Does it have a projector? Are there work computers with internet access which can be used to collect their job task ratings? Does this need to be reviewed through a human subjects board (HSB) and the formal institutional review board (IRB) process).

Once a job analysis has identified the most critical and frequently completed job tasks, the KSAOs, and the tools/software used to complete the task, then an organization is able to use these factors to effectively hire the best candidates. These factors can be used to tailor a formalized recruitment and selection (hiring) process, or they can simply be used as factors to properly weight resume items for comparison purposes. As an additional benefit, the job analysis can support additional human resources (HR) and training & development (T&D) department efforts such as writing job descriptions, identifying targeted recruitment opportunities, creating competency models, updating forms used during 6-month performance reviews, updating employee promotion criteria, and even revising employee exit interviews.

Legality. A brief note. Before making any personnel decisions, always review all local and federal laws to ensure compliance. Special attention should be paid to Title VII of the Civil Rights Act of 1964, the Americans with Disabilities Act (ADA), the Rehabilitation Act, the Fair Labor Standards Act, the federal Equal Pay Act, Age Discrimination in Employment Act (ADEA), and the Immigration Reform & Control Act. The U.S. Equal Employment Opportunity Commission (EEOC) is responsible for enforcing these laws and ensuring protected classes are not discriminated against in the workplace. Their webpage on EEOC Regulations is a good resource [6]. An excellent resource is the Uniform Guidelines on Employee Selection Procedures [7]. In Section 14.C.2 these Uniform Guidelines state that a job analysis utilizing specific criteria should be used as a content validity study for selection procedures. Similarly, Section 14.D.2 states that the same job analysis should be conducted to establish construct validity related to selection procedures. Trained I-O psychologists are taught to review and incorporate local and federal laws into their methodology.

Supporting Job Analysis Tools. In the most basic cases, paper-based job analysis forms can be used. Several software solutions are also available to conduct job analysis, such as Automated Guidelines Oriented Job Analysis (AutoGOJA) or Position Analysis Questionnaire's (PAQ) Occupational Assessor. Microsoft Excel or Access database forms are also common solutions based on their mass-availability, even if they typically offer less usability/process flow. Sandia National Laboratories created flexible job analysis software called Job Task Linker (JTL) in order to conduct job analyses with SMEs. This software walks SMEs through a series of tasks including, but not limited to, verifying the currency and accuracy of job tasks; identifying duplicate tasks; rating tasks on the factors of difficulty, importance, frequency, duration, and complexity; linking the tasks to all relevant organizational competencies, knowledges, skills, abilities and other factors. Job Task Linker is currently undergoing updates, but may be released as open source software in the future.

2.2   Cognitive Task Analysis (CTA)

Cognitive Task Analysis (CTA) has become a popular methodology to assess job performance and job-fit in recent years. CTA was developed to assess the non-observable, cognitive aspects of jobs (e.g., decision making, analysis, problem solving) as well as the cognitive workload (mental workload) associated with those tasks. CTA is the systematic process of identifying all of the cognitive tasks and functional goals related to the job.

The gold standard for a CTA is the National Aeronautics and Space Administration's Task Load Index (NASA-TLX) [8]. Other methods include the Subjective Workload Assessment Technique (SWAT) and the Workload Profile (WP), though these have received much less attention. While it exceeds the scope of this paper to cover the differences between the three methods, research by Rubio et al. highlights the various strengths and weaknesses of each of these [9].

It is important to use a CTA to identify cognitively demanding aspects of the job because it is this cognitive load which can, over time, lead to cognitive fatigue (mental fatigue). Cognitive fatigue has been linked to decline in job task performance, reduced motivation to complete tasks and an increase in the number and severity of errors [10].

The CTA is a helpful process for identifying cognitive tasks which cause a high cognitive workload and are executed under time pressure which can lead to errors. Areas of the job, which are more prone to errors, may need additional training; tools to handle the additional cognitive load and time pressure; or the job tasks may need to be redesigned in order to reduce errors/risk. Certain tasks which cause increased cognitive load, and where critical errors could be damaging, may warrant changes to the candidate selection criteria in order to ensure a candidate is hired who has expertise - prior to receiving on-the-job (OTJ) training. The importance to identifying job applicants with expertise is based upon Antonenko et al. finding that experts experience less intrinsic cognitive load [11].

NASA-TLX. Briefly, the NASA-TLX (Task Load indeX), created by Hart and Staveland begins by identifying the work tasks [8]. Then, while they are completing the task or directly following their completion of that task, SMEs or incumbents rate the tasks on six factors: mental demand, physical demand, temporal demand, performance, effort and frustration. The SMEs or incumbents then provide a rating from zero to 100 in increments of five on each factor, for each task. In the final step, SMEs provide weights for each task to allocate how much each factor matters for each task. To read the detailed instructions see Hart and Staveland's article [12]. To support these efforts, NASA provides free NASA-TLX software, which can be downloaded from their website [13].

It should be noted that the NASA-TLX step of having SMEs weight each factor takes a great deal of time and for this reason, many researchers have abandoned this step. The truncated version, which simply identifies the tasks and collects ratings on the six factors (without collecting factor weights), is called the TLX or Raw-TLX. This is a good alternative when time or access to SMEs doing the job in real-time is constrained [8].

3 Strategic Advantage

The vast majority of threats to national security involve humans. Our nation's cyber defenders and cyber incident responders are people trying to detect, delay, and respond to threats launched by other people. We need the best cyber war fighters available to stand up against our adversaries. To do this, we need to recruit and select the very best personnel for the job. This requires identifying the KSAOs necessary to perform the most important job tasks. Based on the extreme number of cognitive job tasks executed by cyber defenders and cyber incident responders, it is also important to recruit and hire individuals who have expertise in this line of work. This will minimize the degree of cognitive fatigue they experience and by extension minimizes the number and severity of errors they would make. Minimizing these errors represents one strategic advantage.

The second strategic advantage comes from improvements to cyber warfighter's speed. The security vulnerability assessment steps of detecting, delaying, and responding are notably similar to US Air Force Col. John Boyd's Observe, Orient, Decide, Act (OODA) loop (see Fig. 1). The OODA loop was taught to fighter pilots to provide them with a strategic advantage over their enemies during a dynamic combat event [14]. Hiring and training pilots to cycle through this loop faster than their adversary was a strategic advantage then, just as selecting and training the best cyber defenders, who will respond the fastest, is an advantage today.

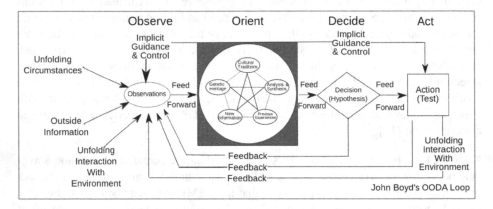

Fig. 1. USAF Colonel John Boyd's OODA loop.

To accomplish this, key decision makers need to be convinced of these strategic competitive advantages, and also of the legal risk mitigation, which these scientific processes yield. For most large organizations, the benefits far outweigh the costs. In some cases one job analysis can cover hundreds or thousands of hires for a single occupation.

4   Conclusion

The cyber defense community and their leadership need to dedicate themselves to elevated levels of personnel selection and analysis. Our cyber defenders have a very difficult job and our adversaries know how to exploit our weaknesses. This nation's government and private industries can fight back by hiring the most intelligent, resilient, diverse, creative, talented, motivated, responsive, and team-oriented cyber defenders, which have the least weaknesses to be exploited.

These elevated levels of personnel selection and analysis will be achieved by conducting proper job analyses and cognitive task analyses which can lead to data driven organizational decisions. Out of the job analysis and CTA new job descriptions can be written, targeted recruitment can be utilized, effective selection (hiring) systems can be created, promotion systems can be linked to key success factors and occupational competencies, new training materials can be created, training material can target key material using a DIF analysis (task difficulty, importance and frequency analysis). In sum, the whole organization's human resource (HR) system (including training and development) can optimize their impact and productivity by applying I-O psychology's JTA and CTA methodologies, maximizing person-job fit and the overall workforce's success [15].

Acknowledgements. Sandia National Laboratories is a multi-program laboratory managed and operated by Sandia Corporation, a wholly owned subsidiary of Lockheed Martin Corporation, for the U.S. Department of Energy's National Nuclear Security Administration under contract DE-AC04-94AL85000, Sandia Report 2015-1424C. Approved for public release; further dissemination unlimited. This research was funded in part or whole by an Interagency Agreement between the Transportation Security Administration and the Department of Energy.

References

1. Lopez, R.A., Denton, T.L.: Aviation Selection Test Battery Component Predictiveness of Primary Flight Training Outcomes Among Diverse Groups. Naval Postgraduate School, Monterey (2011)
2. Chow, C.W., Haddad, K., Singh, G.: Human resource management, job satisfaction, morale, optimism, and turnover. Int. J. Hospitality Tourism Adm. **8**(2), 73–88 (2007)
3. Hoover, L.T.: Trends in police physical ability selection testing. Public Pers. Manag. **21**(1), 29–40 (1992)
4. Williams-Bell, F.M., Villar, R., Sharratt, M.T., Hughson, R.L.: Physiological demands of the firefighter candidate physical ability test. Med. Sci. Sports Exerc. **41**(3), 653 (2009)
5. Wilson, M.A., Bennett Jr, W., Gibson, S.G., Alliger, G.M. (eds.): The Handbook of Work Analysis: Methods, Systems, Applications and Science of Work Measurement in Organizations. Routledge Academic, London (2013)
6. Equal Employment Opportunity Commission. http://www.eeoc.gov/laws/regulations/index.cfm
7. Uniform Guidelines on Employee Selection Procedures. http://uniformguidelines.com/uniformguidelines.html
8. Hart, S.G.: NASA-task load index (NASA-TLX); 20 years later. In: Proceedings of the Human Factors and Ergonomics Society Annual Meeting, vol. 50, no. 9, pp. 904–908. Sage Publications, October 2006
9. Rubio, S., Díaz, E., Martín, J., Puente, J.M.: Evaluation of subjective mental workload: a comparison of SWAT, NASA-TLX, and workload profile methods. Appl. Psychol. **53**(1), 61–86 (2004)
10. Faber, L.G., Maurits, N.M., Lorist, M.M.: Mental fatigue affects visual selective attention. PLoS ONE **7**(10), e48073 (2012)
11. Antonenko, P., Paas, F., Grabner, R., van Gog, T.: Using electroencephalography to measure cognitive load. Educ. Psychol. Rev. **22**, 425–438 (2010)
12. Hart, S.G., Staveland, L.E.: Development of NASA-TLX (Task Load Index): results of empirical and theoretical research. Adv. Psychol. **52**, 139–183 (1988)
13. NASA TLX computer version download. http://humansystems.arc.nasa.gov/groups/tlx/computer.php
14. Coram, R.: Boyd: The Fighter Pilot Who Changed the Art of War. Little, Brown and Company, USA (2002)
15. Thompson, K.W., Sikora, D.M., Perrewé, P.L., Ferris, G.R.: Employment qualifications, person-job fit, underemployment attributions, and hiring recommendations: a three-study investigation. Int. J. Sel. Assess. **23**(3), 247–262 (2015)

Measuring the Effect of Tangible Interaction on Design Cognition

Mary Lou Maher[1(✉)], John Gero[1], Lina Lee[1], Rongrong Yu[2],
and Tim Clausner[3]

[1] University of North Carolina at Charlotte, Charlotte, USA
{M.Maher,jgero1,llee52}@uncc.edu
[2] University of Newcastle, Newcastle, Australia
rongrong.yu@uon.edu.au
[3] University of Maryland, College Park, USA
clausner@umd.edu

Abstract. Recent developments in interaction design provide gesture and tangible interaction as an alternative or complement to mouse, keyboard, and touch interaction. Tangible user interfaces provide affordances that encourage and facilitate specific actions on physical objects. There is evidence that gesture and action affect cognition, and therefore it is hypothesized that the affordances of tangible interaction will affect design cognition. In this paper we report on the analysis of experimental data in which participants are asked to make word combinations from a set of six nouns and give them meaning. The task is presented as a design task with references to function, behavior, and structure of the word combination meanings. The participants performed the task in two conditions: one in which grasping the words was afforded and one in which pointing at the words was afforded. We segmented and coded the verbal data using the function-behavior-structure coding scheme to compare the participants' references to design issues across the two conditions. The results show that the two conditions differ in the phase in which they search for word combinations and the phase in which they described new meanings.

Keywords: Tangible interaction · Cognition · Creativity

1 Introduction

Creative people are unrestrained, appear to lack discipline, and display a great deal of curiosity about many things. Children, to some degree, are the embodiment of creativity [1, 2]. To think of innovative ideas and solutions, there are tools and techniques that creativity experts use to help people think differently, and problem-solve more creatively. We believe that Tangible User Interfaces (TUIs) may provide new approaches to support creativity.

TUIs are a type of human computer interaction design based on graspable physical objects that are shifting the actions required for interacting with digital information from pointing and clicking to holding, grasping and moving physical objects. TUIs are the coupling of physical objects and digital information, and eliminate the distinction

© Springer International Publishing Switzerland 2016
D.D. Schmorrow and C.M. Fidopiastis (Eds.): AC 2016, Part I, LNAI 9743, pp. 348–360, 2016.
DOI: 10.1007/978-3-319-39955-3_33

between input and output devices, such as mouse and display [3, 4]. For example, Fig. 1 illustrates Sifteo™ cubes, a type of TUI, and Fig. 2 illustrates children using the cubes.

Fig. 1. Sifteo™ tangible user interface cubes

Tangible interaction takes advantage of how people typically interact with physical objects in the world and brings those affordances to interactions with digital environments. Recent studies of TUIs, and physical objects more generally, and creative thinking have lead us to explore two hypotheses: 1. Tangible interaction increases the quantity of creative ideas. 2. Tangible interaction encourages the development of creative concepts.

TUIs have been shown to affect designers' cognition during a design task [5, 6]. Kim and Maher [7] compared TUI and GUI on a floor plan configuration task: They found an increase in epistemic actions and through a protocol analysis were able to observe an increase in the cognitive processes typically associated with creative design. The affordances of TUIs such as manipulability for physical (re-)arrangements may off load cognition to the tangible objects and reduce cognitive load associated with spatial reasoning. Brereton and McGarry [8] studied the role of objects in supporting design thinking as a precursor to designing tangible interaction. They found that design thinking is coincident with gesturing with objects and recommend that the design of tangible devices should consider a tradeoff between exploiting the ambiguous and varied affordances of specific physical objects. If TUIs offer greater opportunity for epistemic actions, then they may improve creativity by affording creative exploration through physical action.

Most studies of TUIs have been undertaken from a HCI technology viewpoint, which aims to describe fundamental technical issues and implement prototypes. Typically, initial user studies are conducted on prototypes focused on functionality only. Prototypes have not been evaluated from a cognitive perspective, which can be used to guide the development of new technology and applications. While many researchers have argued that TUIs improve spatial cognition, there has been no empirical evidence to support this [5, 6]. Although some researchers have reported on the users' perception of TUIs using survey questionnaires or designer comments, the subjective nature of self-reports calls into question their validity as measures of cognitive ability [9]. Technology-oriented studies, anecdotal views and subjective measurement are also insufficient as measures of cognitive ability leaving a gap in our knowledge. Our research addresses this gap on the effect of TUIs on cognition by reporting on an experiment design and coding scheme for comparing design cognition in two conditions that are distinguished by the affordances of pointing and grasping.

There is evidence that gesturing aids thinking. There is extensive evidence that gesturing with our hands promotes learning [10, 16], and aids problem solving [11], but few studies have explored actions with objects [12], and none have compared tangible object and intangible interaction. When children are learning to count, the learning is facilitated by touching physical objects [13, 14]. Kessell and Tversky [11] show that when people are solving and explaining spatial insight problems, gesturing facilitates finding solutions. Goldin-Meadow et al. [15] found that children who were instructed to imitate a teacher's gestures learned a strategy for solving math problems compared with children who did not gesture. Goldin-Meadow and Beilock [17] summarize these and related findings as "gesture influences thought by linking it to action" (p. 667), and "producing gesture changes thought" and can "create new knowledge" (p. 668). These studies show that gesture, while originally associated with communication, is also related to thinking. Tangible interaction design creates an environment that encourages actions on objects and therefore induces more gestures and actions than traditional GUIs. This paper provides an experiment design that can be used on learning tasks for a better understanding of the impact of tangible interaction on learning.

Studying creative processes provides insight into creative cognition. The processes for generating potentially creative solutions are described generally by Boden [18] as: combination, exploration, and transformation where each one is described in terms of the way in which a conceptual space provides a basis for producing a creative solution and how the conceptual space changes as a result of the creative solution. Gero [19] describes processes for generating potentially creative designs, including combination, transformation, analogy, emergence, and first principles. These processes explore, expand or transform the relevant conceptual space. Maher et al. [20, 21] identify characteristics of creative products as being new, surprising and valuable. These characterizations of creative processes and products provide a basis for comparing the effect of TUIs and GUIs. In this paper, we use the concepts of new and surprising to compare two conditions: pointing and grasping.

In this paper, we describe an experiment design [20] and a coding scheme to measure how graspable tangible devices differs from pointing in a creative task of combining words and giving the combination a meaning. Ultimately, our goal is to study how interfaces based on physical objects (i.e., TUIs) engage human cognition differently than traditional computer interfaces that do not include grasping within a design context. In order to see how TUIs change cognition, we segmented and coded the verbal protocol data using the function-behavior-structure coding scheme [22] to compare the participants' references to design issues across the two conditions. We show how the two conditions differ in the number of new and surprising concepts introduced as well as the characteristic design reasoning processes in the two conditions.

2 Experiment Design for Studying the Effect of TUI on Cognition

This section describes an experiment design for comparing TUI, with a focus on the grasping affordance, and GUI, with a focus on the pointing affordance. The experimental task is conceptual combination as a design task, where the design task is a synthesis of prescribed components (words) and the creation of a meaning for selected combinations. We adapted a conceptual combination task based on Wisniewski and Gentner [23] using nouns that varied semantic dimensions: natural kinds/artifacts (e.g., frog/box) mass/count nouns (clay/candy). The participants performed the task in two conditions: a poster condition and a cubes condition. We carried out a protocol analysis: we collected audio/video data while the participants were engaged in the task, then coded and analyzed the data. We expected that rearranging cubes would generate more word combinations and thus more creative meanings than reading words on a poster. We also expected that grasping cubes would engage spatial cognition and spatial metaphors more than reading words from a poster.

2.1 Experimental Environment

In the experiment, the participants are asked to combine words from a given set of 6 words, and then describe meanings for the combined words. In the instructions, the participants are asked to think about the function, behavior, and structure of the combined word when creating its meaning by giving them examples of function (what is it for?), behavior (how does it work?) and structure (what it is made of or look like?). The visual display features of the word stimuli were similar in font, size, and layout in a square border, and we varied whether words were displayed on tangible user interface cubes or printed on a poster board. In the Cubes Condition (Fig. 2, Left) words were graspable and rearrangeable because each word was displayed on a tangible cube. In the Poster Condition (Fig. 2, Right) words were printed on a poster board, and thus intangible.

Fig. 2. Experimental design left: cubes condition/right: poster condition

In pilot studies with words displayed on computer tablets we found that even when participants were instructed that words could not be moved they tried to manipulate them by attempting dragging and tapping gestures and grasping the tablet. We designed the cubes and poster conditions to avoid these potentially confounding variables and to limit the change in the two conditions to varying human interaction affordances while maintaining the same visual features of the word stimuli across conditions. Participants could point at the poster in the poster condition and pick up cubes in the cubes condition while reading word stimuli and speaking their responses.

2.2   Participants

Forty 6th grade children (aged 11–12) participated in the experiment. This number of participants provided data for 20 pairs of participants. We chose 6th grade children because of their more developed ability to compose creative meanings while engaging them in a task that would be received as age-appropriate, which was supported by the middle school's faculty. Due to procedural errors we were able to use the data from 14 of the 20 pairs of participants.

2.3   Words as Design Elements

Two sets of words were constructed to serve as stimuli for the word combination task, designed to form compounds, which would promote creative definitions. The two word sets consisted of six words each, matched within and between sets on a variety of psycholinguistic properties so they could serve as counterbalanced stimulus sets in both experimental conditions, while minimizing potential psycholinguistic effects between conditions unrelated to our hypotheses. All words were one syllable nouns representing concrete basic-level category objects. Each noun represented one of six disparate semantic categories: food, furniture, tool, clothes, vehicle, and animal. This prevented word combinations from forming same-category meanings, thus promoting creative thinking (Table 1).

Table 1. Word set stimuli by semantic category

Category	Word set 1	Word set 2
Animal	cow	bee
Artifact-tool	phone	rope
Clothes	shoe	shirt
Food	egg	rice
Furniture	chair	desk
Vehicle	bike	car

Six Sifteo cubes were programmed to display one word per cube. The display did not change, and no other cube sensors or capabilities were active. The display screen of Sifteo cubes is housed in a square frame with rounded corners. We designed printed poster words to match cube displays on task relevant perceptual attributes: text font and size; words appeared centered in a rounded square; and initial spatial arrangement of the cubes and printed squares matched. Each cube displayed the same word throughout the session. We printed words on a single poster paper (Fig. 2 Right) after pilot studies explored alternatives, such as sticky notes, and found that a poster board secured to a table served best to match the appearance position and reach of the cubes (Fig. 2 Left). Photo images of cubes were not used to avoid reminding participants of the graspable affordance of real cubes. Two sets of six cubes each were assigned to display words from Word Set 1 and Word Set 2, respectively. Two poster papers were printed containing words from Word Set 1 and Word Set 2.

2.4   Experimental Procedure

The experimental design was within-subjects consisting of an instruction phase followed by two experiment conditions: Poster Condition and Cubes Condition in two counterbalanced blocks. The two Word Sets were counterbalanced by condition type (Poster, Cubes), block order (Block 1, Block 2), and WordSet (Set 1, Set 2).

Participants were assigned to 20 pair groups. Based on pilot studies, working in pairs promoted talking and gesturing, while maintaining focus on the task, because participants had a peer co-engaged in the task with whom to verbalize their responses. The duration of the experiment was approximately 20 min consisting of the instruction phase followed by two experimental blocks of 5 min each. During the instruction phase two participant pairs sat together in a common room, afterward each pair of participants moved to an assigned testing room. Participants were instructed to "combine words and come up with as many creative meanings as you can". The task was presented as a game to encourage the children to explore many word combinations, and verbally describe creative meanings. Instruction consisted of an example: "the word fish and the word car are things everyone knows about, but nobody knows about a fish car". Three questions based on function, structure, and behavior [22] encouraged creative thinking: Who can tell me what a fish car might look like? —what a fish car is for, or what it does? —how a fish car works?

In the experimental phase each participant pair sat at a table with a poster paper (Poster Condition) or Sifteo cubes (Cubes Condition). Participants self-selected their choices of word combinations and how they took turns presenting their creative ideas to their paired partner. Experimental sessions were video and audio recorded.

3   Data Analysis

3.1   Segmentation and Coding

Our analysis of the video stream for each session involves segmenting the video into discrete elements defined by a start time and end time, and assigning a code to each segment. We started by segmenting the verbal stream according to speaker, and then segmenting into smaller segments so that a segment is formed around the utterance of a word combination or around the definition of a word combination. To analyze the participants' consideration of design issues, we had an additional stage of segmentation in which each segment is associated with one "FBS" code using the FBS coding scheme described below. This final segmentation and FBS coding were done simultaneously. Coding was conducted by four of the authors (Maher, Gero, Lee, and Yu) to ensure agreement. Then a single coder coded all sessions twice, separated by a period of several days, followed by an arbitration process to identify and resolve differences in coding. This coding process ensures a uniform coding across all 20 sessions.

3.2   FBS Coding Scheme

The Function-Behavior-Structure (FBS) coding scheme used is an adaptation of the one presented in Gero [22]. We mapped the word combination task onto the components of a design task: the given words are effectively the design requirements and serve as the building blocks for the participants' designs. By asking the participants to create a meaning for word combinations, they are asked to describe the design that results when you put two or more words together. For example: bee shirt, when they talk about what a bee shirt is they talk about what it looks like, how it behaves, and what it is for. This allows us to code each meaning for a word combination as if it were a design description and can be labeled as F, B, or S. Specifically, our FBS codes are:

- R: Requirements. This is when the participant makes a verbal reference to one of the six words printed on the poster or cubes.
- F: Function. This is when the participant talks about the purpose, use, or function when describing the meaning of the word combination.
- Be: Expected behavior. This is when the participant talks about an expected behavior in the meaning of the word combination.
- Bs: Behavior from structure. This is when the participant talks about whether the structure in the meaning of the word combination can actually achieve the expected behavior.
- S: Structure. This is when the participant talks about the appearance, the form, the spatial qualities, and the material properties of the meaning of the word combination.
- O: Other. This is used when a participant repeats a phrase or talks about something that is not relevant to the task.

3.3   New and Surprising

A definition of creativity [24] may focus on novelty as the primary criterion and claim that novelty is expressed as a new description, new value, or a surprising feature of a creative product. Alternatively, many definitions will state that value is the umbrella criteria and novelty, quality, surprise, typicality, and others are ways in which we characterize value for creative artifacts. Maher [21] presents an argument for three essential characteristics of a product to be considered creative: novelty, value, and surprise.

Amabile [25] introduces a Consensual Assessment Technique (CAT) in which creativity is assessed by a group of judges that are knowledgeable of the field. Within this technique, Amabile defines a cluster of features associated with creativity for the judges to rate that are specific to the artistic or verbal artifact being assessed (for example, in an artwork: creativity, novel idea, variations in shapes, complexity, detail). The CAT does not assist in developing a common set of metrics for evaluating creativity but instead provides a common technique for people to judge creativity.

To compare the creativity of the descriptions of the word combinations, we coded when each F, B, or S segment introduces a new and/or surprising idea for that pair of participants. The segment was coded as New if a word in the segment had not been used before in the session. The meaning of surprising is derived from the distinction between novel and surprising in Maher [21]. Surprising ideas are those not normally associated with the function, behavior or structure of the words in the word combination. If a response is possible, viable, realistic, feasible, or if it makes sense, we did not code it as a surprising word. A segment was coded as Surprising if it contained words that introduce unique concepts, different from the inherent function of the requirement words.

For example, when explaining chair egg in session with student pair 3 (P03), Child 2 said "a chair and an egg what if there is like a whole cracked up egg and you can just sleep on it like a vampire or just like be in the egg." A vampire in this context is unexpected and was coded as surprising.

4   Results and Analyses

4.1   Verbal Response

As participants composed word combinations and described meanings they interacted with the stimulus materials by pointing to and touching words on the poster, and by grasping, arranging, and combining the cubes. The length of combinations ranged from two to six words. All pairs of participants followed a two stage response pattern that repeated throughout the session: Search then Description. In the Search phase, the participants verbalized a series of word combinations as they searched for one to describe. In the Describe phase, the participants talked about the meaning of one of the word combinations identified in the Search phase. The two phases repeated until the session ended. Unexpectedly, some participants' initial search responses included additional familiarization with the materials.

4.2   FBS Results

The overall statistical analysis of the FBS coding across all participants is shown in Fig. 3. Figure 3 shows the average of the percentages of the number of segments for each of the FBS codes, with errors bars showing the standard deviation. This analysis shows that there is no significant difference in the average of the design issues across the two conditions.

We compared the number of Search phase segments and the Description phase segments in the two conditions for each pair of participants. For the Search phase we compared the percentage of segments coded as Requirements. For the Description phase we compared the percentage of the sum of the segments coded as F, Be, Bs, and S. For this initial pair-wise analysis we labeled an increase (or decrease) of more than 10 % as an increase (or decrease). Table 2 shows the results of this analysis. The results show that in the Cubes condition 11 of the 14 pairs of participants show an increase in segments coded as Requirements, which we associate with the Search Phase. The results show that in the Poster condition 13 of the 14 pairs of participants show an increase in segments coded as F, B, and S, which we associate with the Description Phase. One possible interpretation is the affordances of the cubes had a positive effect on the number of alternative word combinations considered and resulted in less talking while the participants were describing the meaning of the word combinations. Alternatively, affordances in the Cubes may have negatively influenced the

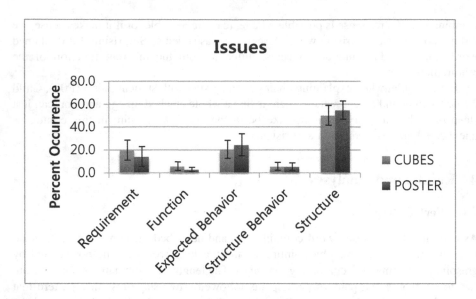

Fig. 3. Average of the percentage of segments for the five FBS codes listed by their design issue labels in the two conditions: poster and cubes.

Search phase, or affordances in the Poster may have positively influenced the Description phase. These data cannot distinguish among these possible interpretations.

4.3 New and Surprising Results

New and surprising ideas are recognized when a new attribute is encountered in a solution, a previously unknown value for an attribute is added, or a sufficiently different combination of attributes is encountered [19]. The participants that produced the most new and surprising ideas displayed a great deal of curiosity about many things and offered unusual, unique descriptions of the meanings of the word combinations.

We counted and compared each pair for an increase or decrease in the number of segments that were coded New or Surprising for each condition, cubes and poster, shown in Table 3. In the cubes condition, 6 out of 14 pairs had more New segments and 11 of the 14 pairs had more Surprising segments. However, the total number of New and Surprising segments showed minimal difference and therefore these are not distinguishing results. The mean value of New segments for the poster condition was 48.4 and the cubes condition was 41.0. The mean value of the Surprising segments for the poster condition was 11.4 and the cubes condition was 12.0. These results indicate that quantity of New and Surprising segment did not differ by condition type.

In this study we assumed that using new words instead of commonly used words in explaining the meaning of a word would lead to surprising or creative meanings and looked into relationship between New and Surprising segments. We found that more New segments does not necessarily mean more Surprising segments. Although more

Table 2. Percentage of number of segments in Search ® and Description (F, B-E, F-S, S) for each pair of participants

Pair	Search ®		Description (F-BE-BS-S)	
	Poster	Cubes	Poster	Cubes
1	21.7	34.8	78.3	65.2
2	33.0	37.3	67.0	62.7
3	6.3	19.9	93.7	80.1
4	16.6	21.1	83.4	78.9
6	6.2	13.7	93.8	86.3
9	12.1	19.7	88.0	80.2
10	27.5	10.7	72.6	89.3
11	13.4	27.2	86.5	72.9
12	11.5	6.1	88.6	93.9
13	11.5	12.8	88.5	87.2
17	2.3	16.3	97.6	83.7
18	13.7	14.0	86.3	86.0
19	11.1	17.1	88.9	82.9
20	6.4	21.0	93.6	78.8

New words are uttered in the poster condition of P06, P11, P13, P17, P18 and P20, for these pairs, the cube condition drew out more novel and surprising meanings.

Table 3. Number of new and surprising segments for each pair of participants

Pair	New[a]		Surprising[a]	
	Poster	Cubes	Poster	Cubes
1	20/192	26/127	3/192	4/127
2	27/177	29/154	5/177	5/154
3	79/229	56/176	21/229	12/176
4	51/196	41/178	9/196	3/178
6	62/213	57/177	11/213	13/177
9	38/167	46/231	9/167	14/231
10	29/142	30/120	5/142	5/120
11	35/181	25/165	8/181	9/165
12	27/123	28/125	15/123	11/125
13	53/163	38/137	7/163	10/137
17	65/185	50/165	2/185	4/165
18	63/223	26/142	10/223	19/142
19	71/290	80/317	16/290	21/317
20	58/159	42/131	38/159	43/131

[a]Number of new or surprising segments/total number segments.

As we noted in Sect. 4.2, 13 of the 14 pairs had more total Description segments in the poster condition. However more total Description segments did not necessarily mean they used more new words or created more surprising meanings. In spite of the fact that total Description segments is higher in the poster condition, we found that P02 and P10 used more New words in the cube condition and P01, P02, P06, P11, P13, P17, P18 and P20 drew out more Surprising meanings in cube condition. The difference in the number of segments is not large, but our results show that the number of segments in the Description phase does not relate positively with the number of New or Surprising words. The indication is that even with the fewer words used to describe the meanings in the cubes sessions, the participants had a higher incidence of New and Surprising words.

5 Discussion

The association of gesture with thinking leads to the possibility that interaction modalities that encourage gesture, and more generally body movement, may affect cognition. In this paper we present an experiment design that compares grasping and touching in a word combination task to explore the affect of tangible interaction on creative cognition. The experiment design isolates pointing and touching through the design of experimental materials that provide the affordance of pointing in the Poster condition and the affordance of grasping in the Cubes condition. In an analysis reported in Maher et al. [26], we analyze pointing, grasping, and gesture in the data collected in these two conditions and show that there is a significant difference in body movement in the two conditions, beyond the simple difference between pointing and grasping. In this paper, we analyzed the same data to compare the two conditions using the FBS coding scheme and an analysis of new and surprising concepts.

Our results show that the two conditions show a difference in the number of segments for Searching (Cubes condition shows increase in segments for searching) and Description (Poster condition shows increase in segments for description). We believe this may be due to the affect of grasping the objects in a TUI, when compared to pointing in a GUI-like session. We also noticed that while there were more segments for the Description phase in the Poster condition, this did not correspond to an increase in the number of new and surprising ideas.

This paper provides an experiment design and coding scheme that is a baseline for future studies of the impact of tangible user interfaces on design and creative cognition. In the future we will carry out additional experiments to determine if a task that requires spatial reasoning (for example configuring blocks) or learning will show a stronger effect on design and creative thinking.

Acknowledgements. This research was funded by NFS grant no. IIS-1218160 to M.L. Maher, T. Clausner, and A. Druin. The author contributions of this paper are: Clausner led the design of the experiment, which yielded data for coding and analysis both by cognitive scientific methods (in preparation), and the FBS coding and analysis (this paper) were led by Maher and Gero, with assistance by Lee and Yu.

References

1. Carlson, S.M., White, R.E.: Executive function, pretend play, and imagination. In: Taylor, M. (ed.) The Oxford Handbook of the Development of Imagination, pp. 161–174. Oxford University Press, New York (2013)
2. Smith, L.H., White, A.J., Callahan, C.M., Hartman, R.K., Westberg, K.L.: Scales for Rating the Behavioral Characteristics of Superior Students. Creative Learning Press, Mansfield Center (1976)
3. Fitzmaurice, G.W., Ishii, H., Buxton, W.A.S.: Bricks: laying the foundations for graspable user interfaces. In: Proceedings of the SIGCHI Conference on Human Factors in Computing Systems, pp. 442–449. ACM Press, New York (1995)
4. Ishii, H., Ullmer, B.: Tangible bits: towards seamless interfaces between people, bits and atoms. In: Proceedings of the SIGCHI Conference on Human Factors in Computing Systems, pp. 234–241. ACM Press, New York (1997)
5. Fjeld, M., Bichsel, M., Rauterberg, M.: BUILD-IT: an intuitive design tool based on direct object manipulation. In: Wachsmut, I., Frölich, M. (eds.) Gesture and Sign Language in Human-Computer Interaction, pp. 297–308. Springer, Heidelberg (1998)
6. Lee, C., Ma, Y., Jeng, T.: A spatially-aware tangible user interface for computer-aided design. In: Proceedings of the SIGCHI Conference on Human Factors in Computing Systems, pp. 960–961. ACM Press, New York (2003)
7. Kim, M.J., Maher, M.L.: The impact of tangible user interfaces on designers' spatial cognition. HCI 23(2), 101–137 (2008)
8. Brereton, M., McGarry, B.: An observational study of how objects support engineering design thinking and communication: implications for the design of tangible media. In: Proceedings of the SIGCHI Conference on Human Factors in Computing Systems, pp. 217–224. ACM Press, New York (2000)
9. Vega, M.D., Marschark, M., Intons-Peterson, M.J., Johnson-Laird, P.N., Denis, M.: Representations of visuospatial cognition: a discussion. In: De Vega, M.M.M., Intons-Peterson, M.J., Johnson-Laird, P.N., Denis, M. (eds.) Models of Visuospatial Cognition, pp. 198–226. Oxford University Press, New York (1996)
10. Cook, S.W., Mitchell, Z., Goldin-Meadow, S.: Gesturing makes learning last. Cognition 106(2), 1047–1058 (2008)
11. Kessell, A., Tversky, B.: Using diagrams and gestures to think and talk about insight problems. In: Proceedings of the Meeting of the Cognitive Science Society, pp. 2528–2537. Erlbaum, Mahwah (2006)
12. Trofatter, C., Kontra, C., Beilock, S., Goldin-Meadow, S.: Gesturing has a larger impact on problem-solving than action, even when action is accompanied by words. Lang. Cogn. Neurosci. 30(3), 251–260 (2014)
13. Alibali, M.W., DiRusso, A.A.: The function of gesture in learning to count: more than keeping track. Cogn. Dev. 14(1), 37–56 (1999)
14. Carlson, R.A., Avraamides, M.N., Cary, M., Strasberg, S.: What do the hands externalize in simple arithmetic? J. Exp. Psychol.: Learn. Mem. Cogn. 33(4), 747–756 (2007)
15. Goldin-Meadow, S., Cook, S.W., Mitchell, Z.A.: Gesturing gives children new ideas about math. Psychol. Sci. 20, 267–272 (2009)
16. Cook, S.W., Goldin-Meadow, S.: The role of gesture in learning: do children use their hands to change their minds? J. Cogn. Dev. 7(2), 211–232 (2006)
17. Goldin-Meadow, S., Beilock, S.: Action's influence on thought: the case of gesture. Perspect. Psychol. Sci.: J. Assoc. Psychol. Sci. 5(6), 664–674 (2010)

18. Boden, M.: The Creative Mind: Myths and Mechanisms, 2nd edn. Routledge, London and New York (2003)
19. Gero, J.S.: Computational models of innovative and creative design processes. Technol. Forecast. Soc. Chang. **64**, 183–196 (2000)
20. Clausner, T.C., Maher, M.L., Gonzolez, A.: Conceptual combination modulated by action using tangible computers. In: Poster Presented at the 37th Annual Meeting of the Cognitive Science Society, Pasadena, CA (2015)
21. Maher, M.L.: Evaluating creativity in humans, computers, and collectively intelligent systems. In: Proceedings of DESIRE 2010: Creativity and Innovation in Design, pp. 22–28. Aurhus, Denmark (2010)
22. Gero, J.S.: Design prototypes: a knowledge representation schema for design. AI Mag. **11** (4), 26–36 (1990)
23. Wisniewski, E.J., Gentner, D.: On the combinatorial semantics of noun pairs: minor and major adjustments to meaning. In: Simpson, G.B. (ed.) Understanding Word and Sentence, pp. 241–284. North Holland, Amsterdam (1991)
24. Csikszentmihalyi, M., Wolfe, R.: New conceptions and research approaches to creativity: implications of a systems perspective for creativity in education. In: Heller, K. (ed.) The International Handbook of Giftedness and Talent, 2nd edn, pp. 81–94. Elsevier, Philadelphia (2000)
25. Amabile, T.: Social psychology of creativity: a consensual assessment technique. J. Pers. Soc. Psychol. **43**(5), 997–1013 (1982)
26. Maher, M.L., Gero, J.S., Lee, L.N., Clausner, T.: Characterizing tangible interaction during a creative combination task. In: Gero, J.S. (ed.) Design Computing and Cognition 2016. Springer (2016)

Psychophysiological Baseline Methods and Usage

Avonie Parchment, Ryan W. Wohleber[✉], and Lauren Reinerman-Jones

Institute for Simulation and Training, University of Central Florida, Orlando, FL, USA
{aparchme,rwohlebe,lreinerm}@ist.ucf.edu

Abstract. There are several different baseline techniques available for completing psychophysiological research, yet no overarching set of guidelines exists to help researchers choose the best method. This review examines several methods used in various fields and highlights the importance and pitfalls of each. As part of this effort we conducted a small study that examines three different baseline techniques. In line with the Law of Initial Value (LIV), outcomes signal a strong positive effect for measures when utilizing a resting baseline, a weaker positive effect when utilizing a baseline directly before tasking, and a nominal effect when calibrating using a comprehensive baseline. The authors caution future researchers to fully assess the needs of their experiment before utilizing comprehensive, vanilla, or resting baselines, and to weigh the consequences of the length and number of baselines utilized. Further investigation of low workload and vigilance tasking is needed to determine whether use of vanilla and compre-hensive baselines provide better contrast than a resting baseline.

Keywords: Resting baseline · Comprehensive baseline · Vanilla baseline · Methods · Psychophysiological measures

1 Introduction

In Human-Computer Interaction, Human Factors Psychology, Neurophysiology, and related fields, psychophysiological measures have become a pillar for research into the human state. For example, recent efforts have employed psychophysiological sensors to create human-robot closed loop systems, [1] test the effectiveness of games [2], and to understand how workload and stress influence performance under various conditions [3]. Psychophysiological measures provide a direct gauge of human state, in contrast to subjective measures, which rely on introspection, and performance measures, which must infer state from behavioral outcomes. As these measures have become increasingly more accessible to researchers due to improvements in technology and reduction in cost, best practices for utilizing psychophysiological measures need to be evaluated. Notably, the use of baselines is an important part of these methods.

Psychophysiology has well over a century of history [4], but is a fairly new formal discipline. A foundational principle of psychophysiology is Wilder's Law of Initial Value (LIV) [5] which stipulates that the direction of a psychophysiological response depends on initial state. If a person's initial arousal is high, then a task designed to elevate arousal may only show a modest increase, if any, when contrasted with the initial state. However, if a person's initial arousal is low, the effects of the same task may appear

© Springer International Publishing Switzerland 2016
D.D. Schmorrow and C.M. Fidopiastis (Eds.): AC 2016, Part I, LNAI 9743, pp. 361–371, 2016.
DOI: 10.1007/978-3-319-39955-3_34

larger and discernable when contrasted to the initial state [4]. This phenomenon is seen in investigations concerning heart rate, respiration rate, and skin resistance (SR), but not in skin conductance (SC) or temperature [4]. In order to best understand this phenomenon and how it effects psychophysiological assessment, an evaluation of various baseline methodologies should be undertaken.

Over the decades, differences in measurement (c.f., [6–9]) have arisen, yet despite the large volume of psychophysiological research conducted over the years, little work has been done to systematically evaluate the available baseline options. From the reports of the procedures used by various researchers, it is evident that these procedures differ depending on the researcher's paradigm, field of study, and experimental content. Unfortunately, these differences in baseline practices have confounded replication efforts as well as efforts to improve methodological approaches [7, 9]. At the root of these issues is the lack of established common practice rooted in sound empirical investigation [4]. Therefore, an examination of baselines for psychophysiological measures is sought and such questions to answer include:

1. What kind of baseline is needed?
2. How long should a baseline be?
3. Where should the baseline be placed?

Answering these questions is the first step to realizing the full potential of psychophysiological measures. The following sections provide a basis for answering these questions and include results from a small investigation which was undertaken to illustrate the impact of baseline choice on the interpretation of psychophysiological outcomes.

2   Types of Baselines

There are several types of baselines for psychophysiological measurement. Among the most prominent are the basal/resting, vanilla, and comprehensive baselines. Within each type, there are multiple variations which can contribute to the difficulties with replicability, validity, and even the ability to generate valid conclusions. These baseline variations are described in subsequent sections and our discussion will include the benefits and shortcomings of each.

2.1   Basal/Resting Baselines

Basal or tonic activity refers to the resting level of activity for a psychophysiological measure. A true basal baseline refers to the absolute lowest reactive state of a participant [10]. Generally, the procedure includes a reduced or simple diet to control any changes in psychophysiological responses due to consumed items. A participant arrives at the testing location and, after being connected to one sensor, is monitored in a supine position that could extend several hours [11]. The benefit of this type of baseline is the use of a highly controlled environment where any variability is due entirely to the participant. However, this baseline also runs the risk of boring the participant, putting the participant to sleep, or exciting the participant by putting him or her in an area devoid of human interaction [8].

While highly controlled, basal baselines enhance and emphasize the individualized responses between participants, making general conclusions based on a sample difficult. Further, these baselines are impractical for obtaining a pre-task resting state.

The shorter resting baseline circumvents the problem of increased individual variability between subjects produced by the basal baseline. By reducing the length of the baseline to ten minutes or less [7], keeping the participant upright but sitting, and requesting that the participant keep his or her eyes open [12], boredom and drowsiness is decreased and the variability between participants is reduced. Although this resting type of baseline addresses some of the problems found in basal baseline procedures, participants still have ample opportunity to lose concentration and let their minds wander; instructions for resting baselines typically do not stipulate what to think about or how to breathe during the baseline (e.g., a participant might increase her heart rate by either thinking of something unpleasant or by taking quick, short breaths). Though a few researchers have been able to determine at which point a baseline stabilizes [7], there remains sizable variability even within the duration of resting baselines. The challenge with using resting/basal baselines is the large variability across participants as well as within the participant that is associated with these baselines.

2.2   Vanilla Baselines

In order to reduce variability between participants when comparing baseline measurements, researchers developed the vanilla baseline. For this baseline, participants are given a low task load activity to complete while connected to a psychophysiological sensor. This procedure involves giving each participant the same activity to think about, resulting in reduced variability between participants [7]. Additionally, Piferi et al. [9] found that systolic and diastolic blood pressure when watching a relaxing video was significantly lower than that during a resting recovery period.

While this procedure is considered a way to standardize participants' psychophysiological response, there can still be substantial variability between studies because researchers can select different low task load activity options that may not be comparable to each other. Many researchers are partial to card sorting tasks or other low task load exercises, while others will use a calming video or a number of shapes on a screen [9]. Because of this variability in vanilla baseline task, differences in mean response to the baseline task may not be comparable across experiments. Nonetheless, the vanilla baseline is able to restrict the range of response in a baseline within a study and can induce a relaxed state in participants that is comparable to that of a true resting baseline.

2.3   Comprehensive Baselines

It has been argued that initial baselines alone, of any kind, are inadequate due to their inability to report the true normal psychophysiological state of the participant [13]. Further, researchers have suggested that the response to some stimuli could be overstated if only a resting value is used for comparison [13, 14]. In order to have a more reliable comparison and to gauge whether a meaningful response to a task has truly occurred, it may be advantageous to use the average response to a variety of stimuli, that is, a comprehensive baseline [13]. Although a comprehensive baseline could refer to a short regimen of various tasks such as that provided by ABM's B-Alert software, for our purposes, we refer specifically to the method of averaging response of all tasks over an entire experimental session, described by Fishel and colleagues as a "gold standard self-calibration period" [13]. By recording and averaging a broader range of responses a participant can have, a researcher may approximate a participant's true average state. Any significant deviation from this comprehensive baseline could be interpreted as a more genuine response to the task in question than would be attained from an arguably artificial resting state.

Despite capturing the full range of responses during an experimental session, comprehensive baselines introduce a large amount of variance in the baseline used for comparison to the experimental task. However, this greater variance may only be seen within the participant response, rather than between participants. Comparisons between the different types of baselines could determine if comprehensive baselines may reduce variability between participants.

The comprehensive baseline highlights important questions for psychophysiological research: is the comparison between a response to a task and an initial resting baseline artificial because participants' psychophysiological response is artificially attenuated to achieve contrast? Typical resting baseline procedures use behavior that may not be a normal part of everyday experience. Additionally, if such procedures are artificial, is the comparative response to subsequent tasking a valid indicator of response to a task? Although there may not be any definitive answer to these questions, a comparison of resting, vanilla, and comprehensive baselines may provide some insights.

3   Baseline Length and Number of Baselines

In addition to the type of baseline, the importance of the length and number of baselines recorded during an experimental session should also be noted. As mentioned in our discussion on resting baselines, a researcher chooses the baseline length based on how long the researcher expects it to take for participants' psychophysiology response to stabilize. The initial portion of a baseline will inevitably contain greater variability than subsequent portions as the participant acclimates to the baseline task. After some time, the participant's psychophysiology reaches some stable state. The length of time required for this acclimation process, and thus the baseline, is often unclear due to the number of different psychophysiological measures, the type of experiment, and the type of equipment.

The use of baselines in-between tasks has also been a matter of debate in the research community. Gauging of psychophysiological response is reliant on contrast with some initial state (c.f., LIV). Adding resting periods between tasking can allow the participant's psychophysiology to return to this initial level and enable researchers to obtain unadulterated assessments of participant's response to multiple tasks [15]. Unfortunately, the introduction of additional baselines may also elicit restlessness, boredom, and mind wandering that results in the corruption of the psychophysiological measurement.

3.1   Length of Baseline

Baseline research is marked by a lack of consensus regarding the length of time for a baseline to stabilize [6, 11, 12, 15, 16]. In the studies just listed, resting baseline length for a heart rate measure ranged from 8 to 15 min; the method for capturing participants' heart rate differed depending on experimental goals and context. Of several methods, Fishel and colleagues [13] used a moving 2 min window when calculating baseline. Jennings and colleagues [7] had a more sensitive apparatus and let their participants rest for over 25 min at the start of the experimental session. They then took the entire time of this baseline and graphed it, noting the time where variability was minimized. While all these methods may be valid, it is important to recognize that instead of standard practices that all researchers must adhere to, there exists a plethora of available baseline practices and generous flexibility of each procedure's parameters (e.g., length), which allows researchers to choose methods that offer them the best chance of showing an effect of experimental manipulations. It may be prudent to consider whether or not such flexibility in practice is advantageous to inquiry or complicates the search for reliable effects.

3.2   Number of Baselines

As mentioned above, some researchers choose to put resting periods (i.e., baselines) in-between tasking in order to reset psychophysiological responses before exposure to new tasking or experimental manipulations. Jennings and colleagues [7] suggest that only a few minutes is required to shed the influence of previous tasking. It might be argued that questionnaires between tasks are sufficient to bring participants back to baseline levels. Others might argue that baselines taken immediately prior to a task provides the most appropriate initial value from which to gauge response to a stimulus [15]. The different perspectives on multiple resting period practice can be summarized thusly: Baselines between tasking are needed to bring psychophysiological response back to the initial baseline levels. Baselines directly before tasking are necessary to gauge true response to a task. Finally, rest times between tasking is irrelevant to psychophysiological response as all psychophysiological responses are relative to some internal constant, basal level. While several articles touch upon these positions [6, 8, 13], no direct comparison of each of these possibilities yet exists.

3.3   Baseline Investigation Summary

Investigation of baseline methods is necessary for improving understanding of psychophysiological response and promoting more generalizable practices that allow for comparison both within and across programs of research. In our review of past baseline research, we identified possible ramifications of varying baseline methods, baseline lengths, and number of baselines. The following sections detail a preliminary effort to help alleviate concerns with baseline practices.

4 Experimental Approach

The present research investigates the differences between different types of baselines: resting and comprehensive. This effort is intended to generate additional inquiry into baseline research. The present experiment follows some of the procedures used by Fishel and colleagues [13] who also investigated multiple baselines types. Specifically, we assessed an initial resting baseline which came first in the experimental procedure and a comprehensive baseline was calculated using every data point throughout the experiment (Fishel and colleague's "gold standard"). Due to the copious number of vanilla baseline methods (calming video, card sorting task, listening to instructions), the authors felt that including a vanilla baseline within this investigation would be beyond the digestible scope of the present research and will be the focus of future research. The goal of this investigation was to compare the two baselines representing the low arousal (initial resting and resting directly before task baselines) and high arousal (comprehensive or gold standard baselines) extremes in a range of baseline options in order to understand the implications of each for different types of research questions and task manipulations [13, 16].

Hypothesis 1: Psychophysiological Responses Across the Various Tasks Would be Different. The materials chosen for this investigation represent a range of possible tasking in human performance research. One task required participants to think about the self and how they would react in different situations. Another required participants to react to changes in a short situation. A third task required them to reflect quickly on intuitive answers. The final task required participants to repeatedly think through a hypothetical scenario and react accordingly to how they expected the scenario to go. Each of these tasks required different processing and were expected to elicit very different responses.

Hypothesis 2: Different Baseline Methods Would Result in Different Initial Value from Which to Compare Psychophysiological Response to Subsequent Manipulations. This investigation compares resting and comprehensive baselines (which tend to indicate different responses to the same task) to the use of a series of baselines taken immediately prior to a task. Fishel and colleagues [13] found that resting baselines showed the greatest bias toward positive response and that a practice (perhaps vanilla) baseline was biased toward negative response. The comprehensive baseline was shown to be a less biased measurement of participant response since it also registered a change in arousal, but did not inflate or deflate responses in relation to other measurement methods. However, a baseline taken directly before tasking was never investigated in relation to these other calibration methods. It was hypothesized that while there would be differences between baseline calibration methods, a baseline taken before the task in question would result in moderate participant response while a resting baseline would show higher response to positive arousal and a comprehensive baseline would show a muted response.

5   Method

5.1   Participants

Seventy-six volunteers from the Central Florida area participated. Due to technical problems with the psychophysiological sensors found after the end of the study, data from two participants were omitted from analysis. Analyses were performed using data from the remaining 74 participants (34 women, 40 men, M_{age}: 21.72 years).

5.2   Materials

Unless otherwise noted, all tasking was administered on a desktop computer.

Everyday Moral Decision Making Task. This task was a mix of two morality measures [17] which asked participants to choose altruistic or egoistic responses to everyday decisions ranging in emotional impact from low to high. Other questions included utilitarian questions that asked participants if they were willing to sacrifice one for the good of many.

Change Detection. A two minute version of the mixed initiative (MIX) testbed [18] asked participants to classify icon changes on a computer screen. The amount of changes varied from the first minute (one change every 8–12 s) to the second (one change every 4 s).

Cognitive Reflection. Fredrick [19] developed the Cognitive Reflection Test that assessed a participant's ability to choose the non-intuitive response to a set of numerical questions.

Paper Game. This task replicates the MIT Beer Game in a computer setting [20] and assesses a participant's ability to make decisions in a supply chain context. The participant played the role of a retailer and had to find a balance between inventory size, orders, and revenue for the entire supply chain over the course of a simulated year.

Electrocardiography (ECG). ECG was monitored using the Advanced Brain Monitoring B-Alert X10 System sampling at 256 Hz. Raw values were Winsorized before analysis. ECG yielded measures of inter-beat interval and heart rate variability, which were recorded using single-lead electrodes placed on the center of the right clavicle and on the lowest left rib.

5.3   Procedure

Participants read an informed consent then completed the initial five minute baseline while keeping their eyes on a dark computer screen and remaining quiet, but alert. Participants then completed pre-questionnaires, the moral decision making task, a resting period, the change detection task, a second resting period, the cognitive reflection task, post task questionnaires, a final resting period, the paper game, and final questionnaires.

6 Results

Each task's percentage difference from baseline was calculated using each of three different baselines: an initial resting baseline taken at the beginning of the study, the baseline immediately prior to the task, and the comprehensive baseline which was the average of all data points in the experiment. The first task's calculation for baseline immediately prior to task used the initial resting baseline.

In order to determine if tasks differed from one another and if baseline methods produced different results from one another (Hypotheses 1 and 2), a 4 (task) by 3 (baseline method) repeated measures ANOVA was run. For psychophysiological response to task, Table 1 shows that for inter-beat interval and for heart rate variability, there was a main effect for task type and baseline calibration method. Planned pairwise comparisons showed that all tasks, with the exception of the comparison between the CRT and the Paper Game, were significantly different from one another for heart rate variability. For heart rate inter-beat interval, all tasks were significantly different from each other with the exception of the change detection task and the Paper Game.

Table 1. Within-subjects 4 (task) × 3 (type of baseline) ANOVA for heartbeat measures

	df	F	η_p^2	p
HRV				
Baseline type	1.629, 118.906	45.289	.383	<.001
Task	3, 219	30.717	.296	<.001
Type * Task	3.130, 228.463	7.705	.095	<.001
IBI mean				
Baseline type	1.296, 94.618	38.327	.344	<.001
Task	2.425, 177.041	27.832	.276	<.001
Type * Task	2.565, 189.461	23.134	.241	<.001

To interpret the difference in response based on calibration method, each response was graphed. Figure 1 shows the difference in percent change from baseline for heart rate variability. With the exception of the first task, which used the initial baseline as the immediately prior baseline (moral decision making), the baseline taken immediately prior to each task resulted in an apparent response that was weaker than the resting baseline based response but stronger than the comprehensive baseline base response. Planned comparisons showed that each difference was significant at the $p < .001$ level.

Figure 2 shows the difference in percent change from baseline for inter-beat interval. With the exception of the first task which used the initial baseline as the immediately-prior baseline (moral decision making), the baseline taken directly before each task resulted in a response between the resting and comprehensive baselines for the change detection task. However, this difference was not seen for Cognitive Reflection or for the Paper Game. In fact, for these two tasks, the use of a baseline directly before the task resulted in a negative response. Planned comparisons showed that the resting baseline calibration method was significantly different from all others at the $p < .001$ level. For inter-beat interval,

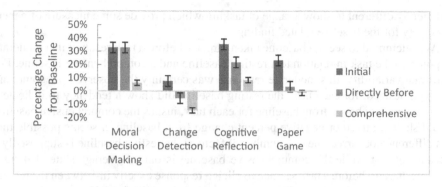

Fig. 1. Heart rate variability percentage change from baseline for each of the four tasks calibrated with the three different methods (Color figure online).

however, the calibration method of taking a baseline directly before the task and the method of taking a comprehensive baseline were not significantly different.

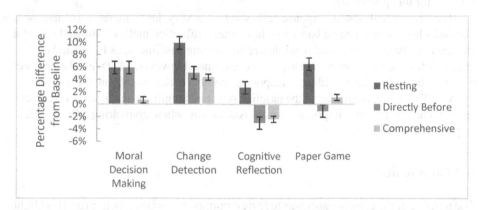

Fig. 2. Inter-beat interval percentage change from baseline for each of the four tasks calibrated with the three different methods (Color figure online).

7 Discussion

The present effort built on that of Fishel and colleagues [13] to determine how baselines taken immediately prior to a task compare to resting and comprehensive baselines. To achieve this goal, each baseline was used to calculate percent change from baseline for four different tasks. The tasks were significantly different from each other with the exception of the Paper Game and the Cognitive Reflection task for heart rate variability and the Paper Game and the change detection task for inter-beat interval. It is possible that the Paper Game shares some aspects of processing with the CRT and the Change Detection Task, though the fact that the rest of the tasks differ was acceptable for the purposes of this research. With these exceptions, we feel that the tasks chosen are sufficiently different to show a range of tasking which provide some measure of generalizability for the baseline related findings.

We attempted to see if a baseline taken directly before a task resulted in a moderate response to the task in relation to a resting baseline and a comprehensive baseline. For heart rate variability, this moderate response was certainly the observed phenomenon. As hypothesized, for each task, the resting baseline did show a tendency to indicate a positive percent change from baseline for each task, just as the comprehensive baseline would show a muted or negative percent change from baseline. It seems possible that this difference occurred due to a number of factors: the resting baseline is supposedly a measure of rest while the comprehensive baseline is one of average state. Taking a baseline directly before a task seemed to elicit a response exactly in-between the resting and comprehensive baseline calibration responses as hypothesized. However, inter-beat interval calibrated using the baseline taken directly before the task, versus the other two methods, was markedly shorter for the last two tasks (CRT and Paper Game). This difference raises the question of whether previous tasking affected participant response to baseline or not. This difference also brings into question methodologies that do not account for this possibility.

Because the calibrated response task showed a very large increase in inter-beat interval when using a resting baseline while other calibration methods showed less of a change from baseline, it seems possible that the resting baseline is, as Fishel and colleagues pointed out, very susceptible to positive response. However, what we did not expect was just how drastically different responses could be depending on the calibration method. Therefore, regardless of the baseline type and length chosen, it seems the intensity of change is most important for consideration when comparing physiological response between tasks.

8   Conclusion

The purpose of the present paper was to review common baseline practices and highlight the challenges involved in choosing an appropriate baseline method when conducting an experiment. The present research indicated that resting baselines are apt to show a large response to a task and that comprehensive baselines show a more muted response, as seen in previous work [13] and as might be predicted by LIV. However, the present research also showed that for a more moderate indication of response, a baseline taken directly before an experimental task may be prudent for showing the effect of the task and not the compounded effect of the entire experiment up to that point in the session. It may be most important to note that the use of any baseline resulted in clear look at participant response to task; a finding that may not have been apparent if no baseline at all had been used. Further research is needed to compare the many different vanilla baseline methods to those reviewed here. Additional research to investigate the effect each of these baselines had on participant response in relation to time on task and session is also needed. We hope that this preliminary effort demonstrated the important consequences of baseline selection and serves as a caution to future psychophysiological work and encouragement for future investigations into baseline methodology.

References

1. Schirner, G., Erdogmus, D., Chowdhury, K., Padir, T.: The future of human-in-the-loop cyber-physical systems. Computer **1**, 36–45 (2013)
2. Mandryk, R.L.: Physiological measures for game evaluation. Game Usability: Advice from the Experts for Advancing the Player Experience, pp. 207–235 (2008)
3. Abich, J., Matthews, G., Reinerman-Jones, L.: Individual differences in UGV operation: a comparison of subjective and psychophysiological predictors. In: Proceedings of the Human Factors and Ergonomics Society Annual Meeting, vol. 59, no. 1, pp. 741–745. SAGE Publications (2015)
4. Cacioppo, J.T., Tassinary, L.G., Berntson, G.: Handbook of Psychophysiology. Cambridge University Press, Cambridge (2007)
5. Wilder, J.: Stimulus and Response: The Law of Initial Value. Wright, Bristol (1967)
6. Cupini, L.M., Matteis, M., Troisi, E., Sabbadini, M., Bernardi, G., Caltagirone, C., Silvestrini, M.: Bilateral simultaneous transcranial doppler monitoring of flow velocity changes during visuospatial and verbal working memory tasks. Brain **119**(4), 1249–1253 (1996)
7. Jennings, J.R., Kamarck, T., Stewart, C., Eddy, M., Johnson, P.: Alternate cardiovascular baseline assessment techniques: vanilla or resting baseline. Psychophysiology **29**(6), 742–750 (1992)
8. Morcom, A.M., Fletcher, P.C.: Does the brain have a baseline? Why we should be resting a rest. Neuroimage **37**(4), 1073–1082 (2007)
9. Piferi, R.L., Kline, K.A., Younger, J., Lawler, K.A.: An alternative approach for achieving cardiovascular baseline: viewing an aquatic video. Int. J. Psychophysiol. **37**, 207–217 (2000)
10. Stern, R.M., Ray, W.J., Quigley, K.S.: Psychophysiological Recording, 2nd edn. Oxford University Press, Oxford (2001)
11. Gerin, W., Pieper, C., Pickering, T.G.: Anticipatory and residual effects of an active coping task on pre- and post-stress baselines. J. Psychosom. Res. **38**, 139–149 (1994)
12. Reinerman-Jones, L.E., Matthews, G., Langheim, L.K., Warm, J.S.: Selection for vigilance assignments: a review and proposed new direction. Theor. Issues Ergon. Sci. **12**(4), 273–296 (2010)
13. Fishel, S.R., Muth, E.R.: Establishing appropriate physiological baseline procedures for real-time physiological measurement. J. Cogn. Eng. Decis. Making **1**(3), 286–308 (2007)
14. Jacob, R.G., Shapiro, A.P.: Is the effect of stress management on blood pressure just regression to the mean? Homeostasis Health Dis. (1994)
15. Piper, S.K., Krueger, A., Koch, S.P., Mahnert, J., Habermehl, C., Stenbrink, J., Obrig, H., Schmitz, C.H.: A wearable multi-channel fNIRS system for brain imaging in freely moving subjects. Neuroimage **85**(1), 64–71 (2014)
16. Stroobant, N., Vingerhoets, G.: Transcranial Doppler ultrasonography monitoring of cerebral hemodynamics during performance of cognitive tasks: a review. Neuropsychol. Rev. **10**(4), 213–231 (2000)
17. Greene, J.D., Nystrom, L.E., Engell, A.D., Darley, J.M., Cohen, J.D.: The neural bases of cognitive conflict and control in moral judgment. Neuron **44**(2), 389–400 (2004)
18. Barber, D., Leontyev, S., Sun, B., Davis, L., Nicholson, D., Chen, J.Y.: The mixed-initiative experimental testbed for collaborative human robot interactions. In: Collaborative Technologies and Systems, IEEE, pp. 483–489 (2008)
19. Frederick, S.: Cognitive reflection and decision making. J. Econ. Perspect. **19**, 25–42 (2005)
20. Kaminsky, P., Simchi-Levi, D.: A new computerized beer game: a tool for teaching the value of integrated supply chain management. Glob. Supply Chain Technol. Manag. **1**(1), 216–225 (1998)

Physiological Measures of Arousal During Soldier-Relevant Tasks Performed in a Simulated Environment

Debra Patton[✉] and Katherine Gamble

U.S. Army Research Laboratory, Aberdeen Proving Ground, Aberdeen, MD 21005, USA
{debra.j.patton4.civ,katherine.r.gamble2.ctr}@mail.mil

Abstract. Deployed United States Army Soldiers operate in dynamic situations, yet there is little known about how to most effectively train Soldier combat skills in a stress-inducing environment prior to deployment. In order to best simulate the experiences of Soldiers in theater, a training environment must be immersive, creating the illusion of "being there," thus providing a heightened level of arousal and encouraging the desire to perform well within the training. A 300-degree immersive simulator was used to examine the potential effectiveness of such a training environment. Participants performed a Shoot-Don't-Shoot task with two types of performance feedback, shock and lifebar loss Levels of arousal were continuously measured through heart rate variability (HRV); psychophysiological measures have been linked to psychological stress and cognitive function. HRV was measured through interbeat interval (IBI), or the peak-to-peak interval of heartbeats, which is linked to cognitive arousal. Higher levels of arousal were seen in the Shock condition compared to the Life Bar condition. IBI was additionally examined in a Baseline session as well as Post-Shock and Post-Life Bar sessions, and results showed that IBI returned to near Baseline levels after both conditions, indicating a recovery from arousal induced during the scenarios. These results show the value of objectively measuring physiology to assess heightened arousal during Soldier-relevant tasks in a simulated environment. Examining the extent to which Soldiers experience arousal, which can often be a proxy for stress, can indicate how immersive or stressful an environment is, and therefore its potential effectiveness as a realistic pre-deployment training environment.

Keywords: Stress · HRV · Simulation · Immersion · Military

This material is based in part upon work supported by the U.S. Army Research Laboratory under Cooperative Agreement No. W911NF-09-2-0053 and by NSF grant IIS-1058132. The views and conclusions contained in this document are those of the authors and should not be interpreted as representing the official policies either expressed or implied of the Army Research Laboratory NSF or the U.S. Government. The U.S. Government is authorized to reproduce and distribute reprints for Government purposes not-with-standing any copyright notation here on.

© Springer International Publishing Switzerland 2016
D.D. Schmorrow and C.M. Fidopiastis (Eds.): AC 2016, Part I, LNAI 9743, pp. 372–382, 2016.
DOI: 10.1007/978-3-319-39955-3_35

1 Introduction

Deployed United States Army Soldiers are frequently required to make critical, time-sensitive decisions in complex and dynamic operational environments. According to U.S. Army Regulation 350-1, the Army will train units and staffs in their core competencies under conditions that accurately and "realistically portray the operational environment" [1]. The extreme tactical environments our Soldiers face in contingencies overseas are unpredictable, mentally and physically challenging, and often insurmountable. These environments pose risk levels that are unacceptable to reproduce for training purposes. Therefore, it is critical to develop training tools that can be used and tested within a safe setting that can simulate extreme environments. To best simulate the experiences of Soldiers in theater, a training environment must be immersive in that it takes into account the emotional factors [2], creating the illusion of "being there," thus providing a heightened level of arousal and encouraging the desire to perform well within the training.

The military uses simulations to train many diverse tactical and social skills, and to test the integration of new systems for future force use. However, current virtual simulations rarely mimic the actual harsh environmental conditions that our military encounters, such as sound, light, smell, or threat of return fire. Thus, because we cannot quantify the stress levels faced in theater, it is difficult to know the extent of comparability that simulations provide in terms of inducing stress in Soldiers.

The U.S. military does employ live training that is able to more closely approximate the battlefield environment than current simulation systems. Survival, Evasion, Resistance, and Escape (SERE) training is both physically and psychologically demanding, and is designed to parallel the stress experienced during real war, captivity, and other combat missions. This type of large-scale, field-based training offers a more realistic experience, but is more amenable to observational studies [3] than controlled experimentation. Immersive Virtual Environment systems that simulate the field-like operational environments allow for good experimental design and control. If these virtual systems were able to provide a more realistic immersive experience, they could provide a low-cost, low-risk way to experimentally measure Soldier response to specific training interventions and lead to more effective military training.

The introduction of stressor threats, such as return fire, in a simulation-based training scenario may induce higher levels of stress that more closely approximate those experienced in battlefield situations. If this is the case, then this newly stressful environment should produce behavior and performance that is more representative of how Soldiers respond in real-world environments. In order to understand the potential effectiveness of such additional stressor elements, arousal must be objectively measured while Soldiers perform real-world tasks in both simulated and live training events.

In order to best match a training environment to situations encountered on the battlefield, Soldiers must be put under stress. One component of the stress response is arousal, which can be caused by both physical and psychological stress [4]. Arousal is linked to learning, and is believed to be a determinant of one's mental capacity to handle the stress of a given situation; that is, arousal levels that are too high or too low work against the trainee [5]. The effects of arousal on cognition and performance follow an inverted-U, such that a certain level of arousal, at the peak of the U, actually improves or even optimizes performance, but arousal beyond that optimal level will begin to hurt performance [6]. Lazarus and Folkman define stress as a state produced when stressors (environmental or social) tax or exceed an individual's adaptive resources [7]. Fatkin and Patton extended Lazarus and Folkman's definition to include that stress is a, "multi-faceted, dynamic, and interactive process with psychological and physiological dimensions" [8]. Because stress has this multifaceted nature, psychophysiological stress measures show how a person is responding to both simulated and real events. The goal of the present study was to assess whether a simulated threat, a return-fire shock, is effective in producing a stress response that may more closely represent stress experienced on the battlefield. We examined arousal, as a proxy for stress and cognitive engagement, through heart rate variability.

Psychophysiological measures have been linked to psychological stress and cognitive function [9]. One such measure, heart rate variability (HRV), provides a non-invasive measure of the autonomic nervous system (ANS). Here, we report on interbeat interval (IBI), which measures the peak-to-peak interval of heartbeats, and is linked to cognition, such that a reduction in IBI is indicative of cognitive arousal [10, 11]. We also examined variability in IBI to determine if arousal levels were more variable as a result of a stressor. Intraindividual variability has been shown to be a marker of neural noise [12], and variability in electrical activity in the brain has been shown to be related to attention regulation in a cognitively demanding task [13].

The present study was designed to assess physiological measures of arousal during a simulated shooting task. The psychological data from this study are described in a previous report [14]; the current report focuses on the physiological responses during two types of feedback (shock and lifebar loss). The lifebar is a form of visual feedback designed to simulate the typical feedback given in the gaming industry, and the shock is a newer type of feedback that is meant to simulate hostile return fire. This effort hypothesized that shock feedback would induce higher levels of arousal than a lifebar loss, as indicated by measures of heart rate variability.

2 Methods

2.1 Participants

A total of 18 male current military, police, and special reaction team personnel volunteered to participate. The age range of participants was 27–48 years ($M = 34$, $SD = 6.5$). After obtaining written informed consent, participants completed a health screening form to identify issues precluding participation, such as pace makers or heart conditions. No participants were excluded. All participants were informed that they could withdraw from the study at any time without penalty; however, all completed the experiment. This study was conducted in accordance with IRB requirements (32 CFR 219 and DoDI 3216.02).

2.2 Design

The independent variable was Condition (Stress or Life Bar). The dependent measure was IBI. Baseline physiological measures were collected before the experimental sessions began. Analysis of HRV was performed using VivoNoetics VivoSense™ software, which follows the European Society of Cardiology and the North American Society of Pacing Electrophysiology [15] procedures set for HRV standards. HRV was derived from a two-channel electrocardiogram. IBI was examined by condition, session, and in an event-related manner, examining IBI at each shock or lifebar loss. Intraindividual variability analyses were also run to provide information about the characteristics of a person's response to stimuli over time [16].

2.3 Tasks and Stimuli

Each condition used all five screens in the Immersive Cognitive Readiness Simulator (ICoRS), a 300° immersive simulator [17] to provide 300° of visibility. Target pairs (friend/friend or friend/foe) were presented in various locations within each scene (e.g., behind a car, wall, building, natural terrain, rocks). The foe targets pointed and fired an M-9 pistol at the participant. The friend targets performed actions such as offering a soda, pulling out a wallet, or making an "I surrender" gesture. Target pairs were presented at the same time on the same screen for 2 s. Participants were instructed to only shoot at the foe targets. Based on subject matter expert input, the 2 s presentation of targets was used to induce a hasty decision. The interval between target pair displays varied between 2, 4, and 6 s. This inter-trial interval was used to minimize a pattern effect.

Based on shooting performance, up to 64 friend/friend and 64 friend/foe target pairs could have been presented. In the Shock and Life Bar conditions, a shock or lifebar loss occurred when a foe was not hit and a minimum of 30 s had passed since the last shock or change in the lifebar status. Therefore, participants could only experience up to 15 feedback events in each condition. Participants were told that even if they shot a foe, it was possible that they might receive a small shock or lose a lifebar because the target had the potential to fire while falling to the ground.

Before target presentation, an indicator sound was activated from the screen on which targets would appear, functioning as a virtual partner, and indicating where the participant should focus his attention. During the Shock condition, participants received a small shock if they missed a foe target. Similarly, in the Life Bar condition, this error caused a lifebar to turn from green to red. A scenario ended when the last (15th) shock was administered or the last lifebar turned red. Each shock and lifebar loss was considered to wound rather than inflict a lethal hit on the participant until the 15th and final feedback presentation. The end of each scenario was indicated by a message presented on the center screen, "the scenario has ended."

2.4 Procedures

For full details of instrumentation and procedures, see [14]. All experimentation was conducted in ARL's Cognitive Assessment and Simulation and Engineering Facility (CASEL) ICoRS [17]. The ThreatFire™ [18] safe return fire system was used to in the Shock condition to induce arousal. The ThreatFire™ system is a wearable belt that uses a rechargeable battery pack to deliver a 50- micro-amp, 200-ms electric shock to simulate the pain of hostile return fire. A modified M4 carbine rifle, fitted with a laser in the barrel and a magazine specially designed to hold CO_2 was used to simulate a similar amount of recoil as one would experience when shooting live rounds on a training range. The LifeShirt™ was used to collect ECG signals during all aspects of the experiment. The shirt is a lightweight (8 oz.), machine-washable shirt with embedded sensors connected to electro pads placed on the wearer's body. Respiratory function sensors are woven into the shirt and provide measurements of heart rate, heart rate variability (IBI ECG signals), as well as a number of other physiological measures. The sensors cycle at 200 Hz every second.

To begin, the participant was asked to stand quietly for 10 min to collect Baseline physiological measures. Next, the participant completed training in the simulator to become familiarized with the equipment and task and to allow aiming adjustment techniques. Each participant completed both conditions (Shock and Life Bar), and was informed of each condition just before it began. Following each condition, participants sat quietly filling out questionnaires; these times made up the Post-Shock and Post-Life Bar sessions.

For the Shock condition, the researcher placed the ThreatFire™ belt on the participant at the waistline. The order of conditions was randomized for each participant.

2.5 Data Analysis

The independent variable was Condition, examining Shock and Life Bar. The dependent variable was IBI. Repeated measures analyses of variance (ANOVAs) were run for all analyses. When assumptions were violated in the analyses of variance, a Greenhouse-Geisser correction was reported.

We compared IBI in the Shock and Life Bar conditions by running a one-way repeated measures ANOVA. We hypothesized that there would be an effect of Condition, with Shock causing reduced IBI.

We investigated recovery from arousal induced in each condition by running a repeated measures ANOVA. We examined Baseline, Shock, Life Bar, and Post-Shock and Post-Life Bar, referred to as Sessions. Paired t-tests were performed to examine if IBI levels returned to Baseline in each Post-Condition session. We hypothesized that IBI would return to near Baseline levels following the two Conditions, in both the Post-Shock and Post-Life Bar sessions.

To investigate if IBI was different in response to the two feedback types (shock and lifebar loss) in the two Conditions, we performed a repeated measures ANOVA on event-related IBI data, looking at the effects of Condition and Event. We hypothesized that

IBI would differ not only by Condition, but also by Event, such that the IBI response would change over the course of feedback events.

To determine whether there were differences in, intraindividual variability (IIV) between the two Conditions, we calculated the coefficient of variation. Coefficient of variation is a measure of an individual's variability that accounts for their mean [16]. A one-way repeated measures ANOVA was performed, and we hypothesized that there would be more IIV in the Shock than in the Life Bar condition.

3 Results

IBI was analyzed at both the scenario level and in an event-related manner. At the scenario level, we hypothesized that there would be lower IBI, indicative of more arousal and cognitive engagement in the Stress than the Life Bar condition. Results showed a significant effect, $F(1,14) = 23.94$, $p < .001$, such that IBI was lower in the Shock than in the Life Bar condition (Fig. 1a).

Because physiology was continuously measured, we were also able to examine IBI both during and Post-Scenarios, with the hypothesis that IBI would return to near Baseline levels after a scenario, indicating recovery. A repeated measures ANOVA was run on Baseline, Shock, Post-Shock, Life Bar and Post-Life Bar sessions, and results showed a significant main effect, $F(2.25,29.30) = 43.53$, $p < .001$ (Fig. 1b). Because we were interested in the IBI levels returning to near Baseline after the scenarios, paired t-tests post hoc analyses were run, and showed that Baseline significantly differed from the Shock $(t(14) = 7.50, p < .001)$ and Life Bar $(t(14) = 5.69, p < .001)$ sessions, but did not differ from Post-Shock $(t(13) = -0.59, p = .568)$ or Post-Life Bar $(t(14) = -1.18, p = .259)$ sessions. Additionally, IBI in the Shock and Life Bar sessions significantly differed from IBI Post-sessions (Shock: $t(13) = -9.57$, $p < .001$, Life Bar: $t(14) = -10.65$, $p < .001$). As can be seen in Fig. 1b, IBI increased in the two Post- sessions, returning to near Baseline levels, which supported our hypothesis of recovery after each scenario.

In the event-related analysis, we were interested in whether the physiological response, IBI, differed between the Shock and Life Bar conditions, and furthermore, if the relationship between the two conditions was sustained across the 15 feedback events during each session. Therefore, we ran a repeated measures ANOVA, which showed main effects of Condition $(F(1,9) = 18.04, p = .002)$ and Event $(F(3.07,27.67) = 7.74, p = .001)$. Visual inspection of the data (Fig. 2) suggests that IBI was lower in response to shocks than lifebar losses throughout most of the sessions.

IIV was measured using the coefficient of variation. Coefficient of variation is a measure of an individual's variability that accounts for their mean [16]. A repeated measures one-way ANOVA was run to compare IBI in the Shock and Life Bar conditions. As can be seen in Fig. 3, there was significantly more IIV in the Shock than in the Life Bar condition, $F(1,14) = 10.86$, $p = .005$.

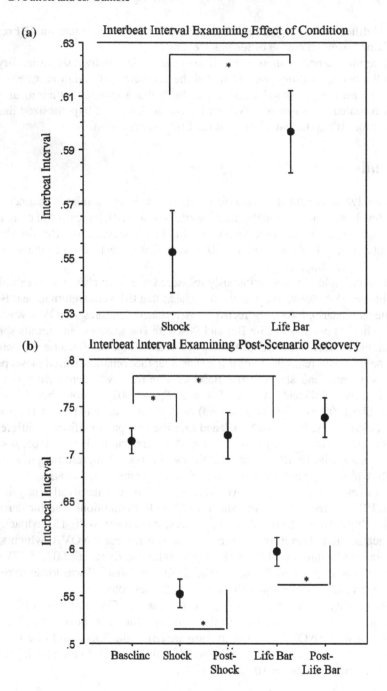

Fig. 1. a. Interbeat interval (mean ± SEM) examining the effect of Condition. b. Interbeat interval (mean ± SEM) examining recovery to Baseline Post-Shock and Post-Life Bar.

Interbeat Interval by Feedback Event

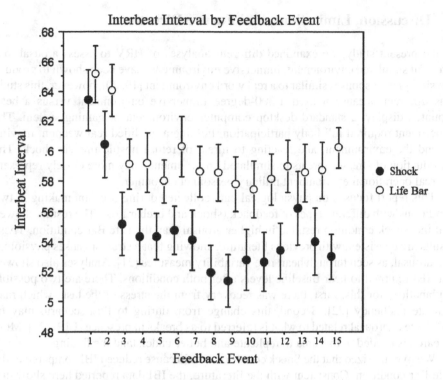

Fig. 2. Interbeat interval (mean ± SEM) in the Shock and Life Bar scenarios by feedback event.

Interbeat Interval Examining Coefficient of Variation

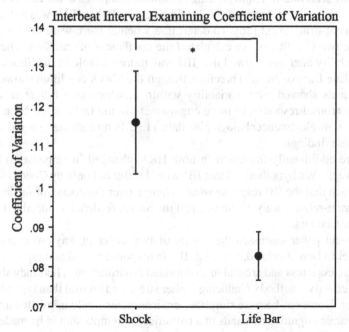

Fig. 3. Coefficient of variation (mean ± SEM) in the Shock and Life Bar scenarios.

4   Discussion, Limitations, and Future Directions

In the present study, we examined different analyses of HRV to assess arousal in a stressful simulated environment. Immersive environments have been shown to produce physiological responses similar to a real word environment [19, 20], however, this study was different because it used a 300-degree immersive environment versus a head mounted display, a standard desktop computer environment or gaming system. The experiment required full body participation, holding a modified real weapon, moving around the environment, and reacting to threat of return hostile fire via shock. The introduction of stressor threats to simulated environments may more closely represent the real operational environment military personnel encounter.

This report focused on physiological data collected during decision making in two conditions with different types of feedback (shock and lifebar loss). The results showed that the Shock condition resulted in higher arousal than the Life Bar condition. These results are consistent with previous literature, showing that a stressor causes physiological arousal, as seen through heart rate variability measures [21]. Analyses also showed that IBI returned to near Baseline levels after both conditions. There are two possible explanations for this. First, there was recovery from the stress of the task, which may indicate resiliency [22]. Second, this change from during to Post-scenario may be reflective of arousal related to what is referred to as breaks in presence (BIP) [23]. More research is needed in this area to replicate and better understand the finding.

We hypothesized that the Shock condition would cause reduced IBI compared to the Life Bar condition. Consistent with the literature, the IBI data reported here show that there was less heart rate variability during the Shock compared to the Life Bar condition [24, 25]. Thompson et al. reported similar findings, such that HRV was reduced during a tactical pistol-firing event [26]. To determine whether there were differences in IIV between the two Conditions, we calculated the coefficient of variation. The intraindividual variability analyses showed that IBI was more variable in the Shock condition than in the Life Bar condition. Therefore, though the Shock condition showed reduced IBI, individuals showed more variability within it, which may reflect an attempt to regulate the arousal response, or more engagement in the task, as has been suggested previously from electroencephalography data [13]. Future studies should attempt to replicate these findings.

We were additionally interested in how HRV changed in response to individual feedback events. We hypothesized that IBI would differ not only by Condition, but also by Event, such that the IBI response would change over the course of feedback events [27]. The event-related analysis showed that the Shock feedback reduced IBI more than the Life Bar feedback.

The present paper discussed the results of two different ways of examining IBI, session-level and event-related, as well as IIV in response to different types of feedback, in order to assess stress and arousal in a simulated environment. This study showed that shock is an effective method of inducing higher stress and arousal than typical feedback, like a lifebar. However, because simulated environments rarely mimic the actual stress and the dynamic cognitive demands of a battlefield, attempts should be made to collect these measures during a live high stress training environment for comparison of stress and arousal levels.

The present results show the importance of objectively measuring physiology to examine the effects of heightened arousal during Soldier-relevant tasks in a simulated environment. Examining the extent to which Soldiers experience arousal, which can often be a proxy for stress, we can know how immersive or stressful an environment is, and therefore its potential effectiveness as a realistic pre-deployment training environment. Future studies should attempt to identify performance metrics of Soldier-relevant tasks and examine how they relate to physiological measures.

References

1. Development, Department of the Army: Army Training and Leader. Goverment Printing Office, Washington, DC, U.S., 18 December 2009/RAR 4 August 2011
2. Huang, M., Alessi, N.: Presence as an emotional experience. In: Westwood, J.D., Hoffman, H.M., Robb, R.A., Stredney, D. (eds.) Medicine Meets Virtual Reality: The Convergence of Physical and Informational Technologies Options for a New Era in Healthcare, pp. 148–153. IOS Press, Amsterdam (1999)
3. Taylor, M., Sausen, L., Mujica-Parodi, L., Potterat, E., Yanagi, M., Kim, H.: Neurophysiologic methods to measure stress during survival, evasion, resistance and escape training. Aviat. Space Environ. Med. **78**(5), 224–230 (2007)
4. Shibasaki, T., Imaki, T., Hotta, M., Ling, N., Demura, H.: Psychological stress increases arousal through brain corticotropin-releasing hormone without significant increase in adrenocorticotropin and catecholamine secretion. Brain Res. **618**, 71–75 (1993)
5. Fowles, D.: The three arousal model: implications of Gray's two-factor learning theory for heart rate, electrodermal activity, and psychopathy. Psychophysiology **17**, 87–104 (1980)
6. Yerkes, R., Dodson, J.: The relation of strength of stimulus to rapidity of habit-formation. J. Comp. Neurol. Psychol. **18**, 459–482 (1908)
7. Lazarus, R., Folkman, S.: Stress, Appraisal and Coping. Springer Publishing, New York (1984)
8. Fatkin, L., Patton, D.: Mitigating the effects of stress through cognitive readiness. In: Performance Under Stress. Ashgate Publishing Limited, Aldershot, UK (2008)
9. Nagendra, H., Kumar, V., Mukherjee, S.: Cognitive behavior evaluation based on physiological parameters among young healthy subjects with yoga as intervention. Comput. Math. Methods Med. **2015**, 1–13 (2015)
10. Taelman, J., Vandeput, S., Vlemincx, E., Spaepan, A., Van Huffel, S.: Instantaneous changes in hear rate regulation due to mental load in simulated office work. J. Appl. Physiol. **111**, 1497–1505 (2011)
11. Mukherjee, S., Yadev, R., Yung, I., Zaidel, D., Oken, B.: Sensitivity to mental effort and test-retest reliability of heart rate variability measures in healthy seniors. Clin. Neurophysiol. **122**, 2059–2066 (2011)
12. MacDonald, S., Nyberg, L., Backman, L.: Intra-individual variability in behavior: links to brain structure, neurotransmission and neuronal activity. Trends Neurosci. **29**, 474–480 (2006)
13. Moore, R., Wu, C.-T., Pontifex, M., O'Leary, K., Scudder, M., Faine, L., Johnson, C., Hillman, C.: Aerobic fitness and intra-individual variability of neurocognition in preadolescent children. Brain Cogn. **82**, 43–57 (2013)

14. Patton, D.: How real is good enough? Assessing realism of presence in simulations and its effects on decision making. In: Schmorrow, D.D., Fidopiastis, C.M. (eds.) AC 2014. LNCS, vol. 8534, pp. 245–256. Springer, Heidelberg (2014)
15. Malik, M.: Heart rate variability. Ann. Noninvasive Electrocardiol. **1**, 151–181 (1996)
16. Wegesin, D., Stern, Y.: Inter- and intraindividual variability in recognition memory: effects of aging and estrogen use. Neuropsychology **18**, 646–657 (2004)
17. Patton, D., Loukota, P., Avery, E.: Validating the ThreatFire belt in 300 degrees: a pilot study. In: 22nd Proceedings of the Behavior Representation in Modeling and Simulation (BRiMS) Conference, Ottawa, Ontario (2013)
18. "ThreatFire," VirTra. http://www.virtra.com/threat-fire/
19. Meehan, M., Insko, B., Whitton, M., Brooks, F.: Physiological measures of presence in stressful virtual environments. ACM Trans. Graph. **21**, 645–652 (2002)
20. Malinksa, M., Zuzewicz, K., Bugajska, J., Grabowski, A.: Heart rate variability (HRV) during virtual immersion. Int. J. Occup. Saf. Ergon. **21**, 47–54 (2015)
21. Chuang, C.-Y., Han, W.-R., Young, S.-T.: Heart rate variability response to stressful event in healthy subjects. In: Chwee Teck, L., James, C.H.G. (eds.) 2008 Proceedings of ICBME, vol. 23, pp. 378–380. Springer, Heidelberg (2009)
22. Souza, G., Mendonca-de-Souza, A., Barros, E., Coutinho, E., Oliveira, L., Mendlowicz, M., Figueira, I., Volchan, E.: Resilience and vagal tone predict cardiac recovery from acute social stress. Stress **10**(4), 368–374 (2007)
23. Slater, M., Edlinger, G., Leeb, R., Pfurtscheller, G., Antley, A., Garau, M., Brogni, A., Friedman, D.: Analysis of physiological responses to a social situation in an immersive virtual environment. Presence: Teleoperators Virtual Environ. **15**, 553–569 (2006)
24. Bernston, G., Bigger, J., Eckberg, D., Grossman, P., Kaufmann, P., Malik, M., et al.: Heart rate variability: origins, methods, and interpretive caveats. Psychophysiology **34**, 623–648 (1997)
25. Bernston, G., Cacioppo, J.: Heart rate variability: Stress and psychiatric conditions. In: Malik, M., Camm, A. (eds.) Dynamic Electrocardiography, pp. 57–64. Blackwell Futura, New York (2004)
26. Thompson, A., Swain, D., Branch, J., Spina, R., Grieco, C.: Autonomic response to tactical pistol performance measured by heart rate variability. J. Strength Conditioning Res. **29**, 926–933 (2015)
27. Moses, Z., Luecken, L., Eason, J.: Measuring task-related changes in heart rate variability. In: Conference Proceeding IEEE Engineering in Medicine and Biology Science, pp. 644–647, (2007)

Theoretical Versus Mathematical Approach to Modeling Psychological and Physiological Data

Lauren Reinerman-Jones[1]([⊠]), Stephanie J. Lackey[2], Julian Abich IV[1],
Brandon Sollins[1], and Irwin Hudson[3]

[1] Institute for Simulation and Training (IST),
University of Central Florida (UCF), Orlando, FL, USA
{lreinerm, jabich}@ist.ucf.edu
[2] Design Interactive, Orlando, FL, USA
stephanie.lackey@designinteractive.net
[3] U.S. Army Research Laboratory, Orlando, FL, USA
irwin.hudson@us.army.mil

Abstract. Variable selection for predictive modeling has traditionally relied on theory in the psychological domain. Given the recent advancements in computing technology and availability, researchers are able to utilize more sophisticated mathematical modeling techniques with greater ease. The challenge becomes evaluating whether theory or mathematics should be relied upon for model development. The presented analyses compared the use of hierarchical and stepwise variable selection methods during a predictive modeling task using linear regression. The results show that the stepwise variable selection method is able to obtain a more efficient model than the hierarchical variable selection method. Implications and recommendations for researchers are further discussed.

Keywords: Cognitive modeling · Perception · Emotion · Interaction · Electroencephalography · Brain activity measurement · Physiological measuring · Human performance

1 Introduction

Psychological researchers have utilized predictive statistical model building techniques to predict, classify, and further understand the true nature of a variety of behavioral phenomenon. While building predictive statistical models, researchers are faced with an assortment of options to consider in order to construct the most appropriate model from their data, such as (1) whether the model is being used for prediction or understanding the relationship between the independent and dependent variable(s), (2) the algorithm being used to build the model, (3) the specific parameters of the algorithm being used, (4) possible data transformations, (5) sampling techniques to build the model, as well as (6) evaluation of the generated models.

One essential consideration to model development is determining how variables are selected [1]. Traditionally in psychological research, variable selection has "relied on informal or intuitive reasoning or historical precedent" [2]. This method of variable

© Springer International Publishing Switzerland 2016
D.D. Schmorrow and C.M. Fidopiastis (Eds.): AC 2016, Part I, LNAI 9743, pp. 383–393, 2016.
DOI: 10.1007/978-3-319-39955-3_36

selection relies strictly on theory, and is efficient and practical when small amounts of well-studied variables are being evaluated as predictors within a model. With improvements in computing power and advancements in measurement techniques, researchers are now able to collect, store, and analyze a much larger amount of data that often times contains an exhaustive amount of potential predictor variables. For example, researchers utilizing physiological measures, most notably the electroencephalogram (EEG), have access to brain activity data from a large amount of sensor sites (sometimes up to 256) over a large amount of frequency bins (1–100+). Physiological variables have been shown to be strongly task dependent [3] and psychophysiological metrics seldom intercorrelate [4], therefore, it may be difficult to assume a predictor for one task type will be applicable to another. Furthermore, more advanced modeling software packages have become available to researchers that allow complex, state-of-the-art statistical methods to be utilized with relative ease. A variety of open source and proprietary software packages are used by researchers for modeling data including SPSS, SAS, R, Python, and WEKA, to name a few. Lastly, the myriad of experimental environments available, including computer-based questionnaires and simulation-based approaches, allow researchers to explore a new range of variables over a large population with fewer cost and resources. As a result, with the influx of large data sets, new variables being collected, and access to more sophisticated modeling tools, researchers are applying objective, mathematical variable selection methods that can be used to reduce the dimensionality of their datasets, facilitate data understanding, discover new patterns or trends in the data, and ultimately improve model prediction [1].

The data and tasks for these present analyses were derived from previous work [5]. The goal for the present analyses is to evaluate a commonly used algorithm by psychological researchers, linear regression, while using a theoretical approach (i.e. hierarchical regression) and mathematical approach (i.e. stepwise regression) for variable selection to develop and compare performance prediction models using subjective and objective measures of workload.

1.1 Workload Metrics

Research has suggested that mental workload plays an essential role in task performance and is an indicator of performance across multiple domains [6, 7]. Although a universally accepted, formal definition of workload does not exist, workload can be regarded as the "perceived evaluation and accompanying physiological response to the experience imposed by task demands" [5]. A significant body of research has investigated the use of subjective and objective methods to quantify an operator's level of mental workload. The subjective and objective metrics described below will be used in the present analyses as each one has been found to contribute to the explanation of performance.

In regards to subjective measures, the Instantaneous Self-Assessment (ISA) [8] and NASA-Task Load Index (TLX) [9] have been extensively used by researchers to capture an operator's subjective level of perceived workload. The ISA is a unidimensional measure that provides an immediate subjective rating of workload during a given task [8]. The ISA has the benefit of being minimally intrusive, is able to be administered in real-time, and has been shown to be a good indicator of workload [10]. Traditionally, the TLX has been used as a "gold-standard" of workload assessment. The TLX is a multidimensional measure that assesses perceived workload during a given task and usually administered post-task [9]. Operators rate their perceived level of workload on six dimensions: three related to the demands on the operator and three related to the interaction with the task [9]. The original measure additionally required pair-wise comparisons to weight the ratings, but research found the weighting is time-consuming and unnecessary [11]. Additionally, the TLX sensitivity is robust to time delays [11]. Although subjective assessment provides valuable insight regarding the operator's perceived impact of task demands, access to unbiased and objective data could provide critical information that might account for more variance associated with task performance.

Psychophysiological measures, such as the electroencephalogram (EEG), electro-cardiogram (ECG), functional near infrared spectroscopy (fNIR), transcranial Doppler (TCD) ultrasonography, and eye tracking, have been extensively used by researchers to objectively assess workload. Several psychophysiological metrics have been identified in the literature to be sensitive to workload variation during task performance [4]. EEG monitors electrical activity in the cerebral cortex. Research found decreased parietal alpha activity [12] and increased frontal lobe theta activity when mental workload increased during a variety of task types [13]. These findings are further supported by functional neuroimaging (fMRI) studies that found psychophysiological responses to workload were associated with both increased thalamic metabolism and a reduction in alpha activity [14], as well as both increased cingulate cortex activation and increased frontal theta activity [15]. Research utilizing ECG to capture cardiac activity found heart rate variability and interbeat-intervals were negatively correlated with workload [16]. The level of regional oxygen saturation (rSO_2) in the pre-frontal cortex gathered from fNIR has been associated with effort [17] and positively correlated with workload [18]. Additionally, research using the TCD to capture cerebral blood flow velocity in the middle cerebral artery found a positive correlation with workload [19]. Finally, eye tracking studies found increased pupil dilation [20], increased randomness in scan patterns as assessed by nearest-neighbor index (NNI) [21], increased fixation durations [22], increased number of fixations [23], and the Index of Cognitive Activity (ICA) [24] were all associated with workload changes. The results of these studies suggest psy-chophysiological metrics might account for unique variance in task performance unaccounted for by subjective metrics, therefore, investigation of such variables should be included in regression model analyses.

1.2   Theoretical Approach: Hierarchical Regression

Hierarchical regression is a method of variable selection in which variables are user-selected and entered into the model in incremental steps based upon their importance for outcome prediction [25]. The variables chosen and the order in which they are entered into the model are based on the specific research hypotheses, under-lying theory, and past research [26]. Within the social sciences, correlated variables are commonly utilized to explain variance on a criterion variable while controlling for other variables, hence justifying the application of a hierarchical regression approach [27]. The adjusted R^2 helps control the amount of variance accounted for in the dependent variable by adjusting the directional impact of correlated and non-correlated independent variables. Consequently, variables that are considered theoretically important contributors to performance or found to be associated with performance in past research are incorporated into the model first, followed by the addition of new exploratory variables [28]. The limitation of this approach relies on the researcher's theoretical knowledge of the relationships among variables and therefore an unbiased algorithmic approach might be more suitable in some cases.

1.3   Mathematical Approach: Stepwise Regression

Stepwise regression is a method of variable selection that accounts for the inclusion and deletion of variables during each step of the model building process [29]. The appeal of this approach becomes apparent when a model aims to explain the variance associated with the dependent variable using the least amount of predictor variables [25], which reduces the likelihood of overfitting the model with variables that can result in misleading predictive power [30]. The method begins by first evaluating all possible one-variable models using the following regression Equation (1):

$$E(y) = \beta_0 + \beta_1 x_i \tag{1}$$

where β_0 is a constant, β_1 is the coefficient for the ith variable, and x_i is the ith independent variable. For each ith independent variable, a t-test evaluating the β_1 parameter is conducted (computed by taking the value of the coefficient divided by standard error of the coefficient), and the variable with the largest absolute t-value is retained [31]. The following regression equation evaluates the remaining independent variables (2):

$$E(y) = \beta_0 + \beta_1 x_1 + \beta_2 x_i \tag{2}$$

where β_0 is a constant, β_1 is the coefficient for the first variable, x_1 is the first selected independent variable, β_2 is the coefficient for the ith variable, and x_i is the ith independent variable. For each remaining ith independent variable, a t-test evaluating the β_2 parameter is conducted, and the variable with the largest absolute t-value is retained. Once the second variable is selected, the t-value of the β_1 parameter is rechecked to determine if it is still significant within the model. If the β_1 parameter is no longer significant, the β_1 variable is removed and replaced with another variable that results in the most significant t-test with the β_2 variable [31]. This procedure continues until no other independent variables are found to be significant within the model. The limitation of this approach falls on to the type of algorithm used by the statistical software [25], therefore to ensure validity of the outcome, researchers must know the mathematical procedure used to achieve any models.

2   Methods

2.1   Participants

Data were collected from 150 university undergraduates and graduates (age: $M = 19.57$, $SD = 3.45$) with 85 males (age: $M = 19.62$, $SD = 3.72$) and 65 females (age: $M = 19.50$, $SD = 3.09$). All participants were required to be right-handed, have normal or corrected to normal vision, and have no experience with the experimental testbed. Additionally, participants were required not to consume alcohol or sedative medications at least 24 h prior to the study, and caffeine and/or nicotine at least two hours prior to the study.

2.2   Experimental Task

Participants completed the experimental task using the Mixed Initiative eXperimental (MIX) testbed [32]. The MIX testbed simulated an operator control unit (OCU) for an unmanned ground vehicle (UGV) that traveled through a Middle Eastern town. During the task, participants monitored an aerial map located on the bottom of the OCU. The icons on the aerial map exhibited three types of changes: appear (icons added), disappear (icons removed), or move (icons relocated). Participants were required to identify and indicate the type of change by left-clicking on the appropriate corresponding change detection button located above the aerial map as quickly as possible before another change event occurred. The icons were derived from a common warfighter symbol database [33], but had no associated meaning. During the experimental scenario, participants received three 5-min conditions comprised of 6, 12, or 24 changes per minute. Each event change consisted of two separate icons changing, but only one type of changed occurred at a time. Event rates and saliency of event rates were derived from previous research [6]. Performance during the experimental task was calculated by taking the total number of change events correctly detected and dividing by the total number of change events presented collapsed across all three change types to give one total performance score.

2.3   Subjective Measures

Participants were administered the ISA and TLX after each event rate condition. The ISA is based on a 5-point rating scale and consists of a single question to assess how an operator felt during the task. The TLX requires participants to rate their perceived level of workload on six dimensions using a 100-point sliding scale. A global workload score was calculated by averaging each of the six subscales. Ratings from all three event rate conditions were averaged to determine an overall score for each subscale of each questionnaire across the entire scenario.

2.4   Objective Measures

Participants were attached to EEG, ECG, fNIR, TCD, and eye tracking sensors that monitored their physiological responses during the task. Similar to the subjective metrics, all three event rate conditions were averaged to determine an overall score for each metric across the entire scenario. Advanced Brain Monitoring's B-Alert X10 EEG nine channel system was used to record participant's brain and cardiac activity. The EEG was sampled at 256 Hz from F3, F4, Fz, C3, C4, Cz, P3, P4, and POz sensors sites using the international 10–20 system with references at each mastoid. Power spectral density analysis was used to extrapolate alpha (8–13 Hz), beta (14–26 Hz), and theta (4–7 Hz) wavelengths from each individual sensor site. Individual sensor sites were further combined to generate values for lobes (frontal, temporal, parietal) and hemispheres (left and right). Participant's heart rate and heart rate variability were calculated using the So and Chan method [34]. Somantics' Invos Cerebral/Somatic Oximeter was used to record participant's regional cerebral oxygen saturation (rSO_2). The fNIR sensors were placed on the participant's left and right hemisphere prefrontal cortex and measured changes in the levels of oxygenated hemoglobin and deoxygenated hemoglobin. Spencer Technologies' ST^3 Digital Transcranial Doppler was used to record participant's cerebral blood flow velocity in the middle cerebral artery. TCD probes were carefully positioned on the participant's temples using the Marc 600 head frame set. Seeing Machine's FaceLAB 5 system was used to record participants' eye tracking data. Two desk-mounted cameras and an infrared light source were positioned in front of the participant, and were individually calibrated for each participant.

3   Results

In the present analyses, each metric previously described will be considered for building the model. In total, a mix of 43 objective and subjective variables are under consideration as contributors to the prediction of task performance. RStudio software was used to conduct hierarchical and stepwise regression analyses. Due to listwise deletions, 107 participants were included in the hierarchical regression analysis, and 94 participants were included in the stepwise regression analysis. Models were evaluated utilizing 5-fold cross-validation to accurately determine their performance with new data.

3.1   Hierarchical Regression

Subjective measures were entered at Step 1 and physiological measures were entered at Step 2 based on the theoretical assumption that subjective measures are more standardized and have been strongly correlated with task performance, specifically the TLX, and should therefore be entered into the model first. The subjective and objective variables entered in each step of the model can be found in Table 1.

In Step 1 of the analysis, the subjective variables resulted in a significant model for each fold that was evaluated with an average adjusted R^2 of .052. The Performance

Table 1. Subjective and objective variables entered into each step of the hierarchical regression.

Variables	Step entered
ISA	1
TLX_mental demand	1
TLX_physical demand	1
TLX_temporal demand	1
TLX_frustration	1
TLX_performance	1
EEG_frontal lobe theta	2
EEG_parietal lobe alpha	2
ECG_interbeat interval	2
ECG_heart rate variability	2
fNIR_left mean rSO_2	2
fNIR_right mean rSO_2	2
TCD_left mean velocity	2
TCD_right mean velocity	2
Eyetracker_ICA	2
Eyetracker_number of fixations	2
Eyetracker_average fixation duration	2
Eyetracker_square NNI	2

subscale from the TLX resulted in a significant coefficient for each of the five folds, and the ISA measure resulted in a significant coefficient for one of the folds. No other subjective variables resulted in significant coefficients.

In Step 2 of the analysis, the inclusion of the objective measures resulted in a significant model for each fold that was evaluated with an average adjusted R^2 of .207. The number of fixations and average fixation duration variables resulted in significant coefficients for each of the five folds. The ICA metric was a significant coefficient for four of the folds. Lastly, the right mean rSO_2 variable resulted in a significant coefficient for one of the folds. No other objective variables resulted in significant coefficients.

3.2 Stepwise Regression

The subjective and objective variables entered into the stepwise analysis can be found in Table 2.

The BIC information criteria was used to determine the addition and removal of variables into the model during the stepwise procedure [35]. According to the results, each fold resulted in a significant model with an average adjusted R^2 of .323. A summary of the variables entered into the model can found in Table 3. Given the nature of the stepwise procedure, each variable entered into the model resulted in a significant standardized coefficient.

Table 2. The subjective and objective variables entered into the stepwise regression analysis

Source	Variables
ISA	ISA
TLX	Mental Demand, Physical Demand, Temporal Demand, Frustration, Performance, Global Workload
EEG	Frontal Lobe Alpha, Frontal Lobe Theta, Frontal Lobe Beta Parietal Lobe Alpha, Parietal Lobe Beta, Parietal Lobe Theta Occipital Lobe Alpha, Occipital Lobe Beta, Occipital Lobe Theta Midsagittal Alpha, Midsagittal Beta, Midsagittal Theta Left Hemisphere Alpha, Left Hemisphere Beta, Left Hemisphere Theta Right Hemisphere Alpha, Right Hemisphere Beta, Right Hemisphere Theta
ECG	Inter-beat Interval, Heart Rate Variability, Heart Rate
fNIR	Left Mean rSO_2, Left Median rSO_2, Right Mean rSO_2, Right Median rSO_2
TCD	Left Mean Peak Velocity, Left Mean Dias Velocity, Left Mean Velocity Right Mean Peak Velocity, Right Mean Dias Velocity, Right Mean Velocity
Eye tracker	ICA, Number of Fixations, Average Fixation Duration, Number of Saccades, Square NNI, Convex-hull NNI

Table 3. A summary of the variables entered into the model based on the stepwise regression analysis.

Variable	Number of times selected
Number of fixations	4
Average fixation durations	4
ICA	3
fNIR_right mean rSO_2	1
fNIR_right median rSO_2	1
Number of saccades	1
Square NNI	1
TLX_frustration	1
TLX_performance	1

4 Discussion

The goal for the present analyses was to evaluate two linear regression approaches, theoretical (hierarchical regression) and mathematical (stepwise regression), for variable selection to develop and compare performance prediction models using subjective and objective measures of workload. The analyses showed that the stepwise method resulted in better model performance than the hierarchical method in terms of adjusted R^2 when investigating the addition of psychophysiological metrics, as well as differing in the number of variables selected within the model. These differences suggest that the mathematical approach was more efficient compared to the theoretical approach for variable selection.

According to the results, the theoretical approach resulted in an average adjusted R^2 of .207 and the mathematical approach resulted in an average adjusted R^2 of .323. Both of these results are deemed to be very weak effects for social science data and potentially due to the ratio of sample size to independent variables [36], however the performance difference between the two models are substantial. The theoretical approach included 18 variables while the mathematical approach included 4 to 7 variables into the final model. With such a high variable set included in the theoretical approach, multicollinearity becomes a concern [26]. Although 18 variables were entered into the final model using the theoretical approach, only three of those variables consistently resulted in significant coefficients including the ICA, number of fixations, and average fixation durations. The mathematical approach resulted in similar findings in which the ICA, number of fixations, and average fixation durations also consistently resulted in significant coefficients, however with substantially less variables entered into the final model. For both approaches, the majority of the variables selected into the final model were eye tracking metrics which is consistent with past research on the effectiveness of using the eye tracker for discriminating between levels of workload during a change detection task [10]. These results suggest that the mathematical approach is consistent with the theoretical approach, however the mathematical approach was more stringent as it was able to objectively identify and ignore non-contributing extraneous variables while selecting only the most relevant variables into the final model.

Variables entered into the model through the theoretical approach were the workload variables that have been backed by a significant body of research relating those variables with task performance. Several of these variables, most notably from the TLX, are considered standard metrics in the workload literature and have been consistently used by researchers to assess performance during a variety of tasks across a variety of domains [6, 9, 11, 37]. Although these variables were entered into the model using the theoretical approach and had the opportunity for being entered into the model through the mathematical approach, none of these variables resulted in significant coefficients for either of the final models. Variables that were selected included those that were associated with task performance, but do not have as much theoretical support compared to the TLX and EEG variables. These results suggest that utilizing a strict theoretical approach for variable selection can introduce bias early into the model building process in which variables are ignored and not properly utilized despite potential for significant prediction. Furthermore, these results suggest using a mathematical approach might help improve and contribute to theory by providing objective outcomes with limited bias to assist in evaluating the potential contribution of new exploratory variables.

Acknowledgements. This work was in part supported by the US Army Research Laboratory (ARL) (W91CRB-08-D-0015). The views and conclusions contained in this document are those of the authors and should not be interpreted as representing the official policies, either expressed or implied, of ARL or the US Government.

References

1. Guyon, I., Elisseeff, A.: An introduction to variable and feature selection. J. Mach. Learn. Res. **3**, 1157–1182 (2003)
2. Hogarty, K.Y., Kromrey, J.D., Ferron, J.M., Hines, C.V.: Selection of variables in exploratory factor analysis: an empirical comparison of a stepwise and traditional approach. Psychometrika **69**(4), 593–611 (2004)
3. Otten, L.J., Rugg, M.D.: Electrophysiological correlates of memory encoding are task-dependent. Cogn. Brain. Res. **12**(1), 11–18 (2001)
4. Reinerman-Jones, L.E., Matthews, G., Barber, D.J., Abich IV, J.: Psychophysiological metrics for workload are demand-sensitive but multifactorial. In: Proceedings of the 58th Human Factors and Ergonomics Society 2014, pp. 974–978. SAGE Publications, Chicago
5. Abich IV, J.: Investigating the universality and comprehensive ability of measures to assess the state of workload. Doctoral dissertation, University of Central Florida, Orlando, FL (2013)
6. Abich IV, J., Reinerman-Jones, L., Taylor, G.S.: Establishing workload manipulations utilizing a simulated environment. In: Shumaker, R. (ed.) Proceedings of the 8th International Conference of HCI International 2013. Springer, Las Vegas, NV (2013)
7. Kohlmorgen, J., Dornhege, G., Braun, M., Blankertz, B., Müller, K.R., Curio, G., Hagemann, K., Bruns, A., Schrauf, M., Kineses, W.: Improving human performance in a real operating environment through real-time mental workload detection. In: Dornhege, G., Millan, J.R., Hinterberger, T., McFarland, D.J., Muller, K.R. (eds.) Toward Brain-Computer Interfacing, pp. 409–422. MIT Press, Cambridge (2007)
8. Tattersall, A.J., Foord, P.S.: An experimental evaluation of instantaneous self-assessment as a measure of workload. Ergonomics **39**(5), 740–748 (1996)
9. Hart, S.G., Staveland, L.E.: Development of NASA-TLX (Task Load Index): results of empirical and theoretical research. In: Hancock, P.A., Meshkati, N. (eds.) Human Mental Workload, pp. 139–184. Elsevier Science Publishers, North-Holland (1988)
10. Abich, J., Reinerman-Jones, L., Taylor, G.S.: Investigating Workload (2013)
11. Measures for adaptive training systems. Proc. Hum. Factors Ergon. Soc. Annu. Meet. **57**(1), 2091–2095. SAGE Publications, San Diego
12. Moroney, W.F., Biers, D.W., Eggemeier, F.T., Mitchel, J.A.: A comparison of two scoring procedures with the NASA-Task Load Index in a simulated flight task. In: Proceedings of the 1992 IEEE Aerospace and Electronics Conference, vol. 2, pp. 734–740 (1992)
13. Ergenoglu, T., Demiralp, T., Bayraktaroglu, Z., Ergen, M., Beydagi, H., Uresin, Y.: Alpha rhythm of the EEG modulates visual detection performance in humans. Cogn. Brain. Res. **20**(3), 376–383 (2004)
14. Smith, M.E., Gevins, A., Brown, H., Karnik, A., Du, R.: Monitoring task loading with multivariate EEG measures during complex forms of human-computer interaction. Hum. Factors **43**(3), 366–380 (2001)
15. Larson, C.L.: Relations between PET-derived measures of thalamic glucose metabolism and EEG alpha power. Psychophysiology **35**(2), 162–169 (1998)
16. Asada, H., Fukuda, Y., Tsunoda, S., Yamaguchi, M., Tonoike, M.: Frontal midline theta rhythms reflect alternative activation of prefrontal cortex and anterior cingulate cortex in humans. Neurosci. Lett. **274**(1), 29–32 (1999)
17. Veltman, J.A., Gaillard, A.K.: Physiological workload reactions to increasing levels of task difficulty. Ergonomics **41**(5), 656–669 (1998)
18. Warm, J.S., Tripp, L.D., Matthews, G., Helton, W.S.: Cerebral hemodynamic indices of operator fatigue in vigilance. In: Matthews, G., Desmond, P.A., Neubauer, C., Hancock, P.A. (eds.) Handbook of Operator Fatigue, pp. 197–207. Ashgate Press, Aldershot (2012)

19. Izzetoglu, K., Bunce, S., Onaral, B., Pourrezaei, K., Chance, B.: Functional optical brain imaging using near-infrared during cognitive tasks. Int. J. Hum.-Comput. Interact. **17**(2), 211–227 (2004)
20. Shaw, T.H., Guagliardo, L., de Visser, E., Parasuraman, R.: Using transcranial Doppler sonography to measure cognitive load in a command and control task. Proc. Hum. Factors Ergon. Soc. Annu. Meet. **54**(3), 249–253 (2010)
21. Beatty, J.: Task-evoked pupillary responses, processing load, and the structure of processing resources. Psychol. Bull. **91**(2), 276 (1982)
22. Di Nocera, F., Terenzi, M., Camilli, M.: Another look at scanpath: distance to nearest neighbour as a measure of mental workload. In: de Waard, D., Brookhuis, K.A., Toffetti, A. (eds.) Developments in Human Factors in Transportation, Design, and Evaluation, pp. 1–9. Shaker Publishing, Herzogenrath (2006)
23. Jacob, R.J., Karn, K.S.: Eye tracking in human-computer interaction and usability research: ready to deliver the promises. In: Hyona, J., Radach, R., Deubel, H. (eds.) The Mind's Eye: Cognitive and Applied Aspects of Eye Movement Research, pp. 573–605. Elsevier Science, Amsterdam (2003)
24. Van Orden, K.F., Limbert, W., Makeig, S., Jung, T.P.: Eye activity correlates of workload during a visuospatial memory task. Hum. Factors **43**(1), 111–121 (2001)
25. Marshall, S.P.: The index of cognitive activity: measuring cognitive workload. In: Proceedings of the 2002 IEEE 7th Conference on Human Factors and Power Plants, pp. 7–9 (2002)
26. Lewis, M.: Stepwise versus hierarchical regression: pros and cons. Paper Presented at the Annual Meeting of the Southwest Education Research Association, San Antonio, TX, 7 February 2007
27. Field, A.: Discovering Statistics Using SPSS, 3rd edn. SAGE, Los Angeles (2009)
28. Pedhazur, E.J.: Multiple Regression in Behavioral Research, 3rd edn. Harcourt Brace, Orlando (1997)
29. Kerlinger, F.N.: Foundations of Behavioral Research, 3rd edn. Holt, Rinehart and Winston, New York (1986)
30. Thompson, M.L.: Selection of variables in multiple regression: part I. A review and evaluation. Int. Statist. Rev. **46**(1), 1–19 (1978)
31. Babyak, M.: What you see may not be what you get: a brief, nontechnical introduction to overfitting in regression-type models. Psychosom. Med. **66**(3), 411–421 (2004)
32. McClave, J.T., Sincich, T.: Statistics. Prentice Hall, Upper Saddle River (2009)
33. Reinerman-Jones, L., Barber, D., Lackey, S., Nicholson, D.: Developing methods for utilizing physiological measures. In: Tadeusz, M., Waldemar, K., Rice, V. (eds.) Advances in Understanding Human Performance: Neuroergonomics, Human Factors Design, and Special Populations. CRC Press, Boca Raton (2010)
34. Department of Defense: Department of Defense Interface Standard: Common Warfighting Symbology (MIL-STD-2525B) (2005)
35. Tan, K., Chan, K., Choi, K.: Detection of the QRS complex, P wave and T wave in electrocardiogram. In: First International Conference on Advances in Medical Signal and Information Processing, No. 476, pp. 41–47 (2000)
36. Beal, D.: Information criteria methods in SAS for multiple linear regression models. In: Proceedings of the 15th Annual SouthEast SAS User Group (SESUG) (2007)
37. Ferguson, C.J.: An effect size primer: a guide for clinicians and researchers. Prof. Psychol.: Res. Pract. **40**(5), 532–538 (2009)
38. Cinaz, B., Arnrich, B., La Marca, R., Troster, G.: Monitoring of mental workload levels during an everyday life office-work scenario. Pers. Ubiquit. Comput. **17**(2), 229–239 (2011)

Monitoring Attention with Embedded Frequency Markers for Simulation Environments

Bartlett A.H. Russell[1(✉)], Jon C. Russo[2], Ian P. Warfield[1],
and William D. Casebeer[1]

[1] Advanced Technology Laboratories, Lockheed Martin, Arlington, VA, USA
bartlett.a.russell@lmco.com
[2] Advanced Technology Laboratories, Lockheed Martin, Cherry Hill, NJ, USA

Abstract. Monitoring both overt and covert attention shifts is critical for the accurate real-time assessment of user state in training or simulation environments. Current attention-monitoring methods predominantly include eye-tracking, but eye-tracking alone is blind to covert shifts in visual attention such as internal distraction and mind-wandering. Steady state visual evoked potentials (ssVEPs) are neural signals that are sensitive to covert attention shifts and offer a means to measure endogenous engagement. Laboratories use ssVEPS to study the dynamics of attentional systems, but the frequencies most often used are causes eyestrain and are highly distracting making them impractical for applied use within simulation or training environments. To overcome this limitation, we examine whether frequencies above the perceptual threshold are similarly sensitive to covert attention shifts. Our qualified results indicate supraperceptual threshold ssVEPs are sensitive to such shifts and should be considered for real-time use.

Keywords: ssVEPs · Simulation · Training · Attention

1 Introduction

Interest in monitoring attention in real-time is growing for use in simulation and training environments, both to learn more about the dynamics of fluid attention during real-world task performance and to monitor, assess and respond to changes in the performer's state such as overload or distraction. The most common tools for such purposes include eye-tracking devices. Though effective, eye-tracking alone cannot account for covert shifts or lapses in attention that are not accompanied by an eye saccade. A neural method for measuring the relative power of steady state visual evoked potentials (ssVEPs) can detect covert attention shifts, offering a potential complimentary capability to traditional eye-tracking methods. ssVEPs have already been used to demonstrate brain-computer interface attention-based control of remote control vehicles [1, 2] yet these methods rely on the use of visual flickers that are distracting and tiring to view. Researchers and training courses use simulation to make experiments and learning environments as ecologically valid as possible and to gather data on the performer that would not

© Springer International Publishing Switzerland 2016
D.D. Schmorrow and C.M. Fidopiastis (Eds.): AC 2016, Part I, LNAI 9743, pp. 394–403, 2016.
DOI: 10.1007/978-3-319-39955-3_37

otherwise be available. In the act of measuring the performer, the simulation instrumentation should affect the student or subject's performance as little as possible. For this reason, though low-frequency ssVEPs are effective, they are impractical for use in training or simulation environments.

High frequency flicker stimuli, however, appear solid to the human eye meaning high-frequency ssVEPs may offer a viable solution for detecting covert attention shifts in simulation and training environments. The ssVEPs these high frequency stimuli generate are more difficult to detect and extract than low-frequency ssVEPs and it is not clear whether higher frequency signals are sensitive to covert attention shifts like their lower-frequency counterparts. For this reason, the present limited exploration examines whether high frequency visual flickers evoke reliable and detectable ssVEPs that are sensitive to attention shifts, so that we may develop the method for monitoring attention in high fidelity simulation and training environments.

2 Background

Steady State Visual Evoked Potentials (ssVEPs) are cortical oscillations stimulated by an external driving frequency such as a visual flicker[1]; electroencephalogram (EEG) can detect the resulting potential evoked in the cerebral cortex. A 12 Hz visual flicker, for instance, will drive a 12 Hz steady-state visual evoked potential (ssVEP) in areas of the extrastriate visual cortex. Any flicker within the visual field should generate an ssVEP of some kind; however, the amplitude and gain of the signal is modulated by attention [3, 4]. When a person attends to the driving frequency, the amplitude of the ssVEP increases, and the amplitude drops as the person shifts attention away (see Fig. 1). Work in primates that record signals directly from active brain tissue suggest the attention-directing frontal eye fields within the frontal cortex direct the dorsal attention network [4, 5] to amplify incoming visual signals from parietal and occipital regions. This "top-down" attention control amplifies signals of interest even without directing the eyes towards the stimuli.

Traditionally the difference between ignored and attended signals is quantified with the Attention Modulation Index (AMI) [8], where:

$$AMI = \frac{(RMS_{attend} - RMS_{ignore})}{(RMS_{attend} + RMS_{ignore})} \tag{1}$$

and

$$RMS = \sqrt{\frac{(x_1^2 + x_2^2 + \ldots x_n^2)}{n}} \tag{2}$$

For EEG measures, $n = (sampling\ frequency \times time_{seconds})$ and x is voltage.

---

[1] Steady state evoked potentials occur in the auditory and somatosensory domains as well. Here we discuss only those in the visual domain.

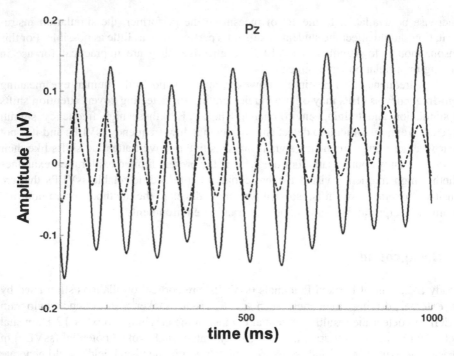

Fig. 1. Difference in amplitude between covertly attended (solid) and ignored (dashed) ssVEP 12 Hz signal. From Russell et al. [7]

A low AMI indicates low engagement, whereas high AMI indicates high engagement relative to an unengaged baseline measure. This type of method has been used with great success to study attention in a variety of ways:

- Mishra et al. used multiple simultaneous ssVEPs to demonstrate that it is not increased focus on task-relevant detail, but the enhanced suppression of potentially distracting stimuli, that underlies superior perceptual performance (speed and accuracy) of skilled video game players [8].
- Over a series of studies, Keil and colleagues [9–12] have demonstrated that emotional stimuli capture attention to a greater degree and are processed preferentially compared to neutral stimuli.
- Russell et al. [7] used this method to examine the simultaneous dynamics of top-down and bottom-up attention control changes in response to threat of shock, showing that increased top-down focus could not overcome the increased distractibility associated with acute anxiety.

Steady State Visual Evoked Potentials are robust enough for applied as well as research applications. For example, roboticists have used attention-modulated ssVEPs to control various kinds of remote vehicles via EEG-based brain-computer interfaces [1, 2].

Critically, because ssVEP amplitude and AMI are sensitive to *covert* attention shifts they are capable of detecting attention lapses (i.e., "zoning out") and when a performer attends peripheral visual fields. Moreover, multiple flicker frequencies can generate corresponding ssVEPs simultaneously [3], offering the ability to distinguish between attention shifts among multiple data streams in complex visual scenes. For these reasons, ssVEPs in combination with traditional eye-tracking, offer a more comprehensive and complete method for understanding the complexities of multitasked, real world environments where attention is divided among many information streams across the visual field.

There are a few technical hurdles however that will have to be overcome before we can realize this kind of capability. In the present paper we discuss our efforts to address one of these challenges and examine the feasibility of using high-frequency, rather than low-frequency ssVEP-driving stimuli to monitor attention. Most research applications use frequencies within the alpha band (8–12 Hz) because those are the strongest and most predominant frequencies in cortical activity, with the highest signal-to-noise ratio [13]. They are also easier to measure in the time domain despite slight phase shifts that occur during visual processing. This poses a problem for applied use however, as frequencies in this range are very noticeable, highly distracting and strain the eyes. Because the purpose of using ssVEPs is to unobtrusively monitor attention habits, shifts and patterns, noticeable frequency flickers in the 8–12 Hz range are too disruptive and will erode the ecological validity of our high-fidelity simulation and training environments.

A potential solution to this challenge is to use frequencies that are above the range of human perception and the critical flicker frequency threshold (CFF) - or the point at which a human can no longer detect a flicker and perceives the flicker as an average of the oscillating stimuli [14] (a black and white flicker will, for instance, appear as solid gray above the CCF). The CCF is roughly 15 Hz depending on factors such as luminance and contrast [14], but under some circumstances humans can detect flicker at much higher frequencies. An unobtrusive, visually complex system would need to present the driving ssVEP stimulus at a frequency far higher than 15 Hz to minimize distraction and disruption. Garcia [15] examined ssVEP frequencies as high as 60 Hz for similar reasons, but because the power of the cortical oscillations in these higher frequency bands are far lower than those in the alpha band, the higher frequencies pose a signal-to-noise-ratio (SNR) challenge.

Here we examine frequencies higher than those reported by Garcia for two reasons. First, in a previous analysis of existing data, ssVEP harmonics of low-frequency ssVEPs (8.6 and 12 Hz) were strongest between 90–110 Hz and exhibited the same attention-related properties as their lower-frequency counterparts. Second, if high-frequency ssVEPs are sensitive to attention shifts, advanced signal processing methods may help us overcome the current SNR challenge. The purpose of this investigation is to explore whether high frequency flicker rates (above 70 Hz) drive ssVEPs that are sensitive to attention shifts to enable development of top-down attention monitoring tools for use in high fidelity training and simulation environments.

3   Methods

For purposes of developing an attention-monitoring system suitable for high fidelity training and simulation environments, we examined the ssVEP electroencephalographic data stimulated by two different frequencies (72 Hz, 100 Hz) during three different attentional states. This pilot exploration included repeated measurements from a single person in a dark room.

In natural environments an operator will shift attention fluidly between attending something he is looking at (foveating on), attending something in the periphery without looking directly at it, and ignoring information within the visual field. We examined the following three attentional states to determine the specificity of this method for distinguishing between them in naturalistic settings:

Foveate: The user is looking directly at, and attending to the driving frequency.

Attend: The user is attending to the driving frequency in his peripheral vision but his eyes are directed away from the driving frequency.

Ignore: The user's eyes are directed away from (in the same location as "Attend") and he is not paying attention to the driving frequency.

In all cases as long as the driving frequency is in the visual field it should generate a cortical ssVEP.

3.1 Display Stimuli

To drive the ssVEP we used Presentation software (version 18.1, Neurobehavioral Systems) to display an alternating black and white square checkerboard (8 squares per side, and each square is 32 × 32 pixels, for an overall size of 2.75 × 2.75 in.) on a gray background in the center of a high frequency monitor (BenQ XL2430T 24-in. gaming monitor). This monitor refreshes at a higher rate than traditional computer monitors to improve the appearance of fast-moving and highly detailed video games, and is similar to the level of fidelity expected in high-fidelity simulations. To test different frequency markers we changed the refresh rate of the screen to 72 Hz and 100 Hz refresh rates, and adjusted the Presentation software code to alternate the checkerboard at the corresponding frame-rate.

3.2 Electroencephalography (EEG) Recordings

We recorded two minutes of EEG data for each condition using Advanced Brain Monitoring Inc. (ABM) B-Alert X24 electroencephalogram with the qEEG Standard Medical Montage sensor strip which arranges electrodes according to the standard 10–20 system [16]. Data were collected at a 256 Hz-sampling rate. For future applications and for examining higher frequency data streams, we would use a system with a higher sampling frequency and that does not impose an on-line bandpass filter.

3.3 Data Processing

All data processing was performed in MATLAB (R2012a).

Filtering. We exported all data into .mat files and processed only the raw data files from ABM. We isolated the frequencies of interest with a linear-phase 257 tap FIR filter, de-trended the data, and applied a Hamming window to suppress frequency sidelobes before performing fast-Fourier transform to quantify power in 0.10 Hz bins.

Averaging. For each condition and frequency we averaged across electrodes closest to the extra-striate regions of the brain (O1, O1, POz, Pz, P3 and P4). These are also the electrode sites most consistent with Mishra et al. and Russell et al. [7, 8]. We then averaged the power from 72–72.9 Hz and 100–100.9 Hz for each band to estimate the relative power of each condition across the 1 Hz frequency bins of interest.

4 Results

Averaged data suggest that both the 72 and 100 Hz ssVEP exhibit attention-related modulation, although the pattern of relative strengths of the signals among the three attentional states was unexpected.

The Attend attentional state, in which the performer was not looking directly at the driving stimulus, generated the largest ssVEP, while the Foveate attentional state, in which the performer was looking directly at the stimulus, generated the lowest power. This is strikingly different compared to results observed in lower frequencies, where foveating on a driving flicker will generate the greatest ssVEP power, and ignoring the driving flicker will generate the lowest ssVEP power. From the averages of these data, it appears that ignoring the high-frequency stimuli in visual periphery generates a larger ssVEP signal compared to looking directly at, and attending to the stimulus (see Fig. 2).

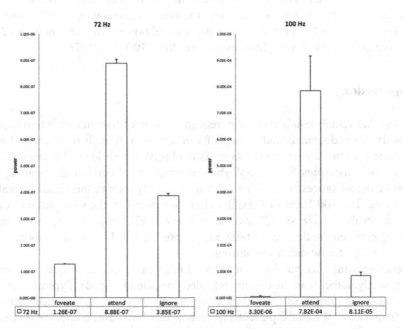

Fig. 2. Relative power of each frequency in foveate, attend and ignore attentional conditions in 72 Hz and 100 Hz ssVEPs in one person. Error bars are the standard deviation for each 0.10 Hz bin averaged across the 1 Hz band of interest. The Y axes are scaled to the relative power of each frequency.

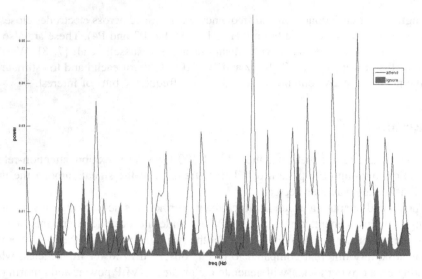

Fig. 3. Detail of the relative spectral power from covertly attending (attend) and ignoring (ignore) the 100 Hz frequency signal at the POz electrode site between 100–101 Hz.

Also somewhat surprising, is that the power of the 100 Hz ssVEP was stronger relative to 72 Hz ssVEP. The power was small in both frequencies but the general trend is that the higher the frequency, the lower the power in neural activity beyond alpha band [13]. See Fig. 3 for a detail view of the spectral power difference between Attend and Ignore conditions at a single electrode site from 100–100.9 Hz.

5   Discussion

We found that visual signals above the frequency range of human perception appear to be sensitive to endogenous and overt shifts in attention, though these limited results suggest the pattern may not be the same as is observed with lower frequencies.

The power measures for the ssVEPs were small in all conditions, meaning a fair amount of online processing will be needed to reliably extract the signal in real-time applications. The 100 Hz ssVEP exhibited greater power in the same amount of time compared to the 72 Hz ssVEP and the 100 Hz ssVEP exhibited a larger relative difference between the three conditions suggesting the 100 Hz may be a more reliable frequency range for attention monitoring.

Most surprising was that the strongest ssVEP appeared in both frequencies emerged in the covertly, rather than the overtly, attended condition (Attend). Typically, foveated signals generate larger ssVEPs, but these trends have been reported mainly in lower-frequencies. While the present exploration was limited in scope, the consistency of the pattern across both frequencies suggests the observation may not be coincidental. One possible explanation may lie within either the uneven distribution of rod and cone cells within the retina, or the relative sensitivity of the magno- and parvocellular pathways to contrast and motion. If so, the mechanisms behind heightened peripheral sensitivity to motion may also underlie our results. In normal daylight conditions the rods responsible for most peripheral vision are saturated, however these data were collected in a dark room. This too has practical implications for ssVEP measurement and suggests different strategies may be necessary for well-illuminated daytime simulations compared to darker nighttime, or theater-like environments. These observations warrant further exploration to determine the consistency and reliability of the observation under various visual eccentricities from center and lighting conditions.

5.1   Limitations and Next Steps

This limited analysis provided an indication that high frequency ssVEPs are attention sensitive, but the unexpected results suggest a full study is needed to examine the consistency and variance across individuals to determine if the effect observed in this exploration is reliable. The curious results warrant further investigation, in particular to test the classification accuracy (sensitivity and specificity) of high-frequency ssVEPs. Given the robust literature in ssVEP research, there are a number of additional considerations that developers should consider when using ssVEP in applied settings.

Individual Differences. Analysis of high-frequency harmonics of low-frequency ssVEPs in a previously analyzed data set (from [7]) showed that there is high variability between individuals in terms of which electrodes exhibit the strongest AMI in response to the driving frequency. This is not surprising given slight individual differences in neuromorphology (e.g., cortical wrinkling) and other features that will affect the dipoles, summation of dipoles, and distortion of the neural signal between the cortex and the scalp electrodes. Those with trait anxiety exhibit phase-shifts in ssVEP entrainment [17]. Though this study included exploratory data from only one person, it holds that any system that intends to use ssVEP signals to monitor attention should account for such differences by either averaging across a series of electrodes where ssVEPs are usually strongest or by determining for each individual which electrodes detect the signals most reliably across the visual field. Though more labor intensive, the latter method directly addresses the SNR challenge, and reduces the number of electrodes needed for reliable ssVEP detection, simplifying subsequent monitoring sessions. Machine learning methods for developing personalized models to interpret complex neurophysiological signals (such as those discussed elsewhere in these Proceedings [18]) will be instrumental for accelerating this kind of personalized approach.

Changes in State. Changes to the performer's state, including perceptual workload and anxiety, can also affect ssVEPs in terms of magnitude and phase. Emotional stimuli can generate a larger ssVEPs compared to those associated with neutral stimuli [9–12]. Similarly, anticipatory anxiety increased the magnitude of a 12 Hz ssVEP during threat of shock [7]. Perceptual workload also decreased the neural response to signals presented in the central regions of a screen while, peripherally presented signals were unaffected by workload manipulations [19]. An applied system will have to account for these state-related effects on ssVEP strength to ensure the system responds specifically to attention rather than arousal.

Frequency-Specific Questions. More than anything, this investigation has highlighted the need to examine the distinct properties of different frequencies used to generate ssVEPs. For instance, though ssVEPs in response to peripheral stimuli may be less sensitive to changes in perceptual load than those from centrally-presented stimuli, given the differences we observed with high frequency ssVEPs it is difficult to know without testing directly whether high frequency ssVEPs would show similar field eccentricity-related differences. There is also evidence that different frequencies tag distinct neural networks [20] posing both an opportunity to target neural networks of interest and potential challenge, as each of these networks may be sensitive to different state and trait-related variables.

Phase Shifts. Beyond frequency-specific and individual differences, ssVEPs also exhibit phase shifts in the "fast pathway" above 15 Hz [21]. This poses an additional signal processing challenge for online collection. Others have found phase-shifts during initial entrainment associated with different stimuli and as a function of trait anxiety [17]. We did not examine phase shifts in this analysis, but future investigations should consider how signal-processing strategies should account for phase shifts in ssVEPs.

In summary, this exploration has demonstrated that high-frequency ssVEPs may offer the kind of attention-sensitivity necessary to detect covert attention shifts for which other methods cannot currently account. While here we have discussed evoked potentials only in the visual domain, steady state potentials also occur in the auditory (steady state auditory evoked potentials, or ssAEPs) and somatosensory (ssSEPs) domains. Monitoring limited auditory attention is similarly important for understanding attention in dynamic environments, yet there are currently no "ear-tracking" correlates to eye-tracking. ssAEPs may thus offer methods for monitoring auditory attention for use independently of, or in conjunction with, ssVEPs in high-fidelity simulation and training environments for more complete real-time and multi-modal attention monitoring.

References

1. Wang, H., Li, T., Huang, Z.: Remote control of an electrical car with SSVEP-based BCI. In: IEEE International Conference on Information Theory and Information Security, pp. 837–840 (2010)
2. Zhang, C., Kimura, Y., Higashi, H., Tanaka, T.: A simple platform of brain-controlled mobile robot and its implementation by SSVEP. In: IEEE International Joint Conference on Neural Networks (IJCNN), pp. 1–7 (2012)
3. Morgan, S.T., Hansen, J.C., Hillyard, S.A.: Selective attention to stimulus location modulates the steady-state visual evoked potential. Proc. Natl. Acad. Sci. **93**(10), 4770–4774 (1996)
4. Müller, M.M., Hillyard, S.: Concurrent recording of steady-state and transient event-related potentials as indices of visual-spatial selective attention. Clin. Neurophysiol. **111**(9), 1544–1552 (2000)
5. Corbetta, M., Shulman, G.L.: Control of goal-directed and stimulus-driven attention in the brain. Nat. Rev. Neurosci. **3**(3), 201–215 (2002)

6. Buschman, T.J., Miller, E.K.: Top-down versus bottom-up control of attention in the prefrontal and posterior parietal cortices. Science **315**(5820), 1860–1862 (2007)
7. Russell, B.A.H., Prosacco, A., Hatfield, B.D.: The dynamics of top-down attention control and bottom-up attention capture during threat of shock: an electroencephalographic investigation (In preparation)
8. Mishra, J., Zinni, M., Bavelier, D., Hillyard, S.A.: Neural basis of superior performance of action videogame players in an attention-demanding task. J. Neurosci. **31**(3), 992–998 (2011)
9. Moratti, S., Keil, A., Stolarova, M.: Motivated attention in emotional picture processing is reflected by activity modulation in cortical attention networks. Neuroimage **21**(3), 954–964 (2004)
10. Wieser, M.J., McTeague, L.M., Keil, A.: Sustained preferential processing of social threat cues: bias without competition? J. Cogn. Neurosci. **23**(8), 1973–1986 (2011)
11. Hajcak, G., MacNamara, A., Foti, D., Ferri, J., Keil, A.: The dynamic allocation of attention to emotion: simultaneous and independent evidence from the late positive potential and steady state visual evoked potentials. Biol. Psychol. **92**(3), 447–455 (2013)
12. Miskovic, V., Keil, A.: Perceiving threat in the face of safety: excitation and inhibition of conditioned fear in human visual cortex. J. Neurosci. **33**(1), 72–78 (2013)
13. Pastor, M.A., Artieda, J., Arbizu, J., Valencia, M., Masdeu, J.C.: Human cerebral activation during steady-state visual-evoked responses. J. Neurosci. **23**(37), 11621–11627 (2003)
14. Ives, H.E.: Critical frequency relations in scotopic vision. JOSA **6**(3), 254–267 (1922)
15. Garcia, G.: High frequency SSVEPs for BCI applications. Computer-Human Interaction (2008)
16. Jasper, H.: Report of the committee on methods of clinical examination in electroencephalography. Electroencephalogr. Clin. Neurophysiol. **10**, 370–375 (1958)
17. Gray, M., Kemp, A.H., Silberstein, R.B., Nathan, P.J.: Cortical neurophysiology of anticipatory anxiety: an investigation utilizing steady state probe topography (SSPT). Neuroimage **20**(2), 975–986 (2003)
18. Ziegler, M.D., Kraft, A., Krein, M., Lo, L.C., Hatfield, B., Casebeer, W., Russell, B.: The use of computational human performance modeling as task analysis tool. In: Human Computer Interaction Proceedings (2016, submitted)
19. Parks, N.A., Beck, D.M., Kramer, A.F.: Enhancement and suppression in the visual field under perceptual load. Front. Psychol. **4**(275), 10–3389 (2013)
20. Ding, J., Sperling, G., Srinivasan, R.: Attentional modulation of SSVEP power depends on the network tagged by the flicker frequency. Cereb. Cortex **16**(7), 1016–1029 (2006)
21. Sharpe, L.T., Stockman, A., MacLeod, D.I.: Rod flicker perception: scotopic duality, phase lags and destructive interference. Vis. Res. **29**(11), 1539–1559 (1989)

Augmenting Robot Behaviors Using Physiological Measures of Workload State

Grace Teo[1(✉)], Lauren Reinerman-Jones[1], Gerald Matthews[1],
Daniel Barber[1], Jonathan Harris[1], and Irwin Hudson[2]

[1] Institute for Simulation and Training,
University of Central Florida, Orlando, FL, USA
{gteo,lreinerm,gmatthew,dbarber,jharris}@ist.ucf.edu
[2] Army Research Laboratory, Orlando, FL, USA
Irwin.Hudson@us.army.mil

Abstract. The evolution of robots from tools to teammates requires a paradigm shift. Robot teammates need to interpret naturalistic forms of human communication and sense implicit, but important cues that reflect the human teammate's psychological state. A closed-loop system where the robot teammate detects the human teammate's workload state would enable the robot to select appropriate aiding behaviors to support its human teammate. Physiological measures are suitable for assessment of workload in adaptive systems because they allow continuous assessment and do not require overt responses which disrupt tasks. Given the large variability in physiological workload responses across individuals, an algorithm that accommodates variability in workload responses would be more robust. This study outlines the development and validation of algorithms for workload classification. It discusses (i) a workload manipulation paradigm, (ii) the evaluation of the algorithms for deriving a workload index that is individualized, and (iii) parameter selection for optimal classification.

Keywords: Workload · Modeling · Physiological measures · Closed-loop system · Human-robot teaming

1 Introduction

Advancements in the technology in past decades have given rise to the development of autonomous agents and robots. Despite being deployed in various domains for specific tasks such as in manufacturing and bomb disposal, robots, being mostly teleoperated and requiring detailed commands, are ineffective with unstructured tasks in novel environments. Nevertheless, there are recent efforts made to develop robots that have task-level autonomy. These robots are capable of multimodal communications through gestures, natural speech, and implicit communication [1]. These communication channels support direct interaction between robots and humans. Direct interaction is often found in human teams and facilitates more dialogue and collaboration, which would help transit robots from being tools to teammates [2].

© Springer International Publishing Switzerland 2016
D.D. Schmorrow and C.M. Fidopiastis (Eds.): AC 2016, Part I, LNAI 9743, pp. 404–415, 2016.
DOI: 10.1007/978-3-319-39955-3_38

1.1 A Closed-Loop System

Implicit communication involves information being transmitted from the human to the robot without the explicit intent of sending a command or instruction. It includes sensing of operator fatigue, workload and other psychological states, which can convey an unarticulated need for assistance with a task. Research has shown that human operators are not always aware of their own mental state and workload and even if they were, they may not be able to assess accurately when they would benefit from aid [3]. In adaptive systems, the use of physiological workload measures is advantageous over self-report measures as physiological measures are more objective, allow continuous assessment of workload state with high temporal resolution, and do not require any overt response from the operator that may interfere with the task.

A closed-loop system that incorporates physiological workload measures would enable a robot to reprioritize its tasks to initiate aid without the human teammate explicitly requesting it. The robot's response to an unstated need would provide relief in cases when the human is in a high workload state and at jeopardy of poor performance.

Information about the human teammate's state can be used as inputs. When workload reaches a level deemed as "high", the robot would adapt its behavior to alleviate the workload. These may include active or passive, direct or indirect behaviors, such as taking over the main task or preventing the operator from being hindered by a secondary task etc. [4]. When the closed-loop system senses that the human teammate's workload level has returned to a level considered to be "low" or manageable, it would trigger robot behaviors that allow the human to resume all duties and full control. This feature is to minimize the performance issues (e.g., loss of situational awareness, skill atrophy, over-reliance issues) associated with having the human "out-of-the-loop" [5].

1.2 Modeling Workload

In order to determine the levels of "high" and "low" workload as assessed by the various physiological workload measures, a workload model is needed. There are several approaches to modeling workload such as using tools like the Improved Performance Research Integration Tool (IMPRINT), or discrete-event simulations [6]. However, these approaches do not clearly distinguish the concepts of workload and task demands, and seem to define workload with respect to the objective demands of the task. This assumes a relatively simple relationship between task demands and workload which may not be true. Instead, in this paper, we view workload as "a mental construct that reflects the mental strain resulting from performing a task under specific environmental and operational conditions, coupled with the capability of the operator to respond to those demands" [7]. Workload is more akin to an operator's dynamic response to task demands. By this definition, the assessment of workload requires inputs from the operator which can be in the form of physiological measures of workload.

1.3 Using Physiological Workload Measures to Classify Workload State

Physiological measures such as heart rate, heart rate variability, brain activity, and pupil size, have been found to index workload and operator state [8] and have been used in adaptive systems that classify workload with some success [9]. Classifiers such as stepwise discriminant analysis (SWDAs) [10] and artificial neural networks (ANNs) [11] have been used to classify workload states. However, although these often result in high classification accuracy, their diagnosticity is limited as their algorithms do not provide much to inform design of adaptive aids [12].

For present study, multiple physiological workload measures were used because different physiological measures assess workload differently [13]. There are measures that tap metabolic responses which reflect a more global state and respond more slowly to changes in workload state (e.g., cerebral blood flow velocity, CBFV), as well as measures which respond to changes in workload more immediately (e.g. eye fixation durations). In addition, given the multidimensional nature of workload [14] and the workload in multi-tasking environments, any single workload measure cannot be expected to capture workload changes in all tasks, because while a measure may respond to a particular task manipulation, it may not respond to other types of task manipulations [14]. Thus, instead of relying on just one or two measures, using multiple workload measures to classify workload state would provide a more complete picture of the workload experienced [15].

1.4   Developing and Validating Models

Two datasets were used to develop and validate the workload classification model: a training dataset from which the model was derived, and a validation dataset to determine if the model was robust enough to classify workload states on a separate sample. The training dataset comprised data from a previous study, Abich [16], while the validation dataset was data from another study, the Validation Study. The Abich [16] study administered two tasks that typified an intelligence, surveillance and reconnaissance (ISR) mission. Hence the present effort sought to model the workload experienced while performing tasks related to an ISR mission. The two tasks administered in the Abich [16] study were (i) a Change Detection task, and (ii) a Threat Detection task. The Change Detection (CD) task required participants to detect and identify changes to icons, representing enemy assets and activities, overlaid on a map of an area of interest (AOI). The second task was a Threat Detection (TD) task in which participants viewed and identified characters who were pre-defined as threats, from a video feed of characters lined along the streets in a geotypical Afghan environment. The task parameters used in both tasks have shown successful workload manipulation in past studies (i.e., Abich [16]). In addition to the suite of physiological measures, workload was also assessed with the NASA Task Load Index (NASA-TLX [17]), which taps six sources of workload as well as a global index of workload.

2   A Novel Approach to Modeling Workload

In the Abich [16] study (training dataset), participants underwent the following four study scenarios in a within-subjects design (see Table 1):

Table 1. Abich [16] study scenarios

	Scenario 1 (single task)	Scenario 2 (dual task)	Scenario 3 (single task)	Scenario 4 (dual task)
Change Detection Task (CDT)	✓	✓		✓
Threat Detection Task (TDT)		✓	✓	✓

The performance and workload responses in the single task scenarios (i.e., Scenarios 1 and 3) were found to be clearly distinct from that in the dual task scenarios (i.e., Scenarios 2 and 4), and the direction of scores showed that the single task scenarios elicited low workload while the dual task scenarios elicited high workload as reported in the NASA-TLX ratings. This was also true for the physiological workload measures, which suggests that the single-dual task manipulation of workload was a robust one. The physiological workload measures[1] included electroencephalography (EEG) tapping brain activity in different lobes, electrocardiography (ECG) measures like heartrate variability (HRV), measures of regional oxygen saturation (rSO_2) from functional near-infrared spectroscopy (fNIRS), cerebral blood flow velocity (CBFV) from transcranial doppler ultrasonography (TCD), and a variety of ocular measures such as fixation duration.

2.1 Matching Difference Scores

Observation of the robust differences in workload found between the single and dual task scenarios led to the computation of difference scores that reflected the change in workload response between a low (single) and high (dual) workload task. For instance, a difference score for HRV was obtained from HRV in Scenario 1 (single task eliciting low workload) and HRV in Scenario 2 (dual task eliciting high workload). Another difference score for HRV was computed from HRV in Scenario 1 (single task eliciting low workload) and HRV in Scenario 4 (dual task eliciting high workload). The correlations of these difference scores, obtained from different pairs of single-dual tasks, were positive and significant ($p < 0.05$), and ranged from 0.299 (Theta at F3) to 0.820 (mean fixation duration). This was further evidence that, for the physiological workload measures, the magnitude of the difference in workload response between single task (low workload) and dual task (high workload) was large and stable enough to be exploited as the basis of determining the level of workload for a new task that elicited an unknown level of workload. If the difference score obtained from the single task (low workload) and new task (unknown workload) matched the difference score

---

[1] The physiological workload measures were computed as percentage change from an initial resting baseline level and all scores were standardized by converting them to z-scores. This allowed different physiological measures (e.g., heartrate, EEG spectral power densities, ocular fixation durations) to be compared.

obtained from the same single task (low workload) and dual task (high workload), then the new task would have elicited the same high workload response as the dual task.

In this approach, there is a *Single Task Baseline* which is a single task condition known to elicit low workload, and a *Dual Task Baseline* which is a dual task condition known to elicit high workload. A *task pair* is the pairing of any two scenarios/conditions to obtain a difference score. The *Benchmark Difference Score* is obtained from a task pair that comprised the Single Task Baseline condition and the Dual Task Baseline condition, while the *Test Difference Score* is computed from a task pair consisting of the same Single Task Baseline condition and the new task condition that elicits an unknown level of workload. If the *Benchmark Difference Score* and *Test Difference Score* matched, then the new task condition would have elicited a similarly high workload response as the *Dual Task Baseline* condition. Given the consistently large differences in physiological workload scores found between Single and Dual task condition, matches are more likely to occur when the *Test Difference Score*, like the *Benchmark Difference Score*, is from a task pair that comprised a Single and a Dual Task condition.

3   Algorithms to Combine Multiple Physiological Measures

Although the matching of difference scores enabled the workload level of a new task to be determined, an algorithm was needed to combine the difference scores from various physiological measures to form a workload index. The workload index would reflect the match of physiological workload responses between the set of Benchmark Difference Scores and the set of Test Difference Scores. A high degree of match would indicate that the physiological workload response to the new task was similar to that of a Dual task, which had been established as eliciting high workload.

Studies suggest that there is sizeable individual variability in the physiological responses to workload [18], i.e., some individuals may show a marked difference in ECG measures between low and high workload-eliciting tasks, whereas other individuals may show a larger change in EEG measures. Hence a robust algorithm would need to account for individual differences in physiological response to workload and allow for a customization based on these differences for computing a workload index. Although several algorithms were explored and evaluated, the two that appeared most promising for accommodating variability in workload responses are described below.

3.1   Algorithm 1: Proportion of Repeated Markers

The physiological markers for workload for the individual were first identified. These were the measures that, for the individual, showed marked difference[2] in response between the Single Task Baseline and Dual Task Baseline conditions, i.e., sensitive to dual-tasking. The markers were obtained from the set of Benchmark Difference Scores, and these were compared to the markers obtained from the set of Test Difference

---

[2] The criteria defining marked difference was an increase or decrease by 0.5 SD or more on the measure, after the z-score conversion to standardize all measures.

Scores. The workload index was the proportion of markers in the Benchmark Difference Scores that re-emerged as markers ("repeated markers") among the Test Difference Scores. A large proportion of repeated markers would mean that the physiological responses evoked by the new task were similar to that elicited by the Dual Task Baseline (i.e., high workload task), and the workload index would approach 1 (Fig. 1).

Workload index (Proportion of repeated markers)

$$= \frac{Markers\ observed\ in\ the\ in\ both\ Benchmark\ and\ Test\ Diff.Scores}{Markers\ observed\ in\ the\ Benchmark\ Diff.Scores}$$

For example:
Workload index (Proportion of repeated markers)

$$= \frac{HRV, IBI, Fix.\ duration}{HRV, IBI, Fix.\ duration, Theta\ frontal\ SPD} = \frac{3}{4} = 0.75$$

Fig. 1. Computation of workload index reflecting proportion of repeated markers

3.2   Algorithm 2: Distance Between All Difference Scores

Similarity in physiological responses (workload index) was quantified as the Euclidean distance between the set of Benchmark Difference Scores and Test Difference Scores. Smaller Euclidean distances denoted a higher degree of similarity between physiological workload responses. There is no set range for Euclidean distance (d) which is computed as follows (see Fig. 2):

$$d(x,y) = \sqrt{\sum_{i}^{n}(x_i - y_i)^2}$$

Where:
x = a physio. measures in Benchmark Task Pair
y = corresponding physio. measure in Test Task Pair
i = a physiological measure
(e.g., $i = 1$ denotes HRV, $i = 2$ denotes IBI etc.)

Fig. 2. Computation of workload index based on Euclidean distance

4   Algorithm Evaluation

The algorithms were evaluated for use in the closed-loop system on the following:

1. For the algorithm, how distinguishable the *mean* workload index values from similar task pairs were from those obtained by chance.
2. For the algorithm, how distinct the *distributions* of workload index values from similar task pairs were from those obtained from random data.
3. For the algorithm, how discriminating the workload index values were in a mock-up of the closed-loop system, and how easily a cutoff for high workload could be set.
4. Use *sensitivity (d')* to fine-tune cutoff parameter.

To validate the model derived from each algorithm, a separate cross-validation dataset from a new sample of participants was used (Validation Study). This sample was also administered tasks that typified an ISR mission, including the same Change Detection task. However, instead of the Threat Detection task, they were administered a Peripheral task as the second task. The purpose was to determine the robustness of the model when applied to workload from tasks within the same ISR context, but not featuring the exact same tasks as the training dataset. The Peripheral task required participants to monitor a video feed of their robot teammate scouting the AOI, and maintain awareness of the robot's whereabouts and the features in the environment. They had to respond to auditory prompts such as "In which direction was the robot heading before the last turn?", and "Did the robot pass any men since the last turn?" The study scenarios for this dataset (Validation Study) were as follows (see Table 2):

Table 2. Validation study scenarios

	Scenario 1 (single task)	Scenario 2 (Dual task Low)	Scenario 2 (Dual task Med)	Scenario 4 (Dual task High)
Change Detection Task (CDT)	✓	✓	✓	✓
Peripheral Task (PT)	-	✓	✓	✓

4.1 Mean Workload Index Values

First, different task pairs were formed yielding various sets of difference scores. The difference scores denoted the changes in physiological responses between the scenarios. Next, pairs of difference scores were formed. The pairs always contained data from the same sample/study because the intent was to have the first set of difference scores reflect the difference in workload response between low (Single Task) and high (Dual Task) workload (i.e. Benchmark Difference Scores), and the second set of difference scores showing the difference in workload response between low (Single Task) workload condition and a new condition that elicited an unknown level of workload. The Benchmark Difference Scores and Test Difference Scores were expected to match when both sets originated from Single-Dual Task Pairs, and not expected to match when the Test Difference Scores involved random data.

The mean workload index values under the two algorithms were computed for different pairs of Benchmark and Test Difference Scores. Using Algorithm 1, when both the Benchmark Difference Scores and Test Differences Scores were from Single-Dual Task Pairs, the mean workload indices were similar, falling within a narrow range of 0.509 to 0.552. This indicated that between 50.9 % and 55.2 % of markers identified from the Benchmark Difference Scores were also markers in the Test Difference Scores, indicating relatively comparable workload responses. On the contrary, when the Test Difference Scores included random data, the mean workload indices, or proportion of repeated markers declined to 28.7 % and 32.3 %, denoting little similarity in workload responses. A similar pattern of results was obtained with Algorithm 2. Smaller Euclidean distances, indicating greater similarity, were obtained when both the Benchmark Difference Scores and Test Difference Scores were from Single-Dual Task Pairs (distances ranging from 4.677 to 4.978), compared to indices that utilized random data (distances were larger at 7.518 and 7.624).

All these findings indicated that as long as the Benchmark Difference Scores and Test Difference Scores were derived from Single-Dual Task Pairs, the workload indices would indicate a degree of match or similarity in physiological responses that was substantially higher than what would be obtained by chance. In addition, for both algorithms, the mean workload index values computed from Validation Study data were comparable to those from the Abich study. As these datasets were from different samples, this provided evidence of cross-validation of the algorithms.

4.2   Distribution of Workload Index Values

Apart from the mean of the workload index values, the algorithms were evaluated on the range and distribution of the index values. This was to check if, in addition to the mean, the range of index values from similar task pairs was also distinct from the range of values obtained by chance. Results revealed that, for both Algorithms 1 and 2, the distribution of index values when both the Benchmark Task Pair and Test Task Pair were similar single-dual task pairs were distinct from the index values where those were dissimilar and included random data. This provided evidence that workload index values yielded from Algorithms 1 and 2 are likely to be sufficiently distinct from values that would be obtained by chance. Hence, if the new task induced a similar level of workload as that of the Baseline Dual task (i.e., high workload), then the workload index computed from these algorithms are likely to be able to reflect that similarity.

4.3   Workload Index Values in Mock-Up of Closed-Loop System

The algorithms were also evaluated in a mock-up of the closed-loop system with the Abich data. From the mock-up, an algorithm would be selected to be used in the closed-loop system and to derive a cutoff point for classifying level of workload.

In addition to Algorithms 1 and 2, a derivative of Algorithm 2 was also evaluated. Instead of using all the physiological measures in the computation of Euclidean distance, Algorithm 2a used the top ten measures on which the individual exhibited the greatest change in physiological response between the Single task (low workload) and Dual task (high workload) conditions (i.e. measures that show the largest absolute difference). This procedure was to further individualize the algorithm as the workload index would include the measures that are sensitive to the workload experienced by the individual, i.e. his markers of workload.

The mock-up simulated the "streaming" of data blocks every 30 s. Each data block or sample comprised data collected over 2 min. This feature was to ensure that there were enough data from the various sensors, all of which have different sampling rates, to compute a meaningful index that reflected the state of workload at that time.

To further examine the contrast between workload index values from similar and dissimilar task pairs, other task pairs were formed from the study scenarios in the Abich

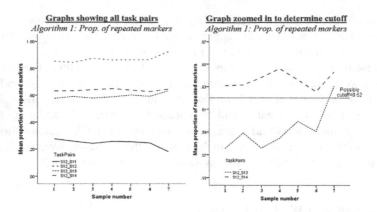

Fig. 3. Workload index values under Algorithm 1 (larger index values denote greater similarity)

study (see Table 2). As the Benchmark Task Pair was always formed from a Single and Dual task Pair (i.e., Scenario 1 and Scenario 2, or S12), greatest similarity would be expected if the Test Task Pair was also a Single-Dual Task Pair (e.g., Scenario 1 and Scenario 4, or S14), and larger dissimilarity would result from Test Task Pair that were a Single-Single Task Pair (e.g., Scenario 1 and Scenario 3, or S13). Based on this rationale, the expected similarity would vary across different task pairs, and this should be captured by the selected algorithm. The task pairs expected to show greatest similarity over all data samples is S12 and S12 or S12_S12[3], followed by S12_S4, then S12_ S13, and lastly S12_S11 were expected to be very dissimilar.

In the mock-up with Algorithm 1 the expected order of task pairs from the most similar (S12_S12) to the most dissimilar (S12_S11) was observed (see Fig. 3). Closer examination of the index values for S12_S13 and S12_S14 (i.e., the middle two sets of task pairs that were the most easily confounded) revealed a sufficient distance between index values for all data samples, except data sample 7. Index values were relatively stable over all data samples, and there was a possible cutoff at 0.62 (i.e., if at least 62 % of physiological markers were repeated with the new task, the new task would be considered to have induced a similarly high workload as the Dual Task Baseline condition).

With Algorithm 2, the expected order of task pairs from most similar to most dissimilar was not obtained (see Fig. 4). The index values for S12_S13 (dissimilar task pair) yielded values that indicated greater similarity than the values for S12_S14 (similar task pair). Moreover, there was greater variability in the index values across the data samples despite a constant level of taskload. Although a cutoff of 7.2 for this algorithm seem plausible, it is likely that the workload levels indicated by data samples 1, 3, and 7 would be erroneously classified (see Fig. 4). Because Algorithm 2 could not correctly identify when workload responses were similar or dissimilar (it showed S12_S13 as being more similar than S12_S14), it was excluded from further consideration.

---

[3] S12_S2 were not completely similar because the Test Difference Score data were streamed as 2-min data samples, but the Benchmark Differences Score data were not.

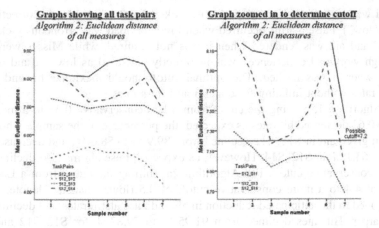

Fig. 4. Workload index values under Algorithm 2 (larger index values denote lower similarity)

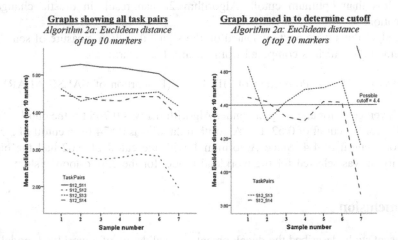

Fig. 5. Workload index values under Algorithm 2a (larger index values denote lower similarity)

Algorithm 2a computed the workload index from the 10 measures that were most sensitive (markers) to changes in the individual's workload. Although the expected order of similarity was obtained, the index values at data samples 1, 2, 5, 6 and 7 are likely to misclassify workload levels with a cutoff score of 4.4 (see Fig. 5).

4.4 Sensitivity of Algorithms

The cutoff scores that were obtained from the mock-up served as decision thresholds that would classify workload in the closed-loop system. Hits, would comprise instances where high workload was experienced and the aid was appropriately evoked (i.e., workload was correctly classified as "high"), Correct rejections were when low workload was experienced and no aid was evoked (i.e., workload was correctly classified as "low"). False alarms occurred when low workload was erroneously classified as "high" and aid was rendered when it was not required, while Misses were cases where high workload experienced was incorrectly classified as low and aid was not provided when it was needed. The optimal cutoff should maximize hit and correct rejection rates without inflating false alarm and miss rates.

For Algorithm 1, moving the cutoff from a less conservative 0.55 to a more conservative 0.62 decreased hit rates as expected, the percentage of the sample who would have been given aid in S12_S12 declined from 89.9 % to 88.6 %, and decreased from 68.5 % to 63.1 % in S12_S14. However, as expected, false alarms also declined with the more conservative cutoff. For Algorithm 2a, shifting the cutoff from a Euclidean distance of 4.4 to a more conservative cutoff of 3.5 (lower distance denotes greater similarity) led to the anticipated reduction in hit and false alarm rates, but declines were much sharper. Hit rates declined from 91.95 % to 79.87 % for S12_S12 and from 75.17 % to 50.34 % for S12_S14/. False alarm rates decreased from 60.13 % to 44.30 % for S12_S13, and from 68.76 % to 40.94 % for S12_S11. This suggest that with a less than optimum cutoff, Algorithm 2a can result in drastic changes in classification.

The algorithms were next evaluated on the signal detection measure of sensitivity, or d-Prime (d'), which is computed from hit and false alarm rates.

$$\text{Sensitivity or } d' = Z(\text{Proportion of HITS}) - Z(\text{Proportion of FALSE ALARMS})$$

The average d' for all task pairs under Algorithm 1 was 0.788 for the cutoff of 0.55, and 0.811 for the cutoff of 0.62. For Algorithm 2a, d' was 0.574 for a cutoff of 3.5, and 0.552 for a cutoff of 4.4. Since Algorithm 1 with the cutoff of 0.62 had the highest sensitivity, it was selected for the workload model for the closed-loop system.

5   Conclusion

The present study described the development and validation of a workload model for a closed-loop system that accommodated variability in physiological workload responses workload across individuals. It defined a systematic method for evaluating workload classification algorithms which includes comparisons with index values obtained by chance. In addition, the study offers a viable approach to developing an individualized workload model and contributes to the direction of future modeling efforts. Future research is needed to implement such a model in a closed-loop system where adaptive robot aiding would be driven by physiological measures.

Acknowledgements. This research was sponsored by the Army Research Laboratory and was accomplished under Cooperative Agreement Number W91CRB-08-D-0015. The views and conclusions contained in this document are those of the authors and should not be interpreted as representing the official policies, either expressed or implied of the Army Research Laboratory of or the U.S. Government. The U.S. Government is authorized to reproduce and distribute reprints for Government purposes notwithstanding any copyright notation herein.

References

1. Barber, D., Abich IV, J., Phillips, E., Talone, A., Jentsch, F., Hill, S.: Field assessment of multimodal communication for dismounted human-robot teams. In: Proceedings of the 59th Human Factors and Ergonomics Society Annual Meeting, Los Angeles, CA (2015)
2. Thrun, S.: Toward a framework for human-robot interaction. Hum.-Comput. Interact. **19**, 9–24 (2004)
3. Neubauer, C., Matthews, G., Langheim, L., Saxby, D.: Fatigue and voluntary utilization of automation in simulated driving. Hum. Factors **54**, 734–746 (2012)
4. Teo, G., Reinerman-Jones, L.: Robot behavior for enhanced human performance and workload. Virtual Augmented Mixed Reality: Des. Dev. Virtual Augmented Environ. **8525**, 117–128 (2014)
5. Endsley, M.R., Kiris, E.O.: The out-of-the-loop performance problem and level of control in automation. Hum. Factors **37**, 381–394 (1995)
6. Donmez, B., Nehme, C., Cummings, M.L.: Modeling workload impact in multiple unmanned vehicle supervisory control. IEEE Trans. Syst. Man Cybern. Part A: Syst. Hum. **40**, 1180–1190 (2010)
7. Cain, B.: A review of the mental workload literature. Report No. RTO-TR-HFM-121-Part-II, Defence Research and Development, Toronto, Canada. Human System Integration Section, Canada, Toronto (2007)
8. Gevins, A., Smith, M.E., McEvoy, L., Yu, D.: High-resolution EEG mapping of cortical activation related to working memory: effects of task difficulty, type of processing, and practice. Cereb. Cortex **7**, 374–385 (1997)
9. Wilson, G.F., Russell, C.A.: Performance enhancement in an uninhabited air vehicle task using psychophysiologically determined adaptive aiding. Hum. Factors **49**, 1005–1018 (2007)
10. Wilson, G.F., Russell, C.A.: Operator functional state classification using multiple psychophysiological features in an air traffic control task. Hum. Factors **45**, 381–389 (2003)
11. Baldwin, C.L., Penaranda, B.: Adaptive training using an artificial neural network and EEG metrics for within- and cross-task workload classification. Neuroimage **59**, 48–56 (2012)
12. Zhang, J.H., Peng, X.D., Liu, H., Raish, J., Wang, R.B.: Classifying human operator functional state based on electrophysiological and performance measures and fuzzy clustering method. Cogn. Neurodyn. **7**, 477–497 (2013)
13. Sciarini, L.W., Nicholson, D.: Assessing cognitive state with multiple physiological measures: a modular approach. In: Schmorrow, D.D., Estabrooke, I.V., Grootjen, M. (eds.) FAC 2009. LNCS, vol. 5638, pp. 533–542. Springer, Heidelberg (2009)
14. Matthews, G., Reinerman-Jones, L., Barber, D., Abich, J.: The psychometrics of mental workload: multiple measures are sensitive but divergent. Hum. Factors **57**, 125–143 (2015)
15. Hankins, T.C., Wilson, G.F.: A comparison of heart rate, eye activity, EEG and subjective measures of pilot mental workload during flight. Aviat. Space Environ. Med. **69**, 360–367 (1998)
16. Abich IV, J.: Investigating the universality and comprehensive ability of measures to assess the state of workload. Unpublished doctoral dissertation. University of Central Florida (2013)
17. Hart, S.G., Staveland, L.E.: Development of NASA-TLX (Task Load Index): results of empirical and theoretical research. In: Hancock, P.A., Meshkati, N. (eds.) Human Mental Workload, pp. 139–184. Elsevier Science Publishers, North-Holland (1988)
18. Johannes, B., Gaillard, A.W.K.: A methodology to compensate for individual differences in psychophysiological assessment. Biopsychology **96**, 77–85 (2014)

Posture Based Recognition of the Visual Focus of Attention for Adaptive Mobile Information Systems

Martin Westhoven[(✉)], Christian Plegge, Timo Henrich,
and Thomas Alexander

Fraunhofer Institute for Communications Information Processing
and Ergonomics FKIE, Zanderstraße 5, 53177 Bonn, Germany
martin.westhoven@fkie.fraunhofer.de

Abstract. This paper presents a method to estimate the visual focus of attention from body posture in a system consisting of a head-mounted display and an arm-mounted smartphone. The approach aims at fast and robust detection without using additional hardware, even when walking. Knowledge about the visual focus of attention can be used to adapt user interfaces. E.g. eye-tracking can yield precise measurements for stationary systems. This it is not always possible using mobile devices due to body movement dynamics. A practical solution is achieved through a combination of orientation information and known anatomical limitations. The approach was parameterized and evaluated, reaching mean detection rates of over 97 %. Generalized parameters allow for usage without individual configuration. Used as a screen unlocking mechanism for smartphones, faster access can be realized in comparison to manual unlocking.

Keywords: Information ergonomics · Mobile HCI · Wearable computing

1 Introduction

With growing number of available wearables and smart devices, the presence of multiple devices on a person is becoming more common. While some devices are designed to supplement each other, e.g. smartwatches and smartphones, most are intended to work standalone. When appliances consist of combinations of different devices, they can leverage single devices' benefits while mitigating possible negative aspects [26]. Chen et al. for example investigate the design space of a smartwatch and smartphone combination to better distinguish gestures and differentiate feedback [4]. The drawback is an increased complexity of the overall system, especially of the UI being distributed across devices. New problems may also surface, e.g. lack of knowledge about the user's intention to interact with a specific device or image overlap when combining see-through displays with normal ones. Potentials and drawbacks are illustrated in the use case of combining a smartphone and a head-mounted display (HMD), e.g. smart glasses. Smartphones are suited for more complex information and offer versatile interaction capabilities. Common UIs require focusing visual attention during interaction, though. Smart glasses provide visual output while allowing to

D.D. Schmorrow and C.M. Fidopiastis (Eds.): AC 2016, Part I, LNAI 9743, pp. 416–427, 2016.
DOI: 10.1007/978-3-319-39955-3_39

observe the environment. The comparatively low display resolution of current smart glasses is less suited for the presentation of complex and extensive data. Also input capabilities are often limited. They complement each other, each offering a workaround to the other's drawbacks. But consider looking through the smart glasses at the smartphone: The displayed data would overlap, possibly leading to loss or misinterpretation of information, which can affect the user's efficiency or cause dangerous situations. This is especially true when regarding professional use, since working environments may require most of the user's attention, leaving only short periods for interaction with a mobile appliance [13, 22]. The user may also be engaged in physical activities, e.g. walking, while interacting [2, 17]. By temporarily disabling information output on the smart glasses, the problem can be avoided. Designing such adaptive UIs requires an understanding of the user's intention to interact in a particular situation. Especially knowledge about the user's attention is needed to adapt to the way the system is interacted with. Human attention in general is complex and is considered a limited resource. In a typical use case, various issues may need attention, the mobile appliance being only one of them. Consequently, users are required to switch attention between appliance and environment. Although several factors influence the cognitive process of attention, human gaze provides hints regarding its actual focus [6, 31]. The user's visual focus of attention (VFOA) can be derived from the eye fixation [8]. To avoid displaying overlapping data, the device holding the user's VFOA should be given preference for presenting visual information. Previous research has brought up different methods to estimate the VFOA in stationary and mobile settings. These are discussed in the following section along with other relevant work. Based on this, an efficient yet simple approach for VFOA estimation for combined mobile devices is presented. It uses the orientation of smart devices to recognize postures associated with a specific visual focus. Head-mounted devices can provide the most valuable information regarding the visual focus of the user. Therefore, we focus on a set-up using such a head-mounted device in a first step. The required parametrization for the approach was obtained in an experiment with 12 participants and evaluated with further 8 participants.

2 Related Work

Recognizing the intention to interact with a device can be based on several aspects. Schwarz et al. e.g. consider body and head posture as well as gestures to determine intention to interact with a wall screen [27]. Interaction with visual displays requires the display to be visible at some point, making the detection of a user looking at the device a primary concern. Information about location and content of what a person is looking at is called the visual focus of attention [19, 30, 32]. It is indicated by the gaze direction, including the head pose. It can be independent of the overall focus of attention, e.g. when the person is in deep thought. When those cannot be measured, pattern recognition on a device's motion sensor data can suffice [1], the lack of head pose information makes this somewhat less reliable though. Similar approaches are used in recent smartwatch designs. E.g., the Galaxy Gear smartwatch[1] and the Apple Watch[2] determine the user's VFOA through pattern recognition on the watches' Inertial Measurement Units (IMU) data to only activate the display when needed. This requires the user to perform a specific movement or to hold a posture for a short time. Sometimes it is possible to measure the gaze direction, e.g. using eye-tracking glasses, eye-tracking being the quantitative recording of eye movements. Most methods are based on image recognition techniques [10]. Eye tracking provides high-quality data, but application to mobile environments is limited. Common systems require a firm fixation, a calibration and in most cases special training [10]. Nonetheless, gaze analysis in mobile applications can be precise, if used in prepared environments. Tracking can be divided into inside-out and outside-in approaches [24]. Inside-out approaches use cameras worn by the user to detect markers in the environment. Outside-in approaches use cameras in the environment to track markers on the user. Both require markers or even cameras to be placed in- or alongside the tracking volume. Also, to compute 3D gaze points, a correct model of the environment is required [9]. Despite the development of automatically calibrating and less cumbersome eye tracking systems, these requirements alongside high costs are some of the reasons the technique is mainly used in scientific context [21]. Detailed visual attention is currently rarely considered in mobile applications. The simpler approach of face detection with the smartphone camera is found e.g. in screen unlocking mechanisms [29], games or screen dimming mechanisms, as in recent Samsung smartphones[3]. Image based methods suffer some drawbacks. They can be sensitive to lighting conditions and thus perform poorly. In the field of Human Activity Recognition, visual methods are therefore mainly used in constrained environments. For dynamic use, body worn inertial sensors are preferred [3]. An alternative is to leverage the orientation of the head which yields a reasonable approximation [16, 30, 32, 34]. Farenza et al. [7] use this to estimate the subjective view frustum, which bounds the portion of the scene a subject is looking at. Possible poses are limited by human motion constraints. This facilitates processing sensor data, e.g. for gait analysis. It is especially helpful for determining relations of poses of different body parts. Seel et al. use knowledge about kinematic constraints in joint movements to determine joint angles and positions [28]. To accomplish this, all involved limbs were fitted with sensors. Using spatial relations between devices is not new (see e.g. [14]). However, the emergence of smart devices expanded possible inter-device interactions considerably. Chen et al. for example study the design space of a smartphone-smartwatch set-up and use Decision Tree learning on accelerometer data [4]. They also give a more general overview of interaction techniques for hand-held/wrist-worn devices and multi-device systems. Our approach also targets multi-device set-ups, albeit focusing on at least one head-mounted device, e.g. smart glasses. It relies on inertial data of two or more devices to estimate the VFOA,

---

[1] http://www.samsung.com/de/consumer/mobile-device/mobilephones/smartphones/SM-V7000WDADBT-support.

[2] https://www.apple.com/watch/technology/.

[3] http://www.samsung.com/de/consumer/mobile-device/mobilephones/smartphones/GT-I9300MBDDBT-support.

specifically the derived orientation. We aim at scenarios where head-mounted devices are already in use or the added weight is an acceptable trade-off for higher precision than found e.g. in the mentioned smartwatch designs. For ease of use, we refrained from adding sensors and used only those already built-in. The data is interpreted considering knowledge about anatomy and device mounting.

3 Approach

The basic idea is to estimate the current VFOA by tracking posture. We demonstrate how posture is used as an indicator for the VFOA in the given context of body worn devices. Subsequently, practical issues regarding collection and interpretation of the required data are discussed. Finally, the algorithm used for the actual recognition is presented. Using VFOA information, it is possible to distinguish between focusing on a mobile device and focusing on the environment. Considering a system consisting of smartphone and smart glasses, the devices and the environment provide possible VFOA targets. As smart glasses are worn to observe the environment and digital information simultaneously, smart glasses and the environment can be treated as a single VFOA target in this case. The problem of VFOA estimation is thus simplified to the distinction whether the smartphone is being looked at or not. Visual perception is mainly driven by the location of the sensory organs as well as size and position of the object in focus [18]. Depending on individual anatomic prerequisites and the target's spatial properties, various postural changes may be necessary to perceive a particular object visually. It may be necessary to rotate the head. If the object to focus on is worn on the own body, one may also need to move respective body parts into view. For a forearm-mounted smartphone, the user has to raise and rotate his forearm. Figure 1 illustrates user postures when wearing smartphone and smart glasses.

A posture where the user's VFOA is likely to be located at the smartphone is depicted in Fig. 1a. The smartphone is positioned in front of the body, screen rotated towards the head. Additionally the user has to rotate and lower his head. As anatomic characteristics restrict the range of motion, it is sufficient to consider relative orientation between head and forearm. If the rotation of either head or forearm differs significantly

Fig. 1. Typical postures (left to right): (a) smartphone focused; (b) environment focus, arm lowered; (c) environment focus, arm raised; (d) environment focus, like a, but arm lowered

(Fig. 1b–d), the smartphone is not visible. The VFOA is then likely to be located in the environment. As Fig. 1c and d show, considering only one component is not sufficient as the remaining information allows for ambiguous interpretation. If only the forearm was considered, Fig. 1a and c would result in the same estimation, although in Fig. 1c the user is clearly not looking at the smartphone. To estimate the users' VFOA target, the position of at least two body parts, namely head and forearm, have to be considered. A tolerance has to be taken into account, due to the varying contexts of motion and constraints in motor control [33]. Motion capturing in mobile environments is usually performed using inertial measurement units (IMU) [25]. In comparison to established videogrammetric methods, they provide less accurate tracking, as static setups are required to achieve this precision. IMUs suffer from accumulated errors by design. To compensate for this, rotation is typically computed from a combination of magnetometer, gyroscope and accelerometer data. One widespread method is the use of Kalman-filters [12]. IMUs are incorporated in smartphones and smart glasses. As the smart glasses are worn on the head, their IMU can be assumed to be a suitable approximation of the head's orientation. Accordingly, the smartphone's IMU can be interpreted as forearm orientation due to its mount. The quality of IMUs found in smart devices is considerably worse compared to dedicated motion capturing systems. Inaccuracies should therefore be taken into account. Orientation in space is typically represented as a rotation around one or multiple axes. Two common notations are Euler angles and quaternions. The former uses successive rotations about three different axes. The latter is based on Euler's rotation theorem, stating that any rotation or sequence of rotations about a fixed point can be represented by a single rotation by a given angle about a fixed axis running through the fixed point. Apart from other advantages, quaternions avoid the Gimbal Lock problem inherent in the Euler angle representation, the loss of a degree of freedom when approaching a yaw angle of 90°. For further reading on representing orientation, see [5]. The orientation of a device is defined by its rotation quaternion $q_{device} = (x, y, z, w)^T$. The rotational difference between devices can be described as the transformation quaternion:

$$q_{\delta_{1,2}} = q_1^{-1} * q_2$$

It contains the information regarding the rotation necessary to rotate from the orientation of the first to those of the second device. In other words, it describes the orientation of the devices towards each other. Be q_{ref} a rotation between two devices, while the VFOA is known to be on a specific device. Let '·' be the inner product. For the current rotation between two devices, the distance to the reference rotation can then be obtained by the metric:

$$\Phi: \mathbb{R}^4 \times \mathbb{R}^4 \to [0, 1], \Phi(q_1, q_2) = 1 - |q_1 \cdot q_2|$$

It was originally developed to describe the difference between Euclidean transformations [15]. Its main advantage is a relatively low computational expense [11]. For the case of two devices, a rotation and thereby a posture $q_{current}$ is recognized if and only if its distance to q_{ref} is below a threshold $\varepsilon \in [0, 1]$:

$$\Phi\left(q_{ref}, q_{current}\right) < \varepsilon$$

Note, that this only requires determining the rotational data of the desired posture and no sophisticated learning. In general this approach can be extended to more than two body parts or respective devices. However, computing the rotational differences naively results in quadratically rising computational effort in the number of devices. For a fixed number of devices, the computational complexity is constant. A common smartphone (Galaxy S3 GT-I 300, Samsung) performs the computation in less than a millisecond. Latency is therefore negligible.

4 Experiment 1: Parametrization User Study

A reference quaternion (q_{ref}), describing the posture of the user when looking at the smartphone and the allowed deviation (ε) have to be determined. The data was gathered in a lab under the mobile usage conditions of walking and standing to get a more dynamic range of motions in comparison to e.g. sitting. Controllability of the environment was of primary concern, although real-world application will likely result in more unrelated movement than lab settings. 12 employees (5 female) of a research institute were recruited as participants. Mean age was 31.25 (SD = 3.34) years. One of four letters was displayed using a wall projection. Each appearance of a letter was announced by audio. The participants had to enter the letter using a software keyboard on the smartphone. Random reordering of the keyboard required looking at the device, so the posture captured at the time of input corresponds to the VFOA being on the smartphone. Each input was followed by random pauses of 5, 6 or 7 s, which allows for completion of a gait cycle and resumption of accompanying arm movement [23]. Two movement speeds were distinguished: Standing (S, 0 km/h) and walking (W, 5 km/h). The sequence of conditions was permuted to avoid learning effects. The assignment of participants to sequences was randomized. All participants completed the task under both conditions on a treadmill, ensuring equal conditions. Both conditions required 60 letters to be processed. The participants were asked to lower the arm after each input. All sessions were tracked by an external motion capturing system (Vicon Bonita, Vicon), to reveal if reduced quality of the built-in IMU's data causes problems. The used devices were fitted with IR-markers. A head mounted display (Lite-Eye LE-750 A, Lite-Eye Systems) with an attached IMU (InertiaCube3, Intersense) was used as a substitute for smart glasses. A smartphone (Galaxy S3, GT-I9300, Samsung) was mounted on the left forearm. This allowed wearing it next to the wrist like a wrist-watch. The IMU data was tracked at 40 Hz. Additionally, the data was logged on every input as well. Each run was recorded on video. Checking the IMUs against external motion tracking, no significant deviations were found. For each participant and condition a reference quaternion was determined, using the mean transformation quaternion [20] between smart glasses and -phone over the first three inputs. All following inputs were compared to this reference. One data set was excluded, as the experimental task was not followed through. A posture was recognized if for the frame captured during input, the rotational difference was below the threshold. To account for

Table 1. Recognition rates and false positives for different thresholds

ε		Recognition rate [%]		False positives [abs]	
		S	W	S	W
0.17	∅	98.73	97.69	5.67	7.45
	SD	2.41	5.63	10.14	10.64
0.18	∅	98.59	98.00	6.25	7.45
	SD	2.38	4.66	11.30	12.2
0.19	∅	98.16	98.15	6.92	7.91
	SD	2.93	4.18	13.06	12.53
0.20	∅	98.02	98.46	7.83	8.00
	SD	2.97	3.26	15.13	16.64
0.21	∅	98.02	98.46	8.83	9.64
	SD	2.88	3.26	17.08	16.4
0.22	∅	97.60	98.46	9.08	10.55
	SD	3.66	2.88	18.08	18.13
0.23	∅	97.6	98.77	9.08	11.91
	SD	3.65	2.16	18.64	21.20
0.24	∅	−97.03	99.08	8.67	19.09
	SD	4.69	1.76	18.83	22.98

visually verifying the input, a tolerance of two seconds after input was given. Before notification or after input this was counted as false positive (*fp*). This includes potentially correct recognitions outside of the task. To get a realistic impression of the impact of false positive detections, coherent sequences were counted only once. This curbs the impact of events such as users looking at the smartphone between the inputs, e.g. to adjust or check the mounting. Only thresholds providing a recognition rate $r > 80\%$ and false positives $fp \leq 15$ were considered. As the exact number of possible negatives is unknown for the experimental task, the false negatives were set into relation to the false positives to determine a threshold providing both a high recognition rate and a low amount of false positives. The resulting quotient is $Q = fp/r$, r being the recognition rate. The recognition rates and false positive detections for each condition are shown in Table 1.

For the condition "standing", Q is minimized by $\varepsilon_S = 0.17$. For "walking", the best results were found for $\varepsilon_W = 0.25$. The stricter threshold for "standing" could stem from the experimental task itself being rather monotonous or from the difference to the walking-induced motion sequence. Video analysis shows that participants produced a greater variety of postures when standing, compared to walking. There were roughly three different types of data. Figure 2 gives an idea of this variety. The charts show distances of the transformation quaternions to the reference. The data set in Fig. 2a shows clear peaks: At the time of input (dashed line) the distance between transformation and reference quaternion decreases sharply. Aforementioned effects for thresholds, 0.21 seems to be a suitable starting point.

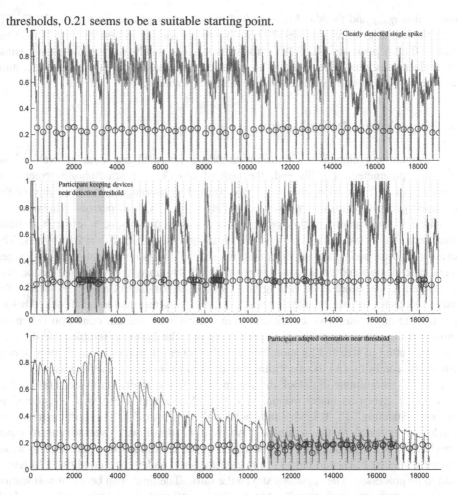

Fig. 2. Exemplary data sets from the parametrization for individual reference quaternions and $\varepsilon = 0.2$. From top to bottom: (a) normal behavior, (b) noise-inducing arm movement and (c) progressive adaption to detection threshold. The graph depicts the distance to the reference quaternion over time. Dashed lines mark input notifications; circles indicate VFOA detections

"standing" can be seen in Fig. 2b. The data is noisy as the participant swung his arms between the inputs. Some participants adapted to the task as depicted in Fig. 2c. The differences between the posture during input and idling in-between steadily decrease. To find a threshold covering both conditions, considering the mean of the thresholds, 0.21 seems to be a suitable starting point.

However, by reduction to $\varepsilon_G = 0.20$ a lower error count is achieved while maintaining the recognition rate. The question arises, if the reference quaternion too can be generalized. We computed the mean of all reference quaternions within both conditions q_{refG}. Applying the algorithm to the measured data, using the generalized reference quaternion q_{refG} and threshold ε_G, resulted in mean recognition rates of 97.18 % (SD 6.27 %) and 4.83 false positives (SD 5.97) while standing and 98.98 % (SD 1.82 %) and 3.80 false positives (SD 5.49) while walking. The results suggest that it is feasible to neglect individual differences to a certain degree, making individual configuration unnecessary. This was evaluated in a separate experiment.

5 Experiment 2: Evaluation

The evaluation's objective was to investigate a practical use case as well as the obtained parameters. To this end, the task of unlocking a smartphone screen was chosen. Apart from task performance, we wanted to investigate the reliability of the obtained general parameters when used to detect the VFOA of persons who were not involved in the parametrization process. Further 8 employees of a research institute were recruited as participants (4 female). Mean age was 30.75 (SD = 2.99) years. The evaluation was performed under conditions similar the parametrization, only logged data, task, design and participant sample differed. Notably, the VFOA detection was computed in real-time. A lab setting was used again for controllability. Basically, the same task as for the parametrization was used, but the screen had to be unlocked before performing any input. Two conditions were used: Under manual condition (M) users unlocked the screen by pressing a specific button. The button resembled the devices' standby button in size and location, being in the upper left corner of the display. Under automatic condition (A) the algorithm was used to estimate whether the user's VFOA was on the smartphone to unlock the screen. In case the algorithm failed, users had to unlock the screen as under manual condition. Movement speed was considered as before: "Standing" (S, 0 km/h) and "walking" (W, 5 km/h). The participants were randomly assigned to the sequences. Again a treadmill was used to ensure equal conditions for the participants. The sequence of the conditions was permuted to avoid learning effects. Each participant completed the task under each condition. 20 letters had to be processed. The apparatus stayed the same. The time span between notification and subsequent input was logged additionally, as well as the interaction with the unlock button under automatic condition. Access times for the different conditions were compared. Data analysis remained the same for recognition rates and false positive detections. Regarding the reliability of the approach for persons not involved in the parametrization, the recognition rates as well as the amounts of false positives were analyzed. For "standing" (S), the screen always unlocked when required, resulting in recognition of 100 %. For "walking" (W), the algorithm failed once, resulting in a mean recognition for all participants of 99.41 %. On average 1.00 (SD = 2.29) false positive detections occurred for "standing" and 1.63 (SD = 2.60) for "walking". We compared the general performance of both parametrization and evaluation by relating the amounts of false positives to the experiment durations (Fig. 3). As can be seen, the approach yields results comparable to experiment 1, even without individual configuration. Using the VFOA algorithm, the times required to unlock the screen were 1.62 (SD = 0.14) seconds for "standing" (S) and 1.66 (SD = 0.2) seconds for "walking" (W). Manually unlocking the screen took 2.29 (SD = 0.31) seconds for "standing"

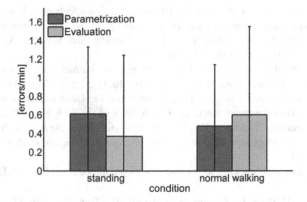

Fig. 3. False positives per minute for both experiments

(S) and 2.38 (SD = 0.48) seconds for "walking" (W). This shows that the automatic screen unlocking is significantly faster compared to manual unlocking.

6 Summary and Outlook

We motivated the value of knowledge about the visual focus of attention (VFOA) for adaptive systems with multiple mobile devices available to the user. User interfaces seeking to avoid problems caused by multi-device usage should consider the user's current VFOA. Image based approaches still have problems when used in mobile contexts. An alternative approach, using device orientation and knowledge about anatomical limitations was proposed. The algorithm recognizes postures associated with the VFOA being on the smartphone. Two experiments were performed to parameterize and evaluate the approach. A general parametrization covering the use while standing nad walking was obtained. A subsequent evaluation investigated the practicability of the proposed algorithm using the identified parameters. The results show that the VFOA can be estimated in real-time, even without individually configured parameters. The approach can be scaled up for more devices, so a future goal is to study the potential of systems comprising e.g. smartphone, smartwatch, smart glasses and or tablets. Additional validation is required to drive the approach towards practical use. The results have to be compared to other methods in an experiment with more participants and also covering a broader population and real-world applications. We currently rely on the mobile devices being mounted to the user's body. An interesting question is, whether good results can also be achieved, when the devices' positions are only roughly known, as is e.g. the case for hand-held devices.

References

1. Abyarjoo, F., Barreto, A., Abyarjoo, S., Ortega, F.R., Cofino, J.: Monitoring human wrist rotation in three degrees of freedom. In: Southeastcon, 2013 Proceedings of IEEE, pp. 1–5. IEEE (2013)

2. Bergstrom-Lehtovirta, J., Oulasvirta, A., Brewster, S.: The effects of walking speed on target acquisition on a touchscreen interface. In: Proceedings of the 13th International Conference on Human Computer Interaction with Mobile Devices and Services, MobileHCI 2011, pp. 143–146. ACM, New York, NY, USA (2011)
3. Bulling, A., Blanke, U., Schiele, B.: A tutorial on human activity recognition using body-worn inertial sensors. ACM Comput. Surv. **46**(3), 33:1–33:33 (2014)
4. Chen, X.A., Grossman, T., Wigdor, D.J., Fitzmaurice, G.: Duet: exploring joint interactions on a smart phone and a smart watch. In: Proceedings of the SIGCHI Conference on Human Factors in Computing Systems, CHI 2014, pp. 159–168. ACM, New York, NY, USA (2014)
5. Diebel, J.: Representing attitude: euler angles, unit quaternions, and rotation vectors. Matrix **58**, 15–16 (2006)
6. Drewes, H.: Eye gaze tracking for human computer interaction. Text. Ph.D. thesis, LMU, March 2010
7. Farenzena, M., Bazzani, L., Murino, V., Cristani, M.: Towards a subject-centered analysis for automated video surveillance. In: Foggia, P., Sansone, C., Vento, M. (eds.) ICIAP 2009. LNCS, vol. 5716, pp. 481–489. Springer, Heidelberg (2009)
8. Frintrop, S., Rome, E., Christensen, H.I.: Computational visual attention systems and their cognitive foundations: a survey. ACM Trans. Appl. Percept. **7**(1), 6:1–6:39 (2010)
9. Hammer, J.H., Maurus, M., Beyerer, J.: Real-time 3D gaze analysis in mobile applications. In: Proceedings of the 2013 Conference on Eye Tracking South Africa, ETSA 2013, pp. 75–78. ACM, New York, NY, USA (2013)
10. Holmqvist, K., Nyström, M., Andersson, R., Dewhurst, R., Jarodzka, H., Van de Weijer, J.: Eye tracking: a comprehensive guide to methods and measures. Oxford University Press, Oxford (2011)
11. Huynh, D.Q.: Metrics for 3D rotations: comparison and analysis. J. Math. Imaging Vis. **35** (2), 155–164 (2009)
12. Kalman, R.E.: A new approach to linear filtering and prediction problems. J. Basic Eng. **82** (1), 35–45 (1960)
13. Karlson, A.K., Iqbal, S.T., Meyers, B., Ramos, G., Lee, K., Tang, J.C.: Mobile taskflow in context: a screenshot study of smartphone usage. In: Proceedings of the SIGCHI Conference on Human Factors in Computing Systems, CHI 2010, pp. 2009–2018. ACM, New York, NY, USA (2010)
14. Kortuem, G., Kray, C., Gellersen, H.: Sensing and visualizing spatial relations of mobile devices. In: Proceedings of the 18th Annual ACM Symposium on User Interface Software and Technology, pp. 93–102. ACM (2005)
15. Kuffner, J.: Effective sampling and distance metrics for 3D rigid body path planning. In: Proceedings of the 2004 IEEE International Conference on Robotics and Automation, 2004, ICRA 2004, vol. 4, pp. 3993–3998, April 2004
16. Lanz, O., Brunelli, R., Chippendale, P., Voit, M., Stiefelhagen, R.: Extracting interaction cues: focus of attention, body pose, and gestures. In: Waibel, A., Stiefelhagen, R. (eds.) Computers in the Human Interaction Loop. Human-Computer Interaction Series, pp. 87–93. Springer, London (2009)
17. Lim, J.J., Feria, C.: Visual search on a mobile device while walking. In: Proceedings of the 14th International Conference on Human-Computer Interaction with Mobile Devices and Services, MobileHCI 2012, pp. 295–304. ACM, New York, NY, USA (2012)
18. Lindsay, P.H., Norman, D.A.: Human Information Processing: An Introduction to Psychology. Academic Press, Cambridge (2013)
19. Liu, X., Krahnstoever, N., Yu, T., Tu, P.: What are customers looking at? In: IEEE Conference on Advanced Video and Signal Based Surveillance, 2007, AVSS 2007, pp. 405–410. IEEE (2007)

20. Markley, F.L., Cheng, Y., Crassidis, J.L., Oshman, Y.: Averaging quaternions. J. Guid. Control Dyn. **30**(4), 1193–1197 (2007)
21. Mayr, E., Knipfer, K., Wessel, D.: In-sights into mobile learning: an exploration of mobile eye tracking methodology for learning in museums. In: Vavoula, G., Pachler, N., Kukulska-Hulme, A. (eds.) Researching Mobile Learning: Frameworks, Tools and Research Designs, pp. 189–204. Peter Lang, Oxford (2009)
22. Oulasvirta, A., Tamminen, S., Roto, V., Kuorelahti, J.: Interaction in 4-s bursts: the fragmented nature of attentional resources in mobile HCI. In: Proceedings of the SIGCHI Conference on Human Factors in Computing Systems, CHI 2005, pp. 919–928. ACM, New York, NY, USA (2005)
23. Perry, J., Davids, J.R., et al.: Gait analysis: normal and pathological function. J. Pediatr. Orthop. **12**(6), 815 (1992)
24. Pfeiffer, T.: Measuring and visualizing attention in space with 3D attention volumes. In: Proceedings of the Symposium on Eye Tracking Research and Applications, ETRA 2012, pp. 29–36. ACM, New York, NY, USA (2012)
25. Roetenberg, D., Luinge, H.J., Baten, C.T.M., Veltink, P.H.: Compensation of magnetic disturbances improves inertial and magnetic sensing of human body segment orientation. IEEE Trans. Neural Syst. Rehabilitation Eng. **13**(3), 395–405 (2005). A Publication of the IEEE Engineering in Medicine and Biology Society. PMID: 16200762
26. Santosa, S. Wigdor, D.: A field study of multi-device workflows in distributed workspaces. In: Proceedings of the 2013 ACM International Joint Conference on Pervasive and Ubiquitous Computing, UbiComp 2013, pp. 63–72. ACM, New York, NY, USA (2013)
27. Schwarz, J., Marais, C.C., Leyvand, T., Hudson, S.E., Mankoff, J.: Combining body pose, gaze, and gesture to determine intention to interact in vision-based interfaces. In: Proceedings of the 32nd Annual ACM Conference on Human Factors in Computing Systems, CHI 2014, pp. 3443–3452. ACM, New York, NY, USA (2014)
28. Seel, T., Schauer, T., Raisch, J.: Joint axis and position estimation from inertial measurement data by exploiting kinematic constraints. In: 2012 IEEE International Conference on Control Applications (CCA), pp. 45–49, October 2012
29. Shen, Y., Hu, W., Yang, M., Wei, B., Lucey, S., Chou, C.T.: Face recognition on smartphones via optimized sparse representation classification. In: Proceedings of the 13th International Symposium on Information Processing in Sensor Networks, IPSN 2014, pp. 237–248. IEEE (2014)
30. Smith, K., Ba, S.O., Odobez, J.-M., Gatica-Perez, D.: Tracking the visual focus of attention for a varying number of wandering people. IEEE Trans. Pattern Anal. Mach. Intell. **30**(7), 1212–1229 (2008)
31. Stiefelhagen, R.: Tracking focus of attention in meetings. In: Proceedings of the 4th IEEE International Conference on Multimodal Interfaces, ICMI 2002, p. 273. IEEE Computer Society, Washington, DC, USA (2002)
32. Stiefelhagen, R., Finke, M., Yang, J., Waibel, A.: From gaze to focus of attention. In: Huijsmans, D.P., Smeulders, A.W. (eds.) VISUAL 1999. LNCS, vol. 1614, pp. 761–768. Springer, Heidelberg (1999)
33. Winter, D.A.: Biomechanics and Motor Control of Human Movement. Wiley, Hoboken (2009)
34. Wright, O.R.: Summary of research on the selection interview since 1964. Pers. Psychol. **22**(4), 391–413 (1969)

Considerations in Physiological Metric Selection for Online Detection of Operator State: A Case Study

Ryan W. Wohleber[1(✉)], Gerald Matthews[1], Gregory J. Funke[2], and Jinchao Lin[1]

[1] Institute for Simulation and Training, University of Central Florida, Orlando, FL, USA
{rwohlebe,gmatthew,jlin}@ist.ucf.edu
[2] Air Force Research Laboratory, Wright-Patterson AFB, Dayton, OH, USA
gregory.funke@us.af.mil

Abstract. The development of closed-loop systems is fraught with many challenges. One of the many important decisions to be made in this development is the selection of suitable metrics to detect operator state. Successful metrics can inform adaptations in an interface's design, features, or task elements allocated to automated systems. This paper will discuss various challenges and considerations involved in the selection of metrics for detecting fatigue in operators of unmanned aerial vehicles (UAVs). Using Eggemeier and colleague's guidelines for workload metric selection as a basis, we review several criteria for metric selection and how they are applied to selection of metrics designed to assess operator fatigue in an applied closed-loop system.

Keywords: Metric selection · Fatigue · Automated decision making aid · Human factors · Supervisory control

1 Introduction

Future military operations may require single individuals to control multiple unmanned aerial vehicles (UAVs) to decrease demand for operators, safeguard human lives, increase efficiency of operations, and increase military capability [1]. To realize this ambition, automated systems must be used extensively to guard against operator overload [2]. For these automated systems to work effectively, operators must rely appropriately on them. Unfortunately, recent work has shown that humans are imperfect at properly calibrating their use of automation [3]. With this in mind, automation researchers have sought to develop closed-loop systems to help operators make proper use of their automated aids [4]. To power such systems, measures must be utilized during operation to continually gauge operator state to inform the system of the proper intervention or interface configuration for a given situation. Recent work in our lab [5] has focused on the problem of fatigue induced by prolonged low workload portions of intelligence, surveillance, and reconnaissance (ISR) missions.

© Springer International Publishing Switzerland 2016
D.D. Schmorrow and C.M. Fidopiastis (Eds.): AC 2016, Part I, LNAI 9743, pp. 428–439, 2016.
DOI: 10.1007/978-3-319-39955-3_40

2   Fatigue

Fatigue is a complex and multifaceted construct about which there is an extensive literature but no single and exacting definition [6]. Figure 1 presents a useful conceptual model for understanding fatigue that distinguishes its trait and state components [6]. The experience of state fatigue emerges over time (i.e. time on task) as a result of a fatiguing agent and the moderating effects of fatigue proneness. The conscious and nonconscious experience of a person's fatigue state can be assessed through subjective measures of self-report and physiological techniques respectively [6]. Additionally, fatigue state is influenced by self-regulation, which along with task performance can serve as a behavioral gauge of fatigue.

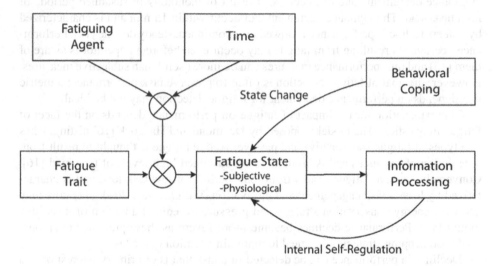

Fig. 1. A simple trait-state model for fatigue. Adapted from [6]

3   Overview of Available Measures and Metrics

In this overview, we refer only to momentary assessments which can be used to gauge fatigue in response to task performance.

3.1   Subjective Measures

Subjective measures are easy to use and provide a more nuanced account of experienced fatigue than can be afforded by physiological or performance based measures alone. These scales can be unidimensional [7] or multidimensional. Typically, state fatigue inventories are administered following task performance and are compared with a version taken prior to tasking. For example, the Dundee Stress State Questionnaire [8] assesses indicators of self-regulation during task performance: distress, task engagement, and worry. These indicators identify different fatigue states such as active and passive fatigue [9]. Subjective fatigue assessments used online are typically simpler than the multi-item post-task assessments, often using a single item to gauge fatigue as a univariate construct. The Karolinska sleepiness scale (KSS) [10] assesses sleepiness on a 9-point scale, and has been used to assess instantaneous fatigue during driving tasks [11]. Subjective fatigue assessments are typically administered via paper or electronically; however, similar measures have been administered verbally [12].

3.2 Performance Measures

There is a long history of using decreased performance with time on task as a gauge of fatigue [13]. In sustained attention research, this decrease is often referred to as the "vigilance decrement" and can occur as a result of monotony or sustained periods of high task-load. The vigilance decrement can occur within 15 min and is characterized by a steep decline in performance followed by a continued, steady decline [14]. Performance decrements resulting from fatigue may occur even before an operator is aware of them [15] and thus performance measures can be more useful than subjective measures. However, the goal of fatigue detection is often to preserve task performance; a metric that depends on performance decrement for fatigue detection may not be ideal.

The explanation for the impact of fatigue on performance depends on the facet of fatigue in question. The model proposed by Desmond and Hancock [16] distinguishes two types of fatigue states: active and passive. Active fatigue is thought to result from a depletion of resources and is brought on by sustained high levels of task-load [16]. Conversely, passive fatigue results from long periods of low task-load and is characterized by loss of task engagement and motivation. With low task-load, operators may adopt an energy conservation strategy and pressure to redirect attention off-task may mount [17]. Performance declines become more severe as these pressures overcome goal based coping strategies designed to maintain attention to the task.

Declines in performance can be detected in a task that is of primary interest or in a secondary task of lesser or even diagnostic importance [18]. The latter method is typically employed to serve as an early warning of the onset of fatigue; compensatory coping strategies can typically sustain performance on a primary task for some time after the onset of fatigue [18]. Examples of performance metrics susceptible to fatigue include reaction time [19], response speed to emergency events [20], and lapses [21].

Probe tasks are another way to measure operator fatigue by testing components not under primary control. Use of a probe in automation monitoring tasks has been demonstrated in several studies [3, 20]. These tasks may assess fatigue by asking operators to recall a certain feature of the task without forewarning them about the question, or by having operators react to an unexpected event. A driving study [20], for example, had participants avoid a van that suddenly appeared in the road. In studies cited here, the probe task was able to discriminate conditions that induced passive fatigue despite participants' success maintaining performance on the primary task.

3.3 Physiological Measures

This discussion will focus on cognitive fatigue measures that can be reasonably used during UAV operation (e.g., we omit functional magnetic resonance imaging; fMRI). Researchers have investigated fatigue and related constructs using several different physiological methods including metrics derived from cardiac activity such as inter-beat interval (IBI) and heart rate variability (HRV) [18] cerebral blood flow velocity (CBFV) [22], electroencephalography (EEG) [23], and eye tracking metrics [24].

Prominent dual process theories have proposed that information processing is supported by two hierarchical levels, a lower level of automatic processing, and a higher level of controlled processing [25]. Whereas controlled processing is characterized by conscious and effortful processing, lower level processing functions effortlessly and largely without conscious awareness. Physiological measures may gauge the impact of fatigue at the lower, automatic level [24] more effectively than subjective measures of fatigue which are more oriented to higher, controlled level processing.

Electrocortical. Thus far, research exploring physiological assessments to gauge fatigue in adaptive automation systems has focused on EEG metrics and event-related potential (ERP) analysis [26]. With the onset of fatigue, EEG registers relatively reliable increases in slow wave activity, related to drowsiness and sleep, and alpha wave activity, inversely related to cortical arousal [23]. These changes in wave activity may occur before performance is impacted [27].

Electrocardiographic. Electrocardiography (ECG) measures have a history of use for detection of fatigue effects with much of the initial work originating in the late 1970s and early 1980s [18]. Typically, fatigue is characterized by an increase in IBI and an increase in HRV. Increase in HRV has been tied to increased self-regulatory effort, or effort to inhibit impulses and persist at difficult tasks [28].

Hemodynamic. Several measures related to blood flow and oxygenation have been tied to fatigue and performance of vigilance tasks [29] but are seldom if ever employed to power adaptive systems. CBFV, as measured by transcranial Doppler sonography (TCD), has been shown to decline reliably with vigilance decrements [22]. Further, declines in left and right hemispheres depend on task characteristics. Interestingly, CBFV on short tasks which may gauge resource availability predicts performance on vigilance tasks, but concurrent measures of CBFV have been less successful in predicting performance [22]. Concurrent CBFV did predict subjective experience of fatigue. Cerebral oxygen saturation, as measured by functional near-infrared spectroscopy (fNIRS), is not commonly used to detect fatigue [29]. One study [30] found that participants performing a three hour drive had lower oxygenation in the left frontal lobe than those in a control group who performed no task. However, there was a relationship between declined oxygenation and reaction time.

Eye Tracking. Like EEG, eye tracking has been evaluated for online state detection in adaptive systems (e.g. workload) [31]. A large body of research has linked eye tracking metrics to states of fatigue [32]. A prominent eyelid closure metric linked to fatigue is percentage of eye closure (PERCLOS), [33] which is considered a standard drowsiness gauge by many researchers. PERCLOS is the proportion of time that a person's eyes are more than 80 % closed and is reflective of slow eyelid closures rather than blinks (<500 ms), which are usually excluded from the computation (e.g., [34]). Lid closures greater than 500 ms are usually defined as microsleeps [35].

Another eye tracking method for gauging fatigue is fixation duration. Eye movements consists of frequent, quick movements called saccades, interspersed with periods of steady gaze called fixations [36]. During fixations, perception and cognitive activity occur [35], and extended fixations can indicate difficulty extracting information [36]. Specifically, as a person struggles to maintain focus and attention with fatigue, fixations lasting 150–900 ms, which are associated with cognitive processing, decrease. Fixations longer than 900 ms, indicative of staring, and less than 150 ms, which may relate to low level unconscious control but not deep processing, increase [35]. Mean fixation duration does not reliably relate to fatigue.

4   Criteria for Metric Selection

Selection of an appropriate metric for any situation requires a high level of regard for the context within which a state is to be measured, and a determination of what state or facet of a state is of particular interest. Criteria used to select metrics are not always explicitly enumerated; however Eggemeier and colleagues [37] identified six properties of workload assessment techniques, of which three were principal: i.e., sensitivity, diagnosticity, intrusiveness. We have framed our discussion of metrics for multi-tasking environments below around these criteria and added one more criterion, robustness. With the presentation of criteria, we evaluate measures and metrics in the context of our lab's current effort to identify metrics for online detection of passive fatigue during multi-UAV operation.

4.1   Sensitivity

Sensitivity may refer to signal to noise ratios as well as the quickness with which a measure can detect changes in state [37]. Concerning the former, sensitivity of the instrument over the entire range or levels of a state (e.g., sleeping to hype-vigilance) is not always an important requirement. Rather, an instrument should be chosen which provides sensitivity within the range of a state that is of interest. In our effort, we were concerned with variance in fatigue while operators were still relatively wakeful so that severe fatigue could be prevented from occurring altogether. Thus, a measure that is very sensitive to variations at higher levels of fatigue (drowsiness), but relatively insensitive to variation at lower levels of fatigue, such as PERCLOS, was not ideal. Further, our aim to detect and respond to operators' fatigue before their compensatory efforts to sustain performance were exhausted precluded the use of primary task performance decrements as a gauge of fatigue.

Concerning sensitivity related to time, an important concept in online intervention or adaptive systems, is the window size of the measure. Window size refers to the amount of time immediately prior to real time from which data is analyzed to determine current state. For example, an online measure may use data from 5 min prior to real time up to real time. Window size is determined by the amount of data required to yield a reliable indication of state. Our effort did not require immediate fatigue detection as might be afforded by EEG (4 s window [38]), but did require detection before operator coping efforts failed and performance was impacted.

One interesting consideration is that subjective measures, which are highly time sensitive, may not be sensitive to fatigue that has not yet reached conscious awareness (implicit fatigue) [15]. Indeed, physiological measures may be capable of detecting onset of fatigue before operators can report it, despite requiring a large window size to provide a reliable signal. Implicit fatigue may be a low-magnitude fatigue state that has yet to reach consciousness, in which case a highly sensitive metric is required. Yet, sleep studies suggest that operators can be highly compromised without realizing it [39], which implies a component of fatigue distinct from subjective tiredness. A test would need diagnosticity to distinguish the two components.

4.2 Diagnosticity

Diagnosticity refers to the ability of the measure to distinguish between different components of a construct.[1] It is especially important for measuring fatigue, which is multi-faceted. One advantage to multivariate self-report measures relative to univariate self-report measures is their ability to distinguish fatigue types. For example, the DSSQ is able to discriminate active fatigue, which is distinguished by an increase in distress, from passive fatigue, which is associated with a loss of task engagement [9].

Generally, task performance decrements may be less severe for active fatigue, which can be bolstered by maintenance of effort, than for passive fatigue which is associated with loss of motivation [40]. A recent driving simulator study to illuminate the relative performance impacts of active and passive fatigue revealed higher standard deviation of lateral position (SDLP), as well as longer braking and steering response times to an emergency event for those in the passive fatigue condition, compared to controls. Unfortunately, relative differences in performance decrement may also signify greater or lesser fatigue which might be difficult to distinguish from differences resulting from fatigue type.

Like performance indices, CBFV is useful for detecting fatigue as it shows a reliable decrease with time on task. Whereas disengagement may indicate either a lack of resources or an unwillingness to allocate resources to a task, CBFV may relate specifically to resource availability [22]. Some work has shown that CBFV decreases as a function of task difficulty, and that changes do not occur without a work imperative, e.g., when monitoring automation that is successfully performing a task [41]. Thus, CBFV might serve as a gauge of resource mobilization, making it a potentially useful gauge of active, rather than passive, fatigue. It is in that regard that CBFV may be useful for multi-UAV monitoring.

In addition to the active and passive fatigue facets discussed above [16], an online gauge of fatigue must be able to detect different types of fatigue expression. One

---

[1] As with Eggemeier and colleague's discussion, we do not discuss selectivity: the ability of a measure to distinguish the target construct from other, related constructs (e.g., fatigue from stress). Instead we consider selectivity a prerequisite for consideration as a candidate metric.

important type is described in driving research as highway hypnosis or driving without awareness (DWA) [39]. Anecdotally this state involves the competent performance of basic tasks without conscious engagement. DWA can be induced by bright points of fixation and highly predictable environments [39], such as monotonous roads. Control stations for UAV operation may be at risk of inducing DWA states, as they offer very little environmental variation and require operators to monitor backlit displays. Although some have questioned the usefulness of eye closure metrics for detecting DWA, this state is purportedly marked by changes in gaze behavior [39]. A binned fixation duration approach [35] might circumvent the diagnosticity problems associated with eye closure.

4.3 Intrusiveness

This criterion refers to the level of disruption caused by the use of a measure. In terms of fatigue, it is important not to use measures that might exacerbate the problem. For example, when operators are actively fatigued, the addition of regular, intermittent subjective fatigue assessments (i.e., instantaneous self-assessment; ISA) may be disruptive to performance [42]. Specifically, they can increase workload when workload is already too high, which can result in task shedding and lack of response. Conversely, passive fatigue may result in acquiescent response bias.

The issue of compounding workload also applies to the use of secondary diagnostic tasking. In laboratory settings the use of secondary tasking requires assigning the secondary task low priority [37]. This prioritization remains constant throughout the experiment which allows secondary task performance to be used as a gauge of workload or fatigue. In practice, evaluating a secondary task in this way is unrealistic as the priority of any secondary task relevant an operation is likely to shift in different situations [37]. Adding a noncritical diagnostic task to operationally relevant tasking presents other problems. Such tasks add workload or, at minimum, a distraction from important tasking. Operators may reject the tasking as artificial or bothersome and blame such tasking for performance deficiencies [37]. Further, such a method is likely to be valid only at lower levels of workload or fatigue as this task would be among the first to be shed in higher workload conditions.

Probe tasks may also be disruptive to task performance and not ideal for providing a continuous online gauge of fatigue level. In the driving fatigue study mentioned above [20], drivers were distressed following the emergency situation probe such that expected stress state differences due to the experimental manipulation may have been masked in a post-task assessment. Less jarring probes may be vulnerable to habituation; the operator may learn to change behavior in anticipation of them [43]. As a result, a probe might only be used successfully one time.

Physiological measures provide mixed potential with regard to intrusiveness. Despite the demonstrated utility of EEG for online detection of fatigue, it is relatively impractical for use in day to day operations supported by closed-loop adaptive systems. For a UAV operator shift, the setup of a capable EEG system would require: an assistant to place electrodes, baseline calibration, and pre-task testing (e.g., impedance checking). During the shift, occasional calibration checks would have to be included to correct electrode drift and/or unsecured electrodes. After the shift, the system components would have to be removed, cleaned, and stored, likely with the help of an assistant. During operations, EEG electrodes would need to be in contact with the scalp, usually in multiple locations. To conduct signals, a cream or gel typically must be used. The operator therefore must maintain a hair style that is conducive to electrode placement, and clean his or her hair after the shift. Further, the electrodes and the unit to relay data may restrict movement during operation and accidental shifts of the equipment may modify the signal or even cause electrodes to lose contact with the scalp. However, future wearable systems may be less intrusive. Similar problems plague set-up and use of TCD which requires head gear and careful set up and calibration with the help of assistants. Specifically, assistants would need to mount the headgear, find an appropriate window through which to locate the mid cerebral artery, and run a baseline assessment. The headgear and wires would restrict movement of the operator during tasking.

Eye tracking shows promise as a solution to the intrusiveness of other available measures. An eye tracking unit may only require a single calibration for each operator, which can be used for all subsequent shifts. Further, that calibration can be done by the operator without assistance. No post-shift cleanup or storage would be required. Eye tracking is restricted in that operators must remain in view of the tracking cameras and must not obstruct large portions of their faces, but these requirements may not be difficult to meet as attention should be focused in the direction of the monitors for task perform-ance and hands on controls.

4.4 Robustness

In a controlled, laboratory setting, many metrics may show promise because noise can be eliminated from the signal which is to be detected. Unfortunately the applied setting does not offer the ability to control for other variables and thus it is crucial to account for the noise added by other factors. For example, gaze pattern-based metrics may be problematic for detecting state due to their sensitivity to the relative spatial distribution and frequency of critical signals, which cannot be controlled in an applied setting. EEG and TCD are disrupted by talking and chewing, and by head movements that might cause the electrodes/probes to lose good skin contact.

Thus, the metric must be robust to quality problems. There are three considerations here. The first issue is whether missing data for a metric tend to be at random or system-atic. In the former case, a measure might provide only 500 out of 1000 possible obser-vations, but nonetheless provide a reliable assessment. However, if loss of data is related to particular events in the scenario, the assessment is much more problematic. The second consideration is how easily the metric loses its ability to detect a state with decreasing data quality. The third and the potentially most problematic situation is whether or not the outcome indicated by the metric changes qualitatively as a result of shifts in quality of the data. One example of this problem came up with our assessment of an eye tracking technique based on the binning of fixations by duration with guidance from a previous effort, which looked at alertness using EOG [35].

Our expectation was that with fatigue, participants would have a decreasing proportion of fixations between 150 ms and 900 ms, the purported cognitive fixation range, to total fixations. Although cognitive fixations declined as expected overall, we found that, at the individual level, our performance and subjective data suggested that those with the lowest proportion of cognitive fixations were the best performers and were the least fatigued. However, the method for identifying fixations we utilized was potentially sensitive to missing data, leading to an underestimation of fixation duration. This meant that the quickest cognitive fixations may have been categorized as express fixations (<150 ms).

Cognitive fixations may have lengthened with diminished perceptual efficiency caused by fatigue. This would cause the incorrectly classified short cognitive fixations to be correctly reclassified as cognitive fixations with the onset of fatigue. Operators more resistant to fatigue would maintain shorter cognitive fixations which would remain incorrectly classified as express fixations. The result is that those who struggled less were less likely to have their incorrectly classified cognitive fixations (those accidentally considered express fixations) reclassified as cognitive fixations; the outcome indicated by the fixation duration binning metric changed qualitatively when data quality was poor. Thus, maintaining reasonable quality for this metric is essential.

5 Conclusions

Using these four criteria in our own effort to identify metrics for passive fatigue, we have concluded that binned fixation duration based eye tracking metrics provide the most promise. Like other physiological measures, these metrics are sensitive to lower levels of fatigue and, therefore, can be used to identify fatigue prior to subjective awareness and performance decrements. Binned fixation duration is diagnostic of passive fatigue whether or not operators are in a DWA state. Finally, eye tracking is noninvasive and easy to set up. Unfortunately, binned fixation duration is not robust to quality problems with our current equipment (a Seeing Machines faceLAB 5 eye tracker recording two 21 in. monitors at 60 Hz). However, systems which are far more capable than that which we used are already available and demonstrate much higher and consistent tracking quality with a dual monitor setup than we were able to achieve. Although other measures may improve with technological advancements, these improvements are currently less promising than those of eye tracking. For example, less intrusive EEG systems lack the quality of the medical grade systems typically used in laboratory settings. In closing, we hope that this elaboration on Eggemeier and colleague's criteria [37] using our work as a case study has provided some guidance for metric selection for operator state assessment in a closed loop system.

Acknowledgement. This research was sponsored by AFOSR A9550-13-1-0016 and 13RH05COR. The views and conclusions contained in this document are those of the authors and should not be interpreted as representing the official policies, either expressed or implied, of AFOSR or the US Government.

References

1. Gertler, J.: U.S. Unmanned Aerial Systems (No. ADA566235). Library of Congress, Congressional Research Service, Washington (2012)
2. Cummings, M.L., Clare, A., Hart, C.: The role of human-automation consensus in multiple unmanned vehicle scheduling. Hum. Factors 52(1), 17–27 (2010)
3. Neubauer, C., Matthews, G., Langheim, L., Saxby, D.: Fatigue and voluntary utilization of automation in simulated driving. Hum. Factors 54(5), 734–746 (2012)
4. Calhoun, G.L., Draper, M.H., Miller, C., Ruff, H.A., Breeden, C., Hamell, J.: Adaptable automation interface for multi-unmanned aerial systems control: preliminary usability evaluation. Proc. Hum. Factors Ergon. Soc. Annu. Meet. 57(1), 26–30 (2013)
5. Wohleber, R.W., Calhoun, G.L., Funke, G.J., Ruff, H.A., Chiu, C.-Y.P., Lin, J., Matthews, G.: The impact of automation reliability on performance and reliance changes with operator fatigue (in preparation)
6. Matthews, G., Desmond, P.A., Hitchcock, E.M.: Dimensional models of fatigue. In: Matthews, G., Desmond, P.A., Neubauer, C., Hancock, P.A. (eds.) The Handbook of Operator Fatigue, pp. 139–154. Ashgate Publishing Company, Burlington (2012)
7. Michielsen, H.J., De Vries, J., Van Heck, G.L., Van de Vijver, F.J., Sijtsma, K.: Examination of the dimensionality of fatigue: the construction of the fatigue assessment scale (FAS). Eur. J. Psychol. Assess. 20(1), 39–48 (2004)
8. Matthews, G., Campbell, S.E., Falconer, S., Joyner, L.A., Huggins, J., Gilliland, K., Grier, R., Warm, J.S.: Fundamental dimensions of subjective state in performance settings: task engagement, distress, and worry. Emotion 2(4), 315–340 (2002)
9. Saxby, D.J., Matthews, G., Warm, J.S., Hitchcock, E.M., Neubauer, C.: Active and passive fatigue in simulated driving: discriminating styles of workload regulation and their safety impacts. J. Exp. Psychol. Appl. 19(4), 287–300 (2013)
10. Åkerstedt, T., Gillberg, M.: Subjective and objective sleepiness in the active individual. Int. J. Neurosci. 52(1–2), 29–37 (1990)
11. Philip, P., Sagaspe, P., Taillard, J., Moore, N., Guilleminault, C., Sanchez-Ortuno, M., Akerstedt, T., Bioulac, B.: Fatigue, sleep restriction, and performance in automobile drivers: a controlled study in a natural environment. Sleep 26(3), 277–284 (2003)
12. Abich, J., Reinerman-Jones, L., Taylor, G.S.: Investigating workload measures for adaptive training systems. Proc. Hum. Factors Ergon. Soc. Annu. Meet. 57(1), 2091–2095 (2013)
13. Warm, J.S., Matthews, G., Finomore, V.S.: Vigilance, workload, and stress. In: Hancock, P.A., Szalma, J.L. (eds.) Performance Under Stress, pp. 115–141. Ashgate Publishing Company, Burlington (2008)
14. Warm, J.S., Parasuraman, R., Matthews, G.: Vigilance requires hard mental work and is stressful. Hum. Factors 50(3), 433–441 (2008)
15. Matthews, G., Desmond, P.A.: Task-induced fatigue states and simulated driving performance. Q. J. Exp. Psychol. Sect. A 55(2), 659–686 (2002)
16. Desmond, P.A., Hancock, P.A.: Active and passive fatigue states. In: Hancock, P.A., Desmond, P.A. (eds.) Stress, Workload, and Fatigue, pp. 455–465. Lawrence Erlbaum Associates, Mahwah (2001)
17. Hockey, G.R.J.: Compensatory control in the regulation of human performance under stress and high workload: a cognitive-energetical framework. Biol. Psychol. 45(1–3), 73–93 (1997)
18. Mascord, D.J., Heath, R.A.: Behavioral and physiological indices of fatigue in a visual tracking task. J. Saf. Res. 23(1), 19–25 (1992)
19. Körber, M., Cingel, A., Zimmermann, M., Bengler, K.: Vigilance decrement and passive fatigue caused by monotony in automated driving. Procedia Manufact. 3, 2403–2409 (2015)

20. Saxby, D.J., Matthews, G., Hitchcock, E.M., Warm, J.S., Funke, G.J., Gantzer, T.: Effect of active and passive fatigue on performance using a driving simulator. Proc. Hum. Factors Ergon. Soc. Annu. Meet. **52**, 1751–1755 (2008)
21. Lee, I.-S., Bardwell, W.A., Ancoli-Israel, S., Dimsdale, J.E.: Number of lapses during the psychomotor vigilance task as an objective measure of fatigue. J. Clin. Sleep Med. **6**(2), 163–168 (2010)
22. Matthews, G., Warm, J.S., Reinerman-Jones, L.E., Langheim, L.K., Washburn, D.A., Tripp, L.: Task engagement, cerebral blood flow velocity, and diagnostic monitoring for sustained attention. J. Exp. Psychol. Appl. **16**(2), 187–203 (2010)
23. Craig, A., Tran, Y.: The influence of fatigue on brain activity. In: Matthews, G., Desmond, P.A., Neubauer, C., Hancock, P.A. (eds.) The Handbook of Operator Fatigue, pp. 185–196. Ashgate Publishing Company, Burlington (2012)
24. Verwey, W.B., Zaidel, D.M.: Predicting drowsiness accidents from personal attributes, eye blinks and ongoing driving behaviour. Pers. Individ. Differ. **28**(1), 123–142 (2000)
25. Smith, E.R., DeCoster, J.: Dual-process models in social and cognitive psychology: conceptual integration and links to underlying memory systems. Pers. Soc. Psychol. Rev. **4**(2), 108–131 (2000)
26. Prinzel, L.J., Freeman, F.G., Scerbo, M.W., Mikulka, P.J., Pope, A.T.: Effects of a psychophysiological system for adaptive automation on performance, workload, and the event-related potential P300 component. Hum. Factors **45**(4), 601–614 (2003)
27. Gevins, A.S., Bressler, S.L., Cutillo, B.A., Illes, J., Miller, J.C., Stern, J., Jex, H.R.: Effects of prolonged mental work on functional brain topography. Electroencephalogr. Clin. Neurophysiol. **76**(4), 339–350 (1990)
28. Segerstrom, S.C., Nes, L.S.: Heart rate variability reflects self-regulatory strength, effort, and fatigue. Psychol. Sci. **18**(3), 275–281 (2007)
29. Warm, J.S., Tripp, L.D., Matthews, G., Helton, W.S.: Cerebral hemodynamic indices of operator fatigue in vigilance. In: Matthews, G., Desmond, P.A., Neubauer, C., Hancock, P.A. (eds.) The Handbook of Operator Fatigue. Ashgate Publishing Company, Burlington (2012)
30. Li, Z., Zhang, M., Zhang, X., Dai, S., Yu, X., Wang, Y.: Assessment of cerebral oxygenation during prolonged simulated driving using near infrared spectroscopy: its implications for fatigue development. Eur. J. Appl. Physiol. **107**(3), 281–287 (2009)
31. DeGreef, T., Lafeber, H., van Oostendorp, H., Lindenberg, J.: Eye movement as indicators of mental workload to trigger adaptive automation. In: Schmorrow, D.D., Estabrooke, I.V., Grootjen, M. (eds.) Foundations of Augmented Cognition. Neuroergonomics and Operational Neuroscience, pp. 219–228. Springer, New York (2009)
32. Stern, R.M., Ray, W.J., Quigley, K.S.: Psychophysiological Recording, 2nd edn. Oxford University Press, New York (2001)
33. Wierwille, W.W., Wreggit, S.S., Kirn, C.L., Ellsworth, L.A., Fairbanks, R.J.: Research on vehicle-based driver status/performance monitoring; development, validation, and refinement of algorithms for detection of driver drowsiness (No. HS-808 247 VPISU ISE 94-04) (1994)
34. Kozak, K., Curry, R., Greenberg, J., Artz, B., Blommer, M., Cathey, L.: Leading indicators of drowsiness in simulated driving. Proc. Hum. Factors Ergon. Soc. Annu. Meet. **49**, 1917–1921 (2005). SAGE Publications
35. Schleicher, R., Galley, N., Briest, S., Galley, L.: Blinks and saccades as indicators of fatigue in sleepiness warnings: looking tired? Ergonomics **51**(7), 982–1010 (2008)
36. Palmer, S.E.: Vision Science: Photons to Phenomenology. MIT Press, Cambridge (1999)
37. Eggemeier, F.T., Wilson, G.F., Kramer, A.F., Damos, D.L.: Workload assessment in multi-task environments. In: Damos, D.L. (ed.) Multiple-Task Performance, pp. 207–216. Taylor & Francis, London (1991)

38. Freeman, F.G., Mikulka, P.J., Prinzel, L.J., Scerbo, M.W.: Evaluation of an adaptive automation system using three EEG indices with a visual tracking task. Biol. Psychol. **50**(1), 61–76 (1999)
39. Briest, S., Karrer, K., Schleicher, R.: Driving without awareness: examination of the phenomenon. In: Gale, A. (ed.) Vision in Vehicles XI, pp. 89–141. Elsevier, Amsterdam (2006)
40. Matthews, G.: Towards a transactional ergonomics for driver stress and fatigue. Theor. Issues Ergon. Sci. **3**(2), 195–211 (2002)
41. Hitchcock, E.M., Warm, J.S., Matthews, G., Dember, W.N., Shear, P.K., Tripp, L.D., Mayleben, D.W., Parasuraman, R.: Automation cueing modulates cerebral blood flow and vigilance in a simulated air traffic control task. Theor. Issues Ergon. Sci. **4**(1–2), 89–112 (2003)
42. Tattersall, A.J., Foord, P.S.: An experimental evaluation of instantaneous self-assessment as a measure of workload. Ergonomics **39**(5), 740–748 (1996)
43. Metzger, U., Parasuraman, R.: The role of the air traffic controller in future air traffic management: an empirical study of active control versus passive monitoring. Hum. Factors **43**(4), 519–528 (2001)

Sensing and Assessing Cognitive Workload Across Multiple Tasks

Matthias D. Ziegler[1(✉)], Amanda Kraft[2,3], Michael Krein[2],
Li-Chuan Lo[4], Bradley Hatfield[4], William Casebeer[1],
and Bartlett Russell[1]

[1] Lockheed Martin Advanced Technology Lab, Arlington, VA, USA
{matthias.d.ziegler,william.d.casebeer,
bartlett.a.russell}@lmco.com
[2] Lockheed Martin Advanced Technology Lab, Cherry Hill, NJ, USA
{amanda.e.kraft,michael.krein}@lmco.com
[3] Drexel University, Philadelphia, USA
[4] Department of Kinesiology, University of Maryland, College Park, USA
{llo,Bhatfiel}@umd.edu

Abstract. Workload assessment models are an important tool to develop an understanding of an individual's limitations. Finding times of excess workload can help prevent an individual from continuing work that may result in human performance issues, such as an increase in errors or reaction time. Currently workload assessments are created on a task by task basis, varying drastically depending on sensors and task goals. Developing independent models for specific tasks is time consuming and not practical when being applied to real-world situations. In this experiment we collected physiological signals including electroencephalogram (EEG), Heart Rate and Heart Rate Variability (HR/HRV) and Eye-Tracking. Subjects were asked to perform two independent tasks performed at two distinct levels of difficulty, an easy level and a difficult level. We then developed and compared performance of multiple models using deep and shallow learning techniques to determine the best methods to increase generalization of the models across tasks.

Keywords: Workload · Cognitive · EEG · HRV · Flight simulator · Neural networks · Predictive models · Deep belief network · Linear SVM

1 Introduction

Over the last decade computational models have gained an increasing presence as techniques to understand human behavior and in linking behavior to physiological measures [1–3]. Studies utilizing computational models have successfully shown links between measures of workload with performance that were not previously apparent due to the large amount of data that current sensors are able to collect [4, 5]. While many studies implement such models they can vary significantly between studies due to the diversity of tasks being tested, number/type of sensors and analysis techniques. This leads to highly specialized models that do not transfer between tasks and individuals.

© Springer International Publishing Switzerland 2016
D.D. Schmorrow and C.M. Fidopiastis (Eds.): AC 2016, Part I, LNAI 9743, pp. 440–450, 2016.
DOI: 10.1007/978-3-319-39955-3_41

A model that is so specialize that any change to the task or individual being modeled requires complete system retraining is impractical in applications outside of controlled experiments. To bring computational models outside of the lab for practical use in real world environments it is important to examine how physiological data can be reliably processed and analyzed in a manner that is beneficial for understanding workload levels and performance across both individuals and tasks of interest.

Recently, studies have shown that cognitive workload levels can be measured using an increasing number of available sensing techniques. Electroencephalogram (EEG) has been one of the most common tools for measuring workload, identifying increased neural activity corresponding to workload levels [6–8]. Eye tracking is also common, as evidence of pupil size and blink rate have been linked to workload levels [9, 10]. Electrocardiogram (ECG) offers another means to assess workload levels via heart rate variability [11]. By combining sensors some studies have been able to show workload levels consistent across multiple physiological sensors [5, 12] and to increase the classification accuracy of any one of these systems alone by accounting for a greater number of physiological systems that respond to changes in workload. In this study we use this combined sensing approach to measure performance in multiple tasks to determine how well general levels of workload are linked to task performance across individuals. While other tools, such as fNIRS, fMRI and biomarkers in particular [13, 14], have also shown to be important measures of workload we do not address these tools in this study.

Understanding the ability of computational models to predict performance from physiological signals is an important tool that could have large number applications in cognitively demanding environments. While many studies have looked at linking workload measures with performance and have even shown success predicting future performance [13], there has been no comprehensive study evaluating the possibilities and limitations of what a combination of physiological measures can predict. Here we start that process by looking at creating a single subject agnostic generalizable model to predict performance based on EEG, eye tracking and ECG. We compare accuracy of a model that is trained based on the performance results over two independent tasks and then tested on a separate hold-out population the model was not trained on. We compare these results with a model that is trained on a single trial from all individuals and tested on the same population over multiple additional trials as well as a model trained and tested on an equal, random distribution of all available data. We posit that subject's physiological signals are unique enough that unless their performance is represented in the training algorithm there will be a decrease in model accuracy of performance prediction. However the exact tradeoff between drop-off in accuracy and individualization necessary for adequate performance is unknown. This study plays an important role in understanding difficulties that occur when trying to use physiological data as a measure of performance without individualized training.

Computational models can vary in complexity of programing, amount of data needed for training, time needed to run the model and number of parameters that need to be adjusted (i.e. layer size, learning rates, etc.) It is important to examine how the accuracy of different modeling approaches affects predictions in an effort to understand the tradeoff between accuracy and time needed to develop/execute the model. In this study we analyzed the results of two types of model, but focus primarily on one a deep belief network using neural networks. We chose a neural networking approach to model human performance, based upon the ability of neural networks to robustly classify nonlinear data. Additionally we did some initial testing comparing the neural network with a linear support vector machine (SVM) model. In each model we did comprehensive cross-validation by randomly distributing the subject pool into training and testing sets and running the model 25 times to ensure accurate reporting the performance of each model. Simply running a model with a single training/testing set may cause skewed results as the training or testing data chosen may not be representative of the overall data. As performance variation between cross-validation runs is an indicator of dataset variability and an estimate for overall method reliability with respect to the data, we will present the models results we tested over the 25 model cross-validation runs and indicate that cross-validation should be standard procedure when testing models.

The result of our study shows that a generalized model with no tailoring performs very poorly when applied to a new individual and that some level of model adaptation or personalization is necessary for any level model prediction to be valid. These findings provide an indication that a comprehensive study is necessary to understand the trade offs between generalized model performances versus the costs of adapting models to individuals.

2   Methods

2.1   Experiment Setup

Participants. A mix of thirty-five right-handed undergraduate and graduate students from University of Maryland were trained and tested on two computer based video games to measure performance over a period of four non-consecutive days. Subjects were trained on the system during day 1 and tested days 2, 3 and 4. Four trials (each from different participants) were disregarded due to errors in recording.

Task Design. We designed two tasks to titrate workload: a simple Snake Game (see Fig. 1) and Prepar3D Flight simulator (Fig. 2), each of which contained multiple levels of difficulty. Subjects received one 45 min training period to become familiar with the tasks and returned for 3 days following the training to perform the tasks. The order of the tasks and difficulty levels were randomized for each day. Each difficulty level lasted for 5 min in both tasks.

2.2   Task Description

Nokia Snake Game. A video game was developed using Presentation programming language to mimic the Nokia Snake game preloaded on Nokia cellular phones. The game, shown in Fig. 1, consists of a "snake" that moves at a constant pace, but the subject controls the snake's direction with keyboard commands, including up, down, left or right. The goals of the game are to avoid hitting any walls or the snake itself (in

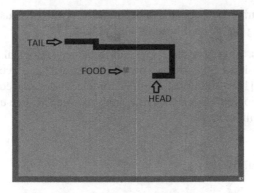

Fig. 1. Example of the "snake game", the subjects control the head to eat the food while avoiding its own tail and the surrounding walls (grey boarder).

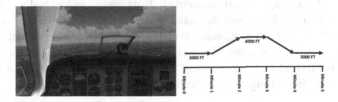

Fig. 2. Example seen from Prepar3D cockpit (left) task instructions (right).

which case the snake "dies" and the level restarts), and to collect as much "food" as possible. When subjects direct the snake to "eat" the food, the food adds a single additional square to the snake's length There is no limit to the snake's length, but as it grows longer, it becomes more difficult to navigate within the maze without hitting a wall or itself. The subjects completed two different levels of Snake: "easy" in which the snake moves at a slow speed (traveling across the screen only once every 100 ms) and a faster "hard" speed (moving once per 38 ms). The game provides an element of automatic titration to player skill; the length of the snake increases the difficulty of the subject's ability to eat food while avoiding itself and the walls of the game. During testing we found that in the "hard" condition the keyboard input latency was delayed such that two fast-sequential keystrokes did not always register as the subject intended.

Prepar3D Flight Simulator. Lockheed Martin's Prepar3D flight simulator was used as a second performance task. Subjects were given control of an aircraft and the task was broken down into 5-one minute subtasks. During minute one they were asked to maintain level flight at an altitude of 3000 ft. with a heading of 180 degrees at speed of 180 knots. In minute two, they were asked to maintain the same direction, but increase their altitude to 4000 ft while never increasing altitude at rate less than 1000 ft/min. They then maintained 4000 ft for another minute before decreasing again to 3000 and maintained that altitude for the final minute. To create multiple difficulty levels the environment in which the plane was flying was changed. In the "easy" condition there was no wind and no turbulence, however in the harder condition winds of over 30 knots and severe turbulence affected the aircraft's position, causing high levels of difficulty maintaining the desired heading and altitude.

Physiological Tools. During testing days subjects' physiological signals were measured using BrainVision EEG system with electrodes arranged according to the standard 10–20 system [15]. Additional BrainVision electrodes placed on the collarbone recorded electrocardiogram (ECG) for HRV analysis. An SMI eye tracker recorded eye movements and pupillometry.

2.3   Computational Models

Model Development and Performance Estimation. We wanted to understand the impact of traditional signal processing methods on our ability to develop transferable human performance models. We baseline corrected the data using the average Welch's Power Spectral Density (PSD) computed from each individual's resting state "eyes-open" session and removed the data for the first and last 10 s for each trial. We computed the PSD for each task, using Welch's method over 1 s interval of data. For each channel and frequency bin, the corresponding baseline PSD average was subtracted from the task PSD. Each resulting 1-second interval was used as a unit of data for training or testing during model development and validation.

The data was tested in two models a Linear SVM model (shallow model) and a neural network model (deep belief network). The deep belief network structures were Gaussian-Bernoulli Restricted Boltzmann Machine (GB-RBM) classifiers based upon Tanaka's code [16]. We estimated appropriate learning rates, learning step sizes, hidden layer sizes, and drop rates based on successive modeling performance during automated model tuning. We tuned models via sequential grid tuning approach; for a particular layer size and drop rate, a grid of step rates (0.1, 0.2, 0.3....) was evaluated. A step rate is then selected based on highest mean AUC and is used for subsequent modeling. The process is repeated for determining drop rates (0, 0.25, 0.5, 0.75...). For all models developed, the layer size chosen for use in determining the optimal learning rate was 100; the drop rate used for selection of optimal learning rate and hidden layer size was 0.5. All human data were standardized via z-score scaling prior to modeling.

Data Analysis. For each of the preprocessing strategies outlined above, Receiver Operating Characteristic (ROC) curves were analyzed and areas under the ROC curve (AUCs) are reported. An AUC of 0 refers to no prediction ability of the model, 0.5 denotes chance prediction, and 1.0 denotes perfect prediction of the model. Here we report the average and standard deviation of AUCs based upon 25 rounds of cross validation. The predictions are based on a binary decision for the model. The model predicts if the current test data that is provided to the model is above or below the median score for the task.

Cross Validation. In one of our approaches to cross-validation, we randomly assign 75 % of the subjects (all trials) as a training set, and withhold the remaining 25 % of subjects as a validation set. This is key to the approach, and reflects the transferability of human performance indicators without prior knowledge. It is important to note that since a developed model here has not been trained on any prior data from the validation set individuals, one would expect modest predictive ability. We compared this to other modeling strategies where data were withheld such that some data from each individual was included in both the training and testing set. We tested this by withholding a single trial from each individual randomly for the validation set (and the rest of the trials were part of the training set). In addition, we performed training modeling experiments where a subset of all subjects trials were included in the validation subject's, the balance of data (75 %) remained in the training set.

3   Results

3.1   Performance

Subjects showed distinct performance differences between the easy and hard levels of both the snake game and the flight simulator. The snake score was determined by adding the amount of time the subject stayed "alive" (avoiding running into walls or other parts of the snake) plus the growth of the snake plus the Manhattan distance from the food.

The average performance difference was 0.5572 ± 0.086 for the easy snake game versus 0.4658 ± 0.0745 for the hard snake game, as shown in Fig. 3. The density value in Fig. 3 represents the number of subjects at a particular score. This scoring system was developed after analyzing each individual measure and recognizing that no one measure alone was representative of the overall performance. The combined mean which was used as the binary output for the model was 0.5115. The Prepar3D flight simulator task showed similar distinct differences in the average subject performance; however there was more variance between subjects and trials within the easy and hard conditions. The mean values for the Prepar3D performance was 0.4517 ± 0.2282 for the easy condition and 0.323 ± 0.2188 for the hard condition with a combined mean of 0.3874. These scores represented a normalized analysis of how far from the desired heading, speed, altitude and vertical feet per minute the subject varied. A score of 1 would have indicated 0 drift from the desired measures.

3.2   Model Results

Deep Belief Network. The deep belief networks showed significant differences in performance based on the type of model used (parameters chosen), type of training performed within the model and the specific task. As outlined in Table 1, all of the deep learning models consistently improved based on the type of training used for the model.

Validating the model on subjects that the model was not trained on showed only around chance levels of performance, 0.49 ± 0.4 accuracy in predicting performance for Prepar3D and 0.54 ± 0.04 predictions for the Snake Game when the best parameters

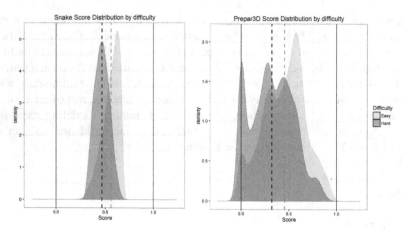

Fig. 3. The snake subject performance (left) on easy (light gray) and hard (dark gray show distinct differences. The Prepar3D task performance (right) had higher variance within a given condition.

Table 1. AUC results for deep belief network and lindear SVM models for varying training/testing datasets (rows) and varying parameters (results of min/max and average shown in the columns

Deep belief network results				
Prepar3D				
	Mean AUC	Min AUC	Max AUC	AUC SD
Split by subject	0.49	0.38	0.58	0.04
Split by trial	0.60	0.57	0.62	0.01
Random split	0.79	0.76	0.81	0.01
Snake game				
	Mean AUC	Min AUC	Max AUC	AUC SD
Split by subject	0.54	0.46	0.59	0.04
Split by trial	0.61	0.58	0.63	0.01
Random split	0.71	0.69	0.73	0.01
Linear SVM				
Prepar3D				
	Mean AUC	Min AUC	Max AUC	AUC SD
Split by subject	0.5234	0.4134	0.6584	0.07
Split by trial	0.4533	0.4027	0.5316	0.05
Snake				
	Mean AUC	Min AUC	Max AUC	AUC SD
Split by subject	0.4981	0.4011	0.5924	0.05
Split by trial	0.4747	0.3966	0.6034	0.07

are chosen (Max AUC). When the training and validation data sets were determined by separation of trials (i.e. inclusion of data from the same three trials for all subjects in the training set and all data from remaining trials in the validation set), the predication ability increased, up to 0.60 and 0.61 when all subjects were included with separate subject trials withheld for validation. The increase in prediction ability peaked with 0.79 and 0.71 when data from all subjects and all trials were represented in both the training and validation of the model.

Linear SVM Model. The linear SVM model was tested as a comparison for only the split by subject training. When training and validation on unique subjects the mean prediction accuracy of the SVM was 0.52 ± 0.07 and 0.4981 ± 0.05 for the Prepar3D and Snake game respectfully. They performed minimally in cross validation of 0.41 and 0.40 for each task and a maximally at 0.65 and 0.59 for each task. There was no significant change in performance when the training was split to including one training session from each subject.

4 Discussion

As scientific researchers push to obtain as much physiological data as possible in order to understand how human performance is holistically defined they will rely on more complex computational models, as traditional data analysis methods will not be sufficient. The results of the experiments in this study show that how the data is processed and modeled can create large variations in overall predictive power. In order to choose the correct computational model, one must take multiple factors into consideration, which we will discuss here.

4.1 Physiological Sensors and Task Design

In this experiment we chose multiple physiological sensors that would record measurements that have been linked to cognitive workload levels. Our original predictions were that as the task became more difficult the workload would increase and performance decrease under the median, while during easy tasks there would low workload and high performance. However the link between workload and performance is not a one-to-one relationship, in fact depending on expertise level it has been shown that two subjects who perform equally may have very different workload measurements [13]. To combat this we trained the subjects for an equal amount of time on multiple tasks in which they had little to no experience in and that drastically differed in necessary levels of workload. For example, during the flight simulator easy task, to maintain constant altitude, heading and speed the subject simply needed to hold the flight stick steady and pull back with minimal force to change altitude. When the flight simulator experiment switched to hard level, independent of expertise, large effort and attention was needed as the winds and turbulence changed the planes course affecting all performance levels agnostic to how well the subject controlled the plane. Similarly the Snake game speed on the easy level was slow enough that avoiding the walls was a simple task and subjects were able to control the snake to gain only enough length that they felt comfortable with the control. When it was switched to hard the subjects not only had to increase concentration based on the speed of the snake, but as an unattended consequence of our task not recording every keystroke, subjects had to change strategies in real time to compensate for keystrokes not responding, theoretically increasing workload levels. The performance graphs of these tasks showed distinct differences in performance between the easy and hard tasks. While the trend comparing model performances was consistent across tasks, there were significantly greater differences in the flight simulator task over the snake task. This difference can be attributed to multiple aspects of the task, first the flight simulator had distinct quantitative goals (altitude, heading, speed, feet/minute) that every subject aimed for. During the snake task subjects had discretion if their priority would be to stay "alive" or to eat as much food as possible and could obtain the same performance measure. The second limiting factor for the snake game was the altered controls in the hard task which may have caused subjects to change their priorities between the easy task in how they approached the food. In the easy task they could take quick turns, but in the hard task they may have elected for larger turns toward the food to compensate for the delay in response to keystrokes and this may have lowered the score or frustrated some subjects, causing workload independent changes to the physiological signals between task difficulty levels.

4.2   Training Method

Given that we saw very similar performance distributions between subjects on the easy and hard levels in both tasks we predicted we would be able to make a single generalizable model for each task that would work to predict performance on novel subjects. However, when we trained both the deep belief networks and the linear SVM on a 75 % subset of the subjects and tested using the remaining 25 % of the subjects the models performed only at a $\sim$50 % prediction accuracy (validation). Under our 25 model runs, altering which subjects were part of the training and which part of the testing the best results were 65 % for the Linear SVM and 59 % for the Deep Belief Networks. These results showed that while some distribution of the subjects caused the model training to be more representative of the larger population, the models were still poor at predicting performance based off of workload measures. The fact that multiple models showed this performance led us to believe that even with similar performance, there was not a standard workload measure that worked consistently across individuals for either task.

To verify if the model could accurately predict performance from individualized workload measures, we trained the deep belief networks in a number of other ways to determine if we could generate a better performing model. When we trained the models using a subset of each subjects' data the models performance significantly improved for the Deep Belief Network, but we saw no improvement in the Linear SVMs. We did this two ways, first by assigning a single session of each subject to train and tested on the remaining sessions (both models), second we randomly chose data points from each subject across all of their data (deep belief only) allowing each subject and testing session to be represented in both the training and testing model runs. While both of these model runs significantly improved the performance of the deep belief network, the later showed the greatest improvement accuracy predicting up to ~ 80 % of the tests in the flight simulator task. The worst cross-validation model performance with this modeling technique was equivalent to or only slightly better than the best general model where there was no training/testing overlap. The model's improved ability to accurately predict performance form physiological workload measures when all subjects are represented in both the training and testing sets illustrates the extreme differences within physiological measures across individuals corresponds to the same behavioral outcomes. Only when a model is personalized for the intended user and possibly to a specific task, will it be reliable and useful as a predictive model.

We posit that the ability of the models to perform best when all sessions are represented in the training session is due to learning that may occur within subject across sessions. Even if performance remains equivalent across sessions, as the subject becomes more familiar with the tasks (and more comfortable wearing all the sensors) their physiological measures may change independent of performance measures. Therefore, not only is it necessary to account for individualized differences when developing a computational model to predict performance or categorize workload, but a model most also account for learning that occurs over time. Even experts in a given field have been shown to change performance and continue learning, albeit at a slower rate, thus models must account for this even in cases when naïve subjects are not being used.

While individualized models show high performance, the time and effort taken to train a new model for every subject is extremely time consuming. To combat this need for individualization, our future work will examine the ability to group subjects based off of current and prior performance and create a set of template models to which a subject can be quickly matched. The template may then be tailored to the individual as the subject improves at the task shortening the overall process. By having not one, but a set of models trained on only subjects that show the same performance trends we posit a high accuracy prediction without a one-to-one relationship between number of models and subjects. This set of models will be the only possibility to create real-time modeling that will be necessary if adjustments to the subjects' performance or tasking are desired in timely fashion.

References

1. Kieras, D.E., Meyer, D.: Computational Modeling of Human Multiple-Task Performance. No. TR-05/ONR-EPIC-16. Michigan University, Department of Electrical Engineering and Computer Science, Ann Arbor (2005)
2. Hugo, J., Gertman, D.I.: The use of computational human performance modeling as task analysis tool. In: Proceedings of the Eighth American Nuclear Society International Topical Meeting on Nuclear Plant Instrumentation, Control, and Human-Machine Interface Technologies, NPIC&HMIT 2012, pp. 22–26 (2012)
3. Meng, J., Wu, X., Morozov, V., Vishwanath, V., Kumaran, K., Taylor, V.: SKOPE: a framework for modeling and exploring workload behavior. In: Proceedings of the 11th ACM Conference on Computing Frontiers, p. 6. ACM (2014)

4. Ke, Y., Qi, H., He, F., Liu, S., Zhao, X., Zhou, P., Ming, D.: An EEG-based mental workload estimator trained on working memory task can work well under simulated multi-attribute task. Front. Hum. Neurosci. 8 (2014)
5. Liu, Y., Ayaz, H., Onaral, B., Shewokis, P.A.: Neural adaptation to a working memory task: a concurrent EEG-fNIRS Study. In: Schmorrow, D.D., Fidopiastis, C.M. (eds.) AC 2015. LNCS, vol. 9183, pp. 268–280. Springer, Heidelberg (2015)
6. Kamzanova, A.T., Kustubayeva, A.M., Matthews, G.: Use of EEG workload indices for diagnostic monitoring of vigilance decrement. Hum. Factors: J. Hum. Factors Ergon. Soc. 56 (6), 1136–1149 (2014)
7. Walter, C.B.: EEG workload prediction in a closed-loop learning environment. Doctoral dissertation, Universität Tübingen (2015)
8. Brouwer, A.M., Hogervorst, M.A., Van Erp, J.B., Heffelaar, T., Zimmerman, P.H., Oostenveld, R.: Estimating workload using EEG spectral power and ERPs in the n-back task. J. Neural Eng. 9(4), 045008 (2012)
9. Bodala, I.P., Kukreja, S., Li, J., Thakor, N.V., Al-Nashash, H.: Eye tracking and EEG synchronization to analyze microsaccades during a workload task. In: Engineering in Medicine and Biology Society (EMBC), 2015 37th Annual International Conference of the IEEE, pp. 7994–7997 (2015)
10. Zheng, B., Jiang, X., Tien, G., Meneghetti, A., Panton, O.N.M., Atkins, M.S.: Workload assessment of surgeons: correlation between NASA TLX and blinks. Surg. Endosc. 26(10), 2746–2750 (2012)
11. Ke, Y., Qi, H., He, F., Liu, S., Zhao, X., Zhou, P., Ming, D.: An EEG-based mental workload estimator trained on working memory task can work well under simulated multi-attribute task. Front. Hum. Neurosci. 8 (2014)
12. Choe, J., Coffman, B.A., Bergstedt, D.T., Ziegler, M.D., Phillips, M.E.: Transcranial direct current stimulation modulates neuronal activity and learning in pilot training. Front. Hum. Neurosci. 10 (2016)
13. Ayaz, H., Shewokis, P.A., Bunce, S., Izzetoglu, K., Willems, B., Onaral, B.: Optical brain monitoring for operator training and mental workload assessment. Neuroimage 59(1), 36–47 (2012)
14. Just, M.A., Carpenter, P.A., Miyake, A.: Neuroindices of cognitive workload: neuroimaging, pupillometric and event-related potential studies of brain work. Theor. Issues Ergon. Sci. 4 (1–2), 56–88 (2003)
15. Jasper, H.H.: Report of the committee on methods of clinical examination in electroencephalography: 1957. Electroencephalogr. Clin. Neurophysiol. 10(2), 370–375 (1958)
16. Tanaka, M., Okutomi, M.: A novel inference of a restricted boltzmann machine. In: 2014 22nd International Conference on Pattern Recognition (ICPR), pp. 1526–1531. IEEE (2014)

Author Index

Printed in the United States
By Bookmasters

Printed in the United States
By Bookmasters